Food and Imagination
Proceedings of the Oxford Symposium on Food and Cookery 2021

Food and Imagination

Proceedings of the Oxford Symposium on Food and Cookery 2021

Edited by Mark McWilliams

Prospect Books
2022

First published in Great Britain in 2022 by Prospect Books, 26 Parke Road, London SW13 9NG.

© 2022 as a collection Prospect Books.
© 2022 in individual articles rests with the authors.

The image on the title page is 'Maillard's Exhibit' from the Trade Card Collection (Col. 9, 04x110.4), courtesy, the Winterthur Library: Joseph Downs Collection of Manuscripts and Ephemera.

The authors assert their moral right to be identified as authors in accordance with the Copyright, Designs & Patents Act 1988. No part of this publication may be reproduced, stored in a retrieval system or transmitted in any form or by any means, electronic, mechanical, photocopying, recording or otherwise, without the prior permission of the copyright holders.

ISBN 978-1-909-248-76-2

Design and typesetting in Gill Sans and Adobe Garamond by Catheryn Kilgarriff and Brendan King.

Printed and bound in Great Britain.

Contents

Foreword
   Mark McWilliams   9

Plenary Papers

Walking through our Gastronomies: Notes from an Imaginary *Flâneuse*
   Janet Beizer   11

'My Dead Miss Eddington': Reader Letters and Early Twentieth Century Food Media
   Emily Martin   20

Symposium Papers

Imaginary Diets, Edible Masculinities: Pirate Food in History and Fiction
   Volker Bach   30

Chaat: Why India's Beloved Snack Is also a Feat of the Imagination
   Vidya Balachander   39

Eat, Lose, Imagine
   Janet Beizer   44

'Imagine an animal enclosure': Surprise Dishes in German Medieval Cuisine, an Homage to the Medieval Chef
   Astrid Böhm, Julia Eibinger, and Helmut W. Klug   59

Delicacies Real and Imagined: Food and Drink as a Diplomatic Gift
   Paul Brummell   69

Greek *támisos* and Provençal *toma*: Etymological Evidence for Ancient Celtic Cheesemaking
   Anthony F. Buccini   79

The Infidels' Drink: Coffee Encounters and Transformations in Early Modern Malta
   Noel Buttigieg   91

Edibly Ever After: The Foods of Seventeenth-Century French Fairy Tales
   Mary Margaret Chappell   101

Imaginative Comparisons
   Rareș Augustin Crăiuț   109

Waterloo Porridge and Plentiful Yorkshire Teas: Food and the Creation of
   Northern English Identities in Mid-Nineteenth-Century Novels
   Gill Eastabrook — 116

Imaginary Feasts: Virtual Meals in a Second World War Prison Camp and in COVID
   Suzanne Evans — 126

Celebrating the Franco-Russian Alliance: French Chefs as Purveyors of Influence
   and Creators of Culinary Imagination
   Caroline Favre — 135

Imagination and Food in the Black Diaspora
   Rebecca Fils-Aimé — 143

Food and Foodways in Science Fiction
   Len Fisher and Anders Sandberg — 152

Saving Food in Bulgaria: Imagining Hopeful Futures through Quiet Food Sovereignty
   Lindsey Foltz — 164

A Conceit of Coney: Philip Harben and Britain's First Television Food History
   Programme
   Kevin Geddes — 174

Feast for the Soul: Food Imaginaries in a South Indian Performance
   Sudha Gopalakrishnan — 184

Sicilian Cheese: A Firm Foundation for Fantasy in the Old Comedy of
   Ancient Athens
   Christopher Grocock — 190

The Curious Case of *Nala's Mirror on Cooking*: Innovation in Medieval Indian
   Cookbook Writing
   Andrea Gutiérrez — 201

Stories Full of Recipes, Recipes Full of Stories
   Adrienne Harrington — 210

Materializing the Culinary Dreamscape: Maps, Guidebooks, and the Role of
   Terroir in (Re)Constructing the Myth of the French Gastronomic Utopia
   Jenny L. Herman — 220

Cogito ergo sum meditate: I Think, Therefore I Imagine!
   Peter Hertzmann — 231

Reconsidering the Culinary Imagination
   Jennifer L. Holm — 238

Food and Imagination

Caste: The Main Character of Indian Food
Ragini Kashyap — 248

Food, the Imagination, and Social Resistance in Sandra Cisneros's *Woman Hollering Creek*
Méliné Kasparian-Le Fèvre — 258

Food and the Irish Short Story Imagination
Anke Klitzing — 267

The Big Cheese: Cheese and the American Imagination
Bruce Kraig — 277

Steak or Salad? Food, Gender, and the Victorian Imagination
Michael Krondl — 286

Imagination and Food (and Drink) in the Novels of Iris Murdoch
Paul Levy — 296

The Hen that Laid a Tofu Egg
Priya Mani — 301

Singapore's Rising Hawkers: Food, Heritage, Imagination, and Entrepreneurship
Keri Matwick — 313

Persian *Tahdig*: A Canvas for Culinary Imagination, Imagery, and Artistry
Nader Mehravari — 322

'Broiling is the poetry of cooking': The Imaginative Symbolism of Gridirons and Broiling in Nineteenth-Century British Food Writing
Lindsay Middleton — 329

The Spiritual in the Sensual, the Sensual in the Virtual: Modern-Day Spirituality through a Community-Supported Farm
Caitlin B. Morgan — 339

The Cookbook Whisperer: How Maria Guarnaschelli's Powers of Imagination Redefined Recipes
James Oseland — 349

New York's Artisanal Oyster Farmers: Creating the Wild(ish) Oyster
Charity Robey — 356

The Birth of a Legend: *Mole de Guajolote* and Mestizo Identity in the Imaginary of Post-Revolutionary Mexico
Ana Karen Ruiz de la Peña Posada — 368

Food and Imagination

Food Reimagined: Diasporic Identity and Authenticity
Shayma Owaise Saadat — 375

'*Bileti*' to '*Desi*': Global Foodways and the Re-Imagining of Bengali 'Modern' Cuisine in Late Colonial Bengal
Samapan Saha — 384

'Coming from a Place of Impossibility': Imagining a World without Taste
Anna Seecharan — 392

Have It Your Way: Elizabeth David and the Problem of Norman Douglas
Laura Shapiro — 402

Making the Ordinary Exotic: The Role of Literary Imagination in the Rise of Gastronomic Tourism in Early Twentieth-Century France
Richard Warren Shepro — 409

Food Looks like a Lady: Designing Gastronomy through Ritualized Seduction
Max Shrem — 420

Incredible Edibles: American History in Chocolate, Cheddar, and Confectionary Forms
Nancy Siegel — 431

Reading the Cookbooks of Communist Romania: An Intimate Defence
Adriana Sohodoleanu — 441

Stirring Up Historical Imagination: Promoting the Teaching of History through Food-Based Pedagogy
Nicholas Tošaj — 450

Food in Sabbath Table Hymns: A Taste of the World to Come
Susan Weingarten — 460

Teaching Cookery Gets Personal: Harnessing Imagination to Feed the Will to Learn
Nikki Werner — 470

A Short History of Science Fiction and Fantasy Tie-In Cookbooks
Shana Worthen — 481

Contributors — 491

Foreword

During the opening keynote to the Oxford Food Symposium's consideration of Food and Imagination, Margaret Atwood insisted on a distinction: 'Let me explain about fiction. It's not real life. Every time you put food in a novel it's for a reason. It's a metaphor. [...] What food does in your life is something else.'[1] While readers may get lost in fiction's created worlds, Atwood clarifies, writers are all too aware of the stakes of each descriptive choice.

In her novel *Cat's Eye,* for example, Atwood compares the young protagonist's porridge to 'boiling mud' that she knows will make her 'stomach [...] contract' and her 'hands [...] get cold', but that she will 'get [...] down somehow, because it's required'. Here porridge stands for rural poverty, drawing on an association with material deprivation that goes back at least to Dickens. In *The Handmaid's Tale*, Atwood depicts wealth just as accurately: describing 'the long table, covered with a white cloth and spread with a buffet: ham, cheese, oranges — they have oranges! — and fresh-baked breads and cakes', the main character's awe captures the access of the elite. Here, as often in fiction, creative prose measures socioeconomic status just as precisely as the surveys and graphs of Pierre Bourdieu's *Distinction*.[2]

But imagining food in fiction does far more than locate characters on scales of various types of capital. The migrants of John Steinbeck's *The Grapes of Wrath* are dirt poor, but the novel's conclusion transcends physical hunger. When Rose of Sharon offers her breast milk to a starving man, she measures not poverty but the very limit of human generosity. As she 'smile[s] mysteriously', she finds agency where there had been none, creates connection when all else has been denied. In *Beloved*, Toni Morrison describes Sethe '[w]orking, working dough' as '[n]othing better [...] to start the day's serious work of beating back the past': preparing food becomes a way to deal with traumatic horrors because sharing meals leads to sharing stories. The importance of that sharing, that 'solidarity' with those Richard Rorty calls 'other, unfamiliar sorts of people', may be what Huck Finn is after when he dismisses meals where 'everything was cooked by itself' in favour of 'a barrel of odds and ends' where 'things get mixed up, and the juice kind of swaps around, and the things go better'.[3]

Huck's implication that we are better together than apart reminds us that things might not be that different in 'real life'. Food is on our own tables 'for a reason' too. The choices we make support industrial systems or build local networks: either way, our participation has consequences. While many of the papers presented at this Symposium analyzed historical moments, symposiasts' discussions often turned to the present and future, to how our shared exploration of foodways might help us imagine better ways to support our communities and our planet. In his keynote, Rob Hopkins pushed symposiasts to move past dreaming about 'What If' to making 'What Is' through our own actions, actions with outsized impacts if taken in solidarity with others.[4] In a moment when all the news seemed bad, we realized that working together toward the Symposium's mission – Change the Conversation, Expand the Table, Improve the Plate – might just leave future symposiasts with developments not only to analyze but also to celebrate. With imagination, we create our own world.

Mark McWilliams
Editor, Oxford Symposium on Food and Cookery

Acknowledgements

Our second all-virtual Symposium was another astonishing success due to many individuals working together: here I want to thank Elisabeth Luard, Cathy Kaufman, Naomi Duguid, Jessica Seaton, Carolyn Steel, and especially Ursula Heinzelmann, David Matchett, and Gamze İneceli. I would also like to express my personal appreciation to those who helped shepherd this volume – the longest yet! – to publication: Cateryn Kilgarriff, Brendan King, Jake Tilson, and all the authors whose virtual papers are here given the physical life they deserve.

Notes

1. Margaret Atwood, 'Fictional Foodies: A Conversation about Food and Fiction with Margaret Atwood and Mark McWilliams', *Oxford Food Symposium*, 22 June 2021 <https://youtu.be/8QjVkvzLi6U> [accessed 27 April 2022].
2. Margaret Atwood, *Cat's Eye* (New York: Anchor, 1988), p. 130; Margaret Atwood, *The Handmaid's Tale* (New York: Anchor, 1986), p. 116; Pierre Bourdieu, *Distinction: A Social Critique of the Judgement of Taste* (Cambridge: Harvard University Press, 1987).
3. John Steinbeck, *The Grapes of Wrath* (New York: Penguin, 1967 [1939]), p. 455; Toni Morrison, *Beloved* (New York: Knopf, 1987), p. 73; Richard Rorty, *Contingency, Irony, and Solidarity* (Cambridge: Cambridge University Press, 1989), p. xvi; Mark Twain, *The Adventures of Huckleberry Finn* (New York: Penguin, 2014 [1884]), p. 10.
4. Rob Hopkins, 'What Is to What If', *Oxford Food Symposium*, 11 July 2021 <https://www.youtube.com/watch?v=uZREoNTC6mY> [accessed 27 April 2022].

Walking through our Gastronomies: Notes from an Imaginary *Flâneuse*

Plenary Address

Janet Beizer

When Cathy Kaufman and Elisabeth Luard invited me to give this summary paper, I was appropriately humbled: I do have a healthy imagination (some might say an overactive one), but my background is in literary studies; I am not formally trained in Food Studies. We each have a story with this vibrant group of people we collectively call the Symposium: here's mine. In 2013 when I was starting intensive work in French culinary culture and literature, I first heard about the symposiasts and the Symposium from Carolin Young, to whom I owe a huge debt of thanks. I've been attending every year since 2014, save one when I had to drive cross-country at the time of the Symposium. It has become a kind of intellectual and social – and even emotional – home for me. My work since then has benefitted from the kindness of those who were once strangers and have now become friends. At my first Symposium, Elisabeth lugged a huge, heavy cauldron all the way from Wales to Oxford for my presentation, and Cathy and others donated their shrimp tails and fish scales and such from dinner the night before so that I could have leftovers for my presentation on recycled food. Since then, I have found nothing but warmth, generous intellectual exchange, and stimulation flowing from this group. So it is a real pleasure to give something back, and I will start by thanking Cathy and Elisabeth, Ursula Heinzelmann, Claudia Roden, David Matchett, Mark McWilliams, Naomi Duguid, Gamze Ineceli, Carolyn Steel, Jake Tilson, Elaine Mahon, and all of the trustees. I hope I won't betray their confidence.

Cathy and I discussed a title for this summing-up before the event had started; we came up with the broad and comprehensive 'Walking through our Gastronomies: Notes from an Imaginary *Flâneuse*'. The idea of the nineteenth-century street nomad seemed apt to describe the experience of wandering through the unexplored phantasmagoria of the

---

This paper is a transcribed oral reflection on the Symposium that seeks to remember, synthesize, and move forward; the tone is therefore informal. Taking the Symposium virtual brought hoped-for and unanticipated benefits – notably expanded access free from travel limitations, restrictions, or cost – but it also spread sessions out across over three weeks, making such a summing up seem especially valuable.

Symposium. But after living the conference day by day, for twenty-three days now, I feel a need to reframe this venture by offering a metaphor that seems better suited to capture the talks we have heard on the walks we have taken together. Rather than the image of an itinerant observer, a person in the street, I want to suggest instead a butterfly, in part for its lightness of being as it suffuses imagination in a world that often feels far from levity. Last year, as we blasted into the then-unknown territory of the era of pandemic Zooming, the dominant metaphor was a kind of Star Trekkian spaceship, with those in Mission Control working hard to keep us all on track as we bravely went where no Food Symposium had gone before. This year, in a kind of throwaway remark very early on – I believe it was before the taping of Margaret Atwood's talk – Elisabeth turned our attention to butterflies, and Ursula followed up by proposing that 'the spaceship might just become a butterfly'. (Never assume you can just throw out a remark that no one will remember: our words come back to haunt us.) For some reason, Ursula's comment stuck in my mind, and as the sessions unfolded, the image of the butterfly kept returning. I saw it in the eye of the camera shooting the salt mines of Peru from way above – so many butterfly's-eye views of the saltfields, which looked to me like an albino butterfly wing, with the residual crystals on the edges forming the veinature that is usually black. I found it baked into savoury biscuits with rosemary and parmesan cheese in the shortbread butterflies that Chef Cordula Peters prepared to garnish her edible flower salad. Less concretely, the butterfly – this embodiment of metamorphosis – became for me the emblem of transformation and transformability, of the possibility of re-imagining the future of food justice and the evolution of eating. I heard a whisper of wings wafting us between the delights of tasting words and foods together – some virtually – and deep concerns for the insecurities of human food and the plight of the natural world. I came to feel that I was listening to the proceedings of the Symposium a little like the proverbial fly on the wall, but more logically here, a caterpillar on a leaf, which had morphed into a butterfly hovering in the ether. So the *flâneuse* has taken to the sky.

If before this year's Symposium had begun, I thought the task of recapitulating it would be humbling, by the end of the first day, I found it absolutely daunting. I decided to be the best listener I could be, trying to hear echoes, rhyming thoughts and concerns, looking for intersections, intertwined threads, and shared feelings. While you can turn to the papers themselves for individual details, I'll be sharing with you now the patterns I noticed, the resonances I overheard, and the spirit that has been carrying all of us through the last few weeks. I'm interested not only in the content of the gathering, but in the ethos and the pathos of the exchanges. If one of the scientists or linguists or lawyers or sociologists or chefs or historians among us were to do the job of listening and echoing our conversations, the words presented would likely be different. My mind tends to work by association and metaphors, so that is the slant I give to what follows.

First, I want to marvel at the breadth of knowledge in diverse disciplines, histories, places, and traditions – though the last has proved to be a very fraught concept (and one to which I will return). Papers took us to Belgium, Belize, Brazil, Bulgaria, Canada, China, England, France, Germany, Greece, Haiti, Ireland, Ghana, Guiana, India, Italy, Iran,

Jamaica, Japan, Malta, Mexico, Pakistan, Peru, Poland, Puerto Rico, Romania, Russia, Turkey, Saint Lucia, Saint Martin, Singapore, South Africa, Spain, Tobago, Trinidad, Turkey, UAE, US, Zimbabwe, and various extra-terrestrial realms: thirty-eight and counting, since I'm pretty sure I missed a few. Panellists covered a vast range of disciplinary topics, most of them in fact interdisciplinary:

- cooking, cookbooks, culinary history, cooking techniques, equipment, and preparation
- fiction: novels, science fiction, fairy tales, fantasy
- poetry, including sacred and secular varieties
- music, again sacred and secular (both foregrounded and backgrounded)
- religion
- history of various sorts
- rhetoric, linguistics, physiology, etymology, grammar (as in 'Meaty Prepositions')
- science and medicine, health and healing, biology, physiology, otolaryngology
- but also, magic
- archaeology, anthropology, geography
- architecture, design (food design, material design, future design), urban planning
- editing and publishing
- agriculture, sustainability, *ostréiculture*
- environmental and climate studies
- fishing and diving
- gender and gender-power relations, pederasty
- race and power
- empire, colonialism, post-colonialism
- socioeconomics
- journalism, advice columns
- politics and diplomacy – and let me emphasize, everywhere, the political: food and its imaginary cannot, ever, be severed from the political

Claudia Roden mentioned in her opening remarks to the Symposium that food was once considered to be a frivolous subject. I want to echo her, though I might even take out the word 'once': in my experience in the Academy, food studies have still not gained the respect of other disciplines. Yet I would challenge anyone harbouring even a vestige of scepticism about the erudition and wisdom shared here to come be another butterfly at the Symposium, hovering in the ether or hanging from a hedge or a tree. The extraordinary wealth of knowledge carried to the table (or the tablet) at this Symposium was complemented by a truly mind-bending curiosity: an immense, intense, devouring curiosity. This is one of the characteristics of the symposiasts that I cannot ever stop admiring, loving, and will never take for granted. It is like the wonder of children who are never ashamed to show what they don't know – an attitude that is in fact a mark of how much they already know or aspire to learn. 'Hearing something new incites a burning desire to immediately learn more,' said one of us.

With that sense of curiosity, I want to move in on the specificities of the 2021 Symposium, and on what it discovered about the imagination in relation to food. A brief word first on my perspective and approach. I will be less dedicated to the attribution of words to individuals than to the intersection of ideas and the collaborative building of vision. This is partly because of how this Symposium unfolded, and, notably, to the important role of the chat (even more so this year). It isn't always possible in rereading notes and chats to know (or remember) where an idea originated, and more importantly it is striking to notice how many of our expressions are collaborative, how they build on each other. So it is in the spirit of respecting this collaboration that I move forward with a focus on the ideas rather than the authors. As it was said and repeated, there may be no keynote speakers, only keynote listeners: the notes become key when the listeners reconstruct and transform them.

We spoke a lot about time and space, to begin with the largest categories. Time, first. The culinary imagination is strung between the past and the future, tethered to tradition – how tightly or loosely generated a lot of conversation – but straining toward innovation. These questions were often connected to the subject of authenticity – a concept that incited much passionate debate. Etymologically, authenticity has to do with origins and with what came first: with the priority and authority of known experience. Authenticity was put forth as a social constraint, as a colonialist trope, as a nostalgic construction by which we think we remember a time and a place that may not exist anymore or that may never have existed as such ('Imaginary Homelands', as Salman Rushdie puts it).[1] The problematics of identity (cultural and individual) often criss-crossed the binary of tradition and innovation and that of authenticity and inauthenticity. Reading across the vast number of papers and discussions that examined culinary evolution across time and space, I might echo a suggestion that came up repeatedly: in diasporic populations (and who, today, does not belong to one of these?) there can be no authenticity, in the strict sense of the term, but only reimaginings, redevelopings, transitions, and transformations.

Closely related to this last cluster of motifs is that of memory. Memory (and forgetting) was invoked on a regular basis by speakers and chatters in relation to recipes that were not always recorded in writing but passed on by hand, voice, or eyes; in relation to tradition, in relation to the tastes of childhood. Chef Skye Gyngell talked about the imagination we use when cooking as 'very definitely based on nostalgia' and childhood memories, while for others that nostalgia, that return to the past, that madeleine – to sum it up in the archetypal Proustian cake – is a lure, a trap, even a falsehood. In a conversation with Richard Burgin, Jorge Luis Borges recalls his father's comparison of memory to a stack of coins piling slowly one at a time, at the base of which he locates the original event. Each successive memory, he says, is like a coin placed on top of the one beneath. By the time we grow old we have amassed a mound, but we are so far removed from the original experience that instead of memories, all we have are memories of memories, distortions, or reconstructions.[2] Panellists and listeners referred to collective memory of recipes and childhood dishes as similarly distanced from an ostensible ur-source, so that any attempt to rely upon remembrance becomes treacherous and any effort to assert absolute fidelity to an origin – that is, authenticity – becomes a fallacy. Memory was also invoked in conjunction with smell and loss of smell; we learned that our brain circuitry connects the ability to remember with the sense of smell, so that, in the case of anosmia, not only are capabilities of smelling and tasting lost, but also, the ability to navigate the world, and even identity itself.

When memory is projected onto a future orientation, its engagement with imagination becomes instead desire: a more forward-looking yearning and motivation for change. From this angle we heard about innovations of tradition; the design of plates, storage, recipes; the redesigning of modes of eating, ways of planting, and ways of cooking (plant-based food: aquafaba and tofu eggs); the reimagining of distribution, determination, and use of resources, ranging from the very tangible such as salt and meat animals to the more abstract such as labour and the environment. (As we've seen, less tangible does not mean any less complex.) We found that we could sometimes get what we want, if we use the Sifter, thanks to Barbara Wheaton and her team.

We also heard and discussed a lot about the perception and transformation of spaces – and with this, I swerve from the temporal to the spatial axis. From Peruvian chef Virgilio Martinez, we heard that 'our geography is like a wrinkled paper [...] containing completely different ecosystems'. *Terroir* and regionality occupied us a lot, especially but not only in France. If opinion was divided on the nature of *terroir*'s reality, it was less so on the commercial exploitation of *terroir*. We also had a flash lesson about the influence of *terroir* on German Rieslings. We were taken on journeys into imagined food in imagined lands and imaginary outer spaces, but also asked to imagine the transformation of inner spaces, by which I mean both our own planetary spaces and the inner places of our individual bodies in which our brains and spirits live in increasingly confined conditions.

We were asked to imagine a revolution of the imagination – and the tautology is intended. Difficult? Yes. Impossible? I'm not sure. I want to say no. Might we start by clearing a space in our lives and in our minds in which we could sleep more, dream more, imagine more? Might we then work outward from this place to the challenges posed to space on the earth and in its atmosphere? We listened to Rilke's observation that '[t]he future enters into us [...] a long time before it happens.' Maybe you looked for the source, as I did, maybe you too were even further intrigued to read the sentence in its entirety in Rilke's *Letters to a Young Poet*: 'The future enters into us *in this way in order to transform itself in us* long before it happens.'[3] So we are not meant to be passive carriers for the future, according to Rilke, and I think also according to Rob Hopkins: we are meant to work the future through our being so that this transformation can happen. And when Rilke says that the future 'enters into us *in this way*' he is referring to the earlier part of the letter, where he spoke of a sadness that must be attended to because it is a harbinger of something that can happen – the future – but only if the sadness is attended to. Might this be a little like what Rares Crăiuț was referring to when he said that 'we should allow for the cracks where the light comes in'?

This time and space of latency – this cocooning of the future, but also, and first, of the space within our minds – call it the imagination, if you will, the space where the future is being prepared – has affinities with the transitional space of the *Zemirot*, the sacred Sabbath poetry we learned about from Susan Weingarten. There, too, there is a transition, through imaginary food this time, from the material world to a sacred space – she calls it a bubble – outside quotidian time and space. I wonder whether in some sense the Symposium works for us 'believers' as just such a place of incubation, a safe transitional space (and maybe there are echoes of Donald Winnicott there too) – a space for the imagination to work. I'll come back to this, but I want first to move on to some recurrent motifs less obviously bounded by my time and space axes.

Literature and life: we talked a lot about fiction. We were cautioned at the start of the conference by none other than Margaret Atwood not to confuse food in literature and life. Her words were memorable: 'Let me explain about fiction. It's not real life. Every time you put a food in a novel it's for a reason. It's a metaphor. Things are in books for a reason. […] What food does in your life is something else.'[4] As someone who reads fiction for a living, I couldn't agree more. Life and literature are discontinuous domains. And yet I was delighted to hear from symposiast Suzanne Evans, about a reader who was so flooded with desire for a Ploughman's sandwich inspired by the unnamed Victorian novel she was reading during the Covid lockdown that she arranged to procure a contactless, mailbox-delivered apple at 10 pm to make a version of the sandwich and satisfy her craving. Here's literature reaching out beyond the pages of the book. I was similarly happy to hear that the revalorization of regional foods might be as much or more due to the influence of late nineteenth-century novelists as it was to Michelin marketing strategies. In the course of the Symposium, we heard of stories full of recipes and recipes full of stories, to the extent that at times the lines were blurred.

Sex and gender came up in the papers and discussions, though perhaps less than in other years. I won't say more about that because I'm not sure what to make of it. A few papers teased out the collective fantasies attached to the gendering of food and cooking and broached the problems inherent to essentializing men as meat and women as sweets. Fantasy, like literature, has implications for life. In the Cooking Lab on Eggs we were entertained by all manner of erotic anatomical allusions in various Portuguese names of Brazilian dishes that blatantly translated visual impressions.

We thought together often throughout the Symposium about the paradoxical connections between imagination and constraints. More than one paper took account of conditions of enslavement under which culinary traditions nonetheless were dispersed from enslaved people out, and how such conditions precipitated innovation, whether in the case of coffee culture in Malta or in terms of the transplanting and recreation of a culture of roots, shoots, and fruits in the African diaspora. I echo Anthony Buccini's awe at 'the genius of people in an impossible situation who create cuisine' with extremely limited resources. Dire limitations such as near-starvation diets in the camps of the Holocaust and various POW camps also led to startling works of the culinary imagination, including recipe performances and inscriptions. Food shortages, due to genuine scarcity or mismanaged distribution, led to intense suffering, but also to ingenuity and art in Romania and practices such as canning in Bulgaria. The uses of constraint were theorized by Rob Hopkins and fellow symposiasts who noted that the imagination needs limits, citing the rigidity of the sonnet form for example, as well as Dr Seuss's fifty-word limitation in *Green Eggs and Ham*. I'll add that seventeenth-century French theatre is another case in point: the tragedies of Corneille and Racine were born in part of the constraints placed on them in terms of what could or could not be shown on stage and the stringent rules of propriety that had to be worked around.

We collectively advanced a series of tentative definitions as we batted around thorny questions. It may be helpful to offer a partial list that I've culled from comments on our double-pronged theme of cuisine and imagination; these can obviously be extended.

Cuisine
- cuisine is what is made in the kitchen (the word in French means both kitchen and cooking)
- cuisine has taken on another meaning outside of France; cuisine = *haute cuisine*
- cuisine = codified ways of eating
- cuisine = food + other meaning (symbolism, aesthetics) (formulated by Eric Rath)

Imagination
- what turns an accident into serendipity
- the most powerful way of understanding geography
- like a patchwork; you see something and you put it together with something else
- a function of privilege; you can't have imagination until you have your basic needs met
- the ability to see things as if they could be otherwise

Hunger of course reared its head above all over the papers, as an unfortunate stimulus to imagination, as a global injustice that still remains to be addressed, as a pain so dire that its mere evocation reduced many of us to silence. Is this the place to mention cannibalism? Hunger is one of the contexts in which it was evoked, but there were many others. It seemed to come up in almost every discussion, in random ways, as did, by the way, cheese, which I will not expand on further here.

One of the less expected but very prominent recurrences were images of hands. I doubt any of us can forget Nilesh Patel's filming of his mother holding a potato about to be peeled, like a parent cradling a new-born's head, or tenderly patting samosa dough. Nor can we forget Gönül Paksoy's ballet of fruits and vegetables, with her fingers gently settling peaches on a plate, and the Tai Chi rhythms of tucking peppers and carrots into graceful cohabitation. Virgilio Martinez's fingers dug into ashes which were then crushed by his fists working the mortar and pestle. The saltworkers of Maras sifted saltwater sumptuously through their worn hands to retain the crystals. And the camera focused on cooking hands as well, and on the anointment of the plated food with a sprinkling of herbs and salt pulverized between thumb and forefinger. We are reminded of the crucial role of our hands in imagination, and that imagination is always embodied, can never be made to reside in the head alone without risking its impoverishment.

Cooking, we know, involves all the senses. The laying on of hands, the cooking by ear that we hear in Junya Yamasaki's food-truck sizzle of fish on the *plancha*, the sound choreography of the samosas gurgling in oil in *A Love Supreme*, all these bits of evidence will not let us forget the synaesthesia put into play by the active senses of a person cooking.

Chat comments during and following *Anay Kashi* and *A Love Supreme* mentioned being brought to tears by the sheer beauty of these two films – and perhaps too by the sense of loss subtly evoked in both. These were not the only moments when many of us allowed emotion to overcome us, as a few of us candidly admitted. So I want to say a few words about this extra-cognitive element of the Symposium, which is maybe in fact an enhancer of cognition. The degree of affect evoked and expressed in our sessions and the freedom to do the same is something that moves me personally. Papers on pedagogy acknowledged not only the importance of knowledge but also of emotion, inspiration, intuition, and intimacy. They jump from cognition to imagination, as in Peter Hertzmann's statement 'I think, therefore I imagine'. We speak, but as David Matchett witnessed, 'we speak through our tears'.

When we chose the theme for this Symposium four years ago, we had no idea we would be living through the pandemic and unable to meet in person. How eerie, then, that we chose, before the fact, to *imagine* our food and our modes of eating when in fact we had no choice but to do just that or to give up on it all. Yet the tone, as Mark McWilliams remarks in his foreword to the proceedings of last year's first V-Symp – the tone was surprisingly intimate, and this year was at least the same. This isn't the place to expound at length on just why this might have been the case. It's tempting to talk about tradition and innovation, and how they work in tandem, and also to remember that what was established over the years at St. Catz is in fact a sort of 'moveable feast', with all the connotations that befit a banquet. It is surely worth mentioning how many papers and how many chat comments, how many questions and breakout sessions, how many reflections on the Cooking Lab referred to Covid, to lockdown, to confinement, to cooking or eating alone or in small 'bubbles', but also to the joys of improvised commensality, conviviality, and intimacy.

It is also worth mentioning and even emphasizing how many comments in the last few days, live or in the chat, have referred to a sense of grief or loss or sadness as we neared the end of what turned into a three-week Symposium. And so in closing, as I too feel this sense of impending loss, I want to go back to my riffing on thinking about our annual meeting as a kind of secular sacred space. Many mentioned at the outset that the Symposium was the high point of their year, and the Kitchen Table gatherings have been a welcome supplement. So, to try to pull together the content and the spirit of what happened this year, and to move that forward into a transitional space, I ask you: what if...? What if we could find a way to keep thinking together and working together and enjoying together before next July? What if we could imagine a way to project our concerns for food justice and sustainability beyond the Symposium proper?

We are busy people. We have others to care for. We have meals to make, wine to drink, books to write, classes to teach, canvases to paint, businesses to run. But what if...? This is admittedly a half-baked idea. Can we get it to the oven together? Is there a way to collaborate, across the globe, to imagine what we could build and to start to build it together? What would it take to do this? What if we could?

Notes

Most quotations come from symposiasts speaking (or chatting) in recorded Zoom sessions over the three weeks of this year's virtual Oxford Food Symposium.

1. Salman Rushdie, *Imaginary Homelands: Essays and Criticism, 1981-1991* (New York: Viking, 1991).
2. Richard Burgin, *Conversations with Jorge Luis Borges* (New York: Holt, Rinehart and Winston, 1968), pp. 10-11.
3. Rainer Maria Rilke, 'Letter Eight', in *Letters to a Young Poet*, trans. by M.D. Herter Norton (New York: Norton, 1993), p. 49.
4. Margaret Atwood, 'Fictional Foodies: A Conversation about Food and Fiction with Margaret Atwood and Mark McWilliams', *Oxford Food Symposium*, 22 June 2021 <https://youtu.be/8QjVkvzLi6U> [accessed 18 April 2022]

'My Dear Miss Eddington': Reader Letters and Early Twentieth Century Food Media

OFS Rising Scholar Award Winner

Emily Martin

When the *Ladies' Home Journal* shuttered its offices in 2016, the choice to close the 131-year-old magazine did not come as much of a surprise. The decision came two years after the magazine's owner, the Meredith Corporation, announced it would become a quarterly, newsstand-only publication. Commenting on the *Journal*'s demise, Sally Koslow, editor of *McCall*'s for its last eight years of existence, reflected on, 'What We Lose in Losing the *Ladies' Home Journal*?' Koslow remembered that the magazine, which published articles on cooking, housekeeping, and other aspects of domestic life, frequently received letters from readers sharing that 'you saved my life'.[1] Allison Pohle, a 2013 intern for the *Ladies' Home Journal,* recalls her role in answering such reader letters,

> *LHJ* kept a copy of every reader letter. The intern responded to every single one. Sometimes readers asked for old recipes, ones they might even remember seeing in 'a spring issue sometime in the '80s'. I would track these down, copy them and mail them free of charge [...]. Most of the time, however, the readers asked us to listen, to read their stories and to make sure they were heard.[2]

Pohle's observations about these twenty-first-century reader letters point to an important part of the larger story of women's magazines, in which consumers responded to and interacted with these publications as a way to share their own stories, shape published content, and express their subjectivities as a part of a larger community of readers.

Reader letters have always been an important part of the *Ladies' Home Journal*'s history and, more broadly, an integral part of women's print media history. As Rachel Ritchie points out in *Women in Magazines: Research, Representation, Production, and Consumption*, recent scholars of women's magazines have recognized that 'readers were not simply passive consumers of these publications and their contents', and that reader letter pages 'provided a virtual community long before the advent of the digital world'.[3] While of value, studies reliant on published letters are limited in what they have to offer as evidence of readers' engagement with a magazine. The challenge for historians is that – published or not – such quotidian letters have seldom been saved or else have been kept out of archives. When it comes to the *Ladies' Home Journal*, Jennifer Scanlon, a historian of the magazine, reports: 'these reader letters no longer exist'.[4] As such, historians interested in women's magazines and women's food writing tend to overlook reader interactions or to rely on published missives – letters written to the editors or to advice columnists or other published reader submissions. Such analyses are necessarily constrained by source material – writers often carefully chose published letters to emphasize certain perspectives, experiences, or concerns.

This paper interrogates the role and importance of reader letters in early twentieth-century women's food media through analysis of a collection of roughly two hundred recently uncovered letters written by readers of the *Chicago Tribune* to Caroline Maddocks Beard or 'Jane Eddington', author of the 'Tribune Cook Book' section of the newspaper from 1910 to 1930. While women's food media around the turn of the century frequently reinforced domestic hierarchies by painting housewives as incompetent or in need of professional help or advice, the informal and unpublished missives written to Maddocks Beard reveal a far less hierarchical idea of professionalism and expertise extended both to reader and writer. I argue that reader letters exist as a more complicated site of identity formation than has been previously recognized. The ways that readers interacted with Maddocks Beard and her work demonstrates reader investment in the professional framework occupied by women's writers and 'professional' housewives. Readers used correspondence to assume this professional legitimacy for themselves and to imagine themselves as part of a larger community of women.

I suggest that this is a significant and worthy example of imagination – not only to imagine recipes or new foodstuffs, but to imagine a culinary world where 'ordinary' housewives were equal to their professional counterparts and were part of a larger community of cooks and homemakers both eager to learn more and share their particular expertise.

Historians who have studied reader letters to women's print media sources frequently note the importance of this reader input in shaping and guiding the messaging and content of women's print media around the turn of the twentieth century. Jennifer Scanlon writes that Edward Bok, editor of the *Ladies' Home Journal* from 1889 to 1919, understood that readers 'should help frame the discussion of housekeeping'.[5] Soliciting reader letters became an important marketing and communications strategy for Bok. And letter writers would be rewarded for their efforts. A notice given on paystubs to columnists guaranteed that 'the author will give prompt and conscientious attention and reply to all letters from the readers of the *Ladies' Home Journal* that may result therefrom, irrespective of the time of receipt of such letters after the publication of the article'.[6] Bok himself sent out decoy letters to the *Journal*'s columnists to ascertain the quality of their replies. In one letter he penned to columnist Christine Frederick, he wrote, 'I wanted to congratulate you not only on the quick reply which you gave to this letter, but upon the full and comprehensive manner in which you gave it.'[7] High-quality responses to reader letters were essential to Bok's business model, which used the promise of personalized advice as a way to entice potential subscribers. During the last four months of 1912 alone, the *Journal* received over 97,000 reader letters; these numbers only continued to climb as the *Journal's* readership increased.[8] As magazine historian Theodore Peterson writes, with this emphasis on correspondence, '[Bok] helped make the women's magazine an organ of service to its readers, a publication keyed to their interests and practical problems'.[9]

While Edward Bok was one of the first to integrate responses to reader letters into his marketing strategy, reader correspondence with print media (and especially women's print media) was generally commonplace at the turn of the twentieth century. Rob Schorman notes that readers regularly bombarded early twentieth-century mail-order catalogues with letters seeking fashion and personal advice, with some mail order catalogues receiving up to 100,000 pieces of reader mail per day.[10] In a 1921 *Scribner's Magazine* commentary on the volume and type of correspondence mail-order houses receive, Viola Paradise described 'a heavy demand for advice and counsel and general information' in addition to the demand for products and product information.[11] Readers were eager to correspond with trusted publications and saw the potential for casual and familiar encounters through their exchanges.

These letters became an increasingly essential part of how women's print media functioned – women's magazines and women's print media more generally were meant to be intimate and encourage readers to feel connected to their favourite publications and columnists. The scarcity of surviving letters to women's publications, however, has limited historians' ability to consider reader engagement with these works. Many historians of women's media have instead focused on the conscious construction of domestic hierarchies that occurred during the home economics movement popularized in the early twentieth century. Glenna Matthews, a historian of housewifery, writes that 'the birth of home economics as a discipline can only be understood as part of the larger pattern of development of the culture of professionalism in the late nineteenth century'.[12] More recent scholars, including Helen Zoe Veit, have built off of this argument, identifying the proliferation of the domestic sciences as part of an 'ethos of professionalization' that pervaded the domestic realm.[13] Women's media played an essential role in selling this new professional image of housewifery, which has in turn led to the suggestion that women's domestic cookbooks and other food media of this era 'adhered to a rigid format and downplayed the author's creativity and sense of humor, presenting in their stead a didactic, matronly persona'.[14] There was certainly a prevailing emphasis on scientific norms in much of the food writing published in early twentieth century women's print media, but contemporary scholars have conflated the emphasis on such norms with an absence of creativity or the presence of only a rigid hierarchy.[15] These letters push back against that framework and help recentralize the personality and agency of the women reading and interacting with early twentieth century women's media.

Reader letters written to Caroline Maddocks Beard, longtime food writer for the *Chicago Tribune*, suggest that women of the time did not view these spaces as particularly unimaginative or strictly hierarchical sites of identity formation. On the contrary, their letters reveal a spirit of collaboration and creativity, where they positioned themselves in conversation with Maddocks Beard's writing. Maddocks Beard's food writing was heavily in line with the scientific standards and norms of the time: the author page of her cookbook, *The Tribune Cookbook,* described her as 'a firm believer in the doctrine that man can prolong life and maintain health over a long period of time by correct eating'.[16] Unlike women who wrote occasional columns for designated women's magazines, she was the singular food writer for the *Chicago Tribune* and was responsible for writing several articles per week for her column.[17] Given the dearth of extant reader letters written to other authors, especially food writers, at other publications, Maddocks Beard's collection is an especially valuable window into how women interacted with favoured authors in reader letters to early twentieth century women writers.[18]

Caroline Maddocks Beard published several letters she received from readers in her column or otherwise referenced them in her published writing. The 8 October 1928 edition of the 'Tribune Cook Book' contained an abridged version of one such letter from Mrs Charles Werro, who explained that Maddocks Beard's column had been such a help in expanding her culinary repertoire and is 'a great help to young housewives'.[19] Maddocks Beard did not include the entirety of the letter: she chose to elide the section where Werro provided details about her own experience cooking a recipe for chicken and dumplings, instead reprinting only the sections that praised her skill as a teacher and writer. In another April 1925 article on baking powder in cakes, Maddocks Beard wrote that 'practically all letters which come to me from one of the cities where my articles are read are simply letters of commendation, no request of any sort being made'.[20] Another article complained of the number of letters she received expecting her to plan in full elaborate parties or weddings, suggesting that readers instead should be careful to be polite and not 'mandatory' in writing to her.[21] These letters or portions of letters that Maddock Beard elected to publish played up her own culinary expertise and provided a suggested model of correspondence for readers interested in reaching her to follow. Letters she received from readers, however, did not strictly follow this preferred deferential norm.

Many readers wrote to Maddocks Beard asking for kitchen help or culinary advice. But even when asking for help, these letters were often very conversational and informal.[22] One of her readers, Margaret Belknap, wrote her in January of 1929 addressing her as 'My dear Miss Eddington' and adding that 'I address you so informally because I've felt acquainted with you for so long!'.[23] This self-referential and informal greeting suggests that some of her readers felt they had an intimate relationship with her because they had spent so long reading her writing about food. Being so acquainted with her work made her an imagined part of their social circles. Belknap was excited to share that she had cooked a goose for New Year's Day 'carefully, according to your instructions', and requested recipes to make use of the remaining goose fat. She closed the letter to Maddocks Beard by asking whether she owned a copy of '*The Belgian Cookbook*' describing it as one of her 'very cherished possessions' and suggesting it might be a good resource for Maddocks Beard's own extensive cookbook library. In the span of two short pages, Belknap established a personal connection, shared her own culinary successes, asked for advice, and offered a suggestion for Maddocks Beard. This letter is fairly typical of others in the collection. Readers certainly sought her advice and saw her as a culinary authority, but they also saw her as a confidante or even a friend. She was a part of a broader network of people they could reach out to for assistance – favourite authors like Maddocks Beard were potential sources of advice and companionship.

Another letter revealing similar qualities comes from Thomas McManus, an eighteen-year-old boy, who disclosed that his mother had passed away several years ago. As a result of his mother's absence from his life, he said he 'looks five years older than I am, which I suppose is due to improper nourishment'; he hoped that Maddocks Beard, 'as a woman', would understand his situation. He revealed that he looks to her 'as a mother' and asked for her advice on proper nourishment, which he is confident she will provide 'as a woman with a mother's heart and understanding'. Thomas was likely not Maddocks Beard's typical reader, but his letter reveals the ways that readers projected their own personal situation and desire for relationships onto writers. Margaret Belknap saw Maddocks Beard as a dear friend, while Thomas saw her as a surrogate mother – both placed her in their social circle by sending such intimate and conversational notes.

Following a similar tone, Nelle J. Muir wrote that 'I'd love to meet you, and better still to work with you'.[24] Another reader, identified in her letter only as 'W.W.R.', wrote: 'My grandmother – descended from Pennsylvania Dutch ancestry taught me to cook when I was not yet twelve years old… Then came years of school, then years of work – never at home, months at a time without hearing a teakettle sing… but recipes have always fascinated me, yours especially'. She compares the knowledge she received from Maddocks Beard's column favourably to the more familial education she received from her grandmother. Belknap, Muir, and W.W.R. imagine a more intimate and familiar relationship with 'Jane Eddington' than they had in actuality. But sharing these thoughts and praises of her work in their letters to her were part of a broader construction of a relationship between reader and author. W.W.R. closes out the letter, not with continued praise of her writing, but with a culinary suggestion of her own – dropping half a dozen marshmallows into a pot of warm apple sauce as it's being removed from the heat.[25] She credits Maddocks Beard and her grandmother together with much of her culinary success, but she is not afraid to offer her own tried and true recipe suggestion in this piece of correspondence. They helped her become a good cook, but she was a good cook in her own right as well. Receiving instruction in the art of cookery does not undermine her own achievements and successes.

Other readers offered up their own recipes in their correspondence. Mrs Cora Mayell wrote to tell her, 'how much I have enjoyed your deep delving into the historical side of cookery', before sharing her own thoughts on making baked ham and offering her recipe for 'Swiss Salad', a warm German-style potato salad.[26] In addition to these occasional one-off recipe suggestions from readers, readers sent in dozens of recipes for designated recipe competitions hosted by the *Tribune*. Several of the nearly '300,000 recipes of more than a thousand varieties' submitted to the Wartime Recipe Contest, including a recipe for a 'white globe cake' and another for 'potato bread sticks', survive in their manuscript forms in Maddocks Beard's collection.[27] While these were more formalized examples of reader interactions with Maddocks Beard's column, they suggest that readers were certainly eager to share their recipes and hoped to gain their publication in the *Tribune* – and win up to $500. The overall winner, Anne Rankin, reportedly entered her recipe for potato rolls because 'she saw in the potato a chance to help her country conserve'.[28] The sheer volume of entries suggests that such opportunities to express their culinary expertise were quite popular and well received; while only a few recipes survive from normal reader letters, the popularity of such competitions suggests that women were eager to have Jane Eddington test their recipes.

Still other readers wrote to Maddocks Beard for networking purposes or to offer up their own ideas and, in one case, inventions. Dorothy Knight wrote her in August of 1918, identifying herself as 'a home economics graduate' with 'two years experience in home economics fields'.[29] She hoped that Maddocks Beard would be 'so kind as to give her an interview' for editorial work in connection with '[her] training and experience'. Knight understood that her professional training overlapped with Beard's, and hoped she might be a resource for her to continue her career. Another reader, who wrote asking for a copy of her cookbook, added, 'I am graduating from the University of Illinois this June majoring in home economics', saying that she was interested in professional work in Maddocks Beard's department at the *Tribune*, since she knew that 'you have another one of our graduates assisting you'.[30] Viola Wright, a student at Iowa State College, sent her a questionnaire on being a woman writer for her thesis in journalism, hoping she might be able to shed light on her career. In these cases, Maddocks Beard was a useful contact because she was an expert in the field they all hoped to enter – but their letters treat her as a potential colleague or resource and not merely as an expert authority. More broadly, that readers so frequently wrote asking assistance – both on professional matters such as these and on more quotidian culinary disputes looking for recipe help – suggests that they saw a large range of questions and conversational topics as being appropriate to send, even as Maddocks Beard wrote about her frustration at the influx of letters she believed were beneath her. The range of letters suggests that readers had their own ideas about what was appropriate to send to such a writer – these were questions they sincerely needed help with, so why wouldn't they ask for help from someone who they already trusted on culinary matters? There was a genuine desire to learn more and solidify their own cooking skills – both by seeking work with Maddocks Beard and by acquiring a recipe for 'candied kumquats' or menu help for a five-course luncheon.[31]

Yet another letter written to Maddocks Beard contained an original invention – a fork/knife combo sent in response to an article called 'the Salad Fork' the reader thought Maddocks Beard might have some helpful feedback on. In addition to the letter describing the invention, the writer included a rough sketch of the device at the bottom (Figure 1), and requested, 'will you let me hear from you as to your opinion?'.[32]

In these letters, the 'imaginative' flair of Maddocks Beard's readers is most clearly on display. Her readers were not just housewives who looked to her only as a culinary expert. They were domestic scientists in their own right: home economics graduates looking for jobs and professional advice, inventors seeking feedback on their products, and cooks searching for another audience for their favourite recipes. In each of these cases, they recognize the expertise of Maddocks Beard but also understand her as an individual who might be interested in their own work and professional interests. They are attempting to open up a dialogue, viewing Maddocks Beard more as a mentor or potential collaborator than as someone who was somehow above them or superior.

There is some evidence that these letters were the starting points for exchanges of correspondence. By her own account in her column, Maddocks Beard did respond to many requests for help, advice, or for copies of clippings. Lorraine Harned wrote back to such a response to say 'you were precious to write so full and kind an answer to my query about cooking under glass'.[33] Another reader wrote, 'You might recall my name as the "codfish lady" – this time I am sending you an S.O.S. and not a criticism.'[34] This reference to an earlier exchange that has not been preserved suggests that Thompson felt comfortable both offering critiques of Maddocks Beard's work and asking for assistance when she ran into trouble in the kitchen. Viewing these letters as exchanges of information, and not merely one-sided requests or praises of Maddocks Beard's column, highlights the reciprocity embedded in these exchanges, reciprocity which is largely erased in Maddocks Beard's published letter excerpts or discussions of reader letters.

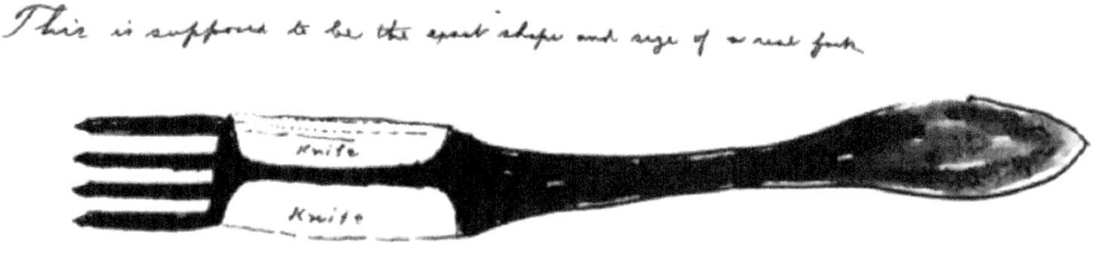

Figure 1. Drawing of fork/knife sent to Caroline Maddocks Beard April 8, 1924.

Despite the displays of culinary skill demonstrated in many of these letters, Maddocks Beard herself was not necessarily a willing participant in her reader's claims to culinary expertise or authority. In one of the few surviving copies of a letter sent by Maddocks Beard to one of her readers, she challenged 'Mrs. Wallace' for criticizing her writing about Creole food. While the original letter sent to Maddocks Beard by Mrs Wallace does not survive, Maddocks Beard responded to the perceived slight on her intellect and understanding of Creole cooking, writing:

> I should never have mentioned the word in the way I did but I am not an ignorant person and I think you are exceedingly rude to say that to anybody. As for me a degree from Wellesley, another from the University of Chicago, a place in *Who is Who in America* and a few other items of the same sort deny any such allegation. Besides I have been in the West Indies, bought Creole books in Cuba, etc. Who are you that you can afford to call anybody ignorant? [...] Tell people that are in error if you want but it is a mighty serious and ugly thing to say to anybody that they are ignorant and nine times out of ten it is a boomerang and the one who says it has but a narrow experience and is rarely an educated person. It is a favorite statement on the ugly lips of the angered illiterate.[35]

Maddocks Beard was evidently quite insulted by the perceived slight on her intellect, responding to her reader not only with a list of her own credentials and accomplishments, but with the implication that Mrs Wallace herself was ignorant and an 'angered illiterate' for distrusting her credentials of authority. Maddocks Beard's response both emphasized her own superior knowledge, both of the topic and in general, suggesting that it was not a reader's place to critique or question her knowledge, especially in such a rude way. Readers were welcome to provide their own suggestions on her column, but she was certainly under no obligation to listen to their suggestions or cede her own authority in any way. There were limitations to her willingness to entertain these non-expert opinions. Status and hierarchy were still of concern to her, even as her readers sent her friendly and familiar letters that emphasized a sense of personal connection over differences in qualifications.

These excerpts come from only a small selection of letters, which are nonetheless indicative of the broader collection, which contains many more requests of clippings, recipes, or menu-planning help. These letters push back against the straightforward narrative that letters offered only one-sided praise of Maddocks Beard's culinary skills. They also push back against the idea that women's food media was uncreative or otherwise undynamic – these letters show a group made up of mostly young women who were eager to build connections, seek advice, and validate their own culinary progress or experiences. Further study of these letters – and a continued search for similar caches of letters – is necessary to construct a more detailed picture of reader interactions with women's food media. This paper is only a starting point, but it suggests that reader interactions with food media are more revealing than has been previously demonstrated.

Notes

1. Sally Koslow, 'What We Lose in Losing *Ladies' Home Journal*', *The Atlantic*, 1 May 2014.
2. Allison Pohle, 'The Last Days of the *Ladies' Home Journal*', *The Hairpin*, 28 April 2015.
3. Rachel Ritchie, 'Introduction', in *Women in Magazines: Research, Representation, Production, and Consumption*, ed. by Rachel Ritchie and others (New York: Routledge, 2016), pp. 1-18 (pp. 17-18).
4. Jennifer Scanlon, *Inarticulate Longings: The Ladies' Home Journal, Gender, and the Promises of Consumer Culture* (New York: Routledge, 1995), p. 244.
5. Scanlon, p. 50.
6. Cambridge, Schlesinger Library, Curtis Publishing Company to Christine Frederick, 16 April 1912, MC 261 fol. 1.
7. Cambridge, Schlesinger Library, Edward Bok to Christine Frederick, 13 January 1914, MC 261 fol. 1.
8. Eventually, the volume of letters became so high that the *Ladies' Home Journal* outsourced the task of answering letters (see Scanlon).
9. Theodore Peterson, *Magazines in the Twentieth Century* (Urbana: University of Illinois Press, 1956), p. 12.
10. Rob Schorman, *Selling Style: Clothing and Social Change at the Turn of the Century* (Philadelphia: University of Pennsylvania Press, 2003), p. 55.
11. Viola Paradise, 'By Mail', *Scribner's Magazine*, 69 (1921), 473-80 (p. 475).
12. Glenna Matthews, *'Just a Housewife': The Rise and Fall of Domesticity in America* (Oxford: Oxford University Press, 1987), p. 150.
13. Helen Zoe Veit, *Modern Food, Moral Food: Self Control, Science, and the Rise of Modern American Eating in the Early Twentieth Century* (Chapel Hill: University of North Carolina Press, 2015), p. 79.
14. Alice Mclean, *Aesthetic Pleasure in Twentieth Century Women's Food Writing: The Innovative Appetites of M.F.K. Fisher, Alice B. Toklas, and Elizabeth David* (New York: Routledge, 2012), p. 2.
15. See McLean.
16. Jane Eddington, *The Tribune Cookbook* (Chicago: Chicago Tribune, 1925)
17. The *Chicago Tribune* enjoyed a circulation of 650,000 in 1925, compared to the *Ladies' Home Journal*'s circulation of nearly 2,000,000 during the same period. In addition to the *Tribune*'s circulation, Maddocks Beard's column was syndicated in a number of smaller regional publication across the Midwest.
18. Maddocks Beard's papers were donated to Wellesley after her death in 1938. Donated after her evidently unexpected death by her brother, the collection was relatively unchanged from its original condition upon donation. The haphazard and disorganized condition of the nearly sixty-box collection, which contained a number of paper scraps, blank pages, and duplicate copies of her work, indicates that the donated papers were not heavily culled or curated upon their donation, which suggests that this sample of letters is fairly representative of those she saved and was not heavily altered for donation to Wellesley. Most letters seem to skew from later in her career and do not address any particular topic. Despite these considerations, however, it is not certain that these are a representative selection.
19. Werro writes in her letter that 'I never kept house, nor cooked, nor spoke English until three years ago when I came to this country', suggesting that Maddocks Beard's column retained some popularity among local immigrant populations in addition to the middle-class, native-born white women typically seen as the readers of such publications (Jane Eddington, 'Learning to Cook', *Chicago Daily Tribune*, 8 October 1929, p. 38).
20. Jane Eddington, 'Baking Powder in Cakes', *Chicago Daily Tribune*, 28 April 1925, p. 22. Of the letters saved, I would not say that 'nearly all' are simply letters of commendation. Whether this is because she saved unusual letters or because this statement is an exaggeration is an open question, though I would

speculate it is the latter, given her evident fondness for sharing the contents of exclusively complimentary letters. It seems unlikely she would save relatively fewer of such letters if they truly made up 'nearly all' of the requests she received; more likely she considered conversational letters not asking for recipe help as strictly 'letters of commendation'.

21 Jane Eddington, 'Clever Hostess Does All Her Own Planning', *Chicago Daily Tribune*, 9 February 1929, p. 9.
22 Since Maddocks Beard wrote under a pen name, a reader's personal familiarity with her can be seen partially through their address. Personal friends seem to frequently address her as Caroline; most letters from readers address her as Jane Eddington. Some address her as 'Jane Edington', suggesting great enough familiarity that they know Jane Eddington is a pen name, though relatively few letters address her as such and not enough information on the letter writers is available to make any firm judgements.
23 Wellesley, Wellesley College Archives, Letter from Margaret Belknap to Jane Eddington, 9 January 1929, MSS-011.
24 Wellesley, Wellesley College Archives, Letter from Nelle J. Muir to Jane Eddington, Undated, MSS-011.
25 Wellesley, Wellesley College Archives, Letter from W.W.R. to Jane Eddington, 18 August 1919, MSS-011.
26 Wellesley, Wellesley College Archives, Letter from Cora Mayell to Jane Eddington, 21 January (no year), MSS-011.
27 'Prize Winners in the Wartime Recipes Contest', *Chicago Daily Tribune*, 25 April 1918, p. B3; See recipes in collection at Wellesley, Wellesley College Archives, MSS-011.
28 'Prize Winners in the Wartime Recipes Contest'.
29 Wellesley, Wellesley College Archives, Letter from Dorothy Knight to Jane Eddington, 18 August 1919, MSS-011.
30 Wellesley, Wellesley College Archives, Letter from Dorothy Styan to Jane Eddington, 5 April 1925, MSS-011.
31 Wellesley, Wellesley College Archives, Letter from Hazel L. Powell to Jane Eddintgon, Undated. MSS-011.
32 Wellesley, Wellesley College Archives, Letter to Jane Eddington, 8 April 1924, MSS-011.
33 Wellesley, Wellesley College Archives, Letter from Lorraine Harned to Jane Eddington 18 March 1929, MSS-011.
34 Wellesley, Wellesley College Archives, Letter from Gertrude Thompson to Jane Eddington 23 August, MSS-011.
35 Wellesley, Wellesley College Archives, Letter from Caroline Maddocks Beard to Mrs Wallace, April 1928, MSS-011. This letter seems to be in response to her article, 'A Creole Stew', published 12 April 1928.

Imaginary Diets, Edible Masculinities: Pirate Food in History and Fiction

Volker Bach

'What Do Buccaneers Eat?'

Among the many things people are eager to learn about the pirates of the Caribbean, what they ate rarely features very prominently.[1] Drink seems a far more immediate concern. Unfortunately, most accounts in modern popular books tend to be rather bleak, influenced heavily by an earlier generation's beliefs about pre-industrial shipboard food. One example reads:

> Food was spoiled or infested with weevils. The water was foul, and to drink it would bring about stomach pains and much worse. One staple meal aboard was hardtack, a flour biscuit made to last months […] The hardtack was soaked and boiled in rum and brown sugar to make it eatable. Pirates would restock their food supply at sea by stealing from other ships. […] One popular dish was Solomon Grundy, which is like a chef salad. The Solomon Grundy contained fish, turtle and meat combined with hearts of palm, herbs and oils. [...] Pirates ate yams, plantains, papayas, pineapples, fruits and vegetables of the tropics. The problem was that food could not be kept on board for long periods before spoilage.[2]

None of this is demonstrably false; water could go off, spoilage was a problem, and there is mention of Solomon Gundy (AKA salmagundi) being eaten by no less than the real Dread Pirate (Bartholomew) Roberts. But very little of this description bears any relation to the food experience of seventeenth-century Caribbean buccaneers we can reconstruct from contemporary sources.

If we delve into these accounts a little deeper, the first voice we encounter is that of Alexandre Olivier Exquemelin, a Huguenot who spent years in the Caribbean and, by his own account, took part in Henry Morgan's raid on Panama before writing the first and by far the most successful history of the buccaneers. His report of their eating habits in the Dutch and German editions is more detailed than in the 1684 English translation. It reads:

> When they have salted as much meat as they think right, they take it onto their ship and store it in a room above the ballast. Of this, they cook twice a day. When the meat is cooked, the fat is skimmed off the top of the cauldron and taken into as many small calabashes to dip as there are wooden platters. And thus they take

their meal of just one dish which often tastes better than the most delicious fare at a lord's table. The captain may not have a better dish than the least among them, or if they notice it is so, they take theirs and put it in the captain's place.[3]

To modern readers, boiled salt pork dipped in pork fat is not a very appealing diet. For the readers of his time, though, it had aspects of wish fulfilment.

Europe in the mid-seventeenth century was suffering from what we know today as the 'Little Ice Age', a dip in overall temperatures that brought crop failure, famine, and disease. At the same time, the continent's population was rising almost everywhere. This was the tail end of the demographic recovery that followed the Black Death, the plague years of the fourteenth and fifteenth centuries, and the convergence of worsening climate and rising populations caused a long-lasting food crisis. To the common people of Western Europe, the post-plague years of labour shortage and open land were a distant but strong memory that still shaped expectations of what a proper life entailed. At that time, meat was commonly served to servants and labourers, and wages could buy ample portions in most years. By the end of the seventeenth century, this state of affairs had ended. Land was in short supply, made worse by enclosures and appropriations. Forestry laws tightened, increasingly banning the poor from hunting, fishing, cutting, or even collecting wood. Work, if it could be had, paid poor wages, nominally often set at reasonably high levels by tradition, but relentlessly devalued by inflationary pressures. And the response of government was often enough draconian, penalizing vagrancy, locking the destitute in poorhouses, or expelling them. These were the people who were brought to the Americas as indentured servants, and their sensibilities coloured views on food both among the colonists and in Europe outside of a small upper class insulated from poverty and dearth.

In the world of Europe's poor, meat was a highly desirable food. It is not coincidental that, around this time, upper-class cuisine moves from conspicuously consuming spices and aromatics to a focus on meat, dairy, sugar, and high-status fruit and vegetables (these, too, feature in the imagined pirate diet). Meat was also associated with status and with masculinity. Soldiers and sailors received daily meat rations even when common workers did not eat meat regularly. The 'roast beef of England' was proverbial not necessarily for its real ubiquity – it was always a middle-class tradition – but for its implications about the national character. Englishmen were meat-eaters, strong, masculine, and rugged.[4] It is in this context we must understand the image of the buccaneer diet.

And it is not just Exquemelin who supports this view. Jean Baptiste Labat, Dominican monk, polymath, and keen observer of all matters culinary, took part in a festivity organized by *flibustiers* in 1698 which he describes in his *Nouveau voyage*. The main course is a roasted feral pig, prepared by enslaved African servants over an open fire. Meanwhile, the *flibustiers* go out to hunt on their own until they are summoned back to the beach by musket shots. The least successful hunter is then punished by having to drink as many glasses of alcohol as the most successful one brought in animals. The only accompaniment to the meat is plantains, and not many because 'the fat and the lean of the pig serve them for meat and bread'.[5]

These descriptions are not purely fictional. Exquemelin and Labat both tell the now-familiar story of the *boucaniers*, hunters who went after feral cattle and pigs in the northern highlands of Santo Domingo in the early decades of the seventeenth century. Cattle were prized for their hides, pigs for their meat which they salted and hot-smoked on a *boucan*, a wooden platform erected over a firepit.[6] They spent months in the forest, in small groups living in temporary camps, before they carried their takings to the coast to sell to planters and merchants. This vision of free hunting, ready access to the bountiful resources of a rich, empty land, also would have contrasted strongly with the limits that Europe's poor faced at every step.[7]

It is telling that Exquemelin places his account of meals in the context of a wider description of buccaneer society. He describes their egalitarian ethos, the way they elect their leaders, jealously guard their independence, and keep order among themselves by a set of mutually agreed-upon rules. This, too, would have been familiar to anyone who lived among the artisans and labourers of Europe who organized in self-governing associations and celebrated their community in shared feasts. Many ordinances regulating these festivities survive. They focus on keeping the peace, defining what food and drink was to be provided, and ensuring everyone had equal or appropriate shares. Buccaneer culture as Exquemelin knows it is the culture of the working class along Europe's Atlantic seaboard, released from the constraints of state and church. The fact that, as he freely admits, the buccaneers keep indentured servants and slaves would not have detracted from that in their eyes.

Though Exquemelin's description was influential in shaping perceptions of the 'pirate diet' in general, it is contradicted not only by other authors, but also by his own eyewitness account of the 1671 expedition against Panama. He lists provisions taken from ships, bought from Native Americans, or plundered or extorted from Spanish settlements, and almost always mentions cassava and maize. This matches what William Dampier writes of a later, ultimately unsuccessful 1679 raid on Panama, though he also mentions plantains as a frequent item in the diet ashore. Jean-Baptiste Labat, a Dominican friar and naturalist who visited the French Antilles in the 1690s, even states that French *flibustiers* subsisted almost entirely on maize that they cooked 'like rice' with meat or fish – and counted themselves lucky to have anything to go with it.[8] Interestingly, in his description of an unfortunate expedition to Costa Rica, Exquemelin describes how buccaneers prepare manatee with maize cooked as *gruit* (groats, i.e. porridge).[9] Perhaps most tellingly, among the descriptions of food preparation that Exquemelin provides, the only recipe that he states with some pride that he prepared himself is roasted shoe leather.[10] How must we imagine their daily fare then?

Food Webs and Food Resources

To try to reconstruct the actual diet of the buccaneers, we need to look at the environment they lived in. This was very different from the natural paradise that pirate romance imagined from very early on.[11] The Caribbean after Columbus experienced one of the few events in history that can rightly be described as apocalyptic. Contact with alien cultures, animals, plants, and diseases had a far-reaching impact throughout the world, but in the Americas it was devastating.[12] The population losses through disease, enslavement, and war are estimated as high as 95%, something very few societies were able to survive. Invasive species, some introduced deliberately by European colonizers, spread across islands and continents, often with destructive results. Social fabrics frayed and established cultural patterns collapsed under the weight of conquest and mass death. The island home of the buccaneer resembled prelapsarian Eden less than it did the world of Mad Max.

What made buccaneering possible was first of all the extremely low population in much of America at the time. The Caribbean is roughly comparable in size with the Mediterranean, but in this world, the seven hundred men Henry Morgan led against Porto Bello were a military force capable of crushing everything in their path.[13] Cities were few, surrounded by large areas of almost empty land. Native communities were small, often reduced to a precarious existence at the margins of the new European-dominated order after the loss of their established relations and resources. Only the territories of the old Pre-Columbian civilizations – Peru and New Spain, especially the highlands around Mexico City – continued to support dense populations. The economy of the Spanish Main was dominated by export-oriented activities that went for low-hanging fruit, resources that could be exploited at relatively low capital cost or yielded high returns.

The business of the *boucaniers* depended on yet another aspect of this environment: feral animals. The deliberate release of European livestock into the American environment had been Spanish policy from the earliest days of colonization. As they entered formerly cultivated, now empty lands with few predators, parasites, or diseases to reduce their numbers, the result was a population explosion. Spanish settlers often managed these populations in a semi-feral state, but across much of the Caribbean, feral cattle and *cochons marons* could be had for the taking.[14] *Boucanier* hunters prowled the forests of Hispaniola, providing dried cattle hides and the preserved meat of wild pigs as trade goods to settled communities in the Americas and passing merchant ships.[15] This background – though in the cases of many individuals, it was a case of fictional shared ancestry – likely goes some way toward explaining the buccaneer diet's emphasis on meat.

Contrary to the assertion made by Exquemelin, the sources agree that buccaneers relied on plant foods for a large part of their caloric intake. They were able to draw on a wide variety of food resources, an emerging 'tropical' crop package that resulted from a number of successful exchanges across oceans. While cassava, sweet potatoes, and maize were native to the Americas (cassava bread is described and remarked on in almost every travel account), plantains, another important food resource, were recent imports from Eurasia, likely via the Canary Islands or West Africa.[16] Coconuts, interestingly, may even have crossed the Atlantic by natural means and arrived in the Caribbean before Columbus. A large number of other fruits and vegetables, too, were European or African imports, a fact that contemporary travel accounts are usually aware of, though they are not always correct on the details.

The sources suggest buccaneers relied on Native Americans to supply the majority of their plant foods. This, too, was not an anomaly. In fact, the focus of many European settlers on cash crops and exportable commodities meant that Native American communities could fill a market niche trading food for European goods. Merchant vessels coming to the Caribbean had relied on this trade as early as the 1550s, and Spanish colonial cities often fed themselves through tributary relationships with surrounding Native communities.[17] There were even established meeting points where ships could signal their interest in bartering for provisions. The degree to which the seemingly primeval village agriculture of the Caribbean was actually an adaptation to this new market is unclear, but it is obvious that a surplus existed and compensation was expected.[18]

A further resource that records mention regularly was seafood. Ship's crews fished and gathered shellfish when ashore, but buccaneer crews – and this appears to have been specific to them – took aboard Native Americans who specialized in fishing, hunting turtles, and harpooning manatees for food. Exquemelin describes them as enslaved abductees, while Ringrose and William Dampier describe more cordial relations. Their 'Mosquito strikers', recruited among the Miskito with whom English colonists had entered into an alliance, move with ease between the two cultures, adopting and shedding English names, clothing, and language at will.[19] These men went into action whenever crews put into anchorages, providing fresh fish and meat. As part of a diet, this was not unusual; turtles, fish, and shellfish were commonly eaten by Natives and colonists alike across the Caribbean.

Buccaneers were in the habit of taking things by force and that applied to food as much as anything else. When we take the trouble to develop a timeline of the expeditions for which we have records, it becomes evident that a good deal of their time was spent robbing the supplies they needed to stay afloat. The frequency with which Spanish colonists approached landing parties to offer maize, cassava, and cattle as ransom to prevent the destruction of valuable property ashore suggests this was as integral to buccaneering as protection rackets are to the Mob.[20] Ships and coastal settlements were also routinely searched for victuals, a practice Ringrose refers to as 'rummaging'. This kind of behaviour was not limited to pirates, either.[21]

These data points lead to the question how victuals thus obtained were prepared. The imaginary pirate diet is strongly coloured by the unhelpful fact that fiction's most famous buccaneer, Long John Silver, is a peg-legged ship's cook lording it over a fully equipped galley.[22] In reality, it is unlikely either was found on buccaneer vessels. Many raiding expeditions were carried out in small, lightly armed craft, sometimes little more than dugout canoes, and cooking equipment was at best rudimentary. Large cauldrons were the most prominent piece of kitchen gear, and when Dampier's crew found themselves underequipped on their South Sea raid, they casually took some from a sugar mill.[23] Cooks, too, are in short supply in our sources. The enslaved Native American cook serving the Spanish commander Manoel Rivera Pardal was taken captive by buccaneers in 1670 and served them in the same capacity afterwards, but that incident has more to do with humiliating an enemy than the usual composition of ships' companies.[24] We know from casual references in our sources that crews often travelled with enslaved African servants whose duties may have extended to food preparation.[25] More likely, the buccaneers themselves, coming from what we would call the food processing business, would have done much of the cooking themselves. By all accounts they were skilled at preparing meat, and very likely their abilities extended to less symbolically charged foodstuffs.

Dietary Distancing

The diet we can reconstruct from a careful reading of the sources – a broad, multifarious food web based on a thorough familiarity with the natural environment, cordial relations with its native inhabitants, and a good dose of defiance in the face of established power – looks very attractive to moderns. It seems to have appeared much less so to writers of the time, or of the subsequent two and a half centuries. The imaginary diet of pork and turtle, rum and salmagundi all but completely displaced the more complex historical reality, and it very likely already did so in the image buccaneers sought to project to the outside world. To try and answer why that was, we should look at another part of Father Labat's work.

In the fourth volume of his *Nouveau voyage*, Labat describes the habits of a group of people living in the French Antilles.[26] Their primary diet was maize, cassava, and sweet potatoes served with salt meat or fish. They enjoyed shellfish and relished fruit. For their festivities, they roasted whole pigs and gathered for long nights of dancing, drinking, and merriment. Liquor was their particular delight, something they were prone to stealing and consuming in copious quantities. Though normally dressed in coarse linen clothes for work, they turned out in ruffled shirts for special occasions, wearing fine hats, gaudy vests, and short, belted jackets made of light, colourful cloth and, if they were rich enough, adorned with buttons of precious metal and gems. These people were the enslaved Africans.

Anyone the least bit familiar with the reality of slavery in the Caribbean will appreciate that this description bears little resemblance to reality. As with the writings of Exquemelin on buccaneering, the details of personal observation give the lie to a generalized tropical idyll. What is striking, though, is to what extent this picture agrees with that of the *flibustier*, the buccaneer, the pirate. This is not entirely surprising since they inhabited the same environment, relied on the same natural resources, and even inhabited a similar social space, remote from the rarefied circles of the ruling class. But for precisely this reason, it is obvious why it would have felt important for the buccaneers – and even more so, for their chroniclers – to emphasize the distance between them.

To the buccaneers themselves, at least initially, the matter may not have been race as much as class. Exquemelin's original Dutch text uses the same word to describe indentured Europeans and enslaved Africans, seeing no distinction in principle between their states. His accounts of the cruelty that especially English masters visited on their inferiors are hair-raising, and starvation features prominently. Meat, eggs, and wine are among the things that they lacked, and that a particularly cruel master on St. Christopher would always place by the body of a deceased servant to prove he had been well provisioned.[27]

Real-life buccaneer society reflected these differences – *boucanier* hunters and logwood cutters used indentured servants for labour, and ships' companies kept slaves. Such social distinctions appear to have mattered less among them than in settler colonies, but they were hardly insignificant. An indentured servant brought from Europe represented a significant investment that a *boucanier* needed to recoup, and a slave valuable property. European servants joining their ranks could expect to rise to full membership if they survived the ordeal – and poor food does not appear to have featured much in that – but the fate of an African fallen among buccaneers seems to have depended on spur-of-the-moment decisions. Some ex-slaves of African ancestry became buccaneers, especially early on. A former Spanish slave known as Diego Lucifer captained a Dutch raiding vessel in the 1630s.[28] At other times, and especially once a ready market existed, slaves were treated as loot. After their victorious return to English waters, Ringrose's account mentions that the crew voted to liberate one slave and gift another to their captain as an extra bonus. The rest were sold off, and the cash distributed.[29]

Imagining a Pirate Diet – Wealth, Masculinity, and Independence

All the elements of the imagined buccaneer diet that contemporary descriptions and later fiction immortalize owe their symbolic significance to this particular situation. It is important to stress here that imagined is not the same thing as imaginary. All its elements really existed, and doubtlessly buccaneers hoped and possibly sought to eat this way. This is not uncommon for the food habits of heavily fictionalized people in general. Police officers on patrol are likely to eat at fast food outlets more often than most of us, and much military food is genuinely bad. Neither coffee-and-donuts nor 'shit-on-a-shingle' adequately represent a more complex reality, but they evoke group identification inside and outside. Buccaneer food likely functioned in much the same way.

Meat, as was already pointed out, had a powerful symbolic pull for Europeans at the time. Interestingly, the same probably was not true for Native Americans in the region, whose intake of animal foods depended far more on seafood. Buccaneers identified as hunters, and skill at processing meat was common enough among their ranks to make not just butchering cattle, but competently preserving all manner of meat something any crew was readily expected to manage. Festivities like that described by Labat had roasted meat as their centrepiece – a turtle might do, but a buccaneer feast of fish and crab, however sumptuous, would be incomplete. Meat, of course, was not just rare and coveted in Europe, but also a foodstuff that was rationed to everyone who had to depend on social superiors to provide it. Slaves, indentured servants, apprentices, and soldiers might have had more of it than the average European peasant, but they did not enjoy the surfeit that Exquemelin paints.

Alcohol was another issue, though one that plays a more prominent role as time progresses. It is interesting that, although Exquemelin and Dampier devote significant space to various alcoholic beverages prepared from manioc roots, plantains, sugarcane, palm juice, honey, and fruit, they almost never mention distilled liquor. Labat describes the production of rum – he refers to it as *guildive*, probably the origin of the English slang term kill-devil – but mainly mentions it as a slave drink. Imported European brandy probably held significant status among the buccaneers – Exquemelin writes that the ritualistic drink of warm marrow from a kill was known as 'taking brandy' – but it was an expensive treat, not daily fare.

The most important aspect of the buccaneer diet, though, is the deliberate absence of power relationships. They were, as Exquemelin writes, allowed to take away the captain's portion if they perceived him having better food than the least among them. Every man was entitled to eat and drink as much as he wanted, with rationing allowed only in times of shortage. Hunting, an endeavour viewed as depending on individual skill and marksmanship, provided meat for the table and proved the individual resourcefulness of these men.[30] They were beholden to no master, dependent on no community, and reliant on their own courage, skill, and tools only. It is probably not a surprise that the legend of the pirate was most influential in liberal, capitalist societies that celebrated a 'bootstrap' myth. It belongs firmly with the trapper and the cowboy among the archetypes of white manliness that tell how the west was won.

Notes

1. 'Pirate' here is shorthand for armed combatants of mainly French, English, and Dutch origin who carried out seaborne raids on Spanish colonial possessions from bases in the Caribbean and colonial North America in the seventeenth and early eighteenth centuries. It may need saying at this point that actual pirates in the Roman law sense probably never existed, and that these men (and occasionally women) certainly were no such thing.
2. Julio Rodriguez, *Cooking Columbus: A History of Cooking in the Caribbean* (Bloomington, IN: Xlibris, 2018), ch. 9.
3. Olivier Alexandre Exquemelin, *Piraten der Karibik* (*Die Amerikanischen Seeräuber*, repr. Königswinter: CloudShip, 2007), I, p. 7. English translation mine.
4. Ben Rogers, *Beef and Liberty: Roast Beef, John Bull and the English Nation* (London: Vintage, 2003).
5. Jean Baptiste Labat, *Nouveau voyage aux isles d'Amerique* (Paris: La Haye [P. Husson], 1722), IV, p. 216.
6. It is interesting that while English derived its word for seaborne looters, buccaneer, from the French *boucanier*, the French adopted the term *flibustier*, probably derived from the Dutch *vrijbuiter*, for the same profession. In French, a *boucanier* was always and only a hunter.
7. The long, bitter conflict between peasant poachers and forestry authorities as it played out in Southwestern Germany is studied in Wilfried Ott, *Ich bin ein freier Wildbretschütz: Geschichte und Geschichten um die Wilderei* (Leinefeld: DRW-Verlag Weinbrenner, 2000). It was not fundamentally different in other parts of the continent.
8. Labat, II, p. 330.
9. Exquemelin, II, p. 7.
10. Exquemelin, II, p. 5.
11. Charles Kingsley's nineteenth-century poem 'The Last Buccaneer' describes golden fruit and tall palms, colibris and parrots, hammocks by the beach, and submissive 'negro lasses', all tropes that were by then already well established. We find much the same imagery used to recruit colonists for early Caribbean ventures, and it still serves to attract tourists to these islands (*A Victorian Anthology, 1837–1895*, ed. by Edmund Clarence Stedman (Cambridge: Riverside, 1895) <https://www.bartleby.com/246/576.html> [accessed 11 May 2021]
12. This field is still contentious in detail, and research continues to advance, but the most influential descriptions are found in Jared Diamond, *Guns, Germs and Steel* (New York: Norton, 1997); Charles C. Mann, *1491: New Revelations of the Americas before Columbus*, 2nd edn (New York: Random House, 2011); and Alfred W. Crosby, *Ecological Imperialism: The Biological Expansion of Europe 900-1900* (Cambridge: Cambridge University Press, 1986).
13. Michel Christian Camus, *L'île de la Tortue au coeur de la flibuste caraïbe* (Paris: Editions L'Harmattan,

1997), p. 79 This was not limited to the latecoming colonists: when the Spanish took Tortuga from the first French colonists, they left behind a garrison of one hundred men to hold it.

14 The concept of '*maron*' – a return to the wilderness – is central to many aspects of Caribbean reality in the seventeenth century. Livestock were '*marons*' if they went feral, escaped African slaves formed communities referred to as '*marrons*' or '*cimarrones*' beyond the reach of Europeans, and '*marooning*' – abandoning in the wilderness – was a punishment used among the buccaneers. The buccaneers themselves can be seen as semi-feral Europeans, and the Caribbean was probably closer to Hobbes' conception of the state of nature than anywhere else on the planet at the time – though still not very.

15 Camus, p. 49. This business should not be imagined as primitive. Some *boucaniers* entered contractual relationships with correspondents in European ports who purchased their goods; provided them with arms, powder, and tools; and contracted for indentured servants to support them. They were part of a monetized, global economy well before they turned to privateering.

16 As early as the sixteenth century, Jean de Léry mentions as a stereotype that Europeans going to America needed to accustom themselves to eating bread made from roots (*Unter Menschenfressern am Amazonas Brasilianisches Tagebuch 1556-1558* (*Histoire d'un voyage fait en la terre du Bresil,* Paris: Antoine Chuppin, 1578; repr. Tübingen: Horst Erdmann Verlag, 1968), p. 58).

17 Both de Léry and Andreas Ultzheimer, surgeon on a number of Dutch ships trading in the West Indies around 1600, describe Natives coming to the shore to meet incoming ships with deliveries of fruit and cassava bread to trade for 'fish hooks, mouth organs, combs and such' (Ultzheimer, *Beschreibung etlicher Reisen* (Gütersloh: Bertelsmann, 1971), p. 72).

18 The Ringrose journal attached to the 1684 English edition of Exquemelin records that buccaneers were welcomed with a gift of two plantains and a piece of sugarcane each, but 'when these were consumed, if we would not truck (i.e. barter), we must have starved' (*Bucaniers of America* (London: William Crooke, 1684), IV, p. 7).

19 See especially William Dampier, *A New Voyage around the Terrestrial Globe* (London: James Knapton, 1698, p. 84). Exquemelin writes that two 'strikers' could supply a thousand men in four hours of fishing. He also describes buccaneers entering into temporary marriages with Native American women and living in their communities for months or years, so the barrier appears to have been porous in both directions (ch. 8).

20 A prominent case of this was 4000 *hanegas* of maize given as ransom for Morgan sparing Rio de la Hacha (Exquemelin, 3, p. 1) and 500 head of cattle as part of the ransom paid to L'Olonois' crews for Maracaibo (Exquemelin, 2, p. 2). Quotidian reality is more likely reflected in the 80 cattle promised (but not delivered) to Captain Sharp's crew for a sugar mill (*Bucaniers of America*, IV, p. 95).

21 De Léry recounts the looting of food supplies from English merchants in times of peace with the flippant dismissal, '*c'est la guerre et la coutume*' (p. 61).

22 The inspiration for this figure likely came at least in part from a famous etching by Thomas Rowlandson. Navy ship's cooks were often invalids in need of a job that did not require the use of all limbs. While buccaneer crews had rules for compensating the loss of limbs, there is no record of them hiring on invalid comrades – or anyone else – as cooks.

23 Dampier, p. 200.

24 Jon Latimer, *Buccaneers of the Caribbean: How Piracy Forged an Empire* (Cambridge: Harvard University Press, 2009), p. 200.

25 Exquemelin mentions two slave women killed as they were sent ashore to fetch water (III, p. 7). Ringrose records the rare data point that a crew of forty-seven travelled with five enslaved African servants (*Bucaniers*, IV, p. 141). We do not know how representative this number is.

26 Labat, IV, p. 151.

27 Exquemelin I, p. 7.

28 Latimer, p. 54.

29 *Bucaniers*, IV, p. 280.

30 The descriptions given by Exquemelin and Dampier suggest actual commercial hunts were a collective operation.

Chaat: Why India's Beloved Snack is Also a Feat of the Imagination

Vidya Balachander

Until the COVID-19 pandemic caused a widespread disruption of urban lives, a scene played out in almost identical fashion across Indian cities. Shortly before dusk, as offices closed for the day, hungry professionals and students disgorged from buildings and huddled at street corners in small groups. Usually, they could be found surrounding a street food vendor with a pushcart.

From a distance, it would seem as if the vendor held their rapt attention like a conductor overseeing an orchestra. His quicksilver hands chopped, tossed, mixed, squeezed, and muddled ingredients with practised ease. In just a few moments, the famished onlookers would have been handed different kinds of *chaat* – sweet-sour-spicy plates of snacks, crowned with a flourish of crunchy toppings. For a few minutes, the clamour of waiting would be replaced with the complete sensory pleasure of eating a plate (or several) of *chaat*.

Widely believed to have been derived from the Hindi / Urdu word *chaatna*, which means to devour or lick clean with one's fingers, *chaat* refers to a genre of savoury snacks that are popular both in India and in neighbouring countries such as Pakistan, Nepal and Bangladesh.[1] There are several theories regarding its origins, including a widely cited story that Mughal emperor Shah Jahan's chief physician ordered the royal cooks to create foods laden with spices to counter a cholera outbreak.[2] Another popular story suggests that *chaat* may have been created as a safeguard against the highly polluted waters of the River Yamuna.

Even though there is little definitive proof that either of these stories has a factual basis, there is evidence to suggest that *chaat* – or at least early versions of it – have been a part of the Indian diet since at least the eleventh century. Colleen Taylor Sen writes about some of the recipes mentioned in the *Manasollasa*, a Sanskrit composition in verse by King Somesvara III, a twelfth-century ruler of southwest India. Even though they are now known by different names, some of the dishes mentioned in the *Manasollasa* could be considered forerunners of ingredients used in modern-day *chaat*. As Sen writes:

> Lentil or chickpea flour mixed with asafoetida, salt, sugar, ground black pepper, cardamom and water was ground into a paste, formed into little discs and deep-

fried to make purika, a forerunner of modern papdi (round crispy wafers used in the popular street food papdi chaat). A fermented paste of ground urad dal and black pepper was shaped into balls and deep-fried to make vadika, which was soaked in milk or yoghurt. A modern incarnation of this is the popular Indian street food dahi vada – fried spicy lentil balls smothered with fresh yoghurt and topped with ground cumin, other spices and a sweet-and-sour chutney.[3]

Like other time-honoured Indian culinary traditions, *chaat* has not just survived but also extended far beyond its traditionally defined contours to become a nationwide phenomenon. In this paper, I argue that, even though *chaat* is often subsumed within the larger and more generic category of street food, it should also be seen as – and its popularity attributed to – a feat of the imagination.

Although it may seem like a random assortment of ingredients, thrown together by the experienced hand of a *chaatwallah* (or purveyor of *chaat*), a good plate of *chaat* demands an imaginative yet intuitive understanding of colours, flavours, temperatures, textures, and how they can be stacked and interplayed to create a memorable mouthful.

Here imagination as it pertains to *chaat* should not just be interpreted literally. With a multitude of iterations of the same dish, made with similar ingredients but distinguished by regional inflections, *chaat* challenges the reductive notion of a pan-Indian uniformity when it comes to cuisine and taste preferences. At the same time, it also serves as a link that demonstrates the elemental appeal of the trifecta of sweet-sour-spicy flavours and the ways in which they are expressed in different parts of the country and the subcontinent.

Disguise or Design?

Although there are simply too many types of *chaat* to list, the most popular kinds usually follow a 'formula' of sorts. This includes a crunchy, deep-fried element, such as hollow spherical *puris* made of semolina, atta, or refined flour; *papdis* or thin, wafer-like discs, or samosas; a tangy-sweet chutney made of dates or tamarind; a spicy chutney made of fresh coriander leaves and mint leaves; and flavouring agents such as *chaat masala*, a blend of freshly roasted and powdered spices that adds an earthy kick. Apart from these, *chaat* also calls for ingredients that lend heft and body, such as boiled chickpeas, potatoes, and dried peas; diced onions and tomatoes; crisp *sev* (thin, deep-fried noodles made of gram flour); and unsweetened yoghurt.

The predilection for deep-fried, carb-heavy ingredients as building blocks for *chaat* has given it a reputation of being unwholesome 'fast food'. But if you set aside questions of how these individual elements are prepared, it becomes clear that *chaat* was never meant to be just a vehicle for indulgence. Traditionally, it was an imaginative and carefully calibrated way to soothe stomachs and aid digestion, especially during the change of seasons. Food writer Anoothi Vishal notes how it is not a mere coincidence that the *pani* (or flavoured water) used in *golgappas* (hollow *puris* filled with potatoes, chickpeas, or stewed dried peas and fiery *pani*) is laden with coriander and mint leaves along with spices such as *zeera* (cumin) and *hing* (or asafoetida):

> Long thought to have curative powers, the cumin-laced water (without bolder spices like chillies but often with other therapeutic ingredients like *hing*) was given to lactating mothers and those whose digestion needed a kick, especially as the weather turned warm in the Indo-Gangetic plain. (It is more than a coincidence that the *chaat* season began with Holi in spring and continued through the long summer.) Because *pudina* (mint) was thought to be cooling, a fistful of dried, crushed leaves would be added to the therapeutic *jal zeera*.[4]

Chaat – at least in its most elemental form – was created with an eye on good health. Its clever packaging of health-giving properties in patently delicious disguise is among its most imaginative feats.

One *Chaat*, Many Iterations

Chaat is often believed to have originated in the northern Indian state of Uttar Pradesh.[5] Cities in Uttar Pradesh, such as the state capital Lucknow, Varanasi, and Prayagraj, boast a robust *chaat* culture furthered equally by entrepreneurs who have been in the trade for generations and customers who are discerning about quality and flavour.

Here, in what can be considered the heartland of traditional *chaat*, it is often made to an exacting standard. The *aloo tikkis* (round or heart-shaped potato patties, sometimes stuffed with *matara* or white peas or fresh green peas) I tried in Lucknow, during a visit in early 2020, were unlike those I had eaten anywhere else. Fried in ghee, they were shatter-crisp yet far from stodgy, offering the unalloyed pleasure of creamy, well-cooked potatoes, topped with a dollop of yoghurt and *saunth*, a sweet chutney flavoured with dried ginger.

But the versatility of *chaat* means that *aloo tikki* has long crossed state lines and acquired nationwide popularity. (The scope of this paper does not extend to northeastern India, which has significantly different dietary habits from the rest of the country). The complexion of the dish varies depending on where you eat it. For instance, in the Chembur area of Mumbai, where there is a significant population of the Sindhi community, the same potato patties are likely to be stuffed with *chana dal* and served with tamarind and coriander chutneys.

Perhaps the best example of *chaat*'s shape-shifting adaptability is *pani puri*. The dish goes by different names across the country; the change in geography also translates to subtle differences in its flavour profile. In Delhi, *pani ke batashe* means flatter *puris* made of atta or semolina stuffed with spiced potatoes and sour-spicy water, whereas in Mumbai *pani puri* implies semolina or refined flour *puris* stuffed with boiled peas or sprouts and a balanced mix of sweet and spicy chutneys. In Bangarpet, in South India, which boasts its own unique spin-offs of *chaat*, *pani puri* may come with hearty boiled, dried peas and the heady kick of garlic-scented water.

Bengaluru resident Ajit Bhaskar, a physicist with an avid interest in food and cooking, told me about the nuances that separate his city's *chaat* scene from that of other cities. He mentioned that the name Bengaluru is in fact derived from the Kannada phrase, '*bendha kaala ooru*' (or the town of boiled beans): 'Traditionally, the weather in Bengaluru used to be cool all year round. So boiled beans provided comfort food.'[6] True to its name, dried and stewed beans and peas feature in many versions of the city's *chaat*, including *masaal puri*, an iconic regional dish that features spicy peas stuffed into *puris*, topped with finely chopped onions, tomatoes, and coriander leaves.

In this way, *chaat* resists narrow definitions of ownership to any state or community. Even when it is tempting to pin it down to a place, such as the world-famous *bhel puri* to the city of Mumbai, one is reminded that *bhel puri*, too, came about from a mélange of cultural influences. As the well-known food writer Vikram Doctor says, 'It's rooted in the mixing together of two culinary trends [… :] the puffed rice snacks that are popular in the south and east, such as Kolkata's *jhal muri*, and the *chaat* ingredients from the country's north.'[7]

The Street and the Showman

Imaginative not just in its physical expression, *chaat* also necessitates a certain rhythm and quality of interaction between the *chaatwallah* and his customers. Often bearers of a legacy that has been passed down from generation to generation, *chaatwallahs* learn the nuances of the trade through observation and experience. But ultimately, even though a carefully calibrated eye on quality can ensure a degree of success, the *chaatwallah* also needs to sharpen an equally – if not more – important prerequisite for success. Constantly vying with other vendors, attractions, and distractions on the streets, *chaatwallahs* must have a flair for showmanship.

Chaiwallahs cannot be aloof or distant if they expect to hold their audience in rapt attention. Some of the country's most famous *chaatwallahs* have an almost theatrical quality, calling out to customers with distinct tunes or juggling plates of *dahi vada* overhead, as the proprietor of Indore's Joshi Dahi Vada (also called the 'Flying Vada House') is famous for doing. In this way, a *chaatwallah* bridges the artistic distance that often separates a chef from his clients, even in the most intimate of settings. The *chaatwallah* draws you into his periphery as you await your turn. In turn, feedback is provided in real time, and tweaks to the dish made accordingly.

In this interaction between a showman and his audience, the street also has a significant part to play. On the one hand, the spectacle of *chaat* effectively converts a shared experience in a public space to a private one. On the other hand, the public nature of the process in turn contributes an air of liveliness to the street. As Harris Solomon notes:

> If the street is both the substance and site of food processing […] then it cannot

only be understood as a location for food's consumption. [...] Studies of street food tend to cast the street as the bit part, with food as the charismatic lead. This approach leaves the street's transformative potential underexamined.[8]

I argue that *chaat* is the conduit for a more joyful experience of the streets, especially against the backdrop of the deep socioeconomic divides of the subcontinent. In that moment when one waits in a tight circle around a *chaatwallah,* awaiting the next round of *pani puri* or *phuchka* on our plates, the street is a powerful equalizing force. In this way, *chaat* becomes imperative to the democratic experience of street life, particularly in the Indian context.

Notes

1. Laura Siciliano-Rosen, 'Chaat', *Britannica*, 2014 <https://www.britannica.com/topic/chaat> [accessed 15 April 2021]
2. Roshni Subramanian, 'Chaats from Around India You Cannot Miss!', *Outlook Traveller*, 5 September 2019 <https://www.outlookindia.com/outlooktraveller/explore/story/69834/chaats-from-around-india-that-you-cannot-miss> [accessed 15 April 2021]
3. Colleen Taylor Sen, *Feasts and Fasts: A History of Food in India* (India: Speaking Tiger, 2016), pp. 139-41.
4. Anoothi Vishal, 'Is Golgappa Better than Paani Puri and Phuchka? That Is the Wrong Question to Ask', *Scroll.in*, 2 February 2021 <https://scroll.in/magazine/984636/is-golgappa-better-than-paani-puri-and-phuchka-that-is-the-wrong-question-to-ask> [accessed 15 April 2021]
5. Vishal.
6. Interview conducted by the author, May 2021.
7. Dan Packel, 'Inside India's Street Food Paradise', *AFAR*, 19 October 2011 <https://www.afar.com/magazine/indias-street-food-paradise--2> [accessed 15 April 2021]
8. Harris Solomon, '"The Taste No Chef Can Give": Processing Street Food in Mumbai', *Cultural Anthropology*, 30.1 (2015) <https://doi.org/10.14506/ca30.1.05>

Eat, Lose, Imagine

Janet Beizer

for Ross Chambers, in memory

Introduction

Imagination, says the OED, is either an action, 'forming a mental concept of what is not actually present to the senses', or a mental faculty 'by which are formed images […] of external objects not present to the senses'. Fundamental to both the act of imagining and the function of the imagination is the notion of absence. This leaning on lack or loss is so basic and so essential to the work of the imagination that I start my meditation on culinary imagining there, even at the risk of underlining the obvious. But my implicit question is what eating and food, whose materiality is patent and which belong to a very distinct province of imagined activity, have specifically to do with loss, lack, and non-presence.

Though I have introduced my paper with a definition and will later call upon the work of theory, the heart of my reflection is lodged in a childhood memory about the inexplicable absence of a particular food-giver, my grandmother, her imaginary reappearance, and the significance of the event in my early consciousness. This memory and its associative threads furnish the initial matter of a short memoir about alimentary pleasure, loss, fantasy, excess, and oppression: in short, a meditation on the peculiarities of eating in my family of origin.

The paper then turns to French filmmaker Anne Georget's documentary films, *Mina's Recipe Book* (2007) and *Imaginary Feasts* (2015), both inspired by the re-emergence of collected recipes that had been rehearsed in whispers by starved prisoners (at Terezín, or Theresienstadt, for the first film, and in diverse locations, for the second) and then transcribed at great risk on cloth or paper scraps.[1] I bring into the conversation also the posthumous publication of the eponymous Mina's cookbook, introduced by Cara De Silva, as *In Memory's Kitchen*.[2] These extreme conjurations of food trace a nexus of nourishment, absence, and imagination in contexts sharply divergent from my own childhood memories. They expose a culinary imagination generated by scenarios of almost unimaginable loss: deprivation of food, family, heritage, dignity, liberty, and life.

In what follows, I then grapple with what it means to think about stories of such different scope, scale, and genre together, and I consider the unexpected revelations of the process of writing the juxtaposition as well as the ethical stakes and intentions of the project. I suggest intersections and rapprochements of the two initial diptych panels, without fully articulating them, in order to pose questions that cannot have clear and tidy answers.

I

Twisting the Grandmother Trope

One Christmas morning I woke early as a child of four or five, brimming with the expectancy of revelation. No religious expectation was involved; we were Jewish, and had recently lit the menorah candles, but like many assimilated Jews in 1950s America, we also celebrated Santa Claus in our idiosyncratic way, with tangerines and walnuts left for him on the eve. In return, on the morn we harvested gifts overflowing our literally interpreted Christmas stockings. From the foil-wrapped nuts and bright citrus globes glinting through the toes of my mother's rent nylons pinned before bedtime to the couch upholstery – one leg per child – up through the bulging calves and widening thighs, an enticing array of eclectic hues and shapes spilled onto the living room carpet. My excitement seems materialistic in retrospect, though it was backlit by the homeliness of family ritual and the anticipation of joining cousins and grandparents for dinner. So it is not entirely odd that in the first moments of awakening on that particular Christmas, I heard my grandmother's voice calling out, wraithlike, drawing me into the day: 'Jaaaaa-net,' she said, 'Jaaaaa-net.' The summoning was quiet but insistent. I slid out of bed to find her. My sister and parents were still asleep; I quickly toured our small apartment but found no one afoot. I looked down the stairwell, under the dining room table, beneath the chairs and couch; no one. But her voice lingered with its come-hither command in the elongated syllables of my whispered name: 'Jaaaaa-net.'

I loved my grandmother. She and my similarly adored grandfather joined us Friday evenings, riding the subway from the far shores of Manhattan out to Queens and then back again a few hours later. My grandfather arrived after work, coat pockets distended with sour pickles filched from the diner where he ate lunch. They were duly plated to join the feast my mother and grandmother would have spent the day preparing. It is possible that Shabbat was the distant avatar of these Friday night dinners, but not a candle or prayer remained as token of such rituals, only the copious table, replete with challah, but also milk for me, whether the meat was chicken, beef, or pork. My grandmother came early for a day punctuated by forays to various supermarkets and finally, Adrian's, the special occasion bakery. There we got golden-crusted challah and an extravagant dessert for dinner: chocolate babka or banana cream pie or cheesecake with chocolatey ripples running through, and thick chocolate squiggles threading through dense buttery crumbs on top. These upper layers could be lifted off and enjoyed, sometimes well before dinner, if I was stealthy enough. The meal would be three courses: an appetizer of cantaloupe crescents or a grapefruit half, then a roast chicken or beef or pot roast, occasionally leg of lamb or pork loin, roasted till crackly with garlic, bedded down in onions, potatoes, carrots, and gravy. And a Bird's Eye brand green vegetable on the side, because it was the '50s. Accompanied by my grandfather's pocket pickles, as we called them, and followed by the bakery cake, however diminished.

In telling this story, I realize that if I am to recall with any measure of fidelity how my past was constructed, I cannot not fall back on what Helen Rosner has called 'the grandmother trope' of food narratives: the assumption that 'our elders are the keepers of domestic wisdom' – and, most crucially, the guardians of the recipes that preserve home cooking and tradition.[3] But the inexorable deviation of this trope from its standard cocooning of home, hearth, forebears, and food might already begin to be clear in the quirky details of its spinning out, even without any elaboration of its later evolution into a trail of roast chickens – sent by US mail – to grandchildren dispersed across the country, relegated to college dorm rooms and otherwise subsisting on cafeteria fare.

But to close the parenthesis that risks circumnavigating childhood: we are still, in fact, many years before the college chicken years, on a Christmas morning in Queens when a small child hears her grandmother's whisper in her ear. Christmas morning was not part of the grandparent ritual, though, and even after the entire household had been wakened, and the underside of every bed checked, no grandmother was in attendance. Despite parental assurances that she could not be found because she was simply not there, I insisted. I knew her voice, and I'd heard my name called. I remember my mother dialling her phone number so I could speak to her: yes, she was home in her Manhattan apartment and even if she had called out to me, because of course she was always thinking about me, I could not have heard her so far away.

This memory stays with me as a watershed; it is probably my earliest remembrance and certainly the most powerful. The sharpness of the combined sense of loss and awe has not dulled, the wonder tempering the absence by a glimmer of something not quite understood but vast in its openness, almost magical in its portent. For the adult looking back, the moment has come to suggest itself – only after many, many years of playback and pondering – as the dawning consciousness of imagination: the inchoate almost-awareness that something can exist in the mind or the heart that is as clear as a sound that falls right into an open ear, and yet not be physically present.

That the advent of imagination – or at least my coming to awareness of it – was coupled for me not only with wanting or lack but more precisely with the absence of the figure most identified with culinary pleasures in my life seems indicative of a potent connection among the workings of eating, suffering loss, and imagining.[4] And yet, and at the same time, this triad flickering at the brink of mourning was connected too with an enthralling sense of discovery and even power, as if I now fathomed that I had within me an arcane faculty that could potentially summon what was lost or too far to reach. The graven acoustic image that has held me in its thrall for as long as I remember is, I suppose, a variation of the grandmother trope. Yet it seems important to note that the scene that brands my memory is not one where my pot-stirring grandmother is reassuringly ensconced in her own aromatic kitchen, nor in ours, though in fact she often was to be found in these places. Instead, I am marked by the instance of her unfathomable physical absence belied by the sound of her voice, disembodied, resonant only within me. I hear it still.

However worn the grandmother trope may be in the collective unconscious, it appears to be more stubbornly unconventional in its actual unwinding: in my experience and, I suspect, more generally, it binds eating, losing, and imagining in a weave that can be as formally irregular as it is mythically familiar. The slipping of my mother's mother from my childhood clasp and the decentring of her voice, the few passing moments that reassigned her to a phantom presence, inaugurates a file of culinary eccentricities that further destabilize everyday kitchen narratives. At what point in family history did unconventional food practices veer into oppressive feedings? Where do I locate the warm light shading into a darkening chill? When does memory effect a transition from the first to the second? Or were they always already one and the same? I cannot forget the urging to eat everything on my plate, and to replenish if I already had, and the reminder, if I protested that I was not hungry, to think about all the starving children in India. I remember a young cousin of seven or eight who cried through most of a Thanksgiving dinner when the turkey, carved into neatly separated joints and slices, was placed on the crowded table, coincidentally right before him. 'Grandma,' he sobbed, 'I can't eat that much!' A funny story savoured by the adults, in retrospect it ushers in a pattern of excess and glut: my grandmother's impressively large purse packed full of plastic bags ready for stashing away the surplus food she helped herself to from restaurant buffets; my grandfather's unabashed grazing on olives and tomatoes from self-serve barrels at the supermarket; the systematic family use of M&Ms as potty training rewards for successive generations of toddlers, as if the bodily parting with food waste needed somehow to be compensated in a never-ending cycle.

As they grew older, my grandparents' feeding behaviours intensified. Every communication with grandchildren at college began and ended with the question: 'Are you eating?' – and the posted roast chickens peppered these queries with emphatic force. What had once been an offering of plenty evolved into an overwhelming surfeit whose effects were only heightened by age and my grandfather's death. In every telephone conversation with my grandmother, a veritable verbal bombardment of daily menus served at the Senior Centre, a litany of reported meals and their evaluations: 'ham sandwiches with swiss on rye, but the bread was stale', 'lasagne, not bad but not hot', 'rice pudding, good but the portions were so small', 'roast turkey with gravy and mashed potatoes; they gave us so much, I brought half of it home'. On every visit to her apartment, an insistence that whatever was in the fridge be placed on the table and consumed. Plied with the leftovers of the past week's meals, some from my grandmother's kitchen but increasingly retrieved from her lunches at the Senior Centre or neighbourhood restaurants, overcome by an existential and often physiological nausea, I could only resist the escalating exhortations to take, and take in, and take some more, and more again.

Cooking with the Mouth

Imaginary Feasts opens with off-camera dogs barking sharply in ominous bursts. Then we hear hushed murmurs against the harsh canine blasts, whispers of initially inaudible speech, women's voices at first, intoning words that we can begin to make out only when they are paired on screen with images of handwriting on scraps of paper and tatters of cloth.[5] Scattered words gradually become audible and then recognizable as a litany of recipe titles: '*profiteroles au chocolat* […] *riz à l'impératrice* […] *flan au fromage* […] *saucisse au vin blanc* […] *charlotte au rhum* […] *coq au vin* […] *croquettes de pommes de terre* […] *blanquette de veau* […] *flan breton* […] *fruits confits* […] *marrons glacés* […]'. These incorporeal voices breathe lists in our ears without origin or context; they make ghosts of food and usher in cooking as a dematerialized concept. Against this background, we are introduced to the clandestine culinary conversations that punctuated women's concentration-camp existence and sometimes led to cobbling together and smuggling away written recipes, scribbled on found or scrounged surfaces and bound pell-mell. Holocaust cookbooks bear witness to human captives barely subsisting on rations of bread, and water thinly flavoured with coffee grounds or vegetable peels; these expiring souls fed their minds and nourished their communality with scraps of food memories recomposed into lavish feasts. Here is a terrible illustration of the generation of imagination through the combustion of food and loss.

In *Imaginary Feasts*, as in Georget's earlier film, *Mina's Recipe Book*, the shocking contrast of the prisoners' stark alimentary reality with their elaborate food fantasies is foregrounded, along with the reactions such disparities elicit from participating and onlooking captives and, in *Imaginary Feasts*, from latter-day theorists as well, ranging from anthropologists to psychologists, Holocaust scholars, food studies specialists, and chefs.[6] Many of the interviewees, survivors and theorists alike, seek to explain the detailed reconstructions of recipes as a distraction from or compensation for the absolute desert of nourishment. Christiane Hingouët remembers 'a different kind of hunger – not what you have when you wake in the morning but the hunger you have after two years of not eating, when you see yourself wasting away, so thin that your bones are poking out, when you have no strength', and she explains the recipe recitations as a moment of respite, 'our fantasy cooking behind barbed wire'.[7] For her as for many of the survivors, the words of the recipes are bred from 'empty stomachs and desperate starvation', as Edith Combus puts it.[8] Another deportee, André Bessière, sums up the phenomenon as a 'gorging on dreams' in which words take the place of sustenance: 'They stuffed themselves with word feasts because they were dying of hunger,' he says, adding that he himself refrained from thinking about food because it was too painful. For others, the transformation of rations sourced in the diluted garbage of SS officers' meals into the verbal facsimile of familiar comfort foods could only be alchemical or magical, or, in the minds of those who were offended by what they experienced as absurdity and escapist mania, simply delusional and even obscene.[9]

Ascriptions of obscenity crop up periodically in discussions of imaginary feasting. I suspect that such charges stem not simply from the stark nature of the oppositions that are put into play by the elaborate culinary rehearsals of those interned in extermination camps, but also, especially, from the fact that they echo the fundamental polarity of death and life. Obscenity, from the French '*obscène*', which some etymologies derive in turn from the Greek *ob skene*, 'offstage', originally alluded to acts and events that could not or should not be shown directly on stage, prime among which was death. Paradoxically, the activity dubbed 'cooking with the mouth' by those who performed it or observed it has often been explained as a defiance of death, an act of life in the face of death.[10] Resistance inevitably acknowledges what it refuses, and so perhaps the perceptions of obscenity have to do with the very blatant staging of the contradiction of life and death, a life-in-death asserted and sustained to the end. Yad Vashem's Yehudit Inbar tells of another phenomenon deemed obscene: children's games. When organizing an exhibition on children's toys in the Holocaust, she initially met with shocked refusal. Yet children played on their way to the gas chambers, she confirms, much like women recited recipes, telling them, like stories, to each other.[11]

In both cases there is a clinging to life from the edge of death; a holding on that is almost a flaunting. For writer Jérôme Thélot, 'meals are a synonym of life'.[12] The evocation of aromatic cakes baking on hearths counters the smoke rising from crematorium chimneys; the rememoration of the intricacies of a recipe (the combining of distinct, pungent spices, the successive steps, the order) restores detail to a landscape of indetermination and chaos. As Rabbi Michael Berenbaum explains, 'We all presume the world makes some sense. That's why when the world does not make sense, it's frightening to us, it's chaos [...]. Primo Levi said: "Here there is no why." It's absurd. And absurdity [...] doesn't allow you a sense of orientation.'[13]

Food scenarios in the death camps did not escape the generalized reign of absurdity. Bianca Steiner Brown recalls that, at Terezín, shelves would be used one day for loaves of bread and the next for corpses; Berenbaum reports that children rewarded with sweets one day would be killed the day after.[14] Slavic Studies professor Luba Jurgenson proposes that imagining recipes defied such a loss of definition and meaning: 'Cooking [...] involves categorization: there's meat, there's fish, there's dessert. Food organizes our life and our time: morning food differs from evening food.'[15] We might say, too, that recipes impose order and system through their narrative form: there is a beginning, a progression, and an end, each instruction unfolding in relation to the others. Recipes have an internal microstructure, and they imply a macrostructure by emerging from a past and opening onto a future.[16]

What we know about 'Holocaust recipes' today has a double dimension. There is the oral practice, in which capacity the recipes were performative, parsing time, creating social communicative space and pockets of meaning within madness. But the fact that the sessions of 'cooking with the mouth' were also transcribed, at great risk to the scribes and to anyone involved with spiriting out the manuscripts, adds another layer of significance to the phenomenon. The written form of recipe-telling in the death camps, the recording, compiling, and rough binding of what would otherwise have remained fragmentary food stories told in passing, indicates that they were meant to reach external eyes and ears, to communicate belatedly with a broader audience, and to be preserved over time. Such collections make recipes into books, whether they exist in manuscript or print form, and they should be read as such.[17]

The cookbook is rarely accorded the status of literature or art, for much the same reason, I suggest, that hunger has been neglected as a philosophical subject; it has been devalued 'as empirical and as a lowly sign of human animality'. With these words Jérôme Thélot explains the scholarly void that inspired his essay on hunger, *In the Beginning there was Hunger: Treatise on the Intractable*. Striving to join literature (and language) to its alimentary sources, he reminds us that many languages use the same word for speech and for the organ that participates in manipulating food as well as words, partaking of the pleasure of both.[18] The tongue – or more broadly the mouth – is the junction of speaking and chewing, the site of an overdetermined need. Hunger leads to language, says Thélot, our language comes from our hunger; from infancy forward, it defines both our subjectivity and our intersubjectivity, our need to receive from and give to the Other.[19] Leaning on Thélot's reinsertion of hunger into the philosophical and the poetic canon, I want to consider cookbooks – and Holocaust recipe collections prime among them – as texts: literary objects, art, writing, even Scripture.[20] This makes a difference in how we read them; it suggests that we pay attention to their wording, their details, and also to what is omitted, as we do with the language of poetry, prose, and dreams.

Chef Olivier Roellinger marvels, in Georget's film, at the degree of precision of the ingredient list in many of the recipes, the careful distinction, for example, between mace and nutmeg, two similar spices (neither of which, of course, would have been materially accessible to the deportees). And there are other aesthetic elements to be noted beyond the level of detail – most readily in Mina Pächter's published cookbook. The recipe writer often remarks on the appearance of the finished product, well beyond practical considerations such as signs of doneness. Plum Strudel, for example, should be '*high and beautiful*', while Chicken Galantine is '*plentiful and pretty*'. There is also a nod toward the pleasures of culinary creation (and perhaps a touch of ironic humour as well) in the instruction for garnishing 'Cold Stuffed Eggs Pächter' to 'let fantasy run free', or in the claim, for a basic dough that is tempered in water, called 'Waterbed Dough', that 'one can do anything with it'.[21]

As in most texts, there are slips of the tongue recorded by the pen in these recipes, blunders or inaccuracies that might have gone unnoticed in the recitation but are conserved in writing. If for Freud a *lapsus linguae* betrays a psychic truth, here there are truths of mind and body; the tongue slips, so to speak, when it is unoccupied, stupefied, unable to perform its normal work of tasting and facilitating the mechanics of ingestion; it slips on an excess of saliva in the absence of food, it trips in the fog of a malnourished head. There are oversights or errors in recipes that give a glimpse of the state of the mind and the conditions of the body and its environment, even reaching back to the ghetto scarcities of pre-Holocaust cooking models. Hirsch makes the case dramatically: 'We cannot cook from these recipes (most leave out ingredients or reflect wartime rationing by calling for substitutions or making eggs optional)', while De Silva details the kind of mistakes consistently made, and survivor André Bessière calls to our attention the impossibly disproportionate amounts of chocolate or sugar, for example, prescribed in certain recipes.[22]

But the most powerful textual element of the recipe books created during the Shoah may well be that of transmission, of connecting the present to the past and to the future. Whatever we can learn from the pages of cookbooks from the Holocaust about the role recipes played in the everyday lives of prisoners confronting probable death, whatever we can intuit from a turn of phrase, an affect-tinged instruction or comment, a detail, or a gap, is amplified by the implications of the written format in the context of its historical reality. It is true, as *Imaginary Feasts* relates, that similar culinary artefacts have surfaced from the Russian Gulag and from Japanese prisoner of war camps: captives in other extreme situations have had similar instincts to rehearse and record culinary memories in moments of extreme crisis. What distinguishes the Holocaust cookbooks, as Michael Berenbaum points out in this film, is the propelling sense of an annihilation extending beyond the individual: 'These people understood they were being destroyed. There would be nothing left.' The recipe compilations were more than an escape, or a therapy, or a catharsis; they were the diffusion of a culinary tradition with all that it might communicate of a disappearing culture, a cancelled way of life. As Marni Reva Kessler reminds us, 'Food has the capacity to tie us […] to our memories, our families, our traditions […] to reveal how the present is always steeped in an enduring past.'[23] These recipes rememorated a perhaps vanished past and recorded it for the future.

When we think about what a legacy is conventionally considered to be (children, money, art – either made or collected – the fruits of whatever bit of earth one has planted and tended), this one is rather extraordinary. It must have been clear to most concentration camp detainees that their offspring could neither receive their inheritance nor be it. Prodigious efforts were made to do whatever was possible to preserve the lives of the interned children: at Terezín, for example, the group compelled by the Nazis to administer the internal business of the camp, the Council of Jewish Elders, decided that children had to be fed more than others, since they represented the future.[24] Yet as Berenbaum explains, the young were usually siphoned off to die quickly, for that very reason.[25] Of the European Jews who were children in 1939, only eleven per cent were alive at the end of the war.[26] Only rarely would the books of the Holocaust dead pass on to surviving children or grandchildren; the heirs were more likely to be anonymous and collective.[27]

II

A Digest of Trivia and Other Essentials

Bellyaching: The activity attributed to my grandmother by my grandfather when she nagged at him to do something, or to not do something that annoyed her. 'Stop bellyaching!' was the refrain of their quarrels, which consisted largely of her complaints and his grumbling protests.

Borborygm: A rumbling or growling sound made in the stomach and intestines by moving fluid and gas, especially when one is hungry. Jérôme Thélot refers to the monosyllabic repetitions – 'Dinn! dinn! dinn! dinn!' – of Arthur Rimbaud's poem '*Fêtes de la faim*' ('Feasts of Hunger') as 'borborygms or mumblings […] the first sounds of hunger speaking'.[28]

Breakfast/Cemeteries: In Mitzi Goldstein's 1996 documentary film *Hatred*, the Australian Jewish filmmaker accompanies her German-born father, Bernard Goldstein, back to his East German hometown of Dessau, from which he fled in 1939.[29] Combing through streets which have all changed name, searching for the house in which he lived fifty years earlier, disoriented, he lapses from English back into German and confuses two words, telling his daughter that they will later go 'to the Jewish breakfast' (*Frühstuck*) when he means to say 'to the Jewish cemetery' (*Friedhof*); realizing his slip of the tongue, he begins to laugh uncontrollably, attributing his mistake in turn to feeling frozen, drunk, in a fog. See **Frühstuck/Friedhof**.

Concentration Camp Survivor: The metaphor used in my family and others to describe the skinny profile of adolescent American girls flirting with anorexia. Used as a scare tactic, it usually did not have the intended result of bringing them back to a full fat diet.

Frühstuck/Friedhof: See **Breakfast/Cemeteries**.

Grandma Cookies: The name we gave to my grandmother's recipe for a confection she often made with her young grandchildren, and later made herself, mailing them in brown paper wrapping to college dorms, alternating with roast chickens. The dough was made of flour, sugar, Crisco, an egg, baking powder, and vanilla, then divided into small balls depressed in the middle with a thumb in whose place a spoonful of jelly was dropped. Mina Pächter's book has a similar recipe (albeit a healthier version, with oatmeal added) for such cookies, there called 'Kisses'.[30]

Robert Jay Lifton: American psychiatrist and author whose work centres on the psychohistory of war, political violence, and other extreme situations. I worked part-time for him in Paris as a translator-assistant when I was a graduate student. We interviewed a number of French-speaking medical survivors of concentration camps, many of them pressed into service under Mengele, for his book *The Nazi Doctors: Medical Killing and the Psychology of Genocide*. The work consisted largely of simultaneous translation of the witnesses' testimony; as I repeated their words to him, changed into English but retaining the first person, there was an uncanny sense of momentarily taking on the experience with the pronoun. See **Mengele**.

M&Ms: Inspired by a candy given to British volunteers fighting in the Spanish Civil War, they were first produced in the United States in 1941 by Forrest Mars, scion of the Mars candy empire. After the US entered the war, the small pill-shaped chocolates encased in hard, coloured shells were sold exclusively to the military for the duration. Distributed as snacks for soldiers, they were prized for their heat-resistant and easily transportable characteristics. Later used in some households as aids to potty training, these tiny remnants of the Second World War were fed to at least a few post-war babies to reward their early losses.

Mengele: Josef Mengele, SS captain and chief physician at Auschwitz, called 'the Angel of Death' for his cool and implacable demeanour during 'selections' that decided which prisoners would be sent to the gas chambers and which retained for work. He was also known for his cruel, often lethal, medical experiments on Jewish and Roma twins. Mengele was infamous for his ability to flip imperturbably from acts of apparent kindness to murder: one day he would give candy to children and the next he would send them to be gassed.[31] See **Robert Jay Lifton**.

Recette: The French word for 'recipe'; same derivation. See **Recipe**.

Recipe: Derived from the past participle, *recepta*, of the Latin verb *recipere*, 'to receive'. A culinary recipe, notes Thélot, is 'what is received. The person who gives us a recipe received it from someone else. And those who invent a new recipe must do so on the basis of a tradition that has no beginning'.[32] See **Recette**.

Starving Children in ... [Place Name]: A common rhetorical device used by food-secure post-war American families in the 1950s and 1960s to encourage recalcitrant children to finish their meals. The full utterance runs something like: 'Think of all the starving children in [Place Name]', with the bracket filled in with the proper name of a non-first world country or continent (India, China, Africa) or a historical referent, such as 'the Holocaust' or 'the concentration camps'. In American Jewish families, the latter terms are frequent, though in my own family, they were not used; India was the comparand of choice.

Stella: The given name of a first cousin once removed, referred to infrequently now and only in lowered voices; the skeleton in the family closet (which here takes the form of a seventh-storey stairwell accessed by a rarely used and barricaded rear door). Stella was my grandmother's niece, the daughter of a much younger sister, close to the grandchildren in age, though since childhood inhabiting a closed and impenetrable world. In her late forties she began living in my grandmother's apartment with her. Stella disappeared after my grandmother's death. Some weeks later the building superintendent discovered her emaciated corpse along with her clothes and a note on the landing. She had starved herself to death.

Talking with the Belly

What was the place of the Shoah in my family of origin? The facile answer is that it lay somewhere outside, distant in space and time. Like Mitzi Goldman, an Australian of Eastern European heritage, I am tempted to say that for me growing up in 1950s and 1960s New York, the Holocaust was 'ancient history, not my life'.[33] I might even add that it had fairy-tale aspects for me; horrific stories of people shoved in ovens coalesced in my child's mind with Hansel and Gretel, and I had terrifying visions of ogres making lampshades of human skin. But they were stories that did not touch my immediate family and their friends. I was born third- and second-generation American on my mother and father's respective sides. No relatives or friends, to my knowledge, had lived or died in concentration camps. I was educated about the Holocaust from an age I cannot pinpoint, beginning perhaps with the diary of Anne Frank, who was for me a legendary heroine, like Joan of Arc – one of a handful of exceptional women whose biographies my mother brought home to me.

But I wonder, now, as I think back through my family's food stories, if my Holocaust education took place also, in less official, unintended ways, around the dinner table. Were the de-ritualized Friday dinners simply end-of-the-work-week celebrations ushering in the weekend, or were they also shadows of ceremonial religious dinners? Was the culinary bounty on the table and in the mail a way of staving off indirect experiences of hunger and malnutrition? How did the alimentary barrage respond to what my family must have known about starvation and other killing regimes in transit barracks and death camps? What did I absorb from my family about the repercussions of famishment during the Shoah, wordlessly, or from ill-chosen metaphors displaced to the effects of weight loss, or from names of sites of famine diverted from Eastern Europe to India, China, Africa? Or were the culinary idiosyncrasies of home distantly tied to much older traditions that might also have had associations with the recipe recitations of the interned Jewish population of the Shoah?

The author/son in Art Spiegelman's graphic novel *Maus* takes in his parents' Holocaust trauma at the dinner table, in a familial space where the past can be transferred, 'internalized without fully being understood', in Marianne Hirsch's words.[34] In her book about the work of 'postmemory' (which other writers have called 'absent memory', 'vicarious witnessing', 'received history', 'haunting legacy'), Hirsch explores 'the relationship that the "generation after" bears to the personal, collective, and cultural trauma of those who came before – to experiences they "remember" only by means of the stories, images, and behaviours among which they grow up'. But their parents' experiences 'were transmitted to them so deeply and affectively as to seem to constitute memories in their own right'.[35] What is at stake is not a legacy of literal memory, but the transmission of affects and psychic effects that attach to such memories.

In borrowing from Hirsch's pathbreaking work, I want to take great care not to make any claims for my own or my family's reception of Holocaust history that would imply an arrogation of memories we do not own or experiences that are not ours. As a daughter of survivors, Hirsch voices a caveat for herself and others, asking 'how can we best carry [the victims'] stories forward, without appropriating them, without unduly calling attention to ourselves, and without, in turn, having our own stories displaced by them?'[36] So let me be clear. I am not the daughter of survivors, and I have no postmemories of experiences my parents and grandparents never lived. But as I try to understand the heritage of my grandparents' life in food I keep returning to the possibility of the reverberations of trauma within our family, like a lateral psychic force pressing upon the table and transmitted across generations.

Ross Chambers introduces the concept of cultural hauntedness in his re-reading of the scandal created by the so-called 'Wilkomirski Affair': the revelation that Binjamin Wilkomirski's alleged Holocaust memoir of 1995 had in fact been written by a man named Bruno Dössekker who did not live the events he describes in the book (including internment in Majdanek and Auschwitz-Birkenau).³⁷ *Bruchstücke* (translated as *Fragments: Memoirs of a Wartime Childhood*) takes its title from the notion of memory scraps, but also, Chambers argues, from an episode in the book in which the interned child is covertly led through the camp to see his dying mother, who gifts him a piece of stale bread.³⁸ In all likelihood Dössekker was suffering from delusions, yet his book and its reception bear witness, suggests Chambers, to the 'hauntedness of a culture of aftermath': one in which 'an individual can mistake the collective consciousness of a painful past for a personal memory'.³⁹

After the discovery of the hoax, the book's publication was suspended, despite its widespread early acclamation as an extraordinary childhood memoir, a masterpiece of Holocaust literature. Chambers proposes that the (fictive) child orphan Wilkomirski, the child who could not speak, stands in symbolically for all the non-survivors, for all the testimony that did not survive. He posits that the Wilkomirskis, or orphaned memories, haunting the collective consciousness *'need a Dössekker* – a "host"' – to be heard and acknowledged as the ghosts of our culture who cannot be laid to rest.⁴⁰ Through pathological self-identification with Wilkomirski, Dössekker takes on 'his' memories derived from collective memory and fosters them in writing. 'Foster writing', for Chambers, both offers a surrogate home to what is homeless and ushers the culturally homeless into culture, making recognizable, through the pain of reading, the memories that collective culture would rather forget, in a broken, fragmented form that lies between imagining and remembering.⁴¹

Might there be such a thing as fostered postmemory? Tapping the broad lines of Chambers's brilliant analysis, I want to submit the possibility of an unintentional handing down of indirectly transferred traumatic experience; that is, a lateral acquisition, through identification, of the extreme suffering of others that would then be transmitted generationally. I think of this process as it might have played out in my family and perhaps in others, *mutatis mutandis*, as a foster feeding rather than a foster writing: a nurturing of ghosts who have lost their place and their sustenance, through more quotidian scenes and modes of nourishment set in childhood around a family table. Of these, only fragments of memory later remain, as small as M&Ms or as broken as *Brüchstucke*, the shards of memory or crusts of bread that Wilkomirski/Dössekker writes into being. These crumbs of remembrance retrieved or reimagined break the fast of oblivion, like the early morning morsel, *Frühstuck*, that a slip of the tongue calls back from the grave, *Friedhof,* in the mouth of German refugee Bernard Goldstein, reminding us that although life and meals may be synonyms (as Thélot contends), death and meals cannot necessarily be kept apart.

Coda

As I was finishing this paper, I joined a remote session in the NYU 'Fast and Famine' series in which Reem Kassis was interviewed by Krishnendu Ray about her new book, *The Arabesque Table: Contemporary Recipes from the Arab World*.[42] Asked about the appropriateness of discussing culinary culture in a time of catastrophic sociopolitical crisis (the latest Gaza war) Kassis responded vehemently in the positive, using arguments that uncannily echoed the analyses of the various experts called to witness in Georget's *Imaginary Feasts* of the Holocaust. She recounted personal communications from friends in Gaza who, amidst the bombings and destruction overlapping with Ramadan, had little access to ingredients called for in the traditional recipes for cakes heralding the end of the holy month. Nevertheless, they adamantly maintained these cultural-familial traditions, altering recipes when necessary but forging ahead with culinary ritual 'to retain a sense of normalcy'. Kassis called this persistence 'an act of resistance' in terms that strikingly repeat, almost word for word, the testimony of Georget's commentators about concentration-camp recipes. The commentary of Georget's interviewees about the relevance of the culinary imagination to surviving and chronicling the catastrophe of Shoah concentration camps, and the replies of this Palestinian author about the pertinence of culinary culture to the Palestinian crisis, concurred in their emphasis on the importance of protecting food traditions for generations to come. A member of the audience referred to the Netflix series, *High on the Hog*, and its witnessing of foodways in African-American history as 'a space of resistance, dignity, creativity, community', even – and perhaps especially – in the case of extended oppression and crisis.[43] In closing, then, I want to juxtapose these Palestinian and African-American examples of gastro-opposition with my own meditation on Holocaust recipes-as-resistance. I will invoke here too Marianne Hirsch's proposition that memory may be harnessed, even generations later, '*and affiliatively readopted across lines of difference* [...] *in a bold* [...] *act of* [...] *connective politics* [...]', to urge us to continue to think these parallel struggles together.[44]

Notes

1. *Les Recettes de Mina* (*Mina's Recipe Book*), dir. Anne Georget, France (2007); *Festins imaginaires* (*Imaginary Feasts*), dir. Anne Georget, France (2015).
2. *In Memory's Kitchen: A Legacy from the Women of Terezín*, ed. by Cara De Silva, trans. by Bianca Steiner Brown, foreword by Michael Berenbaum (Northvale, NJ: Jason Aronson Inc, 1996).
3. Helen Rosner, 'The Best Cookbooks of 2020', *The New Yorker,* 15 December 2020. <https://www.newyorker.com/culture/2020-in-review/the-best-cookbooks-of-2020> [accessed 23 December 2020]
4. In one of the few philosophies of hunger I know, Jérôme Thélot suggests that 'hunger gives rise to consciousness, hunger is the origin of consciousness, and its affect is the foundation of verbalization' (*Au Commencement était la faim: Traité de l'intraitable* (*In the Beginning there was Hunger: Treatise on the Intractable*) (Fougères, La Versanne: Encre marine, 2005), p. 59). Translations are mine unless otherwise indicated.
5. There are a few men's voices heard as well, and the film makes clear that reconstructing recipes was not confined to women, though much more common among them, for the obvious reason that women

have traditionally maintained culinary traditions.
6   Georget's *Mina's Recipe Book* [*Les Recettes de Mina*] documents the retrieval of a single Holocaust cookbook by the family of its deceased author, Mina Stein Pächter, some thirty years after her death, and traces its trajectory from the impulses that prompted it to its eventual emergence in print; her *Imaginary Feasts* [*Festins imaginaires*] is a broader documentation of such cookbooks, and, secondarily, similar compendiums of recipes created in Japanese POW camps and Russian Gulag prisons, interspersed with interviews with survivors and scholars.
7   *Imaginary Feasts*. Hingouët's effort to explain a hunger unlike any most of us have known echoes Primo Levi: 'We say "hunger," we say "tiredness," "fear," "pain," "winter," and they are different things. They are free words, created and used by free men who lived in comfort and suffering in their homes. If the Lagers [camps] had lasted longer, a new, harsh language would have been born; and only this language could express what it means to toil the whole day in the wind, with the temperature below freezing, wearing only a shirt, underpants, cloth jacket and trousers, and in one's body nothing but weakness, hunger, and knowledge of the end drawing nearer' (quoted by Cara De Silva, 'Introduction', in *In Memory's Kitchen*, p. xv. English translations from Georget's films are based on the subtitles, which I have altered when necessary to retain the literality or the flavour of the French.
8   *Imaginary Feasts*.
9   *Imaginary Feasts*. Bianca Steiner Brown, a survivor interviewed in *Mina's Recipe Book*, explains that when she was kept awake at night by the women talking, comparing, for example, how much sugar, how much chocolate went into a Sachertorte, 'I was furious. They lived in their own kind of a fantasy'.
10 De Silva relates that Susan E. Cernyak-Spatz, a survivor of Terezín and Auschwitz, 'describes people in both places as speaking of food so much that there was a camp expression for it. We called it "cooking with the mouth", she says. "Everybody did it"' (pp. xxviii-xxix).
11 *Imaginary Feasts*.
12 *Imaginary Feasts*.
13 *Imaginary Feasts*.
14 *Mina's Recipe Book*; *Imaginary Feasts*.
15 *Imaginary Feasts*.
16 An extreme example of future orientation is pointed out in *Imaginary Feasts* by psychoanalyst Géraldine Cerf: a recipe that advises canning extra portions of a seafood dish so it will be on hand when someone drops in unexpectedly for a visit.
17 That most are not easily accessible does not change my argument, though it complicates our readings. Mina Pächter's book is the only published Holocaust cookbook I have been able to read, though I have seen facsimiles of the handbound manuscript cookbooks used in *Imaginary Feasts*. I am extremely grateful to Anne Georget for sharing these facsimiles, and for her conversation in Paris in July 2015.
18 Thélot, p. 86.
19 Thélot, see especially pp. 25, 59, 63, 146.
20 In *Imaginary Feasts*, Yehudit Inbar compares the recipe recitations to prayers: 'It was the women's prayer. They had no other'. Cara De Silva calls the cookbook 'forceful testimony to the power of food to sustain us, not just physically but spiritually', reminding us that gastronomic traditions, 'the foods and foodways we associate with the rituals of childhood, marriage, and parenthood […] are critical components of our identities' (p. xxvi). In *Imaginary Feasts*, chef Olivier Roellinger is so awed by the connotations of unfurling a large piece of cloth inscribed with a jumbled mass of penned recipes that he compares it to a burial shroud. De Silva argues for considering Holocaust cookbooks as art: 'half a century after the Holocaust, when we thought we were familiar with all the creative ways in which human beings expressed themselves during the long years of the horror, at least one small genre, the making of cookbooks, has gone largely unnoticed' (pp. xxxii-xxxiii).
21 De Silva, pp. 28, 51, 52, 32.
22 Marianne Hirsch, *The Generation of Postmemory: Writing and Visual Culture After the Holocaust* (New York: Columbia University Press, 2012), p. 178; De Silva, p. xli; *Imaginary Feasts*.

23. Marni Reva Kessler, *Discomfort Food: The Culinary Imagination in Late Nineteenth-Century French Art* (Minneapolis, MN: University of Minnesota Press, 2021), p. xvi.
24. De Silva, p. xxxviii.
25. *Imaginary Feasts*.
26. Susan Rubin Suleiman, *Crises of Memory and the Second World War* (Cambridge, MA: Harvard University Press, 2006), p. 181.
27. What allowed Mina Pächter's book to be transmitted to her daughter Anny (albeit three decades later) was nothing short of miraculous. Anny had fled Prague with her family, reaching Palestine in the last transport out, while Mina had declined to leave, believing that her advanced age would protect her. The book reached Mina's daughter thanks to the persistence of a camp survivor and a chain of transmission. Surviving family members who received recipe books of deceased relatives usually donated them to museums, as detailed in the credits following *Imaginary Feasts*.
28. Thélot, p. 60.
29. *Hatred*, dir. Mitzi Goldman, Australia (1996). I am grateful to Hirsch's *Generation* for bringing this film to my attention.
30. *Mina's Cookbook*, in *In Memory's Kitchen*, p. 61.
31. *Imaginary Feasts*. On Mengele, see Robert Jay Lifton, *The Nazi Doctors: Medical Killing and the Psychology of Genocide* (New York: Basic Books, 1986) or, for a summary presentation, 'Josef Mengele' in *Holocaust Encyclopedia* (United States Holocaust Museum) <https://encyclopedia.ushmm.org/content/en/article/josef-mengele> [accessed 27 May 2021]
32. *Imaginary Feasts*.
33. *Hatred*.
34. Art Spiegelman, *Maus: A Survivor's Tale* vol. 1: *My Father Bleeds History* and vol. 2: *And Here my Troubles Began* (New York: Pantheon Books, 1973; 1986); Hirsch, *Generation*, p. 31. When Hirsch suggests that '*Maus* locates the scene of transmission in the bedtime connection between parent and child', she is referring to 'the three-page first *Maus*, published in 1972, [that] begins as a bedtime story [...in] the child's bedroom [...] a seemingly safe scene in which the father can evoke for this son the most brutal stories of wartime violence and persecution, fear and terror' (p. 29). Here I am referring instead to the full-fledged graphic novels *Maus* I and II, which show the son collecting his father's narrative fragments often at the table during meals (and occasionally when the father is on his exercise bike). But the point remains the same: the space is familial, a place where 'the language of family, the language of the body' (p. 34) can take place easily and the past can be transmitted across generations (p. 31).
35. Hirsch, p. 5.
36. Hirsch, p. 2.
37. Ross Chambers, *Untimely Interventions: Aids Writing, Testimonial, & the Rhetoric of Haunting* (Ann Arbor, MI: University of Michigan Press, 2004), p. 194; Benjamin Wilkomirski, *Bruchstücke* (Frankfurt am Main: Suhrkamp, 1995); translated by Carol Brown Janeway as *Fragments: Memoirs of a Wartime Childhood* (New York: Schocken, 1997).
38. Chambers, p. 209.
39. Chambers, pp. 194-95. While acknowledging that Chambers's use of Dössekker as a cultural metaphor has been controversial, I do not believe he is heroizing the man or his pathology.
40. Chambers, p. 197; original emphasis.
41. Chambers, pp. 200-03.
42. Reem Kassis and Krishnendu Ray, 'The Arabesque Table: Exploring the History of Arab Cuisine', *Feast and Famine Series*, NYU Steinhardt Department of Nutrition and Food Studies, 26 May 2021; Reem Kassis, *The Arabesque Table: Contemporary Recipes from the Arab World* (London: Phaidon, 2021).
43. Chat comment by Fabio Paresecoli, 'The Arabesque Table'.
44. Hirsch, pp. 248-49; my emphasis.

'Imagine an animal enclosure ...': Surprise Dishes in German Medieval Cuisine, an Homage to the Medieval Chef

Astrid Böhm, Julia Eibinger, and Helmut W. Klug

'If you want an animal enclosure, take flour and eggs. From this you can make whatever you want. From meat or fish you can make any ten animals, whatever you want, if you want, ten of each kind in this enclosure.' These are the opening sentences of a recipe in the collection of Master Hanns, personal chef to the dukes of Württemberg, which is dated to 1460. The editor of the manuscript, Trude Ehlert, is sceptical about the practicability of the whole enterprise: 'And the last recipe, the animal enclosure, with a castle and knights and ladies who are enjoying themselves in it – all made of edible material – must be relegated entirely to the realm of fantasy, as all this is difficult to realise; it seems significant to me, however, that the author neglects to include the instructions for preparing it [...]'.[1] The recipe describes an elaborate *Schaugericht*, a surprise dish, a common element of festivities during medieval times.

For medieval people the course of the year was sequenced into fast and feast days, according to the church calendar, with the fast days highly predominating. In addition, basic food provision was strongly dependent on weather and climate, so that even during the high times of agricultural production hunger was a constant threat to the whole population. In this context, it is not surprising that the feasts were generally celebrated lavishly by all social classes. The richer the host, the more extravagant were the meals as well as the entertainment offered to the guests. The host most likely had to build up or uphold his reputation and status.

In the Middle Ages, feasts were generally used to celebrate political or social agreements, and the guests had to be impressed accordingly. A medieval feast was a staged event. The planning started with the decoration of the room, included the seating of the guests, and was, of course, continued in the meticulous choreography of the feast itself. The feast was a coordinated series of courses that varied according to the social status of the diners; between courses the guests had to be entertained. For this purpose musicians, jesters, trained animals, dance, or even theatrical plays were included in the feast. But the entertainment of the guests was not limited to the time between courses, chefs wanted to entertain the guests with their food, too.

There were no limits to the cook's imagination! Elements of surprise and entertainment could be added to all kinds of dishes, starting at the basic puree or deceptive names of simple dishes escalating up to elaborate dishes that were planned and implemented like architectural construction projects. Researchers have understandably picked out examples of the last group, as these impressive dishes were also frequently recorded in historical accounts. Looking at this category of dishes from a different perspective by reading the recipe texts that have been handed down in various manuscripts, we can not only experience a greater deal of variation but also receive a more detailed picture of medieval chefs' imagination. The defining elements of surprise dishes generally are found in a combination of factors: clever naming conventions can transform a simple dish like aspic into entertainment. They often provide an extraordinary visual impression, so that guests might not be sure at first glance what they are being served. Most important is the significant transformation of ingredients through grinding, colouring, and/or substitution. And as implied in the name, surprise dishes have to entertain, by having a heightened fun-factor, evoking astonishment and even shock or repulsion.

But while innovative in the different implementations of surprise dishes, medieval cooks were not the first to impress their diners with creativity that goes beyond the concept of a delicious meal. One of the earlier examples, a Roman textual witness of culinary deception, is the description of a wild sow, filled with thrushes to be released when cut open, and its suckling pigs made of pastry being presented to the diners at Trimalchio's feast in the *Satyricon* by Petronius.[2] The different recipe traditions have varying names for these kinds of entertainment dishes: the French term is *entremets*, for something that is served 'between courses'. These dishes equally bridged the gap between courses and allowed for leisure time for the guests. English texts refer to these dishes as *sotelties* ('subtleties'), or sometimes as 'served out of course'.[3] The history of the French word is quite easily traceable through history. It is said to have been first used as a description of a dish in the twelfth century in a satirical chanson in a parody of a noble feast; in another example from about the same time it refers to some kind of theatrical entertainment. This double meaning remains prevalent until a clearer distinction arose during the sixteenth century: in the late medieval food world *entremets* denote elaborate dishes, table sculptures, fantastically arranged plates, or any other kind of entertainment between courses.[4] The English *soteltie* also denoted any 'ornamental figure, scene, or other design, typically made of sugar, used as a table decoration or eaten between the courses of a meal'.[5] Its use was antiquated after the sixteenth century.

Looking at it from the practical side, these intermediary dishes generated some more time for the waiters and kitchen staff to take away one and prepare the next course, as they guaranteed that the guests were engaged. There seems to have been no fixed order when these dishes were served: sometimes creations were even served only to select guests, while the others watched the spectacle.[6]

Edible *entremets* started out small and simple like wheat puree, aspic, or sauces – albeit coloured with saffron – but soon evolved into more and more elaborate dishes, providing the chef an opportunity to impress both his master and the guests.[7] These masterpieces included the famous blackbirds in a pie, roasted peacocks dressed as live birds, *Coqz heaumez* (a roasted, helmeted cock seated on a roasted suckling pig like a knight in a tournament), and the 'Cockentrice' (where the front half of a suckling pig is sewed to the back half of a capon). At the turn of the modern era it became more common or even necessary due to the complexity of the showpieces to also use nonedible pieces like paintings, sculptures, or fountains as elements of the distraction between courses. But the different areas start to overlap and connect in their aim to impress the audience: 'Pie Parma Style' combines culinary skill with architectural elements as it represents castle-like structures filled with a delicious something or other, while gold and silver coated roasted swans call for the skilful hand of a craftsman used to working the fine metal.[8]

There are few to no records in German manuscripts that would prove customs similar to those in France or England, where certain dishes were served between courses. Historical sources of the wedding between Hedwig, the Polish King's daughter and Georg, Duke of Bavaria, at the town of Landshut in 1475, which probably was the most entertaining event of the second half of the fifteenth century in this part of Europe, provide a list of dishes for the wedding feast, but a cradle, manufactured completely from gingerbread, which would have been the *entremets* as well as the bride's dish, is only cursorily listed there.[9] Nevertheless, there are a plethora of recipes describing fancy dishes that go beyond the simple preparation of food. Although such dishes are quite common in medieval German culinary recipes, until now no one has provided historical evidence of contemporary names. Research took up the historical term *Schaugerichte* (or *Schauessen*), that was used in the second half of the sixteenth century to describe dishes, or parts of dishes (e.g. pie heads), that could also be labelled as *entremets* (in both its meanings). The focus, though, according to the historical dictionaries, was rather on the ornamental and entertaining than the edible aspect.[10] Today, *Schaugerichte* is generally translated as 'show dishes', although the historical interpretation of the term as 'dishes that are meant for the guests to look at' would be more to the point. Presently we know of only three sources (all recipes for the famous 'pie with live birds') that provide Early New High German collective names for this kind of recipe: *ein schympfessen* or *Ein gepachens das gehoert zu einer kuerczweil*.[11] The recipe titles could loosely be translated as 'a surprise dish' or 'a pastry that is part of an amusement'. Since the terminology is not consistent in the English research literature and this kind of dish goes beyond what is commonly denoted *entremets* or *sotelties* – as they are also part of regular courses (cf. the list of dishes at the Landshut wedding) – we suggest using the term 'surprise dish', as it most comprehensively describes the character of this kind of dish.

Medieval recipe collections generally hand down the outstanding, or the complicated recipes, that might only have been prepared for special occasions. In this paper we assume a very broad-minded view of surprise dishes, and we will not solely focus on the extremely extravagant preparations but also aim at a categorization of all dishes that fall under our initial definition including naming conventions, visual distinctiveness, transformation of ingredients or food, and an explicit entertainment factor. Table 1 offers a comprehensive summary of medieval cooks' skills and their fabulous imaginations. We will structure the summary according to our definition in order from simple to complex preparations.

I. Naming	a) food unrelated connotation
	b) preparation methods
II. Visual	a) colour
	b) imitation of standard dishes
	c) imitation of objects outside the cooking sphere
III. Transformation	a) substantial manipulation / change of physical condition
	b) imitation of ingredients
	c) substitution of ingredients ('fake' dishes)
IV. Entertainment	a) fancy cooking techniques
	b) extraordinary implementation, complex cooking techniques
	c) surprise elements to entertain, shock, or repulse

Table 1: A systematic characterization of medieval surprise dishes.

Some of the medieval German recipes indicate that the dishes were either presented by name when served or that there was some food-related talk at the table, as one comment in a cooking recipe for 'An Eel Prepared in Two Ways' suggests: the eel is skinned, the skin is filled with egg stuffing, then the eel's head is sewn back to the skin, then this assembly is roasted; meanwhile, the skinless carcass is cooked in wine. Following the serving instructions the author comments: *So mag der herr woll gesprechen von wann chumbt der ainn all* ('This way the master can say: "Now served: *one* eel"').[12] This renders the titles of the recipes (when they are available in the manuscripts) even more important than we consider them now.

This emphasis on surprise might also explain the hilarious naming of certain recipes, like 'Peas Roasted on a Skewer', 'Roasted Milk', 'Cloth Puree', or 'Suspenders Aspic'.[13] Both the titles of the pea and the milk recipe combine ingredients with cooking methods that usually do not go well together. In the diners this evokes wonder, curiosity, and suspense. Both recipes use a similar method: from the peas a sponge dough is prepared, that is baked, cut into squares, covered with batter, and spit roasted; the milk is mixed with eggs, set into hot water to coagulate, cut into chunks, and roasted on a spit. The other two titles seemingly combine ingredients from outside the cooking domain: cloth and suspenders, both associated with accoutrement and clothing. Again, both the host and the chef play with the imagination of their guests and let suspense build up. The first recipe, as medieval recipes often are, is not really specific in its instructions: slices of stale bread are to be cooked in almond milk and served sweet. This takes some interpretation on our side, but if the slices are rather large but thin, they might resemble pieces of cloth. The instruction for the aspic is more detailed: roe deer skin has to be unhaired, cut into medium broad (just as broad as suspenders) strips, boiled, and then finished as a classic aspic, with some tails of the stripes gilded and hung over the edge of the dish. For this recipe, the title is meant to surprise, but the visual appearance is just as important.

The aspect of visual appearance touches, of course, all our categories to some extent, as the imitation of ingredients, dishes, and objects outside the cooking sphere are closely related to the transformation of foodstuffs. The numerous recipes for Lenten roasts in the medieval manuscripts combine these two aspects by replicating the visual image of a roast, oftentimes in impressive detail (e.g. larding the faux roast with egg white or fish filet). One perhaps not obvious example of imitation are the recipes to make chicken leg from chicken breast.[14] This rather refined process requires the breast to be ground, mixed with spices, bacon, and white bread and fitted on the chicken bone to resemble a conventional chicken leg. Recipes to imitate objects outside the cooking sphere do not result from a lack of availability, but rather show the playfulness of the medieval upper-class kitchen in its purest form. Particularly remarkable is the number of recipes describing the creation of a 'Hedgehog', with each recipe featuring a different main ingredient (almonds, raisins, etc.), therefore offering a range of possible colours to choose from. Another example is the replication of a 'Necklace' made of dough and stuffed with apples and grapes.[15]

As these feasts were meant to entertain, medieval cooks created an extremely colourful cuisine. The medieval German recipe collections include many recipes for preparing food colouring and tips on how to preserve them. Perhaps the best known and most frequently handed down recipe for coloured food is *Blanc manger*, found in nearly all recipe collections throughout Europe. The striking fact about this recipe actually is the absence of colour! All ingredients – almonds, breast of chicken, or fish if it is for Lent – aim at producing a creamy white dish. But of course, the *haute cuisine* of the Middle Ages even coloured this dish, for example, blue by adding violet or cornflower petals. Food colourants were mainly derived from herbs, spices, or fruit. The most frequently called for are parsley for green; saffron for yellow; nutmeg, cloves, cinnamon for brown; raspberries for red, and blueberries for a bluish violet. Black was generally produced by excessively roasting gingerbread; white often was simply egg white. With these, all kinds of dishes were coloured: purees, pancakes, aspic, stuffings, etc. The different coloured dishes were also often prepared in a way that the colours were arranged in a check pattern or layered like aspic or pancakes. For example, the base recipe for 'Pancakes in Three Colours' reads as follows: separate the yolks from the egg white; pound parsley and mix it with some egg white; colour the yolks with saffron; prepare white, green, and yellow pancakes; brush the pancakes with egg and stack them; bake it in lard as any other cake. When the cake is brought before the guests and cut into pieces a beautifully coloured cut surface is displayed.[16]

Restrictions on the consumption of food – either imposed by nature or society – encouraged a special kind of culinary creativity: the imitation of certain foodstuffs in times of shortage or fast. Here again the visual presentation of the dishes is crucial, as the illusion relies on each dish looking like something it is not and thereby tricking the diner's eye. Probably the most common type of recipes for imitation dishes are Lenten versions of meat dishes like roasts. By indulging in these 'fake' versions of dishes, one could indulge a fantasy of fasting without any constraints, adding another layer of imagination to the culinary feats of medieval Europe. The visual aspect is clearly important: while taste is hardly ever mentioned (if so, the rather nonchalant *so ist es guet*, meaning 'this is well-prepared', offers no real information in that regard), the desired visual impression is highlighted and emphasized. There was a whole range of tools available to transform food in the Middle Ages, from transforming the substance of ingredients to tricking diners by playing with established conventions, as when a Lenten version of a venison dish was served in the sauce inextricably linked with the actual meat version of the dish. This technique at least combines visual perception and taste.

Surprise dishes often entail a striking change to the properties of the ingredients. These changes can either aim to imitate of other foodstuffs or simply offer a new perspective on everyday ingredients. Changes may affect the physical condition or texture (e.g. grinding meat so fine that it can be formed to resemble something completely different) or the visual appearance (e.g. colouring a dish transforms the appearance). The medieval German recipe collections are rich in puree recipes, most of them coloured in some way. By pounding and grinding the various ingredients into a fine mash, the original physical properties are lost, transforming them into one homogenous dish, often coloured to charm the diner by adding one of the many known food colourings. But transformation is perhaps most important in regards to substitution and imitation of ingredients when their consumption is either forbidden during fast days or impossible due to the season.

One of the most important ingredients for substitution are almonds, which can substitute for a variety of ingredients such as milk, cheese, butter, and even eggs. While almond milk and nut cheeses of various kinds are back in fashion nowadays (in the Middle Ages all kinds of nuts, hemp, or opium poppy seeds were used), almond eggs are a forgotten art. In a recipe for 'Almonds as Poached Eggs', almonds are ground and divided into three parts. The first part is transformed into yolks by colouring with saffron and mixing with white bread, spices, and honey.[17] The second, still white part forms the egg white, which shall hold the yolks, while the third part is liquified a little and mixed with flour, sugar, and again saffron. This unbelievably creative dish is only one of many substitution dishes with almonds playing a central role, each of which proves that necessity is the mother of invention.

In the Middle Ages, consuming particular ingredients was limited not just by the restrictions of the Roman Catholic Church calendar, but also by nature. The seasons inevitably determined which foodstuffs were available, spurring on imitation of ingredients not in season. One resulting dish is 'Fake Morels, Around Christmas Time', in which the morels are formed of dough, covered in batter, and fried in lard.[18] The fake morels can also be made out of choux pastry, dried fruit, or meat paste and filled with various stuffings. The wonder and excitement at receiving something simply not available in a specific season makes these kinds of dishes so intriguing. Both approaches compensate for an absence of foodstuffs, whether self-imposed or environmental.

Some of the dishes handed down in the medieval German recipe collections are entertainment perfected to the optimum, whilst still remaining edible. By applying unusual cooking techniques, medieval cooks created astonishing dishes that ranged from 'simple' roasts to extraordinarily complex architectural food sculptures. Fancy cooking techniques are employed to render normal food preparations exceptional. Some of these include the coating of roasts with colourful batter or crusts, moulding hollowed out roasts filled with aspic, preparing fish by skinning it and stuffing the skin with a farce made of its own flesh, or applying two or three preparation methods on one piece of fish or eel (frying, cooking, roasting). The recipe of 'Fish Prepared in Three Ways' is handed down in several European languages: put it on a roast, flour the head part, wrap the middle part with linen, score the tail part; pour hot lard over the head part until it is golden brown, pour a mixture of boiling wine and water over the middle part, the third part roasts itself.[19] Bringing such a dish before guests would certainly have created awe and surprise, and both host and chef would have received great praise concerning this artful cookery. Another recipe, included in many manuscripts, to produce one giant egg made of thirty or forty normal-sized chicken eggs with the help of two pig's bladders intends to leave diners wondering what legendary creature the host might possess that could possibly lay such huge eggs.[20] Similarly, the result of the numerous *Krosseier* recipes may seem more like a magic trick than a dish prepared by man: the eggs are slightly cooked, so that some of the egg white congeals, then blown out, the yolk is gently warmed and mixed with green herbs, subsequently filled back into the eggshells, the eggs are then hard-boiled and presented as whole, unexciting eggs to the diner – of course the guests are in for a marvellous surprise when peeling and cutting the eggs![21]

But the medieval sense for entertainment at the dining table surpasses what one might consider awe-inducing techniques. At times, the intention behind recipes is clearly to shock or even repulse the guests. For this purpose, quicksilver was oftentimes used to bring movement to the already prepared dishes, thus making animals look alive as they squirm or jump in front of the guests. One example in the German manuscripts is the 'Chicken, Clucking on a Table', which requires cautiously filling the neck of a roast chicken with quicksilver to avoid the neck ripping open.[22] Another is 'Live Fish in Aspic', which calls for small fish to be filled with an amount of quicksilver the size of a pea to imitate them swimming in the aspic next to the fish prepared to be actually eaten.[23] (This recipe also explicitly mentions that it may be served to noblemen.) These recipes show the lavishness in festival cooking, since animals tainted with quicksilver are not fit for consumption.

The most complex surprise dishes combine exceptional cooking techniques with technical or architectural skills. While the dishes described so far are extraordinary, these have all the characteristics to be the climax of a feast: a pig's head spitting flames; a whole egg, or even a whole chicken, served in a pinch bottle; a dish of parsley that actually grows on the table; the pie with live birds in it; a tiled kitchen stove. Even reading the titles shows that these dishes were primarily made to surprise and entertain the guests. With some of these dishes, it is difficult to even imagine how they would have been eaten, as we, in fact, know how to insert the egg or the chicken into the bottle, but we have no sources that tell us how it was taken out! To prepare these dishes, the chef needed to be extremely experienced and skilled. He had to be not only an expert in cooking techniques (skinning the chicken, inserting the skin whole into the bottle, restuffing it with the right amount of meat, and cooking it to the point), but he also had to master some gardening skills (preparing the soil and the parsley seeds), and know his chemistry (igniting the brandy in the pig's mouth with a glowing ember when served, dissolving the calcium in the eggshell to soften it up for insertion into the bottle). Making the tiled oven required extraordinary knowledge and skill. The tiles are deep fried egg dough over a wooden frame, glued to sections of pre-baked gingerbread with a stuffing of apples, raisins, and spices, and ornamented with confectionaries. The gingerbread shapes the body of the stove, the top is a white dough sheet, on which sticks of wood and glowing embers made out of almond puree are placed. The recipe labels this dish as a *praut essen*, a 'bride's dish'.

The most important trait of a medieval chef in a courtly kitchen, however, must have been the vivid imagination needed to plan and implement enormous architectural showpieces made of food. For example, in his *Du fait de cuisine*, the French chef Master Chiquart describes a raised *entremets*, a whole castle. He starts with the wooden construction, on which a castle with four fortified towers is built, lit from within, manned with crossbowmen, decorated with branches bearing flowers, fruit, and birds. At the foot of the towers in the courtyard are a boar's head, a pike cooked in three ways, a glazed piglet, and a swan, all four breathing fire and served with accompanying sauces. The centrepiece is a fountain of love, spewing rose water and mulled wine, beside which are a roasted goose and peacock, redressed with their feathers. All around are roasted birds and men as well as animals moulded from meat and legume paste. Chiquart closes the recipe describing how the wooden construction needs to be devised to hide several musicians.[24] Similar, albeit not so extravagantly outfitted, castles are described in the *Forme of Cury* and a Lower German recipe collection.[25]

Just as impressive is the architectural surprise dish handed down in the recipe collection of Master Hanns from 1460. What he names an 'animal enclosure' is actually a whole edible hunting party in a typical medieval setting: an extended compound, enclosed with walls and fences, filled with greenery and fruit trees; a tower surrounded by a moat with fish in it; the compound holds ten kinds of game; on the tower there are ladies, girls, knaves, and knights who look out for game to hunt. In the vicinity of the tower is a kitchen and a feasting party. The description of the dish's layout is interspersed with fragmentary cooking instructions: men and animals are to be made from meat and fish paste, the fences and walls from different bread doughs, the greenery from parsley coloured egg paste, and so on.

Researchers have often dismissed this recipe as a corrupted text or outright phantasmagoria due to the text's rather confusing structure. However, in the light of medieval cooking recipe transmission in general and compared to Chiquart's castle recipe in particular, this seems a perfectly sane and structured recipe – at least for people who are experienced in medieval cookery, as of course medieval chefs were. But above that, it can simply be seen as a great inspiration for cooks who love an imaginative approach towards cooking, as a practical attempt to implement this recipe by the society Medieval culinary art Graz has shown.[26] As soon as the idea of surprise dishes and the design of Meister Hanns's hunting party was properly communicated, these cooking enthusiasts began churning out ideas – the results of this endeavour have been captured on video.[27] Watching it conveys the awe, suspense, and entertainment medieval surprise dishes must have evoked with contemporary diners!

Notes

1. Trude Ehlert, *Maister Hannsen des von Wirtenberg Koch* (Frankfurt: Tupperware, 1996), p. 336; translations by Helmut W. Klug.
2. Titus Petronius Arbiter, *Satyricon*, ed. by Michael Heseltine (London: Heinemann, 1913), Petr. 40, in *Perseus Digital Library* <http://data.perseus.org/citations/urn:cts:latinLit:phi0972.phi001.perseus-eng1:40> [accessed 27 May 2021]
3. Paul Freedman, *Food: The History of Taste* (London: Thames & Hudson, 2007), p. 192.
4. L. B. Ross, 'Beyond Eating: Political and Personal Significance of the entremets 145 at the Banquets of the Burgundian Court', in *At the Table: Metaphorical and Material Cultures of Food in Medieval and Early Modern Europe*, ed. by Timothy J. Tomasik and Juliann M. Vitullo (Turnhout: Brepols, 2007), pp. 145-66 (p. 146-47).
5. Oxford English Dictionary, 'subtlety', 4.b. (Version 12/20) <https://www.oed.com/view/Entry/193191?redirectedFrom=soteltie#eid> [accessed 27 May 2021]
6. Ken Albala, *Cooking in Europe, 1250-1650* (Westport, CT: Greenwood Press, 2006); Freedman, pp. 30, 192; Melitta Weiss Adamson, *Food in Medieval Times* (Westport, CT: Greenwood Press, 2004), p. 74.
7. Adamson, p. 74.
8. Bruno Laurioux, *Tafelfreuden im Mittelalter*, trans. by Gabriele Krüger-Wirrer (Augsburg: Bechtermünz, 1999), p. 132; Freedman, p. 192; Adamson, pp. 74, 164.
9. Roman Deutinger and Christof Paulus, *Das Reich zu Gast in Landshut* (Ostfilder: Thorbecke, 2017), p. 68.
10. Jacob Grimm and Wilhelm Grimm, '*Schaugericht, Schauessen*', in *Deutsches Wörterbuch*, digitalisierte Fassung in *Wörterbuchnetz des Trier Center for Digital Humanities* (Version 01/21) <https://www.woerterbuchnetz.de/DWB> [accessed 27 May 2021]
11. Helmut W. Klug (with the help of A. Böhm, J. Eibinger, and C. Steiner), 'Pie with Live Birds', *CoReMA – Cooking Recipes of the Middle Ages. Corpus – Analysis – Visualisation* <http://hdl.handle.net/11471/562.10.1029>, <http://hdl.handle.net/11471/562.10.358>, <http://hdl.handle.net/11471/562.10.1486>

12 Klug, 'Eel, Boiled and Roasted', *CoReMA* <http://hdl.handle.net/11471/562.10.999>
13 Klug, 'Peas Roasted on a Skewer', *CoReMA* <http://hdl.handle.net/11471/562.10.427>, <http://hdl.handle.net/11471/562.10.704>, <http://hdl.handle.net/11471/562.10.1552>; 'Roasted Milk': <http://hdl.handle.net/11471/562.10.1233>; 'Cloth Puree': <http://hdl.handle.net/11471/562.10.593>; 'Suspenders Aspic': <http://hdl.handle.net/11471/562.10.331>, <http://hdl.handle.net/11471/562.10.642>, <http://hdl.handle.net/11471/562.10.1003>, <http://hdl.handle.net/11471/562.10.1461>
14 Klug, 'Fake Leg of Chicken from Chicken Breasts', *CoReMA* <http://hdl.handle.net/11471/562.10.1454>, <http://hdl.handle.net/11471/562.10.1633>
15 Klug, 'Necklace', *CoReMA* <http://hdl.handle.net/11471/562.10.983>
16 Klug, 'Pancakes in Three Colors', *CoReMA* <http://hdl.handle.net/11471/562.10.960>, <http://hdl.handle.net/11471/562.10.557>
17 Klug, 'Almonds as Poached Eggs', *CoReMA* <http://hdl.handle.net/11471/562.10.889>
18 Klug, 'Fake Morels, at Christmas', *CoReMA* <http://hdl.handle.net/11471/562.10.1187>, <http://hdl.handle.net/11471/562.10.1235>
19 For example Klug, 'Fished, Prepared in Three Ways', *CoReMA* <http://hdl.handle.net/11471/562.10.761>
20 For example Klug, 'Egg, Giant', *CoReMA* <http://hdl.handle.net/11471/562.10.1206>
21 For example Klug, '*Krosseier*', *CoReMA* <http://hdl.handle.net/11471/562.10.531>
22 Klug, 'Chicken, Clucking on the Table', *CoReMA* <http://hdl.handle.net/11471/562.10.944>
23 Klug, 'Fish, Living, in Aspic', *CoReMA* <http://hdl.handle.net/11471/562.10.945>
24 Terence Scully, *Du fait de cuisine par Master Chiquart 1420* (Sion: Archives Cantonales, 1985), p. 137-45.
25 Chastletes, No. 197, in *Curye on inglysch*, ed. by Constace Hieatt and Sharon Butler (Oxford: Oxford University Press, 1985); Klug, *CoReMA*, recipe collection W05, recipes 39 and 77 (available soon: <https://gams.uni-graz.at/o:corema.w05>).
26 KuliMa – Kulinarisches Mittelalter an der Universität Graz <http://kulinarisches-mittelalter.org/>
27 Kulinarisches Mittelalter Graz, *Mittelalterliche Schaugerichte – Medieval Surprise Dishes*, YouTube, 29 October 2021 <https://youtu.be/QsvcS8LakNs> [accessed 29 October 2021]

Delicacies Real and Imagined: Food and Drink as a Diplomatic Gift

Paul Brummell

The giving and receiving of diplomatic gifts dates to prehistory as a part of diplomatic engagement across the world. For French sociologist Marcel Mauss, whose 1925 study *The Gift* is a seminal text on gift exchange, the gift economy has a social function. Mauss distinguishes between two forms of exchange.[1] In gift exchange, a social relationship is created and maintained by gifting, an act binding giver and receiver together.[2] In commodity exchange, the relationship between buyer and seller generates no enduring link.[3] The need for diplomacy arises when two geographically separated and distinct groups must conduct business. This business is facilitated by an ongoing social relationship between the groups, and diplomatic gifts are an important means of establishing and maintaining such a relationship.

Mauss identifies three obligations underpinning the gift exchanges he studied, from the Trobriand Islanders of Melanesia to indigenous peoples of the northwest coast of America. These are the obligations to give presents, to receive them, and to repay gifts received.[4] If these obligations are not met, the social relationship with the other party is repudiated.[5] Gifts, then, require reciprocation, building a system of exchange that while voluntary in outward appearance is in fact obligatory.

The choice of gifted object is usually that of the giver and serves their objectives. These are not necessarily benign. The citizens of Troy would have done better to look their gift horse in the mouth. Gifts may be used to underline authority and power, for example in lavish gifting to a recipient unable to match its beneficence. They may be offered in the expectation of a greater return. A gift offered as a bribe would fall into that category. Or they may reflect insecurity about a relationship and be used as an attempt to fortify it.

An enormous range of objects has been deployed as diplomatic gifts, from armour to zebras. They tend to stand out from items of quotidian exchange, as objects intended to generate wonderment in the recipient. In a study of gift exchange with the Mamluk Sultanate of medieval Egypt, Islamic art expert Doris Behrens-Abouseif identifies the Islamic concept of *tuhaf*, or 'marvels', as an essential attribute of the chosen gift.[6] The use of exotic animals as diplomatic gifts, from the elephant gifted to Charlemagne by Abbasid Caliph Harun al-Rashid to the 'panda diplomacy' of modern-day China, speaks to the capacity of such creatures to enrapture the recipient.

A gift might also be chosen as a calling card of the gifting polity, highlighting its technological sophistication or cultural achievements. The gifting of Meissen porcelain by eighteenth-century Saxon rulers underlined that country's success in uncovering the secrets of hard-paste porcelain manufacture where other European courts had failed.

Gifts might support export ambitions, by showcasing a product the gifting polity hopes to sell in the receiving one. This potentially jars with the aim to create a sense of wonder, and the export-promotion intent of diplomatic gifts tends to be limited to luxury items. Lord Macartney's ill-fated mission to China of 1793 aimed to open the Chinese market to British exports. Believing that the mission's gifts could showcase the best British goods to the Chinese, manufacturer Matthew Boulton provided recommendations of fine examples of British wares, from buttons to candlesticks.[7] However, Macartney wanted to distinguish the king's gifts to the emperor from simple trade goods, and such items were sidelined in favour of gifts intended to speak to British achievements in science and technology.[8] The most eye-catching gift was a glass-cased planetarium, incorporating three clocks and embellished with ormolu pineapples. Macartney presumably glossed over the fact that this remarkable object was not British, but the work of a pastor and clockmaker from Württemberg.

Food and drink play a distinctive role as diplomatic gifts, which arises in part from their necessary place in diplomacy. Visiting envoys must eat. Dining occasions provide informal settings for discussions, more relaxed than audience halls or negotiating tables, with the act of breaking bread together serving as a mark of friendship.[9] Depending on the historical and cultural context, the host polity may be required to provide gifts of food and drink in various forms, whether offering a single meal or underwriting the full expenses of the visiting mission.

The role of food and drink as diplomatic gifts is not restricted to their place as gifts necessary to the functioning of a diplomatic mission. They enjoy further advantages as gifts. Luxurious and unfamiliar food and drink products can inspire awe and wonder. They can be repositories of *tuhaf*. They can showcase the cuisine and agricultural wealth of the gifting country: their use as diplomatic gifts parallels the current focus of many countries on gastrodiplomacy, in which a national cuisine is used as a form of soft power.[10] Seasonal food gifts such as fruits lend themselves to repetition, becoming an annual tradition that can be an effective and low-cost means of reinforcing a social relationship, seen for example in the gifting of mangoes by South Asian political leaders.[11]

Because of the association of eating and drinking with friendship and conviviality, diplomatic gifts of food and drink may also be intended to hint at a warmth in the relationship between the two polities. Gifts of food that allude to their home-made or home-grown nature can similarly suggest a personal, friendly relationship between giver and receiver. Thus Giovanna d'Austria, the wife of Francesco I de'Medici in sixteenth-century Florence, sent home-made jams and pastes to both the Pope and Holy Roman Emperor.[12] A twenty-first century equivalent came in the visit to Washington of British Prime Minister Theresa May in 2017, when she gifted First Lady Melania Trump a hamper of produce from Chequers, her official country retreat, including apple juice, damson jam, and marmalade.[13]

One further quality of gifts of food and drink is worth comment. As objects designed to be ingested, acceptance of a gift of food or drink requires trust.[14] Gifts of food and drink may serve therefore not just as symbols of a warm relationship, but also as tests of it.

Has the use of food and drink as a diplomatic gift changed over time? To explore this question we will look at the examples of sixteenth-century Venice and the twenty-first century United States of America.

Diplomatic Gifts of Food and Drink in Sixteenth-Century Venice

Food and drink were used as diplomatic gifts by the Republic of Venice in the sixteenth century both to provide hospitality and sustenance for visiting diplomatic delegations and as luxury gifts to foreign rulers. Cheese provides an example of its use in both contexts.

In common with many other powers at the time, the Venetian government viewed the provision of hospitality to visiting diplomatic delegations as its duty, covering accommodation, entertainment, and food and drink. The latter in part took the form of elegant banquets. The hosts aimed to impress visitors with Venetian wealth and power through the impressiveness of food, spectacle, and venue. Thus a banquet organised in honour of a Muscovite embassy visiting Venice in 1582 *en route* to Rome was held in the Arsenal, providing a visual statement of Venetian maritime power.[15]

Food and drink also came in the form of a gift package provided to the visiting envoy on arrival, known as *refrescamenti*, or 'refreshments'. Its contents were luxurious in character, with a strong showing of Venetian specialities. This would typically include sugar, nuts, spices (including cinnamon and pepper), a range of fish or meat, fresh fruits, and a barrel of Moscato wine, as well as sweet confections such as the sugar-coated fruits or nuts known as *confetti*.[16] The Venetians provided all the food required for the twenty-three-day stay of the Muscovite delegation – and threw in the services of the doge's chef to prepare it. This was no small undertaking: the hospitality given to the Muscovite delegation cost Venice some 589 ducats, with food the largest component.[17] This sum pales though against the Venetian expenses for their spectacular reception for the future King Henri III of France in 1574, estimated at 100,000 ducats.[18] Venetian records show that the *refrescamenti* provided to the Muscovite delegation included four cheeses: mozzarella; the soft *giuncata*; *marzolino*, a sheep's cheese made from spring milk; and *piacentino*.[19]

Venice did not just deploy cheese in *refrescamenti* packages for visiting envoys. It was also a prestigious gift to foreign rulers. Turning back to the early sixteenth century, the relationship between Venice and the Mamluk Sultanate provides an example. The spice trade had long fuelled an interdependence between the two powers, though one always subject to stresses, such as over a policy introduced in the 1420s by Sultan Barsbay requiring Venice to buy some of the pepper at the heart of the trade from the sultan's warehouses. This was offered, of course, at inflated prices.[20] Despite such squalls, the lucrative nature of the trade meant that it had continued for centuries.

The landing in India in 1498 of Portuguese explorer Vasco da Gama would change Venetian and Mamluk fortunes irreparably. Portugal could now bring spices to Lisbon by the new maritime route. This was not the only headache facing Egypt and Venice. The Ottoman threat loomed large, and indeed Venice was at war at the turn of the century. The response to these external challenges provoked further disputes between Venetians and Mamluks. Attempting to make up the declining income from the spice trade, the sultan sought to force Venetian merchants to buy more pepper at an even higher price from his warehouses.

Attempting to both agree a common response to the external threats and to sort out the bilateral squalls, Venice despatched a mission in 1502 led by Benedetto Sanudo to Sultan Qansuh al-Ghawri in Cairo. Sanudo had two principal aims: first, to persuade the sultan that it was in the mutual interest of the two powers for Egypt to lower tariffs on spices and other goods imported from India in order to improve Venetian competitiveness against Portugal, and, second, to underline the seriousness of the Portuguese threat and hint, in a way that did not however provoke charges of Venetian conspiracy with a Muslim power against a fellow Catholic one, that he should take direct action against the Portuguese.[21]

Sanudo only reached Cairo in spring 1503 after a challenging journey. His gifts to the sultan included textiles, furs, and, yes, cheese, and he was given return gifts for the doge, including porcelain, incense, sugar, and civet musk.[22] The sultan did despatch a fleet against the Portuguese, but this did not have the desired effect, ending with Mamluk defeat in 1509 in a naval battle at Diu. Portuguese maritime control was firmly established.[23]

Another Venetian mission, headed by Domenico Trevisan, thus arrived in Cairo in 1512 against a worsening backdrop. Trevisan was tasked with sorting out ongoing disputes over the pepper price, resolving an issue of access to the Holy Land and securing the release of Pietro Zen, Venice's consul in Damascus, who had been detained in Cairo around suspicions related to contacts with the Safavids.[24] Venice had cause to be pleased with the outcome of the visit, securing what would prove to be their final commercial treaty with the Mamluks. Zen was not only released, but even received a parting robe of honour from the sultan.[25] However, this success had little lasting benefit: the Mamluk Sultanate had only five years left before being swept aside by the Ottomans in 1517.

Paralleling the Venetian practice in respect of visiting envoys, the sultan was keen to impress, providing the Venetian party with fine lodgings in a palace that had belonged to a wife of the former sultan. On their arrival, he sent them a gift of provisions including twenty geese, forty-four sugar-loaves, and five jugs of

Indian honey.[26] Trevisan's gifts for the sultan included 150 gowns, some of velvet, some satin, others threaded with gold. He also presented a huge quantity of furs, including 4500 squirrel furs, as well as sables and ermine, and fifty cheese blocks.[27]

Present in the gift packages to the sultan from both Sanudo and Trevisan, cheese was clearly an important component of Venetian gifting to Mamluk sultans in the early sixteenth century. What were these distinguished cheeses? Historian Jesse Hysell proposes that the cheese presented by Sanudo was *piacentinu*, a Sicilian cheese named for its pleasing taste.[28] With its golden hue created by the addition of expensive saffron, this cheese does appear to offer the quality of wonderment looked for in a prestigious diplomatic gift. It is also tempting to identify the peppercorns added to *piacentinu* cheese as a symbol of the pepper trade that underlay the close relationship between Venice and Egypt. Perhaps the cheese in question was however not *piacentinu* but *piacentino*, cheese from the Italian region of Piacenza. Historian Kenneth Meyer Setton identifies the gift made nine years later by Trevisan as 'cheeses from Piacenza'.[29] As we have seen, these were among the cheeses given in 1582 to the visiting Muscovite embassy. Piacentine cheese was also gifted by Venice to the Ottoman court.[30]

The cheese in question might have been a hard, crumbly, parmesan-like product, something like the Grana Padano produced in Piacenza province today. Parmesan-type cheeses were popular diplomatic gifts from various Italian courts. In gratitude for the support of the young King Henry VIII of England for his 'Holy League', Pope Julius II not only conferred on him a Golden Rose, the prestigious papal award to favoured sovereigns, but also gave him a hundred parmesan cheeses.[31] Parmesan was so highly prized in England that when, in 1666, the Great Fire of London threatened the property of diarist Samuel Pepys, his parmesan cheese was one of the items placed in a pit in a neighbouring garden for its protection.[32]

Diplomatic Gifts of Food and Drink to Twenty-First Century US Presidents

Diplomatic gifts were viewed with concern by the founding fathers of the United States of America, built on the ideals of the Enlightenment. They seemed to represent the corrupting influence of the Old World and its absolute monarchies, a threat to the very survival of the new state.[33] In drawing up the US Constitution they built on Article VI of its forerunner, the Articles of Confederation, devising an Emoluments Clause providing that 'no Person holding any Office of Profit or Trust under them, shall, without the Consent of the Congress, accept of any present, Emolument, Office or Title, of any kind whatever, from any King, Prince, or foreign State'. These rules attempted to guard against corruption through an over-arching framework that, in embracing all gifts, did not require corrupt intent.[34]

Such concerns were not unknown in the Old World, and indeed the sixteenth-century Venetian Republic had rules in place preventing individual acceptance of valuable diplomatic gifts from foreign powers. The gift to the doge of a diamond ring from the future Henri III at the end of his stay in 1574 occasioned debate in the

Venetian senate about what to do with it. The eventual decision was to mount it in a specially made gold lily, commemorating Henri's goodwill towards the republic, and place it in the treasury of St Mark's.[35] However, provisions as sweeping as those adopted by the United States were uncommon. They had the effect of changing diplomatic gifts from personal to regulated transactions.[36]

Congress is not of course required to deliberate on every foreign gift a US official would like to keep. Rather, the Foreign Gifts and Decorations Act of 1966, and subsequent amendments, give effect to the Emoluments Clause. This legislation allows officials to accept and keep gifts worth less than a statutorily defined 'minimal value' – $415 from 1 January 2020.[37] Costlier gifts may be accepted if refusal would cause offence or embarrassment, or otherwise be harmful to US foreign relations, but such gifts cannot be retained personally by the recipient. They are accepted on behalf of the US and passed to the National Archives and Records Administration, unless the recipient pays the US government the appraisal value of the gift in order to keep it.[38] They rarely do. Gifts to US presidents from foreign leaders are generally transferred to the presidential library museum collection, itself under the purview of the National Archives and Records Administration, after they have left office. Gifts of food, drink, and other perishable items such as perfumes are 'handled pursuant to US Secret Service policy', which appears to mean that they are simply disposed of.[39]

The rules around the acceptance of gifts by US officials give rise to the annual publication in the United States Federal Register by the Office of the Chief of Protocol of the US State Department of a list of the reported gifts from foreign government sources received by US federal employees. This serves as a useful source of information on the diplomatic gifts given to US presidents. This paper surveys the foreign gifts received by US presidents George W. Bush and Barack Obama, covering the sixteen years from 2001 to 2016, exploring the place of food and drink items in these gifts.

There are some limitations in the information set out in the annual list. It says nothing about the gifts given by the US president during the gift exchanges. Attempts to draw conclusions from the overall figures are challenged by the changing methodology used to compile the list. For example, presentations involving more than one gift are usually grouped as one entry, but in 2007 and 2008 are more often separated out. Most importantly, the list covers only gifts valued above the statutorily defined 'minimal value'. This means that food and drink items on the list generally fall into one of three categories: items gifted as part of larger presentations incorporating other gifts; food or drink gifted in particularly large quantities, such as the 300lb of lamb gifted to President Bush in 2003 by Argentinean President Néstor Kirchner; or items presented in an expensive container, such as the wooden box incorporating an American flag and eagle design made of precious and semiprecious stones in which President Mahinda Rajapaska of Sri Lanka gifted six pouches of coffee to President Obama in 2011.[40]

Over the sixteen-year period, 1099 gift packages received by the president, including gifts made jointly to the president and first lady, are listed in the returns. Eighty-seven include one or more items of food and drink, around eight per cent of the total. Food and drink are not then among the most common components of expensive gift packages to the president. Gifts involving food or drink come from forty-one countries, with eight countries offering three or more food or drink-related gifts over the sixteen-year period: France (9), Algeria (8), Brunei (8), Tunisia (4), the United Kingdom (4), Italy (4), Morocco (3), and Poland (3). Wine is the most frequently gifted food and drink item (mentioned in 31 gift packages), followed by spirits/liqueurs (15), chocolates (15), dates (11), biscuits (8), and fruit (7). Items mentioned just once include banana chips, beer, panettone, popcorn, peanut butter, and cheese, the sixteenth-century Venetian favourite.

What can be discerned from the State Department lists about the gift strategies underpinning the choice of food and drink items? Most obviously, items chosen as diplomatic gifts are generally products associated with pleasure and luxury, particularly wine, spirits, and sweet food products, rather than with sustenance. No gifts of vegetables are recorded.

The most consistent gift strategy in evidence is that of showcasing food and drink products for which the gifting country is particularly known: Haut-Médoc wine from France, ice wine from Canada, Turkish coffee, tequila from Mexico. In some cases, the gifts highlight the culture of the gifting country through its food and drink, as with a gift of maté to President Bush in 2006 from Tabaré Vázquez, President of Uruguay, gifted together with the traditional silver drinking straw and container.[41] Gifts may also highlight products for which a country would like to be better known internationally, supporting the export ambitions of local food and drink producers by associating the product, whether Angolan coffee or Croatian wine, with the president of the United States.

Gift packages offered to visiting heads of state and government attending international summit meetings often use food and drink items characteristic of the summit venue to convey a sense of 'place' that can otherwise prove elusive in tight-packed programmes of intensive negotiations in conference rooms. Gifts to President Obama from British Prime Minister David Cameron at the 2013 G8 summit held at the Lough Erne Resort in Northern Ireland included Co Couture chocolates, the work of a luxury Belfast producer, and a bottle of whiskey, alongside other gifts providing geographical markers, including books about Northern Ireland and a pair of porcelain cups decorated with shamrocks.[42]

Not all food and drink gifts to US presidents have a specific association with the gifting country. A different gifting strategy is in evidence in respect of the Lady McDuffies lemon cheesecake, the work of a bakery in Clarence, New York, gifted in December 2003 to President Bush by the Sultan of Brunei. This was part of a package full of pleasant holiday-season gifts, from a mahogany jewellery box to a CD entitled *An Old English Christmas*, as well as two dozen McDuffies shortbread cookies in a glass jar.[43] Such gifts of generic nice presents can convey an impression of a friendly, familiar relationship between the two leaders.[44]

The presence of dates as the fourth most frequently gifted category of food and drink items to US presidents owes much to the holiness accorded to the date within Islam and to the tradition of breaking Ramadan fasts with dates, specifically that of distributing dates at Ramadan among friends and family. Regular gifts of dates to US presidents account for the prominent place of both Algeria and Tunisia in the breakdown of food and drink-related gifts by country. The importance placed on munificent gift-giving in Islamic societies may also lie at the root of the lavishness of some individual gifts. In 2013, King Mohammed VI of Morocco gifted President Obama a basket of Godiva chocolates valued at $2484, suggestive of a considerable quantity of chocolate.[45]

Conclusion

In sixteenth-century Venice, the food and drink given as a diplomatic gift was intended to be consumed, whether as the *refrescamenti* provided to visiting delegations or as the large quantities of luxury cheeses presented to foreign courts. However, fears of poisoning meant that it would not always be enjoyed, at least by the intended recipient. It seems for example that Henri III refrained from eating at the lavish banquets held in his honour.[46]

While real gifts of food in sixteenth-century Venice thus sometimes became only imagined ones for the intended recipient, this is the norm in the regulated environment surrounding gifts to twenty-first century US presidents. Here, the recipient is destined never to consume the gifted item, which is instead handled 'pursuant to US Secret Service policy'. Rather than a gift intended to be tasted, it functions as a diplomatic signal. It can highlight the prized food and drink of the gifting country and potentially promote exports, as well as take advantage of the specific qualities of food and drink as gifts: their associations with friendship and conviviality serving as a metaphor for the desired warmth of the relationship between the two leaders.

At a less exalted level than gifts to the US president, today's diplomatic gifts of food and drink are of course frequently consumed, and with pleasure. The limits on the value of gifts that may be accepted and retained by government officials adopted by many countries, including the US, promote the attractiveness of food and drink as gifts. Their relatively low cost means that small gifts of consumable products may be offered in the reasonable expectation that the recipient will be allowed to retain and enjoy them. For the giver, they both underline a desire to continue a relationship and serve as a calling card for their country's luxury food and drink products, part of a wider strategy of gastrodiplomacy. The gifting of jars of maple syrup by Canadian diplomats, or bottles of wine by their Georgian counterparts, are examples.

A sixteenth-century practice embodying similar considerations is described by historian Sarah Bercusson in her account of three Austrian archduchesses who married into Italian courts. She found that food gifts were used extensively by her subjects to develop and maintain their own social relationships, including with foreign rulers: being both informal in nature and low cost, food items did not conflict with the rather different gifts used by their husbands as assertions of their status.[47] This example highlights the roles of different actors in diplomatic gifting, and suggests that, in this context at least, food and drink gifted as acts of personal relationship building by the consorts may have helped to reinforce wider diplomatic ties.

Notes

1. Marcel Mauss, *The Gift: Forms and Functions of Exchange in Archaic Societies*, trans. by Ian Cunnison (London: Cohen and West, 1966).
2. Emma Mawdsley, 'The Changing Geographies of Foreign Aid and Development Cooperation: Contributions from Gift Theory', *Transactions of the Institute of British Geographers, New Series*, 37.2 (2012), 256-72 (p. 258).
3. James Carrier, 'Gifts, Commodities, and Social Relations: A Maussian View of Exchange', *Sociological Forum*, 6.1 (March 1991), 119-36 (p. 123).
4. Mauss, p. 10.
5. Carrier, p. 123.
6. Doris Behrens-Abouseif, *Practising Diplomacy in the Mamluk Sultanate: Gifts and Material Culture in the Medieval Islamic World* (London: I. B. Tauris, 2016), p. 17.
7. Maxine Berg, 'Britain, Industry and Perceptions of China: Matthew Boulton, "Useful Knowledge" and the Macartney Embassy to China 1792-94', *Journal of Global History*, 1.2 (2006), 269-88 (p. 283).
8. Berg, p. 272.
9. Paul Brummell, 'Gastrodiplomacy and the UK Diplomatic Network', in *Food and Power: Proceedings of the 2019 Oxford Symposium on Food and Cookery*, ed. by Mark McWilliams (London: Prospect, 2020), 67-72 (p. 68).
10. Brummell, 'Gastrodiplomacy', p. 67.
11. Muhammad Saleh Zaafir, 'FO Sending Mangoes for Heads of over 32 Countries', *The News*, 10 June 2021 <https://www.thenews.com.pk/print/847404-fo-sending-mangoes-for-heads-of-over-32-countries> [accessed 17 October 2021]
12. Sarah Jemima Bercusson, 'Gift-Giving, Consumption and the Female Court in Sixteenth-Century Italy' (unpublished doctoral thesis, Queen Mary College, London, 2009), p. 217.
13. Jon Craig, 'Theresa May's Presents to Donald Trump: A Scottish Cup and Jam', *Sky News*, 26 January 2017 <https://news.sky.com/story/mays-presents-to-trump-a-scottish-cup-and-jam-10742783> [accessed 17 October 2021]
14. Bercusson, p. 219.
15. Laura Mesotten, 'A Taste of Diplomacy: Food Gifts for the Muscovite Embassy in Venice (1582)', *Legatio*, 1 (2017), 131-62 (p. 143).
16. Mesotten, pp. 136-37.
17. Mesotten, p. 146.
18. Evelyn Korsch, 'Diplomatic Gifts on Henri III's Visit to Venice in 1574', trans. by Nicola Imrie, *Studies in the Decorative Arts*, 15 (Fall-Winter 2007-2008), 83-113 (p. 87).
19. Mesotten, p. 142.
20. Benjamin Arbel, 'The Last Decades of Venice's Trade with the Mamluks: Importations into Egypt and Syria', *Mamlūk Studies Review*, 8.2 (2004), 37-86 (pp. 37-38).
21. Bailey W. Diffie and George D. Winius, *Foundations of the Portuguese Empire, 1415-1580* (Minneapolis:

University of Minnesota Press, 1977), p. 231.
22. Jesse Hysell, 'The Politics of Pepper: Deciphering a Venetian-Mamluk Gift Exchange', *AHA Today*, 6 July 2016.
23. Diffie and Winius, p. 240.
24. Deborah Howard, 'Venice and the Mamluks', in *Venice and the Islamic World 828-1797*, Institut du Monde Arabe/Metropolitan Museum of Art (New Haven: Yale University Press, 2007), pp. 72-89 (p. 84).
25. Kenneth M. Setton, *The Papacy and The Levant (1204-1571), Vol. III, The Sixteenth Century* (Philadelphia: The American Philosophical Society, 1984), p. 33.
26. Setton, p. 30.
27. Behrens-Abouseif, p. 110.
28. Hysell.
29. Setton, p. 31
30. Eric R. Dursteler, '"A Continual Tavern in My House": Food and Diplomacy in Early Modern Constantinople', in *Renaissance Studies in Honor of Joseph Connors,* ed. by Machtelt Israëls and Louis A. Waldman (Cambridge: Harvard University Press, 2013), pp. 166-71 (p. 169).
31. Garry Wills, *Why I Am a Catholic* (Boston: Mariner, 2003), p. 170.
32. A. Lloyd Moote and Dorothy C. Moote, *The Great Plague: The Story of London's Most Deadly Year* (Baltimore: The Johns Hopkins University Press, 2004), p. 264.
33. Paul Brummell, 'A Gift for a President', *The Hague Journal of Diplomacy*, 16.1 (2021), 145-54 (pp. 145-46).
34. Zephyr Teachout, *Corruption in America: From Benjamin Franklin's Snuff Box to Citizens United* (Cambridge: Harvard University Press, 2014), p. 4.
35. Korsch, pp. 93-95.
36. Teachout, p. 2.
37. General Services Administration, 'Revision to Foreign Gift Minimal Value', *Federal Register*, 17 March 2020.
38. Jack Maskell, 'Gifts to the President of the United States', *Congressional Research Service,* 16 August 2012, pp. 1-6 (p. 5).
39. Robin Wright, 'Presidential Swag and the Gift Horse', *The New Yorker*, 20 May 2016 <https://www.newyorker.com/news/news-desk/presidential-swag-and-the-gift-horse> [accessed 17 October 2021].
40. Office of the Chief of Protocol, US State Department, 'Gifts to Federal Employees from Foreign Government Sources Reported to Employing Agencies in Calendar Year 2003', *Federal Register,* 2 August 2004; 'Gifts to Federal Employees from Foreign Government Sources Reported to Employing Agencies in Calendar Year 2011', *Federal Register*, 26 April 2013.
41. Office of the Chief of Protocol, US State Department, 'Gifts to Federal Employees from Foreign Government Sources Reported to Employing Agencies in Calendar Year 2006', *Federal Register,* 7 December 2007.
42. Office of the Chief of Protocol, US State Department, 'Gifts to Federal Employees from Foreign Government Sources Reported to Employing Agencies in Calendar Year 2013', *Federal Register,* 12 November 2014.
43. Office of the Chief of Protocol, US State Department, 'Gifts to Federal Employees from Foreign Government Sources Reported to Employing Agencies in Calendar Year 2003', *Federal Register,* 2 August 2004.
44. Brummell, 'A Gift', p. 151.
45. Office of the Chief of Protocol, US State Department, 'Gifts to Federal Employees from Foreign Government Sources Reported to Employing Agencies in Calendar Year 2013', *Federal Register,* 12 November 2014.
46. Michael Krondl, 'Sugar and Show: Power, Conspicuous Display, and Sweet Banquets during Henri III's 1574 Visit to Venice', in *Food and Power: Proceedings of the 2019 Oxford Symposium on Food and Cookery*, ed. by Mark McWilliams (London: Prospect, 2020), pp. 167-76 (p. 171).
47. Bercusson, p. 226.

Greek *támisos* and Provençal *toma*: Etymological Evidence for Ancient Celtic Cheesemaking

Anthony F. Buccini

On the basis of classical texts and archaeological evidence for early Celtic pastoral practices, Kindstedt – with no mention of linguistic evidence – concludes: 'it was Celtic cheesemakers who were first (or among the first) to experiment with the making [of] large cheeses.' Further:

> It seems likely that the Celts brought their technologies for producing durable, long-lived cheese wherever they migrated across Europe, which may account for the extraordinary geographic range of Celtic cheeses that were exported to Rome, extending from Toulouse in far southern France to the Menapii region of Belgium and far northwest France, to the alpine regions of eastern France and the Massif Central, to Switzerland and Austria, to Dalmatia in the Balkan peninsula. (2012: 108, 109)

My research has led me independently to very similar conclusions, but central to my reasoning is the linguistic evidence presented below.

Specifically, I consider some words of considerable antiquity relating to dairy production which shed light on the early history of cheesemaking in Europe, words which have hitherto received remarkably little attention from linguists and food historians. One is Gallo-Romance *toma 'cheese' (French *tomme*); another is Greek τάμισος, attested in Classical Greek with the meaning 'rennet'. I demonstrate that these words, like other dairy-related words of the western Alps, are of Continental Celtic origin and point to the early development of rennet-based cheese production already in the second millennium BC.

Toma: A Gaulish Word for 'Cheese' in the Western Alps

In the centuries preceding and following the Roman conquest of the Western Alps (i.e. from western Switzerland south to the Mediterranean in Provence and northwestern Italy), this region was one whence emanated important innovations in the processing of milk into formed, aged cheeses, as evidenced by descriptions in classical texts and later by the rise of the term *formaticum* for a technological innovation for pressing and shaping processed curds. After the spread of *formaticum* throughout Gallo-Romance territory, it spread secondarily into central and southern Italy, where reflexes of Latin *caseus* 'cheese' survive but in more specialized uses alongside the intrusive *formaggio*.

In modern times, at the level of the standard languages, one finds throughout almost all western Europe reflexes of but two terms for 'cheese': *caseus* and *formaticum*. At the level of the dialects, however, one also finds in Romance territory a third term occurring throughout an area that corresponds largely to the Western Alpine region, namely *toma*.[1] This word appears with a range of specialized local senses from modest-sized, aged cheeses to fresh cheeses to curds produced by means of rennet (Wartburg 1928: v.13/2, 20-21) and, as with *caseus* in central and southern Italy, *toma* appears to have been ousted by reflexes of *formaticum* in its older role as generic word for 'cheese'.

It appears then that in the Latin/Romance of the Western Alps *toma* was quite plausibly a regional equivalent of *caseus* in the time before the rise of *formaticum*. Yet this word is attested neither in other Romance-speaking areas nor anywhere in the vast body of Latin writings, nor does it have any obvious etymological connexions within Latin. Given its restriction to a formerly Gaulish-speaking region and further to a region with a pre-Roman tradition of cheesemaking, I conclude that in all likelihood it is a Gaulicism which survived the linguistic switch from Gaulish to Latin/Romance.

This conclusion is supported by the occurrence of other dairy terms of likely or certain Gaulish origins which survived in Gallo-Romance varieties and especially those of the Western Alps. Indisputably of Gaulish origin are, for example, dialectal French *mègue* 'whey' (stFr. *petit lait*), from Celtic **mezgo-*, cf. OIr. *medg*. Similarly, a well-known cheese of the Western Alps (Savoie), *reblochon*, has as its root a Gaulish element. Though the name of this cheese is surely not ancient, it points us to a verb formerly widespread in the northern part of the Western Alps which is ancient and Gaulish in origin: *bléchier* 'to milk' goes back to Gallo-Romance *bligicare, derived from Gaulish **mlig-o-* (cf. OIr. *mligid*; Welsh *blith*, Ir. *bleacht* 'milk') (Maurice-Guilleux 1995). Similarly, French *claie* 'wattle, hurdle, etc.', attested in Medieval Latin as *clida* and with reflexes throughout Gallo-Romance territory in various specific applications, is a Gaulish loanword (Celtic *klēta), with direct cognates in Insular Celtic (e.g. Irish *cliath* 'wattle, hurdle'). Though we cannot date the beginning of its technical application in cheesemaking, where it means 'rack on which cheeses are dried' (Fr. *claie/claion à fromages*), this usage could well go back to pre-Roman times. Other such Gaulish survivals in Alpine Romance (and German) varieties have been adduced by Hubschmied (1936).

We conclude that Gallo-Romance *toma* 'cheese', which lacks dairy-related correlates in Greek or Latin and is thus unlikely to have been borrowed from those languages, has a dialectal distribution that suggests a Gaulish origin, a theory which is supported by the demonstrable presence of other dairy terms of Gaulish origin in Romance (and Germanic) dialects of the Western Alps.

Greek τάμισος

Since classical times, when discussions of dairy production are first attested in Greek, the primary word for 'rennet' has been πυτία (with variants πυετία, πιτύα). In the *Geoponika*

18.19 (Dalby 2011: 331), a tenth-century Byzantine text based on much older sources, we are told that πυτία, especially from kids, was the most widely used coagulant for making cheese, and this clear statement accords with what we can glean directly from classical sources. This word indicated in particular the curdled milk (and accompanying mucus and gastric juices) taken from the stomach of a suckling animal, and this sense fits well with the likely etymology. Beekes (2009: 1259) sees πυτία as a straightforward derivative of πυός 'beestings', i.e. the rich milk produced by the mother immediately after giving birth, which makes sense both semantically and morphologically. Yet the deeper etymology of the root, as noted by both Beekes and Chantraine (1968: 956), most likely goes back to an IE root *pu(H)- 'to rot, decay', represented in English *foul*, *filth* (Germanic), *putrid*, *pus* (from Latin), and reflected clearly in Greek πύθομαι 'to putrify', πύον/πύοσ 'pus'. To my mind, the derivation of 'beestings' directly from a root denoting 'pus, rot' makes little sense, but if we consider how the curdled beestings and especially the mucus – the πυτία – from the stomach of a just-born kid looks, we can see a reasonable association with pus. I therefore suggest that πυτία was derived from πύον 'pus, putrifaction' and that πυός 'beestings' was backformed from πυτία, given that the curdled milk (used as rennet) was often enough curdled beestings.

There was another word in Classical Greek that meant 'rennet', namely, τάμισος, attested especially in medical texts, most notably of Theophrastus (born on Lesbos, fl. fourth century BC) and Nikander (born in Ionian Anatolia, fl. third century BC), where it seems to overlap in meaning with πυτία 'rennet' yet refers to something somehow distinct; in Hesychius (sixth century AD) it appears with a simple gloss of 'πυτία' (Schmidt 1867: v.4, 127).

Greek τάμισος is an odd word that has been treated only briefly in the etymological dictionaries (e.g. Chantraine 1968, Beekes 2009) with no clear solution to its origins having been proposed. The basic oddity of this word resides in that what appears to be suffixal material (-*is*-) does not look in a Greek context like the reflex of an inherited Indo-European suffix, a point duly noted by Chantraine and taken by Beekes to be indicative of the word originating in his non-Indo-European 'Pre-Greek' substrate language. Yet the root of τάμισος looks very much like it might derive from a widely attested and semantically appropriate Indo-European verbal root, namely *$temh_1$- 'to cut, separate', which was particularly productive in Greek. The apparent combination of an IE root with a non-IE suffix seems, however, impossibly backwards – one would far sooner expect a non-IE root fitted out with a native Greek suffix inherited from Indo-European. Another peculiar characteristic of τάμισος is the fact that it is a feminine *o*-stem (2nd declension) noun, a relatively small and moribund category in Greek with regard to inherited Indo-European vocabulary which otherwise includes numerous loanwords (some of substratal origin, some Semitic) (Morpurgo Davies 1968: 19-20). A last noteworthy fact about τάμισος is that it was considered a Doricism, i.e. a word identified with the Doric dialect(s) of Greek; its marginal survival in Greek in the dialects of the Aspromonte (Calabria) and Tsakonia (Peloponnese) accords with that claim. Considering these facts, we cannot deny the possibility that τάμισος may be a borrowing into Greek from Beekes's Pre-Greek substrate or some other unidentifiable non-IE ('Mediterranean'?) language with which the Greeks were in contact: the suffix -*is*- seems to point strongly in that direction and its membership in the category of feminine *o*-stems, along with other loanwords, perhaps lends further support to that view.

Another possible explanation of τάμισος, one left unconsidered in the etymological dictionaries, is suggested, however, by the plausible relationship of this word's root with IE *$temh_1$-: perhaps τάμισος can be analyzed as a loanword from another branch of Indo-European. From this perspective, the membership in the class of feminine *o*-stems with other loanwords maintains its possible relevance and the seemingly non-IE suffix -*is*- might find a plausible explanation. In addition, the identification of the word as a Doricism may rise in significance: the Doric dialects of the Peloponnese and southern Greek islands are closely related to the Northwest Greek dialects and are generally believed to have spread southward from a northwestern homeland in the aftermath of the collapse of Mycenaean civilization (*c.* 1050 BC). Northwest Greek, centred in the mountainous region of Epirus by the Adriatic, was the neighbour to the south of the Indo-European Illyrian language and possibly of other such 'Palaeo-Balkan' Indo-European languages; unfortunately, these extinct languages, including Illyrian, are very poorly attested and understood. In this location, however, the common ancestor of the attested Northwest and Doric Greek dialects may, through trade or unknown population movements around the Ionian and Adriatic seas and their hinterlands, have been in direct or indirect contact with other Indo-European languages of Italy and the eastern Alps.

As we have seen, the Alps constituted an early centre of innovation in dairy production, but how early might cheesemaking have developed there? Could Greek τάμισος ultimately be of Alpine origin?

French/Provençal *tamis*

To my knowledge, no one has hitherto seen a connexion between Greek τάμισος and a French word known to professional cooks the world over, namely, *tamis* 'sieve'. Before its modern global success, the word was largely limited in distribution to the Gallo-Romance dialects of France, northern Italy, and western Switzerland, with the earliest attestations in French and Provençal (both *tamis*) starting from the twelfth/thirteenth century (Wartburg 1928: v.13/1, 73ff.); the word is also attested in Medieval Latin as *tamisium*, perhaps before 1000 AD in the Lyon region (Whatmough 1970: 586). We note, however, that the word appears also to have been borrowed into West Germanic at a very early date, before the operation of primary umlaut of ă (*c.* sixth/eighth cent. AD), the High German Consonant shift (*c.* sixth/seventh cent. AD), and probably even well before the Anglo-Saxon conquest (fifth/sixth cent. AD): Eng. *temse* (OE *tæmes*- *c.*1050 AD), Dutch *teems*, Frisian *têms*, German (dial.) *Zims*, all meaning 'sieve'.

Two things stand out about the Romance and Germanic reflexes of this word:

Greek *támisos* and Provençal *toma*: Etymological Evidence

1) there is generally great uniformity (allowing for local phonological peculiarities) of form; 2) there is also great uniformity in meaning as a kind of fine sieve. Already in the Middle Ages this kind of sieve had a close association with the sifting of flour, but this association need hardly be original and/or exclusive, as in parts of England it is also associated with beer-making and in France a *tamis* has also always been used to separate solids from liquid. Interesting in this regard is that in a large swathe of Germanic territory, extending through the western dialects of Dutch northward into Frisian and Low German areas, the *teems*, etc. is a traditional tool in cheese and butter making. I suggest that this usage may well be relictal and that the use of sieves bearing cognate names may have been the rule in dairy production in early Latin/Romance varieties of Gaul. It seems quite possible that the early borrowing of the word *caseus* into West Germanic (Eng. *cheese*, Dutch *kaas*, etc.) and spread of the knowledge of making aged cheese into Germanic territory was the very context in which an effective tool of cheesemaking, a specialized sieve, was also diffused northward.

We will return below to the historical details of the Gallo-Romance form *tamis*, etc. but, assuming the word is ultimately of Indo-European/Celtic origin, it seems most likely a derivative of the IE root *$temh_1$- 'to cut/separate', as mentioned above with regard to τάμισος. Though reflexes of this root are not directly attested in our limited Continental Celtic material, cognates are found in Insular Celtic, e.g. OIr *tamnaid* 'to cut', *taman/tamun* 'stump'. The primary sense of 'cut' seen here is reflected in many cognates in other IE branches though we see in some cases the secondary sense of 'separate'. Consider, for example, these Greek derivatives in all three ablaut grades: 1) e-grade: τέμενος 'domain, sanctuary'; 2) o-grade: τόμος 'section, piece', τομός 'cutting (adj.) sharp', τομή 'cutting, thing cut off'; 3) zero-grade: τμῆσις 'division', Doric/Ionian τάμνω 'to cut' (analogically reshaped in Attic τέμνω).[2] Greek τέμενος 'land set off, separated (as domain or divine sanctuary)' clearly bears the secondary sense; a differently formed Latin derivative of IE *$temh_1$-, *templum* 'temple', shows a parallel semantic development. The sense of 'separate' also lies behind Latin *(con-)temno* 'despise' (cf. Eng. *contempt*) which presumably started as 'to separate (socially)/shun' and became 'to scorn/despise'.

Gallo-Romance *tamis*, an instrument by which things are separated, fits well here. Interestingly, a connexion of reflexes of IE *$temh_1$- with dairy production is perhaps found in Greek γαλατμόν, which appears to be a compound of γαλα- 'milk' and -τμόν, perhaps a zero-grade derivation. Hesychius glosses this word as λάχανον ἄγρον 'wild herb', presumably indicating a plant used as vegetable rennet and called 'milk-separator'.

An Etymology of τάμισος/*tamis*

The formal near-identity of and clear semantic relationship between Greek τάμισος and Gallo-Romance *tamis* are quite sufficient to justify an attempt to seek a common origin and, as noted above, the evidence inclines us to consider a Celtic source. Assuming that τάμισος/*tamis* is ultimately of Indo-European origin, the root involved must have been *temh₁- 'to cut/separate'. Taken at face value, the root vowel points to a zero-grade, *tm̥h₁-, which by Celtic sound laws with a following vowel (-i-) would have indeed regularly yielded *tam-, as opposed to (e-grade) *tem- or (o-grade) *tom-.

As with any attempt to analyze τάμισος as an inherited IE form in Greek, the real problem is the suffix, as -is- did not exist as a simple derivational morpheme in Indo-European. That is not to say that a suffix of this form did not occur; rather, it did occur as the zero-grade of the ablauting suffix *-yos-/-yōs-/-yes-/-is-, which is reflected in several IE branches, particularly in the formation of the comparative grade of adjectives. None of the comparative formations attested, however, align with the apparent formation behind τάμισος/tamis, for they all reflect a root in full-grade and the base forms (nom./acc.) have *-yos- or *-yōs-; of direct relevance here is that the regular comparative in Celtic had full-grade of the root and *-yōs-, as in OIr. sen/siniu 'old/older' (siniu < *sen-yōs-) (Jasanoff 1990: 171).

While a Celtic ancestor of τάμισος/tamis cannot have been an inherited comparative, it can have been, and perhaps was, a related kind of form, specifically, a forerunner of what is attested as the superlative in Indo-Iranian (Ved. -iṣṭ(h)a), Greek (-ιστος), and Germanic (Go. -ists, Eng. -est). It is widely agreed that Proto-Indo-European did not possess morphologically-marked categories of adjectival gradation and that the comparatives and superlatives attested in the core Indo-European branches arose only in the late PIE period and their development was completed in the subsequent period of early dialectal diversification (Cowgill 1970: 114-15). Also generally agreed is that these new adjectival categories grew out of what are referred to as 'elatives', derived adjectives expressing that the thing described had the quality of the base adjective to a great degree. For example, from an adjective PIE *h₁wér-u-s (nom.)/h₁ur-éw- (wk) 'broad', the elative could be derived with the *-yos-/-is- suffix: *h₁wér-yos- (str.)/hur-is-' 'exceptionally broad' (Ringe 2006: 64; cf. Meillet 1964: 270). With differences of detail, the elative gave rise to the comparative formations attested in Indo-Iranian, Greek, Germanic, Balto-Slavic, Italic and Celtic (Rau 2014: 327-28).

Secondary to these Proto-Indo-European elatives was a further formation which ultimately gave rise to superlatives in Indo-Iranian, Greek, and Germanic, apparently derived by addition of the zero-grade of the elative suffix *-is- and a further individualizing suffix *-tó- (cf. Cowgill 1970: 124). Opinions differ as to the original ablaut grade of the root and place of accent in this formation. In the attested superlatives the evidence clearly points to accented full-grade root, but a number of scholars have argued that originally the root was in the zero-grade and the accent on *-tó-; Van Beek (2013: 86) calls this view 'communis opinio' (which he rejects) with multiple references. From this perspective, the accent and ablaut pattern of the attested superlatives were analogically reformed according to the pattern of the comparatives, leaving only a few marginal relic forms with the original shape (cf. Rau 2014: 329).

This formation in *-is-tó-, I believe, lies behind τάμισος/tamis, thus *tm̥h₁-is-tó-, built either directly from the verbal root *temh₁- or from an intermediary adjectival derivative (cf. Gk. τομός 'cutting, sharp') but with the secondary sense of 'separate/separating'. Nominalized, *tṃh₁-is-tó- would have meant 'that which separates exceedingly well' and was perhaps thus coined to designate a form of animal rennet. Semantically parallel deverbal constructions are attested in Indo-Iranian: Vedic hán-iṣṭha 'best at killing', Avestan nas-išta 'best at destroying' (Rau 2014: 332).

The phonological development of such a suffix in Gaulish is clear: -st- yielded a sound which in Gaulish attestations was represented graphically in a variety of ways with unknown phonetic value, called by linguists *tau gallicum*, but in some inscriptions it was also rendered simply with «-ss-» or «-s-»: the development was then from -st- > -SS- (*tau gallicum*) > -s(s)- (Eska 1998). Thus, an early Celtic *tam-isto- (< *tṃh₁-isto-) would have yielded unproblematically a late Gaulish *tamisso- and ultimately *tamiso-, the form seemingly borrowed into Gallo-Romance.

A possible objection to my etymology is this: while superlatives in *-is-tó- are attested in Indo-Iranian, Greek, and Germanic, they are not found in Italic and Celtic. These last two branches show superlatives built with a different complex suffix, namely *-is-m̥mo- Lat. -issimus, Proto-Celtic *-isamo- (Cowgill 1970: 125, Jasanoff 1990: 171); indeed, this innovation is central evidence for an Italo-Celtic stage after the dissolution of late Proto-Indo-European. It is then generally assumed that *-is-to- was a PIE formation that was eliminated in Italo-Celtic, of which traces could nonetheless theoretically have survived in those branches. That reflexes of *-is-to- are not attested in Celtic is a further possible objection and, to be sure, unassailable reflexes are wanting, but this fact must be relativized: with our extremely limited knowledge of the Continental Celtic lexicon and the relative lateness of our robust attestations of the Insular Celtic languages (many centuries after the borrowing into Gallo-Romance posited here), it is quite possible that clear relict forms with *-is-to- have simply not survived in the existing material. In this regard, a comparison with Italic, the other Indo-European branch which rejected *-is-tó- for superlative formation, is relevant. There too reflexes of *-is-tó- are exceedingly few, with but three recognized out of all of the attested Latin corpus, of which only one survived into Romance; two of these forms were archaisms related to religious practices (Watkins 1975) and the third, perhaps an old elative form, *iuxta* 'very closely yoked' (< *yugistā, with root in zero-grade), which had been lexicalized as a new adjective and thus survived in morphological isolation (i.e. was not reformed as a superlative in *-is-m̥mo-) (cf. Weiss 2020: 380). For Continental Celtic, there are some attested Gaulish personal names that might reflect formations in *-is-tó-, e.g. *Elvissa, Clarisso* (de Bernardo Stempel 1999: 423, De Goede 2014: 24-25). In my view, τάμισος/*tamis* are ultimately indirect reflections of a Gaulish archaism parallel to the Latin *iuxta*.

More on the Origins of Gallo-Romance *tamis* and *toma*

As we have seen, Greek attestations of τάμισος, from the fourth century BC to the modern dialects, can all be glossed as 'rennet', whereas all the Gallo-Romance forms, *tamis* etc., mean 'sieve', and while the semantic and contextual connexions between the two referents – each a means of separation and the two used sequentially in cheesemaking's crucial process of separating curds from whey quickly and thoroughly – are very close, one wonders how to account for the apparent shift of referent from 'rennet' to 'sieve' in Gallo-Romance, including the dialects of the Western Alps, the area where in my view the original Continental Celtic form *tam-isto- (< *tm̥h₁-isto-) 'rennet' likely arose. I say 'apparent shift' because, in fact, the family of forms that mean 'sieve' do not go back directly to the Celtic word for 'rennet' that was borrowed into Greek but rather to a similarly ancient Celtic derivative of *tam-isto- that survived as a borrowing in Latin/Romance and thence passed into West Germanic.

A detailed exposition of the Romance material is warranted but must be left for another time; here, it must suffice to state that the relevant Gallo-Romance forms for 'sieve' go back to a derived form with the suffix *-yo-, thus late Gaulish *tamisyo-. This form is clearly reflected in the Medieval Latin attestations of the word, *tamisium*, and, if we take *tamisium* as the starting point for the attested Gallo-Romance forms, the developments are fairly straightforward. Of particular interest is the development of the sequence *-Vsyu, in which the cluster -sy- has yielded widely a voiced and often palatalized sibilant (-z-, -ž-) with either loss of the yod or its metathesis into the preceding syllable where the vowel in *-Vsyu was non-front (a, o, u), e.g. regional Lat. *pertusium* 'hole' > Fr., Prov. *pertuis*. An unambiguous exact parallel of *tamisium* is wanting but a close parallel is found in late Latin *camisia* 'shirt' > OProv., Piedmontese *camisa*, Fr. *chemise* (»s«=[-z-]), Genoese *camixa* (»x«=[-ž-]); *tamisium* and *camisia* appear to have differed only with regard to gender and the final vowel, with -*a* long preserved in Gallo-Romance whereas -*u(m)* was lost in many varieties (incl. French and Provençal). In those dialects which preserved the final -*u*, the modern dialects show *-ísyu as -izo (Venetian *tamiso*, »s« = [-z-]) or as -*ižo-* (NIt./Tusc. *tamigio* [*tamižo*]). In many Gallo-Romance varieties, the final -*u* was lost and the then word-final sibilant was in many areas devoiced (and itself often subsequently lost), yielding Fr./Prov. *tami(s)* (dialectally also [tamiš]) (Wartburg 1928: v.13/1, 73ff.).[3]

We have then evidence from Greek τάμισος for a possible Celtic *tam-isto- 'rennet' and from Gallo-Romance *tamis*, etc. for a very likely late Gaulish *tamisyo- 'sieve (for curds?)', possibly from earlier *tam-ist-yo-. The relationship between our reconstructed forms seems clear both from a Celtic and the broader Indo-European perspective. There is abundant evidence across the family for a Proto-Indo-European suffix *-yó- (with a variant *-iyó-) which was used to derive adjectives and nouns from both verbal and nominal roots and also from nouns formed with suffixes (Weiss 2020: 294ff.). This suffix *-(i)yo- remained productive in Celtic and is attested in a wide array of semantic functions (Pedersen 1976, v.II: 16-17), an array so wide that the meaning of the suffix was clearly fairly bland, something along the lines of 'related to' or 'pertaining to'. In the present case, *tam-ist-yo- must have originally been coined with a sense of 'the thing used in conjunction with rennet (for separation of curds from whey)' and was a neuter noun, thus *tam-ist-yo-m giving late Gaulish *tamisyon, which was adapted upon borrowing into Latin, giving the attested *tamisium*.

The existence of the Gallo-Romance sieve word, tied to a formerly Gaulish-speaking area in which innovation in cheesemaking is demonstrable in early historical times, lends strong support to the analysis of Greek τάμισος as an early borrowing from Continental Celtic. If my proposal is correct, we have, moreover, a basis for interpreting the origin of the otherwise mysterious Gallo-Romance word for cheese, *toma*. The simplicity of this word, lacking any substantial suffix to aid in identification, allows for little analysis on its own: is it pre-Indo-European? Ligurian? The fact that this word occurs, however, essentially only in the Western Alps, the area to which *tamis* and, quite plausibly, τάμισος are also linked, allows us to more confidently propose that *toma* 'cheese' is in origin also Gaulish, a Celtic derivative of the IE root *$temh_1$-* ; it is then a Celtic analogue of Greek τομή 'a cutting, thing cut off' but with the secondary sense of 'the thing separated', i.e. 'drained curds', a sense attested in some modern Gallo-Romance dialects and easily the starting point for the other attested meanings of specific kinds of cheese and the generic meaning of 'cheese'.

In support of my claim that it is *$temh_1$-* that is reflected in these Western Alpine words is the fact that in Irish the word for rennet is *binid*, derived from another verb originally meaning 'to cut/strike' but in this context clearly also 'separate' (Buccini 2022). The Celtic rennet words share this semantic sense, focussing on the achievement of the action, and in this regard contrast with rennet words in Germanic (Eng. *rennet–run* 'run together'), Romance (Fr. *présure–prendre* 'take') and Latin (*coagulum–coagulare* 'drive together') which clearly focus on the initial stage of gel-formation. In effect, the Irish word seems to reflect a very old and peculiarly Celtic way of looking at the process of curd-production.

Conclusion

On the basis of the linguistic evidence, I date the coining of Continental Celtic *tam-isto- 'rennet' and *tam-ist-yo- 'sieve' to an early stage of the branch, when Celtic phonology and morphology were still close to the late Proto-Indo-European stage and, crucially, to a time when the elative formations discussed above had not yet fallen completely into disuse; conceivably, this could correspond to the brief Italo-Celtic stage, which Cowgill (1970: 114) dates very roughly to *c.* 2000 BC ±500, at a time when I believe Proto-Celtic was most likely taking shape in the general area of modern northeastern France and southwestern Germany, as Sims-Williams (2020) has proposed. Of central interest to our discussion is the archaeological evidence, which possibly indicates that, in this period around 2000 BC, a new population began to expand into higher areas of the Western Alps and perhaps began to exploit through transhumance higher elevated pasture lands (Walsh and Mocci 2016: 189). Transhumance implies increased seasonal milk production which, in turn, would be of little use without efficient means to turn the milk into storable and transportable products, i.e. aged cheeses (cf. Pearce 2016).

In such a context, one imagines the societies involved would be highly motivated to experiment with technologies to improve dairy processing, and new forms of rennet and tools for draining whey from curd would be primary desiderata. Considering all the evidence, I believe the coining of **tam-isto-* 'rennet' and **tam-ist-yo-* 'sieve' took place sometime in the early second millennium BC in the Western Alps.

If τάμισος is a borrowed word in Greek, it seems impossible to account for its transmission in the context of the historically documented expansion of the Celts in the Balkans (fourth century BC) or their subsequent attack on Greece (third century BC) without the contemporary Greeks being aware of its Celtic origins. It is, however, interesting that τάμισος was identified as a Doricism and the Doric dialect originated in the far northwest of Greek territory. This fact suggests the possibility that the word might have indeed first been borrowed into Northwest Greek at a very early time, even perhaps before the spread of the Dorians southward (from *c.* 1100 BC), through contact with speakers of one or more intermediary Palaeo-Balkan languages. Again, if a borrowing, τάμισος could well have been originally a commodity, something that could travel, and as a form of rennet, we think not of the fresh stomach or its pus-like contents but rather of the salted, fermented, and desiccated stomach of a young animal, an invention that has considerable advantages over πυτία in some situations, especially in the context of transhumance involving summertime high pastures. From this perspective, τάμισος may be the only attested form of what linguists refer to as a 'Wanderwort', a word that had diffused through a number of languages. It is hardly inconceivable that, with the innovation of a new form of animal rennet, the thing and its name could have spread throughout the Alps, thence down the Carnic and Dinaric Alps of the western Balkans to the edge of the Greek world.

Back in the Western Alps, Gaulish **tamisyon* 'sieve' survived the language shift to Latin/Romance but **tamiso-* 'rennet' did not; with the new language, the Latin word for rennet, *coagulum*, was taken up and ousted the Gaulish term, though there is no way to judge the speed of the process. Perhaps already at the time of language shift, the referents of the two words were not different. In the case of *tamisyon*, however, it must be the case that the specific kind of sieve to which it referred was distinct from that to which the old Latin term *cribrum* referred; late Latin *saetacium* (It. *staccio*), as a fine sieve made with animal hair, was perhaps coined as a new word, equivalent to (inspired by?) the Gaulish fine sieve **tamisyon/tamisium*.

With these points in mind, it is not surprising that an apparently old word for cheese, *toma*, managed to survive to the present day in the Western Alps, a place with particularly propitious conditions for milk-production, especially when the rich upland pastures became available through transhumance, and with ample supplies of salt near at hand. And while other peoples in other parts of the Alps may well have played an important part in the prehistoric development of cheesemaking in this region, the linguistic evidence indicates that the Celts of the Western Alps played a central role.

Greek *támisos* and Provençal *toma*: Etymological Evidence

Notes

1 Forms of *toma* occur outside the Western Alpine region in neighbouring parts of Occitan-speaking areas. In addition, reflexes of this word are found in much of Sicily and parts of Calabria and Basilicata (alongside reflexes of *formaticum* and *caseus*), which others have uncritically taken as relics from pre-Roman times. I see them instead in the context of dialectological and historical evidence demonstrating that the word arrived in the Mezzogiorno in the Middle Ages, when under Norman and Angevin auspices colonies of Gallo-Romance speakers from the Western Alpine region were established there, a topic which I have addressed in different culinary contexts (e.g. Buccini 2015: 58ff.).

2 A few notes on the IE forms discussed here are warranted. First, *-h-* is used to indicate a 'laryngeal' consonant, of which there were three, each indicated with a subscripted number. Laryngeals were lost in almost all the daughter languages, though they often left traces of their former presence on neighbouring sounds.

Second, an important morphological element in IE is called 'ablaut', which refers to patterned (grammatically, derivationally) alternations of vowels. Theoretically, a given morpheme (root, suffix, desinence) could appear under certain conditions in the e-grade (with the vowel *-e-*, 'full-grade'), o-grade (with *-o-*) or zero-grade (with no vowel); there were also lengthened grades. Grammatical conditioning of ablaut can still be observed: e.g. English *sing-sang-sung* (reflecting in order the three basic grades). In nominal categories, different ablaut and accentual patterns occurred in 'strong' cases (nom., acc.) and 'weak' cases (gen. etc.).

Third, in IE the glides *y, w* and resonants *l, r, m, n* could function as vowels in some environments. This change of role arose frequently in zero-grades: *y, w* were realized as *i, u* and resonants as *l̥ m̥ n̥ r̥*.

3 I must leave for elsewhere my discussion of the Breton evidence, especially Vannetais dialect *tanouiz* 'sieve', which lends further support to my argument.

References

Beekes, Robert. 2009. *Etymological Dictionary of Greek*, 2 vols (Leiden: Brill)

Buccini, Anthony F. 2015. 'The Merchants of Genoa and the Diffusion of Southern Italian Pasta Culture in Europe', in *Food and Markets: Proceedings of the Oxford Symposium on Food and Cookery 2014*, ed. by Mark McWilliams (Totnes: Prospect Books), pp. 54-64

—— 2022. '*Cé a bhog mo cháis*? The Celtic Origins of Irish Cheesemaking', Dublin Gastronomy Symposium 2022, forthcoming

Chantraine, Pierre. 1968. *Dictionnaire étymologique de la langue grec*, 4 vols (Paris: Klincksieck)

Cowgill, Warren. 1970. 'Italic and Celtic Superlatives and the Dialects of Indo-European', in *Indo-European and Indo-Europeans*, ed. by G. Cardona and others (Philadelphia: University of Pennsylvania Press), pp. 113-53

Dalby, Andrew (trans.). 2011. *Geoponika* (Totnes: Prospect Books)

de Bernardo Stempel, Patrizia. 1999. *Nominale Wortbildung des älteren Irischen* (Tübingen: Max Niemeyer)

De Goede, Tim. 2014. 'Derivational Morphology: New Perspectives on the Italo-Celtic Hypothesis' (unpublished doctoral thesis, Leiden University)

Eska, Joseph. 1998. 'Tau Gallicum', *Studia Celtica*, 32: 115-27

Hubschmied, Johannes. 1936. '*Ausdrücke der Milchwirtschaft gallischen Ursprungs*', *Vox Romanica*, 1: 88-105

Jasanoff, Jay. 1990. 'The Origin of the Celtic Comparative Type OIr. *tressa*, MW *trech* "stronger"', *Die Sprache*, 34: 171-89

Kindstedt, Paul S. 2012. *Cheese and Culture. A History of Cheese and Its Place in Western Civilization* (White River Junction, VT: Chelsea Green)

Maurice-Guilleux, Nicole. 1995. '*Étymologie synchronique et diachronique: le cas de reblochon*', *Cahier des annales de Normandie*, 26: 347-54

Meillet, André. 1964. *Introduction à l'étude comparative des langues indo-européennes* (University: University of Alabama Press)

Morpurgo Davies, Anna. 1968. 'Gender and the Development of the Greek Declensions', *Transactions of the Philological Society*, 67: 12-36

Pearce, Mark. 2016. 'Hard Cheese: Upland Pastoralism in the Italian Bronze and Iron Ages', in *Summer Farms*, ed. by J. Collis and others (Sheffield: J.R. Collis), pp. 47-56

Pedersen, Holger. 1976 [1913]. *Vergleichende Grammatik der keltischen Sprachen*, 2 vols (Göttingen: Vandenhoek & Ruprecht)

Rau, Jeremy. 2014. 'The History of the Indo-European Primary Comparative', in *Das Nomen im Indogermanischen*, ed. by N. Oettinger and T. Steer (Wiesbaden: Reichert), pp. 327-41

Ringe, Don. 2006. *From Indo-European to Proto-Germanic* (Oxford: Oxford University Press)

Schmidt, Mauricius (ed.). 1867. *Hesychii Alexandrini Lexicon*... Sumptibus Hermanni Dufftii, 4 vols

Sims-Williams, Patrick. 2020. 'An Alternative to "Celtic from the East" and "Celtic from the West"', *Cambridge Archaeological Journal*, 30: 511-29

Van Beek, Lucien. 2013. 'The Development of the Proto-Indo-European Syllabic Liquids in Greek' (unpublished doctoral thesis, Leiden University)

Walsh, Kevin, and Florence Mocci. 2016. 'Driving Forces and Variability in the Exploitation of a High-Altitude Landscape from the Neolithic to Medieval Periods in the Southern French Alps', in *Summer Farms,* ed. by Collis and others, pp.183-201

Wartburg, Walther von. 1928-. *Französisches Etymologisches Wörterbuch*, 25 vols (Bonn: Klopp)

Watkins, Calvin. 1975. 'Latin *iouiste* et le vocabulaire réligieux indo-européen', in *Mélanges linguistiques offerts à Émile Benveniste* (Leuven: Peeters), pp.527-34

Weiss, Michael. 2020. *Outline of the Historical and Comparative Grammar of Latin* (Ann Arbor: Beech Stave)

Whatmough, Joshua. 1970. *The Dialects of Ancient Gaul* (Cambridge: Harvard University Press)

The Infidels' Drink: Coffee Encounters and Transformations in Early Modern Malta

Noel Buttigieg

In 1633, Inquisitor Martino Alfieri (1631-1634) issued a search order for a slave who was eventually apprehended in a shop where Muslims regularly gathered to drink coffee.[1] The shop formed part of the slaves' prison complex, one of the earliest references to a coffee-house in the small Mediterranean archipelago of Malta.

This lesser-known Maltese case presents several opportunities to explore interesting coffee-related trajectories. This study provides a brief overview of the nature of coffee drinking during the seventeenth and eighteenth centuries, followed by an exploratory attempt to understand how the drink gained popularity among all sections of Maltese society at a time when the brew was relatively unknown to large parts of Europe. The concept of 'embodied imagination' is employed as an analytical tool to investigate three different but interrelated vectors that shed light on Malta's early modern coffee experiences: material culture, social meanings, and sensory perceptions.

The Context

The Maltese islands are strategically located in the narrow channel separating Sicily from North Africa. Prior to the sixteenth century, Malta's state of isolation characterized its archaic cultural behaviours, with its own unique language and customs.[2] A fortunate change in the rule of the archipelago ushered a period of sustained growth and progress. In 1530, the Order of the Knights of St. John took control of Malta. Until their sudden departure in 1798, the Hospitaller Knights transformed the geographical and cultural landscape of the islands, as Malta's domestic and foreign policy came to reflect the ebb and flow of Mediterranean affairs.

New urban settlements surrounding the Grand Harbour altered Malta and the life of its inhabitants. By the first half of the seventeenth century, the harbour towns became multifunctional and cosmopolitan. The urban conglomerate of fortified towns, constituted by Valletta, Vittoriosa, Senglea, and Cospicua, represented almost a third of the island's population. The narrow streets and the main thoroughfares became theatres of transcultural experiences as people of a foreign denomination, the Maltese, and a sizable slave community shared a common space.

The sea that defined Malta's isolation was gradually transformed into a bridge, linking

Malta to the rest of Europe. The Order's naval prowess, coupled with fantastic harbour facilities, relocated Malta within Mediterranean affairs.

Malta's Early Encounters with Coffee

Inquisitor Alfieri introduces the researcher to some of the earliest coffee discourse in Malta: '*in apotheca ubi Infideles solent bibere herba vulgo dicta cafè*' ('a shop where Muslim slaves regularly go to drink an herb popularly known as coffee').

Cursory analysis of the discourse sheds interesting light on the early days of coffee consumption in seventeenth-century Malta. Apart from a clear marker of Arab and Ottoman identity, coffee appears to have offered important respite to a considerable Muslim slave community during their forced stay in Malta. Coffee smells and tastes generated a sense of home-away-from-home among the slave community, eventually even transforming the slaves' prison into a coffee destination for the Maltese.

Although Alfieri knew where the coffeeshop was located, he appears to be less informed about the infidels' brew since he describes it as an herb rather than a bean. However, he informs us that the word *café* had already become part of the common vernacular by 1633. What remains certain is that the drink of the slaves equally seduced the spirits and the imagination of the working class as well as people of rank.

While coffee was still an exotic curiosity throughout Europe, the slaves' prison became a destination for the knights and other persons of quality too. Travellers experiencing Malta as part of their Grand Tour visited the slaves' *bagnos* for a taste of the exotic brew. One distinguished guest was Baron Georg Friedrich zu Eulenberg, who in 1663 was accompanied by some knights to watch a slave prepare the ingredients for the brew he then enjoyed.[3] It appears that some slaves excelled in the art of preparing coffee and possibly had an element of control over the supply of the coffee drink.[4] Amid sparse evidence, the earliest coffee experience in Malta seems to lack a high-class noble setting. The first coffee-house recorded in the documents was no centre of enlightened thought and lacked the exquisite forms associated with other contemporary coffee-houses in leading European cities such as Paris, London, Rome, or Vienna.

Another important source was published in 1665 by the Maltese cleric, erudite scholar, and traveller, Domenico Magri. His lesser-known scientific treatise *Virtu del kafè* was published again in 1671 with a special dedication to Cardinal Francesco Maria Brancaccio.[5] The latter is better known for being assigned responsibility to provide the Pope with all necessary information about another novel stimulant in Europe – chocolate. The Cardinal's interest in Magri's work becomes rather obvious, especially since even the cover of the pamphlet indicates how coffee had just been recently introduced in Italy. However, when referring to Malta, Magri states how the brew was a '*bevanda molto pratticata in questa mia Patria*' ('a drink commonly consumed in my country').[6]

By the closing decades of the seventeenth century, coffee-houses became the new destination within Malta's urban fabric. Privately owned coffee-houses gradually substituted the service offered by the slaves' prisons. In 1663, the Frenchmen Albert

Jouvin de Rochefort noted that some Greeks sold coffee in the harbour towns. Thirty years following this observation, the experienced French traveller Françoise Deseine again remarks that the coffeeshops of Vittoriosa and Valletta were serviced mainly by Greeks.[7] By the second half of the eighteenth century, coffee became an interesting business venture for several coffee-house owners. In 1784, coffee drinkers could taste the brew from any of the fifty-two licensed shops in the harbour towns. Valletta alone had twenty-five coffee shops, an average of one shop for every seven hundred inhabitants in an area of 0.61 km² (0.23 square miles). This density probably explains why the Norwegian priest Pavels, the Danish secretary of the frigate *Tetis*, and the young sculptor Bertel Thorvaldsen were sipping on coffee as soon as they entered the Grand Harbour in 1796, claiming that 'the coffee-houses in Valletta are easy to find'.[8]

Evidence of popular consumption was also reflected through the regular importation of coffee to Malta. During the second half of the seventeenth century, coffee became common among the wares that reached Malta.[9] The availability of the bean became more pronounced during the eighteenth century. In 1791, captain Gaetano Cini imported 800 kg (1764 lbs) of coffee from Castellammare di Stabia within the city of Naples.[10] Apart from brisk supplies of coffee beans reaching the island, a 1776 Chamber of Commerce report indicates that Malta exported coffee to other destinations including Sicily and Calabria.[11]

Coffee also entered the realm of sophistication around aristocratic tables.[12] The Grand Master employed a *garzone di cafè* [coffee maker] among his Palace retinue.[13] Receipts of the Magisterial Palace contain references to payments for quantities of coffee beans supplied through specific contracted merchantmen.[14] This attitude justifies the observation of the traveller De Bray, who described Grand Master Emanuel de Rohan [1775-1797] as a coffee addict.[15] A series of recipes, probably penned by a Sicilian chef who served the Knights, includes coffee as the main ingredient. Apart from the *Modo di fare cafè in cafè* (a type of mousse) and *Biscotti di cafè* (lit. coffee biscuits), the 1748 *Libro di Secreti per fare cose dolce di varii modi* caters for those refined tastes interested to indulge in a coffee sorbet and a coffee ice-cream.[16]

Coffee was more than a drink. Coffee was also an idea.

Embodied Imagination

Food is intense. The need for food is so compelling that we are often 'consumed' by what we eat. In fact, cooking and eating could be viewed as a series of mental processes. Food is loaded with many abstractions, confirming Clifford Geertz's statement that 'man is an animal suspended in webs of significance he himself has spun'.[17]

The main aim of this study is to attempt to unpack aspects of these 'webs of significance' through the manifestation of 'embodied imagination'. Robert Bosnak coined the term to explain how people experience their dreams both in the mind and their entire body.[18] Research in the field of neurogastronomy compliments Bosnak's theory, since the perception of taste is a culmination of complex interactions of sensory and cognitive experiences. This aligns again with Geertz's understanding of how culture is 'a system of meanings embodied in symbols', providing people with opportunities to understand reality and animate their behaviour.

In search for novel experiences, humans become inspired by their need to satiate their curiosity, the need to discover new experiences, and the urge to imagine new ideas and translate these aspirations into realities. With every moment that a food is experienced, human imagination invariably influences those cultural meanings that generally aggregate food as prominent or despised. The need to imagine forms part of the restless human psyche, the need to know the unknown, while seeking ways of perfecting the known. Against this background, an attempt is made to explore aspects of that process by which new products, in this case coffee, become, as Sidney Mintz explains, 'transformed into the ritual of daily necessity and even into the images of daily decency'.[19]

Material Culture

Recently, a renewed interest in material culture has become evident in European food studies, with a focus on human behaviours and relationships with the material world. Along with the shift of focus to everyday practices, the kitchen has gained prominence as a topic of analysis. Contextualizing objects within their existing environments provides a confluence of meanings and shared values between the object, the person, and the food prepared for consumption. Understanding the meanings behind the 'ecosystem of goods' highlights another aspect of the pronounced transition of Malta's coffee culture from the infidels' prisons into the broader public and private realm.

The transformation of a coffee bean into a drink does not necessarily require specialized tools, although specific equipment was developed to roast, boil, and serve coffee. Early seventeenth-century descriptions of coffeeways by Westerners visiting Ottoman territories often limit their references to coffee pots and drinking receptacles, the latter generally described as China dishes or porcelain cups.[20] Probably, these early encounters with coffee receptacles refer to fine Turkish fritware. In 2017, fragments of a coffee cup of a Kutahya origin were discovered within an unstratified layer of earth in the Inquisitor's Palace. A similar fragment was also found in a sealed archaeological context in a Valletta residence.[21] Another interesting find from the Inquisitor's Palace includes various fragments of a coffee drinking set delicately painted with a scatter of strawberries and sprigs. The set consists of cylindrical coffee cups and two types of saucers – possibly a *sous-tasse* and a dessert plate.[22]

Trying to understand how such objects travelled to eighteenth-century Malta remains quite obscure due to the relative absence of archival evidence. The island's maritime activity, especially corsairing, allowed such products to reach the Maltese market. Such objects, possibly destined for other countries, were redirected to Malta through the activities of ship captains, such as Giuseppe Briffa. In 1793, at the helm of a corsairing vessel that had just returned to Malta following operations in the Levant, Briffa listed all the goods plundered from a Russian passenger sailing on a Greek ship. The list of confiscated items included two cups and two coffee pots.[23]

Culinary objects are strongly connected to culture. 'The importance of any kitchen technology,' argues Bee Wilson, 'goes beyond function and enters the realm of symbol.'[24] Therefore, any personal interest to own coffee utensils should also be viewed through the consumer's ability to imagine and recognize novel experiences.[25] According to Pietro Verri, those seeking the newest trends were also harbingers of the 'science of *savoir vivre*'.[26] Malta's aristocratic settings immediately introduces the researcher to those embodied meanings associated with coffee as an intangible form of culture through the tangibility of kitchen equipment. A 1759 inventory of the Inquisitor's Palace in Malta includes references to several coffee pots, a coffee grinder affixed to the kitchen wall, and a coffee roaster. The Inquisitor also owned four *cuccumelli*, a maiolica receptacle that introduced a novel way of how to prepare coffee.[27] The eighteenth-century Neapolitan novelty poured the boiling water on the coffee powder resting on a fine sieve. The filtered liquid collected at the bottom of the *cuccumella* was then served, reducing the gritty feeling one experienced when drinking coffee. Similar to the Ottoman fritware, the porcelain cups and saucers, these culinary objects became symbols of sophistication.

The utensils used to prepare and serve coffee are characterized both by their utilitarian and their symbolic meanings. Beauty and finesse enhanced the consumption experience. The glamorous objects reflected the socio-political position of their owners. The quality of the coffee service transcended the practical purpose of containing the dark liquid. Even the aesthetic nature of the equipment, especially the coffee service, stressed the importance of the host. In the case of Malta, the refined utensils came to overshadow the origins of coffee in Malta. The drink of the enemy was poor, drab, cheap, and within the reach of many. Sophisticated tastes elevated the drink to a unique experience. Indeed, the 'ecosystem of goods' within the private realm of an aristocratic setting became another symbol of distinction.

Social Meanings

Coffeeways provide interesting avenues to analyze the development of discourse, revealing how coffee could generate a sense of conviviality while also being a weapon in power relations, a medium of social distinction. Understanding the social dynamics associated with the novelty of the infidels' drink in Malta is a great place to start looking into those connections between coffee and the politics of identity.[28]

An important component of Malta's urban society was formed by a considerable slave community, the most valuable goods seized during corsairing activity. Slaves in Malta either belonged to the Order of the Knights of St John or to private individuals. Slaves could reside in one of the three *bagnos* found in Valletta, Vittoriosa, and Senglea. Within these spaces, slaves could build their own refuges supported by their own mosques and priests.[29]

The presence of slaves within the harbour towns could be easily discerned. The Maltese working class constantly found themselves sharing the same urban spaces. As Dumont observed, by the end of the seventeenth century slaves roamed the streets of the city freely from sunrise to sunset.[30] Slaves were even permitted to earn some money of their own, including by selling coffee as a drink.[31]

During the first half of the seventeenth century, the *bagnos* became a destination for those interested in experiencing a drink not readily available on the market. In this case, to what extent did the *bagno*'s coffee experience resemble the social experience of equality among the coffee drinkers in the coffeehouses of Constantinople? It is possible that during those fleeting moments of coffee drinking, the prisons became a site of social and political rapprochement when the knight and the aristocrat were briefly decentred. However, one should approach such arguments with caution, especially since the rituals of the coffeehouse culture of Constantinople must have contrasted sharply with the visitors' experience of the coffee service offered at the slaves' prisons in Malta.[32]

Social distinction was much less clearly defined when considering the urban commoners. Many Maltese coffee drinkers existed on the fringes of urban society. Especially for the deserving poor, the coffee drink was less of a sensory experience and more of a temporary relief from hunger pangs. Furthermore, the popularity of the drink among the lower classes may have provided the slaves with some sense of belonging. When considered in combination with other opportunities toward 'integration', sharing coffeeways with the Maltese lower class provided an element of temporary relief from the hardships associated with slavery. This argument aligns with Sidney Mintz's conclusion with regards to slave societies in the Caribbean where the choice of culturally meaningful foods afforded slaves an element of human dignity and some sense of freedom.[33]

Nevertheless, the sale of coffee by members of the slave community was fraught with challenges. The prisons' coffee makers operated in an environment open to haggling with potential coffee drinkers trying to strike a good business transaction. To a certain extent, this behaviour represented a ritualized exchange. An accord had to be achieved between the coffee makers themselves, but also between the coffee maker and the customer. Potential coffee drinkers could go through several price negotiating sessions. These challenges were further accentuated when privately-owned coffeeshops started to increase in the harbour towns. Thus, the slave coffee maker was exposed to situations rather different from those generated by licensed coffeeshops. The coffeeshop owner had a better sense of privacy and enjoyed the confident support of a regular clientele. The slave coffee vendor was more open to public scrutiny especially by the customers who sought any opportunity to take advantage of social distinction. With little sense of 'social bonding', any business-minded coffee drinker could have posed a threat to any slave using coffee as a means of generating some money. This also means that while coffee had generated some opportunity for identities to be blurred, socio-cultural meanings were constantly checked, used and possibly abused especially when contracting business with slaves.

The primacy of the slaves' prison as the main supplier of coffee grew significantly weaker by the end of the seventeenth century. The coffeeshop became another distinct feature of the urban streetscape. After the slaves' prisons democratized coffee drinking in Malta, coffee started to lose its identity as the drink of the infidel. Slaves themselves even met in the public coffee-houses rather than the *bagnos* during the eighteenth century.[34] Gradually, coffee became daily fare, a transcultural experience for the cosmopolitan population of Malta's urban towns.

The Infidels' Drink: Coffee Encounters and Transformations

Sensory Perceptions

When the natural philosopher Leonhard Rauwolf travelled to Aleppo in 1573, he described his first encounter with the drink 'as black as ink'. For the English traveller George Sandys, coffee 'does not taste better than soot: burnt, bitter and gritty'. There was no good smell to the drink, argued diplomat George Manwaring, although he admitted its wholesomeness. According to William Parry, coffee tasted like medicine. The English preacher William Biddulph held a similar opinion, concluding that the drink was not adequate to the tastes of his fellow countrymen.[35]

Although taste is highly subjective, discourse employed in archival documents shed interesting light on the physical sensation of flavour and how this impinges on our food likes and dislikes. Sensory perceptions are culturally determined, interesting sites of study that inform another aspect of 'embodied imagination'.

Elisabeth and Paul Rozin adopted a psychological perspective when exploring the concept of acquired taste.[36] Flavour is influenced by the familiarity of a community to a particular combination of ingredients found in the cuisine of a locality. Familiar tastes, argued the Rozins, facilitated the historical introduction of exotic crops. Based on this reflection, it is here suggested that there were several culturally determined sensory perceptions that facilitated the adoption of coffee drinking among the Maltese lower classes.

Black appears as an unwelcome sight when related to food among early modern society. The colour has been associated with soot, ink, mould, and burnt food. Black has also formed an integral part of contemporary discourse as another marker of social hierarchy. Food products, such as black honey or black bread, produced from poor and unrefined processes have been associated with the world of the lower classes. These culturally determined meanings must have also influenced the food-choice decision making process when presented with the dark drink. In the imagination of the lower classes, the colour of the brew appears less of a determining factor in the consumption of the infidel's drink.

The gritty feeling when drinking coffee seems to have produced an unwelcome sensation among all coffee drinkers. Magri informs the reader that, after pouring the hot brew in a cup, one had to recite the Apostles' Creed before sipping the drink to allow any particles suspended in the liquid to settle at the bottom. This appears to have been important for the refined tastes of the elite. In fact, the preparation of coffee in the Neapolitan manner was driven less by the exploration of new tastes and more by the need to eliminate the gritty feeling experienced by coffee drinkers. The development of the *cuccumelli*, similar to those found in the kitchen of the Inquisitors' Palace in Vittoriosa, provide another clear example of how acquired tastes influence food-related behaviour among various consumers.

The addition of sugar and spices to imported stimulants, especially coffee and chocolate, generated an interesting debate among researchers. Anthropologist Ross Jamieson argues that any attempts by Europeans to exactly emulate indigenous practices was primarily a reminder of European colonial greatness.[37] Marcy Northern claims that such additives were not adopted by Europeans to domesticate the bitter taste, but rather were an attempt to emulate indigenous consumption and as substitutes for ingredients unavailable to the consumer in Europe.[38] Both observations, amid their contrasting nature, cannot really fit the Maltese case-study. First, the Maltese have always been part of a foreign system, and thus any claims for colonial greatness are impossible to put forward. Secondly, Malta's culinary experience was primarily a product of the Mediterranean context, especially since the island depended on significant amounts of imported food products. The limited nature of the local varieties in coffee preparation is again clearly evinced in *Virtu del kafè*. In fact, Magri suggests to anyone about to be initiated to the drink to consider the addition of sugar as a sweetener and cloves to improve the smell of the drink. Both products were available for coffee consumers, especially those with refined tastes.

It appears that the Maltese urban working class had a favourable sensory perception, positioning them as better consumers of the unadulterated brew. There is consensus on the nature of food consumed by the majority of the urban populace, considered as drab and monotonous, limited in imagination and unrelated to the refined tastes and culinary interests of the more sophisticated classes. The availability of an additional means of sustenance was important for any urban community, where many invariably experienced hunger on a regular basis. Even though we have no evidence to indicate the cost of a cup of coffee brewed by a slave, the likelihood is that the cost was low. Any service offered by an infidel carried with it an amount of stigma and the potential to engage in lucrative business was simply made impossible. Evidence indicates that the sale of food and drink involved cheap products, mainly catering for the needs of the working society.

Even if the product was devalued because of the service provider, it appears that the lower classes enjoyed an acquired taste that explains why they did not question the qualities of the drink. First, the lower classes often consumed foods with textures that generated a similar feeling to the grittiness one experienced when drinking coffee. Bread made from poorly milled mixed grains already familiarized a gritty sensation, especially in a diet that depended almost exclusively on coarse wholemeal bread. The second aspect was related to colour. As stated earlier, several dark food textures were associated with the lower classes. For instance, the colour of bread was an important marker of a person's social and economic standing. In Malta's early modern hospital, the lower classes were served brown bread, while black bread was exclusively reserved for the infidels. Consequently, the sight of the drink and its gritty sensation did not necessarily detract from the utilitarian primacy of the brew. The drink was wholesome, and thus it was considered as another cheap and filling experience, serving well the purchasing power of Malta's urban working class. These observations, coupled with the daily interaction between the slave community and the working class, provide a possible explanation to Domenico Magri's 1665 observation regarding coffee's well-established popularity in Malta at a time when the rest of Europe was still being introduced to the drink.

Conclusion
Coffee drinking became a phenomenon of consumption in Malta at a time when large

parts of Europe associated coffee with the 'Turkey merchants' of the Levant. When the medical properties of coffee were being considered as an effective marketing tool, the Maltese had already acquired a taste for the drink that transcended beyond their humoral needs.

Clearly, food is an important marker of identity, especially when considered within a broader context of socio-cultural values and norms. In the case of coffeeways in early modern Malta, the bottom-up approach discussed here appears to have transformed the exotic beverage into a normal dietary practise. The slave community introduced the experience, willingly sharing the brew with the many people with whom they commonly co-existed. Having their personhood and even their identity as human beings largely denied because of their social and political standing within a Catholic community, Muslim slaves inevitably tended to seek any possible opportunity to relate to their owners. The early years of coffee drinking could be seen as a reaction to as well as a self-affirmation of this transcultural experience. This was especially the case for coffee makers since they played an emotional part in the lives of their masters.

On the contrary, the knights would gradually continue to enjoy the stimulant mainly in a private setting. While emulating European trends, the Maltese nobility sought ways to establish distinction through material culture. The private ownership of coffee utensils continued to reaffirm the aristocracy's sense of its own cultural and biological superiority. This cultural mindset screened a rather ambivalent attitude: one wonders to what extent coffee was seen as exclusive to the enemy. Irrespective, apart from a means of distinction from the rest of society, it was as another form of perpetuating the social stigma against the slave.

Similar to the rest of Europe, coffee-houses popularized the brew as a public affair. This development transformed the coffee experience from the drink of the Muslim slaves into a drink effaced of any culture, religion, social standing, or identity. By the end of the eighteenth century, the direct association of coffee with the Muslim world in Malta seems to have faded away.

The process of change and continuity indicates how embodied imagination could become a medium of analysis to help us better understand how individuals and groups use food as an indicator of identity formation as food is enshrined in meanings influenced by social, economic, political, and cultural norms and behaviours. At the same time, food meanings also affect the social, economic, political, and cultural expectations of identity making.

Notes

1. Kenneth Gambin and Noel Buttigieg, *Storja tal-Kultura ta' l-Ikel f'Malta* (Malta: PIN, 2003), p. 153.
2. Carmel Cassar, *Society, Culture and Identity in Early Modern Malta* (Malta: Mireva, 2000), p. 2.
3. Thomas Freller, *The Cavaliers Tour and Malta in 1663* (Malta: PIN, 1998), p. 172.
4. Godfrey Wettinger, *Slavery in the Islands of Malta and Gozo* (Malta: PEG, 2002), p. 543.
5. Domenico Magri, *Virtu del kafè* (Rome: 1671).
6. Giovanni Bonello, 'The Maltese Who Pioneered Coffee in Europe, 1665', *Histories of Malta: Figments and*

    Fragments (Malta: PEG, 2001), pp. 48-52.
7. Thomas Freller, *Malta and the Grand Tour* (Malta: Midsea Books, 2009), p. 512.
8. N[ational] A[rchives] M[alta], M[agna] C[uria] C[astellania], PA 92/04, Box 460.
9. Dominic Cutajar, 'The Malta Quarantine Shipping and Trade, 1654-1694', *Mid-Med Bank Report* (Malta: 1987). N[ational] L[ibrary] M[alta], Libr[ary]. M[anuscript]. 267, f. 152-53.
10. NLM, Libr. Ms. 628, 1A, ff. 469-70.
11. NLM, Libr. Ms. 1020.
12. A[rchives] O[rder] M[alta], 1068, f. 20; AOM. 1072, f. 17.
13. AOM, 1087, f. 23.
14. AOM, 1079, f. 21; AOM. 1068-79.
15. Freller, *Malta and the Grand Tour*, p. 513.
16. NLM, Libr. Ms. 1242, ff. 29, 121, 73.
17. Clifford Geertz, *The Interpretation of Cultures* (New York: Basic Books, 1973), p. 5.
18. Robert Bosnak, *Embodiment: Creative Imagination in Medicine, Art, and Travel* (New York: Routledge, 2007).
19. Sidney Mintz, 'Time, Sugar and Sweetness', *Marxist Perspectives*, 2 (1979), 91-103 (p. 56).
20. Markmann Ellis, *The Coffee House: A Cultural History* (London: Weidenfeld & Nicolson, 2004), pp. 8-9, 17, 24.
21. Nathaniel Cutajar and Mevrick Spiteri, 'Ottoman Coffee Cups from 18th Century Birgu and Valletta', *Tesserae*, 8 (Malta: Heritage Malta, 2019), 38-45 (pp. 39, 40-42).
22. Nathaniel Cutajar and Kenneth Cassar, 'The Inquisitor's Porcelain in 18th-Century Malta', *Exhibition Catalogue* (Malta: Heritage Malta, 2019).
23. Liam Gauci, *In the Name of the Prince – Maltese Corsairs (1760-1798)* (Malta: Heritage Malta, 2016), p. 110.
24. Bee Wilson, 'Sorks, Pestles and Peelers: Why Kitchen Technology Matters', *Food and Material Culture: Proceedings of the 2013 Oxford Symposium on Food and Cookery*, ed. by Mark McWilliams (London: Prospect Books, 2014), pp. 20-32 (p. 21).
25. Caroline Young, 'The Soup that Went into the Tureen: Connecting Dots between Food and Material Culture', *Food and Material Culture: Proceedings of the 2013 Oxford Symposium on Food and Cookery*, ed. by Mark McWilliams (London: Prospect Books, 2014), pp. 33-47.
26. Piero Camporesi, *Exotic Brew: The Art of Living in the Age of Enlightenment*, trans. by C. Woodall (Cambridge: Polity Press, 1998), p. 1.
27. NLM, Libr. Ms. 1429, ff. 20.
28. Fabio Parescoli, *Bite Me: Food in Popular Culture* (Oxford: Berg, 2008), pp. 103-25.
29. Peter Earle, *Corsairs of Malta and Barbary* (London: Sidgwick & Jackson, 1970), p. 176.
30. Earle, p. 170.
31. Earle, p. 176; A[rchives] I[nquisition] M[alta], Crim[inal]. Proc[eedings], 72B, 4 November 1665; AIM, Crim. Proc. 107B, f. 433.
32. Ellis, pp. 8-9.
33. Sidney Mintz, *Tasting Food, Tasting Freedom: Excursions into Eating, Culture, and the Past* (Boston: Beacon Press, 1996), Chapter 3.
34. Wettinger, p. 145.
35. Ellis, pp. 16, 17, 5-7, 11.
36. Elizabeth Rozin and Paul Rozin, 'Culinary Themes and Variations', *Natural History*, 90 (1981), 6-14.
37. Ross Jamieson, 'The Essence of Commodification: Caffeine Dependencies in the Early Modern World', *Journal of Social History*, 35 (2001), 269-94.
38. Marcy Norton, 'Tasting Empire: Chocolate and the European Internalization of Mesoamerican Aesthetics', *American Historical Review*, 111 (2006), 660-91.

Edibly Ever After: The Foods of Seventeenth-Century French Fairy Tales

Mary Margaret Chappell

Once upon a time, a French writer named Charles Perrault included a pumpkin in his version of a well-known folk tale. It was a clever addition, sure to delight the savants and socialites that frequented seventeenth-century Parisian literary salons, where fairy tales were all the rage. Little could Perrault have known that his pumpkin would grow so huge in readers' imaginations that it would define all versions of *Cinderella* ever after.

'Princes and queens, palaces and castles dominate the foreground of a fairy tale, but through the gold and glitter, the depth of the scene is filled with vivid and familiar circumstances,' writes Marina Warner in *Once Upon a Time: A Short History of Fairy Tales*.[1] *Cinderella* is not the only fairy tale to use food as a 'vivid and familiar' element to enhance the story. Bitter greens, baskets of goodies, cakes with hidden surprises, banquets that magically appear – these are just a few of the delectable details found in the tales by Perrault and his contemporaries. Certain particulars have vanished from all but the original versions. Others, like Perrault's pumpkin, have captivated our collective imagination and survived in adaptations that span hundreds of years.

The French fairy tales of the seventeenth century represent the genesis of the genre. Their authors – Charles Perrault, Marie-Catherine d'Aulnoy, Charlotte-Rose de Caumont la Force, Marie-Jeanne L'Héritier and Henriette-Julie de Murat – were literary trailblazers. Angela Carter calls Perrault's *Histoires ou contes du temps passé* (*Stories or Fairy Tales from Past Times*) 'one of the first self-conscious collections of European fairy tales', essentially establishing him and his contemporaries as the very first European folklorists.[2] Madame d'Aulnoy is credited with coining the term 'fairy tale' (*conte de fée*) when she published a collection of her stories under that title in 1697.[3] All these authors were famous, well-educated writers and members of the French bourgeoisie and aristocracy. And they knew their craft.

J.R.R. Tolkien alludes to the importance of craft in 'fairy-stories' when he describes the essence of the genre: 'We may say that the Pot of Soup, the Cauldron of Story, has always been boiling, and [.... i]f we speak of a Cauldron, we must not wholly forget the Cooks. There are many things in the Cauldron, but the Cooks do not dip in the ladle quite blindly.'[4] The 300-year-old stories recounted by these seventeenth century French authors had staying power and are among the best-known fairy tales of all time:

Cinderella, Little Red Riding Hood, Puss-In-Boots, Rapunzel (*Persinette*)*, Donkeyskin, The White Cat, Sleeping Beauty*. They remain the subject of countless iterations. In one form or another – a bedtime story, an animated film, a TV series, a musical theatre production, a blockbuster movie, or an art film – they, and the foods they include, have infiltrated our own, individual imaginations.

That Pumpkin

Charles Perrault may have conjured a pumpkin from his imagination for *Cinderella*, but that pumpkin did not magically appear out of nowhere. Its source can be traced to one enchanted garden: *Le Potager du Roi*, Louis XIV's fruit and vegetable garden at Versailles. Designed by Jean-Baptiste de la Quintinie, *Le Potager du Roi* took five years to complete (1678 to 1683) and remains to this day a marvel of form and function.[5] Within the twenty-nine enclosed gardens, La Quintinie developed ways to ripen fruits five to six weeks ahead of time, so the king could enjoy asparagus and lettuce in January, strawberries in March, and peas as early as April.[6]

Madame d'Aulnoy invokes this astonishing bounty in her fairy tale, *The White Cat*. She enumerates the fruits a coven of wicked fairies conjure from their garden for a hungry queen: 'apricots, peaches, nectarines, cherries, plums, pears, melons, grapes, apples, oranges, lemons, redcurrants, strawberries, raspberries.' The queen, perplexed, notes that all the fruits mentioned are harvested in different seasons. 'Not so in our garden,' the fairies explain. 'We grow every fruit in the world and they are always ripe, always delicious, and never go bad.'[7]

Charles Perrault would have known La Quintinie's garden even better than Madame d'Aulnoy. As Premier Commis des Batiments (Minister for Building Works) under Louis XIV, he actively participated in the garden's creation. Perrault was a mega-fan of *Le Potager du Roi*, devoting a full page of verse to the garden's wonders in his poetic ode to Louis XIV, *Le Siecle de Louis-Le-Grand*.[8] And what lay at the heart of the garden in one of the sixteen plots that make up Le Grand Carré? Pumpkins. La Quintinie made a point of including the relatively new vegetable in both *Le Potager du Roi* and in his treatise on gardening, *Instruction pour les jardins fruitiers et potagers*.[9]

A pumpkin patch must have seemed even more magical in seventeenth-century Europe than it does today, especially one in a palace garden. Is it any wonder that Perrault would seize on the image for his *Cinderella*? He tempers the magic, though, and draws his audience deeper into the scene by putting that pumpkin into an everyday context. Cinderella's Fairy Godmother doesn't just turn a pumpkin into a coach with a wave of her wand. First, she hollows it out herself – as any cook would. Perrault prefaces the magical with something real and tangible – the act of prepping a pumpkin for soup. (Soup was the most common way to cook pumpkin in the seventeenth century.)[10]

Over the centuries, Cinderella's pumpkin has endured and evolved. Gone is the hands-on hollowing-out step, however. In its place, and indeed in most of our imaginations, you will find a magic wand which Cinderella's Fairy Godmother waves over the bright orange gourd in the 1950 Disney animated feature as she sings, 'Bibbidi Bobbidi Boo'. The animation sequence, said to be one of Walt Disney's favourites, is so sublime that it has become a touchstone for all generations since. The omission of any culinary context is perhaps due to the animation process, which was artistic and technical, and involved using a wood-and-wire pumpkin model instead of the real thing.[11] The shift could also be attributed to the changing perceptions of pumpkins in 1950s America, when children were far more familiar with pumpkins as Halloween decorations than as recipe ingredients.

'The fairy tale is in a perpetual state of becoming and alteration,' explains Philip Pullman in his introduction to *Fairy Tales from the Brothers Grimm*, adding, 'To keep to one version or one translation alone is to put a robin redbreast in a cage.'[12] The Walt Disney Studios certainly adhere to that belief as they remake their animated fairy tales as live-action feature films. In Disney's 2015 *Cinderella*, the 'Bibbidi Bobbidi Boo' scene is replaced by an exchange in which the Fairy Godmother selects a pumpkin for her magic from a list of garden vegetables that Cinderella gives her. And just like that, with some help from a humour-seeking screenwriter, Cinderella's pumpkin is firmly replanted in the kitchen garden once more.[13]

Food Fit for a King

For the twenty years that Perrault was the Minister of Building Works, his whole world orbited around Louis XIV and Versailles. He got to watch the magic unfold as pavilions were built, gardens were dug and decorated, and the Sun King's court was installed in the palace. It is only natural that he should season his stories with all he saw there, as Perrault's biographer, Patricia Bouchenot-Déchin, confirms. She points out that the castle the prince enters in *Sleeping Beauty* 'looks exactly like Versailles would have the day after a great ball that Perrault would been on hand to help to orchestrate'.[14]

Louis XIV's passions and preferences were well documented by courtiers at the time, which makes it easy to connect the dots between life at his court in Versailles and the fairy tales written during his reign. So, when a king is renowned for loving the game served at his table almost as much as he enjoys the act of pursuing it, and when his palace (Versailles) was originally his father's hunting lodge, what better way to curry favour with him (or his fairy-tale counterpart) than by presenting him with gifts of fresh-snared rabbit and a brace of partridges? And that is just what Puss-in-Boots does in Perrault's tale.[15]

Game – and a cat's hunting prowess – appear at the table in Madame d'Aulnoy's *The White Cat* as well.[16] When the prince first dines with the White Cat, he is served squab bisque, a dish that just so happens to have been on one of the King's menus at Versailles.[17] (His hostess, ever the cat, enjoys a bisque of her own, laced with big, fat mice.)

King's cake (*gâteau des rois*) was another of Louis XIV's favourite dishes, and he was a particular fan of the merriment that surrounded finding the prize (*la fève*) baked inside it. At the time, king's cakes were served at baptisms and other special occasions, not just for Epiphany. An article in *Le Mercure galant* (a magazine devoted to the goings-on in court) reported in 1684 that at one king's cake fête held by Louis XIV, 'The King enjoyed himself so much that he wanted to hold another one the following week.'[18]

In Perrault's tale, *Donkeyskin*, the ring that slips off Donkeyskin's finger as she is preparing a cake for her prince is reminiscent of the dessert game. All at court – and elsewhere – would have understood the significance of finding the prize.

Donkeyskin offers an example of a seventeenth-century food reference that has stood the test of time. Indeed, the hidden ring has become the best-known element of the tale, thanks to 'Le Cake d'amour,' a song-recipe composed by Michel Legrand for filmmaker Jacques Demy's musical adaptation of the tale. The princess (Catherine Deneuve) sings it as she prepares the cake. To this day, many French people, young and old, know the tune and most of the words. However, there is one notable difference in Demy's adaptation of *Donkeyskin*: the princess places the ring in the cake herself. (It was the seventies, after all!)[19]

In other instances, the specificity of food detail has lost all meaning as times changed and the tales' audience shifted from educated adults to innocent children. The hunted game references in *Puss-in-Boots* and *The White Cat* have been simplified so that all that remains are Puss-in-Boots's clever skills and the White Cat's penchant for mice.

A similar phenomenon occurs with a '*sauce Robert*' that pops up in Perrault's *Sleeping Beauty*. His version of the tale does not end happily ever after with a Prince's kiss. Instead, Sleeping Beauty goes on to be a married mother-of-two, who must contend with a child-eating ogress of a mother-in-law. At one point, the Ogress-Queen Mother tells her chef she wants to eat her granddaughter, and she wants her served '*à la sauce Robert*'.[20] Few children would get the reference to a white wine vinegar sauce traditionally served with grilled meat; most would quail at the grisly turn of events. This is perhaps why the Grimm's version and subsequent adaptations have been truncated to omit this plot twist entirely.[21]

Greens, Greens and Nothing but Greens

Whenever a fairy tale is retold, its food specifics are embellished and reimagined to suit a given audience and time. Nowhere is this more apparent than in *Persinette*, Mademoiselle La Force's precursor to *Rapunzel*. Mademoiselle La Force reimagines a sixteenth-century Italian tale by Giambattista Basile, where a pregnant young woman craves parsley from the garden of a fairy who lives next door. The narrator explains, 'At the time, parsley was rare; the fairy had imported it from India and the only place it was found in the country was her garden [...]. Back then, the taste of parsley must have been excellent.'[22]

Excellent-tasting or no, parsley had another reputation: as an abortifacient.[23] Mademoiselle La Force's readers would have understood the inference, for, in addition to being a love story about a maiden in a tower, *Persinette* is all about pregnancy. The tale begins with a pregnant woman's cravings. These lead to her having to relinquish her newborn daughter to the fairy, who names her Persinette. Just as Cinderella has 'cinders' in her name, Persinette has parsley in hers; *persil* is parsley in French. The story continues on to the fairy's relentless sequestration of the girl. But in Mademoiselle La Force's version, the fairy is not evil, just misguided. All she wants to do is protect the girl from a foretold (and assumed unwanted) out-of-wedlock pregnancy, which comes to pass anyhow when she's visited by the prince.

Over a hundred years later, the Brothers Grimm published their version of *Persinette* as *Rapunzel*. There, parsley is replaced by *rapunzeln* (rampion), a blue-flowered bitter green (*Campanula rapunculus*) that was popular at the time. Once the implication of pregnancy and potential abortion were eliminated along with the parsley, the herbs stolen from the fairy witch's garden are wide open to interpretation, as is the entire tale itself. Philip Pullman points out, 'Wilhelm Grimm bowdlerized the exchange between Rapunzel and the witch that had existed in all previous versions, and indeed in the Grimms' own first edition of 1812. Instead of revealing her pregnancy by saying that her clothes no longer fit, Rapunzel asks the witch why she is so much harder to pull up than the young prince.'[24]

Fast-forward to modern times: when rapunzeln (the herb) has faded from common memory and use, storytellers must modify its description. In *The Complete Fairy Tales of the Brothers Grimm*, Jack Zipes translates it as rapunzel lettuce, for clarity.[25] Philip Pullman calls it lamb's lettuce in his adaptation. Author Kate Forsyth refers to the plant as 'bitter greens' in the title of her fantasy novel. But the award for the most evocative of all the *Rapunzel/Persinette* greens references is to be found in the lyrics of 'The Witch's Rap', a song written by Stephen Sondheim for the musical *Into the Woods*. The Witch tells the baker how his pregnant mother craved

> Greens, greens, and nothing but greens:
> Parsley, peppers, cabbages and celery,
> Asparagus and watercress and
> Fiddleferns and lettuce!
> He said 'all right,'
> But it wasn't, quite,
> 'Cause I caught him in the autumn
> In my garden one night!
> He was robbing me,
> Raping me,
> Rooting through my rutabaga,
> Raiding my arugula and
> Ripping up the rampion
> (My champion! My favorite!)[26]

The sophistication of Sondheim's reference is right up there with those of the seventeenth-century French writers. It's all there – the seventeenth-century parsley, the nineteenth-century rampion (rapunzel), the sexual innuendo, plus two very twentieth-century culinary allusions to arugula and fiddleferns. For when *Into the Woods* was first staged in 1986, both arugula and fiddlehead ferns were new, hot-ticket items in New York restaurants.[27]

Something Lost, Something Gained

The story arc of food in fairy tales is akin to that of fairy tales themselves. Whenever a reference is lost, a new one is gained. Perrault's Cinderella shares oranges and lemons with her stepsisters at the ball (citrus was another favourite of Louis XIV); these become 'sugared oranges and lemons' in a 1971 British version retold by Jane Carruth.[28] By then, oranges and lemons were available year-round, in every supermarket, and the gift needed to be sweetened up, so to speak. In the same collection, Little Red Riding Hood's basket is filled with 'eggs, jam tarts, thick honey, and a pound of fresh creamy butter' rather than the more meagre 'cake and pot of butter' Perrault described in his original.[29]

When Jean Cocteau reimagined *Beauty and the Beast*, in his 1946 film, he borrowed the magical, disembodied hands from the similarly-themed *The White Cat*. Those hands in turn became the animated servingware in Disney's *Beauty and the Beast*. Lumière, Mrs. Potts, Chip, and the others invite Beauty to the table with the musical number, 'Be Our Guest':

> Be our guest! Be our guest!
> Put our service to the test
> Tie your napkin 'round your neck, chérie
> And we'll provide the rest
> Soupe du jour, hot hors d'œuvres
> Why, we only live to serve
> Try the grey stuff, it's delicious
> Don't believe me? Ask the dishes…
> Beef ragout, cheese soufflé,
> Pie and pudding 'en flambé'
> We'll prepare and serve with flair
> A culinary cabaret![30]

A Neverending Story

And so, the French fairy tale food tradition goes on. This paper is by no means a definitive overview. Even if it were, even if it covered every food reference in every tale written by Perrault *et al.* along with every modification to those tales made ever since, it would already be obsolete. Somewhere, at this very moment, someone is retelling one of them and incorporating his/her own delectable take on the food. It could be a father adding peas to a fairy tale banquet to get his daughter to eat them. Two friends reenacting *Little Red Riding Hood* and filling her basket with candy. A novelist tapping into the stories of her childhood. A young girl singing along to 'Le Cake d'amour' and making up some of the words. Or the venerable Andrew Lloyd-Webber adding a coda to the Cinderella Bake-Off he YouTubed at the end of 2020.[31]

Fairy tales, French or otherwise, are in a constant state of flux and reimagination with, as Marina Warner says, 'scores of storytellers and inventors gathering, interpreting, revisioning the material [...] losing themselves in the forests of fairy tale in order to come back with baskets of strawberries picked in the snow'.[32]

Even fairy tale scholars cannot resist the urge to embellish their narratives with food imagery. From Tolkien describing Cooks who dip their ladles in the Cauldron of Story to Angela Carter saying that determining the true source of a fairy tale is like asking, 'Who first invented meatballs?', food is imagery that continues to speak to us all and offer endless possibilities where storytelling is concerned.[33]

The only thing to do, then, is to join in. Revisit the stories. Invent, embellish, add, omit. See where your imagination takes you when you imagine the foods in French fairy tales for yourself. For as Philip Pullman concludes in the introduction to his version of Grimms' fairy tales, 'You are at perfect liberty to invent other details than the ones I have passed on, or invented, here. In fact you're not only at liberty to do so: you have a positive duty to make the story your own.'[34]

Notes

1. Marina Warner, *Once Upon a Time: A Short History of Fairy Tales* (Oxford: Oxford University Press, 2014), p. 74.
2. Angela Carter, *The Virago Book of Fairy Tales* (London: Virago Press, 1991), p. xi.
3. Jack Zipes, 'Madame d'Aulnoy, the mysterious fairy tale queen,' Princeton University Press blog, 17 March 2021 <https://press.princeton.edu/ideas/madame-daulnoy-the-mysterious-fairy-tale-queen> [accessed 30 May 2021]
4. J.R.R. Tolkien, 'On Fairy-Stories,' 1938 <https://coolcalvary.files.wordpress.com/2018/10/on-fairy-stories1.pdf> [accessed 30 May 2021]
5. 'Création du Potager', *Le Potager du Roi Versailles*, 2019 <http://www.potager-du-roi.fr/site/pot_histoire/index.htm> [accessed 5/30/21]
6. Luc Menapace, 'Jean-Baptiste de La Quintinie, *créateur du Potager du roi*', *Blog Gallica*, 6 November 2019 <https://gallica.bnf.fr/blog/06112019/jean-de-la-quintinie-createur-du-potager-du-roi?mode=desktop> [accessed 30 May 2021]
7. Charles Perrault and Madame d'Aulnoy, *Contes: Suivis de Contes de Madame d'Aulnoy* (Leipzig: Grund, 1989), p. 171.
8. Charles Perrault, *Le Siècle de Louis-le-Grand* (1687 BNF Collection), p. 16.
9. La Quintinie, Jean de, *Instruction pour les jardins fruitiers et potagers*, 1700, Bibliothèque Nationale de France <https://gallica.bnf.fr/services/engine/search/sru?operation=searchRetrieve&version=1.2&collapsing=disabled&rk=85837;2&query=%28gallica%20all%20%22la%20quintinie%22%29%20and%20dc.relation%20all%20%22cb30740584n%22> [accessed 30 May 2021]
10. François Pierre La Varenne, *Le Cuisinier françois* [1651], in *The French Cook; The French Pastry Chef; The French Confectioner,* trans. by Terence Scully (London: Prospect, 2006)
11. 'Behind the Scenes Interview: Cinderella's Coach', *Cinderella Diamond Edition* (Disney Studios, 2012).
12. Philip Pullman, *Fairy Tales from the Brothers Grimm* (London: Penguin Books, 2012), p. xix.
13. *Cinderella*, dir. By Kenneth Branagh (Disney Studios, 2015).
14. Patricia Bouchenot-Déchin, *Charles Perrault* (Paris: Fayard, 2018), p. 127.
15. André Castelot, *L'Histoire à Table* (Paris: Librairie Jules Taillandier, 1973), p. 41.
16. Perrault and d'Aulnoy, p. 171.
17. Castelot, p. 117.

18 S.J. Sender and Marcel Derrien, *La Grande histoire de la pâtisserie-confiserie française* (Geneva: Minerva, 2003), p. 91.
19 *Peau d'âne,* dir. by Jacques Demy (Marianne Productions and Parc Film, 1970).
20 Andrew Lang, *The Blue Fairy Book* (London: Longman, Greens, and Co, 1885), p. 61.
21 Jack Zipes, *The Complete Fairy Tales of the Brothers Grimm* (New York: Bantam Books, 1992), p. 189.
22 Charlotte-Rose de Caumont La Force, *Les Fées: Contes des contes* (Amsterdam: [n.p.], 1785).
23 Pullman, p. 64.
24 Pullman, p. 63.
25 Zipes, *The Complete Fairy Tales,* p. 47.
26 Stephen Sondheim, 'Witch's Rap', *Into the Woods* (Rilting, 1986).
27 David Kamp, *The United States of Arugula* (New York: Broadway Books, 2006), p. 227.
28 Jane Carruth, *The Giant All-Colour Book of Fairy Tales* (London: Hamlyn, 1971), p. 440.
29 Carruth, p. 281; Perrault, p. 40.
30 Howard Ashman, 'Be Our Guest', *Beauty and the Beast* (Wonderland Music Company, 1991).
31 'A Cinderella Bake-Off', *Andrew Lloyd-Webber's Cinderella*, 27 November 2020 <https://www.youtube.com/watch?v=MM83rxVypmI> [accessed 30 May 2021]
32 Warner, p. xxii.
33 Carter, p. x.
34 Pullman, p. xix.

Imaginative Companions

Rareș Augustin Crăiuț

In the Shadow of a Cake

10 May 1971. Sigi Krauss Art Gallery in London. A human-size outline made from waffles is resting on the gallery floor. Each waffle has a note attached to it with a small string. During the evening, audience members each receive a baked slice of the human sculpture. The disembodiment ceremony could remind one of a Eucharist of sorts, one difference here being that audience members can choose to eat the offering on the spot or to take it away. In any case, no one leaves empty-handed; if nothing else, they have the paper notes commemorating the event.

This is the work of Romanian refugee artist Paul Neagu. The work, entitled 'Cake Man', is part the 'Antropocosmos'; a series of drawings, installations, sculptures, and performances dealing with the relationship humans have to the cosmos. The work marks a period of creative freedom. After escaping the restrictions of the Romanian Socialist regime, the artists worked with different materials, producing figurative and abstract works, culminating in the consumption of art objects: eating as a form of artistic participation. The motive of this artistic practice is not about owning something, but instead about being part of something.

Paul Neagu is not singular in his use of food in performance art. There is an entire history of artists basing their works around sourcing, cooking, serving, and eating food as forms of artistic expression.

Around the same time as Neagu's 'Cake Man' performance, we see a number of artists dealing with food as a medium in performative settings. In Paris, Gina Pane is performing her piece '*Action Nourriture/Actualités télévisées/Feu*', which explores alienation and animal cruelty, through force re-feeding herself ground meat, watching the nightly news, and extinguishing flames with her hands and feet. In Zurich, Daniel Spoerri is presenting 'Eat Art', a series of events where entire dinner tables, together with their leftovers, cutlery, and napkins, are fixed and mounted as art pieces, sometimes by request by private clients, and sold as works of art. Around forty kilometres from Vienna, Hermann Nitsch starts his performance series 'Orgy-Mystery Games', making ceremonial use of animal blood and carcases. Meanwhile in New York, Gordon Matta-Clark is opening 'Food', an artist-run restaurant, where the performance of restaurant life will also become the object of a film. And last but not least, Tom Marioni has just started performing his series 'The Act of Drinking Beer with Friends is the Highest Form of Art', enacted in various museum and galleries. Still in 1971, at the San Francisco Zoo, Bonnie Ora Shrek is performing 'Public Lunch', a performance where the artist, in her own cage, is fed by zoo visitors in parallel with tigers having their lunch. In other parts of the United States, Dennis Oppenheim is documenting himself eating a 'Gingerbread Man', and artist Alison Knowles has just published the *Journal of the Identical Lunch*, the documentation of her recently completed performance series. For our investigation, we don't even need to go too far from Paul Neagu's place of performance, London, as Gilbert and George are in full swing around the English capital, performing their drunken binges for the 'Drinking Sculptures' series.

The Trouble with Food

The year 1971 is not singular regarding the richness of food's use as a medium or theme in live art. There is a considerable lineage of connecting food and performance. But official histories of art are largely devoid of food performances. This is not incidental, as there has always been an issue with food in art generally, not just in performative contexts. And unfortunately, as Korsmeyer would say, 'food does not qualify as a fine art; it does not have the right history, to make a complex point in shorthand'.[1]

Throughout the history of aesthetics, the qualities associated with food are actually its constitutive elements, such as taste and smell. Elizabeth Telfer, Carolyn Korsmeyer, and Michel Delville are some of the main authors deliberating on the philosophy of art and food. In his 2008 book *Food, Poetry, and the Aesthetics of Consumption: Eating the Avant-Garde*, Delville maps out the main reasoning and counter arguments, articulated by some of the Western world's leading food-disgruntled philosophers. It turns out that the main detractors are Plato, Hegel, and Kant.

In my work with other artists, conversations with curators, and negotiations with art institutions, reformulations of the arguments belonging to these three thinkers invariably find their way into discussions around why cooking and food-related practices cannot be considered with the canonical field of live art. These include:

- 'Food is not a serious enough subject.' Here, I see similarities with Plato's argument that the body, and most anything related to it, is nothing but an endless distraction to the soul.
- 'Food cannot be contemplated from a rational distance.' This relates to Hegel's exclusion of taste, smell, and other senses, from the appreciation of art, privileging sight and sound.
- 'Food is something very personal and too subjective.' This relates to Kant's argument that smell and taste reduce the field of attention to the individual experience of the body.

Despite these objections, the past ten years have seen an increase in the number of publications, dealing not just with food and art in general, but particularly with food in and around performance. In the early 2000s, the main article on the topic was

Barbara Kirshenblatt-Gimblett's 'Playing to the Senses'. Published in a food-themed edition of the journal *Performance Research*, the article set the cardinal points on how to think about food in and as performance: the history of the concept, leading artists, examples of performance works, thematic categories, influences, and ingredients. Since then, books, journals, articles, and exhibition catalogues have been put into circulation, each approaching the topic of food and performance from different viewpoints and disciplines.[2]

Regardless of the advancements in research, there is still a heavy past, one relying on the supremacy of sight and sound, above other senses. This also relates to the mechanisms of the art market and the impracticality of food performances as particular artistic practices. Generally speaking, live arts cannot be stored and bought, so they also cannot be stored and collected. When they involve food, things become even more problematic because there is no standardization in conservation practices. Even if someone gave us the rights over staging a reperformance of Paul Neagu's 'Cake Man', for instance, it would always be devalued because it can never be anything other than a copy. Even if pieces from the original installation existed, they would probably not be fit for consumption. From an art market point of view, an original sketch from the event, with the artist's signature, would always be more valuable. Food is difficult to preserve in an artist's studio or art gallery conditions.

In terms of the practice of working with food in art, there is also an inconvenience related to the controllability of the medium. Food *per se*, not just as a theme, was quite present at the beginning of European theatre, when the processions dedicated to Dionysus included eating and drinking, along with song, dance, and poetry. It was perhaps the equivalent of what we would today call an immersive experience. Later, Greek comedy included scenes re-enacting Symposia on stage, and audiences were allowed to eat and drink during performances.[3] Over time, food and drink were dropped, mainly due to practical reasons like storage, preparation, and cleaning at venues. But also, and more importantly, because while sound and light can be switched on and off, taste and smell tend to linger and combine. And rightly so, since, as an audience member, it's rather hard to focus on the action taking place in act two's forest, when you can still smell the roast from act one.

Helping Us to Imagine Ourselves

Since 2013, through projects of artistic research and art as research, I have worked with food in performance art. My investigations were carried out through re-enacting other artistic works including the Futurist manifestos, the Fluxus cookbook, or Matei Bejenaru's 'Strawberry Fields Forever', as well as through producing original food performances based on affective memory and imagination surrounding the food of 1980s socialist Romania – AlimenTARA, GOSPOdina, CofetARia. The process of re-enactment required that each element be investigated individually: the artist, the individual context, the performance protocol/score/scenario, and also the food. It was a process of reconstruction that put the food forward, and from time to time the ingredients, the cooking, and the serving; they were all asking for attention. Swinging between my own original creation and re-enacting works of art conceived by others, I found myself pondering the role that we give food in art making and artistic research.

One of the early questions for reflection was around how we attribute ourselves the central role, even when food in artistic creation is sometimes more than just a medium or theme. In the culinary world, we are also used to considering humans as the ones endowed with intelligence and creativity.[4] From heritage dishes to *haute cuisine*, everything is described in terms of the chef's skilful control of taste and matter, or masterful arrangements of symbolic meaning attributed to ingredients, production processes, or presentation.

Maybe food does not imagine *per se*, or maybe we don't know how to question its imagination. But food undeniably supports us in imagining ourselves and others. Food supported the artistic and political manifesto of the Futurists through exemplary dishes. Food aided Marina Abramović, Martha Rosler, and Suzanne Lacy to make feminist statements through eating practices. Working as a conceptual device, food improved the works of Vito Acconci and the Romanian group subREAL. Food fed Allan Kaprow's project dedicated to distorting the lines between art and life. In collaborations with Paul McCarthy or the Viennese actionists, food shocked audiences into action. The materiality of food helped investigate new dimensions of sculpture and live action in the works of Paul Neagu, Daniel Spoerri, and Joseph Beuys. Félix Gonzalez-Torres used candy to create an elegy to his lover in 'Untitled (Portrait of Ross in L.A.)'. Freshly cooked food supported Gordon Matta-Clark, Lee Mingwei, and Rirkrit Tiravanija in developing collaborative aesthetic strategies. Through this universe of food accompanying artists in their practices, we see that we never perform truly alone.

The field of critical

Figure 1. 'Diplomat cake', from the CofetARia collage series, by Rares Crăiuț and Xavier Gorgol.

posthumanities and the increasing interest in thought and research decentring the human subject, together offer us a framework for considering how agentic faculties can be extended to food.[5] The works evoked in the context of food performances are complex networks of human and nonhuman agents, networks that exceed the traditional understanding of 'food as medium' or 'food as thematic inspiration'.

Can we argue for a reconsideration of food as a non-human performer? How and what can/does food support the imagination of in art (i.e. performance art) alongside and together with the human artist/author? How does the food and artist coloration disrupt assumptions of artistic control and authorship? How are work and research produced in such a collaboration? How far does this artistic collaboration apply to food, in the case of non-human performativity? When do we (just) imagine that food imagines? What does this consideration of 'food imagines' enable and open in other, non-artistic domains, such as food sourcing or food preparation?

Creating the Conditions for Others to Perform Alongside Humans

We need artists to imagine and to continue performing on food-centred topics. Food is not only highly problematic but also mind-numbingly complex. It is difficult to visualize and understand the problems that food production and consumption bring about, and to recognize how they can disrupt the existence of living beings. Art doesn't need a utilitarian teleology. However, it is worth considering that some artists can help us feel and think differently with food. We can imagine our individual nostalgic pasts in solidarity, or we can dream of sustainable shared futures. We cannot change the practice and politics of food by science alone. We also need ways to imagine and engage around the food-related problems we create and the solutions we still must discover.

A clear example that artistic practice has moved on, well beyond the existing theoretical frameworks, was the participation of Ferran Adriá in 'Documenta 12' (2007). The transplantation of his 'El Bulli' restaurant, from afar, to Pavilion G did not raise too many eyebrows or lead to substantial discussions. The Art Basel banana incident caused more debate and discussion about food in/and art.[6]

But artists and their new credos should also take into consideration food itself: how we talk about human-nonhuman collaborations as well as how we set up these collaborations. In her article, 'Non-humans and Performance', Finish theorist Tuija Kokkonen talks about how, in order to invite others to perform alongside humans, we need to change our relation to time and the intensity of how we contribute, basing her performance collaborations on '"weak (human) action", which is a prerequisite for the perception and participation of non-human agents'.[7]

We find ourselves on a 'damaged planet' because we prioritize our actions and our interests above those of others.[8] The projects of 'Banquets in the Dark Wildness' (2014) by Dana Sherwood and 'Sleeping with Cake' (2011) by Diane Borsato show the way in which we could work on developing attention paying to otherness and negotiating the conditions for others to perform alongside us.

Of course, an obvious opening question in this investigation is whether food can perform or if we just imagine that it performs. From my artistic research and production, I believe that depending on the audience, cakes, for instance, offer a concrete answer when looking for a performative collaborator. Cakes are more performative than other dishes; they are colourful, expected to be sweet, and usually on display, so our attention can pass from one to another, anticipating the consumption. They make us imagine. Because of the relation we develop over time with them as products, they have a power of attraction. They are also more contained culturally, and some are even attributed superstar status, with names and background stories. But cakes can perform outside of our cultural projections: movements and changes indicating transformations like the actions of raising agents on dough, shrinking in volume when cooling down (visible also through infrared), falling as a physical movement, or deformations when they are going stale.

Around the time of leaving Romania in 1969, Neagu launched the 'Palpable Art Manifesto'. His text is a call for a type of artistic practice that still holds today: 'Let there be one, public, palpable art through which all the senses, sight, touch, smell, and taste will supplement and devour each other so that a man can possess an object in every sense'. As a performance artist researcher, I would add that we need an art through which sight, touch, smell, and taste supplement and devour each other so that we can be aware how otherness can also possess humans in every sense.

Notes

1. Carolyn Korsmeyer, *Making Sense of Taste: Food and Philosophy* (Ithaca, NY: Cornell University Press, 2014), p. 144.
2. A short overview of publications on food and performance art since 2010 includes: Silvia Bottinelli and D'Ayala Margherita Valva's *The Taste of Art: Cooking, Food, and Counterculture in Contemporary Practices* (Fayetteville, AR: University of Arkansas Press, 2017; Mélanie Boucher, *La Nourriture en art performatif: son usage, de la première moitié du 20e siècle à aujourd'hui* (Quebec: Éditions d'art Le Sabord, 2014); Michel Delville, *Food, Poetry, and the Aesthetics of Consumption: Eating the Avant-Garde* (New York: Routledge, 2013); Lindsay Kelley, *Bioart Kitchen: Art, Feminism and Technoscience* (London: I.B. Tauris, 2016); Cecilia Novero, *Antidiets of the Avant-Garde: From Futurist Cooking to Eat Art* (Minneapolis, MN: University of Minnesota Press, 2010); Athena-Hélène Stourna, *La Cuisine à la scène: boire et manger au théâtre du XXe Siècle* (Rennes: Presses Universitaires de Rennes, 2011); Joshua Abrams and Richard Gough (eds.), *Performance Research: On Taste*, 22 (2017); Alexandra Alisauskas and Paula Pinto (eds.), *Invisible Culture. Aesthetes and Eaters – Food and the Arts*, 14 (2010); Julia Csergo, *L'Artification du culinaire* (Paris: Publications de la Sorbonne, 2013); Allen S. Weiss and Ivan Magrin-Chagnolleau, *CUISINE & PERFORMANCE*, 3 (2016); Raz Weiner and Julia Peetz (eds.), *FEASTING – Platform: Journal of Theatre and Performing Arts*, 10.1 (2018); Antje Baecker and others, *Amuse-Bouche – the Taste of Art Interdisciplinary Symposium on Taste and Food Culture* (Ostfildern: Hatje Cantz, 2020); Nicolas Bourriaud (ed.), *Cook Book: l'art et le processus culinaire: exposition du 18 octobre 2013 au 9 janvier 2014, Palais des Beaux-Arts, Paris* (Paris: Beaux-Arts de Paris, 2013); Season Butler, *Food & Performance: A Study Room Guide on Eating and Dining as Explored in Performance* (London: Lada Publishing, 2016); Dorothy Chansky and Ann Folino White, *Food and Theatre on the World Stage* (New York: Routledge, 2016); Mimi Oka and others, *Festins orphiques: expérimentations culinaires ou*

l'autobiographie d'une collaboration artistique = Experiments in Dining or the Autobiography of an Artistic Collaboration: Entretiens (Paris: Les éd. de l'épure, 2011); Stephanie Smith, *Feast: Radical Hospitality in Contemporary Art* (Chicago: Smart Museum of Art, University of Chicago, 2013); Thomas Howells, *Experimental Eating* (London: Black Dog, 2014); Agnieszka Gratza, 'Spiritual Nourishment: Food and Ritual in Performance Art', *PAJ: A Journal of Performance and Art*, 32.1 (2010), pp. 67-75 <https://doi.org/10.1162/pajj.2010.32.1.67>; Francis Maravillas, 'The Unexpected Guest: Food and Hospitality in Contemporary Asian Art', *Contemporary Asian Art and Exhibitions: Connectivities and World-Making*, 2014 <https://doi.org/10.22459/caae.11.2014.09>; Christina Normore, *A Feast for the Eyes* (Chicago: University of Chicago Press, 2015); David Andrew Szanto, 'Performing Gastronomy: An Ecosophic Engagement with the Liveliness of Food' (unpublished PhD thesis, Concordia University, 2015); Yael Raviv, 'Food and Art: Changing Perspectives on Food as a Creative Medium', in *The Bloomsbury Handbook of Food and Popular Culture*, ed. by Kathleen LeBesco and Peter Naccarato (London: Bloomsbury Academic, 2018).

3   John Wilkins, *The Boastful Chef: The Discourse of Food in Ancient Greek Comedy* (Oxford: Oxford University Press, 2000).
4   Frédéric Zancanaro, *La Créativité culinaire: les trois étoiles du Guide Michelin* (Tours: Presses Universitaires François Rabelais, 2019); Nicola Perullo, *Taste as Experience: The Philosophy and Aesthetics of Food* (New York: Columbia University Press, 2016); Korsmeyer.
5   On critical posthumanities, see Gilles Deleuze and Félix Guattari, *A Thousand Plateaus: Capitalism and Schizophrenia* (London: Bloomsbury, 2019); Donna Haraway, *The Companion Species Manifesto: Dogs, People, and Significant Otherness* (Chicago: Prickly Paradigm Press, 2003); Karen Barad, *Meeting the Universe Halfway: Quantum Physics and the Entanglement of Matter and Meaning* (Durham, NC: Duke University Press, 2007); Jane Bennett, *Vibrant Matter: A Political Ecology of Things* (Durham, NC: Duke University Press, 2010); Rosi Braidoti, *The Posthuman* (Hoboken, NJ: Wiley, 2013); Anna Tsing, *The Mushroom at the End of the World* (Princeton, NJ: Princeton University Press, 2015).
6   At the 2019 Art Basel in Miami Beach, a member of the audience removed the banana from Maurizio Cattelan's installation 'Comedian', an installation comprised of a banana duct-taped to a wall. The 'Comedian', initially estimated at 120,000 US dollars, made an incredible international career after the incident, and finally finding a place in the collection of the Solomon R. Guggenheim Museum in New York City. The audience member in question was not a simple vandal, but artist David Datuna, who claimed that he had merely repurposed the banana for an impromptu performance art piece, he would title 'Hungry Artist'.
7   Tuija Kokkonen, 'Non-Humans and Performance: A Performance with an Ocean View (and a Dog/ for a Dog) – II Memo of Time', *Journal for Artistic Research*, 2011 <https://jar-online.net/en/exposition/abstract/non-humans-and-performance-performance-ocean-view-and-dogfor-dog-ii-memo-time> [accessed 30 March 2022]
8   The concept of 'living on a damaged planet' is broadly inspired by Anna Tsing's *Arts of Living on a Damaged Planet: Ghosts and Monsters of the Anthropocene* (University of Minnesota Press, 2017).

Waterloo Porridge and Plentiful Yorkshire Teas: Food and the Creation of Northern English Identities in Mid-Nineteenth-Century Novels

Gill Eastabrook

Benedict Anderson's ideas of 'imagined communities' are crucial to our understanding of national identity, but they are equally relevant to other place-based identities.[1] In this paper I look through the lens of food at the way northern English identities were understood in the mid-nineteenth century and seek to bridge a gap between three areas of the existing historiography. Social and cultural historians have increasingly recognized the significance of food in the construction of national identity and other facets of identity including class. At the same time, northern regional identities have been examined in relation to aspects of elite and popular culture such as sport, music, and literature. In addition, there is much descriptive writing about food in and of the North ranging from locally focused material on specific towns to discussion of regional differences in work with a broader canvas. However, relatively little has been written about the way food has been used to imagine northernness or indeed other regional identities in England.

To fill this gap, I explore three themes showing how food contributed to the construction and reflection of northern identity in the period. First, although by the mid-nineteenth century wheat had largely replaced oats as the staple grain of most people in the North, oatcakes and porridge still symbolized a homely and wholesome North. Second, in what subsequently became known as the Hungry Forties, there was a perceived link between the North and hunger despite probably equal rural poverty in the south of England and urban squalor in London. Third, there was a converse trope in the national discourse: the North as a place of plenty and extravagance. So the idea of the North holds three very different characteristics in tension.

These characteristics can be seen in some non-fiction of the time, but I will concentrate here on how works of the imagination played both a reflective and a constitutive role, looking particularly at five novels by archetypal northern writers: *North and South*, *Mary Barton*, and *Sylvia's Lovers* by Elizabeth Gaskell; *Wuthering Heights* by Emily Brontë; and *Shirley* by Charlotte Brontë.[2] All these works were published between 1840 and 1870, so reflecting the attitudes of that period. However, several are set earlier suggesting there may be an element of nostalgia for an earlier, rural, imagined northern community in these Victorian depictions. I will also make occasional reference to other novels and to non-fiction writing of the period.

Before looking in detail at my three themes I need to say what I mean by 'the North'. The idea of an English North/South divide resonates in the contemporary political discourse but has deep roots.³ One can link this divide to geological time with fertile lowlands to the south and east of a line from the Tees to the Exe and pastoral higher lands to the north and west. Quite when the term came to have more than purely geographical meaning is contested. It arguably predates the Norman Conquest but some see it as a nineteenth- or even twentieth-century construction.⁴ Although the North is bounded on three sides, by other countries or the sea, the southern edge is not well defined; indeed some scholars see this elusiveness as attractive.⁵ Where definition is needed I follow that of the journal *Northern History* in taking 'the seven historic northern counties' of Cumberland, Westmorland, Northumberland, Durham, Yorkshire, Lancashire, and Cheshire.⁶

The Homely and Wholesome North

Mid-nineteenth century novels use oatcakes and porridge to construct and reflect an image of the North as a homely and wholesome place. Climate and elevation affect what cereals can be grown in different parts of England. As early as the Norman Conquest differences in staple grains influenced the way people saw the North-South divide.⁷ John Burnett suggests that by 1815 wheat had become the universal bread corn of England but other writers imply that while oats may no longer have dominated across the North in the nineteenth century they did survive as an important component of the diet in some areas.⁸ So we might expect them to play a part in the expression of northern identity.

In *Sylvia's Lovers*, Elizabeth Gaskell uses oatcakes to represent plain, wholesome northern food at several points. The novel is set on the North Yorkshire coast where Sylvia is the daughter of local farmer Daniel Robson and his Cumberland-born wife Bell. An account of the autumn tasks of good housewives on bleak northern farmsteads refers to 'great racks for oat-cake' (p. 85). At one level, this is a simple description of food and of the lived experience of northern farmers' wives as Gaskell believes they had been at the time she is writing about – during the French Revolutionary Wars. But it is also an account of how half a century on, in the mid-nineteenth century, a middle-class urban woman saw a distinctive northern identity reflected in food. Later references to a great chest for oatcakes and to cold bacon and coarse oatcake bought by the recruiting sergeant carry the same implication (p. 132). The specifically 'plain' nature of oatcakes is reinforced by Daniel's comment to Sylvia that they (unlike Bell and her nephew Philip Hepburn, whose family were socially superior) are 'oat-cake folk, while they's pie-crust' (p. 36).

Emily Brontë's first mention of oatcakes in *Wuthering Heights* is similar to many of Gaskell's. When Lockwood, the framing narrator of the tale, visits Heathcliff, his new landlord, at Wuthering Heights on the Pennine moors for the first time, he sees in the family sitting room a 'frame of wood laden with oatcakes' along with legs of beef, mutton, and lamb, noting the room and contents would have been 'nothing extraordinary as belonging to a homely northern farmer' (p. 3). On another visit, later in the book but earlier in time, Nelly Dean accompanies young Catherine to Wuthering Heights to see her estranged cousin. They find the servant Joseph 'in a sort of elysium alone, beside a roaring fire; a quart of ale on a table near him, bristling with large pieces of toasted oat cake; and his black, short pipe in his mouth' – a slightly different more rugged and masculine picture of northern homeliness, perhaps with plainness dominating (p. 208).

In *Shirley*, set in a Yorkshire mill town during the Luddite disturbances but again reflecting its author's mid-century perspectives, Charlotte Brontë's symbolism of oatcakes is more directly about simplicity and wholesomeness, with northernness coming partly from the location of the story but also from the reactions of those involved. Shirley is toasting oatcakes for her young semi-invalid cousin Henry when Mr Hall, the rector, and Louis Moore, Henry's half-Belgian tutor, return from a walk and are invited to join them for this schoolroom lunch with the warning they 'will be restricted to new milk and Yorkshire oat-cake'. Louis rejects oatcakes, speaking partly in French. As Henry explains, 'He cannot eat it […] thinks it is like bran, raised with sour yeast' (p. 439). Here northern (or to be more precise in this case Yorkshire) identity is being reinforced by the 'otherness' of the foreign tutor – who is socially of ambiguous status. At the same time he is asserting his own identity, coming from a nation that prides itself on its cuisine, and his right to reject strange food.

In these examples we have seen specific Yorkshire settings stand for the North as a whole, but Mrs Gaskell also uses oatcakes to highlight intra-regional differences, in particular between what is now Cumbria and more southerly parts. She links these to feelings of home and homesickness. In *Mary Barton*, set in Manchester, Alice Wilson offers her precious 'oat bread of the north, the clap-bread of Cumberland and Westmoreland' (that is the two traditional counties forming most of modern Cumbria) as a special treat, taken from her old deal box, when she introduces Mary Barton to Margaret Jennings (pp. 30-32). The two girls' enjoyment of this dainty provides the prompt for Alice's account of how she left home further north and moved to Manchester in search of work. Although her migration, initially in service, is a relatively short distance in modern terms, she had never been able to return home while her mother was still alive, or even go to her funeral, but she now hankers after one last visit to her birthplace while she herself still lives. So for her it is county, or even more local, roots that have an emotional pull. Bell Robson, in *Sylvia's Lovers*, has also moved from her Cumbrian birthplace, but in this case to marry a Yorkshireman and settle on a farm near the east coast. She too attaches importance to the clap-bread of her youth. In this case she has a 'great rack of clap-bread' hung in her house symbolizing how she thinks she is a better housekeeper than – and generally superior to – the Yorkshire women among whom she now lives and who make the 'leavened and partly sour kind' of oatcake (p. 35-36).[9] Later in the novel, while waiting for news of her husband Daniel's trial for attacking press gang collaborators, she encourages Sylvia to make clap-bread 'for him', thus demonstrating a bond within the family but also asserting her Cumbrian identity (p. 313).

So far I have focused on oatcakes, but porridge too appears several times in *Sylvia's Lovers* to reinforce a picture of domestic peace and comfort in a northern farmhouse, often implicitly contrasted with the wild northern outdoors. When Daniel Robson is confined to the house, by a combination of weather and his resulting rheumatism, he interferes in 'the boiling of potatoes, the making of porridge, all the work on which [his wife] specially piqued herself' (p. 45). At a different time, Robson shares a supper of porridge and milk with Kester, his farm servant, after returning from a tough day's work pasturing sheep on distant moors – in contrast to the more urban, and perhaps urbane, cousin Philip who is trying to teach the young Sylvia to read after a day working indoors at Fosters' shop (p. 94). Later in the story, the first two men again share porridge, this time for breakfast, as Robson recovers from his encounter with the press gang (p. 269). So, although it represents comfort and domesticity, porridge can also reference a rugged masculine form of domesticity, chiming with the male and working-class characterization of northernness noted by, for example, Dave Russell.[10]

So I would argue that, although by the mid-nineteenth century wheat had largely replaced oats as the staple grain of most people in the North, oatcakes and porridge retained a symbolic association with northern identities in a variety of ways. Oatcakes offered an image of northern simplicity and wholesomeness that was often tinged with nostalgia. Closely related to this were the ideas of northern homeliness and domestic peace. While this included an element of 'good housewifery' it also had a masculine aspect. The local variation underpinning northern identities could be seen in different types of oatcake for different districts. This difference could have real emotional charge for people who had migrated within the north. Porridge could carry a similar message of comfort often implicitly contrasted with the wild northern outdoors.

The Hungry North

In an urban setting, however, porridge was sometimes related not to comfort but to poverty and hunger. This takes us to my second theme: the construction of the North as a place of hunger. The period 1840 to 1870, and in particular what later became known as 'The Hungry Forties', was one in which food, or perhaps more usually the lack of food, was prominent in public and political discourse. Two contrasting political campaigns of the period were relevant to food and hunger. The Anti-Corn Law League (ACLL) opposed laws preventing imports of wheat until its home-grown price reached a very high level. For many of its adherents, repeal was not simply a matter of cheaper and more plentiful food. That was clearly a direct concern both for working-class supporters and for manufacturing employers who saw low food costs as helping keep wages low. But for many it was part of a wider issue of free trade – an almost religious enthusiasm.[11] At the same time, the Chartists' specific demands were concerned with electoral reform, but the movement as a whole had economic and cultural aspects. For some Chartists the suffrage was 'a knife and fork question [...] a bread and cheese question', and they drew on partly invented tradition to describe their vision of a 'moral economy' where basic necessities such as food were not left entirely to an unregulated market.[12] Both these campaigns had links with northern cities that may have fed into the trope of northern hunger.[13] However, it is far from clear that people in the North were in general worse fed than in other parts of the country. When Jane Cobden Unwin brought together accounts of how people remembered the years before Corn Law repeal in her 1904 book *The Hungry Forties*, she saw a nationwide issue.[14] Modern analyses of data from slightly earlier periods suggest northerners may even have been better fed.[15]

Gaskell's *Mary Barton* describes two incidents where porridge (or the type of or want of porridge) is not related to comfort as described above but to poverty or hunger. When Alice Wilson invites Mary Barton and Margaret Jennings to a small tea party, Margaret entertains them by singing the 'Oldham Weaver' – a dialect song about the weaver's hard lot. He had to live on nettles and 'Waterloo porridge the best o'eawr food, Oi'm tellin' yo' true' (pp. 35-37). Waterloo porridge is a dialect term for oatmeal porridge made with water only. None of the three women is well off so this ties in with their own experience. In a more direct reference to porridge as subsistence food, a widow, who cannot afford to send her son to school, regrets that he was not allowed to work under the Factory Act, complaining 'this law o' theirs, keeping childer fra' factory work, whether they be weakly or strong. There is our Ben; why, porridge seems to go no way wi' him, he eats so much' (p. 88). The way this is expressed in dialect reinforces an overall picture of northern urban poverty. Charlotte Brontë makes some similar use of porridge (and its lack) as a sign of poverty. In *Shirley*, the family of William Farren who has been thrown out of work by mechanization, have 'only porridge, and too little of that' (p. 158).

Porridge was not the only way to depict the North as a place of poverty and hunger. Frances Trollope's 1840 *The Life and Adventures of Michael Armstrong, The Factory Boy* is probably the first 'industrial' novel – defined as one that attempts to depict the great transformation of the industrial revolution or to grapple with its significant social dislocations.[16] In a factory near a fictionalized Manchester, pauper apprentices exhibit 'the frightful spectacle of young features pinched by famine' and suffer the 'misery of incessant labour, with strength daily failing for want of pure air and sufficient food'.[17] These hungry apprentices are archetypal figures of the industrial North.

Gaskell portrays a close relationship between hunger and the North in *Mary Barton*. John Barton and a friend visit a family who are even worse off than they are. The father is laid off from the mill but he is ill too and they have had 'no money fra' th' town' because they fear that claiming relief under the Poor Law would risk them being sent back to Buckinghamshire where he was born (p. 64).[18] The two men have taken some food they can ill spare and after giving some to the children Barton offers some to the mother:

> She took the bread […] but could not eat. She was past hunger. She fell down on the floor with a heavy unresisting bang. The men looked puzzled. 'She's well-nigh clemmed,' said Barton. 'Folk do say one mustn't give clemmed people much to eat; but bless us she'll eat nought.' (p. 61)

The dialect word 'clemmed', meaning starving, reinforced the northern context. The scene is in stark contrast with that at the mill owner's house. There his wife has ordered 'breakfast upstairs […] the cold partridge as was left from yesterday, and put plenty of cream in her coffee'. Meanwhile 'at the well spread breakfast-table, sat […] father and son' (p. 68). In this vignette the North is a place of hunger but of hunger made all the worse by the plenty alongside.

So we can see, in what subsequently became known as 'The Hungry Forties', there was an implicit association between the North and hunger, despite probably equal rural poverty in the south of England and urban squalor in London. Sometimes this was portrayed via the traditional northern food of porridge but at other times more directly as a simple lack of food. Sometimes the relationship between northernness and hunger was explicit, but at other times it appears implicitly via the northern location of the tale. The intersection with class is unavoidable, but sometimes they are so intertwined as to be hard to distinguish.

Before moving on to my third theme I would like to mention that this interest shown by writers and readers of fiction in northern hunger appears to have worked its way out after the 1840s. There were periods of economic downturns or food shortages during the 1850s, but it was the Lancashire 'Cotton Famine' of the early 1860s that next gave hunger in northern England the same traction in the national discourse as it had in the 1840s. This was reflected in the press and also in 'Cotton Famine Poems', but I have found little reference in the novels of the time.[19] Clare Pettitt suggests that *Sylvia's Lovers* (written during the Cotton Famine but set around 1800 and on the coast of Yorkshire well away from the textile areas) was influenced by Gaskell's experience of the way a distant war impacted on life in Manchester.[20] However the famine of 1800 described in *Sylvia's Lovers* does not seem to have any regional dimension. It is attributed explicitly to harvest failure, war (with France), and the Corn Laws (p. 481).

Conspicuous Consumption and Wholesome Plenty

The last theme challenges the idea of a hungry North. Elsewhere in these novels the North, perhaps particularly the industrial North, was associated with extravagance of various kinds. It was a place where money was being made, and specifically 'new money', as the successful mill owners were often self-made men. At the same time factories and mines provided some relatively highly paid work. There was also more work for women and children meaning that, whatever the downsides, some families had higher incomes than if they had only one breadwinner's wage. The combination of social mobility and inequality provided the opportunity both for conspicuous consumption and for the disapproval of its showiness.

In Gaskell's *North and South*, Mrs Thornton (the mill owner's mother) gives a sumptuous dinner party, attended by Margaret Hale and her father who had moved to Milton from the south of England.

> Margaret, with her London cultivated taste, felt the number of delicacies to be oppressive; one half of the quantity would have been enough, and the effect

> lighter and more elegant. But it was one of Mrs Thornton's rigorous laws of hospitality, that of each separate dainty enough should be provided for all the guests to partake, if they felt inclined. (p. 213)

A rather different contrast, though again suggesting northern extravagance, is provided by Mr Hale's comment after he visits the house of a striker earlier in the same day:

> I hardly know how to compare one of these houses with our Helstone cottages. I see […] food commonly used which they would consider luxuries; yet for these very families there seems to be no other resource […] One had need to learn a different language, and measure by a different standard, up here in Milton. (p. 212)

For both middle and working classes, we are presented with a more extravagant lifestyle in the North. However in neither case is the 'delicacy' or 'luxury' named, still less described. Despite this coyness about detail we can recognize a version of conspicuous consumption that is not only extravagant but demonstrates a lack of sophistication verging on the uncivilized.

A more flamboyant version of Mr Hale's view appears in Charles Dickens' *Hard Times*. Bounderby the banker and manufacturer claims that 'There is not a Hand in this town, sir, man, women, or child, but has one ultimate objective in life […] to be fed on turtle soup and venison with a gold spoon'.[21] Bounderby is asserting that the mill workers of Coketown had unreasonably extravagant dietary expectations and, while Dickens may not have agreed, he presented it as an extreme expression of a common view.

A simpler plenty that sits between this extravagance and the homeliness described earlier is linked to traditions of hospitality. In one scene in *Shirley* young Caroline Helstone, who lives with her uncle at the Rectory, finds herself obliged, by the conventions of Yorkshire hospitality, to give an impromptu tea party for an uncomfortably mixed group of guests. The three curates (who follow each other round the neighbourhood in search of hospitality throughout the book) have called to see the Rector. She is hoping that they will not stay for tea when Mrs Sykes and three Misses Sykes arrive to 'see her "in a friendly way", as the custom of that neighbourhood' (p. 131). So Caroline has to cope with the twin challenges of keeping conversation going with this ill-assorted group and the practicalities of feeding them when the cook had 'put off the baking today because […] there would be bread plenty […] while morning' (p. 135). The evening is indeed a social trial for her but after hurried consultation and the despatch of the maid to buy baked goods from the village a suitable spread is provided:

> Yorkshire people, in those days, took their tea round the table; […] essential to have a multitude of plates of bread and butter, varied in sorts and plentiful in quantity: […] the tea was spread forth in handsome style, and neither ham, tarts, nor marmalade were wanting […] The curates, summoned to this bounteous repast, entered joyous. (pp. 135-36)

While this scene of simple but generous hospitality is framed as specifically Yorkshire (if not even more local) it can be seen as standing for the North in general. By placing the scene 'in those days', Brontë brings in an element of nostalgia, although as Laura Mason points out it is not clear how much she was influenced by her own childhood memories of the 1820s. While the specific foods offered are not uniquely northern, both ham and curd tarts had some Yorkshire associations by this time.[22]

In these examples different sorts of culinary extravagance and plenty are associated with the North. Some, such as from the self-made mill owner, or the factory worker who is now relatively well-paid, can be seen as associated with a lack of sophistication, or even a lack of prudence. Others however seem to have been rooted in nostalgia for a North where traditional English hospitality thrived.

Conclusion

The treatment of food, its consumption, and its lack in mid-nineteenth century novels contributed to the construction and reflection of an English North and northernness in several ways. First, although by then wheat had largely replaced oats as the staple grain of most people in the North, oatcakes and porridge held symbolic associations with northern identities. Overall they offered an image of northern simplicity and wholesomeness that was often tinged with nostalgia: the way different types of oatcake were favoured in different districts could have real emotional charge for people who had migrated within the north. Second, in what subsequently became known as the Hungry Forties, there was an implicit association between the North and hunger despite probably equal poverty in the south. However, during the Lancashire Cotton Famine of the early 1860s, fiction offered little to reflect the association in the public imagination between hunger and the distressed areas seen in the contemporary press. Third, there was a converse trope in the national discourse: the North as a place of extravagance verging on vulgarity and/or imprudence, often associated with new money, whether the riches of mill owners or the good wages, by the standards of the time, of factory operatives. A different aspect of plenty can be seen in simple northern hospitality. So we have an emerging northern identity characterized by a three-way tension between homeliness, hunger, and extravagance. This tension is often linked to more specific place-identities within the North, and there is some ambiguity about whether counties took the primary place-identities themselves or were standing for the North as a whole.

Notes

1. Benedict Anderson, *Imagined Communities*, 2nd edn (London: Verso, 2006); Karl Spracklen. 'Theorising Northernness and Northern Culture: The North of England, Northern Englishness, and Sympathetic Magic', *Journal for Cultural Research*, 20.1 (2016), 4-16 (p.10) <http://dx.doi.org/10.1080/14797585.215.1134056>
2. Elizabeth Gaskell, *North and South*, ed. by Dorothy Collin (London: Penguin, 1970 [1854-1855]); Elizabeth Gaskell, *Mary Barton – A Tale of Manchester Life*, ed. by Macdonald Daly (London: Penguin,

1996 [1848]); Elizabeth Gaskell, *Sylvia's Lovers,* ed. by Andrew Sanders (Oxford: Oxford University Press, 1982 [1863]); Emily Brontë, *Wuthering Heights,* ed. by Ian Jack (Oxford: Oxford University Press, 1995 [1847]); Charlotte Brontë, *Shirley,* ed. by Andrew and Judith Hook (London: Penguin, 1974 [1849]). Subsequent references to these works will be cited parenthetically.

3   This paper is concerned with the North of England and implicitly its relationship to the south of the country. For simplicity it does not attempt to consider the broader context of the United Kingdom of Great Britain and Ireland, which in this period included the whole of the island of Ireland. For discussion of the relationship between Englishness and Britishness in the eighteenth and nineteenth century see, for example, Linda Colley, *Britons: Forging the Nation 1707-1837* (London: Pimlico 1994), pp.13-14, 322-23, 372-73.

4   Helen M. Jewell, *The North-South Divide: Origins of Northern Consciousness in England* (Manchester: Manchester University Press, 1994), p.206; Neville Kirk, 'Introduction', in *Northern Identities: Historical Interpretations of 'The North' and 'Northernness',* ed. by Neville Kirk (Aldershot: Ashgate, 2000), pp. ix-xiv, (p.ix).

5   See, for example, Stuart Rawnsley, 'Constructing "The North": Space and a Sense of Place', in *Northern Identities,* ed. by Kirk, pp. 3-22 (p. 3); Dave Russell, *Looking North: Northern England and the National Imagination* (Manchester: Manchester University Press, 2004), p. 16.

6   *Northern History,* 5 (1970), front matter.

7   Jewell, p. 36.

8   John Burnett, *Plenty and Want* (Harmondsworth: Penguin, 1966), p. 16, p. 53; Peter Brears, *Traditional Food in Yorkshire* (Totnes: Prospect Books, 2014), p. 98; Peter Brears, *Traditional Food in Cumbria* (Carlisle: Bookcase, 2017), pp. 161-77; Marie Hartley and Joan Ingilby, *Life and Tradition in the Yorkshire Dales,* 50th anniversary edn, ed. by Gillian Cookson and Kirsty McHugh (1968; Leeds: Yorkshire Archaeological and Historical Society, 2018), pp. 28.

9   A wide range of different types of oatcake were made in different places and at different periods but there were two main types. Unleavened clap-bread, made in much of Cumbria and the adjacent more northerly Yorkshire dales, was rolled or patted ('clapped') flat in the same way as modern Scottish oatcakes. Leavened oatcakes or riddlebread were made further south and in a few areas of Westmorland with a yeasted batter. See Hartley and Ingleby, p. 30; Brears, *Yorkshire,* pp. 106-07; Brears, *Cumbria,* pp. 161-70.

10 Dave Russell, 'Culture and the Formation of Northern English Identities from c.1850', in *An Agenda for Regional History,* ed. by Bill Lancaster, Diana Newton, and Natasha Vall (Newcastle upon Tyne: Northumbria University Press, 2007), pp. 271-88 (p. 273).

11 Peter Gurney, *Wanting and Having: Popular Politics and Liberal Consumerism in England, 1830-70* (Manchester: Manchester University Press, 2015), pp. 7-8; David Cannadine, *Victorious Century: The United Kingdom, 1800-1906* (London: Penguin, 2018), pp. 208-09.

12 Edward Royle, *Chartism,* 2nd edn (Harlow: Longman, 1986) pp. 24, 95; Gurney, *Wanting,* pp. 3, 54.

13 Cannadine, pp. 209, 205.

14 J[ulia] C[obden] U[nwin], 'Introduction', in *The Hungry Forties: Life Under the Bread Tax: Descriptive Letters and Other Testimonies from Contemporary Witnesses,* ed. by Cobden Unwin (London: T. Fisher Unwin, 1904), p. 54.

15 Sara Horrell and Deborah Oxley, 'Bringing home the bacon? Regional Nutrition, Stature, and Gender in the Industrial Revolution', *Economic History Review,* 65.4 (2012), 1354-79 (p. 1359).

16 'The Industrial Novel', *The Oxford Encyclopedia of British Literature,* ed. by David Scott Kastan <https://www.oxfordreference.com/view/10/1093/acref/9780195169828-e-0231> [accessed 9 June 2020]

17 Frances Trollope, *The Life and Adventures of Michael Armstrong, the Factory Boy* (London: Henry Colburn, 1840), pp. 178, 186.

18 This trope of northern industrial workers being reluctant to seek help for fear of being returned to their rural parish of birth also appears in non-fiction works of the period.

19 See, for example, John Simpson, Secretary, Wigan Mechanics Institution 'Lancashire Distress' letter to the editor, *London Evening Standard,* Friday 22 May 1863, p. 3; Simon Rennie, 'Poetic Responses to the

Civil War', *Journal of Victorian Culture*, 25.1 (2020), 126-143 (p. 128) <http://dx.doi.org/10.1093/jvcult/vcz024>

20 Clare Pettitt, 'Time Lag and Elizabeth Gaskell's Transatlantic Imagination', *Victorian Studies*, 54.4 (2012), 599-623 (p. 599) <https://www.jstor.org/stable/10.2979/victorianstudies.54.4.599> [accessed 29 March 2021]. At the time the 'Cotton Famine' was largely perceived as the result of accepting the Unionist blockade on cotton during the American Civil War, and so supporting both the abolition of slavery and Britain's strategic interests but this also masked an economic depression. See, for example, John Walton, 'The North West', in *The Cambridge Social History of Britain 1750-1950: I: Regions and Communities*, ed. by F.M.L. Thompson (Cambridge: Cambridge University Press, 1993), pp. 355-414 (p. 386).

21 Charles Dickens, *Hard Times,* ed. by Kate Flint (London: Penguin, 1995 [1854]), p. 130.

22 Laura Mason, 'Everything Stops for Tea', in *Luncheon, Nuncheon and Other Meals*, ed. by C. Anne Wilson (Stroud: Alan Sutton, 1994), pp. 71-90 (p. 80); Laura Mason with Catherine Brown, *Traditional Foods of Britain: An Inventory* (Totnes: Prospect Books, 1999), pp. 221-22, 291-92.

Imaginary Feasts: Virtual Meals in a Second World War Prison Camp and in COVID Times

Suzanne Evans

During the Second World War, in the spring of 1942, small groups of ravenous women began gathering each afternoon in Singapore's notorious Changi Jail, where they had been imprisoned by the Japanese since March of that year. They talked of food, of all the sweet and savoury dishes they could only dream of eating and sharing. The words seemed to quell their hunger, if only briefly. While a majority of the women were British, there was one very bossy Canadian in the group, Ethel Mulvany. Mul, as she was known, organized these gatherings and in time, insisted the women keep a written record of their food dreams. She collected their recipes and brought them back to Canada after the war. Over the next year she had 20,000 copies of the resulting cookbook printed up which she sold, raising money to send food to former prisoners of war hospitalized in England where rationing was still in effect.

In 2010, while working at the Canadian War Museum in Ottawa, I discovered a copy of Mulvany's *Prisoners of War Cook Book* in the museum's library.[1] Her collection of prison camp recipes is fascinating, but not unique. In the Second World War starving prisoners around the world, men and women, were dreaming and writing about food.[2] In fact, at this Symposium, twenty-one years ago, two papers were presented on the subject of prisoners of war and their food memories.[3]

Compelled to find out more about Mulvany, I burrowed down into years of research about prison camp life. The written result of my work is a biography, *The Taste of Longing: Ethel Mulvany and Her Starving Prisoners of War Cookbook* (2020). However, not quite sated on the subject, I decided to further explore the stories that arise when we talk about food that is meaningful to us. In the spring of 2019 I joined Alchemy, an Art Residency program on Toronto Island that focuses on the intersections between food, art, and community. For my project, I invited the artists in residence to an Imaginary Feast and asked them to describe a dish or meal they would want if they were painfully hungry.

The results were poignant and led to a second Alchemy Imaginary Feast four months later. The latter became the subject of a CBC radio documentary aired on Thanksgiving Sunday, October 2019.[4] These Alchemy dinners provided the groundwork for a subsequent series of six Imaginary Feasts conducted over Zoom during the pandemic. Ranging in groups of six to thirteen people, aged twenty-something to seventy plus, the guests came from diverse backgrounds and genders. They joined in from Newfoundland to California and as far afield as Brunei, each eager to share a story of a meaningful meal or dish in response to open invitations sent out via word of mouth, local newspapers, email contacts, and Facebook. Some of these miniature autobiographies were funny, others intimate and painfully tender. A few grappled with the pandemic, but most served, as did the recipes for the women in Changi Jail, as an escape hatch leading away from a world unravelling. I will compare a selection of the more than fifty stories collected with the recipes and experiences of the women from Changi Jail and explore their overlapping themes.

Tradition

Our invitation to consider 'Food and Imagination' for this year's Symposium stated that 'imagination implies challenges to tradition'. Certainly the food the Changi Jail prisoners found to augment their rations was very inventive. They ground up eggshells for calcium, dined on slugs and live baby mice. They even tried snacking on talcum powder. However, for their imaginary meals, what Ethel Mulvany called their tea parties, the women relied on the comfort foods of home. In much the same way, the attendees of the pandemic feasts mostly focused on very simple or traditional dishes. The challenge to tradition in both cases was the use to which the virtual meals were put: instead of broadening the belly, they fed the mind and the heart.

Let me begin with the early days of hunger in Changi Jail. The women gathered in the hot, crowded cement courtyard and began their imaginings by conjuring chairs to sit on and a dining table, covered with linen, decorated with flowers, and set with cutlery. Ethel Mulvany claimed that these parties usually began with someone serving up the food they came to yearn for most, bread. After this, the mainly British women turned to the plain dishes of home: colcannon, pork pies, kidneys on toast, and steamed puddings galore. They recorded over 450 recipes, some repeated, all loved.[5]

Few of the POW recipes incorporated elements of the cuisine of Singapore and Malaya where the women had lived, some for years. Instead, their dream foods reflected their culinary heritage.[6] A majority of the approximately sixty-three contributors to Ethel Mulvany's POW recipe collection identified as housewives, a role intimately tied to food. In this role, women are often weighted with the responsibility of maintaining traditions, culinary and otherwise, across generations. While many of the prisoners were bereft of family members to whom they could pass on their recipes, they shared stories of food and loved ones with their prison family.

During the virtual feasts, a number of the participants described dishes that had been passed on by mothers and grandmothers. In the case of Adrian, though, she had to reconstruct a culinary tradition after the death of her family's matriarchs.[7] Adrian's family had immigrated to Canada from Iceland four generations ago. They brought with them a cherished recipe for vinarterta, a multilayered cake filled with spiced plum jam. The cake had held great status in Iceland at the time, having migrated from the pastry capital of Vienna, hence the name Vienna Torte, to Copenhagen and from there to the Danish colony of Iceland. The dessert was reserved for celebrations and the Icelandic communities of Manitoba held tight to that tradition.[8]

Each year at Christmas Adrian's family drove eight hours north from Winnipeg to Flin Flon knowing that the vinarterta would be served at the climax of the feast. She remembered the flavour from when she was very young, but was never taught the recipe because unlike the girls in her family she had grown up as a boy. After the death of both her mother and grandmother in quick succession, Adrian had come out as transgendered. With that transition she became the eldest daughter of the eldest daughter, a position which for her meant taking on the mantle of family matriarch. She felt it her duty to strengthen the family ties that had loosened while her mother and grandmother had been sick and was convinced that this process had to begin with hosting Christmas dinner and serving the symbolic vinarterta. With a recipe saved by a cousin and a memory of what the final product tasted like, she forged ahead. Each step of the process was new to her, never having been instructed to stir the jam or pull the cake layers out of the oven as a young girl might have been asked to do. The vinarterta was a success, and with it Adrian took on a new role.

The pandemic feasts were held in November and December so it is not surprising that there were a number of Christmas foods, particularly desserts, that were discussed. They were rooted in British, Norwegian, Icelandic, Swedish, and even Chinese-fusion traditions. Even if these events had been held at a different time of year, aspects of the Christmas feast would likely have arisen. It is, after all, an annual affair often attended by many family members and requiring concentrated effort in the kitchen. Certainly the Changi prisoners discussed a number of Christmas fruit cakes that were eventually included in Mulvany's cookbook.

Wartime

Not surprisingly, another prominent category that emerged in the modern stories dealt with war, during which any experience is intensified and thus made more memorable. This was true of the Christmas pudding that Karen's British grandfather wrote about in a letter to his mother when he was at the front in the First World War. He missed it terribly. After the war, he immigrated to Canada and took the recipe with him. He never cooked it, but made sure to give it to his Canadian wife. In time she passed it on to her new daughter-in-law just before she headed off to live on Cape Breton Island, Nova Scotia with her husband. That young woman, Karen's mother, set up house on a Royal Canadian Mounted Police outpost, miles from any store. Unable to buy dried fruit to make the pudding, she improvised. The surrounding cranberry bogs provided her with a plentiful harvest and from then on the pudding has been made with dried cranberries. It is still served with a moment of silence in respect for the young man who fought in the trenches and yearned for the taste of home.

War circumscribed the heart-shaped Norwegian waffles that Fay held up to show us via her Zoom screen. She makes them every year in November in memory of her Norwegian grandmother. During the Second World War when German-occupied Oslo was being bombed by the allies, civilians were asked to shelter in basements. Over time, when Fay's grandmother realized that her neighbourhood was not being directly targeted, she invited her normally reserved neighbours into her windowless front hall where they could safely wait out errant explosions without fear of shattering glass. Being the consummate hostess, she went into her kitchen, braving the dangers of a big window. There she cooked up waffles and brewed coffee. Over the months, when stores of coffee beans ran out, she roasted peas and made ersatz coffee. Carrying on these coffee klatches became a form of resistance supported by imagining the flavours and settings of former peaceful times while in the company of new friends.

During the same war, farther south, a young Canadian RCAF flight engineer had his plane shot down on 8 July 1944 near Beauvais, France. A farmer in the area noticed the allied pilot walking along the road in front of his farm. He hurried over to him, explained the danger he was in, and rushed him into his barn. For three weeks the whole family took care of the young man, feeding him and keeping him hidden until he was able to escape to England with the help of the French Resistance. Many decades later, in 2000, the engineer, now too old to travel, gave his daughter Pauline and her family the airfare to go to France. He wanted them to meet the French family and thank them properly for what they had done. The two families had a week-long visit which culminated in a grand meal. A casserole brimming with ratatouille was served outdoors at a table just long enough to seat the assembled crowd. Pauline cherished her hosts' respect for the food, their delight in sharing it, and the time they took to savour what had brought them together.

Brands and Convenience

Many of the Changi recipes and the pandemic stories included brandname and convenience foods. The products of Misters Lea & Perrins, Heinz, Kraft, Campbell, Libby, and Nestlé were summoned into the land of make-believe dining by the prisoners. Specific brands of salmon, evaporated milk, beans, and soups were incorporated into recipes. For both groups, the products acted as landmarks of another time and place. The pandemic feast stories that referred to mothers' use of tinned soups were a great source of laughter and memories shared by people who had never met. The products most enjoyed were Campbell's tomato soup and cream of mushroom soup. In John's Irish Catholic family of nine, his mother's cooking was all about stretching resources. The great unifier of all her meals was Campbell's cream of mushroom soup. It spread over and thickened everything from tinned green beans to meatloaf, and any left in the can, she was told by a neighbour, could be used as face cream.

The anonymous woman who contributed a recipe to the POW cook book for 'Chili Con Carne with Spaghetti' was definite that it required a tin of Libby's Con Carne. In contrast, Mike, in one of the modern Imaginary Feasts, did not remember the brand of the most important canned chilli that he ever ate. He was twelve years old at the time, the eldest of six children being raised by a single mother in San Jose, California. His mother's new boyfriend, Ken, a biker and ex-convict, took Mike to visit his old neighbourhood, a shanty town in a drought-dry river bed in an industrial part of town. Mike thought this would be a place of freedom with no rules, but was quickly disenchanted with this impoverished world. Tarped roofs protected make-shift furniture, and TVs powered by a web of cords siphoned electricity off a local street lamp. Ken took the young Mike straight to Sugar, the matriarch of this enclave, who presided over inhabitants of all ages and backgrounds. She welcomed them, as she did everyone, with hugs and a glass of cool, clean water.

It was not long before Mike started grumbling to Ken. He was hungry and had his heart set on having two Burger King cheese burgers. Overhearing him, Sugar offered him something from her pantry instead. Half-heartedly he chose a can of chilli from her metal utility shelf stacked with tinned goods. She opened it and directed him to put it on the fire, handing him a pair of vice-grips for the job. When it bubbled, he clamped onto the tin and dipped his spoon in. Ken leaned over and asked how it tasted.

'It isn't cheese burgers.'

'You'll get your burgers', Ken replied, 'but now the kids here won't get any chilli.'

Those words left a permanent mark on Mike, 'hit[ting] my heart harder than anything else had before'. For the first time he was able to imagine the hunger of others.

Pain and Politics

The near-starvation rations in Changi exacted a physical and emotional toll on the prisoners. The hunger they experienced during the war was painful. In her unique way, Ethel Mulvany described it as a 'going-down-the-valley-one-by-one pain of hunger'. She asserted, 'There is nothing stronger. There is nothing where the body is more vulnerable to absolute capitulation, to any vice.'[9] Hunger caused some to sell their bodies for food while others stole to alleviate the pain.

Food and pain can be united by more than hunger. This was the case for Seema when she was growing up in Calgary, Alberta in the 1980s. She was the only child of East Indian origins in her class, and neither her teachers nor her fellow students had ever seen the dal and roti she brought for lunch. Told she was dirty because her fingers were yellowed, it took years before she realized that the stain was from turmeric. Inside her home she felt equally pressured to fit in, in this case to be a traditional Indian daughter. The weight of that pressure followed her even after she left home to live in Montreal. She felt it with each package of homemade roti her mother sent her. Seema wondered, "If you can taste the love in food, can you taste the manipulation and guilt?"

Erin might well have asked the same question. She had been living in India with her husband in a marriage that was coming apart under the weight of the emotional abuse he exerted upon her. Since their early days together food exploration had always been a shared source of delight for them. As their relationship fractured, that joy slipped away from Erin to the point where she lost her sense of taste. She felt the texture of the food, but it had no flavour. That changed when she escaped from her husband and flew back home to the United States. Once settled in her seat on a Korean airlines flight, she felt safe. The dish of bibimbap she was served combining rice, vegetables, and meat was something she had come to love while living overseas, and it was served with her favourite condiment, gochujang red chilli paste. With joy she squeezed the whole tube over her meal in the shape of a heart and then took a bite. All the flavour she used to relish in her food returned at that moment. It was only an airline meal, but it was spiced with freedom.

In a gentle but clear act of resistance, one of the women imprisoned in Changi Jail shared a recipe for mint humbugs with her fellow prisoners. Her list of ingredients specifically states that the peppermint oil to be used must be English not Japanese. When even the smallest defiance could result in punishment by the Japanese, this modest request stands out and surely would have been much appreciated by the other women in the jail.

A similar note of resistance came to the fore in a pandemic story that Namitha, a woman of colour, told about the bake-off conducted by her two roommates for her twenty-first birthday. Knowing her well, they both baked cakes that reflected her tastes and character. One made a three-tiered cake, each layer representing a favourite book with *The Catcher in the Rye* on top. The other roommate baked a cheesecake decorated with blueberries and strawberries depicting a police car on fire. While she chose the book cake as the winner, she noted that at the moment, 'most of my identity is hating cops'.

A story of hatred in remission was told by Jeanette, a Canadian diplomat. She was on posting in Zagreb, Croatia early in her career in 1996 just after the Bosnian war had ended. It was a delicate time in statecraft when tensions were running high. When she and her husband, who loved to cook, had been there long enough to take a measure of the atmosphere, they hosted a brunch. With hutzpah and diplomacy they invited a selection of people from across the political spectrum. All accepted and came with their young children. Jeanette made sure the guests had plenty on their plates and in their glasses while her husband did the cooking. Tension was palpable at the outset, but gradually subsided over time as the talk continued, which it did for twelve full hours. Jeanette cannot remember anything about all the dishes they served over that time span. She acknowledged, 'The food is super important, but the conversations are also what makes a feast a feast.'

Fiction Coming to Life

The characters who add to those conversations are also important, even if they are fictional, as happened in the prisoners' recipes. Dickens's character Oliver Twist, who had the temerity to ask for more food, made it into the cookbook in the guise of a cake named in his honour. The inhabitants of J.M. Barrie's Never Never Land lingered around the biscuit recipe for Peter Pans. The recipe for Mikado Pudding came with memories of the then-popular Gilbert and Sullivan comic opera. In one of the pandemic feasts, Uma, a writer of children's books, described how fiction became real. One of her books features a cook who makes a delicious curry puff with a secret ingredient. After the book's publication Uma was asked to talk to a group of children and share the recipe with the secret ingredient. Having only imagined the curry puffs, Uma had to spend days in her kitchen experimenting with possible secret ingredients. It would have to somehow appeal to the funny bone and the taste buds of children. In the end, a little bit of cocoa did the trick. Uma summed up her experience, 'When you make stuff up it can sometimes turn real in ways you didn't expect.' Surely this was true for the hungry prisoners of war who felt nourished just by imagining their favourite foods.

Like Uma, Ken shared a fanciful world drawing on the culture of his island home. He did what Newfoundlanders are famous for: he told a very tall tale. This one was about an old woman named Nan from the outport town of Raison Arm. Nan was famous for her Christmas cakes and decided to make a really big one that year to feed the community. None of her pans were big enough, so she took out the seats of the old tin boat stored in her shed. She lined the boat with grease paper and poured in the batter. There wasn't an oven on the island that could handle a cake that size so she left it where it was and lit the shed on fire. Soon the fire brigade arrived, but when they saw there was no need for hoses, they set up their chairs and put on a kettle. The local accordion player arrived not long after, and then others turned up, drawn to the music and aroma. When the shed finished burning the tea was poured and Nan served the warm fruit cake to all assembled.

Casey, another virtual Zoom participant, found her community expanded and her culinary imagination inspired by the hunger of a fictional character. Her story was one of the few that dealt head-on with the pandemic. Seattle, Washington, where Casey lives, was ground zero for the pandemic in the United States. Just before COVID hit she anxiously stocked her cupboards and freezer. Thereafter she limited herself to one grocery shop a month. As her social life shrank away, she increasingly spent time reading. She was deep into a novel set in Victorian England, when she came to a part where a desperately hungry character was eating a ploughman's sandwich. Instantly she was struck with a craving for that sandwich. Her well-stocked kitchen had all the ingredients except for apple chutney. Never mind, she would make it, except that she didn't have an apple. It was 10 pm and the stores were closed. Her only recourse was to make a request online to her *Buy Nothing* neighbourhood group. She was messaged back immediately, 'We are a symptom-free household. I can put it outside on the box which has been disinfected. Do you need it now?' She felt embarrassed but admitted that she did. The house was just three blocks away. She didn't know the owners but had passed it almost daily while going for her pandemic walks and talking on her phone. It was one of the few streets in her neighbourhood where she could get cell reception. That night Casey ran, picked up the apple, and made the chutney. She ate her sandwich at midnight, taking joy in its flavour and feeling grateful for her pandemic community.

Great pleasure comes from feeding a community whether that be with imagined food or with the real thing. Amanda found this to be true when she and her mother decided to throw a party for friends and neighbours. Amanda, an only child, and her single mother moved from New York City to Toronto in the early 1970s. Soon after, these self-described 'scrap and scrabble city girls' bought a farm in Perth County near Stratford, Ontario and called it Flat Broke Farm. The house was old, droopy, and had little in the way of amenities. The wealth of the place was found in the soil of the kitchen garden. 'All we had to do was wave a packet of seeds over it,' said Amanda, 'and it would produce!' Based on the garden's powers they decided to host a party and call it 'The First Annual Perth County Slumgullian Festival'. Understanding slumgullian to be a gold rush term for a stew with anything and everything in it, in their case whatever the garden could provide, they thought the name fit.

City friends arrived in jeans and t-shirts, and Dutch immigrant neighbours came in their Sunday best. Then strangers began turning up. They had heard in town that there was going to be a Perth County Festival. Being fans of the then-famous rock group, Perth County Conspiracy, they mistakenly thought this was going to be Canada's answer to Woodstock. It wasn't another rock festival for the ages, but no one was disappointed. Guests brought food, and many took turns cooking in the big farm kitchen. The party went on all night, and somehow unplanned-for breakfast foods appeared the next morning. 'It was,' said Amanda, 'a case of the loaves and the fishes.' For her, the festival was a turning point, where she went from poverty and loneliness to abundance and friendship.

Conclusion

The women of Changi were deprived of both food and family, but it was their hunger that was most immediate. For those who came to the virtual table in the pandemic, it was the absence of family and friends that was felt most acutely. While the prisoners focused on the intense savouring of culinary delights, both groups viewed particular dishes as signposts leading to a world inhabited by unreachable friends and family. The imaginary feasts held during the pandemic were shaped by memories of simple and traditional foods, much like the recipes that Ethel Mulvany collected in Changi. Women and housewives as keepers of the family traditions dominated the stories. Brandname convenience foods, and the nostalgia that they carried with them, played a part during both time periods. While war, pain, and politics were the backdrop to the POW recipe collection, they also featured in the stories told during the Imaginary Feasts. Food, the lack of it, the production of it, and the sharing of it, has become a major topic of interest during this pandemic. It seems that, in a world divided eighty years ago by war and now by disease, talking about what we eat can help shrink divisions.

Notes

1   A digital copy of Ethel Mulvany's *Prisoners of War Cook Book* is available at the Canadian War Museum <https://collections.historymuseum.ca/public/objects/common/webmedia.php?irn=5523402> [accessed 24 February 2022]

2. Two examples of unpublished recipe collections of imagined dishes are Lily Casey, *The House Wife's Dictionary and Suggestions* IWM LBY 90/1859, and Helene Marcelle Chambon, *Diary of Helene Marcelle Chambon* CWM ARCH DOCSMANU 58A 1 89.11. A selection of published collections include: Cara De Silva (ed.) *In Memory's Kitchen: A Legacy from the Women of Terezin*, trans. by Bianca Steiner Brown (Northvale, NJ: Jason Aronson Inc, 1996); Col. C. Fowler, *Recipes Out of Bilibid* (New York: George W. Stewart, 1946); P.C.B. Newington, *Good Food* (Ipoh, Malaya: Charles Grenier, 1947), and Edith Peer, *Fantasy Cooking Behind Barbed Wire: Recipes* (Sydney, Australia: Edith Peer, 1986). A well-illustrated and tested collection of recipes by a number of Dutch women imprisoned by the Japanese in Indonesia during the Second World War is found in Cathelijne Van den Bercken, *De Smaak van Verlangen: droomrecepten en verhalen uit bezet Nederlands-Indie* (Amsterdam: Artemis BV, 2007).

3. Sue Shephard, 'A Slice of the Moon', in *Food and the Memory: Proceedings of the 2000 Oxford Symposium of Food and Cookery*, ed. by Harlan Walker (Totnes, Devon: Prospect Books, 2001), pp. 223-27; Jan Thompson, 'Prisoners of the Rising Sun: Food Memories of American POWs in the Far East During World War II', in *Food and the Memory*, ed. by Walker, pp. 273-86.

4. 'How a Canadian Woman's Imaginary Feasts helped starving World War II Prisoners', *Sunday Edition*, CBC, 14 October 2019.

5. The original log books with the handwritten recipes are held in the Pioneer Museum, Mindemoya, Manitoulin Island, Ontario.

6. The men on the other side of Changi Jail also discussed food. Intriguingly, a collection of their recipes published after the war in Malaya did include many Asian recipes. This difference may be due in part to the fact that the cooking facilities were all on the men's side of the jail, hence they learned how to cook with local ingredients (Newington, *Good Food*).

7. The participants are presented by first names only to preserve their privacy.

8. For a fascinating discussion on the symbolism and fractious history of vinarterta in North America, see Laurie K Bertram, 'Icelandic Cake Fight: History of an Immigrant Recipe', *Gastronomica*, 19.4 (Winter 2019), 28-41.

9. Ethel Mulvany to Sidney Katz of *Maclean's* magazine, tape #10 interview, April 1961, Pioneer Museum, Mindemoya, Manitoulin Island, Ontario.

Celebrating the Franco-Russian Alliance: French Chefs as Purveyors of Influence and Creators of Culinary Imagination

Caroline Favre

As the nineteenth century drew to a close, an unexpected alliance was formed between two political regimes which seemed irreconcilable in their essence. In 1894, the French Republic and the Russian autocrat Alexander III ratified the Franco-Russian Alliance that would last until the outbreak of the Russian Revolution in 1917. This coalition came into existence after years of arduous negotiation and not without strong reluctance on both sides. This hesitation was hardly surprising given the diametrically opposed interests and ideological differences of the two nations. Until the 1880s, the idea of a political alliance between France and Russia would have seemed ludicrous for most people.[1] Yet, the heightened isolation that the two countries experienced on the political stage brought them closer. Eventually, the threat posed by the growth in power of Germany along with the rampant rumour that Great Britain would be joining the Triple Alliance sealed their rapprochement.[2] When the announcement of the Alliance was made, it was embraced by both societies. However, defiant voices were soon heard, which denounced the formation of this abnormal union and its political consequences.[3] In order to render the Alliance popular and gain the support of public opinion, the two states mobilized culture through the festivities and the artefacts produced for these occasions. These collective cultural endeavours fostered a sense of shared values among groups whose self-image was quite different.

For many years, scholars have written extensively on the political and diplomatic aspect of the Alliance, overlooking the cultural dimension of the rapprochement, all to the credit and benefit of the small diplomatic corps who had upheld the national interest above all else. As Faith Hillis has argued in her article on the Franco-Russian Marseillaise, 'these studies suggest that diplomacy was driven by its own logic, protected from the pressures of domestic and public opinion. Yet it was not preordained that the general public would accept this diplomatic fait accompli.'[4] Independently from the authorities, numerous men and women in favour of the Alliance became unofficial mediators between Russia and France and consequently helped to reconcile the cultures of the two nations. In recent years, the development of cultural studies prompted scholars to focus more on the cultural facet of the Alliance and the different networks that helped to promote the rapprochement outside the political sphere.

This study proposes to explore one particular network that has often been overlooked: the cooking profession. French chefs felt very much concerned by the events as they had maintained close ties with Russia since at least the eighteenth century when French influences had swept into Russian culture.[5] The employment of French chefs became a status symbol among the Russian nobility, and as a result these men found many opportunities in the Empire. Most of them remained in Russia for years, working in the richest households or opening restaurants in large cities.[6] Others frequently went back and forth between the Empire and their homeland. The movement of these professional cooks created an intricate network and ensured the circulation of recipes and culinary knowledge. They became formidable intermediaries at the crossroad of two culinary cultures. These exchanges were further strengthened by the political context of the Franco-Russian Alliance which saw the birth of new recipes. Through their creations, chefs brought together Russian and French cuisine – or gave that illusion. Not only did they engage with the imagination of the eater, but they played with the stereotypes surrounding Russia to make their dishes more appealing. The present study, then, intends to look at these culinary artists and their contribution in familiarizing French opinion with a culture which until then had been discredited.[7] It argues that French chefs played a significant role in the cultural climate of their time, thus facilitating the rapprochement and its popularity.

The sources regarding these men are unfortunately rather scarce, and little material remains that discusses their lives. However, an important documentary source endures in the thriving nineteenth-century culinary press. One particular periodical stands out for our study. Called *La Cuisine française et étrangère*, it was the official newspaper of the Culinary Philanthropic Union, and its successive editors were all members of the *Académie de Cuisine* of Paris. This publication was written by and mainly for the professionals, even though they aimed to attract a broader public. Whereas culinary newspapers were characterized by a relatively short lifespan, our source was published monthly from 1891 to 1927. The format of the paper persisted throughout the period with sections dedicated to French and foreign recipes and articles that touched upon various culinary matters. While determining the reach and the influence of this periodical is particularly difficult due to the lack of statistics for its distribution, we know that French chefs who lived in Russia could subscribe to it. Furthermore, archival documents from Carcassonne in the South of France give us an indication as to the wide circulation of the periodical. Thus, this culinary press is a valuable source to assess how these ingenious chefs made a significant contribution to the cultural relations between France and Russia in those particular years of the Alliance.

French Chefs: 'the very first to define the Alliance'[8]

The first articles regarding the Franco-Russian Alliance published in *La Cuisine française et étrangère* immediately drew attention to the general sentiment of disaffection felt among the cooking profession. There had been no mention on the part of the authorities or the press of the significant role French cuisine and its chefs had played

Celebrating the Franco-Russian Alliance

in forging ties between France and Russia. In the issue of July 1892, the food journalist Barthemely wrote:

> So far, we have invoked all the reasons more or less plausible that could have prepared the ground to this Franco-Russian Union. Only the influence of French gastronomy, that has continued to be exerted in Russia, has been overlooked or ignored. As a journalist, I must claim, in favour of the French culinary art, its rightful part in the formation of this brotherhood.[9]

It is reasonable to infer that French chefs left an enduring imprint upon Russian culture. To counter Barthelemy's claim would be omitting the cultural dimension of food but also denying the impact of the lives of countless men and women who left France to practice their craft in Russia.

At the time, the Russian nobility had pledged allegiance to the Western perceptions of refinement that included cuisine. In making French chefs the masters of their kitchens, the nobility was part of a cosmopolitan elite bound by a common set of cultural practices and experiences. These French men were then in a position of direct influence on the domestic culture of these wealthy households. However, beyond the apparent lack of recognition of the work accomplished by the French chefs in Russia, what Bartelemy's comment reveals is a deeper issue related to the ambiguous status of cooks during the period. If certain chefs were regarded as culinary artists, most in the profession were still considered as household staff by society. Dreadful working conditions and meagre pay were the common lot for most of these professionals.[10] Furthermore, despite the stellar reputation of French cuisine, France had shown so far a remarkable callousness towards these professionals.[11] Many chefs, from Carême to Escoffier, expressed over the years their disappointment regarding the manifest ingratitude shown by French society for their trade.[12] The first chef to be awarded the Legion of Honour, the highest order of merit in France, was Auguste Escoffier in 1928.

By contrast, the Russian Sovereigns openly expressed their appreciation for the work done by their French chefs. During the course of their careers, these chefs received diverse honours and medals, such as the Order of Saint Anna and the Cross of Serbia.[13] They also held, more often than not, the highest charge in the imperial kitchens as *kamer-fourrier* and were the highest paid employees at the Court, a privileged position the chefs never failed to mention in *La Cuisine française et étrangère*.[14] In October 1896, chef Besnard published a column celebrating the official visit in France of Nicholas II. In an exalted poem, he praised the Imperial family for recognizing the talents of French chefs and having made them the masters of their kitchens. Besnard concludes that the rapprochement between the two nations had begun years before, when chefs had gone to Russia and brought together the two cuisines. It was only natural that professionals be given the credit they deserved.[15]

Besnard's poem is not only an ode to the legacy of the men who left their homeland to spread the French *savoir-faire* in Russia, but it also represents the growing desire for a long-awaited recognition. The chefs who wrote for the periodical showed a remarkable self-awareness and as they sought to improve their social rankings, the culinary press became an important tool of expression for them. The press offered a way to assert their authority, to have their work acknowledged by as many people as possible, and to gain public appreciation. The Franco-Russian Alliance thus became the occasion to remind the public of the involvement of the chefs in the rapprochement. More importantly, it gave them the opportunity to honour their profession.

As a result, *La Cuisine française et étrangère* followed closely the festivities of the Alliance. Every time the two nations gathered around a table, the newspaper shared with its readers the menu served on the occasion. Occasionally, an entire article was dedicated to detailing the course of a party, which allowed the writers to praise the author of the feast. For instance, on 31 January 1894, the Russian nobility gave a reception for the Count of Montebello, Ambassador of France. The periodical reported that the food for the 460 guests had been provided by the French restaurant *Contant*, one of the most prestigious establishments in Saint-Petersburg: 'Mr Contant is one of the men who have contributed most to maintaining the prestige of our national art in Russia.'[16] After the festivities, chef Contant received from the organizers a pansy-shaped pin made with a sapphire surmounted by two diamonds. The article implied that the success of the evening was partly due to Contant's ability to serve a delicious dinner. On another occasion, it was proudly announced that the chef of Nicholas II, Pierre Cubat, had served a dinner for 3800 guests, the fourth largest dinner hosted by the Sovereigns during the month of January 1900.[17] These types of articles emphasized cuisine as a powerful diplomatic tool but also enhanced the figure of the chef. In other words, the culinary press, in celebrating the rapprochement, was in fact honouring the chefs and the work they had accomplished in Russia.

Imagining the Franco-Russian Alliance

The Franco-Russian Alliance proved a creative catalyst for the chefs who used this political moment to invent or reinvent dishes. The new recipes that sprang up in *La Cuisine française et étrangère* were mainly featured in the 1890s, after which they tended to wane in favour of the publication of more traditional Russian recipes. This shift suggests that the creative process of these chefs was very much tied to the fashion of the time, ebbing and flowing partially in response to the popular fervour surrounding the Alliance.

While observing the new recipes of the first feverish decade of the rapprochement, one could obviously expect dishes that associated French and Russian cuisines. However, a closer examination of these recipes shows that French chefs took rather shy steps towards Russian cuisine. The dishes might have been called '*Franco-Russe*' or have a Russian element in their name, but they were often made from several culinary influences while remaining mostly French in their craftmanship. Nevertheless, from the food they used down to the design and names given to their creation, chefs called upon the imagination of the eater. For instance, the cake '*Cronstadt*', created in 1891, was made from blanched almonds, mandarin peel, and a hint of Maraschino.[18] Its name evoked one of the most significant events that led to the formation of the alliance: the visit of the French squadron under Admiral Gervais to Kronstadt in July 1891.

In memory of this visit, other recipes bearing the name of the imperial town were created in the following years. In 1893, pastry chefs Pierre Lacam and Antoine Charabot introduced in their baking cookbook their creation named '*Bombe Cronstadt*' which appeared soon after in *La Cuisine française et étrangère*.[19] The '*Bombe*' was shaped from various culinary influences and consisted of a Champagne zabaglione with an ice cream made with Russian kummel. The zabaglione was a Neapolitan dessert, traditionally composed with egg yolks, sugar, and marsala. French chefs had incorporated this *entremets*, dating back to the fifteenth century, in their daily practise and called it *sabayon*. The author of the '*Bombe*' then provided further instructions on how the sweet confection should be presented. Placed upon a sculpted block of ice that gave the impression of an explosion, a candle was to be added in a small hollow carved into the base of the sculpture. To complete the effect, some pistachio ice cream and small tricolour bouquets were to adorn the bottom of the impressive piece. The decoration was an essential element of the recipe as it was crucial that the practitioners 'vary the scents and colours, so as to delight the eye before the palate.'[20] This '*Bombe Cronstadt*', which celebrated the union between France and Russia, was then a combination of French and Italian cuisines with only the alcohol as a Russian ingredient.

In similar fashion, there was the dessert named '*La Czarine*' (1896). It resembled a rum baba with its savarin dough, but a few drops of Russian kummel along the inscription in buttercream of *Czarine* made it Franco-Russian. We find almost the same approach in other recipes with one specific ingredient evoking Russia. For example, the common thread between the recipes '*Escalopes de veau à la Russe*' (1892), '*Cervelle de veau à la Orloff*' (1898), and '*Tournedos à la russe*' (1910) is the presence of mushroom stew. Mushrooms were an essential component of the Russian table, and it enhanced many of the national recipes.[21]

Another distinctive feature of Russian cuisine that held a prominent place in the Franco-Russian recipes was fish. It was prepared in several ways. In the recipe '*Oeuf à la russe*' (1895) the practitioners recommended blending the vésiga, the sturgeon spinal cord, with buckwheat and eight eggs. In '*Filets de Turbot au Tzar*' (1898), the fish was accompanied by a purée of ceps and a velouté that joined the French sauce *Suprême* to a sturgeon cream. Another creation of the period that employed fish was the '*Saumon à la Nicolas II*' (1901). This dish's elaborate design was meant to impress its beholder. The recipe prescribed cooking the salmon in a court bouillon and then laying it on a wooden base representing the deck arch of a bridge. Russian salad cast in small dariole moulds embraced the salmon while various shrimps and crayfish were displayed on the bridge alongside an unctuous mayonnaise and Tatar sauce. The finishing touch to the grand piece was the presence under the bridge of five carafes with little fish in them. This creation bore the mark of French cuisine with its bouillon and different sauces but also emphasized Russian influences with the products of the sea and its décor.[22] The design most likely referred to the time, in 1896, when Nicholas II laid the foundation stone of the Pont Alexander III in Paris.

Occasionally, the only Russian element in these new recipes was in the name, such as in the '*Diplomate Moscovite*' (1900). It was a variation on the classical French Diplomat confectioned with biscuits, fruits, and cream. In this recipe, the delicate dessert was accompanied with a rich berry sauce or a zabaglione made with rum.

This brief overview of the recipes created in honour of the Franco-Russian Alliance shows the parsimony with which French chefs incorporated Russian cuisine in their creations. Many mainstays of the Russian diet were overlooked such as porridges, sour cream, pies, pickled vegetables, and the like. The combination of sour, sweet, and salty tastes that is so representative of Russian cuisine was left out. Nevertheless, if these new dishes bore prominently the mark of French cuisine with their techniques, sauces, and bouillon, one could always find a nod to the Russian Empire whether in the use of a particular ingredient, design, or name. This pattern could be the result of various reasons: the unavailability of certain ingredients, the lack of knowledge concerning Russian cuisine since not all new recipes came from chefs who were well acquainted with Russian culture, as well as the culinary fashion of the time. Chefs constantly borrowed from different culinary cultures to create or reinvent dishes. Furthermore, these recipes were curated for a European audience and had to agree with their tastes. Ultimately, the *tour de force* of these French chefs was to imagine dishes that made the unknown familiar.

Naming Dishes: Unlocking the Imagination

Another culinary effect resulting from the Franco-Russian Alliance was the rise of new recipes named *à la Russe*. Readers of *La Cuisine française et étrangère* could find a myriad of recipes bearing this appellation, to mention only a few: '*Langoustine à la Russe*' (1899); '*Fricandeau à la Russe*' (1902), a *fricandeau* being either a speciality from Switzerland or the French region of Aveyron; '*Omelette soufflée à la russe*' (1893); or even '*Rissolés de volailles à la Russe*' (1893), which according to the author should be served with a Béarnaise sauce.

One can wonder what was Russian about these dishes since they all carried the signature of French cuisine. Nevertheless, the extensive use of this misleading appellation brings attention to the cultural and political climate of the period, especially the perception France had of foreign countries. The custom of giving dishes geographically based denominations like *à la russe, à l'anglaise, à l'italienne,* or *à la grec* was not recent. Along with honorific and historical names, it was part of the French pantheon of names given to gastronomic dishes. However, it is interesting that these recipes flourished according to the cultural environment of the period. A telling example can be found in the nineteenth century's lingering fascination with Greece which influenced architecture, fashion, literature movements, and food named *à la grec*.

One of the reasons French chefs tended to overuse the appellation '*à la*' stemmed from the effect it produced upon the expectant eater. For it all begins when the guests sit down and open the menu. By carefully choosing the names of their dishes, chefs conjured up images and sensations that played with the imagination of the eater. The simple evocation of a particular place could either arouse appetites or repulse them. This response is personal, since a place can evoke a memory or a sensation, but it is also a matter of collective perception that revealed how a society perceived the other, the foreigner. Considering the anti-Russian sentiment that prevailed in France during most of the nineteenth century, the turnaround that occurred in the *fin de siècle* is astonishing – astonishing but necessary in light of the political context.[23]

As the valorization of Russia rose from the depreciation of Germany, new mediators emerged who proposed a new vision of the Empire.[24] Russia, which had been once viewed as backward, even barbaric, appeared in a new light. Books, songs, prints, and food products served to remind the French public of this new, devoted friend of the Republic. In confectioners' shops, every detail of the attractive wrapping of the candies used stereotypical Russian imagery to charm the Western customers. The boxes in which they were sold appealed to the imagination with decorative scenes depicting troikas, women in traditional costumes, Orthodox churches, and the like. Such details emphasized the difference between Russia and the West, making the Russian Empire a captivating land for the consumers in search of new horizons. The increasing number of recipes *à la russe* in periodicals hence fulfilled a demand from the public, confirming the growing interest for Russia.

The influence of public campaigns conducted by the authorities and by private citizens such as our chefs with the culinary press shows in the personal cookbooks of François Maniel.[25] This precious textual archive from the 1890s also provides us an opportunity to shift from the usual Parisian focus since Maniel was a cook from the city of Carcassonne in Southern France. Even though he had never been to Russia, he recorded various Russian or Russian-sounding recipes that piqued his interest from *La Cuisine française et étrangère*. Among them we can find: '*Potage à la Czarine*', '*Tapioca à la Czarine*', '*Omelette franco-russe*', '*Œufs de foie gras à la Néva*', '*Hors-d'œuvre*' (the traditional Russian appetizer called *zakouski*), '*Truite de rivière à l'Ermitage*', '*Ours à la Sibérienne*', '*Filet d'ours à la russe*' and '*Suprêmes de Volaille à la Nicolas II.*' In addition to these recipes, Maniel also copied three menus from the various Franco-Russian festivities that the newspaper had printed.

These pages from his personal cookbook attest to his curiosity for the Alliance, but, more importantly, the choices he made while selecting the recipes reveal a great deal about how Russia was perceived at the time. Four of them revolve around the theme of the Russian sovereigns: '*Potage Czarine*', '*Tapioca à la Czarine*', '*Suprêmes de Volaille à la Nicolas II*', and '*Truite de rivière à l'Ermitage*'. The 1896 visit to France by Nicholas II and Empress Alexandra Feodorovna had been a great success. Despite representing an autocratic power, the young imperial couple captivated the French.[26] Monarchs were political actors as well as symbolic ones: they could arouse collective emotions, and as such the Russian sovereigns embodied the Franco-Russian Alliance, hence the many recipes named after the imperial couple until 1917. Two other recipes in Maniel's cookbook are particularly interesting, '*Ours à la Sibérienne*' and '*Filet d'ours à la russe*'. Bear meat was far from being common in the Russian diet, and yet the words 'bear' and

'Siberia' evoked images of exoticism and danger. It alluded to a distant and enthralling land that couldn't have been more different from France.

In naming their new recipes *à la russe*, chefs called upon the imagination of the eaters while still providing the familiarity of French cuisine. Chefs, pastry chefs, confectioners, and others took an active part in shaping and vivifying the imagination surrounding Russia. Ultimately, even if in essence the dishes called '*à la russe*' often had no connection to Russia, they were telling a tale, and the audience was eagerly consuming it.

Notes

1. See for example Paul Cambon, *Correspondance 1870-1924* (Paris: Grasset, 1940), p. 418.
2. Christopher Clark, *The Sleepwalkers: How Europe Went to War in 1914* (London: Allen Lane, 2012), pp. 121-59.
3. Sylvain Bensidoun, *Alexandre III: 1881-1894* (Paris: SEDES, 1990), p. 223.
4. Faith Hillis, 'The "Franco-Russian Marseillaise": International Exchange and the Making of Antiliberal Politics in Fin de Siècle France', *The Journal of Modern History*, 89.1 (March, 2017) <https://www.journals.uchicago.edu/doi/full/10.1086/690124>
5. Jean-Pierre Poussou and others, *L'Influence française en Russie au XVIIIe siècle* (Paris: Presses de l'Université de Paris-Sorbonne, 2004).
6. Julia Demidenko, *Restorany, traktiry, chajnye. Iz istorii obshhestvennogo pitanija v Peterburge XVIII nachala XX veka* (Moscow: Centrpoligraf, 2010), p. 72.
7. Gianni Cariani, *Une France russophile? Découverte, reception, impact la diffusion de la culture russe en France de 1881 à 1914* (Lille: ANRT, 1998), pp. 42-58.
8. E. Besnards, '*Salut au Czar Nicolas II*', *La Cuisine française et étrangère*, October, 1896.
9. F. Barthelemy, '*Ovation à M. Krantz*', *La Cuisine française et étrangère*, July, 1892.
10. Alain Drouard, *Histoire des cuisiniers en France: XIXe-XXe siècle* (Paris: CNRS Editions, 2007).
11. Barthelemy.
12. Auguste Escoffier, *Le guide culinaire: aide-mémoire de cuisine pratique* (Paris: Art Culinaire, 1903), p. 68.
13. Barthelemy.
14. Greg King, *The Court of the Last Tsar: Pomp, Power, and Pageantry in the Reign of Nicholas II* (United States: John Wiley & Sons, 2006), p. 113.
15. Besnards.
16. Constantin Grunwald, *Les Nuits blanches de Saint-Pétersbourg* (Paris: Berger-Levrault, 1968), p. 146; J. F., '*La France en Russie*', *La Cuisine française et étrangère*, January, 1894.
17. *La Cuisine française et étrangère*, February, 1900.
18. J. Morard, *La Cuisine française et étrangère*, November, 1891.
19. Pierre Lacam and Antoine Charabot, *Le glacier classique et artistique en France et en Italie* (Paris: 1893), p. 247.
20. Lacam and Charabot, p. 3.
21. Musya Glants and Joyce Toomre, eds., *Food in Russian History and Culture* (Bloomington, IN: Indiana University Press, 1997).
22. Amy B. Trubek, *Haute Cuisine: How the French Invented the Culinary Profession* (Philadelphia: University of Pennsylvania Press, 2000), p. 7.
23. Cambon, p. 362.
24. Cariani, pp. 158-84.
25. Aude, Departmental Archives, Série J: Commerce, 151 J, Fonds François Gaudérique Maniel et de la Fédération culinaire 21e section de Carcassonne.
26. See for example Edmond de Goncourt, *Journal, mémoires de la vie littéraire* (Paris: R. Laffont, 1989), p. 877.

Imagination and Food in the Black Diaspora

Rebecca Fils-Aimé

The transatlantic slave trade defined and shaped many of the cuisines we know and love today. Africans from various countries on the continent were enslaved and sent to other parts of the world. During the sixteenth and seventeenth century, consequently, approximately fifteen botanical families moved from the continent of Africa to the Americas.[1] It is well documented that enslaved Africans and slave traders carried seeds and plants on the ships that took them from Africa. However, the transport of knowledge and traditions, and how they adapted to the foods of their new environment, is less documented. In the past, Africans and people of the African diaspora were almost notorious for not writing things down for various reasons – not knowing (or being legally barred from learning) how to write or speak in a language that others around them could understand, rules against sharing knowledge during colonization, and the intentional quelling of tradition to force assimilation. As a result, new foods and botanical remedies developed as enslaved Africans exchanged with each other and Indigenous peoples. With so few of their staple foods and plants available, enslaved Africans were guided by tradition and imagination to create many African-inspired cuisines around the world. This paper will connect the dots between leafy greens, watermelons, rice and beans, and okra in Africa to various present-day cuisines around the world. All these countries have one thing in common: many of their present-day staples would not exist without the presence of descendants of African people.

Leafy Greens

Boiling leafy greens is a central cooking technique in African cooking.[2] The evolution of the dishes *sauce feuilles* and *kontomire* stew, from Guinea and Ghana respectively, can be seen in the Caribbean, Latin America, and the US south.

Enslaved Africans were at the forefront of cooking done in the home during colonization. However, they were not allowed to eat much of what they cooked for the plantation owners. They were typically given meagre pieces of meat scraps that slave owners did not want to consume or had to hunt for small wild game to supplement their rations. This meat was then used to flavour the vegetables and vegetable-based stews that were made with the small number of plants they were able to grow for themselves.[3]

Sauce Feuilles, Guinea

Sauce feuilles literally translates to 'leaves sauce'. The dish is traditionally made with sweet potato leaves, red palm oil, aromatics, and cubed pieces of meat, or shrimp or crab for extra flavour. Vegetable stews popular in the Caribbean and Latin America can be seen as not-so-distant relatives to this dish.

When enslaved Africans were brought to what is now Haiti, sweet potato leaves were not readily available. Instead, they used whatever leafy greens they could find, including a type of leaf called *lalo* or jute leaves, which is also found in present-day Guinea and every other country in tropical Africa.[4] This shows how a traditional dish from Guinea stayed the same in method and technique but changed due to descendants using substitutes that were readily available in their new location.

In the English and Spanish-speaking Caribbean, the dish is called *callaloo* and sweet potato leaves are replaced by a variety of indigenous leaves dependent on which country you are in. The green of choice used in the Jamaican and Guyanese versions of *callaloo* is amaranth, which is one of the most widely eaten boiled greens in Africa's humid lowlands. In Trinidad and Tobago, Grenada, and the Dominican Republic, *callaloo* refers to a dish made with taro leaves, dasheen bush, or water spinach. Like Haiti's *lalo*, pork and crab are common additions, but it can also be served as a meatless dish.[5]

Kontomire Stew (Palava Sauce), Ghana

Another technique that originated in Africa is drinking the juices resulting from cooking the greens. In the *Kontomire* stew, cocoyam leaves are used instead of sweet potato leaves, and it includes ground bitter melon seeds or *egusi*, aromatics, red palm oil, and it is usually flavoured with smoked fish and/or dried shrimp, although beef or chicken can also be present. It is served with pounded yam or boiled plantain to sop up the flavourful and healthy liquid.[6] Due to the technique of simmering the greens in water, water-soluble vitamins and minerals like potassium, B vitamins, vitamin C, calcium, folate, and iron are present in the liquid left from the cooked greens.[7] Sopping up the meat-based sauce ensures that these nutrients are absorbed in addition to nutrients in the leaves themselves, a clear demonstration of how African peoples and their descendants used food as medicine. This method of sopping up vegetable sauce may sound familiar to those familiar with greens from the Deep South in the United States.

In the United States, the Deep South is a subregion with multiple distinct cultures. The term was originally used to describe the states that relied on plantations and slavery the most during and following the transatlantic slave trade – South Carolina, Georgia, Alabama, Mississippi, Louisiana, Florida, and Texas. For this paper, however, the Deep South does not include Texas and Florida, as the cuisines and cultures of large portions of those states have been heavily impacted by other peoples (Mexican/Indigenous and the Indigenous/Caribbean, respectively).

Most enslaved Africans brought by the slave trade and their descendants resided in these states from the time they were brought to the US beginning in the seventeenth century until the Great Migration of 1916, when six million African Americans moved out of the rural South to the more urban Northeast, Midwest, and West. As a result, most

African American 'soul food' is seen as inherently southern (or vice versa, depending on one's stance in this contentious debate). Greens are a staple soul food dish in this region.

In the southern US, 'greens' usually referred to simmered collard greens, although kale, beet leaves, turnip leaves, and other greens common in some Native American cuisines like milkweed and marsh marigold were also commonly used. Smoked meat is used to flavour the greens in the same way smoked fish or dried shrimp is used in '*Kontomire* stew'. Since cooking greens for so long compromises some (not all) of the nutritional value, consuming the water-soluble vitamins in the remaining liquid is vital. In this region, that leftover liquid from cooking greens in water slowly for hours has a name – 'potlikker'.[8] Usually, cornbread is served with greens to dip into the potlikker – reminiscent of how West Africans serve pounded yam, also called 'fufu', or boiled plantain with '*Kontomire* stew' for the same reason. Potlikker is full of iron and vitamin C, showing one of the many ways Black people still intentionally and unintentionally use food as medicine – a drastic difference from how most foods of African origin are portrayed in the media, where they are typically labelled as 'poor food choices'. As a result, foods that are inherently nutritious are left out of national and international conversations about healthy foods and foods in general.

Watermelons

Watermelons are large berries that originated in Africa. While the specific origin in Africa is hotly debated, evidence points to northeastern Africa. The original watermelons tasted much different than what we know now; they were less sweet – almost bitter – smaller, and much harder. Watermelon was grown to be used as a portable water reservoir to provide relief from the high temperatures in the area. Besides being high in water content, it is also full of vitamins just like potlikker; again, this shows how African descendants use food to support health. Specifically, watermelon is full of citrulline, an amino acid that helps the body deal with heat-related stress. Through trade, the watermelon travelled to the Mediterranean, then India, China, and later to Spain and the rest of Europe.[9]

In 1576, Spanish settlers and enslaved Africans began growing watermelon in Florida, and the plant spread across the eastern United States. The water content and nutritional makeup of watermelon made it very beneficial for the enslaved Africans to consume and cultivate. Naturally, African slaves were the ones who mostly cultivated watermelons back then.[10] Today, watermelon is, unfortunately, associated with extremely racist tropes that have impacted African Americans, so much that many refuse to eat watermelon in public or at all despite its African origin.

Although the Civil War ended slavery in the US, racism remained in full force, and Black people freed from slavery had to find ways to make money on their own. Given their long involvement in crop cultivation, many began to grow, eat, and sell watermelons – which became a symbol of their freedom. Many southern Whites felt that Black people were flaunting their newfound freedom in their faces. Southern

Whites who felt threatened by this freedom responded by making watermelon a symbol of their various prejudices against Black people. Through plays, movies, minstrel shows, newspapers, and eventually television, Whites made watermelon a national symbol of Black uncleanliness and laziness.[11] This trope took over American popular culture with a vice grip, so much so that the origins of the watermelon are obscured.

Today, watermelon is still primarily grown in the southern US due to favourable weather conditions. Most Black people in the United States still live in the South, but many refuse to eat watermelon to this day. This avoidance demonstrates how hatred and forced assimilation have disconnected many of us in the African diaspora from our own heritage.

Rice and Beans

Rice and beans is a common dish all over the world. However, there are thousands of different types of rice dishes, and in the Western world most are directly influenced by traditional African foods and techniques. The transatlantic slave trade played a big part in the history of rice and beans in the Caribbean, South America, Latin America, and the United States. Not only did enslaved people bring certain types of rice with them when they were brought from the continent, but when Spanish settlers brought other types of rice to various southern states in the US, enslaved Africans knew how to cultivate it. Many of them came from regions that had been producing rice for hundreds of years; after this realization, slave traders went to African regions specifically looking to take Africans who knew how to grow this crop. As a result, rice is extremely popular in countries that have heavy Spanish and African influences. In the United States, many rice dishes considered native to the country originated in the Deep South, where just over half of both African Americans and Black people from other countries currently reside.[12]

Meat played a smaller role in traditional African diets; therefore, beans were used as a primary source of protein and additional nutrition. *Waakye* is Ghana's national dish, and it uses black-eyed peas in a method like Hoppin' John from the US south. The black-eyed pea came to the United States from Central Africa by way of the Caribbean. Field peas or cowpeas – also native to Africa – were used in the original versions of Hoppin' John, but over time that changed to black-eyed peas due to cost and availability.[13] Some historians believe that the beginning of the successful cultivation of rice in the US started when an enslaved African woman taught her owner how to grow the crop in the South Carolina Sea Islands. This area has a subculture of African Americans called the Gullah-Geechee, whose ancestors were some of the most proficient cultivators of rice in continental Africa. South Carolina was one of the richest colonies in the nineteenth century, due largely to the extensive rice cultivation being done by these enslaved Africans.[14] In the present day, the Gullah-Geechee maintain strong ties to their West African roots, unlike many other African descendants in the United States. While they do speak English, they use similar words, ingredients, and spiritual traditions as their West African ancestors.[15] Rice remains an integral part of the Gullah-Geechee culture.

A direct line can be drawn from West Africa to Haiti to New Orleans just by looking at red beans and rice, a dish which remains quintessential in New Orleans cuisine today. Haiti has at least a dozen variations of *diri ak pwa*, or rice with beans. The kidney bean version went on to influence New Orleans's red beans and rice after free Black people from the country emigrated to French-speaking Louisiana after the Haitian Revolution. Coupled with White slave-owners who also fled Haiti around this time with their enslaved Africans, the Black population in the city doubled, which contributed to many of the foods and culture popular in New Orleans today.[16]

The method of making rice and beans, sometimes flavoured with small pieces of seafood or meat, is one of Africa's biggest impacts in the food world. Many, if not all, of these rice and beans dishes remain largely unchanged apart from subtle aromatics and choice of meat that, again, vary by location and history of colonization. This re-imagining of old traditions by adapting to new environments is the crux of most Black cuisine throughout the Americas.

Okra

It is believed that okra was first cultivated in Ethiopia in the twelfth century BC. Okra was grown along the entire 3500 miles of African coastland where most enslaved Africans were taken from. So, it was a common ingredient across tribes. As historian Michael W. Twitty states, 'To the Wolof people it was "*kanja*", to the Mandingo, "*kanjo*", to the Akan it was "*nkruman*" and to the Fon, "*fevi*".'[17] The English word 'okra' comes from the Igbo language of Nigeria, where okra is referred to as okuru. It is also called gombo in several West African languages, and it is eaten across the continent of Africa, throughout the Caribbean, and the Americas. There were two main historical preparations of okra, and both consisted of a peppery stew served with carbohydrate-heavy sides like rice, pounded yam, or millet. The difference was the addition of other ingredients – the stew was either made with onions and tomatoes in a sauce or boiled on its own, as Twitty explains.

Okra was first introduced to the Americas through Brazil in the 1500s, where approximately five million enslaved Africans were taken before the country abolished slavery in the late 1800s. Many of them came from the West African Bantu region, and they introduced okra to Brazil as a thickener and a vegetable. The Brazilian word for okra is *quiabo*, which comes from a Bantu language name for okra – *kigombo*. The oldest recorded African dish in Brazil, *caruru*, dates to the 1600s and describes a spicy stew made with okra, onions, peppers, palm oil (another ingredient introduced by Africans), and smoked fish or shrimp.[18]

Soon after being introduced to Brazil, okra was introduced by the same method in the 1600s to the West Indies where approximately forty per cent of all enslaved Africans were taken.[19] Almost every Caribbean country uses okra in their cuisines, either in a soup or as a thickener in a stew. In Haiti, okra is commonly boiled in its own peppery stew or in one with meat. The Haitian Kreyol word for okra is *gombo*, from the name in Angolan languages that call it *ngumbo*.[20] The country of Barbados uses okra to help thicken cornmeal in its signature dish, coucou and flying fish.[21] In Belize, okra, or okro, is commonly added to stewed beef or to oxtail. St. Martin, Trinidad, and St. Lucia each have variations of *callaloo* that add okra to the boiled greens of the dish. Both the Dominican Republic and Puerto Rico prepare okra boiled in its own stew (*molondron guisado* and *quimbombo guisado*, respectively). These examples show just a small piece of West Africa's strong impact on the Caribbean cuisines so many of us know and love.

Historians guess that okra may have arrived in mainland North America in the eighteenth century. Okra was cooked early in Charleston, South Carolina and New Orleans, Louisiana due to their close relations with the Caribbean colonies. Many plantation owners moved from the West Indies to New Orleans and the coastal areas of South Carolina due to the similarities in weather. In fact, when okra recipes started showing up in the United States, the dishes were initially referred to as dishes from the West Indies.

In the Lowcountry of eastern South Carolina and surrounding states, enslaved African cooks, who were cooking for their slave masters, made dishes that were strongly influenced by Senegambia. Many plantation owners living there came from the Caribbean and were generally used to that kind of fare, including its use of okra.[22] As time passed and these dishes were made and tweaked, they began making African-inspired dishes that the region could call their own. Simultaneously, New Orleans went through a similar 'Africanization' as mentioned earlier.

Both cities developed cuisines in which okra played a huge part. In the Lowcountry, okra is cooked in a peppery soup with tomatoes, onions, and meat and served with rice. This dish, known as okra soup, can be seen as the cousin to New Orleans's gumbo, which means okra in French. Okra is the star ingredient in traditional gumbo, serving as both a vegetable and a thickener in the peppery stew. Okra appeared in other recipes too – okra and shrimp and Limpin' Susan in the Lowcountry, smothered okra in New Orleans, as well as other versions of gumbo in other cities. There are also versions of Brunswick stew from the southeastern coastal states and burgoo from Kentucky that include okra, tomatoes, onions, and peppers. There is a version of okra soup from Baltimore, Maryland that adds crab to the mix to create their 'crab gumbo'. Once okra began to appear in American cookbooks in the nineteenth century, it was clear that enslaved African cooks had a major impact on white American housewives and their food preferences.

The history of okra also demonstrates how enslaved Africans and Native Americans interacted and shared with one another. Gumbo was originally made with okra as the thickener until some Black cooks were introduced to file powder made by the local Choctaw Native Americans. File powder is a thickener made by grinding up sassafras plants, which are indigenous to the southeastern United States. While okra was readily available in the West Indies and South America due to favourable weather conditions, the weather in parts of the southern US was not as tropical year-round. It is assumed file became popular as a stand-in in recipes when okra was out of season.[23] Enslaved Africans began using sassafras in traditional healing methods when okra was out of reach – boiling the leaves in water to use for skin conditions,[24] encouraging diarrhea and vomiting,[25] and as an abortifacient.[26] Conversely, the Choctaw began using okra as a thickener in place of sassafras occasionally after okra was introduced to the United States.[27]

The use of okra as medicine also shows how strong the connection is to the various countries of the African diaspora. Both West Africa and the greater Caribbean are tropical, and they share approximately eighty-five floral families as a result.[28] Enslaved Africans were just as foreign to the land as the Europeans who forcefully brought them there. However, many Africans were already familiar with tropical weather, tropical plants, and tropical diseases in a way that aligned with Amerindian knowledge. As a result, enslaved Africans used flora familiar to them, or to their forebears, and became experts in the use of new plants learned from the Amerindians.[29] Historically, Egyptians used okra to prevent kidney stones. It was also used in other African countries to soothe skin conditions, and the seeds were ground and used in food and as a coffee substitute. There is evidence of okra seeds being used as a coffee replacement in continental Africa, the Caribbean, and the US south.[30]

Okra, along with watermelon, was one of the few plants of their homeland that enslaved Africans grew for themselves to make up for foods enslavers refused to provide.[31] Despite being surrounded by Africans from various tribes who didn't speak the same languages, okra became a unifying crop that went on to solidify Africa's historical role in world history.

Diaspora Pathways Post-Slavery

Black food continues to be re-imagined as diasporic migrations continue to occur. In addition to African techniques influencing cultures around the world, some Afro-descendant cultures went back to Africa and continued to create new cuisines. Soon after slavery was abolished in Cuba and in Brazil, some of the formerly enslaved decided to go back to Ghana and Nigeria, respectively. These Afro-Brazilians in Lagos, Nigeria, called *Maro, Agudas, Tabom,* or *Amaros*, re-created a Brazilian dish called *Mingau*. In Brazil, it is a porridge made from corn, tapioca pearls, or rice. In Lagos, these Afro-Brazilians use tapioca granules or cassava, which is the tuber that tapioca comes from.[32] They also further adapted an African-inspired Brazilian black beans and meat dish called *Feijoada* into *Frejon*, blended black beans spiced with coconut milk and cloves, traditionally accompanied by fish stew and pepper sauce.[33]

Many foods that are central to various cuisines and cultures can be traced back to African foods, plants, and/or traditions. Despite this fact, Africa, particularly West and Central Africa, is largely unvalued in the Western mainstream culinary world. The spread of watermelon and okra across the world occurred because they were important to African diets, and, as a result, they are now important to the diets of many others. Africans from the more tropical parts of the continent were accustomed to cultivate rice in similar weather, which made them invaluable during the transatlantic slave trade. Now, rice and beans is a staple dish across the world in many of the countries that relied on enslaved Africans.

The traditional methods of boiling/simmering leafy greens and consuming the remaining liquid/sauce and the methods of cooking okra have been passed down across generations, from ancestors who have been cooking this way much longer than had been documented. African cultures and cultures of African origin have always relied heavily on oral knowledge sharing and storytelling. As a result, the rigid Western definitions of 'acceptable sources' can inherently put any research on cultures like these at a disservice. It can be difficult to share nuanced and specific information about these cuisines when limited to the Western definition of literacy and fact-checking. I challenge food institutions and food historians to keep this in mind when discussing or researching food pathways of non-Western cultures.

Food historians and chefs who descend from these various countries are continuing to highlight traditional foods with African roots at the forefront. In the future, I hope to see more recipes and plants get their proper accreditation from culinary professionals outside of the global Black community. If we start treating all foods and recipes with value, we can ensure that certain regions and cultures receive the historical and societal credit and respect that they deserve.

Notes

1. Londa Schiebinger, *Secret Cures of Slaves: People, Plants, and Medicine in the Eighteenth-Century Atlantic World* (Stanford: Stanford University Press, 2017), p. 16.
2. Jessica B. Harris, *High on the Hog: A Culinary Journey from Africa to America* (New York: Bloomsbury, 2011), p. 11.
3. Harris, p. 95-98
4. Luís Catarino and others, 'Edible Leafy Vegetables from West Africa (Guinea-Bissau): Consumption, Trade and Food Potential', *Foods*, 8 (2019) <https://www.ncbi.nlm.nih.gov/pmc/articles/PMC6836000/> [accessed 28 April 2021]
5. Cynthia Nelson, 'A Guide to Callaloo in Caribbean Cuisine: Differing Takes on Callaloo Depending on the Caribbean Country', *The Spruce Eats*, 3 July 2020 <https://www.thespruceeats.com/what-is-callaloo-2138166> [accessed 1 May 2021]
6. Freda Muyambo 'Palaver Sauce Recipe', *The Spruce Eats*, 3 December 2021 <https://www.thespruceeats.com/palaver-sauce-recipe-39553 > [accessed 10 March 2022]
7. Franziska Spritzler, 'How Cooking Affects the Nutrient Content of Foods', *Healthline*, 7 November 2019 <https://www.healthline.com/nutrition/cooking-nutrient-content> [accessed 21 October 2021]
8. Christina Regelski, 'The Soul of Food: Slavery's Influence on Southern Cuisine', *U.S. History Scene* <https://ushistoryscene.com/article/slavery-southern-cuisine/> [accessed 4 May 2021]
9. Mark Strauss, 'The 5,000-Year Secret History of the Watermelon', *National Geographic*, 21 August 2015 <https://www.nationalgeographic.com/history/article/150821-watermelon-fruit-history-agriculture> [accessed 24 October]
10. Liz Smith, 'Forbidden Fruit', *The New York Times Magazine*, 30 March 2003 <https://www.nytimes.com/2003/03/30/magazine/forbidden-fruit.html> [accessed 24 October 2021]
11. William R. Black, 'How Watermelons Became a Racist Trope', *The Atlantic*, 8 December 2014 <https://www.theatlantic.com/national/archive/2014/12/how-watermelons-became-a-racist-trope/383529/> [accessed 12 May 2021]
12. Bach Pham, 'Hoppin' John and How African Slaves Influenced Bean-and-Rice Culture', [Columbia, SC] *Post and Courier*, 7 November 2019 <https://www.postandcourier.com/free-times/food/hop-

pin-john-and-how-african-slaves-influenced-bean-and-rice-culture/article_2ceafcd1-8c0c-5430-8b29-0d68c7e99336.html> [accessed 3 May 2021]
13. Amethyst Ganaway, 'Hoppin' John Recipe', *Serious Eats*, 1 February 2021 <https://www.seriouseats.com/hoppin-john> [accessed 10 May 2021]
14. Harris, p. 68-69.
15. Samin Nosrat, 'A Dish that Reflects Our Nation: Okra Soup', *The New York Times*, 22 September 2020 <https://www.nytimes.com/2020/09/22/magazine/samin-nosrat-okra-soup.html> [accessed 12 May 2021]
16. Eater Video, *In New Orleans, Mondays Mean Red Beans and Rice*, 12 March 2017, <https://www.youtube.com/watch?v=jm1sckNY2DQ> [accessed 13 May 2021]
17. Michael W. Twitty, 'The Secret History of Okra – Okra Soup', *Tori Avey*, 27 August 2013 <https://toriavey.com/history-kitchen/history-okra-soup-recipe> [accessed 29 April 2021]
18. 'Food in Brazil Afro-Brazilian', *Food by Country* <http://www.foodbycountry.com/Algeria-to-France/Brazil-Afro-Brazilian.html> [accessed 10 May 2021]
19. Henry Louis Gates, Jr, 'How Many Slaves Landed in the US?', *The Root*, 6 January 2014 <https://www.theroot.com/how-many-slaves-landed-in-the-us-1790873989> [accessed 30 April 2021]
20. Steven Raichlen, 'Okra: Beyond the Slime', *Los Angeles Times*, 16 June 1994 <https://www.latimes.com/archives/la-xpm-1994-06-16-fo-4864-story.html?> [accessed 5 May 2021]
21. 'Cornmeal Coo Coo', *Immaculate Bites*, 1 April 2021 <https://www.africanbites.com/cornmeal-coo-coo/> [accessed 11 May 2021]
22. Harris, p. 70-72.
23. Robert Moss, 'The Real Story of Gumbo, Okra, and Filé', *Serious Eats*, 10 August 2018 <https://www.seriouseats.com/history-new-orleans-gumbo-okra-file-powder> [accessed 1 May 2021]
24. 'Mid-19th Century Plant Uses', *U.S. Department of the Interior: National Park Service* <https://www.nps.gov/bowa/learn/historyculture/upload/THE-FINAL-Plant-Uses-site-bulletin.pdf> [accessed 2 May 2021]
25. Erin Brooke Hamby, 'The Roots of Healing: Archaeological and Historical Investigations of African-American Herbal Medicine' (unpublished doctoral dissertation, University of Tennessee, 2004).
26. Joseph E. Holloway, 'African Crops and Slave Cuisine', *Rice Diversity* <http://ricediversity.org/outreach/educatorscorner/documents/African-Crops-and-Slave-Cuisine.doc> [accessed 29 April 2021]
27. Hilde G. Lee, 'Okra Has an Interesting Food History', [Charlottesville, VA], *Daily Progress*, 20 September 2017 <https://dailyprogress.com/okra-has-an-interesting-food-history/article_b49d5bf3-30d6-5ae2-aa15-3de9450ae1be.html> [accessed 30 April 2021]
38. Schiebinger, p. 45-64.
29. Lee.
30. Hannah Bauman and Allison Porter, 'Food as Medicine: Okra (*Abelmoschus esculentus, Malvaceae*)', *American Botanical Council* <https://www.herbalgram.org/resources/herbalegram/volumes/volume-12/number-8-august/food-as-medicine-okra-abelmoschus-esculentus-malvaceae/food-as-medicine/> [accessed 1 May 2021]
31. Amethyst Ganaway, 'Black Communities Have Always Used Food as Protest', *Food & Wine*, 4 June 2020 <https://www.foodandwine.com/news/black-communities-food-as-protest> [accessed 4 May 2021]
32. Alaba Simpson, 'The Politics of Culture and Diaspora Settlement in Lagos: Ethnographic Presentation of the African Brazilian Fanti/Caretta Carnival', *The African Diaspora Archaeology Network: June 2007 Newsletter* <http://www.diaspora.illinois.edu/news0607/news0607-6.pdf> [accessed 24 October 2021]
33. Solimar Otero, *Afro-Cuban Diasporas in the Atlantic World* (Rochester: University of Rochester Press, 2010), p. 94-110.

Food and Foodways in Science Fiction

Len Fisher and Anders Sandberg

Introduction
The imagination of science fiction writers has given us galactic travel and adventures, alien species and civilizations, unusual ethical dilemmas, and whole new worlds to explore. What might such creative minds have to offer when it comes to the subjects of food and drink?

The answer in the majority of cases is not very much. As with the characters in conventional fiction, those in science fiction seem seldom to eat and even more seldom to take an interest in their food. Even authors who have had a real-life involvement with food often seem to forget its existence when it comes to their novels. E.E. (Doc) Smith, the originator of the 'space opera' genre, was a food scientist who gave us bleached flour, but food seldom appears in his space-devouring novels.[1] Jason Sheehan, restaurant critic by day and science fiction writer by night, produces novels of giant killer robots, radioactive mutants, mad scientists, and rampant nanotechnology, but still steers clear of what or how his characters eat.[2]

Luckily for our present theme, some sci-fi authors have boldly faced the fact that their characters need to eat and drink. Here we explore where the authors' imaginations have led them, and we ask whether their solutions may have relevance for our real-life present and future. We divide our investigation into two parts: (1) types of food, and (2) food ethics, etiquette, and manners.

Types of Food
Normal Earth Meals
We begin in 1865, when Jules Verne, considered by many to be the father of science fiction, wrote *From the Earth to the Moon*. His heroes, housed inside a giant cannon shell (complete with sofas, windows and a kitchen!) have been shot out of an equally giant cannon towards the moon. The journey takes them 97 hours and 20 minutes – plenty of time for breakfast:

> The breakfast began with three bowls of excellent soup, thanks to the liquefaction in hot water of those precious cakes of Liebig, prepared from the best parts of the ruminants of the Pampas. To the soup succeeded some beefsteaks, compressed by an hydraulic press, as tender and succulent as if brought straight from the

kitchen of an English eating-house. Michel, who was imaginative, maintained that they were even 'red'. Preserved vegetables ('fresher than nature,' said the amiable Michel) succeeded the dish of meat; and was followed by some cups of tea with bread and butter, after the American fashion. The beverage was declared exquisite, and was due to the infusion of the choicest leaves, of which the emperor of Russia had given some chests for the benefit of the travelers. And lastly, to crown the repast, Ardan had brought out a fine bottle of Nuits, which was found 'by chance' in the provision-box.[3]

The 'precious cakes of Liebig' (an extract of meat) were a real thing. Liebig was a well-known chemist, responsible for the modern science of organic chemistry, and also for promoting the myth that searing the outside of meat 'seals in' the juices. His 'extract of meat' was 'a thick, dark syrupy beef extract paste', sold in glass bottles, and later rebranded as OXO.[4]

Verne had his characters eating what was essentially a normal Earth meal. To some extent, this is possible in the real environs of space, as we see in a menu from the 1965 *Gemini 7* space mission (Figure 1).

Menu I (Calories: 2315)	*Menu II (Calories: 2304)*	*Menu III (Calories 2322)*	*Menu IV (Calories 2297)*
Days 1,5,9,13	Days 2,6,10,14	Days 3,7,11	Days 4,8,12
Meal A Grapefruit drink Sausage patties Banana pudding Fruit cocktail	Meal A Chicken and gravy Beef sandwiches Apple sauce Peanut cubes	Meal A Salmon salad Pea bar Gingerbread Cocoa	Meal A Bacon squares Ham and apple sauce Chocolate pudding Orange drink
Meal B Beef and vegetables Potato salad Cheese sandwiches Strawberry cubes Orange drink	Meal B Orange-grapefruit drink Beef pot roast Bacon and egg bites Chocolate pudding	Meal B Grapefruit drink Bacon squares Chicken and vegetables Apricot cubes Pineapple fruitcake	Meal B Beef and gravy Corn chowder Brownies Peaches
Meal C Orange-grapefruit drink Tuna salad Apricot pudding	Meal C Potato soup Shrimp cocktail Orange drink	Meal C Spaghetti and meat Cheese sandwiches Orange drink	Meal C Coconut cubes Cinnamon toast Apple sauce Grapefruit drink

Figure 1. 'Food for US Manned Space Flight', M.V. Klicka and M.C. Smith, Technical Report NATICK/TR-82/-19, 1982 <https://apps.dtic.mil/sti/pdfs/ADA118316.pdf>

The menu offers familiar foods that one might find at home back on Earth. The same stricture applies to the food on more recent missions.[5] It seems that, just like most science fiction authors, the planners of real space missions (or perhaps the astronauts themselves) were simply not interested in applying their imaginations to the problem of food. More likely, perhaps, plain and familiar foods would have provided comfort in an environment that was otherwise startlingly unfamiliar.

The meal of beef with vegetables, pork and potatoes, and bacon and apple sauce reputedly consumed by Neil Armstrong and Buzz Aldrin during the 1969 moon landings fits into the same category.[6] Admittedly, the components would have been reconstituted, and there was also the undoubtedly unfamiliar fact that they had spare meals stuck to the inside of their helmets in case of emergencies.

Familiar foods continue to be a theme in science fiction and in real life. In E.E. Smith's *Lensman* series, the hero Kimball Kinnison at one stage grills himself a thick, juicy steak after a fight with an alien monster.[7] Reality trumped fiction when, in 2001, the Pizza Hut chain delivered a pizza to Russian cosmonaut Yuri Usachov on the International Space Station.[8] NASA is now working to grow fruit and vegetables in space.[9] So 'normal' Earth meals may also become normal in space – at least for vegetarians.

Food Pills and Blocks

One problem with 'normal' Earth meals in space is just that – space. Storage on spacecraft is likely to be highly limited.

The problem is often resolved by compressing the food. Isaac Asimov in *Prelude to Foundation* had 'flavor spheres,' which were raw dainties, flavoured for the outside market, but eaten unflavoured ('slightly sweet and [...] a faintly bitter aftertaste' with a 'main sensation that eluded [description]') by the natives of the planet Mycogen.[10] Nat Schachner, in *Redmask of the Outlands*, produced a follow-up to these rather chunky objects, about the size of a table-tennis ball, with tiny rose-red cubical wine pellets, which brought 'a sparkle into the eyes with the coursing of concentrated stimulant through the veins'.[11]

Cubical pellets of various types and sizes are a mainstay of science fictional food. The first mention of such 'food tablets' was probably in an 1879 novel called *The Senator's Daughter* by Edward Page Mitchell, where just a small box full, scarcely larger than a watch, could sustain a person for more than twenty years (J.R.R. Tolkien in *The Lord of the Rings* would later ascribe similar properties to the fictional elvish *lembas*, or 'waybread').[12] Among the advantages of the tablets in *The Senator's Daughter* were 'an end to the evils of gluttony [...] and [...] the brutal murdering of fellow animals and brother vegetables' – presumably also an end to the Oxford Symposium as we know it.

There are, of course, real-life equivalents of these space-saving space foods. Here on Earth many dried foods, from OXO cubes to Kendall mint cake, come as cubes or rectangular prisms, since these are an efficient, space-filling way to pack the material. In space, the US *Gemini* mission (1965-1966) astronauts and those from the early *Apollo* moon missions (1968-1972) were provided with bite-size food cubes and food squeezed from tubes, although those on later missions (up to the present day) were also provided with pouches, cans, and eventually food trays with more-or-less normal implements.[13]

But the astronauts still had to carry water, although in the Space Shuttle (1981-2011), the fuel cells provided water as a by-product. Here the fiction writer has an advantage, since in fiction the necessary water may be collected from any passing comet or planet.

Microorganisms

With microorganisms we come to a point where fiction and reality become difficult to distinguish. Plankton, yeast, algae, and bacteria were being discussed as foods of the future by science fiction writers at around the same time as their use was being seriously considered by earth-bound food scientists. Arthur C. Clarke's *The Deep Range*, for example, tells of a world where plankton is farmed underwater for human food, with whales being used as farmers.[14] Isaac Asimov is one of a number of authors who favour yeast as a source, with yeast farmers being distinguishable by their distinctive aromas.[15]

Algae are another possibility, making their first appearance in Fred Pohl and Cyril Kornbluth's *The Space Merchants*, where they are harvested by the process of 'scum skimming'.[16] Algae, being considered for today's space programme, also feature in James Blish's *Cities in Flight* – the successor, perhaps, to today's seaweed-based gastronomic delicacies. Unfortunately, the algae in one of Blish's tanks mutates when they pass too close to a source of radiation:

> 'There's been another mutation in the Chlorella tanks; must have started when we passed through that radiation field near Sigma Draconis. We're getting a yield of about twenty-two hundred kilograms per acre in terms of fats.'
> 'That's not bad.'
> 'Not bad, but it's dropping steadily, and the rate of decrease is accelerating. If it's not arrested, we won't have any algae crops at all in a year or so. And there's not enough crude-oil reserve to tide us over to the next star.'[17]

The one fungal food to avoid is mushrooms. As Ray Bradbury points out, aliens may disguise themselves as mushrooms.[18] Eat one at your peril.

Algae, yeasts and other microorganisms are clearly a viable source of food for intrepid space travellers. Many experiments have already been carried out along these lines. Some of the results have been serendipitous, including the discovery of previously unknown bacterial strains aboard the International Space Station. The bacteria concerned were a strain of *Methylobacteria*, which can help to promote plant growth and to fight off infections in food plants growing under stressful conditions.[19]

Perhaps the most imaginative use of bacteria lies in microbial electrosynthesis of complex food molecules – a process whereby bacteria exposed to an electric current are stimulated to synthesize acetic acid from carbon dioxide and water as a substrate for the synthesis of more complex food molecules. This wildly fictional-sounding idea has actually been proposed as a viable approach to help feed the world population in the event of a Sun-obscuring catastrophe such as a super-volcanic eruption.[20]

Another bacteria-based approach to feeding the astronauts, or indeed to feeding the global population in the event of an agricultural catastrophe, is to use hydrogen-oxidizing bacteria – a process whereby electricity is used to split water into hydrogen and oxygen and provide them to hydrogen-oxidizing bacteria as material for their growth.[21] Some such bacteria have been found to contain as much as 50% protein and 25% carbohydrate – an ideal food source!

These various approaches to chemical synthesis of food from CO_2 for space missions and food resilience have been compared by Garciá Martínez and his collaborators and stand up well against the traditional transport of dried foods.[22]

Single Cell Cultures

The use of cultured cell lines to produce meat-like products is now well established.[23] In science fiction it seems to have made its first appearance in H. Beam Piper's *Four Day Planet*, where *carniculture* is the order of the day. The carniculture plant can produce any kind of animal tissue – Terran pork and beef and poultry, Freyan *zhoumy* meat, Zarathustran veldtbeest. 'You can get all the *paté de foie gras* you want here,' says the protagonist. 'We have a chunk of goose liver about fifty feet in diameter growing in one of our vats.'[24]

More recently, the wonderful *Bistro in Vitro* offers us something that is really in tune with the times: 'Celebrity Cubes', made from celebrities' stem cells.[25] Eat your favourite star. The fictional bistro offers them dipped in a whiskey glaze and describes them as 'deliciously addictive.'

Food in Television Series

With television series such as *Red Dwarf* and *Star Trek*, we finally come to some truly imaginative ideas about food in science fiction.

Star Trek began conventionally enough with the routine concentrated food blocks, but the franchise progressively introduced so many unusual foods and food ideas that there is now a whole cookbook devoted to them.[26] Perhaps the most unusual is the onomatopoeic Klingon delicacy *gagh* (live worms): 'the actual taste of *gagh* is revolting and it is eaten solely for the unique sensation of the *gagh* spasming in one's mouth and stomach in their death throes.'[27] Heston Blumenthal, beat that.

Star Trek also solves the food problem in a more general way with its iconic food replicator, which can synthesize from scratch any food that your heart desires, including stewed *bok* rat liver.[28] Fred Pohl takes us one step further with the Oort Cloud Processor, which processes icy pieces of space debris into food.[29]

Red Dwarf features food extensively, including a whole episode where food occupies centre stage. The food situation is dire. 'We've no meat, no pulse and hardly any grain,' says the mechanoid Kryten, 'and space weevils have eaten the last of the corn supply.' Kryten decides to grill the weevils ('at least they are corn fed'), which Lister devours avidly, taking them for crunchy king prawns. Shades of contemporary discussions on insect-based diets! Enter the character Legion, appearing from a swirling mist. He offers them a 'traditional 24th century Mamosian banquet.' We are not told what the food consists of, but the tools to eat it are literally out of this world. Kryten, 'programmed to be proficient in all known off-world eating techniques, including Jovian Boogle Hoops, and the often-lethal Mercurian Boomerang Spoon', is also versed in Legion's antimatter chopsticks. The design of the first two is left to our imagination, but the antimatter chopsticks are presented rather unimaginatively as whirling devices, rather like egg whisks with the ends cut off.[30]

No matter. The point of the chopsticks is that they never touch the food, which rises by itself when the chopsticks are brought near. This is not quite as silly as it sounds. Animal tissue (a frog) has indeed been levitated in a magnetic field, although it has to be admitted that the magnet was rather larger than can be conventionally accommodated in a spaceship.[31] The Mamosian telekinetic wine that accompanies it is contained in glasses that are fixed to the table, so that there is no chance of knocking them over. One simply wills the liquid into the mouth, and then telepathically decides on its flavour. Robert Heinlein offers a similar idea when his characters land on a planet inhabited by friendly aliens who can read your mind and modify local fruits and vegetables to your taste.[32]

Mind control is closer than one might think. Taste sensations on the tongue have been stimulated electrically, although stimulating the olfactory bulb may be a trickier proposition.[33] There is also an implant that can read the brain waves of people and convert them into written words.[34]

Hybrid brain-computer interfaces and neuroprostheses are now a practical reality.[35] One possibility for the future, operating on a simpler level, is to translate electroencephalographic signals from the brain to direct a 3-D printer to produce 3-D printed food.[36] Many other possibilities for the use of digital technology have also been proposed, including the fully digital kitchen where food shapes and flavours may be controlled at will.[37]

Humans

Some of the most powerful ethical questions of all revolve around the question of cannibalism. To what extent is it permissible? Under what circumstances?

Soylent Green is a well-known example.[38] Less well-known, and more extreme, is the Larry Niven short story 'Bordered in Black'.[39] The title itself is a black joke, since death notices are frequently bordered in black. But the story is worse. Far worse.

Two space explorers have discovered a planet that has been terraformed, but then apparently abandoned. There are lakes on the planet, full of algae. It appears that the planet was developed as a food source.

But there is a wavy black line around each lake. Close approach reveals that it consists of people, struggling to reach the algae. It seems that they are the descendants of farmers left on the planet to harvest the algae before it was abandoned. But recognition strikes. It wasn't the algae that was the food source; it was the *people*, kept as food animals and fed on the algae.

Sometimes a writer's imagination can take him or her a bit too far!

Designer Animals

Douglas Adams offers us:

> a large fat meaty quadruped of the bovine type with large watery eyes, small horns and what might almost have been an ingratiating smile on its lips.

> 'Good evening,' [it says], 'I am the main Dish of the Day. May I interest you in parts of my body?' [....]
> 'Something off the shoulder perhaps? Braised in a white wine sauce?'
> 'Er, your shoulder?'
> 'But naturally my shoulder, sir,' mooed the animal contentedly, 'nobody else's is mine to offer.'[40]

Adams is challenging us in a number of ways here, not least in the way that we often treat food animals in real life, and in the idea of 'designer animals' bred exclusively for food. In doing so, he elevates the role of science fiction which, like other forms of fiction, can be used to raise and investigate distinctly uncomfortable ideas.

In the case of designer animals, the uncomfortable ideas extend well beyond using the animals for food. Margaret Atwood, in the fictional *Oryx and Crake*, explores the ethics of transgenic animals, such as the 'pigoons' used for growing human organs in pigs for xenotransplantation.[41] Traci Warkentin uses Atwood's novel as a foundation for the exploration of this whole ethical area, while Sherryl Vint shows how animals have often appeared as 'the other' in science fiction, with lessons to be drawn about our ability to relate to 'the other', including aliens and other humans.[42]

Food Ethics, Etiquette, and Manners
Ethical Conundrums

The problem of designer animals leads us into more general questions of food ethics. Many of the ethical conundrums explored by science fiction writers are exaggerated versions of real-life situations.[43] N.K. Jemisin's *Broken Earth* trilogy, for example, deals with food rationing in a world that is facing disaster.[44] A community's careful calculations of food rationing are thrown out when a woman gets accidentally pregnant. The solution is grim; it is determined that the woman will get no extra food to support her yet-unborn child until someone else in the community dies.

Another extreme example is Ray Bradbury's *Here There Be Tygers*.[45] Human space explorers discover a planet where anything may be had merely by imagining it. Water becomes wine for the asking. Fish swim unwittingly into hot springs, cooking themselves for your dinner.

The conundrum comes with the over-exploitation of such an apparently infinite resource. In Bradbury's story, the discoverers can't leave well enough alone. They begin drilling into the ground, only to discover too late that they are injuring what turns out to be a sentient planet. Lakes turn into tar pits, dinosaurs and mammoths appear, and the explorers leave hastily. Their report back on Earth says that the planet is hostile and of no benefit to humans.

Climate change is a frequent subject, even before the issue became such a serious one in real life. Paolo Bacigalupi's *The Windup Girl*, for example, features large food corporations battling over gene banks in a world devastated by climate change.[46]

Capitalist society also takes a battering. The American cartoonist Al Capp is seldom considered as a science fiction writer, but he certainly belongs in the genre with his invention of the shmoo in 1948 as a character (well, species) in his cartoon strip *Li'l Abner,* set in the fictional deep South community of Dogpatch. Shmoos (forerunners of Douglas Adams' bovine animal), are shaped like soft bowling pins, reproduce rapidly, are delicious to eat, and are eager to be eaten. They also lay eggs, their eyes make perfect suspender buttons, and their whiskers can be used as toothpicks. But their free availability threatens to undermine capitalist society ('Wif these around, nobody won't nevah havta work no more.'). Captains of industry become alarmed, and organize to exterminate the shmoos. Dogpatch's extortionate grocer Soft-Hearted Jones is ecstatic: 'Now them mizzuble starvin' rats has t'come crawlin t'me fo' the necessities o' life. They complained 'bout mah prices befo'! Wait'll they see th' new ones!!'[47]

Finally, we must mention George R.R. Martin's *Tuf Voyaging*, where the protagonist has control over an amazing ship that can perform wonders of bioengineering.[48] He is trying to deal honestly with the planet S'uthlam, which is suffering from food scarcity due to overpopulation. Just inventing new food sources merely makes the problem worse in a classical Malthusian manner. The brilliant solution turns out to be a form of manna that inhibits the libido – shades of the urban myth that bromide was added to the tea of British soldiers in the First World War for a similar purpose.

With such powerful allegories, science fiction has occasionally had a similar impact to some traditional fiction on community responses to ethical questions. Mary Shelley's *Frankenstein*, for example, still speaks to questions of science, ethics, and society.[49] It is difficult, though, to think of other specific examples. Perhaps science fiction is seen (incorrectly) by most people as a genre devoted to ideas, but seldom to people.

Etiquette and Manners

Many stories, science fiction and otherwise, use manners and etiquette to tell us lessons about their societies. In Asimov's *The Caves of Steel*, yeast-based meals are served in communal kitchens. In this crowded imaginary world, good manners prescribe that one should not look at one's fellow diners while eating. The fact that two fellow diners keep glancing at our hero gives them away as baddies.

The etiquette of tea-drinking features strongly in Ann Leckie's debut novel *Ancillary Justice* and sequels.[50] Whole planets are devoted to its production. In a complex plot, the way in which tea is prepared and presented distinguishes regional and cultural differences and the supposed superiority of one group over another. The most prestigious teas are used as gifts to those from whom one might need a large favour. In a post-scarcity society, refinement, taking time, and obsessing over details sends social signals far more strongly than any show of material wealth – and are hard to fake. Tea drinking habits are used as clues by our heroine Breq as she seeks revenge against those who treacherously destroyed her starship.

The high point of food etiquette in science fiction is surely Scott Meyer's *Master of Formalities*, centred on the exploration of rigid social hierarchy, political skulduggery, and cultural incomprehension – especially when the food *Skolash* comes in. A favourite on the hero Hennik's home world, it is presented as a dish that he has requested from his captors, whose society is governed by good manners – including preparing any dish that the captive has asked for. But *Skolash* is some dish. Its literal translation is 'surprise,' and among those who are surprised are the chef, the sous-chef, and so on down the line, none of whom are allowed to know what the dish consists of. Nor are the guests at the banquet where it is to be served. The lowest kitchen employee is landed with the job of cooking a shapeless mass supported on a grav-platter (whatever that is). The food turns out to be a rotting carcass, cooked in a hermetically sealed chamber by setting fire to its own gases. The first slice is presented to Hennik as the honoured guest. 'I'm not hungry,' he says.[51] Truly a Space Opera of Manners.

The very real astronauts and cosmonauts on the International Space Station have developed their own etiquette for shared dinners. Astronaut Don Pettit describes how a proper dinner should include 'something special that is not repeatedly eaten on the standard nine-day menu':

> Now is the time to break out those thermal-stabilized pouches of beef steak that you have been hoarding [...]. Perhaps you can share a can of smoked anchovies, New Mexico green chili, or a piece of Old Amsterdam cheese [...]. Being generous now will reap more benefits than eating these delicacies in solitude.
>
> The choice of beverage is rather limited [...]. You can provide a special treat if you have access to one of the research refrigerators. In space, all your food is either hot or at room temperature [...].
>
> For special occasions—perhaps after a space walk or the docking of a resupply vehicle—you can serve your beverages in a 'zero-g' cup [...]. Zero-g cups, unlike bags with straws, are better for social rituals like toasting, and will bring a smile to the faces of your guests [...].
>
> Fresh tape, wipes, and an extra spoon [...].
>
> In space, catching food in your mouth is considered polite. Opening wide and making a clean catch will most always bring cheers from your guests. In one impressive gulp, you can leave them with the image of some sea creature inhaling another. Catching food in your mouth, like belching at the table (considered impolite in most cultures, but a compliment to the chef in others) is rude on Earth but *de rigueur* in space.[52]

This is the politeness of practicality among peers.

The key features of manners and etiquette are (1) that they reflect the social structure of the society, (2) that they offer the humane recognition of other people, and (3) that they provide solutions to the physical constraints involved. As we move further from terrestrial environments these features may shift, yet stay the same, and we may expect some manners to become truly alien. H.G. Wells's 'Man of the Year Million' has a much-reduced mouth and feeds by osmosis. An artist's conception of a dinner party at that remote period 'suggests a group of two-year-old babies crawling about a shallow wading pool'.[53] Greg Egan's *Schild's Ladder* takes us even further when a visitor to a research outpost politely requests an artificial body since demanding the right to eat and excrete would be crass and frivolous.[54]

Conclusion

Science fiction writers have come up with a few truly novel ideas about food and foodways, but in the main their writing has aimed to highlight deep paradoxes and problems of human society and the human condition through a futuristic setting. Unfortunately, these lessons are seldom picked up or even noticed by the vast majority who do not count science fiction as serious 'literature'.

But there is room for more, not necessarily so serious. No author to our knowledge has yet combined food questions with Einstein's relativity of simultaneity. If I am toasting somebody who is approaching close to the speed of light, how do we time the raising of the glasses? If a dinner party is held in a gravitational well so that some participants have gravitational time dilation, how do we determine whom to wait for when starting to eat? If seniority matters, what about time dilated seniors? These and other questions remain to be answered.

Notes

1. 'Smith, E.E.', *SFE: The Encyclopedia of Science Fiction*, 16 August 2021 <http://www.sf-encyclopedia.com/entry/smith_e_> [accessed 11 March 2022].
2. Jason Sheehan, *Cooking Dirty* (New York: Farrar, Straus & Giroux, 2010); *Tales from the Radiation Age* (London: 47North, 2013).
3. Jules Verne, *From the Earth to the Moon* (London: [Various], 1867), pp. 298-99 <https://www.gutenberg.org/ebooks/83> [accessed 11 March 2022].
4. 'Liebig's Extract of Meat', *Cook's Info*, 5 October 2020 <https://www.cooksinfo.com/liebigs-extract-of-meat> [accessed 11 March 2022].
5. 'Apollo to the Moon: Food in Space', *Smithsonian National Air and Space Museum* <https://airandspace.si.edu/exhibitions/apollo-to-the-moon/online/astronaut-life/food-in-space.cfm> [accessed 11 March 2022].
6. Charlotte Edwards, 'Crunch Time: A History of Astronaut Food', *The Sun*, 20 July 2019 >https://www.thesun.co.uk/tech/9522962/astronaut-food-history-moon-landing/> [accessed 11 March 2022].
7. E.E. Smith, *Second Stage Lensman* (New York: Fantasy Press, 1953).
8. Sarah Ramsey, 'Pizza Hut Once Delivered Space Pizza to the ISS', *Wide Open Eats*, 15 June 2020 <https://www.wideopeneats.com/space-pizza/> [accessed 11 March 2022].
9. NASA, 'Growing Plants in Space', NASA, 12 July 2021 <https://www.nasa.gov/content/growing-plants-in-space> [accessed 11 March 2022].
10. Isaac Asimov, *Prelude to Foundation* (New York: Doubleday, 1988), pp. 226-27.
11. Nat Schachner, 'Redmask of the Outlands', *Astounding Stories*, January 1934, pp. 2-30 (p. 6).
12. Edward Page Mitchell, 'The Senator's Daughter', *New York Sun*, 27 July 1879; J.R.R. Tolkien, *The Fellowship of the Ring* in *The Lord of the Rings* (Boston: Houghton Mifflin, 2004), pp. 21-412 (pp. 369-70).

13. M. Perchonok and C. Bourland, 'NASA Food Systems: Past, Present, and Future', *Nutrition* 18 (2002), 913-20.
14. Arthur C. Clarke, *The Deep Range* (London: Frederick Muller, 1957).
15. Isaac Asimov, *The Caves of Steel* (New York: Galaxy Magazine, 1953).
16. Fred Pohl and Cyril Kornbluth, *The Space Merchants* (New York: Macmillan, 1987 [1953]), p. 73.
17. NASA; James Blish, *Cities in Flight* (Woodstock, NY: Ballantine, 2000 [1970]), p. 220.
18. Ray Bradbury, 'Boys! Raise Giant Mushrooms in Your Cellar', in *The Stories of Ray Bradbury* (London: Knopf, 1980 [1962]), p. 884.
19. NASA; Ashley Strickland, 'Previously Unknown Bacteria Discovered on the Space Station Could Help Grow Plants', *CNN World*, 16 March 2021 <https://edition.cnn.com/2021/03/16/world/international-space-station-microbes-scn-trnd/index.html?utm_source=Nature+Briefing&utm_campaign=02e41775a1-briefing-dy-20210318&utm_medium=email&utm_term=0_c9dfd39373-02e41775a1-43732721> [access 11 March 2022]
20. J.B. Garciá Martínez and others, 'Potential of Microbial Electrosynthesis for Contributing to Food Production using CO_2 during Global Agriculture-Inhibiting Disasters', *Cleaner Engineering and Technology*, 4 (2021), 100139.
21. K.A. Alvarado and others, 'Food in Space from Hydrogen Oxidizing Bacteria', *Acta Astronautica*, 180 (March 2021), 260-65.
22. J.B. Garciá Martínez, 'Chemical Synthesis of Food from CO_2 for Space Missions and Food Resilience', *Journal of CO2 Utilization*, 53 (2021), 101726.
23. M.J. Post, 'Cultured Meat from Stem Cells: Challenges and Prospects', *Meat Science*, 92 (2012), 297-301.
24. H.B. Piper, *Four Day Planet* (New York: Ace, 1961), p. 52 <https://www.gutenberg.org/ebooks/19478> [accessed 11 March 2022]
25. 'Celebrity Cubes', *Bistro in Vitro* <https://bistro-invitro.com/en/dishes/celebrity-cubes/> [accessed 11 March 2022]
26. Adam Kuban 'A Primer to "Star Trek" Food and Drink', *Serious Eats*, 10 August 2018 <https://www.seriouseats.com/2009/05/a-primer-to-star-trek-food-and-drink.html> [accessed 11 March 2022]; Ethan Phillips and William J. Birnes, *Star Trek Cookbook* (New York: Prentice Hall, 1999).
27. 'Foods and Beverages', *Federation Space* <https://wiki.fed-space.com/index.php?title=Foods_and_beverages> [accessed 11 March 2022]
28. *Food Replicator*, 2022 <https://foodreplicator.tumblr.com/recipesbyseries> [accessed 11 March 2022]
29. Fred Pohl, *Beyond the Blue Event Horizon* (New York: Ballantine Books, 1980).
30. 'Red Dwarf/Food', *The TV IV Wiki*, 7 January 2007 <http://tviv.org/Red_Dwarf/Food> [accessed 11 March 2022]; 'Red Dwarf Season VI Episode 2 "Legion"', *Červený trpaslík (Red Dwarf)* <http://www.cervenytrpaslik.cz/scenare/EN-32-6_Legion.htm> [accessed 11 March 2022]
31. M.V. Berry and A.K. Geim, 'Of Flying Frogs and Levitrons', *European Journal of Physics*, 18 (1997), 307-13,
32. Robert Heinlein, *Methuselah's Children* (New York: Astounding Science Fiction Magazine, 1941).
33. R.A. Nimesha Ranasinghe, 'Digitally Stimulating the Sensation of Taste Through Electrical and Thermal Stimulation' (unpublished doctoral thesis, University of Singapore, 2012) <https://core.ac.uk/download/pdf/48659289.pdf> [accessed 11 March 2022]
34. John Timmer, 'A New Brain Implant Translates Thoughts of Writing into Text', *Wired*, 14 May 2021 <https://www.wired.com/story/new-brain-implant-translates-thoughts-of-writing-into-text/> [accessed 11 March 2022]
35. M. Rohm and others, 'Hybrid Brain-Computer Interfaces and Hybrid Neuroprostheses for Restoration of Upper Limb Functions in Individuals with High-Level Spinal Cord Injury', *Artificial Intelligence in Medicine*, 59 (2013), 133-42.
36. N. Ninyawee and others, 'Making Food with the Mind: Integrating Brain-Computer Interface and 3D Food Fabrication', *FTC 2019, AISC 1069*, ed. by K. Arai and others (Switzerland: Springer Nature

(2020), pp. 239-47 <https://doi.org/10.1007/978-3-030-32520-6_19>
37 Michele Dantini, 'The Mutant's Food: Design and Science Fiction', in *Arts and Food. Rituals since 1851*, ed. by Germano Celant (Milan: Mondadori Electa, 2015), pp. 624-45.
38 *Soylent Green*, dir. by Richard Fleischer (Metro-Goldwyn-Mayer,1973).
39 Larry Niven, 'Bordered in Black', in *Inconstant Moon* (London: Sphere, 1973).
40 Douglas Adams, *The Restaurant at the End of the Universe* (New York: Ballantine, 2005 [1980]), p. 115.
41 Margaret Atwood, *Oryx and Crake* (New York: Doubleday, 2003).
42 Traci Warkentin, 'Dis/integrating Animals: Ethical Dimensions of the Genetic Engineering of Animals for Human Consumption', *AI and Society*, 20.1 (2006), 82-102; Sherryl Vint, *Animal Alterity: Science Fiction and the Question of the Animal* (Liverpool: Liverpool University Press, 2010).
43 Ross Pavlac, 'Some Thoughts on Ethics and Science Fiction', *The Ethical Spectacle*, March 1996 <https://www.spectacle.org/396/scifi/pavlac.html> [accessed 11 March 2022]
44 N.K. Jemisin, *The Fifth Season* (London: Orbit Books, 2015).
45 Ray Bradbury, 'Here There Be Tygers', in *New Tales of Space and Time*, ed. by R.J. Healy (New York: Holt, 1951), pp. 1-15.
46 Paolo Bacigalupi, *The Windup Girl* (New York: Nightshade Books, 2009).
47 'Shmoo', *Wikipedia*, 12 December 2021 <https://en.wikipedia.org/wiki/Shmoo> [accessed 11 March 2022]
48 George R.R. Martin, *Tuf Voyaging* (Wake Forest, NC: Baen, 1986); '*Tuf Voyaging*', *Wikipedia*, 1 March 2022 <https://en.wikipedia.org/wiki/Tuf_Voyaging> [accessed 11 March 2022]
49 Paul K. Guinnessy, 'The Lessons of *Frankenstein*', *Physics Today*, 2 March 2018 <https://physicstoday.scitation.org/do/10.1063/PT.6.3.20180302a/full/>
50 Ann Leckie, *Ancillary Justice* (London: Orbit, 2013).
51 Scott Meyer, *Master of Formalities* (Seattle: 47North, 2015), pp. 123, 127.
52 Don Pettit, 'An Astronaut's Guide to Space Etiquette', *Air & Space Magazine*, 27 June 27 2012 <https://www.smithsonianmag.com/air-space-magazine/an-astronauts-guide-to-space-etiquette-12934/> [accessed 11 March 2022]
53 G.S. Haight, 'H.G. Wells's "The Man of the Year Million"', *Nineteenth-Century Fiction*, 12 (1958), 323-26.
54 Greg Egan, *Schild's Ladder* (London: Gollancz, 2002).

Saving Food in Bulgaria: Imagining Hopeful Futures Through Quiet Food Sovereignty

Lindsey Foltz

Into the Cellar

When I meet Vasi she is just coming from the elementary school. During her working years she was a primary school teacher and continues to volunteer in retirement. She is wearing a well-tailored dress with an abstract design in muted greens, golds, and tans. Her dress is complemented by formal white shoes with a low heel. We walk down the block to her house, which sits over the small machine shop that she and her husband own. Walking down the sidewalk to her gate she greets many of the children, who are buying breakfast at the corner bakery. She explains to me that she has a Sunday school at the Orthodox church across the street and knows many children from there and from volunteering at the elementary school.

We take off our shoes and stash our bags as we head upstairs into her kitchen. There she is making yoghurt with milk from a woman she knows, which she does twice a week. She unwraps a towel and lifts the lid on the round, enamel pot to reveal the new yoghurt. It is sitting in a warm and draft-free part of the house, next to the stove. She feeds me a large spoonful and it has a pleasant, mild sourness. She says you can buy starter for yoghurt or just start the next batch with some yoghurt from the previous batch mixed in with new milk. She is adamant that you can only use fresh milk to make yoghurt and it is better to buy it from people you know, '*poznati*'. She doesn't trust the quality from the store. She buys milk from *poznati* because, 'You know they won't sell you something bad or that will make you sick […] you know each other, and they will take care of you'. She describes this milk that she buys as 'clean' and 'good quality'.

She has heard I am especially interested in cellars, so she agrees to give me a tour of hers. Even though it is a hot September day, the air is cool as we descend the stairs into the stone and cement basement. She flips on a bare light bulb and opens an old wooden door to reveal a spotless and well-organized cellar. In the deepest, coolest part are wooden wine barrels, thick plastic barrels for fermenting cabbage (which will happen later in the fall), and a square plastic jug with a spigot containing the last remains of a fermented lingonberry drink. 'This is good for the kidneys,' she tells me as she offers me a small glass of the tart and slightly fizzy drink. 'In general, the mountains have them [lingonberries]. But if we don't go to gather them ourselves then we buy them in the market from someone who did gather them [themselves].' There are also dried herbs hanging which she uses for tea and seasoning food.

Along the walls she has several custom-built wooden shelves that go from the floor almost up to the low ceiling. Fabric is hanging in front of each shelf to keep dust off the jars stored there. She pulls up the green, flower-patterned fabric from the first shelf to reveal rows of jewel-coloured jars and bottles. She narrates the contents of each one. She knows by sight what is in each jar. The first shelf is full of compote: raspberries, strawberries (both cultivated and wild), pear, peach, apricot, sour cherry, sweet cherry, cornelian cherry, and plums (both yellow and blue). She picks up a small jar with golden brown contents and describes how to make it, as she has done for many of the jars: 'This is cornelian cherry and apple marmalade. First you clean the cornelian cherries and after that you add peeled and sliced apples and cook them until they are soft. Then you grind them [in a food mill] and return them to the pot to cook until it becomes thick. You know it is ready, this is the way my grandmother taught me, when it becomes dark and is very thick.' She insists that I take this jar with me to eat on bread during my last few days in Bulgaria. We keep up our tour through the fruit jars and after that move on to the vegetables.

We walk up two steps, just outside the cellar, into the garage where she stores her preserved vegetables along the wall. There are sliced cucumber pickles, tomatoes in salt water, marinated cherry tomatoes with spicy peppers, mixed vegetables (*gyuvech*), marinated eggplant, marinated summer squash, a seasoned tomato and pepper puree that she uses as a soup starter (*podpravka*), roasted pepper and tomato chutney (*lyutenitsa*), tomato juice, and ketchup (which she makes because her grandchildren like it on pizza). Most of the *lyutenitsa* is in small, threaded glass jars with screw-on caps that she says are recycled baby food jars. The tomato juice and ketchup are in recycled Queen's brand juice bottles.

There are almost no empty jars at this point in the year. The jars are of different sizes and shapes, and some of them are recycled industrially produced food jars. But most of them are the squat jars with rounded shoulders, common from socialist times, that are sealed by round metal lids that must be crimped over the mouth of the jar with a hand-tool. Many of the jars were bought by her mother when she was five years old, so they are over fifty years old now. Vasi says that she buys new jars from time to time if older ones break.

As we look through the jars in the garage, she makes the comment that her daughter tends to buy fresh but 'plastic' imported fruits and vegetables all winter long. Many people describe these imports as 'plastic' or 'wooden' because, while they look nice, they don't have any smell or taste. Vasi doesn't understand buying this fresh produce since the taste isn't as good, and she thinks it is expensive and unhealthy to buy produce out of season. Most of the produce that Vasi eats and preserves comes from her garden and a few things she gathers from the forest or mountains such as blueberries, strawberries, and herbs. She buys sugar, salt, and oil for making preserves from either a local store or a larger chain store in a nearby town.

'Is this really that useful to you?' she asks with a smirk as we begin more carefully counting and inventorying the jars. She immediately answers her own question, 'I guess it can show how one family feeds itself.' Then she reminds me, 'This isn't all the jars I made.' There are more in the pantries of both her son and daughter who live in their own houses. 'How many do you think you made in all this year?' I ask. 'More or less 400', she replies, not including any alcohol. She gives about one hundred jars each to her children and keeps the rest in her cellar. 'It's a little bit like living in a village house, you know? We have a little of everything, scattered here and there, but it's easier to live and more joyful.'

Introduction and Methods

Fermenting, drying, and jarring food, like Vasi does, for personal and familial consumption are relatively common practices in post-socialist countries, even while they are marginal practices in most Western countries. These home-preserved foods embody a nexus of practices that link material, biological and cultural survival, formal and informal economies, social networks, wild and cultivated foods. As such, they are an ideal subject for investigating how ordinary people engaging in mundane social practices, like saving food for the winter, are creating resilience and meaning in their lives in the context of broader economic and political forces that lay largely beyond their control. Home-based food preservation practices provided resilience in the context of the socialist food regimes of the past and continue to be adaptive as Bulgaria has joined the global market economy and is increasingly integrated into the industrial, corporate food regime.

My ongoing, multi-sited research examines home-based food preservation practices in contemporary Bulgaria through participant observation, formal and informal interviews, cellar and garden surveys, and social media posts from 2018 to 2021 (built upon two years of living and working in Bulgaria from 2006 to 2008). The bulk of the research is conducted in person, though during 2020 due to COVID travel restrictions some work was done virtually. I have taken an open-minded, empirically based, inductive approach to theme generation similar to grounded theory.[1] However, I have diverged from a purely inductive model of theory generation by using a more deductive approach to analyzing existing literature and theories related to the themes identified inductively. This is consistent with what Goldkuhl and Cronholm call 'multi-grounded theory'.[2]

Through this process I am integrating my observations about everyday food saving practices in contemporary Bulgaria with literature emerging from Russia and Eastern Europe theorizing 'quiet food sovereignty'.[3] By using social practice theories as an analytic, I provide a tentative suggestion for how 'Thinking Food like an East European' can contribute to developing and preserving resilient food systems.[4] Finally, I describe evidence of quiet food sovereignty that is not connected with a rights-based social movement or ethical consumerism driven alternative food networks.

Social Practices and the Dynamics of Social Change

I am conceptualizing food preservation in Bulgarian households as social practices that condense in the cellar. Food preservation practices are intrinsically linked to other social practices relating to many aspects of everyday life such as shopping, gardening, gathering, cooking, and eating. Social practices are intentional, though often routinized, activities which consist of interconnected elements such as 'embodiment, physical objects, inner emotions, competences of how to do things, and motivations to do them'.[5] They are performed by carriers of the practices, and, when they are performed, they are 'the routine accomplishment of what people take to be "normal" ways of life'.[6] Accordingly, social practices are performed 'on the basis of what members learn from others, and are capable of being done well or badly, correctly or incorrectly'.[7] They are 'intrinsically connected to and interwoven with objects' and non-human entities.[8]

Practice theory rejects the focus on either individual minds and actors or social structures in studying and understanding social life and how it changes or stays the same; rather, it conceptualizes agency and structure as recursive.[9] According to practice theorists such as Schatzki, what we know and how our social life is organized and reproduced is through action and interaction with practices. This includes how knowledge is advanced and how social life is transformed.[10]

In simplified terms, social practices are composed of three interconnected elements: materials, competences, and meanings.[11] These three elements are integrated when practices are enacted and emerge, persist, shift, or disappear 'as links between their defining elements are made and broken'.[12] These practices are constituted through particular performances but are also entities which exist as long as they are reproduced by a broader community of practice, amongst whom these food preservation practices are recognizable and the competences of others in the community can be judged. Finally, the careers of practices emerge and persist in historical and geographic context. Therefore, I will describe these three basic elements of the social practices related to preserving food. Additionally, I will provide historical context for the social practices of home-based food preservation.

The Bulgarian cellar, seen through the lens of social practice theories related to the dynamics of social change, evidences quiet food sovereignty that does not manifest as a result of a public social movement or the development of alternative food networks based on individual ethical consumption. Foregrounding these everyday practices opens up new opportunities for imagining the maintenance and emergence of just and resilient food systems which are essential for hopeful food futures.

Historical Context

While home-preserved foods have deep historical roots in Bulgaria, and play a significant role in contemporary household strategies for making-do, they are also tied to experiences of living under state socialism.[13] Citizens in socialist countries, like Bulgaria, developed complex and multifaceted strategies to negotiate economies of shortage, secure basic material needs, and pursue something more than just utilitarian survival.[14] Gaining access to food, not only for basic nutritional needs, but also for celebrating; offering hospitality; supporting health; performing personal, local, and/or national identity; and satisfying personal and familial desires and aesthetics required elaborate strategies, networks, and skills. These strategies included the creation and maintenance of extensive social networks and a robust second economy for everyday goods like food.[15] The centrally planned economy in socialist states was not the only economy operating in everyday lives.[16] During socialism, even as most agricultural land in Bulgaria was consolidated and nationalized by the state, many families tended small personal garden plots. These were especially common in small towns and rural areas. However, home-preserved foods that were produced in rural areas circulated far beyond their rural origins; they travelled along networks of extended social relations in what Smollett refers to as the 'economy of jars'.[17] Post-socialist foodways studies demonstrate that while post-1989 entry into neoliberal global economies is a rupture with the centrally planned economy of the past, many of the everyday food related strategies, practices, and networks developed by Bulgarians and other socialist citizens continue to the present day.[18] Home-based food preservation practices in contemporary Bulgaria emerge from long-term daily confrontation with uncertainty and precarity and are exemplary of resilient foodways that have allowed people to negotiate major disruptions and changes such as the end of socialism and joining the European Union.

Elements of Home-based Food Preservation: Materials, Competences, Meanings

Social practice theory emphasizes the inextricable and co-constitutive nature of material 'things' in the social. Many of these things are durable and create a material connection with the past. The materials that condense in the Bulgarian cellar are two-fold: those which are physically present in the cellar and those that are utilized in the production process.

Glass jars are critical in ongoing food preservation practices. While it is sometimes necessary for people to buy new glass jars, many people I interviewed inherited large collections of glass jars from their mothers, mothers-in-law, or grandmothers. I was also instructed on proper jar etiquette; if you receive a jar, it is essential that you return it to its owner after you eat the contents. Many jars in the cellars I inventoried were produced during socialist times. They most commonly have crimp-on metal lids or single-piece threaded metal lids, which can be purchased in almost every outdoor market, shop, and supermarket throughout the country during the spring and summer months. Additionally, many people wash and save the jars from commercially processed foods. Some of these are also from the socialist period, notably small baby-food jars which many people have saved from when their children were small. There are also more recently produced industrial jars from products such as *lyutenitsa*, beans, tomatoes, and juice. Many trips to Bulgarian corner stores and large supermarkets reveal the persistent prevalence of jarred industrial foods compared to tinned foods. These jars are threaded and usually re-used with the original branded lid, so they are easy to identify.

These re-used jars are evidence of a hybrid approach to food provisioning that makes use of purchased, industrially produced food in addition to home-produced and preserved foods. This ongoing hybrid approach was not widely expected by those theorizing capitalist transitions in the nineties. While these hybrid approaches remain common, even among the middle class or upper middle class who don't rely on home-produced food out of economic necessity, they continue to be described by some government documents as 'ineffective' or a 'hangover from the past'.[19] Jars are re-used year after year, though they may not always be in continuous use. Stockpiles of empty jars were a common sight in many homes. However, the glass is durable and is therefore a flexible resource which can be put to use whenever necessary.

Additional materials that are durable and therefore carried over from socialist times include: multiple sizes of kettles for cooking and water-bath canning, food grinders, fire-pits built from brick or concrete blocks, gas burners, and pepper roasters.

The ingredients themselves are acquired each year, and the people participating in my research use multiple sources, methods, and economies for doing so. Some foods are grown by the families in gardens or foraged by them, in other words acquired through production. Other ingredients like oil, spices like ground red pepper or cumin, sugar, and salt are purchased from formal markets such as stores. Some people also buy vegetables from supermarkets and large-scale vegetable producers. Informal or grey markets are also a source of ingredients which can include fruits, vegetables, herbs, milk, or meat. These are often purchased from neighbours or other people that they know, *poznati*, who are not licensed or taxed on this production.[20] Finally, preserve-makers acquire some ingredients through informal transfer from people in their social networks as gifts. Because food flows from exchanges inside and outside formal markets, these producers' relationship with food is not exclusively commodity defined. This connects home-based food preservation practices to social networks, informal markets, cultivated production for self-consumption, and foraging (which incidentally occurs in both urban and rural settings). In summary, exchange (purchase in formal market), production, and transfer (informal exchange) are all common features of the ingredients found in Bulgarian cellars.

Competences in the case of these preservation practices are usually learned from older generations; mothers, grandmothers, or mothers-in-law taught food preservation, and older male relatives passed down skills related to making alcohol. Though I noticed that these stark gendered divisions of labour were more blurry in practice when families gathered to make preserves or alcohol together, interviewees very consistently attributed expertise in these gendered terms. There are competences related to cooking up the preserves, properly sealing them, and safely water-bath canning them. Fermented foods and alcohol require a host of skills in cultivating desired and safe communities of microorganisms in addition to skills related to distillation and aging. Since many ingredients are home-grown, competency in growing and harvesting cultivated fruits and vegetables are evident, as are a wide variety of foraging skills including knowledge of where and when to look, plant identification, and proper harvesting and processing techniques. Interestingly, some people supplement or expand their repertoire through watching videos from other home-preservers on internet sites such as YouTube. Two women that I interviewed converted their knowledge on how to make fermented cabbage into making kimchee using existing knowledge supplemented by internet recipes and fish sauce purchased in a large town nearby. Some younger interviewees indicated that they are the drivers in their household to make certain preserved foods, such as *lyutenitsa*, and that they bring the generations together so that they can learn through doing. In a similar fashion to the jars, these competences may be learned and then lay dormant, sometimes for years, before being pulled back into use. These embodied competences can be flexibly deployed, innovated upon, and called into action when necessary or desirable.

The meanings of home-preserved foods and motivations to make them are varying and, in many cases, overlapping. I have sorted the most commonly identified meanings and motivations into themes illustrated by the following emblematic quotes:

- Tradition: 'Because our grandmothers and mothers did this.'
- Well-being: 'Because it is easier to live and more merry.'
- Food Security: 'I have to eat, don't I?'
- Memory: 'One taste and I was transported to my grandmother's garden when I was a little girl.'
- Safety/Purity: 'You have to buy it from someone you know because they won't give you something that will make you sick.'
- Taste/Aesthetics: 'When you preserve them this way, they stay crunchy and tasty.'
- Health: '*Rakiya* [home-made brandy] is important first of all for health.'
- Preventing Waste: 'What am I supposed to do, throw away the plums?'
- Care for Family: 'My grandchild calls, 'Granny can you make me something please?' Tell me what you desire, and I will make it.'

While I will not extrapolate on it further in this paper, there are a group of people in one village where I worked who are actively recruiting home-made food preservers into a food-based social movement, namely Slow Food. For these participants it was clear that public, political activism was a motivating factor in their home-based food preservation practices. The same materials and competencies are being utilized but motivated and enlivened by new meanings such as preserving agricultural biodiversity, protesting corruption in the government, and participating in an international movement of gastronomes. This provides a contrast to all other interviewees who evidence 'quiet' or implicit politics, that I elaborate on below.

Features of Thinking Food like an East European: Lessons from the Cellar

Bulgarian cellars demonstrate many features identified by Jehlička and others related to 'Thinking Food like an East European', further supporting their claims of the benefit of looking to Eastern Europe for theories and practices related to resilient and just foodways. In particular, many systems often understood as contradictory in Western food studies are non-oppositional in practice in Eastern Europe, including industrial vs. small scale agriculture, cultivated vs. wild foods, formal vs. informal economies, and leisure vs. work.

People who produce home-preserved foods in Bulgaria get their ingredients from a wide variety of sources which include purchased, traded, gifted, and self-produced items which entangle formal and informal economies and markets. There is a non-oppositional relationship between industrial and smaller scale agriculture evident through the integration of ingredients from both systems and, in some cases, generating income through employment in industrial agricultural while the household also makes home-preserved foods. Another point of comparison to their studies is that the middle class continues production. Most of those I have interviewed are squarely in the middle class, highly educated, and have stable employment or income. They have strong familial livelihood networks which include multiple sources of income such as pensions, remittances, and paid employment. This runs counter to 'development' narratives that predicted household food production would decrease with rising incomes and integration in formal markets or that characterize domestic food production as driven by poverty.[21] This is not to say that home-based food preservation is purely a leisure activity. It is important nutritionally and is a way to reduce expenditures. Accessing things like utilities, prescription medications, and complex medical care are still a challenge for many households due to their expense.

There are many environmental and social benefits of home-based food preservation in Bulgaria, linking it with food sovereignty. Though small-scale food production, which provides the bulk of the ingredients, is not always without chemical inputs, they are minimized due to both considerations of care and expense. In some cases, keeping small animals like chickens or goats makes closed-loop nutrient cycles possible. Food miles are also minimized, as is food waste. Some people making home-preserved foods are also specifically saving and propagating rare varieties of agricultural plants and animals that are well-suited to food preservation. Preserved foods that are fermented, dried, or jarred do not require refrigeration. Additionally, they minimize non-reusable food packaging. These foods, and the materials and competences required to produce them, provide food security and resilience in the face of uncertainty. Not only do they diversify foods during the winter and provide calories, they are also gift-able, trade-able, and sale-able and so can be converted into other resources. They are also functional foods which can restore or preserve health and decrease dependency on expensive medicines or care. They preserve materials and competences for future use. Beyond these benefits are the feelings of pride, the pleasure in familiar and valorized tastes, the ability to properly host guests and celebrate, and the connection to familial and national heritage.

Conclusion

Home-preserved foods in Bulgarian cellars are prized as clean and reliable alternatives to industrial food (even while sometimes utilizing industrially produced ingredients), tastes of home and the village, functional foods that preserve and restore health, and essential components in both everyday and ritual life. Bulgarian cellars provide underappreciated evidence of resilient, alternative food networks and suggest how they might be developed in contexts where there are various political and economic barriers to social movement-based change or marketized approaches to alternative food system development. The entanglement of formal and informal economies, domestic and wild foods, smallholders and industrial farms, local and global influences that are visible in everyday food practices in Eastern Europe provide resilience in terms of food security but also the ability to pursue something more than mere survival. Home-preserved foods preserve knowledge and practices related to agroecological food production, traditional ecological knowledge, and self-provisioning at the interstices of the global corporate food regime, which Visser and others characterize as 'quiet food sovereignty'.[22] This concept opens new avenues for understanding and supporting food politics as they are being practiced, particularly outside of Western settings.

For many people worldwide, predominant food systems are bleak. Imagination is critical to the pursuit of future food systems that go beyond mere sustenance and uphold the aspirations of food sovereignty, including the right to food that is desirable, healthy, meaningful, and produced or acquired in an environmentally sound way. Bulgarian cellars inspire me to imagine beyond binaries, expand my vision of food politics occurring quietly in domestic spaces, and preserve my hope in the possibility of abundant and resilient food futures.

Notes

1. Anselm Strauss and Juliet Corbin, *Basics of Qualitative Research: Techniques and Procedures for Developing Grounded Theory*, 2nd ed. (Thousand Oaks, CA: Sage, 1998).
2. Göran Goldkuhl and Stefan Cronholm, 'Adding Theoretical Grounding to Grounded Theory: Toward Multi-Grounded Theory', *International Journal of Qualitative Methods*, 9.2 (2010), 187-205.
3. Oane Visser and others, '"Quiet Food Sovereignty" as Food Sovereignty Without a Movement? Insights from Post-socialist Russia', *Globalizations*, 15.4 (2015), 513-28.
4. Petr Jehlička and others, 'Thinking Food like an East European: A critical reflection on the framing of food systems', *Journal of Rural Studies*, 76 (2020), 286-95.
5. Nicklas Neuman, 'On the Engagement with Social Theory in Food Studies: Cultural Symbols and Social Practices', *Food, Culture & Society*, 22.1 (2019), 78-94.
6. Elizabeth Shove, *Comfort, Cleanliness and Convenience: The Social Organization of Normality* (London: Bloomsbury Academic, 2003), p. 117.
7. Barry Barnes, 'Practice as Collective Action', in *The Practice Turn in Social Theory*, ed. by Theodore R. Schatzki, Karin Knorr-Cetina, and Eike von Savigny (New York, Routledge, 2001) pp. 27-36 (p. 27).
8. Theodore Schatzki, *The Site of the Social* (University Park, PA: Pennsylvania State University Press, 2002), p. 106.
9. Anthony Giddens, *The Constitution of Society* (Cambridge: Polity Press 1984); Theodore Schatzki, 'Introduction: Practice Theory', in *The Practice Turn in Social Theory* (New York: Routledge, 2001), pp. 10-23 (p. 12).
10. Theodore Schatzki, *The Site of the Social: A Philosophical Account of the Constitution of Social Life and Change* (University Park, PA: Pennsylvania State University Press, 2002).
11. Elizabeth Shove, Mika Pantzar, and Matt Watson, *The Dynamics of Social Practice: Everyday Life and*

How it Changes (London: Sage Publications, 2012), p. 14.

12 Shove, Pantzar, and Watson, p. 21; Jennifer Braun, 'The Making and Breaking of Food Preservation Practices in a Rural Albertan Community', *Rural Sociology*, 80.2 (2015), 228-47.

13 Melissa Caldwell, *Not by Bread Alone* (Berkeley, CA: University of California Press, 2004).

14 Elizabeth Dunn, 'Food of Sorrow', in *Food Ethnographic Encounters*, ed. by Leo Coleman (New York: Bloomsbury Academic, 2010), pp. 139-49; Katherine Verdery, *What Was Socialism, and What Comes Next?* (Princeton, NJ: Princeton University Press, 1996); Gerald Creed, *Domesticating Revolution: From Socialist Reform to Ambivalent Transition in a Bulgarian Village* (University Park, PA: Pennsylvania State University Press, 1996); Paulina Bren and Mary Neuburger, *Communism Unwrapped: Consumption in Cold War Eastern Europe* (Oxford: Oxford University Press, 2012); Slavenka Drakulic, *How We Survived Communism and Even Laughed* (New York: Norton, 1992).

15 Alvena V. Ledeneva, *Russia's Economy of Favors* (Cambridge: Cambridge University Press, 1996).

16 Susan Gal and Gail Kligman (eds.), *Reproducing Gender: Politics, Publics, and Everyday Life after Socialism* (Princeton, NJ: Princeton University Press, 2002).

17 Eleanor Smollett, 'The Economy of Jars: Kindred Relationships in Bulgaria', *Ethnologia Europaea*, 19.2 (1984), 125-40.

18 For examples, see Melissa Caldwell, Elizabeth Dunn, and Marion Nestle, *Food & Everyday Life in the Postsocialist World* (Bloomington, IN: University of Indiana Press, 2009); Yuson Jung, *Balkan Blues* (Bloomington, IN: Indiana University Press, 2019); Yuson Jung, 'Ambivalent Consumers and the Limits of Certification', in *Ethical Eating in the Postsocialist and Socialist World*, ed. by Yuson Jung, Jakob A. Klein, and Melissa A. Caldwell (Berkeley, CA: University of California Press, 2014), pp. 93-115; Elizabeth Dunn, *Privatizing Poland: Baby Food, Big Business, and the Remaking of Labor* (Ithaca, NY: Cornell University Press, 2004).

19 Czech government document quoted in Jehlička and others, p. 291.

20 For examples of informal food economies in other post-socialist contexts, see: Diane Mincyte, 'Homogenizing Europe: Raw Milk, Risk Politics, and Moral Economies in Europeanizing Lithuania', in *Ethical Eating in the Postsocialist and Socialist World*, ed. by Yuson Jung, Jakob A. Klein, and Melissa A. Caldwell (Berkeley: University of California Press, 2014), pp. 24-43; Guntra Aistara, 'Good, Clean, Fair and Illegal', *Journal of Baltic Studies*, 46.3 (2015), 283-98.

21 Jens Alber and Ulrich Kohler, 'Informal Food Production in the Enlarged European Union', *Social Indicators Research*, 89.1 (2008), 113-27.

22 Visser and others, pp. 527-28.

A Conceit of Coney: Philip Harben and Britain's First Television Food History Programme

Kevin Geddes

Introduction

Today, we can happily switch on the television and choose from a myriad of options to settle down and watch. Even within genres, there are endless choices and subgenres. If we are interested in watching programmes about food, we are not limited to learning about the preparation of ingredients. We can discover where food comes from, how supermarket products are made, and what effect different foods have on our bodies or watch ordinary people or celebrities compete to produce the biggest, best, worst, or strangest concoctions. We can also choose to watch food history. Indeed, it is hard to imagine the schedules without Annie Gray and Lucy Worsley dressed-up and ready to explore kitchens of the dim and distant past, bringing them to life before our eyes. We are regularly transported back in time to see modern-day families cook, eat, and enjoy (or otherwise) food from the past. It may seem like a relatively new thing, with an explosion in food history programmes since *The Supersizers* went Edwardian in 2007, closely followed by an Elizabethan adventure in 2008.

So, the idea that food history forms part of our televisual habits is not new, but just how old is it? Where did food history on television begin? What elements of food history on television today have been borrowed themselves from television history? Has the mix of television entertainment and education that we can enjoy watching in *The Supersizers*, with Annie Gray and Lucy Worsley or through the eyes of families on *Back in Time for…* been a new twist, or does it have its roots in the past?

Although early television programmes in Britain are often considered to be basic in nature, several of the programmes broadcast after the war were more experimental in nature, attracting audiences who simply enjoyed watching without learning, or realizing that they were being entertained. These were often 'must-see' television broadcasts which would lead Guy Debord in the 1960s to coin the phrase 'Society of the Spectacle' to represent the relationship connecting the audience, and wider society, with the images and messages they were receiving more and more through mass media such as television (1994). Audiences became consumers of media, and society itself became more consumer focused, using the spectacle to convey messages about what the consumers should 'have' and 'want' in their own lives. These cultural changes noted by Debord had a background firmly focused on history, which he proposed was at the heart of culture and society.

This paper will look in detail at one such 'spectacle', broadcast in 1953 by the British Broadcasting Corporation (BBC) to coincide with and celebrate the Coronation of Queen Elizabeth II, to look more closely at the imagined past being explored through television screens and consumed by eager audiences at home. *An Evening's Diversion* (*Radio Times* 1953) included the very first television food history demonstration by the then 'television cook' Philip Harben (Levy 2021a). Did he unwittingly inspire a boom in food history programmes by dressing up in historical outfits, and a subsequent explosion of imaginative interpretations of food from the past?

Context

Reinterpretation of historical events, and historical food, were obviously not new by the time television broadcasts began. Some may argue that all written recipes are historical documents which are then reinterpreted by those who cook at home, recreating what others before them made. The idea of understanding history more through re-enacting events is also well understood as a valuable and performative tool for historians and those interested in history and food archaeology (Gray 2010). As food played a central role in all lives, modern and historic, the re-enactment and re-discovery of food, recipes, and menus from the past has enabled people to understand and define periods of history better (Long 2004). Television cooking shows have been shown to be a capable vehicle for storytelling, sharing and interpreting experiences to entertain and educate simultaneously (Matwick and Matwick 2019).

When television services began again in Britain after the Second World War, the popularity of television sets in the home increased greatly (Scannell 1996). Prior to the war, television services and transmission were limited primarily to London and considered in retrospect as 'experimental' for the BBC, at that time Britain's only broadcaster (Briggs 1985). Television broadcasts had ceased completely in Britain during the war, with radio broadcasts continuing. Radio was considered a vital communication lifeline for the people of Britain, and television much less so. It was only after the war, perhaps, that television would be considered as something useful for households (for a wider discussion, see Scannell 1996). A useful distraction, a source of entertainment, a place to receive information, and also, crucially, a provider of education to a nation focused on family survival and resilience for a number of years.

Television of the late 1940s and early 1950s is often characterized as radio enhanced by visuals, with the assumption that previously tried and tested programmes, formats, and ideas broadcast via radio were simply transferred to the television studio, recreated, and set loose into the homes of Britain as a somehow secondary form of national broadcast (Lyon and Ross 2016). However, most of these early broadcasts are lost to the world, as many were transmitted live, not recorded, and not considered then to be in any way valuable as artefacts to be preserved in archives (Gorton and Garde-Hansen 2019). Television was mostly, at that time, produced, consumed, and even forgotten. In particular, programmes deemed 'ordinary' in their scope (which often in reality meant lifestyle programmes produced mainly for a daytime female audience watching as they completed their housework) were low on the priorities for being recorded, preserved, and even of being discussed (see Bonner 2003 and Sullivan 2005).

Television itself can be seen as part of everyday lifestyle culture, which has grown and developed since the beginning of television broadcasts in Britain (Sullivan 2005). Britain moved from 'television scarcity' in the 1940s, when television was a cultural novelty, to a period when television symbolized a 'new modernity' in the 1950s (Carnevali and Strange 2007). However, it was not until the 1960s, when television was less of a novelty, that a historical understanding of the place of television in lifestyles could be recognized (Benson 2005). This understanding led to a more established genre of lifestyle programming and channels in the decades that followed, but most prominently from the 1990s onwards.

Due to the archiving policies of television companies (see Baker and Terris 1994), and the assumed lack of interest or significance of 'lifestyle' programmes aimed at women (Bell and Hollows 2005), as well as early television programmes being broadcast live (Briggs 1985), complete programmes from before the 1990s are hard to find. Issues of analyzing television programmes prior to the establishment of clear archiving policies from the major institutions have been the subject of several recent discussions (see Gorton and Garde-Hansen 2019, Lison and others 2019, and Scannell 2010).

Fragments of information from programme listings in the *Radio Times,* reviews in *The Listener,* publicity materials, photographs and interviews published in newspapers, and other resources become invaluable in piecing together what programmes may have been like, beyond the basic descriptions often relied upon.

History itself was a popular subject on television from the very beginning, whether as part of the broadcast or a subject within it (Hilmes 2003). From the earliest broadcasts in 1936 on the BBC, examples of 'history' were shown. The BBC had a remit to inform, educate, and entertain, and their early historical output reflected this with variety (Briggs 1985). History featured in drama, such as *The Mask Theatre* in 1936 (*Radio Times* 1936). Musical programmes with a historical background were broadcast, such as *The Orchestra and Its Instruments* (*Radio Times* 1937a). History featured in comedies focused on important historical events: most notable was the early screening of a version of events from 1066 (*Radio Times* 1939). Documentaries followed subjects such as the fire service and provided a historical background (*Radio Times* 1938). Educational programmes such as *Living History* suggested using models and miniature figures to bring the teaching of history to life (*Radio Times* 1937b).

Food and cooking also were quick to transfer to the 'new' medium of television. Marcel Boulestin is often credited as the 'first' television cook, but others appeared in the early months of 1936 before he made his first appearance in January of 1937 (see Geddes 2022). Following the resumption of television broadcasting in 1946, after a seven-year break during the war (Briggs 1985), cooking programmes also resumed their place in the schedules (*Radio Times* 1946a). Some broadcasts included food and advice linked to information from the British Government Ministry of Food, as food rationing was still in place. Cooking presenters such as Marguerite Patten and Joan Robins, who both had food demonstrator backgrounds with the Ministry, began regular presenting duties on cookery and food programmes (Baker 2021 and Levy 2021b).

These programmes reflected their expected audiences with names such as *Designed for Women* (*Radio Times* 1947b), *For the Housewife* (*Radio Times* 1948), and *Housewife in the Kitchen* (*Radio Times* 1947a). However, the ten-year period after the war included a broad range of cookery programming that covered the BBC remit to inform, educate, and entertain, not simply to encourage housewives to cook more efficiently (see Geddes 2022).

In the next section I will discuss Philip Harben who cooked alongside Marguerite Patten and Joan Robins on the BBC from 1946 and who hosted *An Evening's Diversion*.

Philip Harben

Philip Harben arrived on radio at the BBC, and indeed to cooking itself, partly by accident. A series of coincidences led him to first manage and then cook at the *Isobar* restaurant, in the now iconic *Isokon* building in London (Daybelge and Englund 2019). Untrained, he quickly learnt on the job, and his skills were in demand with the British Overseas Airways Corporation (BOAC) as their canteen manager (Bateman 1966: 8). It was during a propaganda press event, with the BBC in attendance, that Harben was called to demonstrate an omelette made from reconstituted egg, which led to him being asked to appear on radio (Bateman 1966: 9). In 1943 he gave a talk about his experiences as a wartime catering adviser (*Radio Times* 1943a), which led to regular appearances for the next few years with *The Kitchen Front* programme, giving talks aimed at cookery beginners (*Radio Times* 1943b).

Philip Harben began his television broadcasting career with a series entitled *Cookery* for BBC television in June 1946 (BBC Genome 2021). Each week, he guided viewers through a different dish, beginning with Lobster Vol-Au-Vents, homemade noodles, and coffee before progressing to how to use dried eggs, make 'emergency' bread, and bottle fruits for the larder (for example, *Radio Times* 1946b).

In 1945, Harben published his first cookbook, *The Way to Cook*, which he insisted was not a recipe book, but rather a book to explain the ideas and principles of cooking, which he would then go on to exploit on television (Harben 1945). On screen, he was presented as a 'lively, tubby, bearded little man in a butcher's apron, who makes difficult dishes look simple in his brisk, well-planned demonstrations' (Bateman 1966). Despite his appearance, presentation style, and lack of formal training, Harben became a 'personality' (Bateman 1966), who was credited with turning food into a form of theatre (Humble 2005). Harben cultivated his personality through appearances on variety shows before moving from the BBC to join the newly formed Independent Television (ITV) in 1955 (Andrews 2012), where he also established consumer culture connections with products, industry, and advertising, establishing his own range of cookware, Harbenware, which had an annual turnover at the time of £100,000 (Bateman 1966). His television cooking programmes, such as *The Grammar of Cooking* and *The Tools of Cookery*, ran regularly on ITV until 1969 (TV Times Project 2021), with associated cookbooks published alongside (Harben 1965, 1968).

Harben chose to wear a butcher's apron tied high over his 'substantial' stomach on screen, with a grey shirt and paisley-patterned tie (*The Liverpool Echo* 1958). His look created controversy, as it was not 'correct' for a cook nor a chef, coming at a time of change in British society. However, Harben later clarified that it was his 'trademark' and chosen as it was right 'for the camera' (*The Yorkshire Evening Post* 1953). Reviews of his demonstrations on television drew attention to his ability to bring things 'down to brass tacks' while other presenters maintained a 'quite maddening air of lofty superiority' (*The Sketch* 1949). By 1951, though, Harben himself claimed to have given over one hundred and twenty television demonstrations (Harben 1951a), rising to over one hundred and thirty in other publications that year (Harben 1951b), and regularly referred to himself as 'the television cook' while other publications referred to him as 'the television chef' (Harben 1951c), which may have indicated a level of cultural capital attached to the growing ownership and consumption of television.

An Elizabethan Evening

On Tuesday, 7 November 1953 the BBC devoted its entire schedule over the course of one evening to one subject, 'An Evening's Diversion', which transported viewers to an imagined studio in Elizabethan times, as if there had been television at that time (*Radio Times* 1953). That year's Coronation of Elizabeth II brought in a new Elizabethan era that revived interest in Tudor times. Costumed announcers explained that the evening was 'Proffered On The Anniversary Of The Session Of Her Majesty Queen Elizabeth I', setting the scene with the words 'Now we ask you to imagine that in 1596 the Elizabethans had a television service of their own, and join us as we put back the clock', inviting those at home to engage their imaginations to view events and entertainments presented historically and for modern eyes simultaneously. The 'News' became a 'Chronicle of the Times', entertainment was provided in the form of song and dance, documentary-style information was presented on 'new inventions' of the time, and 'concerts' were given, purely for leisure, featuring fashion, shopping, comedy, and song.

Befitting such a historic and Royal occasion, the entire evening was telerecorded. This was unusual at the time, although this of course now means that the programme still exists today in the Alexandra Palace Television Society archive. This thankfully allows us to see directly how the television of the time in the 1950s sought to portray history, and, in this particular early example, food history.

The cookery segment of *An Evening's Diversion* was provided by BBC resident 'television cook' Philip Harben, styled as 'Master Harben' 'the cook' who contrives a Conceit of Coney. The BBC studio set contained one grand kitchen where Harben swapped his usual cooking outfit for something more Elizabethan, and talked the audience through the cookery demonstration, as he imagined it would have been presented in Elizabethan times. The next section considers his broadcast in the context of the first glimpses of food history on television in Britain, and considers what, if anything, this innovation lends to television food history programmes today.

A Conceit of Coney

Suspension of Imagination

The Mistress for the evening (Jeanne Heal, the usual Alexandra Palace continuity announcer who normally appeared on screen, in the studio, to provide live links between programmes) dressed as a courtier – perhaps as an imagined Elizabeth I herself – and introduced Master Harben following the Interlude in the evening. She later reminded the audience that 'rightly is Master Harben known as the Epicure of Cooks', establishing him as an authentic voice for both food and history. Harben invited the audience to suspend belief and imagine they were watching him as an Elizabethan cook, holding a pair of rabbits high in one hand. The scene was set for an instruction in food history, blending the familiar vision of Harben with the unfamiliar setting, dress, and ingredient list.

Setting the Scene

Harben set up his cookery table, in front of a grand brick fireplace within the studio, to resemble the imagined kitchen of a palace or castle where he might have been cooking and broadcasting from had this really been Elizabethan times. Behind him and across the table are an array of cooking equipment, wooden bowls, pewter plates, and apothecary bottles, placed more to conjure up the times than for any historical accuracy or reference. Harben tends to the cooking conies (rabbits) throughout: setting a three-legged iron pot 'upon' the fire, he reassured the audience that 'there it will keep hot and there it will thicken'.

Image 1: Philip Harben presenting his Conceit of Coney on television. With kind permission of the Alexandra Palace Television Society Archive.

Harben is dressed in an Elizabethan ruff and outfit more suited to court than kitchen, with puffed sleeves and a tightly tied apron. Harben traditionally wore a striped butcher's apron while on television, itself an imagined representation of a cook's outfit; however this switch of outfit maintains his style, remaining easily recognizable as the familiar face of cookery on television at the time. Harben looks directly down the camera lens and speaks in his usual clipped, clear, and precise voice. His hands motion towards the audience at home to ensure that they remain engaged with all he had to say. Harben begins by reading out the ingredients for the recipe he would demonstrate, in the same familiar way that he would during normal broadcasts, signifying that this too was a 'normal' cooking programme, albeit set in the imagined world of Elizabeth I.

The cookery segment was broadcast live, as the entire evening was. Harben was skilled at presentations, and worked between two cameras, often directing a camera to focus on details by signalling 'if we look closely here' while completing a task. Harben modulates his language and voice throughout the demonstration, using scripted phrases such as 'bear with me my fair gentles if I seem ware of this work', 'mark you gentles', and 'this pie crust is as frail and insubstantial as a young man's vows' for entertainment value as well as for perceived historical phraseology.

Harben ultimately creates a castle from pastry to encase his conies, now in a stew. Building the castle walls from pre-prepared pastry cut to resemble turreted walls with windows and doors, Harben admits that 'this work is fraught with possibilities of danger'. Although at one point it seems as if 'disaster has overwhelmed' Harben with a breakage, it allows him to reassure the audience that he has spare parts prepared just for this occasion, stating, 'fear not, I have another yet' in place of 'here is one I prepared earlier'.

Harben-isms – Was this Broadcast about History, or about Harben?

Harben cannot, however, resist including a few trademarks of his own style and persona to the demonstration. From the outset he is honest with the audience that this 'conceit of coney' is by his 'own devising', swapping the instruction to 'take four chickens' from the supposedly real original recipe, declaring boldly 'I am using coney' without any given explanation. Harben carved a particular niche on television for cooking using a frying pan (which he later would go on to develop his own range of, known as Harbenware, with other kitchen equipment, for sale) and during this segment instructs his audience to 'put them into the frying pan' and 'place them on a baking sheet' out of character and time, but as Harben would have during an ordinary modern-day broadcast.

Any illusions of historical accuracy are gone when the time comes to beat eggs to add to the dish, as Harben does with an ordinary kitchen fork, folding them into the pot with an ordinary domestic wooden spoon, both common utensils in a modern-day kitchen.

Harben keeps a long, pointed knife tucked into his apron belt. He brings this out performatively to chop parsley with more than exaggeration before slicing a lemon with vigour. Harben pours wine (for the recipe) from a small 'fair round brass pot' which he says his daughter Jenny had bought him as a present when she visited the Isle of Guernsey, more in line with the added commentary he might add to a more normal broadcast than offering anything of historical accuracy, being unlikely that the daughter of an Elizabethan cook would make such a journey.

Philip Harben and Britain's First Television Food History Programme

History or Entertainment – Was Harben Aiming for Authenticity?

Harben lends an air of authenticity to his broadcast by referring to supposedly real-life characters from history, whom viewers may recognize or at least would recognize as sounding probable. The conies which Harben holds aloft at the outside are described as coming from 'My Lord Oxford' for Harben to prepare. Lord Oxford may have been the real-life courtier in the Elizabethan era most prominently linked as a potential alternative author for the works of Shakespeare, although no defining details of him are given during the broadcast. Harben prepares his dish to 'lay before Lord Oxford and those who he may honour' signifying a different role for the food than merely for enjoyment. The Elizabethan meal was as much theatre as Harben's demonstration of it was.

Harben states that he has devised this 'conceit of coney' for Lord Oxford, but also that he has made some changes to the original recipe to include a few things Harben thought 'my Lord Oxford would prefer' – things which are richer and sweeter. Harben holds an old book in his hands, and looks as if to read the recipe from it as he mentions that it has long been a 'favourite in my Master's family' to emphasize to viewers the perception that this recipe – which he refers to as a receipt to signify the language of Elizabethan times – is historic, established and authentic. Harben puts the book down, again emphasizing that he is now in control of the recreation, and tells viewers, 'up until now I have faithfully followed my Master's recipe … from now on this is where my conceit shall start.'

Harben adds several herbs and spices to his dish, many of which evoke historical connotations. By using 'thyme, winter savoury, sweet marjoram, cloves, and mace' and also pepper, bashed to a ground in a pewter mortar, and powdered nutmeg from a large jar, he gives the impression of history to the viewers by underlining the unfamiliar.

At the end of the demonstration, Harben breaks open his pastry castle 'conceit' and tastes a piece of the pastry to show viewers how delicious it was. This felt more like a 'normal' end to a Harben cookery programme than the way in which an Elizabethan cook would act.

Conclusion

In this paper I have discussed interpretations of food history, and although these undoubtedly took place prior to the arrival of television in Britain, I have shown that their own history stretches back much further into television history than those of recent memory. Philip Harben presented the first television historical interpretation of food and cookery in 1953 as part of a wider celebration of the Coronation of Queen Elizabeth II, itself an important and historic occasion. Harben's imagined culinary tourism to Elizabethan times was part fantasy, part entertainment, part self-promotion, and part inspiration, perhaps encouraging audiences to gain a mere flavour of the past enabling them to explore more.

Like most innovations, there was no blueprint or example to follow; instead Harben's broadcast shares many familiar aspects of television food history today, elements which we would expect to see if we watched *The Supersizers*, Annie Gray and Lucy Worsley, or the *Back in Time For…* programmes. He set his performance in a credible location, indicating 'history'. His usual studio and performance setting was replaced with artefacts and items which again suggested 'history'. Harben's costume was instantly recognizable as Elizabethan, albeit in more of a fancy-dress way than as an authentic cook's outfit of the time. He performed using dialogue and phrases which conjured up images of the past while still connecting himself to, and not alienating himself from, his present-day audiences. Harben referenced books, recipes, and people from history to give his performance some legitimacy and authenticity.

Ultimately, Harben's performance and demonstration would be unlikely to stand up to close scrutiny and standards by historians who may be part of, or acting as consultants on, the programmes we consume today, nor would his broadcast fool 'serious' historians watching for a documentary type of food archaeology. The programme was intended to inform, educate, and entertain as per the founding principles of the BBC. It succeeded in firing the imagination of audiences at the time and of subsequent writers, presenters, and consumers of food history on television, who have more to thank Philip Harben for than they realize.

References

Alexandra Palace Television Society (APTS). 2021. *An Evening's Diversion,* from 17th November 1953.
Andrews, Maggie. 2012. *Domesticating the Airwaves* (London: Continuum).
Baker, Anne Pimlotte. 2021. 'Robins [*neé* Godfrey], Joan Rafferty', in *Oxford Dictionary of National Biography* (*ODNB*) <https://doi.org/10.1093/ref:odnb/55647>
Baker, Simon, and Olwen Terris (eds.). 1994. *A for Andromeda to Zoo Time – Television Holdings of the National Film and Television Archive, 1936-1979* (London: BFI).
Bateman, Michael. 1966. *Cooking People* (London: Leslie Frewin).
BBC Genome. 2021. <https://genome.ch.bbc.co.uk/> [accessed 15 May 2021]
Bell, David, and Joanne Hollows. 2005. *Ordinary Lifestyles* (London: Open University Press).
Benson, John. 2005. *Affluence and Authority: A Social History of 20th Century Britain* (London: Hodder Education).
Bonner, Frances. 2003. *Ordinary Television* (London: Sage).
Briggs, Asa. 1985. *The BBC: The First Fifty Years* (Oxford: Oxford University Press).
Carnevali, Francesca, and Julie-Marie Strange (eds). 2007. *20th Century Britain: Economic, Cultural and Social Change* (Harlow: Pearson Education Limited).
Daybelge, Leyla, and Magnus Englund. 2019. *Isokon and the Bauhaus in Britain* (London: Batsford).
Debord, Guy. 1994. *The Society of the Spectacle* (New York: Zone).
Geddes, Kevin. 2022. '"The Man in the Kitchen": Boulestin and Harben – Representation, Gender, Celebrity and Business in the Early Development of Television Cooking Programmes in Britain', in *Food and Cooking on Early European Television*, ed. by Ana Tominc (London: Routledge).
Gorton, Krysten, and Joanne Garde-Hansen. 2019. *Remembering British Television – Audience, Archive and Industry* (London: Bloomsbury).
Gray, Annie. 2010. '"The greatest ordeal": Using Biography to Explore the Victorian Dinner', *Post-Medieval Archaeology,* 44.2 (2010), 255-72.
Harben, Philip. 1945. *The Way to Cook* (London: John Lane The Bodley Head).
——. 1951a. *The Pocket Book of Modern Cooking* (London: News of The World).

——. 1951b. *Television Cooking Book* (London: Odhams Press).
——. 1951c. *Entertaining at Home* (London: John Lane The Bodley Head).
——. 1965. *The Grammar of Cooking* (London: Penguin).
——. 1968. *The Tools of Cookery* (London: Hodder and Stoughton).
Harbenware. 1958. *The Harbenware Range of Non-Stick Pans* [catalogue].
Hilmes, Michele. 2003. *The Television History Book* (London: BFI).
Humble, Nicola. 2005. *Culinary Pleasures: Cookbooks and the Transformation of British Food* (London: Faber and Faber).
Levy, Paul. 2021a. 'Harben, Philip Hubert Kendal Jerrold', in *ODNB* <https://doi.org/10.1093/ref:odnb/60050>
——. 2021b. 'Pattern [neé Brown, (Hilda Elise) Margaret' in *ODNB* <https://doi.org/10.1093/odnb/9780198614128.013.110493>
Lison, Andrew, and others. (2019). *Archives: In Search of Media* (Minnesota: University of Minnesota).
Long, Lucy. 2004. *Culinary Tourism: A Folkloristic Perspective on Eating and Otherness* (Kentucky: University of Kentucky Press).
Lyon, Phil, and Liz Ross. 2016. 'Broadcasting Cookery: BBC Radio Programmes in the 1920 and 1930s', *International Journal of Consumer Studies*, 40.3: 327-35.
Matwick Kelsi, and Keri Matwick. 2019. *Food Discourse of Celebrity Chefs of Food Network* (London: Palgrave Macmillan).
Radio Times. 1936. 'The Mask Theatre', 685 (15-21 November): 94.
——. 1937a. 'The Orchestra and Its Instruments', 692 (3-9 January): 62.
——. 1937b. 'Living History – The Use of Models in The Teaching of History', 705 (4-10 April): 46.
——. 1938. 'Fire-Fighting', 778 (28 August-3 September): 38.
——. 1939. '1066 and All That', 800 (29 January-4 February): 17.
——. 1943a. 'The New Cooking Comes to the Canteen', 1043 (26 September-2 October): 6.
——. 1943b. 'The Kitchen Front', 1048 (31 October-6 November): 10.
——. 1946a. 'Cookery – How to Make Lobster Vol au Vent', 1184 (9-15 June): 26.
——. 1946b. 'Cookery – How to Bottle Fruit and Make Jam', 1196 (1-7 September): 26.
——. 1947a. 'Housewife in the Kitchen', 1249 (21-27 September): 35.
——. 1947b. 'Designed for Women', 1255 (2-8 November): 32.
——. 1948. 'For the Housewife – Rabbits', 1273 (7-13 March): 26.
——. 1953. 'An Evening's Diversion – Proffered on the Anniversary of the Session of Her Majesty Queen Elizabeth I', 1566 (15-21 November): 26-27.
Scannell, Paddy. 1996. *Radio, Television and Modern Life* (Oxford: Blackwell).
Scannell, Paddy. 2010. 'Television and History – Questioning the Archive', *The Communication Review*, 13.1: 37-51.
Sullivan, Tim. 2005. 'From Television Lifestyle to Lifestyle Television', in *Ordinary Lifestyles: Popular Media Consumption and Taste*, ed. by D. Bell and J. Hollows (Maidenhead: Open University Press), pp. 21-34.
The Liverpool Echo. 1958. 'Better Cooks Than French: Mr Harben Praises Our Housewives', 19 March: 7.
The Sketch. 1949. 'A Disappointing Fortnight', 22 June: 440.
The Yorkshire Evening Post. 1953. 'I Never Said I Was a Chef – TV Harben', 7 December: 8.
TV Times Project. 2021. TVTiP <http://bufvc.ac.uk/tvandradio/tvtip/> [accessed 1 May 2021]

Feast for the Soul: Food Imaginaries in a South Indian Performance

Sudha Gopalakrishnan

I am going to tell a story about a glutton.

But first I have to provide the context of the glutton's story. A fantasia – an imagined universe – on food and eating comes alive in an oral performance called *Ashanam* (Sanskrit: food; literally, 'eating') from Kerala in South India.[1] A *tour de force* on the delights of food, *Ashanam* is a gourmet's journey from the perspective of a glutton who holds forth on the virtues of a vegetarian feast, properly served and relished. The next best thing to savouring good food is dreaming about good food, they say. Using the context of a grand feast on the first anniversary of the death of the ruler of the land, *Ashanam* is an oral performance celebrating time-honoured traditions around creating and serving foods. It considers the appropriate occasions for eating, invokes a full regalia of dishes including the names of vegetables and a typology of how they are procured and prepared, explores the conventional methods of serving a feast, classifies people according to their tastes, and defines the characteristics of a good gastronome.

From all historical records, it seems plausible that the performance of *Ashanam* and its larger repertoire called *Purushartha Kuttu* may have originated around the fifteenth or sixteenth centuries. It is possible that it may have evolved into its present form over centuries, and it remains popular with audiences among the Malayalam-speaking people of Kerala. *Purushartha Kuttu* performance is itself part of the Sanskrit theatre of *Kutiyattam*, with a long history of stage performance and an elaborate mode of acting that takes several days to complete a story. *Purushartha Kuttu* is a segment of a ninth-century Sanskrit play called *Subhdradhananjaya* that tells the story of two lovers, Subhadra and Dhananjaya. A delightful digression from this main story involves a comic character, called by the generic name of *Vidushaka* (clown), who holds the stage singlehandedly for four days. The *Vidushaka*, a philosopher-fool and friend of the play's hero, speaks in the vernacular Malayalam language and entertains the audience with seemingly silly, farcical dialogue. While the theatrical grammar of the codified art of *Kutiyattam* remains less accessible to most people, the speech and actions of the *Vidushaka* are directed towards more popular tastes.

Purushatha Kuttu is a subversion of the concept of the four '*purusharthas*' ('goals of life'), one of the basic theories of classical Indian philosophy. The accepted codes of ethical living are classified as fourfold: *dharma* (doing righteous action), *artha*, (acquiring material wealth), *kama* (indulging in sensual pleasures), and *moksha* (attaining spiritual liberation). The five-day monologue *Purushratha Kuttu* twists the moral rigour of the concept of the *purusharthas* through an irreverent, deliberate inversion of these ideas in a parodic format.

In *Purushartha Kuttu*, the *Vidushaka*, is depicted as belonging to a high-class Brahmin community, though he has fallen onto hard times and now lives a life of penury. Over the years, members of his community have lived impoverished and decadent for so long that they have become totally anarchic: with a collapse of morals, they argue endlessly between themselves and fight over silly matters. The *Vidushaka* initially tries to mediate and settle disputes in his community, but he finally sees that there is no alternative than for him to take refuge with the king, serving as a courtier and as his friend-in-mischief. Driven by self-interest and a powerful survival instinct, he identifies an alternate set of four life goals of his own: *vinoda* (seeking sensual pleasures), *vanchana* (swindling/cheating others), *asana* (enjoying a good feast), and *rajaseva* (serving under a king for a carefree life). The re-articulated tinkering of dharmic injunctions, while apparently light-hearted, silly, and mostly lovable, underpin symbolic meanings barely openly expressible in a world whose values seem farcical.

Ashanam, a one-day segment of this five-day performance sequence of *Purushartha Kuttu,* is about how a glutton imagines and enjoys good food. It opens up an accumulated and preserved body of culinary knowledge which perhaps might have otherwise disappeared from cultural memory. In *Ashanam*, the *Vidushaka* narrates stories and episodes from the lives of gods and humans that all deal with food and eating. Within the broad framework of the narrative, the performer has the challenging task of improvising and elaborating on the story by citing verses and anecdotes, creating a rich world of imagination consistent with the times in which the play was choreographed, but also adapting it to suit the taste of his contemporary audience. The monologue is in a conversational and argumentative mode, as though two people are talking to each other, which offers the chance to give multiple points of view through exaggerated commentaries, nonsensical speech, parodies, and illustrative sub-stories. The pleasure of knowing the inquisitorial role of the *Vidushaka* and the flair of his narration in the familiar setting of the *koottu* stage has made him a favourite with audiences down the centuries. Using a language that intersperses the elite Sanskrit and the local Malayalam, he moves forward and backward in time, connecting the contemporary setting to epical space. He interprets complex ideas in an entertaining manner blended with humour, satire, and mockery, making them accessible to all people.

The whole performance is about food, in this case a grand feast held by a prominent Brahmin family on the occasion of the first anniversary of death of the head of the family. The *Vidushaka* lusts after the fabulous vegetarian feast about to be served. He is a connoisseur of good food and has an insatiable appetite. However, the *Ashanam* discourse is not merely about what happens during the feast; it is about more than gourmet fantasies of good food. It is an encyclopaedia of culinary information, abundant illustrative examples of food items are framed or packaged in the parodic mode. The *Vidushaka* elaborates various incidents and stories that deal with food and eating.

The performance tells about the joys of eating seen through a glutton's eyes. To the *Vidushaka*, it is about delicious food in multiple courses, served in prodigious quantities – filling up to the throat, choking the nose, and cramming till it reaches the head! The *Vidushaka* warns at the outset that it is not easy to understand food: one needs to know many things, such as the different occasions for a feast, the different types and characteristics of hosts, the varieties of foods, the manners of serving, and the correct amounts to be served. Comparisons are brought out between rice – the supreme food – and a king, the supreme ruler. Just as a king is accompanied by his ministers, feudatories, and other aides, rice has its accompanying dishes which are served in the right order of their importance. In another comparison, a well-prepared meal is like a beautiful woman: for just as it is difficult to keep away from a lovely woman, it is difficult to abstain from good food.

It is not easy to define what constitutes good food, because of variables in context, perspective, and taste. For example, food served by one's mother, even if it is made with the humblest ingredients, tastes delicious. A simple meal in one's own kitchen can be extremely fulfilling, but there are also grand social occasions like birthdays, death anniversaries, and weddings when elaborate feasts are served, in which all the skill of the cooks is reflected in the quality and taste of the meal. However, according to the *Vidushaka*, these cannot qualify as '*ashanam*'. Throughout his performance, the *Vidushaka* considers the defining characteristics of *ashanam*.

The Best Occasion for a Feast
A birthday? A grand wedding, perhaps? The *Vidushaka* disagrees. The best social event for a feast, he says, is the celebration of the anniversary of the death of the head of a family.

On such an occasion, all the people of the Anadhitimangalam village set out for the house where the feast is being held. There is great excitement in the air. Once the group reaches the venue, they are a bit dismayed by the large crowds, but are reassured when they tour the storehouse and granary inside the house, where they see ample food is being prepared. (In case it bears remembering: the *Vidushaka* acts this entire tableau himself.) Many verses are devoted to describing each element of the feast: large mounds of rice, huge piles of vegetables, enormous pots of oil, heaps of fruits, towers of coconuts, and massive cooking vessels. With the depiction of each item in graphic, elaborate terms, the crowd's craving for food increases. There are charged accounts of how the food is served. When the distribution of the food starts from the first row, the anticipation grows, and the *Vidushaka*, picturing himself in the story, almost swoons in excitement by the time the food reaches him.

The Ideal Place and Ingredients for a Feast
A place for preparing a grand feast has to be chosen according to the importance given

to the occasion by the family members. In an ideal situation, a temporary yet spacious kitchen would be constructed, with different areas marked out for the preparation of different dishes and storerooms for grains, pots of oil and clarified butter, lentils, plantains, yam, coconuts, eggplants, long beans, cucumbers, mangos, jackfruit, yoghurt, milk, and sugar. There are pickles (*upplilittatu*), chips (*upperi*), side dishes and pastes (*puliyinchi, madhurakkari*) and soups (*rasam*) described with great relish, and in minute detail. Many descriptions are supplemented with evocative verses in Malayalam.

Rice, Sustainer and Nourisher of the World, Is Like a King

Just like a king is loved by all and has an honoured position among his people, rice is undeniably the king of foods. Just as a king's arrival is accompanied by drumbeats, when rice arrives on the scene during a feast, the announcement comes first, when tinkling vessels cause a pleasurable sensation all around. Comparable to a king's retinue, rice is accompanied by main dishes and side dishes. It is not possible to imagine a situation without a king, just as it is impossible to think of a world without rice. Just think of a situation when someone consumes all accompanying dishes – different types of curries – without the overall predominance of rice. Everything gets jumbled up in the system, exactly like how a country becomes anarchical without a ruler.

A Feast Is Like a Beautiful, Well-Adorned Woman

Now the imagination of the *Vidushaka* goes wilder. He speaks passionately about the aesthetic aspects of food, and this fervour leads to his second major statement. It is not a mere assertion, but is established with every detail, with minute comparisons brought out to acknowledge the virtues of each and every food item. For example, the *Vidushaka* asks, when fresh white butter melts slowly over a mound of steaming rice, if you keep gazing at it, you can detect a glow, like the soft smile of a lovely woman, can't you? Now come closer, he asks: softly fried eggplant, shining, luscious like her lips, yes? The fantastical comparison builds and builds, becoming absurd by the minute as the *Vidushaka* catalogues minute comparisons between aspects of food and the details of a woman's body.

The Varieties of Hosts

The *Vidushaka* then turns to the next point: who serves food, and how? Not everyone who invites you for a feast is a good host, so he proceeds to analyze the characteristics of an ideal host.

Don't ever go for a meal at invitation of the first category, the gracious-churlish host, who appears to be gracious but in effect not welcoming or offering food. If you are really in need, perhaps you could go to the home of the second type, the churlish-gracious host, who appears inhospitable but in the end gives a good meal. The third type must be refused: the churlish-churlish host, needless to say. Of course, visiting the house of the fourth type, the gracious-gracious host, is always a delightful experience. To support his taxonomy, the *Vidushaka* reels off anecdotes about the experiences of visiting the houses of each of these four kinds of hosts. For example, the gracious-gracious host tells his guest:

> Great, come, come in. I'm delighted you are here with us today. You look a bit tired, please rest for a while… Here's some water, please wash your face. You came at the right time. The meal is just about ready. Do you need to take a bath and freshen up before that?

These words are heard so often at his home that even his child and his caged parrot can repeat them!

The Grand Feast

Now we come, finally, to the feast itself. Many people are gathered to enjoy the great meal, and large quantities of food are prepared to their satisfaction. The *Vidushaka* chooses a comfortable place, away from distractions, and waits expectantly. A plantain leaf, which serves as a plate, is placed in front of him, and the servers swing to action. Rice is already served in the tenth row. His feverish anticipation grows as he observes the slow progression from row to row until, at last, it's on his plantain plate! It is a mountainous quantity, but who is complaining?

Let us see what happens next:

> The food is ideally served on a neat plantain leaf which has not been dirtied by crows. In the subsequent narration, the Vidūṣaka describes the turmoil of the feast from the point of view of a Brahmin guest called Mūssad. In his eagerness, Mūssad is described as demanding that leaves should be placed on all sides around him. The leaf is to be sprinkled with water and washed. Thereupon, clarified butter is to be served, followed by plantain fruits and jaggery. The Vidūṣaka portrays the nearly delirious ecstasy of the Brahmin guest when the rice is being served. He almost passes out from excitement, much to the amusement of the onlookers. The warm rice served is white like the flower of the medicinal plant called *tumba* (*Leuca indica*.) The gentleman demands clarified butter to be poured like a female elephant urinating (*hastinīmūtrapāta*), followed by a handsome serving of lentils. Next arrive all kinds of chips roasted in ghee, made of banana, jackfruit, elephant yam, tuber, and catmint. The next items are sautéed vegetables consisting of bitter gourd, drumstick leaves, *Cassia tora*, aubergines, bitter aubergines, plantain, and tender jackfruit.[2]

The *Vidushaka* praises the dishes one by one. He speaks directly to the bitter gourd:

> *Young babies of bitter gourd clusters, birthed by creeper mothers!*
> *Spattered with green along the fields as an embellishment to the hedge*
> *Wafting and billowing in the breeze, like blessed gifts*
> *crushing the arrogance of nectar – please come, come to my hands now*

He pays homage to a mixed vegetable curry called *olan*:

Pumpkin, cucumber and eggplant
combining with fresh string beans –
Ah, if lovely blue-eyed women served them
Olan, olan is enough – why look for a hundred other things?

He loves *ataprathaman*, a steamed, thick rice paste flake cooked in a sweet gravy of milk, jaggery, coconut milk, and spiced with cumin and dried ginger. He worships *pāyasam*, Kerala's much beloved dessert:

When superb sugar mingles exquisitely
with purest milk, payasam is born.
When heavenly nectar sought a contest
payasam was judged superior
and nectar fled in shame.

By the end of the feast, our gluttonous brahmin is so full to the brim that he can barely rise and stand straight. When the grand feast concludes, he is so pleased that he blesses – or, rather, curses – the eldest member of the family to 'conduct another such event in the house exactly twelve months from now'.

Conclusion

Sophisticated, witty, and powerful, *Ashanam* is an invaluable resource of information on food and food culture, handed down from the semi-urban Brahmin community of Kerala presumably of the fifteenth and sixteenth centuries. While there is a pronounced Kerala-Malayali flavour to the narration and performance, *Ashanam* offers both philosophical insights and a set of practical recommendations to the world at large, on how to eat, live, and survive in a harsh world where deceit and self-interest reign supreme. Delightfully, these complex ideas are articulated in *Ashanam* in the most light-hearted, silly, and lovable manner.

Notes

1. My essay is drawn mainly from seeing *Ashanam* performed several times in Kerala. A transcript of one oral performance was compiled by V.R. Krishnachandran in Malayalam (*Purusharthakkkotthu* (Trichur: Kerala Sahitya Akeademy, 1978, rpt. 1994).
2. C. Rajendran, 'From Fast to Feast: The Aśana Discourse of the Vidūṣaka in Kerala's Traditional Sanskrit Theatre', in *A World of Nourishment: Reflections on Food in Indian Culture*, ed. by Cinzia Pieruccini and Paola M. Rossi (Milan: Ledizioni, 2016), pp.111-120 (p. 116).

Sicilian Cheese: A Firm Foundation for Fantasy in the Old Comedy of Ancient Athens

Christopher Grocock

In two passages from his fifth-century BC comedies, *Peace* and *Wasps,* Aristophanes makes rapid references to Sicilian cheese. In *Peace*, these remarks are central to part of the comic (and geopolitical) points he is making, but the scene in *Wasps* is a throwaway, incidental almost, and yet it is there. Aristophanes wrote comedies, but, as every comic playwright knows, comedy is a serious business; more so for Aristophanes, since his aim was not just to make an audience laugh, but to make them laugh more at his work than at that of his rivals in a drama competition. He wanted to win, and every word had to count. So why mention 'Sicilian' cheese? Was there something intrinsically funny about that for an ancient Athenian audience? It made me wonder.

I also wondered what sort of cheese he and his audience might have had in mind. Wild flights of imagination were a bedrock of ancient Athenian comedy, seen in both the plays of Aristophanes and numerous fragments of others (principally in the second-century CE writer Athenaeus). Several scenes in the surviving plays use foodstuffs and foodways to make comic points, especially in Aristophanes's *Knights, Wasps,* and *Peace.* These passages have often been discussed from a literary viewpoint, emphasizing the symbolism of the foodstuffs and envisaging a mainly imaginary context for the scenes. Could it be equally likely that real foodstuffs might have lain behind these scenes, as the basis for the fantastical in the imagination of the authors? This paper therefore seeks to 'start from the other end', as it were, looking at the basic processes of initial production of the types of food referred to and the distribution routes suggested for some of the specific items mentioned in the plays (cheese being the most obvious). Geophysical contexts of fifth-century Athens such as terrain and available transport links are balanced against political context(s) in which fifth-century BC Athens found itself during its protracted war with Sparta from 431 BC onwards. In short, how likely was it that one of the core ingredients in two typical comic scenes – the Sicilian cheese – was a real product, actually transported to fifth-century Athens in sufficient quantities for it to be a comic staple? Unlike purely theoretical literary approaches, this requires combining an examination of ancient texts and archaeology with current farming practice to establish what kinds of cheese might have been referred to in the ancient application of invention to everyday realities.

Let us turn to the two scenes. First, *Wasps*, produced in 422 BC.[1] This scene is

Sicilian Cheese: A Firm Foundation for Fantasy

ridiculous and fantastical enough without the cheese course: to satisfy his lust for passing stiff sentences in the lawcourts (an obsession of which his son Bdelykleon wishes to cure him), the old man Philokleon is presiding at home over the trial of his dog Labes (Snatcher), accused of theft by another dog:

Philokleon	Who's the accused?
Bdelykeon	This fellow.
Philokleon	What a big fine he'll get!
Bdelykleon	Now hear the charge: it is alleged by Dog, of Cydathenaea, that Labes of Aexone feloniously consumed the cheese all by himself, the Sicilian cheese: penalty, a collar of sycophant – sorry, sycamore-wood.
Philokleon	No, death – a dog's death! once he's convicted.
Bdelykleon	And here is this 'Snatcher', the accused.
Philokleon	What a filthy brute! Doesn't he just look like a thief! So he thinks he'll bamboozle me, grinning like that. But where's his accuser, Dog of Cydathenaea?
Dog	Woof! woof!
Bdelykleon	Here he is.
Xanthias	This one's another 'Snatcher', Only good for barking and licking the dishes clean!
Bdelykleon	Sit down, be quiet. You, come up here and start prosecuting.
Philokleon	Right then, and while he does, I'll pour some soup out and slurp it down.
Dog	You have heard for yourselves the charge which I have brought, Gentlemen of the jury, against the defendant. For he has done The direst deeds both again and against every man jack of you. He sneaked off into a corner and – well, he ensicilized Loads of cheese and woofed it down in the dark.
Philokleon	By Zeus, it's clear he did! He's just now belched cheese most evilly at me, the loathsome creature!
Dog	And he didn't give me any when I asked for some. Think about it – who'll be able to do you a good turn, Is somebody doesn't throw a bit to me, your watchdog?

And later, 'Dog' adds this further accusation:

Dog	And don't find him innocent – why, of all the dogs he's by far the most eat-it-by-yourselfing man there is, he's sailed right round the mortar in a circle and gnawed the hard rind off the city-states.[2]

There is an element of total fantasy here – as so often in Aristophanes – as one dog prosecutes another in a makeshift Athenian-model courtroom scene set in a humble domestic setting; later, witnesses called include a dish, a pestle, a cheese grater, a brazier, a cooking-pot, and other half-burnt kitchen equipment. Moreover, the scene is a political satire on two leading politicians of the day: the Greek word for 'Dog', *kuōn*, recalls Aristophanes's principal target, the demagogue Kleon, who styled himself as 'the people's guard-dog'; *Labēs*, or 'Snatcher', sounds like another politician, Laches. The cheese represents their ill-gotten gains – and one of 'Dog's' main accusations is that 'Snatcher' wouldn't share it when asked!

But what about the cheese? Is this equally part of the fantasy? It is defined as Sicilian – the adjective is placed at the start of a line in an emphatic position, and comes at the end of the charge, which might more literally be rendered 'cheese – alone – he ate up/ – the Sicilian stuff'. Later, 'Snatcher' is accused of 'ensicilizing' it. And finally, in a glorious confusion of realities and fantasy, he 'went round gnawing the hard rind off all the city-states'. So hard cheeses, which have developed a solid crust, are implied: the Greek *to skiron* is 'the hard part', which Sommerstein translates as 'rind', while Barrett interprets it as 'plaster' and claims in a note (oddly, I think) that 'cheeses were encased in plaster to keep them fresh'.[3] We are dealing with a mature, hard cheese; the presence as a witness in a later scene of a 'cheese grater' or *turoknēstis* also implies than the cheese was hard enough to be grated (Figures 1 and 2). The situation Aristophanes creates is utterly fantastical, but one of his building blocks seems to be a product familiar to his audience – a hard cheese with a rind, from Sicily. The cheese need not be regarded as fantasy at all: it is used to implant in the audience's mind the idea that the greedy politicians had helped themselves to some of the cities' precious revenues. The idea that 'he's sailed right round the mortar in a circle and gnawed the hard rind off the city-states' is a glorious conflation of concepts which leaves the mind reeling, though one can easily imagine a

Figure 1 (left). Cheese grater in the form of a goat; Asia Minor, 5th-6th century BC. Figure 2 (right). Etruscan cheese grater with wooden lion's head; 5th century BC. Drawings by Dan Shadrake.

Sicilian Cheese: A Firm Foundation for Fantasy

dog nibbling off the accessible parts of a cheese within reach (our old dog Winston once did exactly this to a very large piece of pecorino).

The second scene from Aristophanes comes from *Peace*. In this satire, produced in 421 BC on the eve of a peace treaty being signed between Athens and Sparta, the deity War is watched by the hero Trygaeos as they demonstrate their powers of destruction by putting ingredients, which sound like or remind the audience of different ancient Greek states, into a giant mortar, ready to be pounded together to make a *muttōtós*, a paste often served with fish (Figure 3):

War:	Alas for you mortals, mortals, mortals, much-suffering ones.
	How much your jaws will ache, and soon!
Trygaeos:	O Lord Apollo, look at how wide that mortar is!
	What an evil thing it is, and look how War is scowling!
	Is this the one we try to flee from,
	The terrible one, the shield-bearer, the one who makes us shit ourselves?
War:	Alas Prasiae, city of leeks, three times wretched, yes, and five times,
	and ten times, how you'll be smashed up today!
Trygaeos:	At least, gentlemen, this doesn't affect us yet:
	For this trouble is Sparta's.
War:	Alas Megara, Megara, how you will be mashed up at once,
	Thoroughly beaten into a paste (*muttōtós*).
Trygaeos:	Oh no Oh noooo, what great and odiferous wailings
	He's thrown in for the people of Megara!
War:	Alas for Sicily, how you are ruined too!
Trygaeus:	What a wretched community will be grated up!
War:	Come on, let me pour on some Attic honey as well.
Trygaeus:	Hey you, I suggest you use some other honey.
	That's the four-obol kind; go easy with the Attic stuff![4]

The mention in lines 250 and 251 to Sicily being dragged into the pan-Hellenic conflict uses the verb *diaknaisthēsetai*, meaning 'will be grated up'. Elsewhere, Aristophanes uses it to refer to a bad actor ruining a play, but its root *diaknaiō* means 'to grate' or scrape away', and a *knēstis* was a grater, which (in its compounded form *turoknēstin*, 'cheese-grater') we saw as a witness in the courtroom scene in *Wasps*. The reference to Sicilian cheese must have been an easy mental leap for the audience to make. War was pounding the four Hellenic areas mentioned like leeks, garlic, cheese, and honey: behind the pantomime-like scene lay a contemporary political reality, since all these areas had been badly affected by the war between Athens (and its allies) and Sparta (and its allies), and the suffering was real. The association of Sicily and a hard, grateable cheese is once again plain to see. The fantasy is built on familiar household objects, of which this cheese is one.

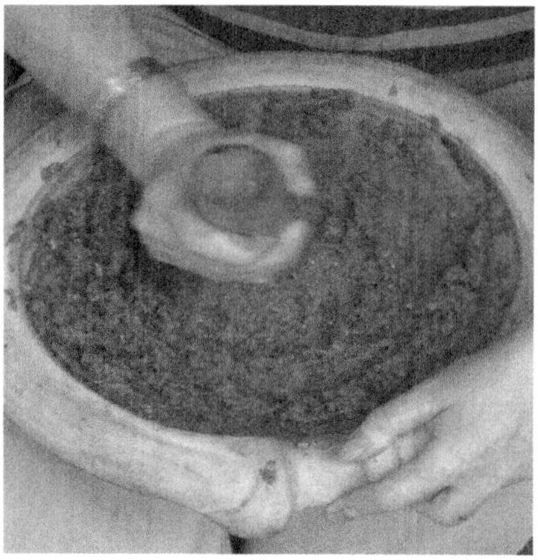

Dairy produce, and cheese in particular, was an essential part of ancient foodways, and the fact that the raw material – milk – can be turned into a nourishing, valuable, lasting, and transportable product was not lost on either Greeks or Romans; recent finds show that it was valued in Asia Minor and Egypt as well.[5] Its appeal, arising from its manufacture, of 'aroma, bacteria and serendipity', is discussed by Sarah Freeman and Silvija Davidson in their helpful explanations of the complex factors involved.[6] Its dietetic benefits and dangers were well appreciated by the Hippocratic writers: the treatise *On Ancient Medicine* assures us that 'cheese does not harm all people who can eat as much of it without the slightest adverse effects [...] but others suffer dreadfully'.[7]

Figure 3. Muttōtós *being pounded in a mortar. Photograph by Sally Grainger.*

Sicily, 'land of plenty to archaic Greeks and Carthaginians' as Andrew Dalby so neatly puts it, was a source not only of luxury foodstuffs but also of ideas, in the shape of both cooks and cookbooks, by the fifth century BC, and Sicilian luxuries made the term '"Sicilian tables" a synonym for gastronomic pleasures'.[8] Its terrain was more extensive and more fertile than those found in Greece; recall the limited availability of level ground for farming in Greece (though sheep were grazed in mountain ranges) and the difficulties of transport, except by sea (Figures 4 and 5).

The potential of such luxuries may even have stimulated ancient Greek (and especially Athenian) expansion in the area. Sicily was certainly an attractive target for Athens, as Thucydides' account of the Sicilian expedition recorded in Books 6 and 7 of his *Histories* makes plain: Athens had several allies on the island, but were also (by 415 BC at least) opposed by Syracuse. Other ancient references to Sicily as a source of luxury provender comes from the comic poet Hermippus, who indicates the extent and volume of commerce across the Greek world in this period: 'Tell me now, Muses whose dwellings are on Olympus, how many good things Dionysus has brought here to men in his black ship since he plied

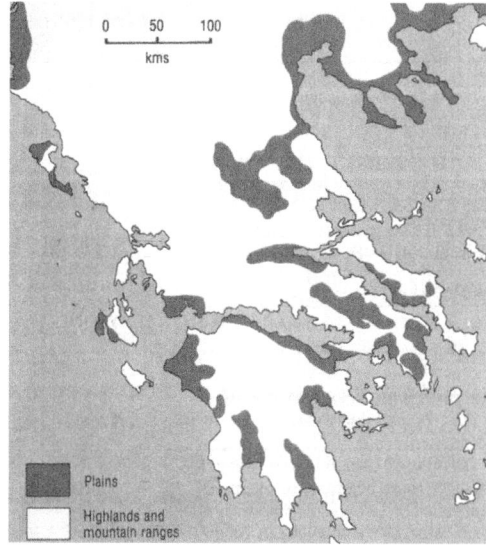

Figure 4. Land use potential in mainland Greece. Drawing adapted by C. Grocock.

the wine-dark sea: [...] the Syracusans send us pigs and cheese; and the Corcyreans, may Poseidon damn them in their slick ships, for they have shifty thoughts [...].'[9]

'On the basis of this and other sources of the sixth and fifth centuries' comments Andrew Dalby, 'one may distinguish some true local contributions to the developing gastronomy of the Aegean coast and the wider Greek world.'[10] He goes on to confirm, as we have already suggested in this paper, that:

> Sicilian cheese was quite a commonplace of Athenian comedy. It crops up often enough to show that its reputation is more than a literary reminiscence of the Cyclops episode of the *Odyssey*, which later readers universally pictured as taking place in Sicily. The Cyclops was certainly said to make goats' milk and ewes' milk cheese (*Od.* 9. 218-33), as Athenian comedies and satyr plays often recalled.[11]

Antiphanes 233 [*Epitome* 27d] lists 'a cook from Elis, a jug from Argos, Phliasian wine, bedspreads from Corinth, fish of Sicyon, flute girls of Aegium, Sicilian cheese, perfume from Athens, Boeotian eels' in a combination that Dalby suggests may be 'a satirical feast for some temporary political alliance'.[12] From the fourth century, we have confirmation from Aristotle (*History of Animals*, 522a22) that '[g]oat's milk is mixed with sheep's milk in Sicily, and wherever sheep's milk is abundant'.[13]

There is no detail in the Greek sources about how cheese was manufactured, but later Roman ones provide us with helpful information on ancient storage, and production techniques, if not methods of using the cheese, were probably little changed since Aristophanes's day. Cato provides us with a recipe for *placenta* involving fourteen pounds of sheep's cheese, but this is clearly fresh – he says it must be *ne acidum et bene recens*, 'not

Figure 5. Terrain and land-use in Sicily. Drawing by Dan Shadrake.

sharp and nicely fresh' – and there is a similar reference to 'freshly-set salty cheese' in a first-century BC poem by Philodemus.[14] Such cheese might not have been suitable for long-distance trade. Varro tells us that the period for making cheese extends 'from the rising of the Pleiades in spring until the Pleiades in summer', which the Loeb editors interpret as from 10 May to mid-July (*De Agricultura* ii. 11. 4). Columella lists several 'things which ought to be collected and stored during the summer about the time of the harvest or even when it is over', of which cheese, *usibus domesticis*, 'for use in the home', is the last, on the grounds that in this season the cheese produces very little whey (xii.10–13).[15]

Columella's exposition of cheesemaking in Book vii section 8 is by far the most extensive: the quality of the milk and methods of curdling are set out in great detail, and he notes the practice of the *rustici* to press the fresh cheeses with weights to squeeze the whey out. Once removed from its basket, the cheese is put in a shaded storeroom and sprinkled with salt. Then it is pressed a second time with weights for nine days, before being washed in fresh water and stored in wickerwork trays to dry out under controlled conditions. At vii. 8. 6, he says *hoc genus casei potest etiam trans maria permitti*, 'this type of cheese can even be exported overseas'. This description seems to fit most closely with the kind of cheese Aristophanes was suggesting, though it is worth noting that Columella's detailed account of cheese-making comes straight after his discussion on keeping goats, not sheep, and goats are clearly indicated in the discussion about fresh cheeses in the same chapter, immediately following the comments about cheese for export.

Pliny the Elder, a contemporary of Columella, lists all the cheeses which he knew or had heard came to Rome in his *Historia Naturalis*: the most highly-praised came from the districts of Lozère and Gévaudan, in the region of Nîmes (but it had a short shelf-life); from Alpine pastures came two sorts of cheese; but more useful is Pliny's comment that from the Apennines came 'Coebanum cheese, mostly made from sheeps' milk', and from the lands bordering Tuscany and Liguria, came 'Luni cheese, remarkable for its

Figure 6 (left). The merchant vessel Kyrenia II. Figure 7 (right). The maritime trade route from Sicily to Athens – under Athenian naval control. Drawings by Dan Shadrake.

size, since individual cheeses weigh up to 1,000lb.' Finally, we should note *trans maria vero Bithynus fere in gloria est*, '(among cheeses) from overseas, the Bithynian cheese is practically put on a pedestal'.[16] Bithynia (southern Turkey in modern parlance) is a longer voyage from Athens than Sicily ever was. The ancient world transported cheeses over long distances as a matter of routine.

The type of ship used for trade round the Mediterranean has now been researched thoroughly from numerous archaeological wreck sites, exemplified by the reconstructed vessel Kyrenia II (Figure 6).[17] About 14 m in length, the vessel displaces some 25 tons and has an average speed of 4-5 knots depending on sailing conditions. A confirmation of a trade route comes from Thucydides's narrative about the Athenian expedition to Sicily in 415 BC: the naval force sailed from Corcyra and crossed to Iapygia and Tarentum, then followed the coast down to Rhegium before crossing the straits of Messina and reaching Sicily (*History* 6.44). On a return journey from Sicily to Athens, it was at Thurii that Alcibiades jumped ship to avoid a political trial (*History* 6.61). In addition, evidence of shipwrecks showing likely routes confirms the accepted pattern of ancient trading – namely, that ships' captains tended to hug the coastlines as far as possible, and kept a 'weather-eye' open in case they needed to make port in a hurry.[18] The availability of the so-called Diolkos, or overland ship crossing, saving the long (and potentially hostile) route around the Peloponnese, is questionable; David Pettegrew has cast doubt on the logistics of colportage, and in any case Corinth was in the enemy camp as far as the Athens of Aristophanes's day was concerned. The longer route seen was probably the one taken (Figure 7).[19] It is some 1000 nautical miles in length, as opposed to the direct distance of about 400 nautical miles from the eastern littoral of Sicily to Athens. The winds and weather were also limiting factors: to the west of the Peloponnese, the prevailing winds come from the northwest, favouring the route from Sicily via Calabria and then crossing over to Corfu. Sailing at 4-5 knots over a 12-hour day, a sailing vessel could have covered 50-60 nautical miles without too much trouble.[20] Thus, a journey round the southern Peloponnese from Sicily to Athens might have taken about twenty days, perhaps less, but often more.

Such a journey would probably not have affected the quality of the cheese by the time it reached Athens. A ship's hold would have been shaded and at a relatively ambient temperature, and the salinity of the sea-voyage would probably not have added to the saltiness of the cheese as it was prepared for transportation. It is generally accepted that trade by sea was carried out from mid-spring to mid-autumn; cheese made in one year might well have been stored prior to early sailing in a subsequent year. Matching this to the seasonality of cheese production, it also seems practicable for cheese made in the early season (i.e. from mid-May) to have been ready after three month's maturing for shipment in mid-August; it might even have been shipped in mid-July, and the time spent in the ship's hold could have expedited its final maturation. This certainly seems to have been the case with the transportation of ancient *liquamen* or fish sauce.[21]

It struck me during the writing of this paper that a consideration of modern cheese production in Greece and in Sicily might offer some parallels with ancient practice, though I do not pretend to be an expert. The differences in regional varieties are interesting; in particular, I found it fascinating that cheese production in the Athens region is nowadays dominated by the manufacture of feta, which forms a central plank of modern culinary offerings for visitors.[22] Of course, feta is far from being the sole type of cheese produced in Greece, as Aglaia Kremezi helpfully reminded us: there is a range of artisanal cheeses from Epirus including *kefalotyri* and *graviera*, which are made in other regions too, as Diane Cochilas notes: 'there are approximately 70 distinct cheeses produced in Greece today, although many are similar and fall into one of several broad categories.'[23] *Kefalotyri* is also made in Macedonia, Sterea Hellas, the Peloponnese, Thessaly, Crete, and in the Ionian and Cycladic islands; *graviera* of Naxos and of Crete are well known; and a mixture of the two last kinds, the *kefalograviera* made in Epirus, Etolokanania, and Evritania and the *formaella* of Parnassos are worthy of note. These are all sheep's and goat's milk cheeses; the Greek landscape does not lend itself to cattle grazing. These cheeses are all ripened for at least three months (at least five, in the case of *graviera* from Crete) and have a moisture content of 35-36% and fat content varying from 28.8% in the *kefalotiri* type, to 40% in the *graviera* of Crete.[24] 10 litres of sheep's milk will produce about 2 kg of cheese.[25] The setting time of sheeps' milk cheese is less than 45 minutes. Presswork (shaping the cheese and squeezing out whey) takes place on the second to fourth days, and the cheese can then be put into storage. In temperatures over 12°C, ripening is fast.[26]

If cheeses like these were also made in the fifth-century BC, we may wonder why Sicilian cheeses seemed to have figured so prominently in Athens. It is possible that regional production from the islands under Athenian control was simply not enough to meet market demand, due to their limited terrains. It is also likely that any possibility of importing cheeses from regions such as Epirus had been ruled out by the Spartan (and Theban) blockade in force since 431 BC. This might have been especially symbolic when the plays were produced – in 422 and 421 BC, when the protracted war with Sparta looked as though it might finally end, relieving the economic hardship which had afflicted all the Greek states so dearly (something which Aristophanes had exploited to the full in his play *Acharnians* of 425 BC). Sicily's terrain was capable of much more extensive production, and trade with it seems to have been unimpaired, as Athens 'ruled the waves'.[27] In addition there may have been a greater 'cachet' associated with a luxury, foreign, imported products, easily added by enterprising merchants to a ship making the regular trip from Sicily to Greece. A number of sheep or sheep/goat cheeses produced nowadays in Sicily would serve as the rind-covered, grateable type Aristophanes seems to have had in mind. These are the *Pecorino Siciliano* and *Pecorino Pepato*, both aged 2-4 months, and often used grated; the *Piacentinu Ennese*; the *Calcagno*, aged up to 10 months, and also often grated; and the *Maiorchino* from Messina and the northern coastal regions, which is aged from 6-8 months, can be matured up to a maximum of 24 months, and can weigh up to 20kg.[28]

In conclusion, despite the utterly fantastical, off-the-wall scenes which Aristophanes

Sicilian Cheese: A Firm Foundation for Fantasy

(and Athenian Old Comedy generally) made a staple of his plays, it can be seen that they were built around everyday, familiar objects – one of which was Sicilian cheese. Likely types of this cheese, of which a pecorino would be a likely modern type, made mainly from sheep's milk, still form a major part of high-quality Sicilian agricultural produce, and would have been readily available even as a 'luxury' product. Its production, preservation and conveyance in the fifth century BC over the long sea-route to Athens was not a fantasy at all, but was one of the 'hooks of realism' around which the comic fantasies revolved.

Notes

1. For commentaries on *Wasps*, see Alan H. Sommerstein, *Aristophanes Wasps: The Commentaries of Aristophanes Volume 4* (Warminster: Aris & Philips, 1983) and Zachary P. Biles and S. Douglas Olson, *Aristophanes, Wasps* (Oxford: Oxford University Press, 2015).
2. Aristophanes, *Wasps*, lines 892-926: see fine, helpful translations in the Loeb Classical Library series by Jeffery Henderson (*Aristophanes: Clouds, Wasps, Peace* (Cambridge, MA: Harvard University Press, 1998)) and David Barrett (*Aristophanes: The Wasps/The Poet and the Women/The Frogs* (Harmondsworth: Penguin, 1964)). Here I have re-allocated the speaking parts, which are a matter of confusion in the manuscript tradition, to make more sense of the final outburst. 'Ensicilized' is Sommerstein's rendering of Aristophanes's invented verb κατεσικέλιζε (one of his favourite tricks), rendered 'sicilized' by Olson in the Loeb and 'siciliated' by Barrett in the Penguin.
3. Sommerstein; Barrett, n. 33, p. 217.
4. Aristophanes, *Peace*, lines 236-254: for a good translation, see Henderson; for commentaries see S. Douglas Olson, *Aristophanes, Peace* (Oxford: Oxford University Press, 1998), pp. 117-21 and Alan H. Sommerstein, *The Comedies of Aristophanes; vol. 5, Peace* (Warminster: Aris & Philips, 1990), pp.144-45. On *moretum*, see Christopher Grocock and Sally Grainger, 'Moretum – a Peasant Lunch Revisited', in *The Meal: Proceedings of the 2001 Oxford Symposium on Food and Cookery*, ed. by Harlan Walker (Totnes: Prospect Books, 2002), pp. 95-103. Carol A. Déry suggests that the cheese used in the poem is a 'round cheese' and 'evidently a hard [one] stored up against times of want' ('Milk and Dairy Products in the Roman Period', in *Milk: Beyond the Dairy: Proceedings of the 1999 Oxford Symposium on Food and Cookery*, ed. by Harlan Walker (Totnes: Prospect Books, 2000), pp. 117-25 (p. 119)).
5. For a helpful survey, see Joan P. Alcock, 'Milk and Its Products in Ancient Rome,' in *Milk*, ed. Walker, pp. 31-38, pp. 31, 33. There is a useful history of cheese in Harold McGee, *On Food and Cooking: The Science and Lore of the Kitchen* (London: Harper Collins, 1991), pp. 3-6. For the Asia Minor find, see *Cheese Grater in the Form of a Goat*, Late Archaic Period, bronze, 7.7 cm, the Israeli Museum, Jerusalem <https://www.imj.org.il/en/collections/431984>; for the Egyptian find, see Niraj Chokski, 'Archaeologists Find 3,200-Year-Old Cheese in an Egyptian Tomb, *The New York Times*, 16 August 2018 <https://www.nytimes.com/2018/08/16/science/oldest-cheese-ever-egypt-tomb.html> [accessed 27 March 2022]
6. Sarah Freeman and Silvija Davidson, 'The Origins of Taste in Milk, Cream, Butter and Cheese', in *Milk*, ed. by Walker, pp. 161-67.
7. VM 20 cited by Elizabeth Craik, 'Hippokratic Diaita', in *Food in Antiquity*, ed. by John Wilkins, David Harvey, and Mike Dobson (Exeter: University of Exeter Press, 1995), pp. 343-50 (p. 347).
8. Andrew Dalby, *Food in the Ancient World from A to Z* (London: Routledge, 2003), p. 302; see also Mario Lombardo, 'Food and "Frontier" in the Greek Colonies of South Italy', in *Food in Antiquity*, ed. by Wilkins, Harvey, and Dobson, pp. 256-72, especially his discussion of 'Sybaritic Luxury' (pp. 267-69).
9. Hermippus 63 [*Epitome* 27e], trans. by Andrews Dalby, *Siren Feasts* (London; Routledge, 1996), p. 105; for the original text, see *P C G: Poetae Comici Graeci*, ed. by R. Kassel and C. Austin, 9 vols (Berlin: De Gruyter, 1983-[2022]).
10. Dalby, *Siren Feasts*, p. 105

11 Dalby, *Siren Feasts*, p. 108 and n. 51.
12 Dalby, *Siren Feasts,* p. 125.
13 Dalby, *Food in the Ancient World*, pp. 80-81.
14 Cato 76; Philodemus, *Anthologia Palatina* 9. 412 <https://attalus.org/poetry/philodemus.html#9.412> [accessed 16 October 2021]
15 Cato and Varro, ed. and trans. by William David Hooper, rev. by Harrison Boyd Ash, Loeb Classical Library (Cambridge, MA: Harvard University Press, 1935); Columella, *On Agriculture,* ed. and trans. by E. S. Forster and Edward H. Heffner, Loeb Classical Library, 3 vols (Cambridge, MA: Harvard University Press, 1968).
16 Pliny the Elder, *Natural History*, ed. by H. Rackham, Loeb Classical Library, 2nd edn (Cambridge, MA: Harvard University Press, 1983), xi, 97.240.
17 For information on Kyrenia II, see 'Life on Board a Mediterranean Merchantman in the 5th and 4th Centuries BCE', Joukowsky Institute for Archaeology, *Brown University* <https://www.brown.edu/Departments/Joukowsky_Institute/courses/maritimearchaeology11/files/19115628.pdf>; 'Kyrenia Shipwreck Museum', North Cyprus, 1994–2014 <http://www.cypnet.co.uk/ncyprus/city/kyrenia/castle/shipwreck/index.html>; and 'Kyrenia Shipwreck', Learning Sites, 4 November 2019 <http://www.learningsites.com/Kyrenia/Kyrenia_home.php> [all accessed 11 May 2021]
18 J. Strauss, 'Shipwrecks Database', *Oxford Roman Economy Project*, 2013 <http://oxrep.classics.ox.ac.uk/databases/shipwrecks_database/> [accessed 11 May 2021] – thanks to Sally Grainger for help in navigating to this; for a wealth of clear, fascinating information about ancient ships and shipping routes, see Arthur de Graauw, 'Ancient Sailing', *Ancient Ports*, 2021 <http://www.ancientportsantiques.com/ancient-sailing/> [both accessed 11 May 2021]
19 See Diederik Willemsen, 'Corinth Canal, Diolkos', *Sailing Issues*, 2000–2021 <https://www.sailingissues.com/corinth-canal-diolkos.html>; David F. Pettegrew, 'The Diolkos of Corinth,' *American Journal of Archaeology* 115 (2011), 549-74 <https://www.academia.edu/7948794/The Diolkos of Corinth> [both accessed 22 March 2021]
20 Citation and map details from de Graauw.
21 See Sally Grainger, *The Story of Garum: Fermented Fish Sauce and Salted Fish in the Ancient World* (London: Routledge, 2021), pp. 168-69.
22 See for example 'Gastronomy', *Attica* <https://athensattica.com/things-to-do/gastronomy/>; 'Costelaros Cheese Factory', *Greek Gastronomy Guide,* 2021 <https://www.greekgastronomyguide.gr/en/item/kostarelos-cheese-dairy-markopoulo-attica/>; and 'History of Feta', *Real Greek Feta*, 2021 <http://www.realgreekfeta.gr/history-of-feta/> [all accessed 16 April 2021]
23 See 'Cheeses', Vlachian Mountains, 2019 <https://www.vlachianmountains.com/en/cheeses> [accessed 20 October 2021]; Diane Kochilas, 'Greek Cheeses – A Short History', *Diane Kochilas* <https://www.dianekochilas.com/intro-to-greek-cheeses/> [accessed 22 May 2021]
24 Pascalis Kastanas and Mario Papadakis, 'The Greek Cheese Page', *Hellas*, 1996 <http://www.greece.org/hellas/cheese.html> [accessed 22 May 2021]
25 K. Biss, *Practical Cheesemaking* (Ramsbury: The Crowood Press, 1988), pp. 8, 29.
26 Biss, pp. 81, 105-110. See also the detailed description of production methods in Columella, *De Re Restica* 7.8 1-4, and the summaries in Alcock, pp. 36-37 and Déry, pp. 118-19.
27 See R. Ross Holloway, *The Archaeology of Ancient Sicily* (London: Routledge, 1991), pp. 49-54; Stephen Ashley and others, 'The Resources of an Upland Community in the Fourth Millennium BC', in *Uplands of Ancient Sicily and Catalonia: The Archaeology of Landscape Revisited,* ed. by Matthew Fitzjohn (London: Accordia Research Institute, 2007), pp. 59-80.
28 Information taken from '10 Most Popular Sicilian Cheeses', *TasteAtlas*, 2021 <https://www.tasteatlas.com/most-popular-cheeses-in-sicily>; see also Giuseppe Barbara and Sabastiano Cullotta, 'An Inventory Approach to the Assessment of Main Traditional Landscapes in Sicily (Central Mediterranean Basin)', *Landscape Research*, 31.1/2 (October 2012), Figure 3 <https://www.doi.org/10.1080/01426397.2011.607925>

The Curious Case of *Nala's Mirror on Cooking*: Innovation in Medieval Indian Cookbook Writing

Andrea Gutiérrez

Nala's Mirror on Cooking (*Nala Pākadarpaṇam*), of unknown provenance within South Asia, is no doubt the most curious example of culinary writing from India, an understudied cookbook composed in Sanskrit that yields more mysteries than it resolves. Comprising chapters on *dals*, rice dishes, buttermilk preparations, vegetable sides, snacks, drinks, milk sweets, yoghurt, and more, it is one of the earliest extant single-standing recipe collections in book (manuscript) form from South Asia, offering a rich glimpse into the region's historical culinary practices. Since there has been little scholarly work on this cookbook, I will first introduce this text's dating and compositional milieu before presenting one special feature, an example of a 'clever deception' *trompe l'oeil* recipe. Then I will explore this cookbook's innovation in terms of its style, including narrative passages, and the extent of the cookbook's innovation in culinary terms. Next I come to the heart of my discussion: the less conventional technologies practiced and mentioned throughout *Nala's Mirror*, which also sometimes feature in the creative narrative passages. What is significant in the example I share is that the narrative describes what appears to be a regionally – or historically – specific culinary technique. I will describe how these techniques using betel (or perhaps areca) leaf seem anomalous in the overall Indian culinary record, illustrating my point using the same narrative example from this cookbook. I will conclude by asserting the cookbook's anomalous status overall, which further confirms the originality of *Nala's Mirror* within the corpus of South Asian historical culinary writing.

With its author unknown (the work was composed under a pen name) and the milieu of its composition also unknown, prior studies on *Nala's Mirror* have generally established its dating to before 1600 or 1700 CE due to the textual absence of chilli pepper, tomato, and other New World foods brought to the subcontinent as part of the Columbian exchange following the arrival of Europeans to South Asia.[1] This is dating by *argumentum ex silentio*; as always, using absence or lack of evidence is not fully reliable for dating a work. Dating by what is missing from a text is even less conclusive here, because *Nala's Mirror* is incomplete in all of its extant manuscript versions. The cookbook abruptly cuts off in what appears to be a very short chapter without a concluding verse to end the chapter, so we cannot know with all certainty the entirety of what this text might have once contained.[2]

My own study has fixed the cookbook's dating to *c.* twelfth to fifteenth centuries CE based on evidence including language, style, and the use of the word 'mirror' (*darpaṇa*) in the title, indicating a literary mirror for princes, i.e. a royal manual.[3] Further justifying my dating, there was a boom of culinary writing in South Asia from the eleventh to fifteenth centuries, with other recipe collections written then as well as a subgenre of cookbooks that called themselves *sūpaśāstra*, manuals or treatises on cooking, with *sūpa* being a generic term for *dal*-type dishes, thus generically referring to food.[4] My study of *Nala's Mirror* has also determined that it was composed in a royal setting as entertainment to be read in courts for the literary pleasures of amusement and aesthetic delight as well as for edification on the subject of cooking, as cooking was one of the elite 'arts' or domains to be mastered by those in the upper echelon aiming to impress.

While not much is known about the cookbook's provenance (let alone the kingdom in which it was composed), *Nala's Mirror* offers many delights upon reading as well as invaluable information on culinary methods. This work was, without a doubt, the most imaginative of the historical South Asian recipe collections, and not only for its disguised dishes, the contrived visual *trompe l'oeils* that ended up in the stomach. One such disguised dish involves plantain stems, the edible core of the banana or plantain plant stem. In this recipe, the stem core is cut three different ways to mimic the ingredients of a rice pilaf-type dish, although it is not called such. The chef cuts the inner core into rice grain-sized pieces, into channa-shaped pieces, and into circular shapes (presumably like fried vada pieces or meat chunks[5]) before combining the cooked shapes and serving the dish, fooling the eye but not the palate or stomach. This very recipe also provides my example of another sort of innovation that *Nala's Mirror* exhibits: rejecting some of the traditional, normative rules of food service laid out in earlier Sanskrit works (not only in cookbooks).[6] Because this innovative divergence from traditional food service appears in this same *trompe l'oeil* plantain recipe, I include my translation of it here (bracketed words added to the original for clarity):

> *Trompe l'oeil plantain stem* [rice pilaf]:
> To extract the core from the middle of the royal plantain plant, one [first] removes the outer 'skin.' Also cutting off the tip and root [of the plant] with a rounded boti knife, a wise person throws [these parts] away. Make pieces the size of your thumb from the innermost stalks and cut [them] again like rice grains. Repeating [this method], cut more stalks like small pieces of rice grains. A very clever chef will cut additional stalks into the shape of pieces of channa. Then, make circular shapes out of [the rest of the material] from the plantain plant stalk [suggesting fried vada or chunks of meat].
>
> A wise [chef] puts these different shapes into [three] different vessels, adds salt and also adds turmeric so they take on a nice appearance, and, adding sour citron, cooks these on the flame. Then, one puts the seasoning ingredients [into a pan] and toasts them, removing them from the flame after heating.

Then put [all of these components] in betel (*pūga*) leaves, and make them fragrant [i.e., fumigating with flowers and aromatics] as in the previous [recipe]. And then a wise cook would wrap [these] little bundles and put them on a tiered tray for serving. When the hour of dining arrives, serve these finest of plantain stems.⁷

Besides clever disguised dishes and the alternative technique of service discussed below, what makes *Nala's Mirror on Cooking* foremost in innovation is that this is the only South Asian cookbook, historical or modern, to utilize a narrative framework to showcase its author's creativity in offering tasteful royal entertainment while promoting the palace chef's skills and fame. With poetic flourishes, chapter endings in verse conforming to the rules of high Sanskrit literature (following *alaṅkāraśāstra*), language style imitative of older epic writing, and entertaining dialogues along the way, it is clear that the aims of this text were as royal entertainment beyond instructing on culinary *śāstra* (system of knowledge).

Determining Innovation in Medieval Indian Culinary Writing

This particular medieval culinary manual might not rank as South Asia's most innovative in terms of variety of culinary techniques, especially if we compare *Nala's Mirror* to the recipe section of the twelfth-century *Mānasollāsa* of the Cāḷukyan kingdom, with its various types of breads both sweet and savoury, its roast fish and even turtle, its tandoori-style cooking methods, and its 'toasting' using the heat that emanates from the top of covered pots. *Nala's Mirror on Cooking* might also appear to lack originality because of its repetition of the same styles of preparation within a section. For example, a seasoned vegetable dish recipe may be listed once as an archetype, with virtually identical variations or ectypes given using a number of different vegetables, repeating much the same preparation instructions (e.g. wash, peel, cut, season, and sauté the vegetable). Such repetition does not actually indicate a lack of imagination, however, as listing identical or similar methods and cases was common practice within this style of Sanskrit writing (i.e. *śāstra*) and in related Sanskrit genres.

What makes *Nala's Mirror on Cooking* so fascinating in terms of its creativity is that the rationale given for this cookbook's divergence from traditional food service is explained in playful passages of original narrative. The frame story that provides the context and the reason for writing this cookbook largely paraphrases the famous Indian epic the *Mahābhārata* (MBh). The Nala who is the supposed eponymous author of this cookbook is a legendary prince in the MBh who was famous for his gambling with dice and his horse-riding prowess but who also had prowess in the kitchen. In fact, when Nala is forced into the disguise of a dwarf in this epic's substory, Nala's wife (from whom he has been separated) is able to locate her missing Nala and recognize his presence by identifying the taste of roasted meat produced in the palace kitchens as unmistakably her husband's cooking. It is in the guise of dwarf Bāhuka ('Little-Arms') that this cookbook's backstory transpires, with the whole of *Nala's Mirror* recounted in the voice of the dwarf (really Prince Nala) describing his extensive culinary knowledge to King Ṛtuparṇa to convince the king to take him on as palace chef so he can be gainfully employed (in the epic he is successful). Incidentally, Nala's fame as a master chef extends far beyond the MBh and this cookbook. We find this legendary Nala described in a wide number of texts as an excellent cook and cookbook author, as well as finding recipes attributed to him cited in a variety of works, including in the *āyurvedic* (medical) tradition.[8]

In *Nala's Mirror*, many dialogues between Nala (as Bāhuka) and the king paraphrase actual passages from the famous epic with phrases similar enough that one can identify them with actual verses from the MBh. This is the case for the sections that present the cookbook's general framing and the occasion for the cookbook's composition: convincing the king of Nala's cooking skills.

While some passages paraphrase the epic closely, practices that diverge from other historical South Asian cookbooks are explained in narrative passages of this author's own invention. These newly imagined dialogues between expert chef Nala and the king do not appear anywhere in the massive MBh, a work which, incidentally, itself claims to contain a recorded account of everything there is and has ever been.[9] These dialogues are purely invented, playful episodes inserted in the cookbook to explain why certain cooking techniques are superior to other culinary technologies as well as to 'play up' Prince Nala's cooking expertise. As it would happen, these invented 'excerpts' from the MBh describe instances of what appear to be regionally- and historically-contingent practices of cooking and service that we can uniquely glimpse in this cookbook. While I have not been able to pin down *Nala's Mirror on Cooking*'s region of origin at this time in my investigation, I call these techniques historically-contingent because they are not found described elsewhere and appear specific to time and place. They also provide details and rationale specific enough to suggest actual practice in historical reality, meaning that the cookbook is not only one of theory on cooking nor the type of coffee table cookbook with recipes seldom if ever produced in a kitchen.

Justifying Divergent Technologies

The cookbook author, in fact, had to rely on his own invention to account for these original practices: because they diverged from the convention described in other manuals (whether religious, legal, royal, or culinary), this author had to explain why these techniques were superior to others commonly practiced. This necessitated the composition of original writing to justify non-normative techniques. Of course he also had to invent these passages because the MBh did not enter into such great detail regarding culinary techniques. The brief passage from *Nala's Mirror* that I present below rejects the usual gold and silver vessels for serving kings and their retinue in favour of betel-leaf wraps for steaming, storing, and serving dainty individual portions to the king and the elites in his court. The advantage of betel envelopes is that they also protect the food from contamination by dust, dirt, and insects and impart a delightful fragrance to the food, especially true for food cooked in betel. The plantain core recipe did not utilize betel wraps for cooking but countless other recipes in Nala's collection do. Using leaf or plant matter to cook and serve food in South Asia is not at all a historical anomaly. We find textual attestations of using lotus-plant matter, bamboo tubes, palash (*Butea Frondosa*), and other tree leaves and plant materials for plates and vessels.[10] Palash, areca spathe, and banana leaves are still commonly used today in India for disposable and biodegradable plating and food service, for example in temples.

What is unique in this cookbook is its repeated use of this particular type of leaf for packaging and wrapping food: *pūgapaṭṭa*, literally areca (*pūga*) 'cloth' or strips (*paṭṭa*). I argue that this was more likely betel leaf than areca plant material that was indicated to be used in so many recipes as a wrapper or envelope for cooking, storing, and serving morsels of food in individual packets, as one might serve hors d'oeuvres today. This usage of a (betel) leaf envelope appears unique to this cookbook. I have found no other historic or modern textual description of food cookery, storage, and service involving betel leaf wraps as Nala indicates (nor any culinary references to *pūgapaṭṭa*) within the subcontinent, although cooking in betel leaf packets is still practiced in Southeast Asia today. Betel leaf is better known in India as the digestive leaf chewed after a meal or at a special function like a wedding, also given as an offering to temple deities and to guests in one's home. The stimulant betel has also historically been offered and chewed, typically with areca nut and other flavourings, to 'seal a deal', as well as to mark one's status as subservient to another if one willingly receives a betel leaf roll from a more powerful figure such as a king or husband.[11] In these situations, the betel leaf preparation is chewed as a stimulant and digestive, often after a meal, and is not itself swallowed. In *Nala's Mirror*, betel is used as an envelope to wrap and contain morsels of food but is not meant to be chewed or eaten as part of the final dish (only imparting its aroma), although I have encountered a rare handful of dishes in present-day India where betel leaves are eaten.

While I do not think it is indicated in Nala's recipes, we do find areca spathes among plant materials used for making plates and vessels in the historical period and up to the present. The spathe, often informally (and incorrectly) called the areca leaf, is the dried sheath of plant material surrounding the flowering part of the areca palm tree. Nineteenth-century documentation indicates that such technology was used to make plates, cups, and dishes for holding various foodstuffs, including plantains, sweet preparations, and fish.[12] While *Nala's Mirror on Cooking* usually uses a term that literally describes areca (*pūga* = areca) 'cloth', the cookbook indicates that the cook should use the material to wrap an envelope or bundle around a portion of food on the spot, in the moment after cooking the other ingredients. Dry areca spathe is less flexible than supple betel and does not lend itself to fold on the spot as a pliable material. Typically the spathes are moistened by soaking for hours and are pressed together firmly, often using heat (nowadays with machines) to 'glue' leaves together and fashion plates or bowls long prior to their use; such dishes are brittle after assembly.[13] This is a further indication that *Nala's Mirror* is referring to betel; the soft, delicate, and tender leaf of the betel plant is easy to fold, commonly used as a wrap for *paan*, and imparts a floral-like fragrance to everything it touches. Finally, the Sanskrit word *pūga* is also occasionally used as a synecdoche to refer to a wrapped betel roll or quid (*paan*) as a whole, so there is already some slippage between the idea of *pūga* as areca and *pūga* as betel.[14]

The following passage recorded in *Nala's Mirror on Cooking* and 'imagined' to be an excerpt from the MBh illustrates the cookbook author's creativity in inventing narrative to teach about this exceptional culinary technique. Appearing near the end of the beverage chapter, King Ṛtuparṇa questions Nala (Bāhuka) about why he uses betel leaf (*pūgapaṭṭa*) so frequently for preparing and serving fine food and drinks for a king, when luxurious gold and silver vessels are available to royalty:

> *King Ṛtuparṇa's question regarding vessels:*
> The King says: "Tell me, O Little-Arms [Bāhuka], when there are golden vessels and more [at the king's disposal], why are all sorts of foods prepared using betel cloth [*pūgapaṭṭa*]?!'
>
> And Nala (Bāhuka) [replies]: 'Nice aromas like of flower blossoms will be released from this food [cooked in *pūga*], and worms, moths, and similar bugs don't like this. Such cooking keeps all sorts of insects away from sweet and tasty items.'[15]

As I indicated, using leaves and other plant material to cook and serve food has never been a rarity in South Asia. However, using fragrant betel leaf for such purposes appears to be a novelty of this cookbook, not appearing elsewhere in the Indian culinary corpus although featuring extensively throughout this text.

Nala does not use the more expected justification for why he repeatedly cooks using betel leaf: single-use leaf containers mean that servers and consumers do not have to worry about washing dishes or purifying them after and between uses. Purification is a major concern in Indian religious law, but leaf dishes are disposable and only touched or sullied by the consumer, so the reader might theoretically expect this sort of reasoning for using betel wraps here, especially, for example, when royalty are entertaining many guests, as at a garden party. Instead, Nala uses explanations that are meaningful for the culinary realm and for the *śāstra* (body of knowledge) of cooking: 1) this sort of leaf imparts a fine fragrance to the food, and 2) this form of packaging for cooking and service keeps insects out because of the smell, also likely repelling them with this particular leaf's chemical properties.[16] Both flavouring and keeping food free of contaminants are priorities for chefs, as well as keeping food soft, moist, and warm for serving. These concerns take precedence over any religio-legal emphasis on purification and avoidance of contamination due to saliva that we find in other literature. Interestingly, the king's worry is that plant matter vessels do not appear royal enough (why not use gold? he asks). Nala's response assuages the king, with the implication that adding fine floral fragrances to food is an elite royal mode of cooking; fumigating and making fragrant with flowers appears in numerous other royal recipes in this collection.

Conclusion: *Nala's Mirror* in the Context of Medieval Indian Cooking

In analyzing this exceptional use of a different leaf for storing and service, one must bear in mind that *Nala's Mirror on Cooking* is in itself an anomalous cookbook. Much of the recipe content described in this book appears in no other historical Indian cookbook except for later royal manuals and cookbooks that copy directly from it.[17] The content from *Nala's Mirror* that is most often repeated in later culinary sources is the theoretical content, that is, the common errors that a chef makes or the basic rules of rice-making. The *Mirror on Cooking* is also anomalous for what it leaves out: there are no recipes for the variety of flatbreads that appear in other royal cooking manuals from the medieval period. Additionally, recipes detailed in Nala's cookbook vastly differ from other versions of such dishes; for example, Nala's recipe for tamarind rice unusually calls for garlic, a pairing I have not encountered elsewhere in the historic record.[18] The spice and flavouring combinations used in this cookbook include some seasonings and aromatics widely known from other Sanskrit literature, but which do not typically appear in other Sanskrit culinary manuals.

In addition to this cookbook's exceptional culinary details, we should also consider its literary merit. *Nala's Mirror* was meant as courtly literature of entertainment as well as a text of culinary learning; both situations also apply to other royal writing on cooking. While the MBh does have descriptions of feasting, roasting, and butchery, the epic obviously does not contain historical recipes. Naturally, any narrative passages in *Nala's Mirror* describing culinary preparations have to be of the cookbook author's own invention. Thus we find a fortunate happenstance when culinary wit and imagination parallel literary wit and imagination. The author reveals his literary flair, and the palace chef (if not in fact the same person as the scribe recording the content) reveals his culinary flair. These instances with narrative justifying cooking techniques 'step out' of the more cosmopolitan mode of writing in Sanskrit, also the mode for writing *śāstra*. These playful passages of narrative imagination, of which I have discussed just one, are also where the author steps away from (re-)recording the traditional rules of cooking, with rules and lists being a common feature of *śāstric* technical writing in Sanskrit. Such lists and rules, which are also found in *Nala's Mirror*, likely indicate older content repeated from earlier sources, since these tidbits of culinary knowledge and theory need to be imparted and preserved over the centuries. In contrast to the lists and rules that are traditionally re-copied, these narrative passages record other types of information, likely more historically contingent, and these passages do not appear re-copied in the later culinary manuals that do copy from *Nala's Mirror*.

No true conclusion is possible here due to the sparsity of the cookbook record for the pre-modern period in South Asia. We sometimes have gaps of a few centuries or more between extant cookbooks, meaning that much is left out from a full understanding of the royal art of South Asian cooking, especially in terms of what might be considered anomalous and what commonplace. Further, there are a few fragments of Sanskrit cookbooks in Newari script and a couple of medieval Kannada cookbooks that I have not been able to analyze to date due to my own limitations in reading only a few South Asian scripts and languages. Perhaps this technique involving betel is not anomalous or exceptional in other cookbooks and we simply do have not enough research to support another conclusion.

Finally, although this is purely speculation on my part, the exclusion of betel leaf wrapping from the broader historical cookbook record might not be a result of the sparsity of extant cookbooks but might rather stem from this technique appearing more humble than royalty might have liked it to appear. Wrapping exquisite food items fit for a king in tropical 'jungle' leaves might not confer the prestige and status that a king's elite food service – typically in gold and silver vessels – ought to convey. That said, it is also not the case that betel is a lowly substance. It is a dietary product imbued with lofty ritualistic significance across various echelons of South Asian life, including royal ritual practices involving betel leaf rolls. Betel therefore does ride a fine line in terms of conveying status, but it cannot communicate the same luxury as fine gold and silver serving vessels. Whether the use of betel leaf wraps and cups was a technology in restricted historical or regional use in South Asian cuisine or not, I am confident that *Nala's Mirror on Cooking* as a whole and through its narrative framing certainly is the most imaginative cookbook of the South Asian corpus, in terms of its entertaining stories, its elaborate and ornate verses of 'high' prosody, and, likely, in terms of its culinary technologies and flavouring methods. Nala's book without a doubt in my mind well merits the descriptor of the most innovative cookbook in India's history.

Notes

1. These studies include Heike Gilbert's monograph, largely comprising her translation of the work into German rather than of historical analysis (*Das Pākadarpaṇa, ein altes indisches Kochbuch (Digitaler Nachdruck der Dissertation*, Marburg 1995), *Monumenta culinaria*, February 2012, Giessen: Giessener Elektronische Bibliothek, 2012) and Jan Meulenbeld's concise study that fixed an earliest possible date for *Nala's Mirror* not earlier than 1200 CE due to terms used for two particular plant foods (*A History of Indian Medical Literature* (Groningen: Egbert Forsten, 2000), IIa, p. 417; IIb, p. 427, n. 50).
2. As an example of what is missing, this text lacks some staples of South Asian cuisines seen elsewhere in culinary writing by the twelfth century, particularly the preparation of flatbreads.
3. Mirror literature was popular worldwide in the medieval and Renaissance period, with its height from the twelfth to sixteenth centuries in both Europe and greater Asia. The notion of the literary mirror and the mirror genre in general likely entered Indian culture via Persian influence from the eleventh century onwards, with the genre popular in Persia from the eleventh century although not yet using the name 'mirror' in Persian until later. See Richard M. Eaton and Phillip B. Wagoner, *Power, Memory, Architecture: Contested Sites on India's Deccan Plateau, 1300-1600* (Oxford: Oxford University Press, 2014), p. 23 and elsewhere.
4. *Nala's Mirror on Cooking* can be classified as a *pākaśāstra* or *sūdaśāstra* (both meaning a manual or treatise on cooking) although all three terms, *sūpaśāstra*, *sūdaśāstra*, and *pākaśāstra*, are synonymous. Any of these terms can also refer to the genre of writing on cooking, just as *śāstra* can be an umbrella term for technical instructions on a subject, referring to a body of knowledge.
5. I suspect the round pieces are meant to resemble meat chunks due to related words appearing in other recipe collections of a similar period.

6   For example, see the Sanskrit description of royal food service in the *annabhoga* (enjoyment of food) section of *Mānasollāsa* 3.13.1585-1587, etc. *Mānasollāsa* of Someśvara III, ed. by G. K. Shrigondekar (Baroda: Central Library, 1925-1961), II, pp. 134-35.
7   *Nala Pākadarpaṇa* 1.211-17. *Pākadarpaṇam*, Mahārājanala, Sanskrit text with translation in Hindi, ed. by Vāmācaraṇa Bhaṭṭācārya and Indradeva Tripāṭhī (Vārāṇasī: Caukhambhā Saṃskṛta Samsthāna, 1983), pp. 31-32.
8   As far as I have ascertained, recipes attributed to Nala in other works do not cite this text or redaction of *Nala's Mirror on Cooking*, although this does not exclude the possibility that there were other historic cookbooks that claim authorship by a supposed 'Nala'.
9   MBh 1.56.33 and 18.5.38 (critical edition): 'When it comes to *dharma*, *artha*, *kāma*, and *mokṣa*, what is here is elsewhere – but what is not here is not anywhere else' and similar verses in the MBh. I thank Nell Shapiro Hawley for help locating this verse.
10 P. V. Kane, *History of Dharmaśāstra*, Vol. 2, Part 1 (Poona: Bhandarkar Oriental Research Institute, 1941), pp. 761-62.
11 See also Andrea Gutierrez, 'Modes of Betel Consumption in Early India: Bhoga and Abhoga', *Scripta Instituti Donneriani Aboensis*, 26 (2015), 114-34 <https://doi.org/10.30674/scripta.67450>
12 See George Watt, *Dictionary of the Economic Products of India* (Calcutta: Superintendent of Government Printing/Authority of the Government of India, Department of Revenue and Agriculture, 1889): 'The spathe which covers the flowering axis may be used for paper-making […]. The spathes are largely used in India for packing and in the preparation of small articles for personal use' (I, p. 298). Also: 'The soft, white, fibrous flower-sheath [i.e., spathe], called *kācholi* or *poy*, is made into skull-caps, small umbrellas and dishes; and the coarser leaf-sheath, called *viri* or *virhati*, is made into cups, plates, and bags for holding plantains, sweet-meats, and fish' (I, p. 301, citing the *Gazetteer of the Bombay Presidency*, XV, Pt. 1: Kanara (Bombay: Government Central Press, 1883), p. 300). I thank James McHugh for locating this record.
13 Nahla Nainar, 'Biodegradable Plates Make a Splash', *The Hindu*, 17 May 2019, <https://www.thehindu.com/sci-tech/energy-and-environment/biodegradable-plates-and-bowls-made-from-areca-palm-spathes-are-making-a-big-splash/article27161523.ece#comments_27161523> [accessed 27 May 2021]
14 See Monier Monier-Williams, *A Sanskrit-English Dictionary: Etymologically and Philologically Arranged with Special Reference to Cognate Indo-European Languages* (Oxford: Clarendon Press, 1899), p. 641: *pūgapātra* (lit., areca container) as the betel box for keeping betel leaves fresh, *pūgīlatā* (lit., areca creeper) as actually referring to the creeping vine plant (betel) and not to the areca palm tree, and *pūgapīṭha* as the spittoon for spitting out the whole betel roll (*paan* or *tāmbūla*) or the saliva produced from chewing the betel roll.
15 *Nala Pākadarpaṇa* 5.23-24. *Pākadarpaṇam*, p. 90.
16 Betel leaf is also a natural insecticide: see for example Ma. C.B. Gragasin, 'Essential Oil from Betel Leaf, a Promising Insecticide', *Postharvest News*, 13.4 (2006); Made Sritamin and I. Dewa Putu Singarsa, 'Utilization of Betel Leaf Extract as Botanical Pesticides to Control Meloidogyne spp. and Tomato Plant Production', *Advances in Tropical Biodiversity and Environmental Sciences*, 1 (May 2017).
17 For example, see the *Śivatattvaratnākara* of Basavarāja of Keḷadi, II, ed. by R. Rama Shastry (Mysore: Oriental Research Institute, University of Mysore, 1969) and *A Chapter on Cookery, Extracted from an Ancient Sanskrit Work Called 'Basavarajeyam'*, Tamil trans. by S. Tirunarayanayyanger, English trans. by Ramasawmi Sastia and others (Madras: Gantz Brothers, 1873).
18 *Nala Pākadarpaṇa* 7.12-15. *Pākadarpaṇam*, p. 97.

Stories Full of Recipes, Recipes Full of Stories

Adrienne Harrington

Recipes and cookery books are more than a set of instructions on how to cook a dish. Floyd and Forster argue that the recipe 'illuminates the cultural worlds in which it appears'.[1] This paper examines a seminal Irish cookery book, *Full and Plenty: Maura Laverty's Complete Guide to Better Cooking*, written by the Irish writer Maura Laverty and published in Dublin in 1960.[2] It explores not only how the recipes contained in the book shine a light on the Ireland of the 1960s but also how the stories that introduce each chapter allow Laverty to highlight the changing role of women at the time, as well as exploring women's agency arising from their cooking role.

It is useful to position the publication of this cookery book in the Ireland of the time. Ireland was still a relatively young country, having only gained independence in 1922. It was just over a century since the Great Famine (1845–1848) when approximately one million people died from starvation and disease, and another million are estimated to have emigrated. The 1950s had been a decade of economic hardship, with over 400,000 people immigrating during that time.[3]

The early 1960s signalled a time of change in Ireland. Seán Lemass became Taoiseach (Prime Minister) in 1958, heralding a new progressive era for Ireland. The Whitaker Economic Plan of the same year promised a new Ireland, one that was outward-looking, leaving behind the protectionism that marked previous decades.[4] Electrification, running water and kitchen appliances such as cookers and fridges had become a feature for many in towns and cities, though many parts of rural Ireland were yet to see this progress. By 1965, 81% of the country had been electrified, with 99% connectivity by 1975.[5]

Despite these economic changes, Ireland remained a socially conservative country. Articles 41.1 and 41.2 of the Irish constitution dealt with (and continue to deal with as these Articles remain in place today) the place of women in society:

> 41.1 In particular, the State recognises that by their life within the home, woman gives to the State a support without which the common good cannot be achieved.
> 41.2 The State shall, therefore, endeavour to ensure that mothers are not obliged by economic necessity to engage in labour to the neglect of their duties in the home.[6]

The Catholic church exerted a strong influence over government policy and directly ruled family and women's lives. It ran most hospitals and schools. A marriage bar in place across many sectors, including banking and the public sector, forced women to resign upon marriage. Contraception was illegal. Despite these restrictions, Ireland could not be protected from the significant changes that the 1960s brought. By 1963, almost half of the population could receive British television stations and could see at first-hand the cultural revolution that had begun, even if for many it was still to directly impact their lives.[7]

Ireland today is an acknowledged centre of food excellence. However, for many in rural Ireland in the 1960s, their diet had not changed significantly in decades, while for those in towns and cities, outside influences were beginning to be felt. Looking at Laverty's cookery writer contemporaries, Fanny Cradock had at that stage become a famous TV cook in the UK, and a year before Laverty wrote *Full and Plenty*, Julia Child co-authored *Mastering the Art of French Cooking*.

Figure 1. Maura Laverty

Laverty was born in 1907, in Rathangan, a small Irish village in County Kildare, as one of nine children. When she was nine years old, Laverty was sent by her mother to live with a Dublin couple for several years.[8] This move may have been for financial reasons; Laverty's father died when she was very young, having been a poor provider in his later years due to his gambling problem. Laverty left Ireland at the age of seventeen, moving to Spain to work as a governess, an independent move at a time when many of her contemporaries chose to emigrate to the UK. While in Spain, she began writing and developed an interest in food, often submitting articles for publication in both Spain and Ireland. Returning to Ireland in 1928, she worked in radio, presenting her own woman's programme, while also working as editor of the magazine *Woman's Life* and as a playwright.

Laverty was a prolific author, writing cookery books; children's books; novels and plays, with her play *Tolka Row* becoming RTE's (Ireland's public sector broadcaster) first soap opera. Laverty wrote four novels, with two of these, *Never No More* and *No More than Human*, presenting a fictional character named Delia, based on the author herself, telling of Laverty's early life and her time in Spain. Two of her novels were banned in Ireland, with copies rumoured to have been publicly burned in her hometown.[9] What distinguishes her novels is the detailed attention paid to food and recipes throughout, with many traditional Irish recipes and techniques highlighted. Richman Kenneally describes Laverty's writing by saying her 'stories are full of recipes, her recipes full of stories.'[10]

Her first cookbook, *Flour Economy*, was published in 1941, commissioned by the Irish government to encourage people to use potatoes and oatmeal as substitutes for wheat at a time of wartime scarcity. 1946 saw her second cookbook published, *Maura Laverty's Cookery Book*, with *Full and Plenty* published in 1960.

As a genre, *Full and Plenty* is part cookery writing, part improvement literature, and part fiction. The first edition ran to 473 pages, and included illustrations and full-colour photos, an unusual feature at that time. The book contains fifteen chapters, with many of these common to cookbooks of the time, such as eggs, meat, and vegetables. More unusually, Laverty included a chapter on *canapés* and another on homebrewed elixirs in which she advises on the health benefits of fermented milks. The book also includes a chapter entitled 'French Cooking Made Easy', with Laverty's daughter Maeve Carney credited with the writing of this chapter, having been a student at Le Cordon Bleu, Paris. This chapter was not universally praised: on her copy of the book, Elizabeth David wrote, 'the kind of pretentious rubbish that has brought French cooking into disrepute as a snobs [sic] preserve'.[11]

Figure 2. Cover of Full and Plenty.

It is informative to look at the context in which *Full and Plenty* was commissioned. Bread had been a staple of the Irish diet for generations, but as Bryan highlights, bread rationing had been introduced in 1947, brought on by post-war economic plight and consistent bad weather.[12] By the late 1950s, the decreasing level of bread consumption was debated by the Irish Parliament; the price of flour had continued to rise while its quality fell. These changes led to a backlash against the flour millers, who in response mounted a PR campaign entitled 'Eat More Bread'. The Irish Flour Millers Association commissioned Laverty as a trusted household name to write a cookery book: *Full and Plenty* was to be a key element in their campaign. The millers subsidized the cost of the book, with their aim being that every household in the country could afford a copy – in 2021 terms, the book would have cost the equivalent of approximately €10, good value for a hardback book with hand-drawn illustrations and colour photos. Prior to this, the only cookbook in most Irish households was the book provided free by the suppliers of the electric cooker. The Irish Flour Millers Association had not misplaced its optimism for book sales. The first run sold out, and the *Irish Times*, reporting on a Dublin reception held in Jury's Hotel to mark the publication of a second edition that brought the total to 75,000 copies, noted 'one of the largest editions of a book ever produced in this country'.[13] The book was a major success and today holds a place in the hearts of many Irish families as a cherished reminder of their mothers and grandmothers.

Laverty took her brief from the millers very much to heart. The chapter on bread opens the book, and begins with the following: '"I believe in breadmaking" is the first and the most important article of my culinary Credo. I applaud every effort to revive this kindliest of domestic arts. My enthusiasm is not based on health reasons alone. I believe in the traditional goodness of bread. I believe that the woman who bakes her family's bread brings this goodness into the kitchen' (p. 1). This last line is a strong endorsement from a woman who, at the time, was what we would today call an influencer. She placed bread-making at the pinnacle of the housewife's duties and, with the use of the word 'Credo', gives it a religious undertone. The chapter brings together a combination of traditional and modern recipes and ingredients, the everyday as well as treats, and includes the regular use of spices as well as recipes from abroad.

Apart from its recipes, *Full and Plenty* distinguishes itself in its use of anecdotes that introduce each chapter. Each story involves the key ingredient of that chapter and, on first reading, can appear as winsome and trivial. The anecdotes are often repeated between her books and also vary slightly between different editions of the same book, with some stories based on previously-published works of fiction. Given the role that this book played in the flour millers' campaign, the chapter on bread deserves particular attention. Laverty's anecdote in this chapter deals with the widow Feeney whose only son Brian, at thirty-five years of age, starts to date a girl, Anna. The widow's delight is short-lived when she hears that her prospective daughter-in-law is a domestic economy instructress whom, her neighbour fears, is a 'high-falutin lassie with strings of letters after her name. A college-trained cook with class notions about dressed-up dishes who'll come in here and make little of your cooking, and who'll make your son wonder how he ever managed to reach manhood on the food you fed him'. Mrs Feeney 'realized now that her happy acceptance of Brian's courtship had been based on visions of herself imparting all she knew of home-making to a girl who would look up to her and respect her and treat her as an oracle' (p. 3).

What to serve when Anna comes to tea is the widow's dilemma, as she is 'the worst hand in the world when it comes to making fancy cakes'. The narrative confirms this to be true – 'As was the case with most of the farming women of Ballyderrig, the making of fancy cakes was as foreign to Mrs. Feeney as going upstairs is foreign to a tinker. Plain bread was a different story' – with Mrs Feeney's plain soda bread extolled for the remainder of the paragraph. However, 'while good soda bread was all right in its way, it would not suffice of itself to make an attractive tea table'. There is an added misfortune as Mrs Feeney lives in rural Ireland, 'a backward place [...] where a nice fancy cake is not to be bought', especially given the suspicion that a shop-bought cake may be stale or 'of the cheapest quality'. The widow begs her neighbour to make some cakes for the occasion. On the day, the table is laid with 'a sponge cake with a swirl of white icing to crown it' and a 'marble cake [that had] risen nicely', as well as Mrs Feeney's soda bread 'for those who might like a bite of something plain to start'. When tea is served, Anna begins with the soda bread: 'She took a slice, and then another slice, and another slice after that.' When offered cake, she replies, 'I'd rather have this delicious soda bread … I've never tasted the like of it in my life. It would win a prize anywhere. How on earth do you make it Mrs. Feeney?' Mrs Feeney gives her recipe, with Anna continuing:

> 'I always think it's in the cooking of plain food that a real cook proves herself [.... A]ny girl could make a sweet cake that will pass [.... I]t's only after leaving college that a girl like myself finds out all that she has to learn. Anyone at all can cook in a city kitchen where there is nothing to be done but look after the stove. But the cook who really deserves admiration is the woman who can turn out good food in a farmhouse kitchen in between churning and feeding calves and fowl.'

Mrs Feeney responds that 'All any young married woman needs is to have someone experienced at hand to give her advice now and again and to show her the way' (p. 3).

This anecdote places value on what has been handed down by generations, the inherited skills and recipes of traditional Ireland as represented by the widow. Soda bread is the traditional, iconic bread of Ireland made with flour, bread soda, buttermilk, and salt. It became popular in the Victorian era when a Frenchman, Nicolas Leblanc, first produced sodium carbonate (a precursor to today's sodium bicarbonate or baking soda) in 1791.[14] Soda bread was well suited to Irish-grown wheat, and, with buttermilk being a by-product of butter-making, it allowed for a cheap bread to be made with readily available ingredients that could be cooked in a pot, over a fire, without the need for an oven.

Furthermore, as Sexton identifies, soda bread is significant in the Irish foodscape as one of the few foods of Ireland that developed outside the influence of British food culture.[15] Laverty eulogizes soda bread in one of her early books, *Maura Laverty's Cookery Book*:

> Every time Ireland is put in the dock, I feel our diplomats are sadly lacking as a counsel for the defense [sic] that they don't bring forward in mitigation of our crimes the fact that we have given a four-leaved shamrock to the world. One leaf is W.B. Yeats, another is boiled potatoes in their jackets, another Barry Fitzgerald. The fourth is soda-bread. And the greatest of these is soda-bread. Spongy white soda-bread with a floury, brown crossed crust…flat sweet griddle-bread with an inch-and-a-half of tender well baked dough sandwiched between the thin crisp crusts… wholesome brown bread with growth and health and energy in its rough nuttiness […]. The queer thing is that in its native habitat soda-bread is never so called. We call it 'cake' or 'cake-bread'. A loaf of bread comes out of the baker's van, but a cake of bread comes out of the pot-oven.[16]

In *Full and Plenty*, Anna's readiness to praise the 'plain bread' and value the country housewife simultaneously reinforces and privileges the importance of the Irish food tradition and the rural way of life. Yet as a trained home economics teacher, Anna represents a modern, educated Ireland. In a time of transition in Ireland, Anna personifies this transition. She is a modern professional woman, about to wed Brian. Yet despite her professional training, in marrying she will be required to resign her teaching position. The homemade is also valued over the 'fancy cake' bought in the shop, the traditional over the modern. The equal status between the two women shows when Mrs. Feeney shares her own recipe for soda bread: 'just take the form of the little blue jug of milk, as much as you think of flour, the taste of salt and a suspicion of bread soda' (p. 5). There is no need to set out exact amounts or weights of ingredients. There is an assumed knowledge between the widow, with her recipe handed down through the generations, and her formally educated, soon-to-be daughter-in-law. This is a meeting of equals. The widow's valuable traditional skills are recognized; Irish cooking heritage is something of which to be proud, to be embraced and included in the new modern Ireland.

The chapter on meat also demonstrates this meeting of the two Irelands. It begins with the story of the almost forty-year-old Statia Dunne, who is 'not the type to catch a man's eye' and who lives with and cares for her bedridden father and three brothers. Dr Crowley moves to the village, 'at the age when a man who is not married begins to show the needs of a woman who'll [...] make sure that he eats good regular meals'. Statia's stew, with 'a tantalizing smell, made up of twenty different fragrances', tempts Dr Crowley to accept an invitation to stay for dinner one night, and, '[i]n the way that one thing leads to another, Dr Crowley got acquainted with Statia's stuffed steak, her coddled rabbit and her baked liver loaded with scalloped potatoes. Before he was halfway through her culinary repertoire, they were engaged'. Once married, they take Statia's father to live with them, which allows one of Statia's brothers to marry his girlfriend of sixteen years, who in turn takes Statia's place as the household cook: 'So that she might do this adequately, Statia brought a twopenny copybook and wrote out the rest of her recipes for her' (p. 197).

Again, this story is imbued with significance. As in the bread chapter, the ability to cook well leads to achievement and advancement. Statia Dunne is spared a life of spinsterhood, and service to her male relatives, 'at an age where she had almost given up hope of ever having a man of her own to cook for' (p. 197). Cooking for her husband rather than her father and brothers is a step up the social ladder for Statia, now the doctor's wife rather than a spinster. Similarly, Dr Crowley marries a woman who can look after him in a manner fitting a professional man in a small village. The domino effect is that her brother is now in a position to marry, so in effect, Statia's stew leads to two marriages. This was significant in the Ireland of the 1960s where emigration rates were still high, with so many single men and women leaving the country that finding a suitable marriage partner was challenging. In 1966, 45.7% of all Irish men were single.[17] These are not the only marriages that occur in the book. Four other chapters – fish, pudding and dessert, vegetables and salads, and cakes – all end in a marriage facilitated by good cooking, with another marriage saved by good food in the sauces chapter.

The meals that Laverty decides to highlight in the meat chapter are worthy of attention, namely stew, steak, rabbit, and liver. With the exception of the steak, the meats are day-to-day and ordinary, with the rabbit most probably caught in the fields by her brothers. Even the steak is stuffed to make this more expensive cut of meat go further. The message is clear – good food does not have to be expensive food if the cook has the right skills. And as in the case of Mrs Feeney and Anna in the bread chapter, Statia passes her recipes to the soon-to-be sister-in-law, again highlighting and preserving the Irish food heritage for the next generation of home cooks. Laverty herself researched traditional Irish recipes at the National Library of Ireland in writing her novels and, as a result, would have been familiar with many older recipes.[18] In her novel *Never No More*, she acknowledges the Irish cookery writer Florence Irwin, and Clear writes that Laverty 'seems to have used some recipes from Redington's economic cookery book' which had its first edition in 1905 and was privately published in Dublin in 1927.[19]

The rewards of good cooking are reinforced throughout *Full and Plenty*. In the introduction, 'Cooking for Health and Happiness', Laverty is explicit about these rewards: 'It does your nerves the power of good.' Rubbing water into flour for scones 'is something I would recommend to neurotic people as a better tonic than anything their doctors could give them'. The value of cooking is further emphasized in the introduction where Laverty states, 'Cooking is the poetry of housework. But it is satisfying in twenty other different ways as well. There is a grand warm companionable feeling to be got out of the thought that every time you baste a roast or beat an egg, or do any other little ordinary kitchen job, you are making yourself one with the Grand Order of Homemakers, past, present and to come' (np).

The use of the words 'Grand Order' is worthy of commentary, echoing the tradesmen's guilds of the time where power was vested in skills and qualification. These skills are as important in the kitchen as they are in the workshop. In describing the gravy that is the basis of Statia's stew, Laverty writes, 'Years of practice had gone to finding the exact amount of mustard that should be added for tanginess, of sugar for the faint underlying sweetness and of vinegar for a teasing sharpness' (np). This alchemy is no accident, but rather the result of the accumulated wisdom and skill of an expert who has learned and honed her craft. The kitchen is seen as the woman's realm and domain, her centre of power where men rarely entered – and then only to eat. The use of the word homemaker rather than housewife is also significant as it incorporates all of the female duties. It applies equally to both married and single homemakers (and equally to all genders, though this would not have been a consideration in 1960s Ireland). The term 'homemaker' may also reference the work of the Commission on Vocational Organizations of the 1940s, which included a proposal for a National Council of Home-Makers, a term put forward by Irish women's organizations of the time.[20]

It is also useful to consider the banning in Ireland of several of Laverty's novels. As Clear notes, in a letter to an American newspaper in 1947, Laverty writes that her book *Liffey Lane* had been banned:

> on the grounds that it is 'in general tendency indecent or obscene'. No reviewer outside Ireland took this attitude – and only one within it. In America, even such religious periodicals as the Jesuits' 'America' and the Passionists' 'The Sign' found no fault with the book on moral grounds. I can only conclude, therefore, that

the ban is due to the fact that in 'Liffey Lane' I tried to show the slum conditions which have become intensified during 15 years of misrule.'[21]

Clear argues that the books were banned 'above all [for] their frankly sensual, joyous and subversive celebration of what the 1937 Constitution called women's "physical, and moral capacity and social function" – women's work in all its forms'.[22]

Laverty appears to have used *Full and Plenty* as a vehicle for conveying a message about the place of women in the home in the transitional period of 1960s Ireland. The book highlights and praises the role of women in the home, their expertise, their skills, and most particularly their being part of an inter-generational movement whereby the recipes and traditions that they learned from their mothers and grandmothers are, in turn, passed onto the next generation, thus finding a place in the emerging modern Ireland.

The ingredients used in Laverty's recipes are everyday foods, with little exotic or imported. In the introduction to *Full and Plenty*, she tells us that '[g]ood ingredients are more readily available in Ireland than in any other country in the world' (np). Many of her recipes are for foods with a rich Irish heritage such as soda bread, colcannon, and stew. She also introduces some foods and recipes that at the time were new in Ireland, such as Spaghetti Bolognese, chop suey, and paella, thus again reinforcing the message that the old and the new both hold a place in this transitory phase of Irish history.

The men in Laverty's stories are usually passive recipients of the food, be they father, brother, boyfriend, husband, or professional figure. Only in the vegetable and salads chapter do we read of a man cooking, but even here the stuffed onions he cooks evoke memories of his mother. These stories reinforce the central role of the woman in the kitchen but in a manner that elevates this role. Cooking is a source of agency, not one that suppresses or undermines the role of the woman. At a time when women were beginning to find more work outside the home, Laverty has taken the woman's traditional role and imbued it with a significance. The role of the homemaker is one that merits appreciation and respect. Additionally, cooking is presented as a means of empowerment, not repression; there is a worth and value in the role of the woman, with her being in the main responsible for the food economies of the house. Yet certain stories retain a more traditional view of the woman's place in the home. The sauces, fillings, icings chapter opens: 'The Foleys were nearly a year married before Sheila discovered that a wife's first duty to her husband is to cook him the kind of meals he likes, and that no marriage can be really happy unless a man is satisfied with his table treatment.' This old-fashioned view of marriage is further underscored when the husband receives advice that 'woman won't ever be happy till you let her see who's boss' (p. 369). The husband takes this advice; his wife sees the error of her cooking ways, and they live happily ever after. Perhaps 1960s Ireland was not quite ready for equality in all marriages.

Ireland was at a crossroads in the early 1960s. Few knew this better than Laverty who had suffered from the conservative views resulting in her books being banned. In her work as an agony aunt, she would have heard the range of issues and challenges faced by the Irish woman, and, rather than risk her messages not being heard in a novel, Laverty cleverly used the cover of a cookery book to advance her subversive message. Women were resourceful. They were adapting to a changing Ireland, to a new modernity in the home characterized by electricity and modern kitchen equipment. The benefits of good cookery were intrinsic in the twenty different ways in which she tells the reader that it is satisfying but she also makes it explicit. Feeding one's family was a role of which to be proud, and it contributed to the growth of the nation. As Richman Kenneally writes, women could 'take command of the kitchen, and, by extension, gain respect as a pivotal, dynamic member of the household, and, by further extension, the nation.'[23] That is an ambition worthy of any citizen, woman or man.

Notes

1. Janet Floyd and Laurel Forster, *The Recipe Reader: Narratives – Contexts – Traditions* (London: Routledge, 2003), pp.1-10 <https://doi.org/10.4324/9781315237480>
2. Maura Laverty, *Full and Plenty: Maura Laverty's Complete Guide to Better Cooking*, 2nd edn (Dublin, The Irish Flour Millers Association, 1960). Subsequent references are cited parenthetically.
3. Irial Glynn with Tomás Kelly and Piaras Mac Éinrí, *The Re-Emergence of Emigration from Ireland: New Trends in an Old Story* (Washington, DC: Migration Policy Institute, 2015) <https://www.migrationpolicy.org/sites/default/files/publications/TCM-Emigration-Ireland-FINAL.pdf> [accessed 14 April 2021]
4. *Programme for Economic Expansion Laid by the Government before Each House of the Oireachtas, November 1958* (Dublin: Stationary Office, 1958) <http://opac.oireachtas.ie/AWData/Library3/Library2/DL006590.pdf> [accessed 2 April 2021]
5. 'The Process of Rural Electrification', *ESB Archives* <https://esbarchives.ie/2016/03/21/rural-process/> [accessed 2 April 2021]
6. 'Constitution of Ireland', *Electronic Irish Statute Book* (*eISB*), January 2020 <http://www.irishstatutebook.ie/eli/cons/en/html#part13> [accessed 14 April 2021]
7. Edward Brennan, 'Television in Ireland before Irish Television: 1950s Audiences and British Programming', Shared Histories Conference 2016, National Library, Dublin, Ireland, 6 July 2016 <https://doi.org/10.21427/D79772>
8. Sean Kelly, *The Maura Laverty Story: From Rathangan to Tolka Row* (Naas: Naas Printing Limited, 2017), p. 42.
9. Kelly, p. 34.
10. Rhona Richman Kenneally, 'Maura Laverty: Ireland's First Celebrity Chef Still Dishes Up Food for Thought', *Irish Times*, 31 August 2016.
11. Tim Hayward, 'The Most Revolting Dish Ever Devised', *Guardian*, 1 July 2009, p.40.
12. Ciaran Bryan, 'Rationing in Emergency Ireland, 1938-48' (unpublished doctoral thesis, National University of Ireland Maynooth, 2014), p. 103.
13. 'Cookery Book into Second Edition', *Irish Times*, 8 July 1960, p. 9.
14. 'The Origins of Irish Soda Bread', *Kells*, 2022 <https://kellswholemeal.ie/the-origins-of-irish-soda-bread/> [accessed 12 March 2022]
15. Regina Sexton, 'Food and Culinary Cultures in Pre-Famine Ireland', *Proceedings of the Royal Irish Academy: Archaeology, Culture, History, Literature*, 115C (2015), 257-306 (p. 298).
16. Maura Laverty, *Maura Laverty's Cookery Book*, 3rd edn (Tralee: The Kerryman Ltd, 1948), p. 70.
17. Brendan Walsh, 'Trends in Age at Marriage in Postwar Ireland', *Demography*, 9 (1972), 187-202 <https://doi.org/10.2307/2060632>
18. Kelly, p. 176.
19. Caitríona Clear, '"The Red Ink of Emotion": Maura Laverty, Women's Work and Irish Society in the

1940s', *Saothar*, 28 (2003), 90-97 <https://www.jstor.org/stable/23199766> [accessed 6 April 2021]
20 Caitriona Clear, *Women of the House: Women's Household Work in Ireland 1921-61: Experiences, Memories, Discourses* (Dublin: Irish Academic Press, 2003), pp. 40-42.
21 Laverty quoted in Clear, *Women of the House*, p. 95.
22 Clear, *Women of the House*, p. 95.
23 Rhona Richman Kenneally, 'Memory as Food Performance: The Cookbooks of Maura Laverty', in *Ireland and Quebec: Multidisciplinary Perspectives on History, Culture and Society*, ed. by Margaret Kelleher and Michael Kenneally (Dublin: Four Courts Press, 2016), pp. 166-82 (p. 182).

Materializing the Culinary Dreamscape: Maps, Guidebooks, and the Role of *Terroir* in (Re)Constructing the Myth of the French Gastronomic Utopia

Jenny L. Herman

Introduction

Despite the wide diversity of regional specificities in culinary practices and among varying populations, the sense of identity arising from the production and utilization of local products reflects the consummation of an effort to unify a nation through food, thus evoking Brillat-Savarin's famed dictum: '*Dis-moi ce que tu manges, je te dirai ce que tu es.*'[1] By consuming the homeland, in all its territorial richness, from a round of Brie de Meaux to a bottle of Champagne or a Saucisson de Lyon, the French issue forth from a self-styled culinary utopia, a materialized *pays de cocagne*. What, then, contributed to the construction of *terroir* as an integral element of French identity, imbuing culinary products with the power of cultural representation? The analysis of gastronomic maps, culinary guidebooks, and labels of origin, all of which focus on products and their territorial associations, elucidates the social significance of *terroir* in mythologizing a collective culinary identity. Furthermore, exploring the pervasiveness of *terroir*-based themes in this literary and material culture will aid in understanding the symbolic power of food in France and its permeation into the collective imagination. While France's culinary history can be traced to more distant writings and events, this paper focuses on the early twentieth century, when we see a marked growth of such publications, and the contemporary period when labels of origin emerged.

From classical gastronomic guides and periodicals such as *La France à table* (1928–1978) and *L'inventaire du patrimoine culinaire de la France* (1992–2015), to more creative works such as *L'Almanach de Cocagne* (1920–1922) or *Les Vins de Gala* (1977), we see a rich literary tradition emphasizing the connection between specific products and particular places, citing this rootedness to explain unique regional characteristics. Likewise, gastronomic maps which enumerate geographically linked products reinforce *terroir* and contribute to national unity by displaying the whole country and its gustatory offerings. Whether included in periodicals such as *La France à table* or published separately, such as chef Alain Bourguignon's *Carte gastronomique de la France* (1929), these maps also served as a significant tool in launching gastronomic tourism. Finally, with the creation of food labels signalling protected origin, such as the *Appellation d'Origine Protegée* (AOP), we see the complex intermingling of patrimonial transmission and policy-making to promote and safeguard regional products. The cultural analysis of Priscilla Parkhurst-Ferguson, *terroir*-focused scholarship of Thomas Parker, and socio-geographical work of Jean-Robert Pitte are principally consulted in this research, which is complemented by the application of semiotic theory (Culler, Barthes, Nora) and direct policy analysis. Through this study I propose a hybrid investigation of *terroir* in France, focusing on its interplay with territory and identity through the lens of gastronomic literature, culinary maps, and labels which valorize regional products, with the ultimate aim of questioning the instrumentalization of *terroir* today, as a tool to both (re)construct the myth of the French gastronomic utopia and as a response to contemporary social, cultural, and economic challenges.

Whose Gastronomic Utopia?

As a point of departure into France as a culinary dreamscape, it is necessary to acknowledge the reign of plurality when discussing both *terroir* and nation. Although we may see France today as an inheritor of a timeless gastronomic tradition, the country's wider culinary acclaim hails from the latter half of the nineteenth and early twentieth centuries, alongside the publication of culinary maps, gastronomic guidebooks, and the creation of policies to protect products-of-origin such as foods and wine. It is also necessary to acknowledge how thoroughly the mythology of France's culinary supremacy spread to achieve its reflexive association with high quality cuisine common today.

Echoed by entrepreneurial chefs such as August Escoffier and later Paul Bocuse and authors such as Marcel Rouff and Austin de Croze, profusions of nationalistic praise for France's gastronomy abound. With repetition they have gained the largely unquestioned status of truism; French gastronomy is 'incontestable and uncontested'.[2] Champions of French cuisine such as culinary journalist Curnonsky unhesitatingly declare France a *pays de cocagne*, likening its culinary marvels to a brimming cornucopia. By the late nineteenth century we begin to see the conflation of cuisine and culinary products, and foods representative of *terroir*, or the unique taste of a place, begin to be viewed positively. As Parker notes, a *goût de terroir*, through the eighteenth century, was seen as negative, therefore this transformation helped facilitate new favourable associations.[3] The quality of cuisine itself is attributed to and dependent upon the land itself. These works extol the natural abundance of France and the *savoir-faire* of its peoples, promoting *terroir* to an element of patrimony.

The notion that France's culinary acclaim is linked with its produce is reinforced by the French and foreigners alike. For instance, in discussing their taste, Theodore Zeldin attributes the success of French cuisine to 'the variety of produce they use'.[4] The prevalence of this assessment, which doubles as a marketing tool, has remained largely unchallenged. Geographer and culinary scholar Jean-Robert Pitte, however, in *Gastronomie française: Histoire et géographie d'une passion*, contests this mythologizing tendency, asserting, 'We are gravely mistaken in believing France would be a country where milk and honey flow spontaneously, where one would only stoop down to collect the most exquisite manna fallen from the sky.' Pitte argues that although France may possess 'the *terroirs* which enable the creation of a noble product', much more is owed to a historical matter of supply and demand stemming from the establishment of a court who sought fine foods and wine.[5] Along with the pressure of noble tastes, Pitte also notes the fortuitous placement of transport and trade routes as contributing to France's culinary success. These factors prompted both the development of agriculture and the cultivation of quality products. This balanced approach resists the patriotic enthusiasm of upholding the myth of France as a gastronomic utopia.

In contrast, two fundamental culinary writers of the early twentieth century, Curnonsky and Marcel Rouff, reinforce the divine inheritance narrative, insisting that the art of eating thrived throughout France because the country is 'favoured by the mildness of its climate and by the variety of its regions', which, in nourishing all manner of livestock, fruits, vegetables, is a veritable garden of Eden.[6] Curnonsky and Pitte do both acknowledge the fundamental role of cooks and the demands of a refined audience to appreciate their art. Enforced in the *Anthologie de la gastronomie française*, Curnonsky insists that '[g]astronome and chef are indispensable to each other: for what would come of the gastronomes if they didn't have good chefs, and what would become of the chefs if they didn't have fine gourmets to discuss and taste their cuisine?'.[7] They cite the symbiotic relationships between cook, land, and gastronome in developing France's culinary notoriety. This recognition of socio-cultural, human factors in developing French gastronomy corresponds with today's policy-enforced use of *terroir*, employed by the INAO in defining and regulating products of origin such as AOC wines and AOP foods, which emphasize tradition and *savoir-faire* in their labelling qualifications.[8]

Tracing *Terroir*(s)

While scholars such as Priscilla Parkhurst-Ferguson have evinced the representative power of cuisine, and the likes of Julia Csergo, Marion Demossier, and Amy Trubek have elaborated geographic connections between food, identity, and marketing, a contemporary analysis of *terroir* as a malleable factor, instrumentalized in heritagization, remains underdeveloped. Thomas Parker has especially explored the historic evolution of *terroir* and the term's fluctuating connotations, while Timothy J. Tomasik provides a more theoretical approach to *terroir*, exploring its usage in the works of Michel de Certeau, highlighting the challenges of transferring or 'uprooting' a distinctly French concept such as *terroir* for a broader audience. Significantly, Tomasik and Parker both acknowledge that *terroir* did not develop linearly, but rather, according to Tomasik, it 'oscillates between references to geologic characteristics like soil contents to traits from the classical tradition of descriptive geography such as city/country (or urban/provincial) distinctions'.[9] Parker further highlights that the development of geographic studies in France was influenced by romanticized notions of *terroir* which attributed location-specific characteristics to people and products alike.[10] It is unsurprising then that these mystic ideas of locality are present in gastronomic texts and policies where we see the insertion of the intangible, an important aspect of mythologizing and safeguarding of culinary heritage.

Contrary to the often-repeated belief that *terroir*, being a French idea, is untranslatable, I suggest that, as we will see in the following section, *terroir* is instead a living term which can be uprooted, adapted, and instrumentalized. Whether by strengthening France's gastronomic offer against global competition, sparking nostalgia, or referencing geographically specific tastes, *terroir* holds myriad potentialities. This fluid term can suggest authenticity, foster cohesion between nation and region, and even inspire patriotism. When considering that culinary guidebooks, gastronomic maps, and product-of-origin labels explicitly employ *terroir* as a complex, plural signifier, I argue that we must stretch beyond the synchronic and diachronic treatment of *terroir* to understand its usage today, embracing a hybrid schema that considers plurality and simultaneity. We must also consider the term abstractly, as seen in the subtext of food critic Périco Légasse's reflection on his travels throughout France. Evoking patriotic sentiments paralleled in culinary safeguarding measures, he recalls that upon encountering the gastronomic treasures of France 'the patriotic instinct animates our taste buds, urges us to preserve'. He asserts that 'French cuisine is, above all, a land of plenty'.[11] Recalling Nora's *lieux de mémoire*, Légrasse interestingly refers to cuisine as a place, something of a nostalgic territory where 'the remnants of experience still lived in the warmth of tradition' linger.[12] The utopic situation of *terroir* is therefore central to the following discussion.

Guidebooks, Maps, and Culinary Literature

This sense of tradition being visible, this romanticization of the rural in a renewed pastoralism, plays a central role in the emergence of culinary guidebooks, literature, and maps, which afford consumers the stabilizing sense of upholding tradition, of preserving a collective past. Like *terroir*, regional cuisines and products act as an anchor to liveable patrimony. Mapping, inventorying, and thus maintaining these elements of national heritage became all the more impactful in the sluggish economic wake following the decline of industry and the slumping morale surrounding the wars. As Tomasik observes, 'In a limited literary sense, *terroir* connotes authorial regionalism and generally conservative returns to rural life, wisdom, and culture.' We can infer that these works signal a place where 'enduring values of man and soil are equated with the political ideals of national socialisms or are intended as correctives to the perceived urban values dominating the (Parisian) administrative center of postindustrial France'.[13] Thus romanticizing the rural becomes the antidote for urban exhaustion and disconnection from nature, from roots. Unsurprisingly, then, works of culinary literature such as guidebooks, inventories, and anthologies gained popularity in early twentieth-century France. Cuisine and *terroir* become visible, consumable, marketable. Following Barthes' *Mythologies*, 'the peasant dish' becomes 'the rural fantasy'.[14]

A crucial character in promoting the popularity of regional cuisines and gastronomic tourism was Curnonsky, the pseudonym of Maurice Edmond Sailland. Through numerous initiatives, including the direction of culinary maps, the publication of guidebook series and monographs, and the foundation of the famed dining club, the Académie des Gastronomes, Curnonsky championed a French cuisine which de-centralized Paris and amplified the collective bounty of France's gastronomic offer. Although culinary-centric travel is familiar to a contemporary audience, as Eluard-Valette suggests, Curnonsky launched the identity of the gastronome prospecteur and initiated 'a new way of traveling, for the discovery of a dish'.[15] This food-centric tourism was placed alongside visiting other emblems of French patrimony. As culinary historian Julia Csergo notes, by the 1920s, '[g]astronomy comes together with other objects of patrimony' such as cathedrals and museums.[16] Furthermore, regional culinary highlights not only attracted a new type of tourism, but also promoted a sense of unity in the interwar period.[17]

La France gastronomique, guide des merveilles culinaires et des bonnes auberges françaises (1921–1928), a series Curnonsky co-authored with regionalist and culinary writer Marcel Rouff, reads like a proto-foodie travelogue, recounting romanticized meals and poetic impressions. It promises readers that they would be thusly welcomed across France, from the humblest country inn to the finest establishment. These personal digressions, however, should not be taken simply as cloaked advertising. They also carry an oral tradition paying tribute to one of France's celebrated fathers of cuisine, Grimod de la Reynière, whose *Almanach des gourmandes* insisted that a table should be 'adorned in a wealth of anecdotes, stories and amusing accounts'.[18] This pleasure of recitation reminds us that culinary conviviality is not centred on the concrete aspects of dining alone, but includes the immaterial as well. Thus a technically good meal may not necessarily equate to a good dining experience. As conviviality can arise around any table, we see a democratization of taste which forms a crucial element of culinary unity-building. We see a corresponding shift from elite, exhaustive gastronomic tomes, to lighter guides accessible to a wider public. For example, Curnonsky's subsequent *France, paradis du vin et de la bonne chère*, published in 1933, offers an abridged overview of France's regions. This slim sixty-three-page volume, complete with pastoral illustrations highlighting the charm of the French countryside, marks a notable shift in the accessibility of culinary literature. In comparison with its twenty-four-volume predecessor, appealing to the passionate gastronome, we see the emergence of concise texts with local maps, geared towards the weekend traveller. In opening this volume, Curnonsky upholds the mythology of France as a '*pays de cocagne*' asserting, 'We are forced to recognize that our country is the most habitable on the planet, among other reasons, because it is surely here that we eat and drink the best.' He continues to insist that 'our incomparable regional cuisine [is] born of the diversity within our provinces'.[19] The collective language of 'our' here suggests the text is directed at French readers, fellow citizens who can be proud to partake in France's gastronomic offer, belonging to nation and region simultaneously. As Parkhurst-Ferguson summarizes, 'Traveling spread knowledge of the culinary patrimony of France and made contacts between regions [...].'[20] In terms of territory, *France, paradis du vin et de la bonne chère*, also resists following territorial boundaries, but rather presents cities or regions based on their specialties and culinary reputations.

However, much like the concept of body politic, Curnonsky situates Paris as the governing head, declaring it a *capitale de la gastronomie* or a convening place where all cuisines converge.[21] Politics and economics play a notable role in this presentation of cuisine. For instance, this text opens with the wines and culinary offerings of Bordeaux, Burgundy, and Champagne, regions with a greater offer to affluent, cosmopolitan tourists. These regions, enriched by their famed wine production and trade, are described in urbane terms such as *riche, fine, somptueuse, exquise,* and *délicate,* evidently appealing to a wealthier potential visitor.[22] A sceptical reader can hardly overlook the advertising plugs in effusions like 'the cuisine of Champagne, fine, delicate, and nuanced, borrows its best grace and its most delicious 'spirit' from the excellence of the wines which enter into the preparation of its sauces'.[23] Keen to not exclude any potential visitors, however, Curnonsky assures readers that 'Champagne agrees with all tastes, goes with all dishes and can be drank in all circumstance'.[24] By contrast, poorer regions are celebrated for their virtues of loyalty and for their regional dishes, many of which are now culinary emblems of France. From vaunting the virtues of Languedoc's cassoulet as an 'admirable national dish' to praising the pot-au-feu and cuisine of central France as *auguste* and *rustique*, each location is praised.[25] Regions already associated with cuisine, such as Lyon, or Bresse/Bugey (birthplace of Brillat-Savarin) are labelled as *pays de cocagne*. Additionally, we see descriptions like *savante* or *noble* for regional products like fruits, vegetables, butter, and sausage, which require *savoir-faire* to produce optimally. This language highlights the hybridity of *terroir* as both location-based and cultural.

Another series, rife with imagination-inspiring folklore, is the periodical *La France à table*. Also directed by Curnonsky, and with regular contributors like regionalists Gaston Derys and Austin de Croze, this long-running gastronomic review is firmly rooted in the tradition of culinary regionalism established in the preceding decade. Initially published from 1934 to 1937 and resuming in 1949 after the war, this series features folk songs and maps and alludes to the necessity of protecting the quality of French products

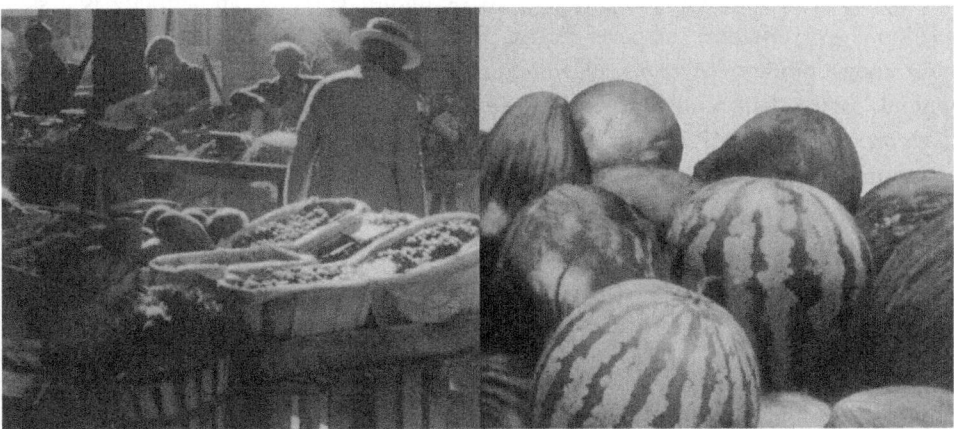

Figure 1. La France à table. *Janvier 1935. p.9. BnF.*

as a duty.²⁶ With the use of high-quality photos and illustrated maps, it marks a visual turn in culinary guides, which, alongside poetic texts, presented a romantic rural life to readers. For example, de Croze paints this florid sketch of Provence, accompanied with idyllic photos (Figure 1), exalting:

> The Provençal soul is exhaled in a composite and very characteristic perfume: it initially smells of verbena and lavender, melons and wheat, the figs which [...] dry on the *canisses* (racks of reed), hot charcoal, fine oil, thyme, fennel, saffron, good, boldly-spiced cuisine, all of this enveloped in the intoxicating odour exuding from the overheated leaves of the fig tree [...]. The plots of soil seem violet where the watermelons flourish, the *lisetto* (Christmas melons), squash and courgette, the peppers, the aubergines, all of the good vegetables of Provence, flavourful and coloured like the sweet-smelling fruits of flowers.²⁷

This evocative segment engages the senses while constructing a multi-layered *terroir*-laden scene, not only listing Provençal products like figs and oil, but also noting the scents of the landscape and local character. Beyond boosting tourism, this text-image pairing would foster pride among locals, and the nostalgia-inducing prose and reassuring rural scenes celebrate a country deeply destabilized by war. In the first issue published after the Second World War, Curnonsky passionately asserts, 'No! The cult of the table is not abolished and France remains the paradise of gastronomy.'²⁸

This series emphasizes the connection between land and people, highlighting photos of farmers, vineyards, and cultivated fields in equal importance to traditional heritage like churches and monuments. The pages are interspersed with poems, folk harvest songs, recipes, and restaurant recommendations, valorized by contributions from esteemed literary figures like Colette, or by doctors and politicians. The covers often display regional specialties as representative elements of local culture. Food items gradually stand as signs of themselves, signalling tourists to the 'authentic'. As semiotician Jonathan Culler writes, 'the authentic is not something unmarked or undifferentiated; authenticity is a sign relation.'²⁹ For instance, the cover for the 'Touraine' issue (Figure 2) displays the area's most-known products of *terroir*, allowing recognition and reinforcement of these culinary symbols for residents and tourists. We see the iconic goat cheese, the *Saint-Maure de Touraine*, a jar of *rillettes de Tours*, and glasses for both red and white wines, which readers can assume are from the surrounding Loire valley. The unlabelled bottle, dusted in soil, recalls a connection with the land. For today's reader, this table-scape is more noteworthy, as each product enjoys established product-of-origin labels.

A more technical cataloguing on products-of-origin is achieved in *L'inventaire du patrimoine culinaire de la France*, a nineteen-volume series initiated in 1992 following aims of the Conseil National des Arts Culinaires and the Ministries of Culture and Agriculture.³⁰ Each region is meticulously documented, listing regional specialties, products, and practices. With a decidedly less-romantic tone, this series nonetheless serves as a gastronomic guide, valorizing products-as-patrimony through

Figure 2 (left). La France à table, *'Touraine' 1949. Figure 3 (right) Detail of Alain Bourguignon's* Carte gastronomique de la France, *1929. https://gallica.bnf.fr/ark:/12148/btv1b525040439q.*

the safeguarding measure of inventorying. Spanning from 1992 to 2015, *L'inventaire* seeks to present a comprehensive list of France's culinary heritage. Each region, bound within its own tome, remains geographically separate. By contrast we can see the benefit of culinary maps in presenting a more unified image of French cuisine.

Unlike guidebook series, which often address regions separately, maps allow a sense of cohesion by displaying France as a whole. Gastronomic maps are inseparably linked with *terroir* as they reinforce associations between places and products. Because of their territoriality, these maps are also inextricably connected with ideas of nationhood. While individual regions may not justify France's reputation as a culinary utopia, the collective bounty displayed in a map can cumulate culinary diversity into a collective patrimony. These maps, especially following the rise in auto tourism, encouraged culinary travel. For example, Alain Bourguignon's 1929 *Carte gastronomique de la France* (detail in Figure 3) emphasizes regional specialties in bold print, and highlights notable wine regions in bright red and yellow. The spatial placement of food items on the land reinforces the link with *terroir* and plays an important role in constructing a French gastronomic identity. Maps could likewise highlight regions singly, often appearing alongside touristic advertisements in guidebooks. An interesting idea arises that unique regions produce their own harmonious pairings.

When considering culinary literature, we must also consider the motivations of the author, be it promoting tourism, safeguarding traditions, or marketing products, which is increasingly the case moving towards contemporary gastronomic literature. Even texts which seem largely imaginative, such as Dalí's wine-centric *Les Vins de Gala* (1977), may foster culinary heritagization. Dalí, whom Pitte praises for his culinary sensibilities in *Diners de Gala* (1973),[31] fills pages with his iconic surrealistic sketches appearing alongside whimsically titled sections like *Vins de joie* and *Vins de lumière* and fictionalized narratives of wine origins such as that of Châteauneuf de Pape. This work seems to be an imaginative tribute to wine by an unexpectedly informed enthusiast.[32] Upon closer inspection, however, a majority of the texts, including the capriciously-titled 'Vins de Gala' are written not by Dalí, but by former general director of the INAO Louis Orizet.[33]

Interestingly, Orizet adopts a poetic style better-suited to a work of Dalí. The wines, with abstract titles like *joie* and *généreux*, recall Curnonsky's emotive labelling of regional foods like *loyale* and *savante*. The '*Les 10 Vins de Gala*' are subdivided into sections such as '*vins de lumière*' listing wines associated with that characteristic. '*Vins de joie*' for instance, includes Beaujolais and Chinon, regions which Curnonsky and Rouff liken to lightness and '*joie paisible*'.[34] A note gastronomique follows each entry with recommended pairings, reinforcing the idea of a natural affinity between local foods and wines. For example, in the section '*Vins de pourpre*' which includes red wines of Burgundy, Orizet writes, 'Thus the meat of Charolles and Morvandelle, the poultry of Bresse, the fish of the Sâone, frame the prestigious Burgundy from Dijon to Villefrance-sur-Sâone.'[35] (This passage directly corresponds with the map selection in Figure 3.) Orizet insists that every gastronomic region of France has propitious soil and geography allowing grapevines to prosper. We see the familiar reinforcement of natural provenance as divine providence in this concept of *terroir*.

What social weight, then, can we attribute to these culinary writings and their treatments of *terroir* in French culture? As Parkhurst-Ferguson asserts, 'The importance and significance to cuisine of language, texts, and representations can hardly be overstated. As much as the foodways by which it is shaped or the actual foods consumed, words sustain cuisine.'[36] Or, as Orizet writes, 'Every school, every religion begins by the establishment of a convention of language. Without this key, there is only obscurity, misunderstanding and conflict'.[37] It is precisely this recognition of the codification of *terroir* implicated in culinary language which leads to safeguarding measures that manifest not only in cultural heritage initiatives, but also in contemporary policies surrounding product-of-origin labels.

Conclusion

While the past century saw the successful construction of a culinary culture in France, today we see the nostalgic utopia evoked to safeguard not only *savoir-faire*, but also *savoir-vivre*. While culinary maps and guidebooks highlighted the culinary diversity of France, today's measures to certify authenticity seek to anchor that diversity both temporally and culturally. The blend of territory and tradition reign in certification guidelines built around *terroir*, subtly excluding changing practices, tastes, or even populations. One of the final volumes of *L'inventaire* includes a preface summarizing its mission to protect traditions and products, stressing the necessity of safeguarding and transmitting culinary patrimony for the future.[38] In other words, product-of-origin labels resist the feared 'acceleration of history'.[39] Recognizing that the hyper-globalization of recent decades brought significant economic competition against France's reputed cuisine, products of *terroir* offer something more difficult to replace. If we consider, as Tomasik proposes, that *terroir* 'carries a strong affective charge,' observing that local products hold representative power, we can see how *terroir* becomes mouldable and moveable.[40] Consumers need no longer travel for a culinary specialty, nor even visit a regional-themed restaurant for 'authentic' tastes. Today, labels for products-of-origin invert the previous century's allure of pastoralism. Rather than seek out rural foodways, one must merely find the nearest supermarket to partake in a certified regional specialty. This result is nearly the antithesis of the actual concept of rootedness upon which *terroir* is based, resulting in the capitalization of the term *terroir* and the mythology surrounding it.

An AOP cheese from Époisses is as close as the local Carrefour; a sausage from the Haute-Savoie can evoke alpine scenes from the comfort of a Parisian kitchen, feeding personal nostalgia with a label of authenticity. A recent ad campaign throughout the metros of Paris asked pedestrians 'How do you eat your *terroir*?' with a #mangerAOP and a picture of *chavignol* goat cheese, reinforcing the idea that *terroir* is a moveable, consumable object.[41] In 2020, a series from the journal *Le Un* focused on three pillars of French culinary mythology – bread, wine, and cheese – delving into their social significance and perpetuating their cultural transmission.[42] A report from the Ministry of Agriculture published in January 2021 notes rising consumption of 'local' products.[43] The general trend towards locality brings *terroir* back into focus as a mutable symbolic concept. As Parkhurst-Ferguson keenly summarizes, 'Every culture has its myths. Neither right nor wrong, neither truthful nor mendacious, myths *are*. Above all, they are useful. Products of a collective imagination, these understandings of the everyday serve individuals as they work for societies.'[44] From the creation of culinary literature and maps to the implementation of safeguarding policies, the concept of *terroir* has shown its adaptability to address social and economic changes and remains an evolving staple of French culinary mythology.

Notes

1. From Brillat Savarin's *Physiologie du goût* (1825), this quote inspired the cliché 'you are what you eat'.
2. Curnonsky (dir.), Gaston Derys (ed.) *La Table; magazine saisonnier de la gastronomie française* (Hiver, 1931–1932), p.12. All translations by the author.
3. Thomas Parker, *Tasting French Terroir: The History of an Idea* (Berkley: University of California Press, 2015), pp.138-40, 176.
4. Theodore Zeldin, 'How to Appreciate Their Taste', *The French* (New York: Vintage, 1984), pp. 289-344.
5. Jean-Robert Pitte, *Gastronomie française: Histoire et géographie d'une passion* (Fayard: 2005), pp. 35, 32.
6. Curnonsky, *La Table*, p.11.
7. Curnonsky and Gaston Derys, *Anthologie de la gastronomie française* (Paris: Delagrave, 1936), p.13.
8. The Institut Nationale des Appellations d'Origine (INAO) is the EU governing body for products-of-origin including the Appellation d'Origine Contrôlée (AOC) label for wines and the Appellation

d'Origine Protegée (AOP) labels for food products.
9. Timothy J. Tomasik, 'Certeau à la Carte: Translating Discursive *Terroir* in *The Practice of Everyday Life: Living and Cooking*', *The South Atlantic Quarterly*, 100:2 (2001), 519-542 (p. 523).
10. Parker, pp. 155-156.
11. Périco Légasse in *Le Repas gastronomique des française*, ed. by Loïc Bienassis and Francis Chevrier (Editions Gallimard: 2015), pp. 54, 55.
12. Pierre Nora, 'Between Memory and History: Les Lieux de Mémoire', *Representations*, 26 (1989), 7-24 (p. 7).
13. Tomasik, p. 520.
14. Roland Barthes, *Mythologies* (Paris: Editions de Seuil, 1957), p. 144.
15. Cécile Eluard-Valette, *Les Grandes heures de la cuisine française* (Paris: Libraries Associées, 1964), p. 176.
16. Julia Csergo, '*Quelques jalons pour une histoire du tourisme et de la gastronomie en France*', *Téoros*, 25.1 (2006), 5-9.
17. This inquiry does not aim to provide a history of regional cuisines nor outline the development of their marketing. For details on culinary commodification, see Julia Csergo's *La Gastronomie est-elle une marchandise culturelle comme les autres?* (Chartes: Menu Fretin, 2016).
18. Grimod de la Reyniere, *Almanach des gourmandes*, quoted in Eluard-Valette, p. 153.
19. Curnonsky, *France, paradis du vin et de la bonne chère* (Paris: Editions d'Art, 1933), p. 5.
20. Priscilla Parkhurst-Ferguson, *Accounting for Taste: The Triumph of French Cuisine* (UP, 2004), p. 127.
21. Curnonsky, *Paradis*, p. 6.
22. Curnonsky, *Paradis*, pp. 8-13.
23. Curnonsky, *Paradis*, p. 18.
24. Curnonsky, *Paradis*, p. 20.
25. Curnonsky, *Paradis*, pp. 33, 48.
26. Curnonsky (ed.), *La France à table* (Provence Méditerranéenne), 1935, p. 45.
27. Austin de Croze in *La France à table*, January 1935, p. 6.
28. Curnonsky in *La France à table* (Touraine), 1948, p. 3.
29. Jonathan Culler, *Framing the Sign* (Norman, OK: University of Oklahoma Press, 1990) p. 6.
30. *L'inventaire du patrimoine culinaire*, "Alsace: produits du terroir et recettes traditionnelles", [sous la dir. de J. Froc, M. Hyman, Ph. Hyman... et al.]; préf. par le président du Conseil régional d'Alsace, (Paris: A. Michel: Conseil national des arts culinaires), 1998.
31. Pitte, pp. 26-27.
32. Dalí, *Vins de Gala* (Paris: Draeger, 1977), pp. 59-70. Although not in the bibliographic information, pp. 16-129 are written by Max Gérard, and the text from pp. 145-290 is by Louis Orizet. For quoting Orizet I will use Dalí/Orizet.
33. Orizet also penned the slogan '*Le Beaujolais Nouveau est arrivée!*' launching the flagging wine region into international fame.
34. Curnonsky, *Paradis*, p. 25; Dalí/Orizet, p. 155.
35. These claims are reinforced with a map of France's wine regions and a guide to its appellations. Dalí/Orizet, pp. 288-89.
36. Parkhurst-Ferguson, pp. 9-10.
37. Dalí/Orizet, p. 145.
38. *L'inventaire du patrimoine culinaire*, 'Région Centre: produits du terroir et recettes traditionnelles', préface par le président de la Région Centre [coordonné par l'] IEHCA, (Paris: A. Michel; Tours: IEHCA, 2012).
39. Nora, p. 7.
40. Tomasik, p. 521.
41. "*Vous le mangez comment votre terroir?*" An alternate version asks "*Vous reprendrez bien un morceau de savoir-faire*"?
42. *Le Un. Le goût du fromage* (19 August 2020); *Le goût du vin* (12 August 2020); *Le goût du pain* (5 August 2020).
43. Rapport n° 20074, '*Les produits locaux*' (Ministère de l'agriculture et de l'alimentation, January 2021).
44. Parkhurst-Ferguson, p. 9.

Cogito ergo imaginor: I Think, Therefore I Imagine!

Peter Hertzmann

For four weeks in June 2016, I was the writer-in-residence at the Edinburgh Food Studio in Scotland. The establishment had existed for about six months by the time I arrived for my four-week commitment. It was started with money from Kickstarter, and I had contributed since I knew one of the two founders. 'Knew' was generous, since four summers earlier, Ben Reade and I had been on the same panel at a Symposium and spent the following hour outside in some amazingly pleasant Oxford weather talking about food.

My expectation before arriving in Edinburgh was that I would spend time observing the restaurant and then spend hours writing. Part of that turned out to be true. I had rented a room in an eighteenth-century stone house a couple of blocks from the restaurant. On my three days off each week, I spent much of my time sitting at the small desk in the dormer next to my bed. As I wrote, I spent as much time looking at the treetops out the small window with its restricted view.

The restaurant had a grand total of three workers plus me. On weekends, an additional guest cook would show up, sometimes just to work for a while and other times to lead the action for the weekend. Most of those passing through were acquaintances of Ben's from his time as director of the Nordic Food Lab. The other workers were Sashana Souza Zanella, Ben's business partner at the time and current life partner, and Philipp Kolmann, an Austrian art student studying in Eindhoven but working in Edinburgh while he explored making bone-based ceramics from some of the restaurant's waste.

Service days started at about ten in the morning with a bacon-sausage-egg roll from the sandwich shop two doors up Dalkeith Road from the restaurant. It ended early the next morning with a splash of Armagnac and a quiet walk back to my room. The hours in between were spent preparing, cooking, plating, serving, and cleaning-up the meals served in the restaurant. Duties were not divided. Everyone did everything.

The four of us gathered in the dining room each morning of service. After the morning roll was downed and the day's first espresso swilled, we created the menu for that evening. Before the 'bidding' for dishes began, it was necessary to take a quick inventory. Someone checked the basement to see what ferments were ready. Someone else surveyed the three mini refrigerators to see what was left from previous orders. The forager was contacted to ascertain what greenery was arriving later in the day. The fishmonger was called to determine if any unusual seafood was available.

Once the palate of ingredients was determined, working course by course, the seven-course meal was imagined. Ben wrote the menu on the whiteboard in the kitchen. Each course was broken into the preparations required before it could land on the diner's plate. During the day, the menu would be adjusted as need be to fit our collective change in imagination.

Each day the dishes were different in most respects. There were limitations built into the kitchen due to size, equipment, location, and the number of workers. Each piece of china was used only once during a service; little was left in reserve. Each course had to have its own plates, and no two courses could use the same plates.

Although the group imagined the entire meal, each person in the group imagined different dishes. When one cook proposed a strawberry soup, each of the other cooks imagined something different. Therefore, the cook who proposed a dish took charge of its preparation and the additional objective to harmonize everyone's imaginations into the finished dish that was plated and served to the diner.

It may be obvious, but I should point out that although the Food Studio had many cookbooks, they were rarely consulted once a dish was imagined. Each cook relied on his or her personal cooking knowledge of methods, techniques, and ingredients. Occasionally, the other cooks were consulted, but rarely a book.

Method I

Over the years, I've become aware of three different methods for imagining dishes. The first method came to me like an uninvited guest. By the early spring of 2011, I was aware that my creative life was in the throes of change. Each morning I awoke with an idea for a new dish. Some concepts came to me fully developed, while others came from remembering some small event from earlier in my life. My imagination followed each remembrance through a series of lateral thoughts until they brought me to a new dish that was most often not related to the original recollection.

The only constraint I placed on each new dish was size. Each had to qualify as an *amuse-bouche, intermède,* or *mignardise*.[1] At the time I was exploring how a series of bite-sized dishes could affect the overall feel of a dinner party. Rather than my standard 'French-style' four-course menu of *entrée, plat,* salad, and dessert, I started with four *amuse-bouche* served individually over a period of an hour or so. These were served in the lounge along with drinks. We then moved to the dining room for the first two primary courses. The salad was bordered on both sides with a single *intermède*. Dessert was followed by four *mignardises* served all at once along with any coffee and *digestifs*. The *amuse-bouche* and *intermèdes* were served individually on small dishes. The *mignardises* were served on a single large plate.

Ginger Ale and Other Sodas

One of the earliest memories I awoke with that spring was my 1960 trip to the National Boy Scout Jamboree in Colorado Springs. It was curious to wake thinking about an event a half century after it occurred. The trip produced many memories, so it was even more curious that the memory I woke with that morning was of Coca-Cola. The grassy area where the Jamboree was held was hot and dry. At any minute, you could imagine

Cogito ergo imaginor: I Think, Therefore I Imagine!

a large herd of longhorn cattle approaching. Spaced around the grounds, which were large enough to hold the tents of 50,000 Scouts, were roped-off areas with enough bunting for a mid-sized town to celebrate Independence Day. In each area was a table where a dime would purchase a paper cup of slightly cool Coke. Prior to the Jamboree, I was not a Coke fan – I still never savour one – but those were different. Like the original soda-fountain drink but without the cocaine, the Coca Cola syrup was mixed with carbonated water to produce the finished drink. The mixing occurred in the soda gun that the server used to dispense the finished Coke into the paper cups. Out there in the heat and dust, the system designed for indoor use produced almost flat, just chilled Coca-Cola. I liked it and spent many dimes there.

As I laid in bed, not yet fully awake, thinking about those 'perfect' Cokes, my mind drifted to a later Jamboree, this time in Greece. No soft drinks were available for purchase at the XI World Jamboree, but in Athens before the event I was introduced to real ginger ale, not the placid stuff available in 1960s America. This Greek ginger ale was spicy, hot, and sweet at the same time. While still in bed, I began to imagine my own ginger ale.

I knew that to make ginger ale, I needed a quantity of ginger syrup. I found a simple recipe online for bartender's ginger syrup. The results were usable, but not great. The flavour was good, but clarification was problematic. I remembered that the process of candying ginger had, as waste, a very nice ginger syrup. So, I candied a couple of pounds of ginger and set the syrup aside.

With syrup in hand, I knew of two ways to make a soda from it. The easiest is to add it one-to-one to soda water. A second method is to dilute it one-to-one with filtered water and then carbonate the mixture. The second method produces bubbles that are sharper on the tongue, so it works best for small portions.

Even before my ginger ale first met an ice cube, I began imaging other sodas based on some other syrups sleeping in my refrigerator. My homemade Meyer lemon syrup was a natural. The bourbon-barrel-aged maple syrup was also handy and delightful. The bacon syrup sample I had recently received made for a curiously interesting soda. The onion syrup I made – because I could – produced a soda with an acquired taste. The ultimate variation was the carrot soda I created when I was playing with Method II for imagining dishes.

Pickled onions

On New Year's Day in 1955, my father's parents celebrated their fiftieth wedding anniversary. Relatives came from all over the country to help them celebrate. The events lasted four or five days, and my seven-year-old self had to attend every one of them. One night at the Palace Hotel in San Francisco, I got parked with a cousin and his wife for forty-five minutes in the Garden Court.[2] Lionel and Anna Schatz drank Beefeater Gibsons, which were, in fact, gin martinis disguised by the substitution of a pickled onion instead of green olives.[3] This made an impression on me. Most of my life, the Gibson has been my cocktail of choice. The idea that came to me that morning on waking was not for the Gibson, but for the onion.

At that time, I'd never pickled any vegetable. A short time earlier I had seen a local high-end French chef pickle a mixture of raw vegetables using a method that included the concoction sitting a specified amount of time in the sun. I took his method and decided it could be significantly simplified.

My brine was two parts white-wine vinegar, one part filtered water, and one part, by volume, granulated sugar. The brine was brought to a boil and then poured over peeled pearl onions in the canning jar. The jar was sealed, while still hot, with a two-piece lid. The actual pickling consisted of sitting on my kitchen counter for five days followed by the onions spending the remainder of their short existence in my refrigerator.

For service, a drained onion or two is placed in a small cordial glass. A few drops of London – Beefeater if you have it – dry gin complete the *amuse-bouche*.

This preparation eventually spawned another where a slightly larger cippolini onion was cut in half crosswise, quick-pickled in the same brine, and the cut edge was grilled before serving. Or in other words, a raw, pickled onion was cooked before serving!

Method I Decoded
This process of creation starts with being semi-conscious during your dream state. I think of it as morphing from a sleep dream to a daydream. When I wake at the end of a dream, especially one about some event in my past, I latch onto the dream's tail with my mind and spin it further. If I'm lucky, the chain of thoughts will move toward food and maybe a new dish. The whole process is not too dissimilar to Freud's concept of free association.

If you can catch your dreams, you can turn them into dishes! With experience, you can gently nudge the path in a direction that seems full of potential. After a while, you no longer need a dream as a catalyst. You'll taste a dish at a restaurant and immediately evolve a dozen dishes from it.

Method II

Unlike the previous method that starts with thoughts, this method starts with a base ingredient. By 'base', I mean an ingredient that is central to the dish, such as a vegetable, meat, or seafood. It is an item that dishes are based around rather than an item that accents another ingredient. Examples could be a potato, a parsnip, a perch, or a pig. With an ingredient as large as a pig, a foot may be a better place to start rather than with the whole animal, although I wouldn't narrow it down to fore or hind leg. Likewise, it's better to start with round onions as opposed to the entire *allium* genus.

Once an ingredient is selected, simply think of different ways to prepare the ingredient or components of the ingredient. When I use this method with groups of cooks as an exercise, the ideas flow linearly for a while and then branch out based on a component of the ingredient, such as its juice. The more experience the cooks have, the easier the process. I've tried the exercise a couple of times with book reading audiences. It went nowhere. They usually lack the required expertise.

The more extensive the participant's knowledge of methods, techniques, and ingredients, the easier it is to devise totally new dishes. One's personal cooking-method familiarity is a matter of experience. Ingredients often benefit from some quick research. Before you attempt to make onion syrup, it's helpful to understand that the average round onion contains about four per cent sugar. You also need a means to extract the juice from the onion. Understanding the structure of the onion can help with this.

Method II Caveats

Since we are only imagining dishes with this method, no recipe testing is required to check our results. Experienced cooks should be able to prepare any dish they imagine, but the results may not justify the effort. Unless you do the exercise and then prepare each dish, you'll never know if an imagined preparation can be realized.

Some of the conceptual dishes produced in this exercise may work just as they are stated, whereas others would require refinement, and some would be a waste of time. For an experienced cook, putting any of the ideas into practise should be simple.

The purpose of the exercise is to expand your cooking range. If your repertoire is expanded, that's nice too.

Choosing an Ingredient

My mother never met a zucchini she couldn't turn into inedible paste. Being an American, I know the courgette as a zucchini. I've chosen the courgette for this example in part because it is one of my least favourite vegetables. No matter how many times I prepare tasty courgette dishes, my disdain remains.

The first step is to better understand the courgette. According to the Oxford English Dictionary, *courgette* first appears in English literature in the early 1930s and *zucchini* in the 1920s. Both were previously referred to as a vegetable marrow. This information can be useful as we pull ways that we've previously prepared courgettes from the depths of our collective, societal memory.

Next, we need to understand the components of a courgette. Most important is that a typical courgette is about ninety-five per cent water. This tells us that high heat cooking methods may be limited due to the cooling effects of evaporating water. The sugar level is less than two per cent, so syrup is a longshot. Likewise, starch is non-existent. The amount of pectin present is unknown, other than it exists in varying amounts in the cell walls of all vegetables. Any thickening will probably require an additional ingredient. The only positive thing about courgettes is that they are high in Vitamin A. One pound is all you have to eat to meet the daily requirement!

Although some preparations may use the whole vegetable, the skin is quite distinct from the flesh of a courgette. While the skin has substantial strength, the flesh is easily mashed. At first glance, there's not a lot to work with with a courgette.

To Cook a Courgette

- Raw courgettes can be cut into shreds and tossed with a variety of salad dressings.

The solo courgette can be accented with other raw vegetables or shredded herbs.
- Raw courgettes can be fermented in salt or a salt-based compound such as miso, fermented in koji, or pickled in an acid. Small specimens can be fermented or pickled whole while larger versions need to be cut into chunks or slices.
- Raw courgette slices can be dehydrated into chips.
- Diced courgette can be dehydrated, fried to crisp, and used like croutons.
- The juice can be used for a soda, consumed plain, or as an ingredient in cocktails.
- The juice can be thickened with a gel to produce a cold sauce for fish or a cold soup. Acidified, the sauce could be used to dress a salad.
- The juice can be solidified with a gel to produce an aspic, or the flesh can be pureed and gelled to make a denser compound that can be diced and used in other dishes, like tofu's uses.
- The juice can be combined with eggs and cornflour to make a savoury pastry cream for use in savoury tarts.
- A cold puree can be fashioned into pearls using agar and a column of cold oil. The pearls can then be used like peas in warm or cold dishes.
- The solid waste produced by juicing can be used as a batter ingredient in cakes and a filling component in pastries.
- The waste can be combined with fish paste to make Japanese-style fried fish cakes (*satsuma age*).
- The waste can be combined with other ingredients to make the filling for raviolis and other stuffed pastas.
- The waste can be dried, ground into a powder, and combined with starch to use as a flour substitute in pasta and crackers.
- Sliced courgette can be cooked in stock and then pureed and served as soup.
- Diced courgette can be cooked slowly in fat and then crushed with a fork for serving.
- Shredded courgette can be pan-fried either alone or with other shredded vegetables.
- Chunks of courgette can be roasted until browned.
- Slabs of courgette can be used as a substitute for flat bread and topped with an array of meats, vegetables, and cheeses before roasting.
- The centres of courgette halves can be scooped out to form elongated bowls for filling, or thick, crosswise slices can be hollowed out and filled.
- Courgette puree can be frozen into a granita, mixed with sugar and frozen into a sorbet, mixed with a sugar syrup and egg whites and frozen into a sherbet, or mixed with milk and cream to make an ice cream.

Method III

The last method partially originated with a word phrase. I morphed the current 'in' dish of 'Chicken and Waffles' into a 'Chicken Waffle'. Macaroni and Cheese became a crispy rigatoni stuffed with goat cheese. I made a Bacon-Marshmallow Lollipop because I liked the way it sounded. I used the same excuse for the Pig's Foot Lollipop and Corn Bark.

The word phrase results from thinking about an ingredient – often one that is left over from another dish or one given to me. The Chicken Waffle started when I found myself the proud owner of fifty pounds of chicken meat. The Macaroni and Cheese started when I had a bowl of puffed rigatoni on hand from an experiment. The Bacon-Meringue Lollipop started when I was given a bottle of bacon-flavoured syrup and wasn't interested in making a bacon-tini. The Pig's Foot Lollipop evolved from an excess of pig's feet. The Corn Bark was the result of my purchasing some freeze-dried corn kernels and deciding they would be better with Aleppo pepper and unsweetened chocolate.

For this method to work, you must be able to imagine a finished dish based on the words in your phrase. If you never eaten ratatouille, what would you imagine upon hearing the name? How about vichyssoise? Or if you're not from the United Kingdom, how about neeps and tatties or spotted dick? Or not from America, scrapple? These last items can conjure up all sorts of dishes, none of which relate to the original.

The process used in this method is not dissimilar to the cook who opens the refrigerator and prepares a meal from the contents. The ingredients provide the opportunity and the cook's experience provides the added 'ingredient'. The difference is whether the effort is conscious or not.

Tying the Methods Together

All three methods, as presented, require a knowledge of how to cook. I define the three elements of cooking as methods, techniques, and ingredients. The more familiar you are with all three, the easier it is for you to cook. (For clarification, braising is a method, stirring is a technique; gelling is a method, clarification is a technique.)

The more you are familiar with the methods and techniques of cooking in your culture or another and knowledgeable about the ingredients available to you, the easier cooking with your imagination will be. Vast knowledge is not required – I've even used these techniques with beginning cooks – but an active imagination and a willingness to dispense with following recipes is required.

Notes

1. *Amuse-bouche, intermède,* and *mignardise* are French terms for small dishes served throughout a formal meal. The meal starts with *amuse-bouche,* or what the English-speaking world would call hors d'oeuvres. *Mignardise* bookmark the meal and are served after the dessert, often with coffee or tea. The term is usually translated as 'petit-fours' but is not limited to small cakes. *Intermèdes* are rarely seen on French menus. In the United States, we would term them as palate cleansers.
2. The Palace Hotel was first built in 1875 as the largest hotel in the Western United States. It was seven stories tall and covered a full city block in San Francisco. In the centre was a large glass-covered courtyard of sufficient size that multiple carriages could enter through an archway on Market Street and discharge or gather their passengers away from the street mud and inclement weather. Around the turn of the twentieth century, the courtyard was converted into a restaurant. The hotel was destroyed in the Great Earthquake of 1906 and rebuilt a few years later, including Garden Court. Until my grandfather's death in 1958, many of our family celebrations were held at the Palace Hotel.
3. At the turn of the twentieth century, a Gibson consisted of equal parts French vermouth and English dry gin chilled with ice and strained. By the 1950s, the ratio was six-to-one gin-to-vermouth. I prefer my Gibson to be made with the vermouth bottle left on the shelf.

Reconsidering the Culinary Imagination

Jennifer L. Holm

In contemporary France, there is a tension between the nation's culinary imagination and reality. The beginning of the twenty-first century marked a period of widespread, nostalgia-induced gastronomic heritagization, capitalizing on the culinary imaginaries of consumers and politicians eager to fortify individual and national identities through ties to the local, the rural, and the land. Today, though, the consequences of engaging these imaginaries are coming to the fore. The gastronomic reality in which the French now live suggests that recent culinary imaginings, despite their creative and emancipatory potential, have resulted in an unsustainable and deleterious gastronomic system. Gastronomic narratives of the past five years have been integral in initiating and promoting a shift from imaginative to realistic thinking. Breaking from their own highly nostalgic bent at the beginning of the twenty-first century and embracing pseudo-documentary forms, these narratives reveal brutal truths and provide necessary critiques of French gastronomic consumption and production. Importantly, though, many of these narratives avoid fatalism, imagining alternative modes of production and consumption, thus calling for a reconsideration of the culinary imaginaries upon which we act. An exemplary narrative in this vein is Paul-Henry Bizon's 2017 novel *La Louve*, which presents a sweeping and unforgiving critique of the French nation's culinary stance, particularly as it takes shape in Paris, while also proposing an alternative gastronomic system in the shape of what sociologist Erik Olin Wright defines a 'real utopia'.

The imagination has occupied a fundamental role in shaping foodscapes over the past three decades. Facing a rapidly changing society, the loss of community structures, and the perceived dilution of culture brought on by globalization, a nostalgic gastronomic reflex marked the turn of the twenty-first century. To orient themselves in the present and establish a trajectory for the future, people turned to food, a preeminent aspect of individual and national identity that is also readily available and easily manipulable. The important food was local and *terroir*-linked, as these nostalgia-laced products offered up the vicarious experience of the 'authenticity' of rural life as well as a connection to the land, to roots, and to perceptibly fleeting values and ways of life. In a compounding of the imagination, people and nations engaged the symbolic values of foods and culinary practices to gain access to an imagined past. This thread of culinary imagination extended across the globe, but was notably influential in France, a country that had a markedly negative response to globalization.[1] Throughout Europe, a series of food safety scares arose at the same time, contributing to French wariness of the global market and industrial food production.² Foods with a connection to *terroir* and small-scale agriculture were not only a direct line to the national rural heritage but also a safe and knowable alternative to the mysteries of the industrial food system. What has developed over the past twenty years is a veritable obsession with the rural and the local. This obsession allows city-dwellers to appropriate and consume rural values and identities, perpetuating the notion that the countryside exists to serve the city in myriad ways.

This nostalgic embrace of the local, the rural, and the traditional in terms of gastronomy extended from individual consumers to the nation. The French government, at the local, regional, and national levels, has embarked on a sustained and far-reaching heritagization effort to protect French culture and values with a particular eye to the nation's gastronomy.³ Demonstrative of the importance of food heritagization is the fact that these efforts cross political and ideological divides. While the list of heritagization efforts is too extensive to discuss here, we can highlight several examples. Internationally, France has engaged in a vast gastrodiplomacy campaign, including, in 2010, availing itself of UNESCO's Intangible Cultural Heritage List to protect and promote the French gastronomic meal. In 2021, France proposed a nomination file to put the baguette on this list. At the local and regional level, protection and promotion came about through local festivals and celebrations dedicated to specific foods and culinary practices. In conceiving of these events, imagination looms large. Many of the origin stories of local products are swathed in myth-making and nostalgic recollection.⁴

French gastronomic narratives – literary and cinematic works in which gastronomy serves as a central structuring device – captured this nostalgic turn in real time, offering it up as a national engagement in which all could take part. Indeed, gastronomic narratives provide valuable windows into contemporary foodways, expressing values, critiquing practices and attitudes, and foreshadowing foodscapes to come.⁵ Films such as *Le fabuleux destin d'Amélie Poulain* (*Amélie*, 2001) demonstrated the ways in which France and the French would harness culinary nostalgia as a tool for self-fashioning in a seemingly unstable world.⁶ Amélie's world was, as the title indicates, fabulous and fantastical. However, it was also indicative of the moment and exemplary of a wider trend in gastronomic narratives and the national gastronomic discourse. In the film, Amélie spends her days dreaming up good deeds and delighting in the small pleasures of food, such as cracking the burnt sugar crust of a *crème brûlée* and sinking her fingers into sacks of grain as she visits her local food vendor. She is an inhabitant of highly charged culinary spaces, working in a café seemingly stuck in the 1960s, whizzing through a busy market street, and often in her kitchen or at the dining table. The foods and culinary spaces of *Amélie* and similar narratives offer up a figurative *retour aux sources*, a return to the land, to the past, and to the perceived values of a time gone by, serving as viable touchstones in the present with the hope of fashioning a better, more stable future.⁷

Over the course of the past five years, however, there has been a marked shift away from the nostalgic, the imaginary, and the fantastical. In gastronomic narratives in the extreme contemporary, a pseudo-documentary form is taking its place. This shift is part of a larger trend in contemporary French literature and film towards the real that has been occurring since the beginning of the twenty-first century but is only recently crossing into gastronomic narratives. There is a general belief that the challenges of our time merit a realistic perspective and a reckoning.[8] In the gastronomic context, authors and filmmakers carefully intertwine truth and fiction to expose and critique the brutal realities of what it means to produce, sell, and consume food in contemporary France. Indeed, the proliferation of these narratives is marked, with over a dozen noteworthy examples and new narratives entering the mainstream each year, some of which I highlight below.

A dominant preoccupation of these narratives is the plight of the modern-day small farmer and the family-owned vineyard. Films such as *Ce qui nous lie* (*Back to Burgundy*, 2017), *Petit paysan* (*Bloody Milk*, 2017), and *Roxane* (2018) shed light on the challenges of owning and running a family-owned farm in the face of European regulation, the threat of multinational corporations, and punitive French tax laws.[9] In this vein, two narratives stand out, each bringing to light the elevated rate of suicide among farmers – Michel Houellebecq's 2019 novel *Sérotonine* (*Serotonin*) and Édouard Bergeon's cinematic hit *Au nom de la terre* (*In the Name of the Land*) from the same year.[10] *Sérotonine* tells of the demise of a farmer, Aymeric, through the eyes of his friend and a former employee of the Ministry of Agriculture who is also the novel's narrator. Enumerating facts and figures that represent the realities of dairy farming in France, the narrator provides the context through which readers understand Aymeric's desperation and eventual suicide. The narrator's own willingness to buy groceries at Carrefour, one of the world's largest grocery distributors, while witnessing the downfall of his long-time friend, provides a reflective and critical mirror through which the reader might view herself. *Au nom de la terre,* depicts a similar picture, drawing the viewer into rural life through an intimate portrait of a farmer struggling to maintain the family farm, eventually succumbing to a multitude of pressures by taking his own life. This film is semiautobiographical: the film's director grew up on a farm, and his father similarly took his own life. The aim of these narratives is to reveal that, even while consuming *terroir*-linked products, attending agricultural fairs and food festivals, and exalting the local, we are painfully unaware of the realities facing those who form the backbone of the food system.

The figure at the heart of heritagization efforts and these narratives is the *paysan*. Though translated as 'peasant', *paysan* refers to the rural inhabitant who has maintained a deep connection to the land and to French agricultural and rural heritage. The *paysan* is not exclusively a farmer, though many are. Traditionally, the *paysan* is considered a guardian of traditional values and an emblem of French civilization. He represents 'the *soul* of the nation, evoking the deep-rooted cultural traditions, attachment to the national territory, and an equilibrium that guarantees the health of society'.[11] Throughout history, the national body has repeatedly and consistently relied on the *paysan* to sustain the nation literally and figuratively and, depending on the moment, to reinvigorate or sustain the national economy.[12] These narratives engage readers and viewers by immersing them in the world of the *paysan* so that he becomes distinct and knowable rather than a distant, minimalized subject in a blurb on the evening news or a symbolic figurehead.[13]

Focusing on hardships, these films and novels break the nostalgic gaze. They expose the gaping chasm between the popular, urban imagination of rural life and its reality, namely the hardship that farmers face. Urban consumers willingly ignore signs of industrial, productivist agriculture such as giant combine harvesters, the use of fertilizers and pesticides, and sprawling warehouse-style barns.[14] It is not only consumers who are to blame, however. Despite numerous opportunities to do so, the French government has repeatedly neglected to address the paradox in which farmers live – they make profound sacrifices to sustain the nation while unable to sustain their own families.[15] This lack of understanding and the paradox of the small farmer are indicative of what historian Venus Bivar describes as a 'collective and voluntary case of misrecognition'.[16] Gastronomic nostalgia and the heritagization of the rural have led to the proliferation of 'fair-weather ruralists', or urban-bound citizens who call upon farmers to protect the landscape and stand as bearers of national values only to either occasionally descend upon the countryside to consume them or otherwise leave them at the mercy of government policy and the industrial food complex.[17]

These paradoxes and moral shortcomings come under the microscope in Paul-Henry Bizon's 2017 novel *La Louve*. An exemplary narrative of its kind, the novel lays out a sweeping assessment of contemporary French food culture, bringing together agriculture and the contemporary urban food scene in a clash of gastronomic values and vision through the interwoven tales of two men: Camille Vollot, an overly idealistic small farmer with dreams of transforming French agriculture and society, and Raoul Sarkis, a smooth-talking charlatan looking to profit off the gastronomic frenzy that has taken over the French capital. Intertwining fiction with journalistic exposé, the novel is a *roman à clef* referencing the Jeune Rue affair, in which Cédric Naudon, a self-described cultural entrepreneur, swindled banks, artists, farmers, chefs, politicians, and, in essence, the entire French nation, all in the name of protecting French cultural heritage.[18] Through Camille and Raoul, *La Louve* exposes the harsh truths that compose the imagined world we (believe to) consume, revealing the whole of French gastronomy to be nothing but artifice – 'a good joke', 'a theatre', 'a scene'.[19]

Through Raoul Sarkis, *La Louve* demonstrates how gastronomy's centrality to the national project renders it easily exploitable. Profiting off the heritagization push described above, investors, politicians, and banks have been eager to throw their weight behind any project aimed at protecting and promoting this national treasure. In the novel, Sarkis claims to be creating a large cultural hub in the centre of Paris, the *Pavillon des Horizons*, where people will engage with the hottest figures in the arts and food. At the centre of the project, he claims, will be French *terroir*. Ingredients for restaurants will be sourced from small-scale farmers practicing ecologically friendly agriculture, because, as Sarkis notes, this is the foundation of the whole of French gastronomic exceptionalism; without its magnificent agriculture, French gastronomy would be 'nothing'.[20] Bringing together farmers from around the nation in the heart of Paris, the Pavillon will impact and represent all of France, Sarkis explains.[21] Speaking as if a saviour, he insists he is creating a 'better world'.[22] Public and private enthusiasm for heritagization projects coupled with Sarkis' smooth talk all but certify his success. Politicians 'could only support him. Public opinion would salute him for his initiative in favour of the land'.[23]

In reality, though, Sarkis is simply co-opting the rural and the local to his own financial ends. His words are just 'ecological smooth-talk'.[24] Sarkis is condescending towards engaged farmers like Camille who truly work for the betterment of the natural world.[25] He is a 'compulsive liar' and an 'opportunist'.[26] He usurps the discourse of land and heritage and steals the fruits of Camille's labour, literally and figuratively, 'to create a brand, a little toy for Parisians and rich tourists'.[27] Sarkis is 'totally indifferent to what is on his plate' or any other, only caring about potential profits to be had.[28] He has no intention of following through on his pretend plans to promote and protect French culture. Once he has enough money in his pockets from banks, investors, and thieving, and just before the walls come crashing down around him, he will cut and run, leaving only financial and cultural ruins in his wake.

The urban co-optation of the rural has become increasingly common with the rise of heritagization and implicates everyone, from everyday consumers to power-hungry politicians. Geographer Claire Delfosse describes the urban and political co-optation and appropriation of rural values, norms, and products as 'post-modern heritagization'.[29] The urban profits off the rural while negating the latter's identity rather than reaffirm it. So eager to believe in something greater than oneself and support a national cause, people are more likely, the narrator in *La Louve* claims, to fall victim to empty promises and deceptive projects like the one Sarkis claims to be leading.[30] Investors and politicians waste money and power while consumers are duped into a false knowledge about what and how they are eating. While Sarkis is at a dinner party with the movers and shakers of the Parisian food scene, another guest explains that people go to restaurants '*believing* that the people who run them are better than their predecessors, that they work towards the happiness of clients, for their well-being and the well-being of all humanity, that they are engaged in a fight for the environment, for farmers, and all that'.[31] A tone of mockery accompanies this exposé, and the dismissive finish of the remark make the reality all the more biting. Parisian restaurateurs are just out to make a buck and do so by playing to contemporary imaginations and desires.

In an interview, Bizon identifies 'post-modern heritagization' and consumer ignorance as a driving force in the novel. The author aims to depict how 'city-dwellers, who are distanced from the soil' forget that agriculture is at the heart of everything they eat.[32] Within the novel, the narrator laments urban consumers who use local products as a way of gaining cultural capital and feeding their fanciful and abstract notions about the countryside, but fail to form any real connection to *paysans* or the land.[33] The entire Parisian gastronomic system, the novel suggests, has devolved into lip service to an ideal that does not exist. In this way, *La Louve* rejects the culinary imagination that birthed and continues to nourish this very system.

While this increasingly derisive take on French gastronomy and the rural turn compounds as the novel progresses, bordering on an altogether fatalistic view, *La Louve* turns back towards the potential of the culinary imaginary at its close in a rethinking of the gastronomic system. After all, imagination is inescapable. It is an integral part of ourselves. It shapes who we are and our understanding of the world. Imagination is necessary for change; how else would we create something new?[34]

A new vision of French foodways comes through Camille Vollot, his farm where he practices agroecology and permaculture, and his cooperative of like-minded farmers. After living for several years in the city of Nantes, Camille and his wife return to the fictional village of Montfort-sur-Sèvre in the Vendée region and purchase his uncle's farm. In just a few years, Camille shows an immense success with permaculture and creates 'a model ecosystem'. The farm becomes 'a stupefying laboratory whose vegetable production [is] *objectively* several times higher than the national average' despite not using agricultural machinery, fertilizers, or pesticides. Not only is Camille's farm 'a nourishing landscape' of 'astounding beauty', it is also a testament to agricultural diversity. One might lose themselves in the 'plant-covered labyrinth where hundreds of varietals and species blossomed in spirals of a mandala-like garden, around ponds, under the foliage of the forest and orchards'.[35] His own farm serves up a healthier and more sustainable alternative to what is in the supermarket – 'the containers of meat wrapped in plastic, the same petrified cheeses and transformed products of all kinds, the same brands of cans and jars and "thingamajigs" to drink, but nothing, really, that seems actually good or edible'.[36] Quite the opposite, the products from Camille's farm 'radiate with a prodigious optimism', 'shine with power and joy', and have unique tastes and textures that linger on the palate and transport the eater.[37] Camille's food is superior. It communicates the land in which it was grown and is imbued with life-affirming values.

For Camille, agroecology provides not only a better way to eat, but also a better way to live. Camille believes this alternative to industrial agriculture is the way forward for France. His greater mission is 'to defend the rural people by freeing them from the overly reductive figure of the "small producer"' and to create an agroecological network of sufficient scale to feed the nation's most vulnerable – children and the elderly.[38] This model will benefit not only the consumer, but also the producer, having a profound impact on the nature of society. Indeed, Camille and his mentor Anne-Marie believe that there is a fundamental problem in contemporary French society – that it has lost the ties that bind it together – that a true connection to the land might resolve.

This loss is manifest in how the nation nourishes itself. According to Anne-Marie, 'our postmodern society, whose model of row crop farming contradict[s] nature's cyclical model that [does] not necessitate the use of fossil fuels or generate waste, neglect[s] a fundamental notion – the necessity of multiple and reciprocal connections between living things'.[39] Undeniably, this passage speaks to the dangers of maintaining the agricultural status quo. It comes in a section of the novel subtitled 'Accusation' and in the middle of a documentary-like exposé on modern industrial agriculture and the harm it inflicts on people and the land. However, removing the subordinate clause, we also understand that postmodern society's blind spot has resulted in the dissolution of multiple and reciprocal relationships between all living things. The gastronomic ecosystem that France has constructed for itself over the course of the past sixty years is on the verge of collapse. Values traditionally associated with French gastronomy including conviviality and agricultural diversity have come to ring hollow in the search for the gastronomic new as both economic and cultural capital. Thus Anne-Marie's, and later Camille's, principal concern is French society's negligence – the forgotten truth that people must cultivate deeply rooted bonds with each other and with the natural world to flourish. It is through the land, figuratively and literally, that Camille believes people can re-establish these links and break down the long-standing, though artificial, divide between nature and culture while simultaneously eating well.[40]

Camille's dream is to create 'rhizome', of which the cooperative will provide the 'central nervous system, linking the soil and its inhabitants, capable of revitalizing all of society'.[41] Bizon identifies Camille's vision as his desired consequence of the novel. Readers should understand they are part of a vast ecosystem in which all people and things interact and are dependent upon one another.[42] The image of the rhizome is particularly important in its emancipatory and creative potential. It is a philosophical and natural form that rejects the verticality of 'rooted' thinking while embracing untethered expansion of connections and possibilities.[43] It is democratic and subversive. Through the rhizomatic cooperative, Camille hopes to create the exact opposite of the 'technocratic utopia' that has driven the French food market since the 1960s. He wants to craft 'the first viable model for virtuous production and for direct sales on a scale much larger than that practiced by the young, locally politically engaged farmers and hippie communities'.[44] In this model, consumers are in direct contact with producers, cultivating real and extensive bonds while also creating economic opportunity for farmers working with alternative forms of agriculture that privilege quality and health for the land and the consumer. It is his fervent belief in the possibility of achieving this new utopia, though, that leads Camille to blindly believe that Sarkis also shares this vision. Camille falls victim to his own imagination.

At the close of the novel, Camille's wife Victoire, an ardent realist and the only person to see Sarkis for what he is, stands alone in the courtyard of what would have been the *Pavillon des Horizons*. Looking at the magnificent building around her, she is struck by its beauty. She sees the potential of creating a gastronomic hub in the centre of Paris, though one that is built by and through her family's agricultural cooperative, not through profiteering intermediaries. If she and Camille can harness their resources and personally take control of the building, then the cooperative could have a promising future, and Camille's rhizomatic ecosystem might flourish.

Ultimately, the novel proposes what sociologist Erik Olin Wright terms 'real utopias'.[45] Wright envisions real utopias as 'viable, emancipatory alternatives to dominant institutions and social structures'.[46] These alternatives balance the fantasies we imagine in utopia with the practical realities and constraints of the world in which we live. Wright's concept of real utopias works on the assumptions that they are generated from the ground-up rather than from top-down approaches and that movement toward greater equality and more democratic societies 'expand the possibilities of human flourishing'.[47] Examples of real utopias include the goal of instituting a universal basic income, urban participatory budgeting, and worker-owned cooperatives.[48] This final example is particularly interesting in the context of *La Louve*. Camille's agroecology cooperative is the backbone for the movement he wants to propagate. Worker-owned cooperatives provide alternatives to contemporary capitalist structures, giving power and agency to workers. These benefits of cooperatives are essential to reforming contemporary foodways, not only in France, but globally. Furthermore, while Victoire is a realist, and her vision at the end of the novel may not completely overlap with that of her husband, her creative thinking provides an important first step on the journey to creating the more viable gastronomic and human ecosystem that her husband imagines. These types of way posts are essential to the real utopia because they provide checkpoints, so that even if the utopic end is unreachable, we 'nevertheless have accessible waystations that help us move in the right direction'.[49] The quest for real utopias, thus, may prove integral to creating real, radical, and rhizomatic alternatives to the status quo.

In the foreword to *Food Utopias* (2015), Frederick Kirschenmann, President of Stone Barns Center for Food and Agriculture and advocate of sustainable agriculture, proclaims that the time has come for a 'creative moment' for engaging new imaginings for our global food system.[50] The French gastronomic system realistically portrayed in *La Louve* is imagined from the top-down. Farmers have long played to the imagination of others rather than cultivate their own visions for the future. The financial constraints and the bureaucratic obstacles they face do not afford them the luxury of realizing their own imaginaries. This system is morally, economically, politically, environmentally, and nutritionally unhealthy. It is also at a breaking point. Gastronomic narratives that question, criticize, and elucidate this system are essential in this moment. Unlike their immediate forebears, gastronomic narratives of the extreme contemporary elevate new ideas and propose change. We would, certainly, be wise to consider the imagined cultural and systemic changes for which they call. As Christy Wampole reminds us, 'the most staggering cultural changes often must happen first in literature, music, and art, which provide the space where new ideas may be tried out without the requirement of apodictic certainty'.[51] In these spaces, imaginative, utopian thinking thrives. In the quest to develop an alternative to the gastronomic status quo, the capacity to imagine and create real utopias proves a necessary faculty, not a fanciful endeavour. If we are to create change and follow the imagination, then, the questions become: Who gets to imagine?

Which imaginative visions do we pursue? Camille and Victoire answer Kirschenmann's call. *La Louve* causes us to reassess the culinary imagination as it has been and as it could be. The novel proposes new imaginations that will fundamentally alter the foodscape while providing direct and meaningful access to the purported values of the nation. The seeds of the gastronomic imaginary must move from the ground up. Only then can imagination lead the development of a real gastronomic utopia.

Notes

1. Philip H. Gordon and Sophie Meunier-Altsahalia, *The French Challenge: Adapting to Globalization* (Washington, D.C.: Brookings Institution Press, 2001), pp. 7-11.
2. Richard F. Kuisel, *The French Way: How France Embraced and Rejected American Values and Power* (Princeton: Princeton University Press, 2012), pp. 181-83.
3. Loïc Bienassis, 'Les Chemins du patrimoine: De Notre-Dame au camembert', in *Manger en Europe: Patrimoines, échanges, identités,* ed. by Antonella Campanini, Peter Scholliers, and Jean-Pierre Williot (Brussels: P.I.E. Peter Lang, 2011), pp. 45-91; Christine Bouisset and Isabelle Degrémont, 'La Patrimonialisation de la nature: Un processus en renouvellement', *L'Espace géographique*, 42 (2013), 193-99 (p. 193-95); Nathalie Heinich, *La Fabrique du patrimoine: De la cathédrale à la petite cuillère* (Paris: Éditions de la Maison des sciences et de l'homme, 2009).
4. Bienassis, p. 86; Pierre Boisard, *Le Camembert, mythe français* (Paris: Odile Jacob, 2007).
5. Amy L. Tigner and Allison Carruth argue that literary criticism provides a valuable contribution to food studies as writers use various literary devices through food to investigate and critique foodways (*Literature and Food Studies* (London: Routledge, 2018)).
6. Jennifer L. Holm, 'Consuming Nostalgia in *Le fabuleux destin d'Amélie Poulain*', *The French Review*, 89 (2015), 69-81.
7. Other narratives include: Muriel Barbery, *Une gourmandise* (Paris: Gallimard, 2000); Philippe Delerm, *La Première gorgée de bière et autres plaisirs minuscules* (Paris: Gallimard, 1997); and Chantal Thomas, *Cafés de la mémoire* (Paris: Seuil, 2008).
8. Lionel Ruffel, 'Un réalisme contemporain: Les Narrations documentaires', *Littératures*, 166 (2012), 13-25; Philippe Vilain, *La littérature sans idéal* (Paris: Grasset, 2016); Christy Wampole, *Degenerative Realism: Novel and Nation in Twenty-First-Century France* (New York: Columbia University Press, 2020), pp. 9-11.
9. *Ce qui nous lie*, dir. by Cédric Klapisch (Studio Canal, 2017); *Petit paysan*, dir. by Hubert Charuel (Pyramide Distribution, 2017); *Roxane*, dir. by Mélanie Auffret (Mars Films, 2018).
10. *Au nom de la terre*, dir. by Édouard Bergeon (Diaphana Distribution, 2019); Michel Houellebecq, *Sérotonine* (Paris: Flammarion, 2019); Pamela Rougerie, 'French Farms Endure a Rash of Suicides', *New York Times*, 21 August 2017, p. A4.
11. Susan Carol Rogers, 'Farming Visions: Agriculture in French Culture', *French Politics, Culture & Society*, 18 (2000), 50-70 (p. 62).
12. Venus Bivar, *Organic Resistance: The Struggle over Industrial Farming in Postwar France* (Chapel Hill: University of North Carolina Press, 2018), pp. 10-12, 174-78.
13. Sarah Waters, *Suicide Voices: Labour Trauma in France* (Liverpool: Liverpool University Press, 2020), p. 2.
14. Bivar, pp. 181-82.
15. Julia Csergo, *La Gastronomie est-elle une marchandise culturelle comme une autre? La Gastronomie française à l'UNESCO: Histoire et enjeux* (Chartres: Menu Fretin, 2016); Elyne Etienne, 'Le Grand débat sur l'alimentation n'a pas eu lieu', *Esprit*, 440 (2017), 30-32.
16. Bivar, pp. 174-75.
17. Bivar, p. 176.

18 David Le Bailly, 'Escroc, mythomane ou visionnaire? Au procès de Cédric Naudon, le créateur de la Jeune Rue', *L'Obs*, 5 March 2021 <https://www.nouvelobs.com/justice/20210305. OBS41019/escroc-mythomane-ou-visionnaire-au-proces-de-cedric-naudon-le-createur-de-la-jeune-rue.html> [accessed 23 October 2021]
19 Paul-Henry Bizon, *La Louve* (Paris: Gallimard, 2017), pp. 101-03. All translations are my own.
20 Bizon, p. 154-55.
21 Bizon, p. 204.
22 Bizon, p. 155.
23 Bizon, p. 142.
24 Bizon, p. 109.
25 Bizon, pp. 154-55.
26 Bizon, pp. 155, 160.
27 Bizon, p. 174.
28 Bizon, p. 89.
29 Claire Delfosse, 'La Patrimonialisation des produits dits de terroir: Quand "le rural" rencontre "l'urbain"?', *Anthropology of Food*, 8 (2011) < https://doi.org/10.4000/aof.6772>
30 Bizon, pp. 216-17.
31 Bizon, p. 103, original emphasis.
32 *Un livre, un jour – La Louve de Paul-Henry Bizon*, France.tv, 11 September 2017 <https://www.france.tv/france-3/un-livre-un-jour/239815-la-louve-de-paul-henry-bizon-gallimard.html> [accessed 26 May 2021]
33 Bizon, p. 188.
34 Peter Murphy, *The Collective Imagination: The Creative Spirit of Free Societies* (London: Ashgate, 2012), ch. 1. ProQuest Ebook Central <https://doi.org/10.4324/9781315614830>
35 Bizon, pp. 66-67
36 Bizon, p. 113.
37 Bizon, p. 188.
38 Bizon, p. 119.
39 Bizon, p. 51-52.
40 Christy Wampole argues that the attempt to break down the divide between nature and culture is a particular concern of the twenty-first century and gives several food-linked examples in her analysis (*Rootedness: The Ramifications of a Metaphor* (Chicago: University of Chicago Press, 2016), pp. 242-49).
41 Bizon, p. 235.
42 *Un livre, un jour*.
43 Wampole, *Rootedness*, ch. 7.
44 Bizon, p. 175.
45 Erik Olin Wright, *Envisioning Real Utopias* (London: Verso, 2010).
46 Erik Olin Wright, 'Real Utopias.' *Contexts*, 10.2 (2011), pp. 36-42 (p. 37).
47 Wright, 'Real Utopias' p. 38; see also Wright, *Envisioning*, ch. 1.
48 Wright, *Envisioning*.
49 Wright, 'Real Utopias', p. 37.
50 Frederick Kirschenmann, 'Foreward: Food Utopias in Perspective', in *Food Utopias: Reimagining Citizenship, Ethics and Community*, ed. by Paul V. Stock, Michael Carolan, and Christopher Rosin (London: Routledge, 2015), pp. xii-xv (p. xiv).
51 Wampole, *Rootedness*, p. 236.

Caste: The Main Character of Indian Food

Ragini Kashyap

Introduction

'[C]aste is ingrained in our taste buds and eating habits. Food snobbery is a part of India, and the food that belongs to upper castes has always been more celebrated. In a caste-sensitive India, labelling your product as Brahmin is a way to communicate that it boasts of the highest form of purity.' – Pushpesh Pant[1]

The access to food is a practical necessity, and perhaps, a rather unimaginative one. In India, however, a wholly imagined construct dictates the details of this access: the caste system.[2] Vedic civilization imposed a caste-based order on society which would go on to form much of the basis of Hinduism, or the way of life of people on the subcontinent. Among a host of other allowances and limitations, food consumption (or the lack thereof) was determined by caste. Food continues to be one of the most visible expressions of hierarchy and power in India today, over three millennia since the composition of the *Manusmriti*.

Subsequent religious and colonial and political incursions have failed to challenge this system, and in fact have most often built upon it, to further their power by pandering to caste sensibilities. This imagined structure has therefore become a defining characteristic of the nation and every community within it. From the *badhraloke* of Bengal in the East to the Tamilian Brahmins in the South, the *Pathare Prabhu* in the West, the *Gangaputra* Brahmins of Uttar Pradesh, and the Kashmiri *Pandits* in the North, caste is truly a national feature of Indian society, culture, imagination, and belonging.

Regional Indian cuisines are a manifestation of this highly stratified system and bound in their '*Indianness*' not by flavour, spice, or technique, but by an adherence to caste-based exclusionary measures. Despite boasting a staggering diversity of highly developed cuisines, this division is, incredibly, one of the few constant features of Indian food along the length and breadth of the country. The ghee-laden curries enhanced with elaborate spice mixtures are primarily the prerogative of the upper-castes, while the curries of the lower castes are often simpler counterparts that maximize available ingredients. In doing so, however, they hinder their upward mobility through the caste-system.

This paper will first discuss the definitions and Vedic origins of the confluence of food and caste identity in India. It will briefly note the impact this system had on Islam and Christianity in the subcontinent, consider the role of modern politics, and finally discuss how these antiquated ideals have moved far beyond national borders to influence Indian food internationally. Today, the international perception of Indian cuisine is primarily that of an upper-caste cuisine, and approximately a quarter of all Indians are unlikely to access the food that several restaurants around the world serve in abundance.[3]

A System Designed to Discriminate

The caste system in India traces its roots back to the Vedic civilization of Aryan invaders who arrived around 1700 BCE. They were intellectual and violent warriors who used caste to subjugate the indigenous populations as they expanded their rule, establishing a structure to classify the population by occupation, placing themselves at the top.[4]

In the first years of the Common Era, the Aryans recorded the Hindu caste system in the early Vedic constitutional document, the *Manusmriti* (*Laws of Manu*). This established the order and occupation of four major caste groups: the Brahmins, who were priests and teachers; the Kshatriyas, who were warriors and law keepers; the Vaishyas, who were the economic engine of society; and, finally, the Shudras who were craftspeople and labourers. These groups were then further divided into thousands of *jatis* based on occupation, family-clan, and ethnic identity.[5] This stratification, which is so deeply embedded through thousands of years of practice, forms the basis of Indian identity, where caste and culture overlap.

A fifth category, previously referred to as the Untouchables, was reserved for those who worked with waste and other tasks considered to be 'polluted' by the upper castes. Today, *Dalit*, a term popularised by activists in the late 1800s, describes those who sit at the bottom of the caste system, or, worse still, outside of it. K.T. Achaya notes *Dalit* comes from the Hindi word *dal* (lentils), which comes from Sanskrit for split or broken.[6] The metaphor of food to denote a community that sees itself as broken is powerful, as food is one of the most common and powerful markers of caste belonging.

Several lower castes are named for what they eat rather than for their occupation, implying that it is their most defining character: the *Mahars* are those who eat carrion, the *Musaharis* named for their consumption of rats, and often the *Valmikis* are called the *jhootan* caste for accepting leftover foods of upper castes.[7] (A nuanced translation of *jhootan* implies that contact with another human being has sullied an item and rendered it impure.) One can safely assume that these were not names that communities gave themselves, and it is difficult to underestimate the impact of these classifications, as they continue to govern social interactions across India today.

The *Manusmriti* has no less than fifty-six verses devoted to food, exalting the purity of ghee and milk; categorizing plants and vegetables; categorizing animal products; and outlining cooking instructions, who to accept food from, and whom to exclude for fear of polluting oneself.[8] Given these texts were in Old Sanskrit and confined to the readership of Brahmins, they brought the system to life through practice for the rest of society. It is the implications of this practice that perhaps led Arjun Appadurai to claim that the convergence of the moral and social implications of food is most clear in Hindu India.[9]

It would be a challenge to speak of Hinduism and not address the two symbols popularly associated with the religion: the cow and vegetarianism. A common misconception in modern times is that the early Vedic Aryans attributed a sacredness to the cow based on a desire for cow protection, thus giving the religion a symbol that is threatened by anyone who consumes beef.[10] As D.N. Jha has claimed however, the holiness of the cow in Hinduism is a politically motivated ideal, which gained prominence long after the formation. While the early Brahmins respected the cow for its value in dairy production and farm work, they routinely sacrificed the animal for consumption. In fact, all of the earliest Indian religious texts, including the Hindu Vedas (1500–600 BCE), the ancient Buddhist texts (1 BCE), and to a lesser extent the early Jain texts (5 CE), reference some consumption of flesh as part of their recommended dietary practice.[11]

The first record of Brahmins abstaining from beef was in response to a famine. As the most powerful caste, they eased tensions with the starving masses by adopting a partially vegetarian diet. This was radical for its time, and despite the nobility they attributed to their own restraint, the *Manusmriti* maintained that 'it is not sinful to eat meat of eatable animals. For *Brahma* has created both, the eaters and the eatables'.[12] Following this, the veneration of the cow went through cycles of Brahminical rigidity and relaxation for centuries. During a period of territorial expansion, in 5 CE, into Southern India, Brahmins travelled with their armies and a small herd of cattle. This was the first time they prohibited cow slaughter for two major reasons: first, they had a lot of land to cover; and, second, they established their Brahminical superiority through a rejection of local dietary practice. They therefore introduced southern India to a version of Hinduism where vegetarian Brahmins led the most meritorious, righteous lives.[13] This would give rise to arguably some of the most conservative Brahmin cultures in present-day Tamil Nadu and Karnataka, whereas in the North, Brahmins continued to consume beef well into the eighteenth century, even requiring it for certain religious rituals.[14] Over the centuries that followed, this system became an accepted way of life across the country, despite certain Brahmin communities maintaining a diet that included fish, like in Bengal, or meat in Kashmir and Kerala.

The Aryan nomads were meat-eating warriors and herders before they were farmers. Conversely, today's popular Hindu discourse idealizes an agrarian lifestyle and the vegetarian Brahmin, making concessions (often patronizingly) for the upper castes who eat meat, but not for anybody who eats beef. The vegetarian ideal in India is myopic, as it exalts the cow while literally milking it for all its worth. The hyper consumption and religious postulation of dairy, specifically of ghee and milk, has facilitated the growth of inhumane and problematic dairy and leather industries.[15] It is noble to revere and protect the cow while the animal is dairy cattle; however, killing, skinning, consuming, or disposing of the animal are considered impure acts.[16]

Further, given that beef is the cheapest protein in India, it is a significant source of nutrition for those unable to afford more expensive meats. Since the caste-system encompasses all aspects of one's professional, personal, and spiritual life, this consumption perpetually keeps *Dalits* who consume beef bound to the bottom of the Hindu system.

Caste: The Main Character of Indian Food

Islam and Christianity in India

'[Originating] in the Hindu social order, [caste] has infiltrated all faiths on the Indian subcontinent. As old as the order of the Indic civilization, the phenomenon of controlling human capacity, creativity and labour has been core to its ideological performance secured by strict legal order. Caste in India is an absolute sanction – of the dominant class over the dominated.' – Suraj Yengde[17]

Although Hindu in its origin, the occupation-based caste system is a South Asian phenomenon and is therefore also a feature of the religions that did not originate in India, namely the subcontinental expressions of Islam and Christianity. Initial Christian and Muslim incursions were minor, but by the time of the Delhi Sultanate in the early thirteenth century, the first large-scale Muslim rule in the subcontinent, the Hindu way of life had persisted for over a millennium.

While some lower-castes converted to escape the tyranny of their birth, many upper-caste Hindus converted to Islam (e.g. Muslim Rajputs), and Christianity (e.g. Syrian Christians) as well. Historically accustomed to significant social capital, caste would prove too significant a benefit for them to forego, so caste-based power and food dynamics persisted. In South Asian Islam, as Zarina Ahmed argues, the social distance between the castes is so great that inter-caste commensality is exceedingly rare and socially unacceptable. The *ashraf* castes, or those who can trace their lineage to non-Indian ancestors (typically either Arab or Persian), hold higher status than the non-*ashraf* castes, who are predominantly indigenous converts.[18]

Colonial Powers, Gandhi, and the New State

As we move towards the twentieth and twenty-first century, it is imperative to note the influence that the British colonial rule and the ultimate rise of Mohandas K. Gandhi had on what M.N. Srinivas refers to as the 'Sanskritization' of caste-based food practices in India.[19] Both these forces legalized and legitimized the caste-system, as well as the idolization of vegetarianism in the Hindu imagination.

As the British looked to bring the numerous Indian princely states under a single administration, Dirks claims, '"caste" became a single term capable of expressing, organizing, and above all "systematizing" India's diverse forms of social identity, community, and organization'.[20] Caste identity, therefore, went on to become a prominent feature of the national administration (the government); not only were citizens demographically categorized by caste, but politicians and states people were overwhelmingly upper caste.

The colonial administration and army primarily employed Brahmins, putting them not only at the top of the religious order, but the administrative order as well.[21] From the time of the Aryans, caste-based politics honoured upper-caste sensibilities, but it was only during colonial rule that the system became a part of modern law and governance, thus moving this wholly imagined system to a legally valid identification, which persists today. This further blurred the lines between caste and class, equating lower castes with lower economic class, since occupation was the basis of division. As we will see in the next section, this dominance had a significant impact on India's national food policy and popular food culture after independence in 1947.

In the years leading up to and after Indian independence, Mahatma Gandhi played a significant role in glorifying an upper-caste Hindu diet, alienating the majority meat eating population of India.[22] Born into the *Vaishya* caste, he was raised a strict vegetarian and upheld the notion of the righteous vegetarian for most of his life. More troubling, however, was his obsession with the self-governing, agrarian Indian village, which is structured on a strict adherence to caste norms.[23] As discussed, these norms are all-encompassing and near impossible to challenge, so implicit in his patronage of the caste system was an acceptance of the food hierarchy. Gandhi has been criticized by *Dalit* scholars for conflating caste with culture, and further cementing the caste-system as the ideal structure of the nation.[24]

Following independence, in the 1950s and 60s Indian food policy and the Public Distribution System (PDS) went on to champion a vegetarian Hindu Brahmin diet. Dr Veena Shatrugna, former Deputy Director at the Indian National Institute of Nutrition, opines that '[o]ne should note here that these experts were upper-caste Brahmins whose personal diet was vegetarian, [and despite] scientific evidence […], it was said that if cereal and pulses are eaten in a ratio of 4:1, in every meal, it will provide sufficient proteins […] justifying the decision to not include milk and other sources of animal protein' in the PDS.[25]

Since the basic Hindu caste order, as identified by Dr B.R. Ambedkar, begins with those who do not eat meat at the top, followed by those who eat meat but not beef, and finally, those who eat beef at the very bottom, the PDS's focus on cheaper grain and pulse rations further encouraged vegetarianism. However, a nutritious, vegetarian diet is simply too expensive for many to maintain. The system was also used as the rationale for reducing the minimum wage, prohibiting those dependent on the rations from purchasing much else, and together these factors contributed significantly to malnourishment, stunted growth, and notably, increased communal and caste stigmatization.[26]

One Nation, Many Castes

> 'Whatever meat could not be consumed, quickly before it got spoilt, she dried it in the sun. After a few days of drying, the sun turned the meat into thin, crackly strips. Those *chanya* were so delicious! Aaee would roast them in the fire for us to eat and for so many weeks, we would beg her for the treat.' – Narendra Jadhav[27]

As Suraj Yengde notes, 'In India, casteism […] affects 1 billion people. It affects 800 million badly. It enslaves the human dignity of 500 million people [….] and [results in the] loss of moral virtuosity for 300 million Indian untouchables.'[28] Further, today, approximately 1500 years after the Vedic civilization, Hindu thought continues to underlie contemporary Indian food practices. Indian law no longer states the required conditions for food consumption, as in the *Manusmriti*. However, food practices are one of the strongest definitions of culture and identity, and meals across the country are still strong statements of caste belonging, exaggerated in recent years by laws against cow slaughter, and the subsequent violence against those suspected of disobedience, most of whom are either *Dalit* or Muslim.[29]

As Yengde points out, the caste system is unique because vertical mobility is not an option.[30] This gives rise to two very specific cultural phenomena. First, since human identity is relative, the rules of food consumption apply as much to oneself as they do to others, making it exceptionally difficult to access foods that society believes one should not have access to. The reasoning is bindingly circular: the Brahmins are at the top of the social order, their diet is pure, and other practices are naturally inferior because Brahminical logic is the pinnacle of morality. Secondly, since inter-caste commensality was religiously implausible, the system has given rise to innumerable micro-cuisines across the deserts, jungles, plains, and mountains of the subcontinent. As a result, we see the Tamilian Brahmin cuisine, the Pathare Prabhu cuisine, the food of the Kayasths of Delhi, the Baniyas of UP, the Nimboodari Brahmins of Kerala, the Mewar cuisine of Rajasthan, and the Ghanchis of Gujarat, to name a handful. The expression of caste (most often described as community) is one of the few common themes across the cuisines, and Marriott describes this phenomenon well, concluding that the Hindu thought runs parallel to the assumptions made by Western social science where rank decreases intimacy. In the Hindu social order, rank increases intimacy within the group and higher castes are likely to insulate themselves for fear of pollution from lower castes.[31]

While the upper-caste communities had the luxury to create elaborate cuisines within the boundaries of their restrictions, *Dalit* food has historically been subsistence-level, with foods permissible to them by other castes. They eat millets where the upper castes eat wheat, broken corn rather than rice, intestines rather than shoulder or breast meat, molasses rather than jaggery or sugar, watermelon seeds rather than white flour, and sun-dried pig skin rather than sundried lentil poppadums; they use animal fat in place of cooking oil or ghee. Though divided by language and geography, *Dalits* are more likely to share food practices across India, including a dependence on chilli and salt for flavouring and the consumption of animal parts rejected by the upper castes. Indeed, the adherence to a caste-based system of food may well be the most common feature of India's 'national' cuisine, and the societal, cultural, and mental capital spent to preserve this divisive structure is so well-ingrained, that upholding it is a reflex for upper-caste Hindus. Though a *Dalit*'s place in society may determine what they eat, it is the imagined narrative of impurity in the minds of upper castes that impose a social narrative on *Dalit* food.[32]

The foods of *Dalit* communities are both understudied and underrepresented in popular discourse, as a cursory look at Indian cookbooks, both in India and abroad, confirms. While community-specific cookbooks have been on the rise since the mid-twentieth century, it has been the prerogative of upper-caste communities who feel pride rather than shame for their diet.³³ A seminal sociological study titled *'Isn't This Plate Indian?'* hosts one of the first collection of *Dalit* recipes published in English.³⁴ The three sample recipes in Figure 1 are samples of Indian delicacies, from a cuisine that has to exist under the radar.

Chunchune	Rakti	Mohol Chi Poli
Ingredients: Beef fat, oil, salt **Process:** Cook the beef fat on a medium flame, allowing the oil of the fat to separate fully. Then take out the dry lump of fat cut it into small pieces. Sprinkle these pieces with salt and deep fry them to a crisp.	**Ingredients:** Oil, goat blood, onion, red chili powder, salt **Process:** Clean the blood well. Dry roast the onion in a pan, adding the blood once the onions have browned slightly. Cook till the blood is thick, then add chilli and salt and continue cooking till it is solid.	**Ingredients:** Bee larvae, sliced onion, and red chilli powder. **Process:** Cook all three ingredients together to the consistency of egg whites. This dish has to be consumed immediately, lest it sticks to the top of your mouth!

*Figure 1: Three recipes from Dalit communities in Maharashtra.*³⁵

Where the Brahmins may define themselves by what they refrain from consuming, *Dalit* narratives note that their strength comes from being able to digest just about anything. After all, it is they who plough the fields to harvest the rice, wheat, and vegetables for other Indians.

In recent decades, increased urbanization has not displaced the Hindu food hierarchy, which persists as the most prominent claim of social superiority.³⁶ An upper-caste, vegetarian landlord in Mumbai will comfortably proclaim that his/her home is available only to vegetarians, immediately excluding people of lower-castes or other religions.³⁷ Broomfield has described the new urban Indian middle-class as '[a] socially privileged and consciously superior group [...] keeping its distance from the masses by its acceptance of high-caste proscriptions and its command of education'.³⁸ Horizontal inter-caste, or inter-community exchanges, although common in urban India, are seen as cultural, rather than caste exchanges. Even the few urban, financially mobile *Dalits* are therefore not able to bring their traditional, lower-caste foods to this exchange, and are more likely to mimic upper caste diets in urban India.

Indian Food Internationally

Appadurai argues that the definition of a national cuisine in India was essentially a postcolonial process initiated by the need for a new pan-Indian identity.³⁹ Until the nineteenth century, regional Hindu culinary traditions were transmitted orally, they were largely domestic, and they were regional in scope. As addressed earlier, the Hindu state was politically, linguistically, and geographically Balkanized, which resulted in innumerable local cuisines.

Indian food has long captured the western world's imagination. Every tradesperson, colonizer, or missionary who has come to India has taken something with them, whether it was a trunk full of spices, the very idea of a 'curry', or an adaptation of Indian recipes. Regional Indian cuisines undoubtedly play a key role in defining the national cuisine, but it was the European colonial expression of Indian food that was the most significant precursor to the internationally emerging Indian cuisine of the twentieth century.[40] The culinary manuals produced for the colonial administration, army, and tradesmen paved the way for Indian food outside India as they traversed the globe. These books were heavily influenced by the extravagance of the Indian royal kitchens and looked to mimic the opulence of the courts. The initial export of 'Indian cuisine' is, therefore, primarily the export of lavish, upper-caste foods.

Later Indian immigrants of the twentieth and twenty-first centuries further propagated the ideals of upper-caste or royal foods as the norm. A quick look at popular Indian restaurants in countries like the UK, US, and Canada reflects this trend, whether through a higher reliance on ghee than on animal fat, through serving primarily vegetarian foods, or by the sheer number of spices required to construct their menus. Since culture and caste have been intertwined for so long in the public imagination, it is plausible that many restauranteurs may be unaware of the caste hegemony reflected in their menus. For example, the restaurant *Dishoom* in the UK, which is positioned as an ode to the Mumbai of yesteryear, only serves the food of certain upper caste communities: the vegetarian street fair delights of Gujarati and Jain traders, the foods of Punjabi and Sindhi migrants, and then finally a classically Mughlai biryani.[41] The menu overlooks the foods of the indigenous inhabitants of the city, the *koli* fishing community and the indigenous *Dalits*, whose *rakti, bhakri, mandeli*, and *nevta* are not on the menu.[42] Ironically, the one menu item that mentions the *koli* people, prawn *koliwada*, is a dish that was invented at a Punjabi restaurant in the 1950s.[43]

This story is common across Indian restaurants and Indian cookbooks in the West and in urban India alike. Unfortunately, Indian food that developed as a means for survival is neither celebrated nor acknowledged. The culture of a few continues to define the many.

Conclusion

On the surface, Indian food is a variety of produce and spices combined with the finesse of highly developed cooking techniques. Many home cooks are highly skilled, equipped with generations of oral, ancestral knowledge. However, it is the narrative in the minds of the cooks and consumers that give us true insight into Indian food culture. Who is cooking? Who is being fed? What are they eating? What are they excluding? And finally, who is forbidden from the table? Answers to these questions tell the story of an imagined structure that has dictated Indian food practices for over three millennia. Today, India's caste-based rules of consumption, preparation, access, and exclusion are more deeply ingrained in the public psyche than perhaps many are comfortable to acknowledge.

Although India is a young country, the caste system has been legitimized repeatedly by history and is now deeply embedded within the fabric of the culture. It has given rise to an incredibly complex food system, rife with symbolism, which has been used to maintain power, status, and notions of religious purity. Despite some changing patterns of consumption in cosmopolitan India, most of the country continues to practise food habits that were prescribed thousands of years ago. Therefore, if *Dalits* continue to eat foods that are accessible and affordable (e.g. beef and pork), upward caste and social mobility is impossible. At the same time, however, a nutritious upper-caste vegetarian diet is unaffordable to them.

Caste is ubiquitous, and that is precisely why it is imperative to consider the role it plays in any study of Indian food. Examining the food practices of those typically excluded from the discourse is the first step to address generations of social conditioning, and to unpack the marriage of caste and culture that surrounds food in India.

Notes

1. Parul Agrawal, 'Caste on Your Plate: A Tale of Food Snobbery in India', *The Quint*, 8 August 2016 <https://www.thequint.com/news/india/caste-on-your-plate-a-tale-of-food-snobbery-in-india#read-more> [accessed 24 May 2021]
2. Nicholas B. Dirks, *Castes of Mind: Colonialism and the Making of Modern India* (Princeton, NJ: Princeton University Press, 2001).
3. Gopal Guru, 'Food As A Metaphor For Cultural Hierarchies', *Center for the Advanced Study of India*, 9.1 (2009) <http://casi.ssc.upenn.edu/index.htm> [accessed 7 May 2021]
4. Reay Tannahill, *Food in History* (New York: Crown, 1988), p. 105-17.
5. Paul Fieldhouse, *Food, Feasts, and Faith: An Encyclopedia of Food Culture in World Religions* (Santa Barbara, CA: ABC-CLIO, 2017), p. 266.
6. Vikram Doctor, 'The Dalit Meanings of Food', *Economic Times*, 4 December 2014 <https://economictimes.indiatimes.com/blogs/onmyplate/the-dalit-meanings-of-food/> [accessed 7 May 2021]
7. 'Dalit Identity And Food – Memories Of Trauma On A Plate', *Homegrown*, 21 November 2018 <https://homegrown.co.in/article/803216/dalit-identity-and-food-memories-of-trauma-on-a-plate> [accessed 24 May 2021]
8. Fieldhouse, p. 268.
9. Arjun Appadurai, 'Gastro-Politics in Hindu South Asia', *American Ethnologist*, 8.3 (1981), 495-511.
10. D.N. Jha, *The Myth of the Holy Cow* (New Delhi: Navayana, 2009), p. 18.
11. Jha, p. xi.
12. Tata Institute of Social Sciences, *Caste on the Menu Card*, 2021 <https://www.youtube.com/watch?v=mQYRinzRGXU> [accessed 30 May 2021]
13. Reay Tannahill, *Food in History* (New York: Crown, 1988), pp. 155-58.
14. WS 10 Class of 2009, *Isn't This Plate Indian? Dalit Histories and Memories of Food*, ed. by Sharmila Rege and others (Pune: University of Pune Press, 2009), p. 62-136.
15. Badri Chatterjee, 'Two-Year Undercover Study Reveals Cruel Side of India's Dairy Industries', *Hindustan Times*, 25 November 2017 <https://www.hindustantimes.com/mumbai-news/two-year-undercover-study-reveals-cruel-side-of-india-s-dairy-industries/story-7icLDyv1Rq2tVV2kbYKccN.html> [accessed 30 May 2021]
16. Sena Desai Gopal, 'Selling the Sacred Cow: India's Contentious Beef Industry', *The Atlantic*, 12 February 2015 <https://www.theatlantic.com/business/archive/2015/02/selling-the-sacred-cow-indias-contentious-beef-industry/385359/> [accessed 24 May 2021]
17. Suraj Yengde, *Caste Matters* (Gurgaon, Haryana, India: Penguin Random House India, 2019), p. 7.
18. Zarina Ahmad, 'Muslim Caste in Uttar Pradesh', *The Economic Weekly*, 14.7 (17 February 1962), pp. 325-36.
19. Guru.

20. Dirks, p. 5.
21. Parimala V. Rao, 'Colonial State as "New Manu"? Explorations in Education Policies in Relation to Dalit and Low Caste Education in the Nineteenth Century India', *Contemporary Education Dialogue*, 16.1 (2019), 84–107 (p. 89) <https://doi.org/10.1177/0973184918807812>
22. Nico Slate, 'Mahatma Gandhi's Experiments with Food', *India Today*, 27 September 2019 <https://www.indiatoday.in/magazine/cover-story/story/20191007/his-experiments-with-food-1603416-2019-09-27> [accessed 30 May 2021]
23. Joseph S. Friedman, 'Mahatma Gandhi's Vision for the Future of India: The Role of Enlightened Anarchy', *Penn History Review*, 6.1 (2008), p. 55.
24. Slate.
25. Abhirup Dham, 'Right to Food: The Politics of Vegetarianism in India', *The Telegraph Online*, 23 November 2019 <https://www.telegraphindia.com/health/right-to-food-the-politics-of-vegetarianism-in-india/cid/1721235> [accessed 17 March 2022]; Bipasha Maity, 'Comparing Health Outcomes Across Scheduled Tribes and Castes in India', *World Development*, 96 (2017), 163–81 <https://doi.org/10.1016/j.worlddev.2017.03.005>
26. Astitav Khajuria and others, 'Digesting Caste: Caste on My Plate, *Lokniti*, 24 August 2020 <https://mpp.nls.ac.in/blog/digesting-caste-graded-inequality-in-food-habits-2/> [accessed 24 May 2021]
27. WS 10 Class of 2009, p. 67.
28. Yengde, p. 2.
29. Meenakshi Ganguly, 'India: "Cow Protection" Spurs Vigilante Violence', *Human Rights Watch*, 27 April 2017 <https://www.hrw.org/news/2017/04/27/india-cow-protection-spurs-vigilante-violence> [accessed 30 May 2021]
30. Yengde, pp. 2-32.
31. McKim Marriott, 'Intimacy and Rank in Food', 10th International Congress of Anthropological and Ethnological Sciences, New Delhi, 10–18 December 1978.
32. 'Dalit Identity and Food'.
33. Appadurai, 'Gastro-Politics'.
34. WS 10 Class of 2009.
35. Radhika Iyengar, 'Blood & Beehives: Culinary Ingenuity of the Marginalised', *Goya*, 16 September 2020 <https://www.goya.in/blog/blood-and-beehives-culinary-ingenuity-of-the-marginalised-dalit-food> [accessed 24 May 2021]; WS 10 Class of 2009.
36. Shraddha Veeranna Chigateri, '"Glory to the Cow": Cultural Difference and Social Justice in the Food Hierarchy in India', *South Asia: Journal of South Asian Studies*, 31.1 (2008), 1–18 <https://ssrn.com/abstract=1030973> [accessed 1 May 2021].
37. Amrit Dhillon, 'In India, Caste System Ensures You Are What You Eat', *Post Magazine*, 26 July 2014 <https://www.scmp.com/magazines/post-magazine/article/1558061/you-are-what-you-eat> [accessed 1 May 2021]
38. James Staples, 'From Caste to Class in Food', in *Sacred Cows and Chicken Manchurian* (Seattle: University of Washington Press, 2020), pp. 140-62 (p. 146).
39. Arjun Appadurai, 'How to Make a National Cuisine: Cookbooks in Contemporary India', *Comparative Studies in Society and History*, 30.1 (1988), pp. 3-24.
40. Appadurai, 'How to Make a National Cuisine'.
41. 'All Day, Every Day', *Dishoom* <https://www.dishoom.com/menu/kensington-all-day> [accessed 24 May 2021]; for more on street food, see Aakar Patel, 'The Caste Guide to Street Food', *Mint*, 6 February 2016 <https://www.livemint.com/Leisure/Ce3gLolc5bfHpXxBp2wtWI/The-caste-guide-to-street-food.html> [accessed 24 May 2021]
42. Local Dalit *Rakti* (coagulated spiced blood) or *bhakri* (a millet flatbread), the Koli *Mandeli* (golden anchovies) or *nevta* (a regional slimy marsh fish).
43. Babita Shringare, 'Koliwada Prawns', *Babs' Projects*, 6 January 2021 <https://rb.gy/goooxz> [accessed 24 May 2021]

Food, the Imagination, and Social Resistance in Sandra Cisneros's *Woman Hollering Creek* (1991)

Méliné Kasparian-Le Fèvre

Chicana writer Gloria Anzaldúa compares the images and metaphors in Chicana literature to the plants and remedies employed by traditional healers, suggesting that literary metaphors could be a way of healing communities and of effecting social change:

> Because we use metaphors as well as herbs or curing stones to effect changes, we follow in the tradition of the shaman. If we are lucky, we create like the shaman images that induce altered states of consciousness conducive to self-healing [...]. From our own and our people's experiences, we will try to create images and metaphors that will give us a handle on the numinous, a handle on the faculty for self-healing.[1]

Such transformative, socially committed use of literary images as a way of healing societal wounds is at the heart of the writings of another Chicana writer, Sandra Cisneros, whose food metaphors perform important political work, denouncing oppressive ideologies and promoting empathy, in texts that are both delightfully whimsical and grounded in the reality of life for marginalized communities in contemporary America.

Sandra Cisneros's prose has a very imaginative and fanciful quality, and her short story collection *Woman Hollering Creek* (1991) is no exception, featuring a striking number of evocative metaphors and poetic images.[2] Another feature of Cisneros's writing that has been remarked upon by critics is the importance of food in her texts. However, no study has focused on the role of food in Cisneros's collection *Woman Hollering Creek* as a whole, or on the intersection between the theme of food and the imaginative, whimsical quality of her prose. This unexplored facet of Cisneros's writing is what this paper seeks to bring to the table, by analyzing food-based metaphors and analogies in *Woman Hollering Creek*. Indeed, food is not only described as a material reality in the collection, but also appears in imaginative associations and metaphorical images.

As this paper will argue, many of the food metaphors in *Woman Hollering Creek* address the politics of the imagination, by gesturing towards, and subverting, the use of metaphors in discourses of exclusion. In the place of stigmatizing metaphors, Cisneros proposes inclusive food metaphors that speak back to cultural discourses that in the US have stigmatized certain communities such as people living in poverty, people of colour, and women.

This reading of some of the food metaphors in *Woman Hollering Creek* will suggest that, in Cisneros's writing, the imagination is highly political and linked to questions of social justice: Cisneros's use of food metaphors exemplifies the idea that 'the issues raised by food and hunger have always been as political as they are poetical', as Sandra Gilbert writes.[3] In *Woman Hollering Creek*, food metaphors are indeed as political as they are poetical, as subversive as they are enchanting. Behind the food images in the collection lies not just an attempt to transform the mundane or to add a poetic touch to the text, but a commitment to address the reality of oppression and domination.

Race and Gender (Re)Imaginings through Food Metaphors

Metaphors are far from flimsy, silly matters. Georg Lakoff and Mark Johnson draw attention to the real-world power of metaphors in people's lives when they suggest that metaphors are not just a question of words but something we 'live by'.[4] As Esther Peeren has shown, metaphors have a political function and are often used to create group boundaries and to denigrate certain social categories by reinforcing negative stereotypes.[5] With regards to the Mexican-American context, which concerns us here, Otto Santa Ana has documented the way certain recurring metaphors in the US media have been a powerful instrument in the stigmatization and dehumanization of Mexicans and Mexican-Americans.[6] In Cisneros's text, food metaphors both point towards, and subvert, this oppressive and excluding use of metaphors.

The collection evokes the frequent use of food images as part of racist discourses, and reflects upon the well-documented role that food plays in the racialized, national imagination of the United States, where racist discourses and representations often associate people of colour with foodstuffs.[7] In racist discourses, food metaphors become racist slurs (as in the case of insults such as 'hot tamales' or 'beaners', which target Latino people), and skin tones are compared to foodstuffs, as Irene López-Rodríguez explains, 'In order to come to terms with people who eat and look differently, the color and shape of foodstuffs have always been at hand. Color terminology has been used [...] to create a taxonomy of human races because of the glaringly obvious differences in skin colors. Hence it seems logical that the color of certain foods be used to conceptualize human groups.'[8]

Cisneros's text reflects on this tendency to use the colour of foodstuffs to create boundaries between certain groups. In the story 'Bien Pretty', the narrator, who is a painter, uses a food-based analogy to describe the colour of her Mexican lover's skin: 'God made men by baking them in an oven, but he forgot about the first batch, and that's how Black people were born. And then he was so anxious about the second batch, he took them out of the oven too soon, so that's how White people were made. But the third batch he let cook until they were golden-golden-golden, and honey, that's you and me' (p. 148). This creation story draws lines between different types of bodies through a food-based analogy, following the logic that has been used to devalue people of colour and to present whiteness as the desirable norm. However, that logic is here turned on its head, as the narrator presents brown skin as desirable: 'God made you from red-clay, Flavio, with his hands. [...] And then he blessed you, Flavio, with skin sweet as burnt-milk candy [...]. He made you *bien* [very] pretty' (p. 148, translation mine). The title of the story, 'Bien pretty', which appears in this passage, insists on Flavio's beauty and counters the dominant norms of beauty within American society, which associate beauty with whiteness.[9] While food-based analogies are often used in racist discourses to denigrate non-white people, here the comparison between this Mexican man's skin and a caramel candy is meant not to disparage but to underline his beauty. Balestrini has identified the same reversal in Cisneros's novel *Caramelo*: 'The novel challenges any essentializing preferences for light skin through the protagonist's fascination with caramel- and chocolate- colored skin and sweets'.[10] This valorization of darker skin through food imagery and more precisely through references to candy also takes place in *Woman Hollering Creek*, which reclaims food-based analogies that have often been used to denigrate ethnic and racialized minorities to affirm the beauty of people of colour.

Food-based metaphors also play an important role in perpetuating sexist stereotypes and norms that oppress women. The analogy between women and edible substances, often associated with sexual connotations, dehumanizes them and associates them with passive substances that have value only as long as they satisfy men's appetites. The trope of the edible woman is pervasive in patriarchal societies, and presents 'women-as-prey, passive and ready to be plucked', according to Antje Lindenmeyer.[11] Cisneros's collection explores this trope of the edible woman to evoke the reality of violence against women and to combat the patriarchal norms that condemn and restrict women's sexual exploration and freedom. Such norms condemn women who seek to fulfil their own appetites and desires freely and suggest that women's sexuality should be controlled and remain in the service of men. As Mary Becker explains, '[i]n patriarchy, men are sexual subjects and women objects: women's sexuality exists to please men.'[12] The trope of the edible woman perfectly embodies this idea that women should remain passive objects, instead of taking on active roles, especially in regards to sexuality. Those women who take control of their own sexuality and pursue their own fulfilment are often punished within a patriarchal society, as Linda LeMoncheck has suggested: 'when women live in a patriarchal society, their sexual exploration, pleasure, and agency become targets for their sexual restriction, repression, and violation.'[13] Cisneros explores this aspect of patriarchal society in 'Eyes of Zapata', a short story set in Mexico during the early twentieth century. In this story, the narrator's mother exemplifies the violation and violence that women often have to face as a reaction to their sexual agency and exploration. After having had a succession of lovers, she is the victim of a collective rape by men who want to punish her for her sexual freedom. Her daughter Ines, who possesses supernatural abilities, sees how the rape happened during one of her visions:

> And I see other faces and other lives. […] My mother in a field of […] flowers with a man who is not my father. […] How, at a signal from her lover, the others descend. […] A machete-sharp cane stake greased with lard and driven into the earth. How the men gather my mother like a bundle of corn. Her sharp cry against the infinity of sky when the cane stake pierces her. […] Eyes still fixed on the clouds the morning

> they find her – braids undone, a man's sombrero tipped on her head, a cigar in her mouth, as if to say, this is what we do to women who try to act like men. (p. 111)

Through the comparison between the mother and a 'bundle of corn', the trope of the edible woman is mobilized to emphasize women's vulnerability to men's violence under patriarchal norms that condemn any woman who does not conform to the strict gender roles meant to control women's behaviour and to limit their agency. Cisneros's story explores the consequences of what Carol Vance has described as 'the traditional bargain women were forced to make with men: if women were "good" (sexually circumspect), men would protect them; if they were not, men could violate and punish them'.[14] Cisneros's story clearly reflects the idea that rape is a tool of control and intimidation, and, as Vance explains, a reminder to women that they are not the ones in power within a patriarchal society and that they should seek to conform to prescribed notions of femininity at all times.[15]

However, Cisneros's collection does not just offer images of vulnerable, oppressed, or violated women, but portrays rebellious women who manage to achieve a degree of freedom and autonomy without being the victims of male violence. As Mullen explains, '*Woman Hollering Creek* offers stories of a variety of women trying various means of escape, through resistance to traditional female socialization, through sexual and economic independence, self-fashioning, and feminist activism, as well as through fantasy, prayer, magic, and art.'[16] One of the main avenues of escape and resistance for the women in Cisneros's text lies in sexuality. According to Rojas, Cisneros 'incorporat[es] a type of female sexuality in her work that declares, "I defy you. I'm going to tell my own story"'.[17] Interestingly, in *Woman Hollering Creek* women's resistance through sexuality is often expressed through food-based analogies that reverse the trope of the edible woman and portray women as active consumers, and men as edible substances to be devoured. Such analogies occur in passages that focus on women who satisfy their own desires instead of conforming to gendered norms according to which women should devote themselves to satisfying the needs of others.

One such character, Clemencia, the narrator in 'Never Marry a Mexican', has affairs with married men: 'Borrowed. That's how I've had my men. Just the cream skimmed off the top. Just the sweetest part of the fruit, without the bitter skin that daily living with a spouse can rend' (p. 72). In this analogy between men and foodstuffs, sexuality outside the confines of marriage becomes a delicacy, as delicious and sweet as any food can be. The food metaphor underlines Clemencia's transgression, which lies in her refusal to abide by the idea that 'female desire should be restricted to zones protected and privileged in the culture: traditional marriage and the nuclear family'.[18] The image of edible men also highlights Clemencia's appropriation of the active, aggressive role usually associated with men, during the sexual act which she describes through an alimentary metaphor: 'I leapt inside you and split you like an apple. […] If I'd put you in my mouth you'd dissolve like snow' (p. 81). As Catherine MacKinnon explains, 'The male sexual role […] centers on aggressive intrusion on those with less power.'[19] In Cisneros's story, it is Clemencia who appropriates this traditionally masculine role of aggression, and the food metaphor, which presents her as metaphorically devouring the men she has sex with, expresses her power, dominance, and resistance to traditional patriarchal roles.

Cisneros's play on the edible woman trope therefore both exposes and undermines the patriarchal hierarchy which subordinates and oppresses women, just like her evocation of the analogy between food and people of colour subverts the racial hierarchy that associates beauty with whiteness. Drawing our attention to, and subverting, conventional food-based metaphors that have been used to exclude and to discriminate against women and people of colour, Cisneros's text validates Pereen's argument that 'literary and other representations can raise awareness of the way metaphors are not just rhetorical ornaments but may be used to oppress and stereotype'.[20]

Cisneros refers to an established vocabulary of food metaphors that form part of a racist and sexist collective consciousness and reclaims those food metaphors in order to denounce and critique the oppressive ideologies they usually convey. But she also proposes new, surprising, and inventive analogies and metaphors based on food. Unlike conventional food metaphors linked to gender and race, these idiosyncratic food images do not participate in excluding discourses but, on the contrary, facilitate connection and subvert stigmatizing discourses about poor people.

Food Images Countering Classist Exclusion

Unconventional food-based analogies in Cisneros's text subvert stereotypes around poverty and erase the artificial distance that is often perceived to separate poor people from the rest of society.[21] *Woman Hollering Creek* offers a realistic depiction of the lived experience of poverty, an experience that Cisneros herself has gone through during her childhood. The text centres on Mexican-American characters, who live in a 'barrio': a socially segregated, marginalized, and majority Spanish-speaking neighbourhood, characterized by overcrowding and underdevelopment. Some of these characters are children, whose lives are marked by unpleasant realities, from rats and hunger to parental neglect and sexual abuse. It is therefore not surprising that these characters should seek refuge in imaginative daydreams, in which foodstuffs frequently appear. Food-based analogies are part of Cisneros's efforts to convey 'the child's voice' in her writing and appear in passages which vividly conjure the imaginative worlds of children.[22] In 'Remember the Alamo', the adult narrator Tristán remembers that as a child, he would imagine that the sound of rice sizzling in a frying pan was actually the sound of an audience applauding him: 'When I was a kid and my ma added the rice to the hot oil, you know how it sizzles and spits, it sounds kind of like applause, right? Well, I'd always bow and say *Gracias, mi querido público* [thank you, dear spectators], thank you, and blow kisses to an imaginary crowd' (p. 67, translation mine). Daydreaming constitutes an essential tool of survival that allows the narrator to escape 'the ugly, the ordinary' circumstances of his life, marred by poverty and abuse (p. 70). The sounds of cooking fuel his playacting and allow him to transport himself into a different reality, in which he is not standing in the kitchen of a dilapidated apartment, but performing on a stage for an adoring public. What food provides is not just physical nourishment but a material for his daydreams, for his visions of a different life and a different future, visions that are as sustaining as any dish could be.

Such passages, in which the motif of food plays a role in children's imaginative worlds, and which may be described as food reveries, reappear throughout the text. Through these food reveries, the characters are presented not as stereotypes but as individual children, with their own idiosyncrasies, dreams, and aspirations, which humanizes them. These food reveries put the emphasis on the creativity and joy experienced by these children thanks to the power of their imagination transcending the very difficult conditions in which they live. They therefore participate in a nuanced portrayal of marginalized members of society that highlights both the violence of their circumstances and their capacity to find pockets of joy, to invent, and to daydream. This allows the text to reflect the full humanity that these marginalized people are often denied. These food reveries suggest that even if survival is a struggle for certain marginalized people, this does not mean that their lives are reduced to survival. To reflect marginalized people's humanity, it is necessary to avoid reducing them to their oppression and struggle, and to highlight, instead, their capacity to feel and create joy, to imagine, and to yearn for something beyond survival, as Chicana writer Ana Castillo suggests: 'We do not simply survive – that would imply that we were no more than drones. We live lives full of meaning.'[23] It is precisely this idea that marginalized people are not drones, functioning purely in survival mode, but humans with rich interior worlds, whose lives are infused with meaning and creativity, that the food reveries in Cisneros's text convey.

Besides highlighting the humanity of people living in poverty, these food reveries constitute an invitation to empathize with them, as they draw the reader's attention to the inner lives of the poor children in the collection, inviting the reader into their inner worlds. The reader's empathy and imaginative connection with those poor children is facilitated by the food-based analogies and images that pepper Cisneros's text, in several ways. First, the very structure of the food image or metaphor can be seen as a facilitator for the empathetic process. Indeed, images and metaphors rely on similarities and invite readers to find connection between objects that were seen as separate, and this process is precisely the one needed in order to empathize despite difference, as Hogan suggests: 'In every case, empathy is based on some sort of similarity. After all, to empathize with someone is to put oneself in his/her place, and that substitution presupposes something that is shared.'[24]

Food-based analogies in Cisneros's text facilitate a connection across class lines not only through their structure but also through their thematic content, because they emphasize what people living in poverty have in common with people of different socio-economic backgrounds. Tristán's food reverie constitutes but one example of food-based daydreams that, in the collection, highlight universal human experiences and traits that cross class lines, such as children's tendency to daydream and imagine. Through food-based analogies and daydreams, Cisneros's text suggests that, apart from their social status, the poor children depicted in the page are like any other in their propensity to dream, to play, to retreat into the world of their imagination. These children's food reveries may therefore remind readers of their own childhoods, a time when they probably experienced the world in the same playful, imaginative way. Since imagining (like eating) is a shared, universal experience, food reveries allow the readers to see themselves in Cisneros's characters, and to practice empathy for those who come from a different background. In that sense, Cisneros's collection reflects the idea that '[l]iterature enlarges our experience, compelling us to enter into imaginative and sympathetic relation with characters and predicaments we would otherwise never encounter'.[25] In Cisneros's text, food-based analogies are central in facilitating the readers entering into such imaginative, empathetic connections with characters whose backgrounds and experiences differ from their own. They make it easier for readers to care for and empathize with people who have had different life experiences from their own by focusing on experiences that can be shared across class lines (such as cooking, eating, daydreaming, or showing affection). Food images in Cisneros's text tend to focus on what connects, rather than separates, poor people from people in different socioeconomic positions, in contrast with the tendency to otherize poor people and to portray them as radically different.

Lastly, when looked at closely, food reveries reveal how Cisneros's text debunks certain representations around poverty. The passages in which food reveries appear speak back to certain dehumanizing and stereotyping discourses about people living in poverty that have profoundly influenced the American culture and the American collective unconscious, as is exemplified by the character of Tristán. Tristán's dream of achieving success on a stage evokes his ambition and his aspirations. His food reverie occurs at the very beginning of the story: Tristán is introduced to the reader first and foremost as an ambitious character who dreams of a better life, which he will actually achieve as he becomes a performer. Tristán's ambition and success goes against a stereotyped view, which has been pervasive in American culture and in the social sciences, of poor Mexican-Americans as passive, lazy, resigned to their lot, and incapable of envisioning a better life for themselves.[26] On the contrary, the characters in Cisneros's collection, like Tristán dream of escaping the 'barrio' and actively seek out opportunity. Far from being content, they look for an escape, even if the only escape to be found is through their imagination.

Through food-based analogies, Cisneros's text also contradicts the stereotype according to which poor families are dysfunctional and fail to maintain stable affective ties. This notion pertains to the 'culture of poverty' thesis, which was first explored by Oscar Lewis in 1959, that has left a deep mark in the American collective psyche. According to Lewis, poor people (and especially Mexican-American people, who were the main subjects of his writings) developed a specific culture which kept them in poverty, a culture that was characterized, among other traits, by a lack of family values and of familial cohesion.[27]

Two food-based analogies which appear in one of Cisneros's stories debunk the idea that poor persons always are pathologically incapable of maintaining functional, stable, affectionate families. In 'Mexican Movies', the narrator, a young girl, describes the delights offered by rare outings to the movie theatre with her family: 'You can put a quarter in the machine in the ladies' bathroom and get a plastic tic-tac-toe or pink lipstick the color of sugar roses on birthday cakes' (p. 22). In the child's imagination, the banal tube of lipstick is associated with a world of colour, beauty, ornamentation, and pleasure, far removed from the rat-infested movie theatre she stands in, and the vending machine becomes a portal towards colourful worlds and visions. The narrator and her siblings always enjoy going to the cinema, even if the movie playing is not particularly interesting: 'We just roll ourselves up like a doughnut and sleep, the armrest hard against our head until Mama puts her sweater there' (23). These two food-based analogies (linking the lipstick with a birthday cake, the sleeping children with doughnuts), not only evoke children's ability to transfigure quotidian life (however drab or difficult that life may be), they also suggest that this young girl has experienced affection, connection, and familial love (evoked through the reference to a birthday cake, often meant to celebrate a loved one, and to the mother's loving gesture of folding up a sweater to put underneath her sleeping children's head). This contradicts the notion that poor people always have dysfunctional families, and suggests that the poor, Mexican-American families who live in the 'barrio' are just like any other.

Unconventional food-based analogies that evoke children's reveries in Cisneros's text speak back to, and resist, dehumanizing, stereotyped views of people living in poverty. They demonstrate the possibility of using metaphors not to exclude (as in the case of the gendered and racialized metaphors Cisneros's text touches upon), but to include, to connect, and to promote empathy and compassion. Just like real food can often be the basis for forming community and connections, food-based analogies and metaphors in Cisneros's text serve as a way to denounce divisive discourses and to foster solidarity based on shared humanity.

In *Woman Hollering Creek*, food-based metaphors and analogies explore different forms of relationality: some inclusive (opening up towards the Other), others excluding and oppressive (excluding and denigrating certain groups). The imaginative and poetic moments in the collection, especially those that feature food-based analogies and metaphors, explore hierarchies of power and promote inclusion and empathy. A close reading of food metaphors and images in *Woman Hollering Creek* reveals that the collection does not shy away from what Carla Cevasco has called 'the dark side of food studies' – issues such as 'scarcity, cruelty, and oppression' – whilst also offering moments of lightness, of whimsy, and of poetry through the idiom of food; perhaps precisely because this mixture of struggle and joy, oppression and creativity, enables Cisneros to provide a more nuanced, less stereotypical portrayal of the lower-income Mexican-Americans she bases her fiction on, one that acknowledges the complexity of their lives and highlights their resiliency and humanity instead of showing them as victims or 'drones, living lives of pure survival'.[28]

Notes

1 Gloria Anzaldúa, 'Metaphors in the Tradition of the Shaman', in *Conversant Essays: Contemporary Poets on Poetry*, ed. by James McCorkle (Detroit: Wayne State University Press, 1990), pp. 99-101 (p. 100).
2 Sandra Cisneros, *Woman Hollering Creek and Other Stories* (New York: Random House, 1991). Subsequent references are cited parenthetically.
3 Sandra M. Gilbert, *The Culinary Imagination: From Myth to Modernity* (New York: W.W. Norton,

2014), p. ii.
4. George Lakoff and Mark Johnson, *Metaphors We Live By* (Chicago: University of Chicago Press, 1980), p. 6.
5. Esther Peeren, *The Spectral Metaphor: Living Ghosts and the Agency of Invisibility* (Basingstoke: Palgrave Macmillan, 2014), p. 5.
6. Otto Santa Ana, *Brown Tide Rising: Metaphors of Latinos in Contemporary American Public Discourse* (Austin: University of Texas Press, 2010).
7. Kyla Wazana Tompkins, *Racial Indigestion: Eating Bodies in the 19th Century* (New York: New York University Press, 2012).
8. Irene López-Rodríguez, 'Are We What We Eat? Food Metaphors in the Conceptualization of Ethnic Groups', *Linguistik online*, 69 (2014), 3-33 (p. 19) <http://dx.doi.org/10.13092/lo.69.1655>
9. Nell Irvin Painter. *The History of White People* (New York: W.W. Norton, 2011).
10. Nassim Balestrini, 'Transnational and Transethnic Textures; or, "Intricate Interdependencies" in Sandra Cisneros's "Caramelo"', *Amerikastudien / American Studies*, 57 (2012), 67-89 (p. 71) <http://www.jstor.org/stable/23509459> [accessed 21 September 2020]
11. Antje Lindenmeyer, '"Lesbian Appetites": Food, Sexuality and Community in Feminist Autobiography', *Sexualities*, 9, 469-85 (p. 471) <https://doi.org/10.1177/1363460706068045>
12. Mary Becker, 'Patriarchy and Inequality: Towards a Substantive Feminism', *University of Chicago Legal Forum*, 1 (1999), 21-88 (p. 28) <https://chicagounbound.uchicago.edu/cgi/viewcontent.cgi?article=1266&context=uclf> [accessed 03 May 2021]
13. Linda LeMoncheck, 'Feminism and Promiscuity', in *Sex, Love and Friendship: Studies of the Society for the Philosophy of Sex and Love 1993-2003*, ed. by Adrienne Leigh McEvoy (Amsterdam: Rodopi, 2011), pp. 9-17 (p. 9).
14. Carol S. Vance, 'Pleasure and Danger: Towards a Politics of Sexuality,' in *Pleasure and Danger: Exploring Female Sexuality*, ed. by Carol S. Vance (Boston: Routledge & Kegan Paul, 1985), pp. 1-27 (p. 2).
15. Vance, p. 3.
16. Harryette Mullen, '"A Silence Between Us like a Language": The Untranslatability of Experience in Sandra Cisneros's *Woman Hollering Creek*', *MELUS*, 21 (1996), 3-20 (p. 8) <http://www.jstor.org/stable/467946> [accessed 21 September 2020]
17. Maythee G. Rojas, 'Cisneros's "Terrible" Women: Recuperating the Erotic as a Feminist Source in "Never Marry a Mexican" and "Eyes of Zapata"', *Frontiers: A Journal of Women Studies*, 20 (1999), 135¬-57 (p. 136) <http://www.jstor.org/stable/3347227> [accessed 21 September 2020]
18. Vance, p. 3.
19. Catharine MacKinnon, *Feminism Unmodified: Discourses on Life and Law* (Cambridge and London: Harvard University Press, 1987), p. 65.
20. Peeren, p. 8.
21. Jean Swanson, *Poor-Bashing: The Politics of Exclusion* (Toronto: Between the Lines, 2001).
22. Juanita Heredia, 'A Home in the Heart: An Interview with Sandra Cisneros', in *Latina Self-Portraits: Interviews with Contemporary Women Writers*, ed. by Bridget Kevane and Juanita Heredia (Albuquerque: University of New Mexico Press, 2000), pp. 45-58 (p. 49).
23. Ana Castillo, *Massacre of the Dreamers: Essays on Xicanisma* (Albuquerque, University of New Mexico Press: 2014), p. 227.
24. Patrick Colm Hogan, *The Mind and its Stories: Narrative Universals and Human Emotion* (Cambridge: Cambridge University Press, 2003), p. 140.
25. Sophie Vlacos, *Ricoeur, Literature and Imagination* (London: Bloomsbury, 2014), p. 190.
26. Octavio Ignacio Romano-V, 'The Anthropology and Sociology of the Mexican-Americans: The Distortion of Mexican-American History', in *Ghettos and Barrios*, ed. by Robert McCabe and Sally Anthony (New York: MSS Educational Publishing, 1969), pp. 89-118.
27. Oscar Lewis, *Five Families: Mexican Case Studies in the Culture of Poverty* (New York: Basic, 1959).
28. Carla Cevasco, 'From the Editor: I Hate Food Puns', *Graduate Journal of Food Studies*, 2 (2015) <https://gradfoodstudies.org/2016/07/01/from-the-editor-i-hate-food-puns/> [accessed 15 June 2020]; Castillo, p. 227.

Food and the Irish Short Story Imagination

Anke Klitzing

Irish writers have been drawn to the short story since it developed out of older short fiction forms such as fairy tales in the nineteenth century, reaching an early peak in Ireland with George Moore's *The Untilled Field* (1903) and James Joyce's *Dubliners* (1914). Influenced by French and Russian short story masters like Maupassant and Chekhov, the form flourished in Ireland more than it did in England, for example.[1] Critics have proposed that short fiction thrived in Ireland because of the long-standing tradition of oral storytelling, which was still vibrant in the nineteenth century, although it suffered – like many other Irish folk traditions – during the Famine and its aftermath, fading away even more with the advent of radio and TV.[2] However, Ingman argues that oral tales, focusing on plot, stereotypical flat characters, and repeating motifs that suit the public performance to an audience, are quite distinct from the modern written short story.[3] At least since Moore and Joyce, Irish short fiction has featured tightly controlled plots with a single focus and often an emphasis on character and mood. Ingman traces the affinity of Irish writers for short fiction to its characteristically sharp, focused insights rather than broad, sweeping social panoramas: these insights suit times of uncertainty, instability, or unfixed identity.

Ireland's history over the last 150 years has been marked by upheavals, repeated searches for identity, and often fragmented community. The Great Famine decimated the population, especially in the rural and coastal areas of the West, taking with it also folk traditions and knowledge. The nineteenth-century Celtic Revival prompted the quest for a pre-colonial Irish identity; however, rooted in an intellectual, mostly urban middle class it failed to thoroughly connect with contemporary rural Gaelic communities. Meanwhile, Anglo-Irish landowners felt alienated and threatened through land reforms and rising nationalism. The struggle for independence brought the revolutionary nationalist streak to the fore, but the subsequent civil war undermined the social unity of newly independent Ireland. Neutrality in the Second World War and decades of protectionism and social conservatism isolated Ireland from much of Europe in the mid-twentieth century; the 1970s saw both the entry to the European Community for the Irish republic and the Troubles in Northern Ireland. The 1980s were characterized by economic recession and a flush of Catholic fervour after Pope John Paul II visited in 1979. The Celtic Tiger brought a boost of confidence from the mid-1990s onwards, but also the new experience of net immigration and a growing multicultural population.

The stranglehold of the Catholic church was broken at the turn of the millennium by a series of harrowing scandals, and a period of social liberation followed, allowing different identities to find their voices. The Good Friday Agreement of 1998 relies on the acceptance of a multitude of identities within the same social space. The recession from 2008 onwards again posed questions of community cohesion and solidarity between those who benefitted from the boom years – some through corruption – and those who were passed by. In a society in flux, such as Irish society has been for over a century, a form of literature like the short story that allows flashes of insight is well-suited to capture and reflect liminal identities and social dynamics as they emerge or disappear.

Gastrocriticism

What role, then, does food play in the Irish short story imagination? This paper takes a gastrocritical approach to investigate this question. Gastrocriticism is an emerging form of literary criticism focused on human relationships with each other and to the natural world through food. It investigates not only the symbolic and rhetorical use of food and foodways in literary texts, but also meaning and context – social, historical, political, or other – of their material or embodied appearance, thus becoming a useful quasi-ethnographic tool for the study of foodways and culinary traditions.[4] Fields such as food history, sociology, folklore, and cultural studies offer a complex understanding of food and foodways, and the gastrocritical approach explores how these meanings are refracted in literary writing.

Representations of foodways in literature may be part of the setting, the background and 'props' to the action. This material reality gives a text verisimilitude, which is of particular importance in realist fiction. It has been much commented that food and foodways are rich in meaning in real life – Appadurai calls food a 'highly condensed social fact'.[5] These layers of meaning translate via representations of food into the meaning of the literary text, making the culinary sign a valuable tool for writers, while inversely also conveying insights into the extra-textual reality. At times, foodways are more densely woven into the fabric of the text and drive the plot, sustain tension, or define characters.[6] The action is moved forward when characters meet and new characters are introduced at meal occasions; also, foodways may chronicle the passing of time.[7] Food preferences and habits of a character can speak to their social and economic status, worldview, and state of mind; through interactions around food, protagonists' affection for each other – or lack thereof – can be succinctly illustrated.

Food representations may provide metaphors, metonymy, similes, or symbols.[8] More broadly, they may provide a theme to the text. Specifically food-related themes include hunger, nourishment, feeding, growth and harvest, communion, appetite, taste, and pleasure. Texts may express emotions, values, or the social status of the author through food and foodways. A text may also exhibit what Jakobson calls the conative function, when it is intended to have a physical, psychological, or behavioural effect on the reader.[9] Many literary representations of foodways are quite literally mouthwatering. Multi-sensory descriptions of food create vivid images, stimulating a sense of pleasure or indeed appetite. This visceral effect also works in the opposite direction, evoking disgust and horror, either simply for the thrill of it or as a call to civic action.

Genres are categories of text that provoke and meet expectations of format, characters, settings – and even plot, mood, or message. In the short story, an important characteristic is the achievement of effects through compression, suggestion, and implication. Epiphanies are also a quintessential element. The multi-layered meanings of food representations prove a useful tool in this case once more.

The Stories

Five stories from the newly published anthology *The Art of the Glimpse: 100 Irish Short Stories* (2020) were selected for gastrocritical analysis, as they feature food and foodways in a particularly significant way.[10] They span almost the entire time period of the collection, from 1880 to 2012. Rosa Mulholland's 'The Hungry Death', first published in Dickens' *All the Year Round* in 1880, depicts the Irish Famine as it befalls a West Irish island community. The story focuses on a love triangle and ends with Brigid sacrificing herself by giving her last morsels of food to her starving rival. Daniel Corkery's 'The Awakening' (1929) tells of a young fisherman who is about to inherit his father's fishing boat and profession. In Emma Cooke's 'A Family Occasion' (1980), grown siblings meet over tea and cake and reflect on the different paths of their lives, as one of the sisters of the Protestant family married a Catholic and is now in thrall to the doctrines of the Catholic church. Maeve Binchy uses a dinner party in 'Holland Park' (1983) to showcase the epiphany of the narrator that she is in love with her female friend. Éilís Ní Dhuibhne's 'Literary Lunch' (2012) takes a rather sinister turn, as a spurned author shoots the chairman of the arts board after the latter's sumptuous lunch. Food – or beverages – fulfil a range of functions in these stories, providing setting but also sketching out character and relationships, providing plot twists, expressing the authors' views, and even involving us, the readers.

'The Hungry Death'

Mulholland's story illuminates the socio-economic situation on the island of Inishbofin before and during the Famine of 1845–1849. The first, pre-Famine, part shows the precarious situation of a community already familiar with 'the hungry death' whenever inclement weather disrupts the potato crop, makes the fishing scarce, or interrupts the lifeline of the supply boat from the mainland (p. 527). Eating seaweed for sustenance is not unfamiliar to the islanders who predict the need for it based on the weather and have opinions on its taste. Fishing brings its own challenges, as fishermen regularly perish. Emigration is a fact of life. The second part, describing the Famine in full force, shines a light on the individual suffering often hidden behind statistics. It shows solidarity, charity, kindness, loyalty, but also baser emotions. Coll struggles to bring a bag of maize meal from the harbour to Moya's cabin, as desperate people try to arouse his pity and obtain a share: 'Hard work I had to carry it from the beach, for the eyes o' the creatures is like wolves' eyes, an' I thought the longin' o' them would have dragged it out o' my hands' (p. 541). Here, for once, the author acknowledges the de-humanizing aspect of starvation, as she likens the starving to 'creatures' and wolves. It is notable, though, how strongly she otherwise affirms the persistent humanity even of the most desperate. There are no vivid descriptions of food in the text, apart from the 'rank-looking' seaweed (p. 540), but it could be argued that the graphic descriptions of starving people, which have been called macabre, aim to rouse sympathy, pity, even horror in the reader.[11] This is particularly effective since the people are never fully disenfranchised of their humanity.

The food items appearing in the narrative fit the time and place. It would have been common in nineteenth-century rural Ireland to produce one's own potatoes, to have chickens and a cow for milk, butter, and buttermilk. Wheat would be nearly impossible to cultivate on Inishbofin due to the meagre soils and wet climate, so flour is bought, along with tea and sugar. Crucially, Brigid also buys 'a sack of meal' at the store (p. 529), and 'meal' features prominently as the only food still available when the potatoes rot. It is 'meal' that Coll and Moya try to feed to the dying mother and that Brigid distributes among the starving, eventually saving Moya from the brink of death. The 'meal' in question is maize or 'Indian' meal, imported into Ireland to fill subsistence gaps from the early 1800s and in considerable amounts during the Famine.[12] As the Famine hits, the islanders persevere 'on a mess of Indian meal once a day, mingled with such edible seaweed as they could gather off the rocks' (p. 539).

Food and foodways are central to the action, particularly in the second part of the story. The search for food drives Coll and Moya about the island just as it drives Brigid's charitable distribution. Food is strongly linked to nature in the text: the struggle to win sustenance from land and sea is ever-present. When the potato blight hits the island, combined with prolonged bad weather and storms, nature is described as a strong and merciless power: 'Earth and sea alike barren and pitiless to their needs' (p. 539). The storms are equally overwhelming as they destroy boats and fishing gear and prevent the provisions boat arriving from Galway. The main conflict in the second part is between humans and nature, rather than each other. For Brigid, though, food embodies a conflict with herself. The 'han'ful o' male [meal] at the bottom o' the bag' becomes the crucible in which she faces her dark feelings, her jealousy, and even hatred of Moya, but it also leads her to overcome those feelings, to reach forgiveness to the point of sacrifice (p. 542). Fischler points out that sharing food turns eating from a mere physiological act into a spiritual one.[13] The reliance on a boat to bring vital provisions, the devastation of the Famine due to a near-total reliance on the potato, and other details are specifically local to a Western Irish island community, but other forces that shape the story such as pride, love, jealousy, or gratitude are universal. Due to the background of the Famine, it is food that throws these universal human traits into sharp relief. The story may be understood as an early specimen of the modern short story – it still shows several characteristics of a tale, with its focus on plot; characters with a touch of the formulaic in the flaming red-haired beauty of Brigid, the tall, handsome male hero, and the innocent wisp of a girl that needs saving; and motifs such as stormy nights, swamps, and love triangles. However, the narrative allows for modern literary traits such as character development and insights into the protagonists' interior life.

'The Awakening'

Corkery's 'The Awakening' is a realist story, and setting, time, and status markers are all given through food. The story opens as the protagonist wakes to participate in the night's mackerel fishing. After the catch and a communal meal, the boat leisurely returns to the harbour to land the fish. Foodways appear in two fundamental ways. On the one hand, food work (fishing) is the setting and prime activity. As their livelihood, it shapes the individual and communal identity of the protagonists. On the other hand, there is the meal, which consists of 'good food' and 'close companionship' (p. 151). The companionship is emphasized again elsewhere in the story, when Ivor repeatedly speaks of the 'real families' of the men who were sleeping on land, indicating another type of family, on the boat (pp. 148, 150). Similar to a so-called 'family meal' in a restaurant, the boat 'family' eats together, bonding over food. They eat boiled fish and potatoes, a simple yet nutritionally complete and typical meal (p. 150).

The story gives insights into the material and social realities of the life and work of a young Munster fisherman in the early twentieth century. It illustrates the fishermen's occupational identity, including their standing with other community members and the community as a whole; their relationships as boat crews in terms of solidarity, hierarchy, roles, and responsibilities; matters of authority, ownership, and inheritance; and also superstition or prejudice, for example about accepting a stranger as a crew member.[14] The meal shines a light on some of these matters, not just companionship but also hierarchies as the cabin boy cooks and cleans while the captain does not partake in the conversation.

The fishing is vividly rendered, the 'dripping, fish-laden', 'fish-spangled net'; the darkness and intermittent 'flakes of wet brightness', where flying drips are caught in lamp light; the mackerel appearing like a 'flight of shining steel-bright daggers' (pp. 146-47). These descriptions are attractive to the reader but also to Ivor, who finds himself enamoured with the work, the companionship, and the thought of running the boat himself. This is his titular 'awakening', the epiphany of the story. Visceral descriptions of food and foodways invoke the conative function, and it is no different here. Multiple senses are employed to describe the work of fishing – wet drips, bright flakes, shining daggers, the clanking of the windlass, the movement of the boat, the smell of smoke and food, the heat of the warm hold as they eat. It glamorizes the fishermen's work and solicits understanding for the 'fisherman's calling' (p. 149). The story praises skilled and hard work, family values, loyalty. While fishing is closely linked with nature and the elements, and the danger of drowning is mentioned twice, nature is not implicated as an opposing force. Even Ivor's father's drowning is presented impassively; rather, Captain Larry's loyalty is emphasized. The text chimes with efforts to capture Irish tradition and heritage in the newly independent country, such as the work of the Irish Folklore Commission that from 1935 recorded a wealth of information on Irish folklore, customs, and heritage. Corkery published several works on the Irish language and Gaelic tradition, as well as a study of Synge who in turn wrote extensively about the Irish peasantry and was involved in the collection of folklore.[15] Indeed, the story resonates with Synge's writings, several of which are set in coastal communities, albeit in the West of Ireland.

'A Family Occasion'

The foods offered at the afternoon tea gathering of the siblings links the story to Ireland. The drink is tea; eaten are (store-bought) 'iced fancies', sponge sandwich cake, and homemade potato cakes (p. 138). The story revolves around family interaction, inter-religious marriage, and women's reproductive rights, but the setting is a food occasion, and a key point of the back story, the meeting of the inter-religious couple, also revolves around food – a meat sandwich that Catholic Seamus accidentally consumes on a Friday, which is a taboo for him. The stroke of midnight turned the meat-containing sandwich from a food to a non-food, an 'offending sandwich'. Seamus' dismay at his transgression underlines his strong Catholic beliefs: '[Beattie] turned round to find Seamus standing staring at a sandwich as if it was about to explode', and, later, he looks at her 'in horror'. The incident provides the first interaction and indeed meeting of Protestant Beattie and Seamus, and had it not happened, neither might the marriage. Beattie alludes to the significance of the sandwich, saying it was 'a joke that she had kept to herself', but that 'in the end, it hadn't been funny after all' (p. 144). While the incident is only remembered and not part of the story action, it can be seen as the story's epiphany. The meat sandwich embodies conflict within Beattie – not at the time but now, as her once treasured memory is a reminder of her bondage to the Catholic doctrine prohibiting contraception that burdens her with many children.

Some food in the story may be read symbolically. When Beattie reflects on how nothing in the family home ever changes, she focuses on a chocolate egg, 'a present from cousins in America', that has been sitting on the shelf, wrapped in cellophane, untouched, since they were children. Beattie recalls that she had been 'wishing and wishing' that her mother would allow the children to taste it, and she closes with the thought that 'it must be mouldy by now' (p. 141). This is a realistic assumption, but it could be read as something extraordinary that was never shared and has gone stale and rotten, much like Beattie's own dreams, stale and curtailed by the realities of her large family and husband who likes a drink.

'Holland Park'

In 'Holland Park', food is an integral part of the action. The central scene is the dinner at Malcolm and Melissa's house, starting with an invitation to the party and going through the evening from pre-drinks at the narrator's flat, then aperitif, dinner, dessert, coffee, and more wine – including an incidence of choking, which can be seen as a form of disordered eating. The narrator gets a piece of food stuck in her throat, guessing that it was 'a piece of something exotic, avocado maybe, anyway something that shouldn't be in a salad' (p. 65). The incident is the story's epiphany, caused by the shock of recognition of the female narrator's attraction to her friend Alice, something that perhaps, in her guilty view, 'shouldn't be there'. The choking embodies a conflict of the narrator with herself, while Alice is strikingly unperturbed and manages to steer the narrator through the difficulty.

Food and drink are repeatedly used to characterize Malcolm and Melissa through their interaction in commensal occasions. Malcolm serves generous aperitifs and also pours the coffee later; Melissa makes everything seem effortless and welcoming, but she does not display false modesty ('There were no cries of praise and screams of disclaimer from the hostess' (p. 65)). Also Jeremy and Jacky, who are organizing the following summer's trip, are characterized by food. Presumably a gay couple, they are thought to be 'madly camp', but when they are suspected to be stereotypically overwrought ('Would they drive everyone mad looking for sprigs of tarragon in case the pot au feu was ruined?'), Alice, who had put forth this thought, is gently admonished for 'typecasting' (p. 67).

Food supports the impression of reality in the text – dinner parties and holiday taverna visits are social settings where people meet, and the different stages of the dinner party serve as time markers. They are also status markers, a display of cultural capital. Expensive now, Holland Park was quite bohemian in the early 1980s. Cultural capital is exhibited in the choice, preparation, and presentation of the foods and beverages. These are slightly rustic yet perceived as sophisticated in their authenticity – the garlic bread is 'fresh and garlicky', neither too hard nor too soggy. The main dish is spaghetti, described as 'excellent' as well as 'mountainous'. The salad 'was like an exotic still-life' (p. 65), alluding to both exoticism and to art. The ice cream is rich, indulgent, and served in 'huge helpings' (p. 66). The text reflects the young intelligentsia of early 1980s London who ate avocado and were able to make their own hummus, feta, and pitta bread. They eat quasi-ethnic but 'authentically'-made food, with mildly exotic ingredients such as a salad with 'everything in it except lettuce' (p. 65). The story illustrates the concept of foodies as later discussed by Johnston and Baumann.[16] Exoticism and authenticity feature in many facets of the chosen foods, and there is the aspect of understated hospitality, of do-it-yourself, unlike the imagined alternative gourmet evening involving 'dinner around a mahogany table with lots of cut-glass decanters, and a Swiss darling to serve it and wash up' (p. 62). Even the invitation is kept informal, talking about 'how many strands of spaghetti to put into the pot' – pots rarely feature in dinner party invitation rhetoric, as the kitchen is kept out of sight (p. 61).

Unusually for fiction, the reader is addressed directly as the narrator declares that Melissa's spaghetti was 'not the kind of spaghetti that you and I would ever make'. The visceral effect continues in the food descriptions of the dinner scene, specifically the garlic bread, which offers smell and taste ('garlicky' does both) as well as texture. Interestingly, the pasta cooking time is mentioned – Melissa seems to be out of the room for only three minutes although, as the narrator adds, 'I know it takes at least eight to cook the pasta' (p. 65). While the actual time span may be different than perceived, underlining the hospitality skills of the hostess, the narrator is trying to reclaim a little cultural/culinary capital herself by showing that she knows how to cook spaghetti.

'A Literary Lunch'

This is the story of two lunches, contrasted in affluence and abundance. The meals show time passing through the various courses and offer a rich backdrop for the story. While some of the setting is specific and real, such as street names, other aspects are invented or semi-invented. There has never been a bistro at Dublin's Usher's Island, but the photographic mural described does exist at an outdoor location further down the river Liffey. The nearly-real locations serve to anchor the story without claims to actual truth. Food and drink also provide period markers, for example through specifying wine vintages.

The choice of foods and eating establishments indicate the social and financial status of the protagonists. The coffeeshop where Francie has his lunch of a baguette sandwich with tuna, sweetcorn, and coleslaw is described as a 'cold little kip' (Irish slang for a place in a bad state of repair, p. 554). The art board members' choice of Gabriel's Bistro indicates a certain level of taste, cultural capital, and snobbery. It trumps their usual choice, a hotel restaurant with a slightly outdated feel and menu: 'alarming starched tablecloths and fantails of melon' (p. 551). The bistro, by contrast, has a 'clever ironic way' that shows in its interior, for example the table set up to mirror a mural of the *Last Supper*, which in itself can be regarded as ironic as it is said to depict 'typical Dubliners eating' (p. 552). Irony also appears in the menu, which lists gourmet foods such as truffles beside hearty dishes like bangers and mash, and in the etiquette: 'Put your elbows on the table, have a good time' (p. 551). This irony can be best appreciated through high cultural capital, as it requires an understanding of what to expect, why the expectation is reversed, and why the reversal of the expectation is arguably more luxurious and sophisticated despite looking the opposite. Cultural capital is not directly tied to financial capital, but indirectly it is, as its acquisition – like becoming a wine connoisseur – often requires money. The board members are not necessarily wealthy – Pam is a writer, for example – but their talent or social capital have led them to be included on the board, which means they can eat and drink expensive victuals gratuitously.

The *Last Supper* appears repeatedly as a motif. The photographic mural is mimicked and mirrored by the layout of the restaurant, and further echoed when the chairman seats himself in the middle and the others to his right and left, divided by gender. The board lunch turns out to be Alan's 'last supper', as he is shot upon leaving the restaurant. In this analogy, Pamela, the new board member, turns out to be Alan's 'Judas', although unlike the original Judas, the betrayal may not have been intentional. Francie's text to

Pam – 'Each man kills the thing he loves…some do it with a kiss' – is another allusion to Judas and his kiss of betrayal.

The lunch at Gabriel's embodies the excesses of the Celtic Tiger era, which witnessed corruption and the nefarious acquisition of wealth at the expense of fellow citizens, a dynamic symbolized in the relationship between Francie and the board. The board members drink copiously and eat sumptuous, expensive dishes, with the exception of the 'soup of the day' that one of the women orders. The eventual bill of €1200 does not perturb the chairman. Gluttony implicates eating in excess while others are starving. Francie is not physically starving, although his sandwich is remarkable neither in quality nor gastronomic satisfaction. However, he is starving metaphorically, consistently excluded from a share of the funding pie as well as recognition, while the board wallows in both, and in never-ending 'meetings and lunches, receptions and launches' (p. 553). This is Pam's first such lunch. When Alan is annoyed with her, he vows to ensure it is 'her first and her last supper' (p. 556). The commensality at the meal at Gabriel's is an exclusive one – literally, as only board members are invited, but also metaphorically, as some people were not 'invited' to participate in the spoils of the Celtic Tiger. It is a localized experience, but it speaks to wider human experiences of access and power; of social, financial, and cultural capital; of frustration and desperation.

Conclusion

The recent publication of a new anthology of Irish short stories, spanning from 1880 to 2020, speaks to the continuing popularity of the genre in Ireland. While the form has seen different trends during the past 140 years – realist, gothic, visionary, modernist, or fantastical stories, written by a diverse cast of authors – it remains a format appreciated by new and established Irish authors to reflect and question social dynamics and identities. A gastrocritical reading of selected stories from the collection shows that through the years, food and foodways have served as valuable tools for Irish short story writers. Food and foodways have provided setting and context, themes and symbols, plot points, conflicts, and characterization. They have expressed loyalty, sacrifice, and humanity; showcased pride in traditional work; captured the oppressiveness of religious doctrine; traced growing sexual self-awareness; and embodied social inequality. As a rich culinary sign, food has also been employed to furnish the quintessential short story epiphanies, allusions, and implications. Throughout its prolific history, food and foodways have always nourished the Irish short story imagination.

Notes
1   Heather Ingman, *A History of the Irish Short Story* (Cambridge: Cambridge University Press, 2009).
2   Rory Boland, 'How the Irish Lost Their Words,' *BBC.com*, 23 May 2016, <http://www.bbc.com/travel/story/20160502-how-the-irish-lost-their-words> [accessed 25 May 2021]
3   Ingman, pp. 2-3.
4   Priscilla P. Ferguson, 'A Cultural Field in the Making: Gastronomy in Nineteenth-Century France',

American Journal of Sociology, 104.3 (1998), 597-641.

5   Arjun Appadurai, 'Gastro-Politics in Hindu South Asia', *American Ethnologist*, 8.3 (August 1981), 494-511 (p. 494); see also Roland Barthes, 'Towards a Psychosociology of Food Consumption', in *Food and Culture: A Reader*, 2nd edn, ed. by Carol Counihan and Penny Van Esterik (New York: Routledge, 2008), pp. 28-35; Peter Jackson, introduction to *Food Words: Essays in Culinary Culture*, by Peter Jackson and CONANX (London: Bloomsbury, 2015), p. 4.
6   Gian-Paolo Biasin, *The Flavors of Modernity: Food and the Novel* (Princeton: Princeton University Press, 1993), pp. 13-16.
7   Biasin, p. 13.
8   Biasin, p. 20.
9   Roman Jakobson, 'Linguistics and Poetics', in *Style in Language*, ed. by Thomas Sebeok (Cambridge, MA: MIT Press, 1960), pp. 350-77 (p. 354).
10 *The Art of the Glimpse: 100 Irish Short Stories*, ed. by Sinéad Gleeson (London: Head of Zeus, 2020). Subsequent references to the stories in the collection are cited parenthetically in the text.
11 Richard Dalby, 'Rosa Mulholland, Mistress of the Macabre', *The Green Book: Writings on Irish Gothic, Supernatural and Fantastic Literature*, 9 (2017), 19-23 (p. 21).
12 Austin Bourke, 'The Irish Grain Trade, 1839-48', *Irish Historical Studies*, 20.78 (September 1976), 156-69 (pp. 163-64).
13 Claude Fischler, 'Commensality, Society and Culture', *Social Science Information*, 50.4-3 (2011), 528-48 <https://doi.org/10.1177/0539018411413963>
14 Shanon Phelan and Elizabeth Kinsella, 'Occupational Identity: Engaging Socio-Cultural Perspectives', *Journal of Occupational Science*, 16.2 (2009), 85-91.
15 Daniel Corkery, *The Hidden Ireland: A Study of Gaelic Munster in the Eighteenth Century* (Dublin: Gill and Macmillan, 1924); Daniel Corkery, *Synge and Anglo-Irish Literature: A Study* (Cork: Cork University Press, 1931).
16 Josée Johnston and Shyon Baumann, *Foodies: Democracy and Distinction in the Gourmet Foodscape*, 2nd edn (New York: Routledge, 2014).

The Big Cheese: Cheese and American Imagination

Bruce Kraig

Nothing fires gustatory imaginations like cheese. Consider the British cheese gourmands Wallace and Gromit, whose hunger for the stuff drives them to build a rocket ship that takes them to the motherlode of all cheeses, the moon (it's not Wallace's beloved Wensleydale). Wallace's and Gromit's turophilia are nothing compared to their American cousins' enduring zeal for quasi-rotted milk. Cheese is for eating, of course, but like other foods it represents ideas that Americans past and present have about themselves. Some of the ideas take political and social expressions; others are embedded in popular culture. The late nineteenth-century expression 'big cheese', meaning someone of importance, a 'big man', refers to large wheels of cheese displayed at state fairs among other venues and might refer to two historical patriotic cheeses. In a broader food sense, cheese tells us about how Americans think it should be produced, sold, and eaten, and what the taste and textures of desirable food should be.

It has become a cliché to call America the land of abundance, a cornucopia of food that makes its inhabitants fat and happy. True in terms of agricultural output, a poisonous falsehood in the hard reality of historic food deprivation among many Americans, the myth has always taken political form. A well-known cheese story of the early republic centres on just this. On New Year's Day 1802, President Thomas Jefferson stood at the door of his official home, the White House, ready to welcome a gift from political supporters: the world's largest cheese, four feet across, eighteen inches high, and weighing more than 1250 pounds. The cheese had been made in the late summer of 1801 by the women of Cheshire, a small community (the 1800 census lists 200 people) in Massachusetts' western backcountry. The effort was led by a charismatic if socially embarrassing preacher named John Leland – he tended to shout and stomp around while preaching. His flock were free-will Baptists resolutely opposed to the hierarchical religious and political establishment of Massachusetts and who thought of themselves as true citizens of a free republic established by God.[1] When Thomas Jefferson (a notable religious skeptic) and his populist Democratic-Republican Party won the presidency Leland's people set to work to celebrate the electoral victory by using the most democratic food produced by an abundant land: cheese. The milk of nine hundred cows from parishioner's farms was turned into curd and placed in a huge vat set on a cider press (cider the usual beverage of ordinary Americans). It was salted, and then transformed by pressing into a big block of cheese.[2]

Most American-made cheeses of the late eighteenth and early nineteenth century seem to have been cheddars, though the people of Cheshire could have made the eponymous cheese. Since these were farmhouse products no records tell us what exactly they were. Cheese was a way to preserve surplus milk, especially during the warm months (milking lasted approximately from April to November), to provide protein over the winter, and to produce something that could be sold in local markets. Farmhouse cheeses were staples of rural America throughout the eighteenth and nineteenth centuries. A cheese that weighed more than half a ton meant a considerable investment in each family's resources and labour since there were no milking machines. Ordinary milk cows of the period were shorthorns of mixed breeds mainly from northern England; not until the 1830s were 'improved' breeds such as Ayrshires and Dutch cows imported for better production.[3] Super producing Holstein Friesians did not appear until 1857. Early cows might have produced 1500 pounds (about 174 gallons) of milk a year.[4] Even at these low milk yields, an average farm with one cow could make 150 pounds of cheese a year, assuming no milk was taken for drinking or butter. Cheshire's dairy was already well-known because of excellent grazing land, so its cows were obviously much better producers than normal – perhaps close to some exceptional yields of 2500 pounds of milk reported in 1800. Large amounts of milk were necessary because the great cheese required 13,000 pounds from the 900 cows in a short time. The American land – and the animals upon it – were clearly abundant as the great cheese was meant to show.

The fame of this huge cheese spread, Leland glorying in the title given to him in the popular press: 'the Mammoth Priest'. But the massive creation was so large and the roads so poor that it could only be shipped in wintertime over snow and ice by sleds and by water routes. It went down the Hudson River by boat to New York City where it was viewed by large crowds of people, then to Baltimore and on to Washington, DC. President Jefferson standing in his doorway welcoming this rare thing seemed mightily pleased by gift. The makers may have known that, in 1792, the village of Norleach in Cheshire, England had created a 1350 pound cheese for America's *bête noir* King George III since it was reported in a United States newspaper. But here was a cheese all the better for being American, as Leland said in his message to the president:

> 'The Cheese was not made by his Lordship, for his sacred Majesty; nor with a view to gain dignified titles or lucrative offices; but by the personal labour of free-born farmers (without a single slave to assist) for an elective President of a free people […].
>
> 'Sir, we had some thought of impressing some significant inscription on the Cheese; but we have found such inconveniency in stamps on paper, that we chose to send it in a plain Republican form.'[5]

For the dairymen and women of Cheshire, the cheese was good publicity, their products well-known throughout the nineteenth century. Even better for Leland, Jefferson paid him 200 dollars (roughly $4,238 in today's dollars).[6]

The Big Cheese: Cheese and American Imagination

The word mammoth had just come into vogue, partly due to Jefferson's own work on America's fauna and flora. Since his tenure as envoy to France he – and before him Benjamin Franklin – had argued successfully with French naturalists that American plants and animals were larger and better than European ones. He succeeded in convincing the greatest one of all, Georges-Louis Leclerc, Comte de Buffon, by sending him a much-decayed moose skeleton and hide. In 1801, with Jefferson's help, famed artist and naturalist Charles Willson Peale had put the skeleton of a mastodon discovered near Newburgh, New York on display at his natural history museum in Philadelphia. Peale declared it 'the LARGEST of Terrestrial Beings', in short a mammoth.[7] John Leland's huge cheese was an edible version of a nascent publicity industry. Peale's skeleton was later brought by P.T. Barnum for his American Museum, showing that bigger and flashier almost always signals superiority in American minds.

Big food was of the moment, and Jefferson's political enemies in the Federalist Party used it to ridicule him in their newspapers. They called it a 'Mammoth' cheese that would soon be filled with maggots that only Democratic-Republican rats would eat. Actually, there is no record of what happened to the cheese once it was brought into the White House, so it is possible that maggots feasted on some of it, because it seems to have remained there for two years. One writer suggested that the women of Lenox, also in western Massachusetts, bake a mammoth apple pie, 15 feet across and 4800 pounds in weight, to accompany the colossal cheese: 'the Apple Pye ought therefore to weigh at least forty-eight hundred as Mr. Jefferson, unless he has a Mammoth appetite for Cheese, will want four pounds of Pye to one of Cheese.'[8] Pie and cheese for dessert was just as American as it was French or British.

Not to be outdone by opposition hyperbole, the party of the people took up the theme with gusto in more than one way. In the spring of 1804, the official bakers of the Navy prepared a 'Mammoth Loaf' of bread presumably to be eaten with the last of the great cheese. Dressed in their best uniforms, the Navy bakers carried it into the Capitol where it was set in a Senate committee room. There is sat beside huge quantities of roast beef, whiskey, and hard cider. Jefferson, normally a fan of French and Italian dining, dressed in a plain old coat, mingled with a large crowd of ordinary people. A critic said that they were 'people of all classes & colors from the President of the United States to the meanest vilest Virginia slave'. The President took out his pocket knife, hacked off a hunk of beef and bread and ate them, washed down with liquor. The 'mob' joined in and spent the rest of the day eating, likely cheese included, and drinking. The event was part of the administration's campaign to raise money for the Navy to fight the infamous Barbary pirates, but it was also a populist celebration of American food and drink.[9]

Thirty years later, another great cheese arrived at the White House, this one dedicated to the self-proclaimed greatest populist president up to that time, master self-promoter Andrew Jackson. This one was made in the summer of 1835, at a time when American agriculture was becoming a main element in the new national market with consequent industrialization. Colonel Thomas S. Meacham was a well-to-do dairy farmer with lands in Salt Creek, New York near Lake Ontario. Although a Whig, opposed to Jackson politically, he was a patriot and nationalist. President Jackson's suppression of South Carolina's attempt at disunion in 1832 was applauded by men such as Meacham, and so in honour of these acts (and to ingratiate himself with political leaders) he created several big cheeses. Three weighing 750 pounds went to the Vice President, the governor of New York State, and New York City's mayor. But the biggest cheese of all went to the big man himself at the White House, on New Year's Day, 1836. Two feet thick, eleven feet in circumference, and weighing more than 1400 pounds the cheese was made in a specially constructed vat composed of twenty-four staves – one for each state of the union – using milk from 150 of Meacham's cows. It took days to fill with curd; no doubt this was an American cheddar since the technique calls for layering of curds. Once pressed it was wrapped in patriotic garb. Proclaimed a gift from 'the whole people of the State of New York', on the cheese was a banner twelve feet long and seven feet wide painted with the motto: 'The National Belt: The Union it must be Preserved'. Twenty-four gold stars and a dedication to President Andrew Jackson came with the banner. A grand procession of boats and wagons carried the great cheese and its smaller fellows down Lake Ontario to Oswego, then by the decade-old Erie Canal and Hudson River to New York City, thence to Philadelphia, Baltimore, and Washington. Throngs of people in cities along the way came out to admire the great creation and to cheer the sentiments on its banner. When the mammoth arrived at the White House, the President accepted it and served up bottles of wine from the White House cellar. Jackson was pleased with the gift and even more with the banner if for no other reason than the phrase about the Union was his own toast (one of twenty-four) given at the White House Jefferson Day dinner in 1830.[10]

The cheese sat in the vestibule until February 22, 1837, when, on George Washington's birthday, the White House was opened to the public for Jackson's last levee. The President announced that anyone could come and take whatever pieces of cheese that they wanted. One writer described coming to the threshold to encounter 'an atmosphere, to which the mephitic gases over Avernus must be faint and innocuous'. Never a people to turn down free food a crowd estimated at 10,000 from across the social spectrum arrived to grab whatever piece of the by now very ripe cheese they could get. Another eyewitness said, 'For hours did a crowd of men, women, and boys hack at the cheese, many taking large hunks of it away with them. When they commenced, the cheese weighed one thousand four hundred pounds, and only a small piece was saved for the President's use. The air was redolent with cheese, the carpet was slippery with cheese, and nothing else was talked about at Washington that day.' The reek of rotted cheese lingered in the White House for months, requiring all the drapes and furniture to be aired out and the walls whitewashed to remove 'an odor which is pleasant only when there is not much of it'.[11] Free, abundant food and drink marked the next political campaign in 1840 along with the hokum and bunkum that shape or reflect Americans' political imaginations.[12]

The Big Cheese: Cheese and American Imagination

Since those days mammoth cheeses have appeared at state fairs and other agricultural exhibitions to show the fecundity of the land and the technical skills of the farmers – and their marketing associations – who create them. Farmers in Perth, Ontario created a 22,000 pound cheese standing six feet tall for the Chicago World's Fair in 1893. It is reported to have crashed through the floor of the railcar carrying it and the stage on which it was shown at the Fair.[13] These giants may have given rise to the satirical phrase 'big cheese' to denote a person of some importance or at least self-importance.

New York State became the major American cheese-making centre, especially in the Mohawk Valley. In the 1820s Herkimer became a centre for cheese production, by the 1860s shipping 25 million pounds or more. The first factory was set up by Jesse Williams in the upriver town of Rome in 1851.[14] Although milking machines had not been invented until the 1870s and even then were not refined until the 1920s, milk production increased. Combined with new types and selective breeding of cows, mechanized hay production and more efficient milk collection and curd making technology allowed dairymen (with the factory system men came to replace women as cheesemakers) to meet the American appetite for cheese. That the factories, some 200 in all, were set along the Erie Canal, built to link the Great Lakes and New York City, shows what the new American dairy entrepreneurs were doing: feeding a growing national market. Farmers in Wisconsin, finding that wheat cops were failing on the state's gravelly soils, turned to dairy farming in the 1870s and soon became the nation's largest cheese producer. By the late nineteenth century, Americans were fully caught up in factory farming ideology. Cheeses were not artisanal farmhouse varieties but, like meat, flour, and canned goods, mass produced to be consumed not by gourmets but by ordinary folks. The quicker and softer – hence more gobbleable – the food, the better.[15]

Most of the early American cheeses were semi-hard or hard. When made at home, some remained fresh, like cottage cheese or farmer's cheese, but cheeses made for storage and for the market were the firmer types. The term 'American cheese' likely referred to the common cheddar or perhaps Cheshire styles. Soft cheeses such as Brie and young Gruyère (most of the latter are now considered to be hard cheeses) were known by the American dairy industry, but they were not popular.[16] By 1905, soft Camembert-type cheeses were beginning to make their appearance in the American market, but limitations on storage made shipping of such European cheeses expensive.[17] Limburger was the most widespread soft cheese, but it is an acquired taste – or at least an acquired smell. A savoury, soft, yet somewhat gelatinous texture was in favour; the popular textures of gelatined meats was applied to cheese.[18]

Health gurus from the nineteenth century on recommended hard and coarse-grained foods as better for digestion – and for Sylvester Graham also taming libidos – but soft cheese is irresistible and, when merged with something a bit chewy or even crunchy, creates a perfect food. This dish, or class of dishes, is melted cheese on bread or toast. Early nineteenth century American cookbooks have recipes for melting cheese on bread in a fireplace or later on a stove using either a tin Dutch oven or a common household utensil, a handheld, grill-like cheese toaster. An English import, Hannah Glasse's popular cookbook gives three versions of the dish, calling them Welsh, Scotch, and English Rabbit. Welsh and Scotch are basically melted cheese on bread, with the English version soaking the bread in wine.[19] All-American grilled cheese sandwiches in their many forms, from lunch counter flat griddled to fancier panini, descend from these early versions. Kraft Foods' single-sliced processed cheeses became the American standard. Like so many other advertisements for factory-made foods, Kraft's has often represented another theme in American food imagination, nostalgia.[20]

The nineteenth century's premier melted-cheese dish was no doubt Welsh rarebit or rabbit – the two names seem used just as often and interchangeably in the US. This familiar cheese sauce made with ale or milk and mustard came in numerous varieties and appeared in restaurants featuring ale and wines. In 1837 New York's Pickwickian Club and The Grotto, were but two of many serving what was considered a British dish.[21] Restaurants from the top of the social scale to the lowest served the dish. Rarebits then moved into polite society when the chafing dish craze gripped American culinary imaginations later in the nineteenth and early twentieth centuries. Beginning among the upper classes, chafing dish cookery and its accompanying cookware moved down the social chain into middling class American homes. Chafing dish cookbooks appeared in large numbers, and general cookbooks all had recipes including Welsh rarebit. The chafing dish was a perfect vessel for melting cheeses in sauces, and numerous variations were created, among them lobster, crab, oysters, mushrooms, Mexican, Golden Buck (with an egg in it), tomato juice, and bean (using mashed cooked beans). In 1898 the Natural Food Company (later Nabisco) promoted its shredded wheat as the base for many varieties of rarebits. So popular was rarebit that a well-known snack food was created to replicate it. Cheese-It, now one hundred years old, was described by its creator, Green & Green of Dayton, Ohio, as 'baked rarebit'. It is still made much the same way with the preferred cheddar cheese and a thin crispy biscuit.[22] Here is an example of food that is democratized in an American way – cheap, nostalgic, uniform, and made in a factory.

But lust for cheese can lead people astray, for gluttony is a deadly sin. Americans are still largely a puritanical (hypocritically so) people who like just desserts meted out at the end of stories. Popular medical knowledge in the period held that rarebit was difficult to digest, indeed dangerous to one's health and sanity. A correspondent to the 26 October 1887 edition of *The Evening World* remarked in response to a question about how to make good Welsh rarebit: 'Editor of Evening World! Tell Mrs. R. that, for mercy's sake. If she loves her husband and has any regard for his friends, not to cook any rarebits at all. They nearly killed me. A Dyspeptic. Brooklyn'.[23]

In 1904, cartoonist Winsor McCay created a comic strip for New York's *Evening Telegram*, called 'Dream of the Rarebit Fiend'. In each strip a protagonist overindulges in Welsh rarebit and then, after going to bed with indigestion, has fantastical dreams, usually nightmares with a moral at the end. McCay influenced generations of illustrators

(Japan's great Studio Ghibli among them) especially with his brilliant *Little Nemo in Slumberland*.[24] He was also a pioneer animator – *Gertie the Dinosaur* (1913) was his most famous character – and he animated one of his rarebit-themed strips in 1921, perhaps the first monster-eats-a-city genre films: *Dreams of the Rarebit Fiend: The Pet*.[25] Another early film based on *Dream of a Rarebit Fiend* is an early live action piece made by Edwin S. Porter for the Edison Company in 1906.[26] With amazing special effects – something like Georges Méliès's – its disgusting eating scene rivals any filmed since. McCay never did say why he chose Welsh rarebit as the subject of his moralizing jokes, but dyspepsia was a common trope, and maybe he had suffered a bout of it from the infamous dish. Sloppy, gooey foods eaten quickly and in excess have always been thought to be funny for varieties of reasons that range from bad manners to unconsciously rude behaviour to satires of supposedly elite food.

Something happened to rarebits during the twentieth century: they mostly disappeared in America, though they did remain in their place of origin, Britain. Not that melted cheese went away, only this particular vehicle for serving it. Soft and melted cheeses hold sway over the American culinary imagination. The texture of warm, silky cheese running down the gullet is a national obsession. It is comfort food, not much to think about, just quick and easy to eat. Behind rarebit's disappearance were changes in cooking fashions that made chafing dishes only vessels for warming party foods, the rise of processed cheeses – and the popularity of pizza.

While pizza's astonishing popularity is beyond the scope of this paper, part of what made it possible has been recognized by historians, who see James L. Kraft as the force behind America's standardized processed cheeses. His pasteurization and emulsifying techniques made cheddar cheeses – made from inferior quality ones – shelf stable.[27] His company bought the Velveeta company (the stuff was invented in 1918) in 1927 and marketed it as a health food: liquid gold, the advertising said.[28] In the US, melted cheese sandwiches seem almost unthinkable without Kraft, or other companys' knock-offs. In 1952, Cheez-Whiz marked a further development of processed cheese, indeed with virtually no cheese in it. It was marketed in the UK as a quick way to make Welsh rarebit and then, like rarebit, migrated to America the next year.

Pizza, once popularized in the 1950s, drove increasing demand for melted cheese since, unlike Neapolitan pizza, American ones are loaded with it. The American culinary theory is more is always better.[29] Today America's most consumed cheese is not cheddar but mozzarella. These cheeses are triumphs of industrialized food processing, just as milk and the animals from which it comes are the end product of a long history of American technical prowess.

The arc Americans' idea of cheese traces through time moves through space too. The earliest cheeses were home-bound, made by farm women for family consumption and local markets. Cheese then entered the wider American marketplace with the rise of factories. Early cheeses were communal, in the sense that makers in each town such as Cheshire, Massachusetts or Little Falls near Herkimer, New York took pride in their local products and linked them to patriotic ideas. Cheese preparations always had class built into them, as seen in the rise of chafing dish cookery. As industrialized food production rose interrelated with urban-centred living, cheese became a commodity, democratized because it was cheap, easy to use, and ubiquitous. No longer community-based, processed cheese represents a different idea of America, one where seventy per cent of the economy is driven by consumer demand and advertising emphasizes individuality over community.

Grab a slice or two of packaged cheese, place it between slices of white bread, and fry it in a non-stick pan until thoroughly melted. Its appeal is constantly reinforced through television food advertising's artfully made, often nostalgic images of gooey cheese: long strands of melted cheese pulling away from a pizza, melted cheese product drenching tortilla chips, vegetables, fries … well, anything. If there is a credo of American cuisine it is this: there is no food that cannot be improved by adding cheese … and a lot of it.

Notes

1. Jeffrey L. Pasley, 'The Cheese and the Words: Popular Political Culture and Participatory Democracy in the Early American Republic', in *Beyond the Founders: New Approaches to the Political History of the Early American Republic*, ed. by Jeffrey L. Pasley, Andrew W. Robertson, and David Waldstreicher (Chapel Hill: University of North Carolina Press, 2004), pp. 31-56.
2. 'Account of the processes employed in the making Cheshire Cheese, from the Agricultural report of the county', *The National Intelligencer and Washington Advertiser* (Washington City [D.C.]), 29 April 1805, p. 1 <www.loc.gov/item/sn83045242/1805-04-29/ed-1/.> [accessed 30 May 2021]; Eliza Smith's cookbook, the first (re)published in the American colonies in 1742, gives a number of recipes for making cheese, including cheddar, and discusses uses for aged Cheshire (*The Compleat Housewife, or, Accomplish'd Gentlewoman's Companion*, 1st edn (London: J. Pemberton, 1727)).
3. Charles L. Flint, *Milch Cows and Dairy Farming* (New York: A.O. Moore, 1858).
4. Alan L. Olmstead and Paul W. Rhode, *Creating Abundance, Biological Innovation and American Agricultural Development* (Cambridge: Cambridge University Press, 2008), p. 335.
5. Leland qtd. in John C. Harriman (ed.), '"Most Excellent – far fam'd and far fetch'd Cheese": An Anthology of Jeffersonian Era Poetry', *The American Magazine and Historical Chronicle*, 2.2 (Autumn/Winter 1986-1987), pp. 3-4
6. *The Papers of Thomas Jefferson, Second Series*, Jefferson's Memorandum Books, vol. 2, ed. James A Bear, Jr. and Lucia C. Stanton (Princeton: Princeton University Press, 1997), pp. 1062-89 <https://founders.archives.gov/documents/Jefferson/02-02-02-0012> [accessed 30 May 2021]
7. Andrea Wulf, 'Thomas Jefferson's Quest to Prove America's Natural Superiority', *The Atlantic*, 7 March 2016 <https://www.theatlantic.com/science/archive/2016/03/jefferson-american-dream/471696/> [accessed 30 May 2021]
8. Harriman, p. 6.
9. Pasley, p. 36; Richard Zacks, *The Pirate Coast: Thomas Jefferson, the First Marines, and the Secret Mission of 1805* (New York: Hachette Digital, 2005).
10. James Parton, *The Life of Andrew Jackson* (New York: Mason Brothers, 1860), III, p. 323, 626; Luther Tucker and others (eds.), *The Genesee Farmers and Gardner's Journal*, vol. 5 (Rochester, NY, 1835).
11. Benjamin Perley Poore, *Perley's Reminiscences of Sixty Years in the National Metropolis* (Philadelphia: Hubbard Brothers, 1886), pp. 196-97.
12. The best modern description of Jackson's cheese is by Robert Remini, *Andrew Jackson* (New York:

History Book Club, 1988), III, pp. 393-94.
13 'Mammoth Cheese Replica Perth, Ontario', *Atlas Obscura* <https://www.atlasobscura.com/places/mammoth-cheese-replicas>; Canada Department of Agriculture, 'The Mammoth Cheese', 23 October 1943, *Lanarck County Genealogical Society Online Resource Library* <http://lcgsresourcelibrary.com/articles/A-CHEESE.HTM> [both accessed 30 May 2021]
14 Milton C. Sernett, *'Say Cheese!' The Story of the Era When New York State Cheese Was King* (Scotts Valley, CA: Createspace, 2011).
15 For the American predilection for softer foods, see Emily J. Arendt's comment on nostalgia and how recipes were changed in 'All Jumbled Up: Authenticity in American Culinary History', *Food and Foodways*, 28.3 (2020), 153-73 (pp. 163-64).
16 *Sixth Annual Report of the American Dairymen's Association for the Year 1870* (Syracuse, NY: American Dairymen's Association, 1870), p. 27.
17 H.W. Conn and others, *The Camembert Type of Soft Cheese in The United States* (Washington, DC: Government Printing Office, 1905).
18 For comments on soft food textures, see Rachel Herz, *Why You Eat What You Eat* (New York: W.W. Norton, 2018), pp. 177-83.
19 Hannah Glasse, *The Art of Cookery, made Plain and Easy*, 2nd edn (London: L. Wangford, 1747); Mrs. M. A. Collins, *The Great Western Cookbook* (New York: Barnes and Company, 1857), pp. 85-86.
20 See Kraft Foods' encomium to melted cheese sandwiches: 'Grilled Cheese Song', *YouTube*, 3 August 2020 <https://www.youtube.com/watch?v=jV_QPBrnHrU> [accessed 30 May 2021]
21 The Grotto was announced as opening '104 Cedar Street, [with] Edward Riley fitting up rooms where he will have Ales, wines, Welsh Rarebits in their season' (*Morning Herald* (New York), 7 September 1837 <www.loc.gov/item/sn83030312/1837-09-07/ed-1/>); *Morning Herald* (New York, NY) 26 Sep. 1837, p. 3 <www.loc.gov/item/sn83030312/1837-09-26/ed-1/> [both accessed 30 May 2021]
22 Leo DeLuca, 'A Brief History of the Cheez-It', *Smithsonian,* 21 May 2021(https://www.smithsonianmag.com/innovation/brief-history-cheez-it-180977777> [accessed 30 May 2021]
23 *The Evening World* (New York), 26 October 1887, p. 3 <www.loc.gov/item/sn83030193/1887-10-26/ed-2/> [accessed 30 May 2021]
24 John Canemaker, *Winsor McCay: His Life and Art* (New York: Harry N. Abrams, 2005).
25 *Dreams of the Rarebit Fiend: The Pet*, written and dir. by Winsor McCay, 1921 <https://www.youtube.com/watch?v=s39jimMyAFI> [accessed 30 May 2021]
26 *Dream of a Rarebit Fiend*, dir. by Edwin S. Porter, Edison Company, 1906 <https://www.youtube.com/watch?v=UhdN7wyK2sY> [accessed 30 May 2021]
27 Melanie Warner, *Pandora's Lunchbox: How Processed Food Took Over the American Meal* (New York: Scribner), pp. 38-43
28 Natasha Geiling, 'There is No Shortage of History When it Comes to Velveeta', *Smithsonian*, 15 January 2014 <https://www.smithsonianmag.com/arts-culture/there-is-no-shortage-history-when-it-comes-velveeta-180949312/> [accessed 30 January 2021]; Paul Kindstedt, *Cheese and Culture: A History of Cheese and its Place in Western Civilization* (White River Junction, VT: Chelsea Green, 2012).
29 See Carol Helstosky, *Pizza: A Global History* (London: Reaktion Books, 2008).

Steak or Salad? Food, Gender, and the Victorian Imagination

Michael Krondl

Introduction

The trouble with fantasy is that it has real-world implications. Once societies invent paradigms, they impose them on flesh-and-blood women and men, who then internalize them and act them out in the real world. Once normalized, these behaviours feed back into the model and, sooner or later, they are essentialized. This is as true of conduct as of appetite. Men become defined by brawn and aggression – throw them red meat and watch them brawl; women are sensitive and dainty – a cup of tea and a plateful of gossip will satisfy their needs.

As anthropologist Mary Douglas, among others, has noted, belief and behaviour are ineluctably joined.[1] Or, as Carole M. Counihan has succinctly summarized when she links food to society, 'Class, caste, race, and gender hierarchies are maintained, in part, through differential control over and access to food. One's place in the social system is revealed by what, how much, and with whom one eats.'[2]

Much of how we define male and female appetites in the West was developed in the nineteenth century by the era's urban bourgeoisie. This was the class that set the tenor for contemporary conversations on diet and decorum; its members were the target of the period's authors and mass media. Arguably, the gendered reality of current American food culture is the outcome of a feedback loop between public expectations and the way people actually performed their gendered foodways. Following Erving Goffman's proposition that people are inclined to perform in ways expected by the social situation, I would suggest that this expected performance is stage-managed by several factors.[3] In this paper, I focus on what might be described as the social imagination, that is the way men and women are portrayed in the popular press, in literature, and in a variety of how-to manuals. These constrain behaviour in at least two ways: first by normalizing or stigmatizing certain actions; second by reproducing observed conduct and, in the process, essentializing it in each sex. To take the thespian metaphor a little further, the actors are taught the script at home, perform it in public, and eventually come to embody each micro-performance. Each bonbon delicately nibbled, each porterhouse ripped apart with gusto, reinforces social constructions of femininity and masculinity. This is then incorporated back into the script reperformed on and on.

Body and Mind

Our current gendered views of food have their roots in the Enlightenment, but it was the nineteenth century that made these ideas omnipresent. In the Victorian imagination, it was men's and women's anatomy that resulted in gendered behaviour. This, in turn, led to gendered foods and gendered dining – tea rooms for ladies, men's clubs for gentlemen – and even the gendered distribution of pathologies – eating disorders among women and cardiovascular disease in men. This idea of anatomy as destiny can be traced to the Age of Reason, when supposedly empirical deductions yielded decidedly imaginative results. Many traced women's actions to their reproductive organs. The presence of a womb predicated motherhood and thus domesticity.

It's not as if earlier generations hadn't trafficked in misogyny, but now it had a supposedly scientific basis. While intellectual activity had once been seen as a distraction from women's domestic duties, now it was seen as a deviation from their biological nature.[4] This fit nicely with the burgeoning industrial revolution with its newly dominant middle class and its need to imagine a new family paradigm where men went out to work and women stayed home to raise the kids. The result was a new bourgeois domesticity, something that would be manifested in reimagined lifestyles, architecture, costume, and foodways. This essentially economic and class transformation needed some sort of moral justification, something that the sermonizers of the day were more than happy to provide.

One such public-spirited scribbler was Thomas Gisborne (1758–1846), a Cambridge-educated Anglican priest and anti-slavery activist. In a text that would echo throughout the coming century he neatly summarizes the roles open to women (at least those of 'higher or [...] middle classes of society'), whose influence 'is like the dew of heaven which descends at all seasons'. This moistening effect was to take the following forms: 'First, in contributing [...] to the comfort of husbands' and relatives 'under every vicissitude'; second, in 'forming and improving the general manners, dispositions, and conduct of the other sex, by society and example'; third, in 'modelling the human mind during the early stages of its growth'.[5]

This virtually doctrinal view of womanhood was periodically tweaked to suit circumstances. In the newly independent colonies, women were to feed their offspring with republican virtue as much as wholesome victuals.[6] Later in the century, some New Englanders feared a decline in domestic virtue could imperil their 'race'. In an 1882 panegyric, Massachusetts doctor N. Allen warned that the danger was especially severe among the members of 'cultivated and refined society', who apparently considered the lives of couples with multiple children as 'vulgar and sensual'. According to the good doctor, the decline of good housekeeping was the culprit here, since '[e]conomy, neatness, order and good cooking are indispensable requisites to the health and happiness of a family'.[7]

Spiritual, or at least moral, sustenance came to be linked to the physical kind. Women were repeatedly instructed (predominantly by male experts) on how to feed their families. Needless to say, a connection between diet and health is hardly spurious, even if we find much of nineteenth-century dietary advice risible. One leitmotif of the mid-eighteen hundreds was that certain foods – highly spiced dishes or intoxicants for example – would lead to sexual excitement, and inevitably masturbation, the latter an activity deemed not only sinful but actually medically hazardous.[8] Accordingly mothers needed to be extra careful when feeding adolescent daughters. The result of all this was that women, not men, became knowledgeable, sometimes obsessively so, about nutrition, especially the nutrition of others. And, arguably, morality still plays a role in diet decisions to this day.

Of course, before a young woman could graduate to moral motherhood, she had to procure a suitable suitor. To this end she needed to learn to perform her gender and her class. And to dress the part – not an easy task in an era of dangerously distorted waistlines. As Thorstein Veblen convincingly argued about his compeers, women's costume was specifically designed to be as impractical as possible, to make it clear that a lady was exempt 'from personal contact with industrial processes of any kind'. If the yards of drapery did not make this abundantly obvious, the corseted waist made any exertion potentially perilous, as was a hearty appetite.[9] The perfect female body, as imagined in fashion plates throughout most of the nineteenth century, had to struggle with actual stomachs, hips, and waists.[10] Even when women weren't purposefully starving themselves to fit into fashionable dresses they could hardly consume more than a couple of dainty morsels before experiencing discomfort.

The corsets were only part of the problem. Young women, especially in any social gatherings, were constantly under surveillance, not merely from potential mates but from other women seeking to police their behaviour. Contemporary authorities were fully aware of this when they condemned young women who starved themselves due to class pressures. Jerome V. C. Smith, a prolific author and professor at New York Medical College (and one-time mayor of Boston), was especially aghast at the fashionable abstemiousness of the socially ambitious, roundly condemning, 'Food most approved and that which carries with it the endorsement of maneuvering mothers anxiously looking forward to the establishment of their children in commanding social positions, even if the intended husband is a baboon, [that] is a slice of dry toast, weak black tea, and an occasional teaspoonful of sweetmeats'.[11] How much, if any, of this advice was followed is an open question. Women – and they were the primary audience of advice manuals then as they are today – received a variety of contradictory information from fashion magazines, cookbooks, novels, and conduct guides, as well as medical authorities. Was at least part of the nervous disorder so noted among affluent women caused by guilt and confusion about food itself?

Dainty Dishes

One point that most Victorian authorities agreed upon was that women should be 'dainty'. Daintiness was especially sought for in women's victuals, and the more delicate the lady's constitution the daintier the fare. In a satirical novel *The Female Sufferer; or, Chapters from Life's Comedy* (1883), Augustus Hoppin depicts an indolent upper-class invalid who lives on little more than 'tidbits of fruit and Jelly', 'a snip of a roll', and 'a wren's leg on toast', though she might occasionally become ravenous for 'dainty' items such as wedding cake, peaches and cream, and freshly cut melon – all this while carrying on a perpetual social life.[12] Dozens of cookbooks published in the latter part of the century are dedicated to 'dainty dishes'.[13] Dainty didn't always mean light and delicate – as we might use the word – as at times it was just a synonym for fancy, but more often than not it did. And suffice it to say that what women liked, men were supposed to disdain.

Dainty dishes were often recommended for lunch, which, along with afternoon tea, had become a de facto homosocial meal by the middle of the nineteenth century. As D.M. Morell pointed out in the food-centred ladies' magazine *Table Talk*, 'The midday meal especially in cities belongs to the ladies and children of the household as few businessmen find it possible to lunch en famille.'[14] Nineteenth-century mealtime had become increasingly segregated as the distance between men's workplaces and homes grew distant. The family might have breakfast together, but husbands now ate dinner, formerly the principal meal of the day, away. Men generally sought out a chop house or other informal restaurant for their mid-day meal, while genteel women took lunch in the modest privacy of their homes and, increasingly, at gender-specific 'tea rooms' and 'lunch rooms' as the century waned.[15]

At home, the lady was permitted a certain latitude in dress 'since the masculine element is almost invariably lacking at that hour'. The meal itself was equally informal. A selection of 'dainty nourishing dishes' from the previous night's supper might prove sufficient.[16] The detail about the clothing is worth noting; women's appetites were literally restricted when in the presence of men. Lord Byron's probably apocryphal quip that 'a woman should never be seen eating or drinking, unless it be lobster salad and champagne, the only truly feminine and becoming viands' was frequently repeated (often with the second clause omitted).[17] Most women were more catholic in their tastes. Mary Alice Brown, in her *Dainty Dining*, has a long list of luncheon menus that do, in fact, feature lobster with some regularity, mostly in the form of lobster Newberg, lobster cutlets, or croquettes. However, chicken, veal, sweetbreads, and fish are popular, as are salads, though sandwiches are relatively few. Except for the occasional inclusion of lamb chops, there is zero red meat in evidence. What there are in superabundance are sweets: ices, ice creams, sherbets, cakes, tarts, marshmallows, jellies, sweetmeats (here meaning candy), even that new-fangled invention, chocolate brownies.[18]

If luncheon was heavy on the sugar, the other female-centric meal offered little else. Tea the meal, as opposed to just the beverage, went through several transmutations prior to its widespread adoption by polite society. Originally formulated in eighteenth-century Britain, where cups of tea really were the focus, in the early years of the following century the concept was exported to the continent in the form of a relatively informal elite get-together. As tea and sugar became increasingly cheap and ubiquitous a second wave of tea enthusiasm in the Victorian era followed, eventually resulting in the 'afternoon tea' visitors to London's posh hotel tea rooms might still recognize.

Whereas, by the mid-eighteen hundreds, in Britain, just about everyone drank tea, in the United States both the beverage and the sweet afternoon repast had specific class and gender associations. Even so, because American women weren't especially fond of the Asian beverage, the tea table might feature coffee, hot chocolate, lemonade, and iced tea, or even champagne and sherry depending on the season and the attendees' social set. Occasionally a clear broth might be offered. There were typically sandwiches and a variety of cakes, tarts, and other sugary nibbles.[19] Hotel and department store teas were even more sweet-centric. A 1914 menu at the Waldorf-Astoria Tea Rooms offered seven kinds of sandwiches, twenty-one pastries, and more than a score of ice creams and ices.[20]

The opinion that women had a predilection for sweet foods had been a Western cultural trope since at least the 1700s, when Rousseau, in his pedagogic manual, *Emile*, critiqued Sophie, the book's supporting player, for her supposedly innate affection for dessert.[21] A century later, the female tooth is invoked so often in period literature that it almost seems a peculiarity of Victorian women's anatomy: 'Women, as a broad and general fact, it may be said, comparatively with men, care very little for eating,' pronounced a columnist in an early issue of *Harper's Bazaar*, 'Their noted "sweet tooth" would prove this if there were nothing else. Women, left to themselves, would really have little other eating than bread and tea, with an occasional sweetmeat or a tart.'[22]

Medical authorities typically ascribed women's appetites to a different part of the anatomy, mainly their reproductive organs. Yale obstetrician Stephen G. Hubbard explained in 1870 that 'given the sympathies with every other part of the female organism', it is 'as if the Almighty, in creating the female sex, *had taken the uterus and built up a woman around it*'.[23] Pretty much any ailment could be traced to uterine distress, from neuralgia to consumption, from constipation to breast cancer.[24] Diet needed to be calibrated to the womb-dominated body and mind. Stimulating foods were especially prone to overtax women's sensitive nervous systems, especially spiced dishes ('highly seasoned concentrated aliment'), alcoholic beverages, and most red meats. New York-based Jerome V.C. Smith explained in 1875 how '[w]omen with us consume too much meat […]. Neither the severity of the [New England] climate nor the necessities of their systems require it in large quantities'. He recommended that '[f]arinaceous articles including an abundance of fruit fresh cooked or preserved should be provided in all well-regulated families especially where there are female children. Eggs and fish are proper and avoiding pork always. Mutton is the most wholesome next to good beef' – though the latter presumably in dainty preparations.[25] Other authorities also contraindicated coffee and tea for being too stimulating and some even forbad sweets.

Manly Appetites

Seemingly men, unless they were paid to do so, didn't fret much about food. That was, after all, a woman's job and, thus, unmanly by definition. And increasingly what nineteenth-century men did fret about was about manliness. The sedentary urban existence of factory accountants and bank managers wasn't likely to engender a society of virile warriors. An earlier, aristocratic definition of manhood seemed in crisis, and all the facial hair grown by the Victorians couldn't quite disguise this. Some men found an antidote in sport, whether in boxing or violent team sports such as rugby at British public schools or the copycat American football at Ivy League universities.[26] In America, the rough and tumble western frontier was supposed to be a cure for the dyspepsia that plagued the industrial east.[27] War and hunting were also options. Or you could roll these last three into one as Theodore Roosevelt did when he ran for New York City mayor as 'the cowboy of the Dakotas', before embarking on a career that included military stunts in Cuba and cynegetic pursuits even further abroad.[28]

Masculine men of action required a manly diet that distinguished them from the feminized epicureans of urban civilization. This imagined male-female duality in diet was best expressed in the semiotic resonance of meat. A character in one of Stanley J. Weyman's stories summarized the opposition evident on his plate: 'You have there the manly beef and the feminine peas, so young, so tender!'[29] The inverse was true as well. Women were seen as disagreeably masculine if they ceased to resemble, or relish, those sweet peas. When women craved flesh, especially bloody, roasted flesh, it wasn't merely unseemly, it broke down the 'natural' order of society. George Eliot references this sort of gendered revulsion in a scene in her 1876 novel *Daniel Deronda*, where a group of gentlemen discuss women's appetites. One recalls a story 'about the epicurism of the ladies, who had somehow been reported to show a revolting masculine judgement in venison, even asking for the fat – a proof of the frightful rate at which corruption might go on in women, but for severe social restraint.'[30] The symbolic connotation of venison was especially manly since it recalled the aristocratic hunt.

Beef was a much more commonplace signifier. Particularly in Britain, beef had long been the most virile of aliments. The British veneration of bovine flesh is perhaps best depicted in William Hogarth's painting *O the Roast Beef of Old England*, where a side of beef, destined for an English inn, takes centre stage even as a weakling Frenchman cowers in the wings.[31] The painting's title references Henry Fielding's popular 1730s ditty that glorified the brawny impact of Albion's meaty appetites, in contrast to tastes in 'effeminate Italy, France and Spain' for 'nice dainties'.[32] The Briton's diet was often linked to his martial prowess. Phillip Stanhope (Lord Chesterfield), a prolific Georgian letter writer, asserted that '[a]n Englishman [...] thinks himself equal to beating three Frenchmen [...]. Roast beef and beer make stronger arms than cold water and frogs'.[33] A half-century later, William Thackeray echoed the sentiment: 'Fancy a hundred thousand Englishmen, after a meal of stalwart beef ribs, encountering a hundred thousand Frenchmen who had partaken of a trifling collation of soup, turnips, carrots, onions and Gruyère cheese. Would it be manly to engage at such odds? I say no.'[34]

If war wasn't in the offing, exercise would have to do. For would-be sporty types, nineteenth-century trainers recommended a diet of broiled, bloody beef or mutton steaks and strong ale – avoiding vegetables at all costs.[35] This advice is reprised over and over on both sides of the Atlantic. One surprising opiner on the topic is Walt Whitman who, under the pseudonym Mose Velsor, wrote a series of advice columns for the *New York Atlas*. 'The man in training,' the famed poet writes, should breakfast on 'a plate of fresh rare lean meat, without fat or gravy, a slice or chunk of bread, and, if desired, a cup of tea' and his dinner 'should consist of a good plate of fresh meat, (rare lean beef, broiled or roast, is best) with as few outside condiments as possible'. Whether he genuinely believed in it or not, this paleo diet seemed no more than a pipe dream, as Whitman admits, sniffing that '[n]ot one out of fifty eats a really wholesome, manly substantial dinner'. Though he doesn't quite put it in those words, his real target seems to be all the dainty, feminine food eaten by most Americans:

> If nine-tenths of all the various culinary preparations and combinations, vegetables, pastry, soups, stews, sweets, baked dishes, salads, things fried in grease, and all the vast array of confections, creams, pies, jellies, &c., were utterly swept aside from the habitual eating of the people, and [...] *an almost exclusive meat diet* [substituted for it] – the result would be greatly, very greatly, in favor of that noble-bodied, pure-blooded, and superior race we have had a leaning toward, in these articles of ours.[36]

As the century progressed, meat-eating didn't merely separate men from women, it also came to denote a racialized virility. This discourse took on a more scientific veneer when medical-sounding 'protein' replaced 'meat' as the manliest of foodstuffs. In a study of potential recruits for the Raj, British doctors evaluated data on 'the different tribes and races of India,' and concluded that 'a high level of protein interchange in the body [is] accompanied by a high development of physique and manly qualities; whilst under the opposite conditions poor physique and a cringing effeminate disposition is all that can be expected'.[37] In America, Maine Senator James Blaine made a similar point – if less scientifically framed – when he explained the negative impact of permitting Chinese workers, since if you work 'a man who must have beef and bread' (i.e. native-born American) next to a man 'who can live on rice' you will inevitably degrade the American down to the standard of the Chinaman.[38]

Not everyone was convinced that meat and Western masculinity were necessarily congruent. In fact, there was a distinct and powerful countercurrent to carnivorous manhood in vegetarian diets promoted by Sylvester Graham, his acolyte John Harvey Kellogg, and others.[39] Yet vegetarianism has never really caught on in America. While plenty of real men did, in fact, subject themselves to Dr Kellogg's regimen at the Battle Creek Sanatorium (Roald Amundsen, Johnny Weissmuller, John D. Rockefeller, and even Theodore Roosevelt all made guest appearances), it appears that most reverted to the carnivorous norm.

The meat-eating man stereotype was certainly alive and well in the nineteen thirties. In *Feeding Father* (1939), a cookbook focused on foods men were supposed to like, author Eleanor Howe summarizes the gendered culinary zeitgeist:

> Just how does [*sic*] a man's food preferences differ from those of women? Well,

for one thing, a man wants more substantial, plainer food. He likes a meal to be composed of only a few dishes, but he wants those to be tasty, full of flavor and perfectly cooked. He likes, also, to know what he is eating, he wants to be able to recognize each main ingredient in its familiar form. In a word, fancy cooking is wasted on the average man but good cooking is appreciated to the limit![40]

By now 'dainty', the adjective, had mostly gone out of style, but men were still supposed to scorn 'fancy cooking'. Even today, meat-eating remains gendered. Multiple studies have shown that vegetarianism and, even more, veganism are much more popular among women than men in the West, and society continues to see a carnivorous diet as more virile than the alternative. Today men still eat steak and women salad.

Conclusion

It's important to note that gender is, or was, (even in the nineteenth century, even among the bourgeoise) hardly the only determinant directing people's dietary choices. Ethnicity, religion, personal preference, convenience, marketing, and, above all, availability have guided what the middle classes have been eating ever since they attained cultural dominance some two hundred years back. Moreover, gender is less of a determinant than it used to be in a society where women's roles are less tied up with domesticity and food preparation now that the culinary industrial complex has taken over most food preparation. This is not to say that society doesn't still expect women to be the primary nurturers, as the Covid pandemic has amply demonstrated.

Does it matter that we keep repeating our gender-delineated roles? Epidemiological data on eating disorders and cardiovascular disease certainly indicate that it does. And from a global perspective, it would be helpful if kale salad wasn't stigmatized as food for soccer moms and sissies. There is another, pernicious effect of men and women embodying gendered behaviour without being aware of it. It is that if society values equality between the sexes and, perhaps even more importantly, the concept of choice, self-awareness of gender-based performance must be a necessary precondition. Of course, our foodways aren't the only way we reproduce nineteenth-century ideas of gender but understanding why we eat what we eat can be used as an indicator of other embodied behaviour that stands in the way of a more equal society.

Notes

1. Mary Douglas, *Purity and Danger: An Analysis of Concepts of Pollution and Taboo* (London: Routledge, 2003), p. 129.
2. Carole M. Counihan, *The Anthropology of Food and Body: Gender, Meaning and Power* (New York: Routledge, 2018), p. 8.
3. Erving Goffman, 'Gender Display', *Studies in the Anthropology of Visual Communication*, 3 (1976), 69-77.
4. See Karen O'Brian, 'Sexual Distinctions and Prescriptions: Introduction', in *Women, Gender and Enlightenment*, ed. by Sarah Knott and Barbara Taylor (Houndmills: Palgrave Macmillan, 2005), pp. 3-7.

5   Thomas Gisborne, *An Enquiry into the Duties of the Female Sex* (London: T. Cadell jun. and W. Davies, 1797), pp. 7, 9, 13.
6   Linda K. Kerber, *Women of the Republic: Intellect and Ideology in Revolutionary America* (Chapel Hill: University of North Carolina Press, 1980).
7   N. Allen, 'The New England Family', *The New Englander*, March 1882, 153-54.
8   Depending on the authority the list also included coffee, tea, chocolate, meat, warm bread and pastry, and confectionery. For more on the topic see Joan Jacobs Brumberg, *Fasting Girls: The History of Anorexia Nervosa* (New York: Random House, 2001), p. 172; Jerome Van Crowninshield Smith, a prominent physician, noted that avoiding 'highly seasoned' food would improve not only a girl's physical attributes but also lead to her 'brighter mental development', promising that this system promised 'with moral certainty to secure for their daughters sound health the foundation for happiness' (*The Ways of Women in Their Physical, Moral and Intellectual Relations* (Hartford, CT: Dustin, Gilman & Company, 1875), p. 129).
9   Veblen perceptively describes the corset as 'substantially a mutilation, undergone for the purpose of lowering the subject's vitality and rendering her permanently and obviously unfit for work' (*The Theory of the Leisure Class* (New York: Macmillan, 1899), p. 121).
10 For more on the obsession on slimness and bodily control, see Anna Krugovoy Silver, *Victorian Literature and the Anorexic Body* (Cambridge: Cambridge University Press, 2002), p. 27.
11 Smith, *The Ways of Women*, p. 115.
12 Quoted by Joan Jacobs Brumberg, 'The Appetite as Voice', in *Food and Culture: A Reader*, 2nd edn (Routledge New York, 2008), pp. 159-79 (p. 164).
13 It would be tedious to list them all, but a couple of notable titles should suffice for illustration: Sarah T. Rorer, the principal of the influential Philadelphia Cooking School, penned *Dainty Dishes for All the Year Round* (1890) featuring 'such Dainty Dishes as Croquettes, Cutlets, Tempting Sandwiches etc. when one's appetite needs to be pampered with something delicate and tasty'. The book was sponsored by the American Machine Company, a manufacturer of ice cream freezers and other kitchen gadgets. Across the Atlantic, Kate Halford, another cooking teacher, authored *Dainty Dinners and Dishes for Jewish Families* (1907), a decidedly aspirational volume of French-influenced recipes for London's wealthier Jewish households.
14 D.M. Morrell, 'The Daily Trio: Breakfast, Lunch, Dinner,' *Table Talk*, May 1894.
15 See Paul Freedman, 'Women and Restaurants in the Nineteenth-Century United States,' *Journal of Social History*, 48.1 (2014): 1-19.
16 Morrell.
17 For example, see the opinion of the 'amiable Lord Brackenshaw, who was something of a 'gourmet'' (George Eliot, *Daniel Deronda* (Oxford: Oxford University Press, 2014), p. 94). According to American George Beard, writing in the 1870s, the romantic teen idol was apparently responsible for girls starving themself to conform to the dead poet's tastes (see Brumberg, *Fasting Girls*, p. 180).
18 Mary Alice Abbott Brown, *Dainty Dining: A Few Simple Luncheons and a Few Not So Simple; But with Tried Reciepts [sic] for Each and All, with a Post-Script for Dinners Added by Request* ([n.p.]: Reed Press, 1908).
19 See, for example, Anna Sawyer, 'Afternoon Tea', *Good Housekeeping*, 10 May 1890, 160; or Mrs. Hamilton Mott, 'Giving an Afternoon Tea', *The Ladies' Home Journal*, March 1893, 4.
20 Rare Book Division, The New York Public Library, 'Waldorf Astoria', New York Public Library Digital Collections <https://digitalcollections.nypl.org/items/c6d5d0ca-df25-54db-e040-e00a18063df6> [accessed 13 December 2020]
21 Jean-Jacques Rousseau, *Emile*, trans. by William H. Payne (New York: D. Appleton, 1905), p. 291.
22 'A Phase of the Cook Question,' *Harper's Bazaar*, 27 January 1877, 50.
23 Martin Luther Holbrook, *Parturition Without Pain: A Code of Directions for Escaping from the Primal Curse* (M.L. Holbrook, 1880), p. 15. The italics are the author's; I am assuming the 'professor Hubbard of New Haven' mentioned in the text is Stephen G. Hubbard, professor of obstetrics at Yale Medical

School from 1864 to 1880.
24 Ann Douglas Wood, '"The Fashionable Diseases": Women's Complaints and Their Treatment in Nineteenth-Century America', *The Journal of Interdisciplinary History*, 4.1 (1973), 29.
25 Smith, *The Ways of Women*, pp. 175-76.
26 See David Kirk, *The Sociocultural Foundations of Human Movement* (Melbourne: Macmillan Education Australia, 1996), p. 210.
27 Colorado was just the place to cure chronic invalids due to its 'more virile, blood invigorating beef, its tempting mountain trout and juicy wild meat' (H.T.F Gatchell, 'Colorado Climate for Invalids', *The Medical Investigator. A Monthly Journal of the Medical Sciences*, 10.113 (May 1873), 279).
28 See Gail Bederman, *Manliness and Civilization: A Cultural History of Gender and Race in the United States, 1880-1917* (Chicago: University of Chicago Press, 2008), p. 171.
29 Stanley J. Weyman, 'Joanna's Bracelet', *The Cornhill Magazine*, 14 (January–June 1890), 211-24 (p. 214).
30 Eliot, p. 94. Coed archery was one of the period's elite's peculiarities.
31 William Hogarth, *O the Roast Beef of Old England* ('The Gate of Calais'), 1748, oil on canvas, 788 X 945mm, 1748, Tate.
32 Henry Fielding, 'The Roast Beef of Old England', in *The Works of Henry Fielding* (London: Henry G. Bohn, 1851), p. 994.
33 Cited in Hippolyte Taine, *History of English Literature* (London: Chatto & Windus, 1880), p. 124.
34 William Makepeace Thackeray, 'Memorials of Gormandising', in *The Works of William Makepeace Thackeray*, vol. XIII (New York and London: Harper & Brothers, 1841), pp. 581-82.
35 Donald Walker, *Walker's Manly Exercises: Containing Rowing, Sailing, Riding, Driving, Racing, Hunting, Shooting and Other Manly Sports* (London: Bohn, 1855), p. 14.
36 Mose Velsor [Walt Whitman], 'Manly Health and Training: With Off-Hand Hints Toward Their Conditions', *New York Atlas*, 12 September 1858, morning edn, p. 1.
37 David McCay, *The Protein Element in Nutrition* (London: Edward Arnold, 1912), p. 206.
38 Quoted in *Great Debates in American History: Economic and Social Questions, Part 2*, ed. by Marion Mills Miller (New York: Current Literature Publishing Company, 1913), p. 251.
39 See for example Kellogg's assertion that a grain-based diet was superior (*The New England Medical Gazette*, 1892, 8).
40 Cited by Jessamyn Neuhaus, *Manly Meals and Mom's Home Cooking* (Baltimore, MD: The Johns Hopkins University Press, 2003), p. 77.

The Imagination of Food (and Drink) in the Novels of Iris Murdoch

Paul Levy

Food and drink have figured in novels at least since Rabelais. In the sixteenth-century French writer's *Gargantua and Pantagruel*, references to food and drink had a clear purpose: they were used to satirize excess. Dean Swift's 1729 *A Modest Proposal*, advocating that the poor should eat their babies, is also patently satirical, and food and drink have found their place in satire from antiquity to the present day. But what about the modern novel in which food and drink figure, but do not have a transparent satirical intent? Rereading Thomas Mann's *Buddenbrooks* (1901), for example, I found this description of a meal given to the would-be suitor Bendix Grünlich:

> He ate mussel ragout, julienne soup, baked sole, roast veal with mashed potatoes and brussels sprouts, maraschino pudding, and pumpernickel with Roquefort cheese – and at each course he offered a new tribute appropriate to the delicacy. For example, raising his dessert spoon, he gazed at a statue woven into the wallpaper and said aloud to himself, 'God forgive me, I can do no other; I've eaten a large serving, but this pudding is just too splendid. I simply must implore my hostess for a second helping.'[1]

The point of this excursus on a mid-nineteenth century meal is not to make the character appear greedy or the hostess generous. It is not poking fun at either of them. It is more to exemplify the *haute bourgeois* setting; if anything, the purpose of the passage is to make some subtle class distinctions between the *nouveau riche* suitor and his old-money Buddenbrook intended.

I also reread a clutch of Dame Margaret Drabble's novels to note her treatment of food, and I recently found a germane piece in the *Guardian*:

> Writers love writing about food, and criticising one another for the manner in which they do it: the only comment a friend of mine made on one of my recent works was 'I think your salade tiède was an anachronism'. Some years ago, I asked the foodie-philosopher Paul Levy for his expert help in planning a repast that was to serve both as a celebration and a last supper for one of my characters [in *The Witch of Exmoor* (1996)]. The menu we devised consisted of ravioli aux trompettes des morts, pieds de porc Sainte-Menehould, and a little

of the soft cheese known as the Caprice des Dieux, which sports pretty cherubs on its packaging.

We didn't get round to naming any wines, surely an oversight on my part, as there must be many heavenly vintages with appropriately suggestive designations.[2]

Part of what I learned from my survey of Dame Maggie's novels is that mere citation, as opposed to more elaborate description of dishes, meals, or menus, is often used as an indication that the novel is in one Realist tradition or another – in other words, that the characters eat breakfast, dinner, lunch, or (especially) tea, because that's what the human frame requires. Ignoring the characters' need for nourishment is unrealistic (as it is to ignore their need to relieve themselves, and I note that, in some of the novels I've been rereading for this paper, a character does occasionally use the loo). The reasons for a novelist citing food can range from the straightforward – indicating that a character is a picky eater, or greedy, or even has an eating disorder – to indicating minute differences of social class, attitudes, or political views. Portraying a character as vegetarian is a venerable but easy way of implying that his political stance is left of centre.

All these dishes, meals, and menus are the work of the imagination, and, rereading Dame Iris Murdoch's fictional oeuvre, I have found there is a good deal of citation of food and drink in her twenty-six novels, from the good sandwiches in *The Bell* (1958) to the cheese soufflé and 'delicate leg of lamb' in her last novel, *Jackson's Dilemma* (completed just before she succumbed to dementia; published 1995).[3] There's poached pheasant and jugged hare in *The Unicorn* (1963). There's *pollo alla cacciatora* in *The Italian Girl* (1964):

> Maggie had left her sewing and was busy at a side table with a dismembered chicken and some vegetables. Now the chicken was sizzling softly in a pan while with quick small fingers Maggie plucked the soiled tattered skins from big mushrooms revealing the creamy fleshy discs within. Then on an oval chopping-board with brisk little movements she chopped yellowish-white fluted stalks of celery and a large moist onion. The sharp smell of it pricked my eyes, while now Maggie was plucking at a greyish-silver papery integument of garlic and peeling the plump yellow clove within. A glass of red wine stood by her on the table.[4]

In *The Sacred and Profane Love Machine* (1974), most of the food and drink cited is in a ten-page scene, set in a restaurant (that, judging from its menu, might be the Restaurant Elizabeth in Oxford). The meal is a dinner given to David Gavender by Edgar Demarny, the new master of an Oxford College. A preference for medium or sweet Sherry is used to indicate Emily McHugh's lower social status. By far the most prevalent meal in the Murdoch corpus is tea; it is also the most common drink, though whisky is pervasive in her novels.

In *The Good Apprentice* (1985) there is, of course, the cult-like vegetarianism:

> 'Now, we have made a feast for you,' said Mother May. 'Every meal is a sacrament, but this is a celebration.'

'A festival,' said Bettina.

'But first we should explain that we are vegetarians,' said Mother May. 'I hope you don't mind?'

'No, no, I'm almost a vegetarian myself, I often feel I should be, I don't mind what I eat – ' [....]

Spooning from various bowls, Mother May put upon Edward's plate a mixture of beans dressed with oil and herbs, lentils in a sweetish sauce, a flat rissole made (as he discovered) of nuts, a concoction of scrambled egg and spinach, and a salad composed of various unidentifiable leaves. All of this (as he also discovered) was delicious. The butter was unsalted and the thick crumbly bread self-evidently home made.

'Will you have wine?' […]

From an earthenware jug decorated with blue and green geometrical patterns, Bettina poured a reddish liquid into his glass. 'Elderberry wine, last year's vintage. We make our own wine.' […]

The wine was delicious too, with a fragrant sweetish taste and quite strong. Edward felt he was drinking flowers.[5]

At Seegard, the house where much of the novel takes place, the vegetarianism serves a narrative function, indicating the belief system of the family.

But Murdoch's writerly use of food has one big exception. Though critics have found the *clef* in several of her *romans,* and identified her characters with their historical models, one such identification stands out from all the others. In one of her best books, *The Sea, The Sea* (1978), the protagonist, Charles Arrowby, is a culinary portrait of Iris's husband, John Bayley (though he has negative traits, especially blind arrogance, that make him unlike John). Rereading it, I see that the food (and wine suggestions) is a compendium of Bayley's 'assembled' (as opposed to 'cooked') meals, which some commentators have found disgusting, and others find merely curious. Charles Arrowby thinks himself not exactly a great cook, so much as a great provider of meals – most of which, in the first two-thirds of the novel, are solitary. He wonders if he will ever get around to writing *Charles Arrowby's Four Minute Cookbook*.[6] The reader will note that the recipes, or rather, assembly instructions, involve very little fresh food, and are heavily dependent on tinned food.

For example, Arrowby's post-swim lunch:

For lunch, I may say, I ate and greatly enjoyed the following: anchovy paste on hot buttered toast, then baked beans and kidney beans with chopped celery, tomatoes, lemon juice and olive oil. (Really good olive oil is essential, the kind with a taste. I have brought a supply from London.) Green peppers would have been a happy addition only the village shop (about two miles pleasant walk) could not provide them. (No one delivers to far-off Shruff End [the sea-side house Arrowby has bought], so I fetch everything, including milk, from the village.) Then bananas and cream with white sugar. (Bananas should be cut, *never* mashed, and the cream should be thin.) Then hard water-biscuits with New Zealand butter and Wensleydale cheese. Of course I never touch foreign cheeses. Our cheeses are the best in the world. With this feast I drank most of a bottle of Muscadet out of my modest 'cellar'. I ate and drank slowly as one should (cook fast, eat slowly) and without distractions such as (thank heavens) conversation or reading. Indeed eating is so pleasant one should even try to suppress thought. Of course reading and thinking are important but, my God, food is important too. How fortunate we are to be food-consuming animals. Every meal should be a treat and one ought to bless every day which brings with it a good digestion and the precious gift of hunger. (p. 8)

This is a typical John Bayley menu: as Iris once said to our mutual friend, the musicologist and psychoanalyst Anthony Storr, 'But this is what John and I eat *all the time.*'[7]

The novel is full of such 'assemblies' by Arrowby/Bayley:

What is more delicious, than fresh hot buttered toast, with or without the addition of bloater paste? Or plain boiled onions with a little cold corned beef if desired? And well-made porridge with brown sugar and cream is a dish fit for a king. (p. 10)

I eat very little meat, and hold in horror the 'steak house carnivore'. But there are certain items (such as anchovy paste, liver, sausages, fish) which hold as it were strategic positions in my diet, and which I should be sorry to do without; [...]. (p. 11)

For lunch I ate the kipper fillets rapidly unfrozen in boiling water (the sun had done most of the work) garnished with lemon juice, oil, and a light sprinkling of dried herbs. Kipper fillets are arguably better than smoked salmon unless the latter is very good. With these, fried tinned new potatoes. (No real new potatoes yet.) Potatoes are for me a treat dish, not a dull everyday chaperon. Then Welsh rarebit and hot beetroot. The shop sliced bread is less than great, but all right toasted, with good salty New Zealand butter. (p. 27)

Felt a little depressed but was cheered up by supper: spaghetti with a little butter and dried basil. (Basil is of course the king of herbs.) Then spring cabbage cooked slowly with dill. Boiled onions served with bran, herbs, soya oil and tomatoes, with one egg beaten in. With these a slice or two of cold tinned corned beef. (Meat is really just an excuse for eating vegetables.) (p. 29)

There are a few cooked dishes, such as the impossible-sounding egg poached in scrambled egg, but this compendium catches the Bayley culinary repertory pretty deftly. Even this last egg-fest is not meant to be the product of imagination, but of recall – it's what the Bayleys ate 'all the time'.

I must conclude by acknowledging that my family and I were close friends of the Bayleys (Iris was godmother to our elder daughter), and we shared dozens of meals at the three addresses where they lived, and the two houses we have lived in near Oxford. It is only fair to say that whatever the Bayleys ate when on their own, John did not normally feed Charles Arrowby's dishes to their guests.

Notes

1. Thomas Mann, *Buddenbrooks: The Decline of a Family*, trans. by John E. Woods (New York: Vintage, 1994), p. 98-99.
2. This *Guardian* article originated as a paper for the 2003 Oxford Food Symposium: Margaret Drabble, 'A Nice Cup of Bovril in Utopia', *Guardian*, 20 December 2003 <https://www.theguardian.com/books/2003/dec/20/featuresreviews.guardianreview34> [accessed 21 March 2022]
3. Iris Murdoch, *The Bell* (New York: Penguin, 1958), pp. 65, 137, 176; *Jackson's Dilemma* (New York: Penguin, 1995), p. 20.
4. Iris Murdoch, *The Italian Girl* (New York: Penguin, 1967), p. 95.
5. Iris Murdoch, *The Good Apprentice* (London: Chatto, 1985), pp. 104-05.
6. Iris Murdoch, *The Sea, The Sea* (London: Vintage, 1999 [1978]), p. 7. Subsequent references are cited parenthetically.
7. Peter Conradi, *Iris Murdoch: A Life* (New York: Norton, 2001), p. 524 and see pp. 414-15.

The Hen that Laid a Tofu Egg

Priya Mani

The millennial pastorals are pushing a new wave of imagined foods as innovators, creators, and consumers of plant-based foods driven by new ethics, sustainability, and wellness ideologies. Food has never been imagined so widely or ever so much in history. Many generations have pioneered new ideas for 'animal-free' food – the singular culinary pursuit of Western ideologies of vegetarianism and veganism.[1] One of the most peculiar, creative, and imaginative trends for better or worse is the rise of plant-based substitutes for animal products. With copious help from big science and most probably produced in a plant, these plant-based foods are catalyzed by one ingredient – imagination.

Imagination is key to culinary mimicry. A completely new set of ingredients, many of which do not belong to the conventional pantry, mimic eggs, honey, meat, and milk products for a complete sensorial experience in appearance, aroma, taste and texture. A deep dive into didactic sources – going beyond cookbooks, recipes, and historic food trends to patents, war, theological diet discourses, and the protein race – shows the rise of the vegan mindset from a fringe movement to the billion-dollar mainstream industry it has become.

Since Nuttose, the first meat analogue, was developed in 1896, most animal-free meat products have followed roughly the same formula.[2] They usually contain a carbohydrate base, assorted proteins, fats, sugars, a source of fibre, antioxidants, emulsifiers, vitamins, minerals to meet nutritional guidelines, colouring agents to render them appealingly authentic, and preservatives. Added probiotics, digestibility enhancers, and enzymes can claim health benefits. Nevertheless, how do we imagine that combining them will lead to a familiar product? What were the key moments inspiring the creators, and what questions did those pioneers ask that led to creating these animal-free analogues?

Many Roads Lead to Rome – Decoding the Creative Process

Imagination and innovation in three distinct areas – the food lab, market-driven food narratives, and food ideologies – have shaped our approaches to dietary ethics and sustainability. The questions posed by actors in these areas spark the nature of their imagination and define their idea's impact. Chefs and cooks are informed by their practice and borrow from each other's kitchen experiences: they seem to ask, '*What if...?*' By contrast, scientists are very imaginative in the food lab, often starting with '*How might we...?*' The events that led to the discovery of aquafaba, a popular plant-based egg white replacement, are a great example.

Asking, '*How might we create a plant-based meringue?*', scientists Kent Kirshenbaum and Alizee Guegan explored the use of saponins in 2011 primarily to address vegan needs. Meringue is prepared from a mixture of saponin, sugar or sugar substitute, and water as a self-sustaining, baked product.[3]

Asking, '*What if a vegetable foam could be whipped like egg whites?*', vegan blogger Joël Roessel discovered, through a systematic investigation into vegetable foams in 2014, that liquid from red kidney beans and palm hearts can be whipped into a foam similar to flax mucilage.[4] Joël built on two important previous developments – Miyoko Schinner's experiments with flax mucilage to replace egg white that she shared on her blog and Kirshenbaum and Guegan's patent from 2013.[5]

Cookbook writers and bloggers have established that whole eggs can be replaced with chia seeds, psyllium husk, bananas, apple sauce, prunes, pumpkin, flax, nuts, and garbanzos in recipes.[6] These work well in recipes that call for whole eggs, but a similar whole-food approach to replacing egg whites in recipes like meringues had been impossible.[7] Commercially available egg and egg-white replacers for home cooks (like products from Orgran, Ener-G, and Bob's Red Mill) contain processed starches, gluten, and concentrated soy proteins with varying degrees of textural and taste acceptance. However, the quest to find a plant-based replacement for egg whites had started on a chat forum seven years before Joël.[8]

Joël posted updates on the bean-liquid-based experiments on his blog. Meanwhile, Goose Wohlt, a software engineer in the US, experimented with existing meringue techniques based on hydrocolloids to replicate egg whites. Inspired by a French video coercing the soaking liquid in canned chickpea to a mousse, Wohlt whipped a stable meringue and concluded that soaking liquid *by itself* can act as a direct egg white replacer.[9] Goose created a virtual space for the experiment on Facebook and called it *aqua faba*, Latin for bean water.

The intense focus on the novelty of creating a plant-based meringue played out in the public sphere fuelled iteration in a participatory design process. Genuine novelty arose from the everyday interactions in the kitchen with cosmopolitan ingredients, techniques, and ideas – not from a scientist or star chef.

Recently, I prepared *batasha*, a traditional Indian sweetmeat popular

Figure 1. Sapindus Mukorossi and sugar is used to make batasha. Photo credit: Priya Mani, 'A Visual Encyclopedia of Indian Foods.'

throughout the Indo-Gangetic plain. Traditionally, the soaking liquid of *aritha* (*Sapindus mukorossi*) is added to sugar syrup to achieve a light, 'brittle', or 'crunchy' texture.[10] Well-made *batasha* looks, feels, and tastes like a meringue, easily achieved without eggs. In a moment of epiphany, I realized that Kirshenbaum and Guegan had inadvertently patented an old, popular Indian sweetmeat. Their patent acknowledged that their heat-stable meringue took reference from a Middle Eastern dessert topping, *natef*, prepared from the saponin-rich roots of *Saponaria officinalis*. However, *natef*, unlike *batasha,* is not heat stable.

Unlocking creative potential in learning from the past as a springboard for the future is crucial – like the potential of plant extracts trapped in unavailable (unrecorded, oral traditions) or inaccessible (due to language barriers) traditional knowledge systems, surely challenging inspiration and appropriation.

Who Were These Skeuomorphic Foods Created for?
Ideology and Markets in the Food Lab

Unlike in ethnically vegetarian groups, the idea of a 'free-from animal source' diet links to strong ideologies that have stemmed from carnivorous societies as a sort of rebellion and refuge. The Western ideology of animal-free foods first emerged as 'vegetarianism' in Victorian Britain. Believers of better health through plant-based food or non-violence to animals followed a diet against the grain of their meat-eating cohort. Meat and dairy were considered essential to strength, vigour, and an aspirational diet, so early vegetarians used hygiene and poor animal husbandry to incite doubt.[11] The dietary ideology was interested not in creating genuinely original food but in changing the ingredients used to prepare dishes people already ate executed in new ways. The most critical factor for converting and staying on a diet seemed to be a struggle between psychological and social factors. Entirely new products would take much effort to educate and explain. Skeuomorphism remains essential to adoption and commerce.

In 1843, a Liverpool native wrote to the editor of *New Age: Concordium Gazette and Temperance Advocate*:

> Quite convinced of the correctness of the principle in every variety of view, I am yet at a loss for substitutes for animal food – for tea, coffee, butter, eggs, milk, & cheese, necessarily precluded by the principles of abstinence from all animal food. The experience of those practically acquainted with this subject, would be of essential service to novices in these matters, who find nothing so perplexing or so difficult as the change of their daily habits in these respects.[12]

It was essential to substitute meat in easy-to-replace, cost-effective ways in known preparations. With no precedence of a meat-free diet, much of the early literature addressed nutrition, protein intake, general well-being, and hygiene concerns on farms. They introduced readers to new colonial ingredients, described ethnically vegetarian cultures to instil confidence, and discussed meat substitution in recipes to encourage a new culture of preparing such foods. By 1896, the *Lancet* reported on the food served at the London Vegetarian Society's press conference: 'various dishes were composed entirely of vegetables and fruit, but such things as macaroni cutlet and dishes prepared *à la Française, à la Normandy*, &c., bore some resemblance to the food eaten by the ordinary 'corpse' eater.'[13]

Imagination Can Stretch Only as Far as People Are Willing to Eat It

For many people shifting to a plant-based diet, the journey starts with a few simple questions. Can we still have milk? Am I getting enough proteins? How can I feel the satisfaction of meat? Such consumer-driven questions forced scientists and the industry to create dietary 'essentials' with new techniques and ingredients.

Novelty in reimagining the archaic

To understand the creative process behind creating the plant-based food alternatives, one needs to delve a bit into how satisfying these different pursuits became drivers for new food industries:

- The pursuit of Godliness for the ethnic and ethical
- The pursuit of plant-based fat & protein for the health-conscious
- The pursuit of the meaty taste and experience for the carbon-conscious

The Pursuit of Godliness for the Ethnically and Ethically Vegans

Religious ideologies use culinary doctrines for community building. Exclusion and inclusion are fundamental to this mechanism. In India, where vegetarianism is a reasonably significant practice, there are two different culinary approaches: one in which plant-based diets rooted in theology and non-violence are integral to ethnic identity, and the other that offers plant-based meat analogues for people who periodically abstain from meat. Among most Brahmin communities from the subcontinent, vegetarianism has lasted many generations, and there may be a complete loss of collective memory of meat-eating, if it ever was practiced amongst them.[14] Strong kinship supported by a highly evolved culinary ecosystem allows for a shared culture and culinary identity.

Many mock-meat dishes have evolved for periods of religious abstinence or as vegetarian options in convivial gatherings. In east Maharashtra, *maaswadi* is a snack made to look like bone, with an outer covering of chickpea flour, and the 'marrow' mimicked with spices and lichen. The Nattukottai Chettiars of South India have used banana flowers to replace spiny loach (*Lepidocephalus thermalis*) in *ayira meen kuzhambu*. A paste of black-eyed peas is steamed in the shape of a fish on a banana leaf and added to *meen kuzhambu* curry to replace mackerel. The Jain community follows a more rigorous approach to non-violence that includes avoiding root vegetables to preserve microbial life forms. Thus, different types of bananas replace starchy tubers, and asafetida satiates the need for alliums. Today, *paneer* and soya chunks have become the de facto replacement for meat in many curries.

A different concern over substitution is found in kosher dairy laws that forbid the consumption of dairy and meat in the same meal. Judaism advocates serving *pareve* foods – those made without milk, meat, or their derivatives – that uphold the dietary laws. *Pareve* foods are not vegan, for it allows the inclusion of fish. While the laws of *marit ayin* forbid eating a *pareve* food that appears as if dairy is being served with meat or vice versa, today such resemblance is permitted, given the wide commercial availability of *pareve* imitations of both dairy and meat foods. Since the demand for foods free of dairy or meat among kosher-keeping Jews is high, this dilemma led David Mintz, an Orthodox Jew, to start his famous line of soy-based dairy-free alternatives, Tofutti, in 1981. Tofutti has found a vast following among vegans as the diet continues to grow in popularity.

The modern ideology of animal-free diets gained momentum with the Seventh Day Adventists, who were shaped by the visions of one of the founders, Ellen G. White. The Church became actively involved in vegetarianism by 1863 and, three years later, opened the Western Health Reform Institute in Battle Creek, later known as the Sanitarium.

In a parallel development, vegetarianism evolved as an idea, gaining a foothold in 1842 with the Manchester Vegetarian Society (UK). The idea of eating a plant-based diet was also coming to seem less alien as colonial life exposed the Western world to new ingredients, cultures, and markets.

The Adventists pioneered these efforts either by the Church directly owning institutions and factories like Battle Creek Sanitarium (USA), Nutana (DK), and Sanitarium Food Company (AU) or by individual Adventists investing in their ventures, seeing the market potential for plant-based analogues as vegetarian reforms went

 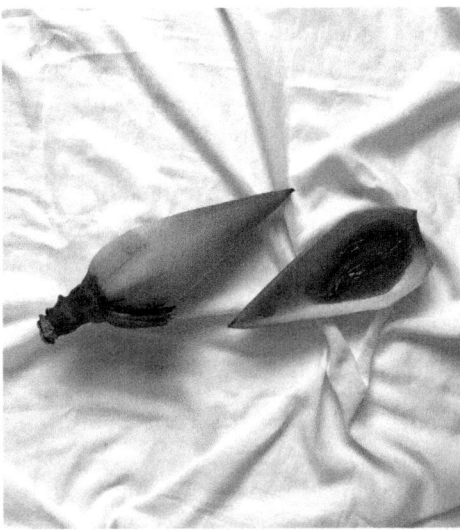

Figure 2 (left). Maaswadi, a mock bone snack. Figure 3 (right). Ayira meen kuzhambu uses banana flower to mimic Indian spiny loach, and Meen kuzhambu uses black-eyed beans to mimic mackerel. Photo credit: Priya Mani, A Visual Encyclopedia of Indian Foods.

mainstream. Adventist John Kellogg's vegetarian ideologies set the commercial stage for new foods and new ideas beyond the Church's fold. He cooked out the preaching in the kitchen of the Battle Creek Sanitarium and established The Sanitarium Food Company to commercialize products that include cornflakes, granola, and nut and peanut butter (Kellogg's patent), spurring competition and patent wars.

In the 1930s, Rastalogy evolved in Jamaica as a calm, peaceful way of life with a dietary focus on cruelty-free eating called *ital* – from 'vital' – an approach to natural foods that discouraged meat substitutes. Interestingly, religious restrictions have long forced people to make an alternate preparation in the historical context instead of 'substitution or mimicry'.[15]

Tofu is used as a meat substitute by Buddhists in Taiwan. Vegetarianism became prevalent among Chinese Buddhists in the sixth century when Emperor Wu urged monastics to stop eating meat. 'Faux meat' emerged catering to monastery visitors between the tenth to thirteenth centuries. Soy, native to the region, forms the base of this cuisine subculture, and those who cook at the monasteries have a deep understanding of its material properties. With limited technology, imagination has fired the flavours in bland tofu or seitan – from beef to pork and eel, monastic cooking fakes it all.

The Pursuit of Plant-Based Fat and Protein for Health-Conscious Vegans

Kellogg developed 'Nuttose' in 1896 for the Sanitarium's patients suffering from intolerance to starch, a condition he describes as 'amylaceous dyspepsia'.[16] In Nuttose, he found the perfect cognate for meat protein. Nuttose was inspired by tofu making – dried soybeans are soaked crushed, boiled, and separated into solid pulp (*okara*) and soy 'milk'. Added salt coagulants separate curds to make tofu. Kellogg soaked and ground peanuts into a paste before processing it with coagulant salts and shaping it in cans. The cans were steamed for three to four hours to 'set' the meat before using it. Kellogg wrote of Nuttose:

> For many years we dreamed of such a product but had little hope of ever seeing the thing accomplished. A discovery, almost accidental, made some years ago, put us in the possession of the key to the situation, and long-continued experimental effort gradually perfected the method, until at last we have really mastered the art of meat making, and can compete with nature so successfully as to be able to produce not only the real thing, but a better thing than the natural product.[17]

Kellogg declared it the 'perfect substitute for flesh food', and said it resembled 'cold roast mutton'.

Kellogg did not patent Nuttose, but, his patent for peanut butter (1895), Protose (1907), and other literary sources, show a familiarity and frenzy for nuts had set in.[18] Nut-based mock meat products flooded the market owing to the Sanitarium's wild popularity. Grains, fruits, and nuts find mention in Ellen White's writings too.[19] She writes of its rising popularity but is quick to warn of excessive consumption.[20] Nuts have since been the primary 'healthy' choice in replacing animal-based products. In 1896 Kellogg famously said, 'Nuts are unquestionably the vegetable analogue of meat and other animal foods.'[21] Protose became the first commercially available meat substitute and was on the market until 2000.

Soy-based products were also one of the early alternatives for plant proteins. Soy is versatile, suited to diverse regions and attractive to farmers and industry. Soy first arrived as tofu and later fermented tofu in the Western world, imported mainly by Asians and made in the US starting in 1878.[22] The pioneering work of Li yu-Ying, who arrived in Paris in 1903, brought Western food semantics to this Asian ingredient. Soy-based roquefort, parmesan, gruyère, kefir, and yoghurt consciously mimicked the familiar tastes of France, and suitable ferments were patented. In 1908, he established the world's first soy dairy, the Tofu Manufacturing Co. Li served vegetarian ham (*jambon végétal*), soy cheese (*fromage de Soya*), soy preserves, soy bread, and so on at the annual lunch of France's national *Société d'Acclimatation* in 1911, keeping with its tradition of introducing new foods from little-known plants.[23]

The growing discomfort among Western vegetarians about inhumane emotions in using animal by-products like milk and eggs led Donald Watson to start the 'veganism' movement in 1944, defining their people as those who avoided milk and other animal products like leather, eggs, and honey. The search for an alternative to milk and meat only intensified. Early vegans were committed to generating knowledge and sharing best practices in the *Vegan Magazine*, published quarterly since 1944. Lively discussions of new ingredients to understand their potential as 'replacements' [nuts for meats regained popularity], taste enhancers [e.g. widespread use of nutritional yeast, miso], new options for coagulants and binders, probiotics [Rejuvelac, kombuchas etc.] were all shared, forming a culture of collective 'vegan practice'.[24]

The Pursuit of the Meaty Taste and Experience for the Carbon-Conscious Vegan

Historically, after soy products supplanted peanut/wheat gluten blends, simulating the 'chewiness' of meat became the next technical frontier in the 'meat-like' challenge. Robert Boyer patented a method to make imitation meat, summarizing the problem in his patent of 1954: 'The stumbling block up to this point has been in the reproduction of the texture and appearance of natural meat, the texture of course involving a factor of "chewiness." [… W]heat gluten [offers] a certain amount of "chewiness," but [… does] not duplicate the fibrous character of meat […] and [… the] satisfaction that comes from […] the mastication of a piece of meat.'[25]

'What makes meat taste like meat?' Pat Brown of Impossible Foods says of his moment of epiphany:

> Humans have been eating meat from animals since we were living in caves. So, I was shocked to discover how little we knew about how and why we crave meat. Our team spent five years studying meat at the molecular level and were able

to make fundamental discoveries before launching a product. Our archive of knowledge on this subject is one of the company's biggest assets.[26]

Seven out of Impossible Foods' fourteen patents address the meat-like taste components.

A new category of lab-reared, plant-based meat alternatives is on the rise that can be defined only by their lack of animal origin components. The Impossible approach takes a gene encoded with the characteristics of heme, a hemoglobin-like compound found in lentils and soybeans, and transfers it onto the common yeast, *S. cerevisiae*. It is a powerful vehicle for flavours and characteristics suited for large-scale replication and production of leghemoglobin. Replicating the mouthfeel of muscle, the texture of meat has been another area of intensive competition.

Imagination in the Blogger kitchens

Plant-based eating found its millennial readership in food blogs, and the influence of vegan food bloggers as recipe developers has spurred a new food culture. They echo a sentiment of personal health and discovering 'cleaner eating'. Over a decade, this rhetoric has given way to eating the 'vegan way'. Plant-based food from hyper-local traditional kitchens inspire their modern renditions, often questioning the meaning of food within its geography. Sarah Britton set off a frenzy for chickpea tofu inspired by Burmese Shan tofu.[27] Her recipe for nut bread became one of the biggest trends to change the way home bakers made bread, introducing nuts to replace grains in bread. The nut-and-seed bread echoes Florence George's nut roast and many Battle Creek-era recipes but fit right in with today's needs of high protein, gluten-free foods.[28] Food bloggers of the last decade have borrowed heavily from the vegetarian and vegan literature of the last century, in part appropriating the efforts of many generations of pioneers – the Seventh Day Adventists, the early vegetarians in England, the vegans of the 1950s, and the Hippies of the 1960s and 1970s. Nevertheless, their contribution to the visual appeal of food through digital photography and social media is the most powerful, bringing plant-based foods from a fringe culture to mainstream consumption.

New Frontiers in Plant-Based Foods
Imagination Sparked by New Questions
An essential part of food science today is that most ingredients are broken down to functional building blocks – starch, fibre, and protein – often using a process called fractionation. Each plant-based ingredient can thus be a catalogue of derivatives and isolated compounds that have physical and chemical properties distinct from the whole. These isolated parts are then selectively picked to fill in for the formula of a plant-based analogue.[29]

Now scientists are also asking, 'Could we just change the process and not the food?

What If One Could Make 'Animal-Based' More Efficient?

Eric Östman set out to make a vegan-copy of cheese for the booming vegan industry. Observing traditional cheesemakers, he stumbled upon a conversation on casein with a cheesemaker: 'If you could give me a bag of casein, it would help small farmers like us compete with giant cooperatives. Just give me a bag of casein!' This sparked Eric to design a super-efficient cheese. Synthesizing dairy protein by fermentation, Eric's casein is structurally identical to milk casein, just animal-free, and its addition increases cheese yield by 50%. Eric is not alone. Hours after the idea hit him; he realized ReMilk, PerfectDay, and many others across the globe are pursuing it. With a valuable intermediary product, Eric and his competitors have markets beyond food.[30]

Imaginative Code for AI Can Keep Additives 'Plant-Based'

Companies such as Brightseed Bio, The Live Green, and NotCo are actively scanning the plant kingdom to identify bioactive compounds identical to synthetic additives that have defined alternative foods from its start. Using AI, their algorithms can scan thousands of plant-based compounds based on threshold values and qualitative terms to identify potential replacements. I dug deeper to understand how the algorithm worked. NotCo 'plant-based' whole milk using its AI has these ingredients:

> Water, Pea Protein, Contains less than 2% of: Chicory Root Fiber, Sugar, Pineapple Juice Concentrate, Coconut Oil, Sunflower Oil, Virgin Coconut Oil, Cabbage Juice Concentrate, Natural Flavors, Salt, Gum Acacia, Gellan Gum, Calcium Carbonate, Monocalcium Phosphate, Dipotassium Phosphate, Vitamin B12, Vitamin D2. Contains coconut.

An array of flavour compounds mimics the taste of whole milk. The programmatic output feeds kitchen experiments that tweak the final recipe to taste. The method allows for exploration of untapped plant isolates.

Oatly, today's leading plant-based milk, uses diverse salts for the enzymatic action required for fluidity. It lists ingredients as:

> Oat base (water, oats 10%), rapeseed oil, calcium carbonate, calcium phosphates, iodised salt, vitamins (D2, riboflavin, B12). Free from lactose, milk protein and soy.

A comparison between the tastes of Oatly and NotCo frames the dilemma of our time: Are we seeking plant-based alternatives or replacements?

Conclusion

The rigorous journey to find analogues to animal-derived foods has food science, novel processes, production techniques, and unusual combinations of ingredients that do not belong to the conventional kitchen. Ideologies from religion to personal health to fighting climate change have driven this thirst for substitution. However, one essential, secret ingredient is the incredible imagination of the unseen influencers who conjure up these seemingly impossible recipes or formulas to fulfil the need for ideological substitution. It is also worth noting that these creative processes are predominantly preoccupied with matching known concepts in animal-based derivatives, including taste, texture, aroma, and cooking processes. Worries about mass appeal or presumptions of being assertively weird hamper imagination into unknown frontiers of unique foods with new forms, tastes, and feel.

These imaginative foods follow a pattern:

- finding innovative substitutes for protein, fats, fibres and binding agents – driven by the need for systematically scanning for scalable yet novel feedstock.
- innovative deconstruction and re-combination of supplemented material by proprietary processes or novel catalyst ingredients – driven by the need to mimic known tastes, mouthfeel, and form.
- imaginative conceptual packaging of the outcome as a valid food for mass appeal – driven by the need to gain ideological acceptance often with the end goal of marketability and commercial success.

These are not apparently discreet and have significant overlaps, but the general notion seems to hold true in most of the cases I have investigated. Temporal variance in ingredient availability, technology to synthesize a subcomponent, and skills of the people driving the process – i.e. food scientist vs. marketing guru – emphasize which aspect of the process gains importance.

It is also worth noting that the quest for imaginative synthesized food seems irrelevant to ethnically multi-generational vegetarians or vegans whose culinary repertoire has no need for mimicry. Food rationing during the Second World War years in Europe and America greatly reduced people's access to meats. The ingenuity of the home cook and opportunistic entrepreneurs is evident in the skeuomorphic meat and dairy alternatives of war-era cookbooks and commercial food products. However, as the global economy improved in the post-war era, we see fewer examples of such foods at commercial scale.

The unsettling truth about these impossible foods is the drive to consume a 'guilt-free' diet that allows us to take pleasure in eating things, and in quantities, that we would never want to eat otherwise. Food is a unique creative offering in that it needs to be eaten by people. It has an emotional and psychological impact far beyond its function. The development of new animal-free and plant-based foods will remain a tussle between retro-vation and innovation. The unending, vivid, chemical diversity of this culinary mimicry shows that food, like the mouth, is a victim of preadaptation.

Acknowledgements

Thanks to Claude Shehadi (www.claudecooks.com) for explaining making *natef* to me, to Elin Östman of Good Idea, Eric Östman, Ragini Ashok, Sasikanth of Live Green who agreed to be interviewed for this paper, and to the Vegetarian Society and the Vegan Society for providing information.

Notes

1. The expression *vegetarian* first appeared in *The Healthian* magazine (April 1842). There is etymological disagreement on whether the English word *vegetarian* comes from *vegetable*, or Latin *vegetus* (strong, vigorous). *Vegan* first appeared in the initial issue of Donald Watson's newsletter ('*The Vegan News*', 1 (1944), see p. 2).
2. John Harvey Kellogg, 'Nuttose: A new food for brain and muscle building', *Good Health,* (July 1896), 195-96. The is the first instance the term 'substitute for flesh!' refers to a meat alternative.
3. K. Kirshenbaum and A. Guegan. 'Meringue Composition And Methods Of Preparation', WO 2013/022750 A9, 13 Feb 2013. (Patent filed on 2 August 2011.) (PCT)
4. Joël Roessel, 'Mousses végétales', *Révolution Végétale* <http://www.revolutionvegetale.com/en/> [accessed 13 March 2021]
5. Miyoko Schinner writes, 'I think the star of the week was my flaxseed meringue, which […] can be folded into mousses and terrines and piled on top of pies, just like the stuff made from egg whites […]. Basically, flaxseeds are simmered for 20 – 30 minutes, strained, and the resulting goop chilled. Afterwards, it whips up just like meringue' ('Intensely Baking', *Artisan Vegan Life*, 2 March 2011 <https://www.artisanveganlife.com/intensely-baking/> [accessed 11 April 2021]).
6. Many cookbooks discuss such alternatives; see for example: Fay K. Henderson, *Vegan Recipes* (London: H.H Greaves, 1946); M.R.L. Sharpe, *The Golden Rule Cookbook: Six Hundred Recipes for Meatless Dishes* (Boston: Little Brown & Company, 1912); Ella Kellogg, *Science in the Kitchen* (Michigan: Health Publishing Company, 1892); and Amanda Lambert, *Guide for Nut Cookery* (Michigan: J. Lambert & Co, 1899).
7. Abu-Ghoush and others, 'Comparative Study of Egg White Protein and Egg Alternatives Used in Angel Food Cake Systems', *Journal of Food Processing and Preservation*, 34 (2010), 411-25.
8. 'History', *Aquafaba* <http://aquafaba.com/history.html> [accessed 9 April 2021]
9. Le Défi FUDA – BONUS #1 Mission Pois Chiches <https://www.youtube.com/watch?v=aIIp_FUINZI&ab_channel=ONGFUDA>; Facebook conversation archive between Joël, Goose, and other vegans reveals the development of aquafaba <https://www.facebook.com/groups/VeganMeringue/permalink/383004105220595/> [both accessed 15 April 2021]
10. Modern-day recipes listed online on various blogs and in cookbooks use soda bicarbonate to create the foamy structure.
11. For the most famous case, see Upton Sinclair, *The Jungle* (New York: Doubleday, Page & Co., 1906)
12. John Davis, 'Extracts from Some Journals 1842-48 – The Earliest Known Uses of the Word "Vegetarian"', *International Vegetarian Union* <https://ivu.org/history/vegetarian.html>. [accessed 3 April 2021]
13. William Shurtleff and Akiko Aoyagi note that '[t]his is the earliest English language document that mentions a meat alternative in the form of a "cutlet"' (*History of Meat Alternatives* (965 CE to 2014): *Extensively Annotated Bibliography and Sourcebook* (Lafayette: Soy Info Center, 2014), p. 36).
14. Saraswat Goud Brahmins, Kashmiri Pandits, and Brahmins of Bengal and Orissa permit meat eating.
15. The national meat bans in Japan imposed gradually from AD 675 to AD 872 still allowed fish.
16. Kellogg, 'Nuttose'. By 1896, seitan, tofu, and casein-based mock meats had been explored.
17. John H. Kellogg, *Healthful Living: An Account of the Battle Creek Diet System* (Michigan: Kellogg Food Company,1908), p. 46.
18. John Kellogg, '*Food Product*' US Patent No. 869371, 29 October 1907 (Patent filed on February 2, 1906); Ellen G. Smith writes, 'Brazil nut meats eaten with beans are an excellent substitute for pork' (*The Fat of the Land and How to Live on It* (Amherst, MA: Carpenter and Morehouse, 1896), p. 132; see also p. 144).

19 Ellen White, *Counsels for Diet and Foods* (Washington, DC: Review & Herald Publishing, 1938), p. 92.
20 Ellen White, *The Ministry of Healing* (Washington: Review & Herald Publishing, 1905), p. 298.
21 John H. Kellogg, *Modern Medicine and Bacteriological Review* (Battle Creek, MI: Battle Creek Sanatarium, 1896), V, pp. 220-23. This is the first use of the word 'analogue' for meat-alternatives.
22 Doufu-ru (Fermented tofu) was first made in the Western world in San Francisco by Wo Sing and Co. in 1878.
23 William Shurtleff and Akiko Aoyagi, *History of Soybeans and Soyfoods in France (1665-2015)* (Lafayette: Soyinfo Center, 2015), p. 6.
24 On nutritional yeast, see: The Farm, *Yay Soybeans! How You Can Eat Better for Less and Help Feed the World* (Tennessee: The Book Publishing Co,1974); Rejuvelac is a kind of grain water invented and promoted by Ann Wigmore in the 1980s.
25 Robert Boyer and Harold Saewert. 1953. 'Method of Preparing Imitation Meat Products,' US2730448A, Jan 10 1956. (Patent filed on 2 February 1953). This is the first use of term 'synthetic meat'. See also 'Patenting the Quest for a More Perfect Veggie Burger', *Lane Powell*, 20 June 2016 <https://www.lanepowell.com/Our-Insights/122560/Patenting-the-Quest-for-a-More-Perfect-Veggie-Burger> [accessed 20 May 2021]
26 Mary Allen, 'Impossible Foods: The Flavour of Meat', *gfi.org*, 2018 <https://tinyurl.com/5f69nu7w> [accessed 21 April 2021]
27 Sarah Britton, 'Genious Chickpea Tofu', *My New Roots*, 2014 <https://www.Mynewroots.Org/site/2014/04/genius-Chickpea-Tofu/> [accessed 29 May 2021]
28 Florence George, *Vegetarian Cookery* (London: E. Arnold, 1908).
29 The formula is protein+fibre+texturizer+emulsifier+binder+probiotic+enzyme+protection.
30 Personal interview with Eric Östman, 2021.

Singapore's Rising Hawkers: Food, Heritage, Imagination, and Entrepreneurship

Keri Matwick

This paper describes Singapore's food scene at hawker centres, open-air complexes with food stalls serving local food. Hawker centres illustrate how 'heritage' is being reimagined as familiar foods and old techniques are being transformed by changing palates and modern technology. The recent UNESCO inscription of hawker centres on the Intangible Cultural Heritage of Humanity list has led to international exposure and revived local interest. Called to preserve their 'community dining rooms', Singaporean youth have responded, setting up food stalls at hawker centres and bringing with them their business drive and tech skills. With modern production and marketing plans, these new hawkers include next generation hawkers who take on their family stall, professionally trained chefs, burned-out corporate workers, and others willing to enter the labour-intensive occupation. An entrepreneurial spirit leads, resulting in hawker entrepreneurs, or 'hawkerpreneurs', entrepreneurs that have turned to food vending.[1] The following analysis of these hawkerpreneurs is meant to open the discussion of how food, along with its preparation and marketing, is imagined as a 'living heritage', and what the UNESCO inscription means within this shifting context. The paper argues that the essence of heritage is conserved by these new hawkers, who now must be savvy in business, digital marketing, and social media. The research draws upon ethnographic observations of hawker centres (old and new), government material, historical documents, local media, and documentaries.

Tiong Bahru Market & Food Centre

Early lunchtime, I am at Tiong Bahru, one of Singapore's oldest housing estates. Central to the neighbourhood is Tiong Bahru Market with its hawker centre on the upper deck, an open-air food court with cafeteria tables covered from the hot sun. The stifling heat from the tropical climate and hot woks is kept breezy with large fans (Figure 1). Scanning the food stalls, I try to decide among the wide array of appetizing dishes. Though just after 11am, queues are becoming long for Hong Heng Fried Sotong Prawn Mee (yellow noodles stir-fried with squid and prawns) and Tiong Bahru Hainanese Boneless Chicken Rice (poached skin-on chicken served with oily rice and cucumber, chilli sauce, and dark soy sauce). Peeling stickers of past Michelin Bib Gourmand awards are reminders of the glory days of these unassuming stalls,

Figure 1 (left). Tiong Bahru Hawker Centre, an open-air food court serving traditional Singaporean food. Figure 2 (right). Tiong Bahru's popular Hong Heng Fried Sotong Prawn Mee hawker stall specializes in a yellow noodle squid and prawn dish. Michelin Bib Gourmand awards are on display.

whose hawker chefs are too intent on their woks to peer through the grease shield at the long queue (Figure 2). Steady orders are coming out from the stall Tiong Bahru Braised Duck, serving Roasted Duck Rice. Bjorn Shen, chef and judge of *MasterChef: Singapore*, describes duck rice as a 'sleeper dish' on a travel food show, noting that the dish is commonly eaten by Singaporeans but not 'one of those top things to eat' like chicken rice or *laksa* (spicy coconut noodle soup).[2] There are other sleeper dishes too, such as the Western dishes being served one stall over.

New to Tiong Bahru hawker centre, Skirt & Dirt sells burgers and fries (Figure 3). This modern offering may be surprising, given that hawker centres are known for their traditional Singaporean dishes. However, Tiong Bahru has long been gentrified. In the early 1990s, the construction of a shopping mall, Mass Rapid Transit station, and new public and private housing brought an influx of new residents, changing the greying population to a more youthful, diverse group.[3] Tiong Bahru is also popular for internal tourism, and weekend visitors cross the island to visit the market, hawker centre, and sprawl of cafes and bakeries. High-end burgers and craft seasoned hand-cut fries would appeal to Western expatriates, youth, and middle-aged professionals.

After the initial survey of the scene, I *chope*, or reserve a seat with a tissue packet, which also comes handy later as napkins are not provided. Then I join the queues for the self-service chicken rice and prawn mee dishes, gaining respect for the patience and passion Singaporeans have for good food. The last order is a burger from Skirt & Dirt, which offers table-service, giving me a buzzer as I take my seat. I begin the meal, alternating bites between tender chicken, spicy yellow noodles, prawns, and the juicy burger. Never had queueing, ordering, and eating seemed so delicious,

Figure 3 (left). Tiong Bahru's Skirt & Dirt hipster hawker stall serves artisanal burgers and fries and has strong branding and marketing. Figure 4 (right). Tiong Bahru's Tow Kwar Pop has been serving rojak salad since 1965.

delightful, and, for an expat like me, entertaining, and for Singaporeans, ritualistic, as at a hawker centre.

I could see that there is more to just picking a stall to satisfy hunger cravings. Yet the addition of a new stall and cuisine offered at the hawker centre signals changes. Is it the place or the food that makes a hawker centre? or maybe the people? I began my eating and exploring of Singaporean food in an attempt to figure out what was happening in Singapore's hawker culture.

Hawker Centres as 'Living Heritage'

In December 2020, the UNESCO committee made a unanimous decision to inscribe hawker culture in Singapore on the Intangible Cultural Heritage of Humanity List. UNESCO refers to 'intangible culture' also as 'living heritage' and 'living culture', the 'practices, representations, expressions, knowledge and skills handed down from generation to generation'.[4] Of Singapore's proposal, the evaluation body noted: 'As a social space that immerses people from diverse socioeconomic backgrounds, hawker centres play a crucial role in enhancing community interactions and strengthening the social fabric.'[5] The space created by hawker centres is emphasized, but the food is also important because serving food is the very function of hawker centres. Stalls such as Tiong Bahru's Tow Kwar Pop have been specializing in *rojak* for over fifty years, a food that has become a metaphor for the ethnic mix of people. Sweet, spicy, and crunchy, *rojak* is a salad of peanuts, green mango, cucumber, and fried tofu, ingredients combined in the same bowl but remain separate. Further embellishing the metaphor, culinary historian Nicole Tarulevicz explains that 'the government binds the chopped salad together, and the dressing is part global culture and part cosmopolitanism'.[6]

Similarly, hawker centres 'bind' the people together, now wrapped even tighter in the UNESCO label.

The 'diversity' of multiculturalism and class, though, may be over celebrated, as historically Singapore hawker centres began as a way to serve the multi-ethnic labour class with affordable, fast food. Chinese Hokkien mee noodles, Indian curry puff, and Malay chicken satay, alongside drink stalls of *kopi* (coffee) and *teh tarik* (pulled tea), satiated the diverse population. Because of this mandated food diversity, Singaporeans often taste the food of their neighbours for the first time, many of whom are of different ethnicity. Like government housing, hawker centres are designed to be representative of Singapore's multi-cultural, multi-ethnic heritage, an image proudly and politically protected by the government with its CIMO (Chinese, Indian, Malay, Other) racial structure. Hawker centres have quotas of drink, halal, and CIMO stalls, yet there is an increasing number of international cuisines that can be found at hawker centres such as Pad Thai, Korean fried chicken, and, yes, burgers. Taking an active role since independence in 1965, the Singapore government continues to regulate, subsidize, and, most recently, renovate the 114 hawker centres sprinkled around the island with a combined total of 6000 stalls. Opened even earlier in 1951, Tiong Bahru Market & Food Centre currently has 83 food stalls, which have been recently renovated with lifts, escalators, and bigger stalls.[7]

However, the UNESCO inscription comes at a time when the hawker food trade is at risk. The average age of hawkers is fifty-nine, and more elderly hawkers are retiring, threatening their specialized food trades. Rising costs are making the business financially less feasible, and the steep learning curve and physically demanding work make it even less appealing to the educated younger generations. Health concerns and demands for more comfortable seating further deter diners. There is a strong preference for international foods, sit-down restaurants, and modern cafes. American BBQ, Taiwanese Bubble Tea, and Korean ramen are among the latest trends alongside the global favourite McDonald's. Even with the latest national and international recognition of traditional hawker centres, there is the reality that Singaporeans, especially the youth, may not be interested in dining there. So, within this generational shift, what does the UNESCO inscription mean? How does an intangible heritage like hawker food remain 'living'? What is being preserved?

Rising Hawkers: Innovation in Food Preparation, Branding, and Marketing

One answer lies in the next hawker generation as younger family members take on their family's hawker stalls. They often seek to preserve the family dish, but sometimes innovate new ones. A highly publicized example comes from the Netflix documentary, *Singapore Street Food* (2019), by the creators of *Chef's Table*, which features Aisha Hashim, a thirty-six-year-old next-generation hawker who continues her family's Malay food stall. The specialty is *putu piring*, steamed rice cakes filled with *gula melaka* (palm sugar), topped with shredded coconut and fragrant pandan leaves. Aisha modernized the labour-intensive method by using machines to grind the *gula melaka* cakes and shred the coconut, speeding up the process from ten hours to two. Forming a central kitchen, Aisha began to grow the business, trucking the Malay snacks to the family stalls around the island. In the film, Singaporean food writer Evelyn Chen reflects about Aisha: 'She found a way to integrate her own ambitions while improving on the traditional methods, and that's really remarkable.'[8] In this case, the hawker food stayed the same. The familiar taste of the *putu piring* remained paramount and that convinced Aisha's parents to support her new methods. Instead, what changed was how the food was made.

This move to centralized, off-site, and mass-produced hawker food is not unlike industrial food, effectively changing the type of labour involved in being a hawker. Historically, manual labour has been the core of food vending, as hawkers have churned out hundreds of the same dishes each day to meet the volume required for profit. Skilled hands make roti crisp, roll out dough for translucent dumplings, and hand-cut curry rice, an art that is increasingly being replaced with industrial substitutes and machines. Instead, a new skill is emerging, one in technology and business.

Besides Aisha, there are other stories of next-generation hawkers who return to help run the family stall and employ innovative methods. A headline in *8 Days* reads, 'Millennial Gives Up $100k a Year Bank Job to Become Sambal Stingray Hawker'. Leaving a steady job, Zhi Jie learned the trade and recipes from his mother and, after six months, opened his own barbecue seafood hawker stall. Initially business was brisk, but slowed down, maybe 'cos the novelty of the new hawker centre wore off', he shrugs.[9] The innovation in his case was marketing and a new way of interacting with customers. Increased marketing efforts led to a steady customer clientele, and now he has taken over his mother's stall.

Indeed, branding and marketing are the 'highest priority' of young hawkers, claims food blogger Seth Lui.[10] For example, Skirt & Dirt's branding is strong, with a modern black and bright yellow design and playful burger logo, a trendy look that has been called 'hipster'. Marketing through social media is also active. A quick check on Skirt & Dirt's Facebook (their handle is clearly posted on the stall front) shows enthusiastic reviews for the Cheese Skirt Beef Burger with its 100% beef patty outsized by a larger patty or 'skirt' of Cheddar cheese. Another dish much liked is Dirt Fries, thick crinkle-cut fries piled with bacon, peppers, pickled relish, and served with cheese sauce and mayo. A distinct and craveable menu is important to compete with chain specialty burger joints on the island, such as Shake Shack and Five Guys.

Yet Skirt & Dirt's menu had to go through several transformations. Led by Fabian Tan, who previously worked as a chef for a restaurant tourism group, the stall had a difficult opening. The initial four months led to mixed reviews – soggy fries, not enough burger-to-cheese ratio, overly salty cheese – prompting Fabian to change his menu multiple times. This ability to change the direction of a business or 'pivot' may be part of the reason why the hipster stall survives beside stalls serving traditional Singaporean dishes of fish balls (fish paste seasoned with soy sauce, stock, and spring onions), *popiah* (spring rolls made of thin wheat skins and filled with cooked turnip, beansprouts, and hardboiled eggs), and chicken rice.

At the same time, I wonder at the business sense for Skirt & Dirt and other new hawkers. Integral to the identity of hawker food is being 'cheap and good food', but this makes it difficult for hawkers to sustain their livelihoods. They are unable to change government-regulated prices, and there is local resistance to any increase in price.[11] So, Michelin-starred hawker stalls still undervalue their dishes, some even less than US$2.00, effectively continuing their role to 'moderate the cost of living' as described by Singapore's National Heritage Board.[12] Yet, Skirt & Dirt's US$5.00 burger would easily go for double the amount at a restaurant. Perhaps hawker centres are just stepping stones for these new hawkers.

Hawkerpreneurs

This priority for business has given these rising hawkers a new title, hawker entrepreneurs, or 'hawkerpreneurs'. As Tarulevic emphasizes, 'What is clear is that hawkerpreneurs are not entrepreneurial hawkers; they are entrepreneurs who have become hawkers.'[13] The low rent makes for an easy entry to gain business experience, test out the menu, get some press and followers, and then move on to their own restaurant. Franchising the concept comes next, further distancing these new hawkers from their predecessors. The dream is to become like Hong Kong's Din Tai Fung.

Yet the Singapore government appears to recognize the ambition of young Singaporeans and makes that part of the appeal to draw them into the hawker culture. One such incentive is a twelve-month Work-Study Certificate in Hawkerpreneurship offered at Temasek Polytechnic, with the first class offered in March 2021.[14] Recent graduates from technical school or national service (notably excluding university graduates) can enrol in the programme to gain classroom and on-the-job training to enter the hawker profession. Part of the application includes the advertisement that hawkerpreneurs can start with one stall but may move into the café and restaurant businesses.

Hipster Hawker Centres

While Skirt & Dirt is embedded in a traditional hawker centre, there is another business model being tested at designated 'hipster' hawker centres. Consider Pasir Ris Central Hawker Centre, a dual dining concept of forty-two food stalls with traditional hawker favourites on the first floor and more eclectic hipster choices on the second floor, cheekily called Fare Ground. At Wild Olive, made-to-order Italian pasta bowls are popular, such as Sambal Seafood Spaghetti, as well as their Mushroom Rice. At Tasty Street: Our Little Red Dot, healthier Singaporean food is offered with mixed grain rice (brown & pearl), sous-vide chicken, onsen eggs, cooked-daily greens, and house-made sauces like wolfberry wine sauce and truffle hotplate tofu sauce. The friendly hawkerpreneur taking my order and preparing the food was also the owner (Figure 5). When asked how she became the owner, she said she had loved the food offered by the first owners and offered to buy it when she heard that the stall was going to close. She was quick to add that this was not her only job; she also runs other businesses.

Another hipster hawker centre, Timbre +, describes itself as a 'food park'. Graffiti and spray paint art splash over the beige-coloured walls of the original hawker centre. Bar stools, wooden tables, and industrial chairs replace hard cafeteria-style orange tables and chairs. Edgy and provocative, industrial-cool, the décor matches the progressive approach taken to the food by the hipster hawker vendors. Two Wings makes chicken wings trendy with a Salted Egg treatment, and, knowing its millennial audience, serves it on an Instagrammable wooden board. This attention to the aesthetics and origin of food are concerns largely absent in traditional hawker centres like Tiong Bahru.

No, lah: Singaporean Youths Push Back

Over an americano at an Australian café, a Singaporean millennial working in the tech industry told me that he rarely eats at hawker centres. Unhealthy food, questionable sanitation, and uncomfortable eating spaces with no air conditioning are all unappealing for business meetings and laptop work, he explains. I asked him about Zion Riverside, a newly renovated hawker centre that added bar tables with electrical outlets. He laughs, 'Too hard, the government is trying too hard.' Trying to modernize an old hawker centre to catch up with Singapore's advancement seems impossible, even a laughing matter.

Other millennials similarly push back from the government's call for new hawkers. 'No, *lah*,' one Starbucks barista told me when asked if he would consider being a hawker, the Singaporean English, or Singlish, particle emphasizing his aversion. 'Insulted,' he continued, explaining his resistance to the government pressure to take up the hawker career. While the youth do not want the hawking profession, they do buy into government rhetoric by perceiving hawker culture as 'culture', a unique 'experience,' and 'Singapore'.[15] Nor is a hawking career desired by their parents who sent them to university. Hawking is seen as a fall-back option, like being a taxi driver, for those who

Figure 5. At Pasir Ris Central Hawker Centre, a hawkerpreneur, entrepreneur turned hawker, serving healthier and house-made Singaporean food.

cannot get a better job. Headlines about millennial hawkers such as, 'Covid 19 Upended His NY Internship, so He is Learning to Make Chicken Rice in Shunfu', frame hawker food as a last resort.[16] The UNESCO inscription may help change the low status of hawking, yet pragmaticism prevails over sentimentalism, highlighting the gap between Singapore youth's career aspirations and their professed passion for hawker culture.

It is not just the youth that push back to these changes in hawking. Older hawkers see this new breed of hawkers and their innovative food as threatening the hawker environment and resulting in a loss of heritage. Soya bean stall hawker Low Teck Seng remarks that he offers a sense of familiarity to his customers. He recognizes their order and knows their names, creating a relationship that makes the food court more than just a place to buy and eat food. (Yet, this feeling of familiarity is not unlike one's favourite café or corner Starbucks.) Appeasing the older generation, Singapore's UNESCO nomination video gives reverence to past hawkers who embody 'culture', 'legacy', and 'Singapore'. How do hawkerpreneurs fit within this image? Can they? *Should* they?

Leaning into the Future

The UNESCO label gives hawker food a certain aura and recognition at local, national, and international levels. There are commercial and ideological reasons to promote hawker food as a statement of identity, national pride, demand for public attention, and social or cultural capital. There is also the attempt to preserve something, which is elusive in a Singapore that has undergone rapid transformation. The rising hawkers are trying to preserve the hawker culture, which has been identified as 'Singapore'. Yet what is Singapore keeps changing. Food too keeps changing. Historically, immigration, global trade, and technology have made hawking an occupation that has never been stable.

The production of food was traditionally the only concern of a hawker; now, new hawkers must be concerned with communicating their food and brand to their customers. The model of a food worker is not a mundane cook or ordinary food service worker but an entrepreneur. One must be 'innovative' and digitally savvy as a food vendor, even if that role is still venerated as traditional.

Whether and how long the UNESCO inscription remains valid, only time will tell. As people change, so must the ways they eat. For food to be 'living heritage', it must be eaten. Rising hawkers are using their imagination to keep traditional dishes current or are inventing new ones for the next Singaporean generation whose palates are increasingly sophisticated, globally informed, and health oriented. Keeping traditional food appetizing to the next generation – keeping it as an everyday food – is perhaps the best nomination a national cuisine can get.

Notes

1   Nicole Tarulevicz, 'Hawkerpreneurs: Hawkers, Entrepreneurship, and Reinventing Street Food in Singapore', *Forum: Journal of Business Management,* 58.3 (May–June 2019), 291-302 (p. 291).

2 *Somebody Feed Phil: Singapore,* dir. by John Bedolis, written and presented by Philip Rosenthal, Season 4, Episode 3 (Netflix, 30 October 2020).
3 Alvin Chua, 'Tiong Bahru', *Singapore Infopedia,* 2010 <https://eresources.nlb.gov.sg/infopedia/articles/SIP_1700_2010-08-11.html> [accessed 3 May 2021]
4 'Intangible Cultural Heritage', *UNESCO* <https://ich.unesco.org/en> [accessed 2 May 2021]
5 'Hawker Culture in Singapore, Community Dining and Culinary Practices in a Multicultural Urban Context', Nomination File No. 01568 for Inscription in 2020 on the Representation List of the Intangible Cultural Heritage of Humanity, UNESCO, 2020 <https://ich.unesco.org/en/RL/hawker-culture-in-singapore-community-dining-and-culinary-practices-in-a-multicultural-urban-context-01568> [accessed 21 December 2020]
6 Nicole Tarulevicz, *Eating Her Curries and Kway: A Cultural History of Singapore* (Champaign, IL: University of Illinois Press, 2013), p. 33.
7 Tiong Bahru Market's original name was Seng Poh Road Market, which was an immediate success for residents during the rapid urbanization after the Second World War. Historical information about hawker centres was gathered for the UNESCO nomination and posted on OurSGHeritage website. Various communities, groups, and individuals were asked to contribute letters of support, including a letter by hawkers from Tiong Bahru Market & Food Centre (<https://www.oursgheritage.gov.sg/wp-content/uploads/2019/07/FMAS-Hawkers-Associations-Jul-2019.pdf> [accessed 2 May 2021]).
8 *Street Food: Asia, Singapore,* dir. by David Gelb and Brian McGinn (Netflix, 26 April 2019). Local reaction was polarized, with some critiquing the Singapore episode as lacking in its representation of local hawker culture. Putu piring was particularly critiqued for being featured as it is a lesser-known Singaporean dish. However, the documentary appeared to emphasize the people themselves more than the food.
9 Jieying Yip, 'Millennial Gives Up $100k A Year Bank Job to Become Sambal Stingray Hawker', *8 Days*, 21 March 2021 <https://www.8days.sg/eatanddrink/newsandopening/millennial-gives-up-100k-a-year-bank-job-to-become-sambal-14458626> [accessed 2 May 2021]
10 'The Big Read: With UNESCO Listing in Sight, will New Breed of "Hawkerpreneurs" Rejuvenate or Erode Hawker Culture?', *Channel News Asia*, 7 December 2020 <https://www.channelnewsasia.com/news/singapore/the-big-read-with-unesco-listing-in-sight-will-new-breed-of-13707580> [accessed 2 May 2021]
11 Annie Tan, 'Commentary: Hawker Food isn't What it Used to Be. And It's Partially Our Fault', *Channel News Asia*, 22 November 2020 <https://www.channelnewsasia.com/news/singapore/hawker-food-singapore-unesco-culture-heritage-list-local-13600612?cid=h3_referral_inarticlelinks_24082018_cna> [accessed 2 May 2021]
12 National Heritage Board, 'Hawker Culture in Singapore', *OurSGHeritage*, 11 February 2018 <https://www.oursgheritage.gov.sg/hawker-culture-in-singapore/> [accessed 2 May 2021]
13 Tarulevicz, 'Hawkerpreneurs', p. 298.
14 'Work-Study Certificate in Hawkerpreneurship', *Temasek Polytechnic*, <https://www.tp.edu.sg/wsphawkerpreneurship#application-entry-req> [accessed 2 May 2021}
15 Daphne Wong and Jocelin Yeo Zhi Ling, 'Understanding Singapore Youth's Perceptions on Hawker Culture', *Pioneer Road: Journal of Undergraduate Research* (Language and Communication Centre, School of Humanities, Nanyang Technological University, 2021).
16 Chua Mui Hoong, 'Covid-19 Upended His NY Internship, so He is Learning to Make Chicken Rice in Shunfu', *The Straits Times*, 20 November 2020 <https://www.straitstimes.com/opinion/the-chicken-rice-seller-and-his-apprentice> [accessed 2 May 2021]

Persian *Tahdig*: A Canvas for Culinary Imagination, Innovation, and Artistry

Nader Mehravari

Persian *tahdig*: the most coveted treat at a Persian meal – the jewel of Persian cooking, or the holy grail of Persian cooking, or the *pièce de résistance* of Persian cooking – is the delicious, buttery, golden, crunchy layer formed at the bottom of the rice pot (Figure 1). For many, however, *tahdig* is much more.

Tahdig is often fought over by family members and guests during meals. It can be life-altering for some first timers, spark fierce competition among Persian home cooks, and disappear seconds after it appears on the dinner table. *Tahdig* has been praised by lovers of Persian food around the world in such eminent newspapers as the *Wall Street Journal*, the *Guardian*, and the *New York Times*; detailed in such culinary guides as *Cooks Illustrated, BBC Good Food, Saveur*, and *Bon Appetit*; discussed on National Public Radio (NPR) and British Broadcasting Corporation (BBC) programmes; seen on such TV networks as Netflix and the Food Network; and studied in international academic forums like the Oxford Symposium on Food and Cookery.

Literally translated, the Persian word *tahdig* (in Persian: ته دیگ) means 'bottom of the pot'. The classic process of making *tahdig* involves long-grain rice going through the stages of being soaked in salted water for several hours, up to a day; parcooked in salted boiling water for several minutes; drained and rinsed with cold water; and then slowly steamed in a buttered pot over low heat, covered tightly, for the hour or two it takes the *tahdig* to form at the bottom of the pot.

In more recent years, though, *tahdig* has become much more than the crunchy layer of rice at the bottom of the pot. Persian cooks – both home and commercial cooks – have

Figure 1. Pieces of tahdig served on the same platter as the rest of the rice from the pot. All illustrated dishes prepared and photographed by the author.

Persian Tahdig: A Canvas for Culinary Imagination

introduced imaginative practices into the process of making *tahdig*. These creative approaches range anywhere from more efficient ways of cooking other elements of the meal (meat and vegetables), integrated with the *tahdig* in the bottom of the same pot, to using more pliable versions of *tahdig* as a bread substitute to make a range of sandwiches, to using the *tahdig* layer to create beautiful edible food art. This paper discusses some of these conscious and imaginative practices.

Historical Background

Some of the earliest references to *tahdig* in Persian cookery date back to the mid-1800s. A translation of an early Persian cookbook, published as a pamphlet in India in 1939, refers to *tahdig* preparation.[1] A recent academic article finds the existence of the word *tahdig* as early as 1848, in the language of Persian people living by the Caspian Sea, where high-quality rice is grown.[2]

Information in these references is consistent with other historical narratives about the origination of *tahdig* and its entry into Persian cookery. *Tahdig* had been present on the royal menus of the fourth and fifth kings of Iran's Qajar Dynasty who ruled the Persian Empire in the 1800s. According to these stories, the servants who worked in the king's residence had their meals using the leftovers after the chef had served the king's table. One day, the servants started arguing loudly over who would get the crunchy rice at the bottom of the pot. When the chef was asked about the commotion, the story of the crunchy rice eventually reached the king, and he ordered that some of it be brought to him. The king enjoyed eating this crunchy, flavourful rice, and ordered that this be served to him in the future as an appetizer before the regular rice that accompanied the main course.[3] These narratives have been confirmed in scholarly works documenting the social life of the period: by the late nineteenth century, *tahdig* had become part of the diet of high-ranking and well-to-do families in Iran.[4]

Two of the earliest cookbooks intended for Iranian urban housewives, written in Persian and published in the early 1900s, include explicit instructions for making *tahdig*. The first of these cookbooks was *Tabākhi-é-Neshāt* (in Persian: طباخی نشاط, literally *Cheerful Cooking*) which was published around the time of the First World War by a woman whose Qajar honorary name was 'Neshāt-al-dowleh' (in Persian: نشاط الدوله, literally, 'the delight of the state').[5] She was the granddaughter of the French adventurer Jules Richard (1816-1891) who served in high Iranian state offices in the mid-1800s.[6] In her cookbook, Neshāt-al-dowleh, whose formal name was Josephine Richard, provides instructions for making basic *tahdig* as well as saffron, yoghurt, and tomato paste variations. The second cookbook, published in 1938, is part of a three-volume set *Āsayeh-é-Zendegāni* (in Persian: آسایش زندگانی, literally, *Comfort of Life*) by J. Tara. In its second volume, the author provides instructions for making basic *tahdig* and for its presentation at a reception.[7]

Imaginative Ways of Taking Tahdig Above and Beyond

The rest of this paper presents a sampling of imaginative ways Persian cooks have taken traditional *tahdig* above and beyond its original form, shape, or purpose. These samplings collectively illustrate some of the drivers and techniques that have resulted in the associated innovations including:

- Creating crunchy dishes other than the original rice-centric *tahdigs*
- Reducing the time and the number of vessels required to make *tahdig*
- Facilitating the incorporation of meat and vegetables
- Meeting dietary restrictions and preferences resulting in, for example, the desire to use more pliable layers of crunchy rice as a substitute for bread
- Satisfying the increasing craving for other (non-rice) crispy and crunchy accompaniments
- Maximizing the amount of *tahdig* generated per cup of rice
- Searching for additional opportunities for Persian cooks to demonstrate artistry and skill
- Gaining finer control of the levels of moisture, oil, and heat used to make *tahdig*
- Using specialty electric rice cookers designed explicitly for Persian rice dishes
- Working with the increased availability of alternative cooking vessels

Matters of Efficiency

Incorporating other components of a complete meal (e.g. meat and vegetables) into the process of *tahdig* making is a clever approach for reducing the required effort, time, and number of vessels used to prepare a meal. In these instances, relatively thin (1 to 2 centimetres) pieces of meat and/or vegetables are arranged at the bottom of the pot – covering all or some of the surface of the bottom of the pot – before parboiled rice is added. Such techniques integrate the cooking of potatoes, eggplants, ribs, or shrimp with the *tahdig* itself (Figures 2-5).

Matters of Texture and Flavour

Satisfying the ever-increasing popularity and craving for crispy, crunchy accompaniments to a meal, without the need for such traditional techniques as deep-frying, pan-frying, or panini griddling, can be achieved by incorporating the relevant ingredients into the *tahdig* making process. These approaches create crunchy flatbread, chicken wings, oriental post stickers, and even lettuce, on the bottom of the rice pot (Figures 6-9). These techniques also enable new texture and flavour combinations not always possible with traditional methods. For example, a chicken wing *tahdig* provides two distinct texture and flavour combinations. One side is golden brown, crispy, with salty and buttery flavours (salted butter having been used on the bottom of the pot) while the other side is soft and moist, capturing the flavours present in the rice.

Matters of Technology

Good *tahdig* making can be time-consuming – as much as ninety minutes to two hours of total cooking. It also requires a lot of practice – good *tahdig* making has traditionally been a measure of an experienced Persian home cook. There are electric Persian rice cookers specifically designed to form basic *tahdig* along with fluffy Persian rice (Figure 10). These specialized rice cookers can produce good, simple *tahdig* within one hour with very little active cooking time (Figure 11).

Tahdig is often fought over by family members and guests during meals because the traditional process does not produce very much of it. Moreover, even under situations where there might be enough *tahdig* for one meal – for example, where there are only two or three diners at the table – there will be lots of leftover fluffy rice. Under the best circumstances, a 20-centimetre-wide pot can generate at most a 20-centimeter disk of *tahdig* from three to four cups of dry rice. In other words, the *tahdig*-to-rice ratio is relatively small. Another advantage of the specialized Persian rice cookers is that they can drastically increase the *tahdig*-to-rice ratio. For example, the author can generate a 17-centimetre-wide disk of good *tahdig* while using only three quarters of a cup of dry rice (Figure 12).

Figure 2. Potato tahdig.

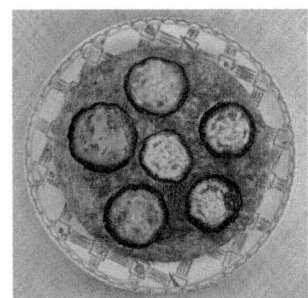

Figure 3. Eggplant tahdig.

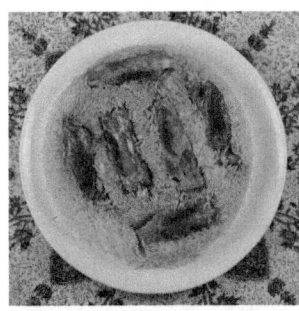

Figure 4. Pork rib tahdig.

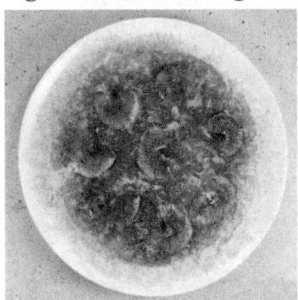

Figure 5. Shrimp tahdig.

Figure 6. Flat bread tahdig.

Figure 7. Chicken wing tahdig.

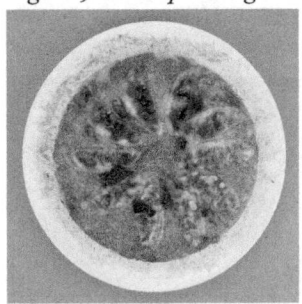

Figure 8. Oriental pot sticker tahdig.

Figure 9. Lettuce tahdig.

Figure 10. Persian rice cooker that generates good tahdig.

Matters of Innovation

By controlling the moisture, oil, heat, and cooking time more precisely in the *tahdig* making process, Persian cooks are able to generate somewhat pliable layers of crunchy rice that can serve as a substitute for bread. These less brittle forms of *tahdig* can then be used to make a range of sandwich-like dishes such as rolls and wraps (Figure 13), taco-like dishes filled with hot or cold fillings (Figure 14), and hamburger-like dishes (Figure 15). Such innovative creations not only serve those with dietary restrictions or personal preferences who want to reduce or eliminate bread from their diet, but also those that seek additional ways to satisfy their craving for *tahdig*.

Matters of Artistry

Persian cooks have been known for elaborate and fanciful ways of decorating their dishes, particularly for special guests and occasions. Recently, the *tahdig*-making process has come to provide yet another opportunity for Persian cooks to demonstrate their skills in creating

Figure 11 (left). Rice and tahdig from a Persian rice cooker. Figure 12 (middle). 'Maximum Tahdig'. Figure 13 (right). Tahdig used instead of bread to make a wrap-type sandwich.

  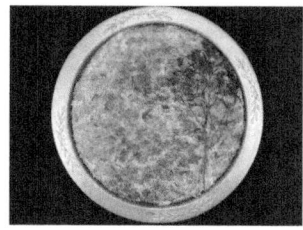

Figure 14 (left). Tahdig used instead of tortilla to make a taco-like dish. Figure 15 (middle). Tahdig used instead of a bun to make a hamburger. Figure 16 (right). Tahdig art mimicking a landscape painting.

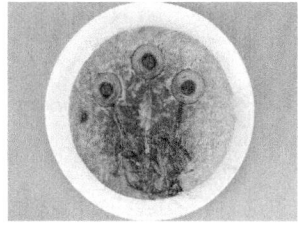  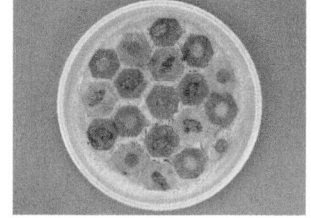

Figure 17 (left). Tahdig art mimicking a flower painting. Figure 18 (middle). Tahdig art creating a lattice pattern. Figure 19 (right). Tahdig art creating a hexagonal pattern.

edible art. A relatively simple set of examples of such *tahdig* range from mimicking paintings (Figures 16 and 17), to generating geometric patterns (Figures 18-20), to taking advantage of natural patterns in plants and vegetables (Figures 21-24), to surprising one's Valentine (Figure 25). Some of this *tahdig* art goes above and beyond just being artistic creations. For example, *tahdig* can be made to resemble popular board game like Settlers of Katan (Figure 19). *Tahdig* can even become an educational tool to teach young children, for example, to identify the leaves of different kinds of herbs (Figure 24). Interested readers can see such sophisticated *tahdig* artistry by searching online with the keywords '*tahdig* art'.

Matters of Kindness

This sampling of the imaginative ways in which contemporary Persian cooks have taken traditional *tahdig* beyond its original form, shape, and/or purpose are relatively new – especially considering how long *tahdig* has been part of the landscape of Persian cookery. There is, however, another imaginative way that Persian cooks have used *tahdig* that has been around for a long time – long enough that it is almost a forgotten practice.

Before there were non-stick cooking vessels, *tahdig* had to be scraped out of the bottom of the pot in small or large pieces. This process always left *tahdig* crumbs

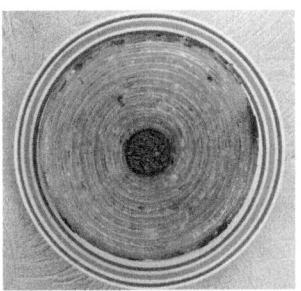 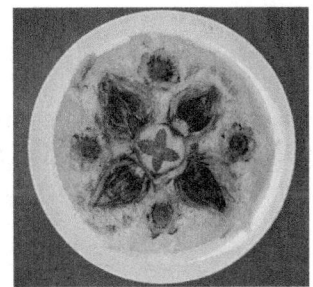 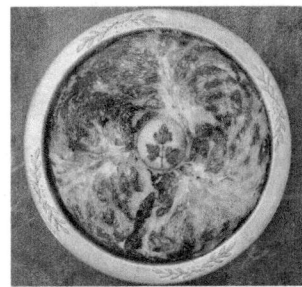

Figure 20 (left). Tahdig art using bucatini noodles to create a circular pattern. Figure 21 (middle). Tahdig art taking advantage of the natural patterns of fennel bulbs. Figure 22 (right). Tahdig art taking advantage of the natural patterns in cabbage leaves.

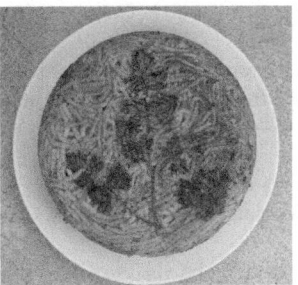  

Figure 23 (left). Tahdig art taking advantage of the natural patterns of parsley leaves. Figure 24 (middle). Tahdig art taking advantage of natural patterns in the leaves of different popular herbs. Figure 25 (right). A Valentine's Day tahdig.

(individual crunchy rice kernels) at the bottom of the pot. Some home cooks, including my maternal grandmother, would throw a fistful of cooked rice onto the bottom of the pot to capture both the *tahdig* crumbs and the remaining butter from the bottom of the pot. The cook would then put a few tablespoonsful of the mixture in the palm of one hand, close their fist, and form an oblong-shaped, delightful snack approximately 2 centimetres wide and 4 centimetres long (Figure 26). In Persian, the common name for this rare creation is '*Changāli*' (in Persian: چنگالی, literally, something formed by closing fingers towards the palm of the hand to form a fist). If there were any *Changāli* made, the cook would come out of the kitchen to the table after the rest of the meal had been served to give these special treats to her or his 'special people' at the table, such as the younger members of the family. Since there would only be at most two or three, these *Changāli* are a double sign of love and caring of the cook – for not letting anything go to waste and for sharing treats with the most loved ones at the table.

Figure 26. *Changāli* – special *tahdig* crumb treats.

Closing

This paper has been a broad but not exhaustive look at various ways Persian cooks have utilized the foundational techniques involved in making *tahdig* to imagine and create other innovative delights, enabling *tahdig* to serve as a canvas for culinary imagination, innovation, artistry, and more.

Notes

1. *The Khwan Niamut: or, Nawab's Domestic Cookery*, ed. by David E. Schoonover (Iowa City: University of Iowa Press, 1992), p. 27.
2. Habib Borjian, 'Neṣāb-e Ṭabari Revisited: A Māzandarāni Glossary from the 19th Century', *Acta Orientalia Academiae Scientiarum Hungaricae*, 63.1 (March 2020), pp. 36-62.
3. Wikimedia Foundation, 'Tahdig', *Persian Wikipedia*, 7 February 2021 <https://fa.wikipedia.org/wiki/ته‌دیگ%E2%80%8C> [accessed 17 May 2021]; 'صاردات گی‌ده‌د‌ا ایرانی,' Tasnim News Agency, 24 June 2018 <https://www.tasnimnews.com/fa/news/1397/04/03/1759266/صاردات‌ه‌ت‌د‌گی‌ا‌یرانی> [accessed 17 May 2021]
4. Abdollah Mostofi, *The Administrative and Social History of the Qajar Period: The Story of My Life. Vol. 1: From Agha Mohammad Khan to Naser ed-Din Shah*, trans. by Nayer Mostofi Glenn (Costa Mesa, CA: Mazda Publishers, 1997), pp. 116, 162.
5. Josephine Richard ('Neshāt-al-doleh'), *Tabakhi-é-Neshāt* (Tehran: Mozaferi Publishers [1920s]).
6. Bert G. Fragner, 'Zur Erforschung der kulinarischen Kultur Irans', *Die Welt des Islams*, 23/24 (1984), 320-360.
7. J. Tara, *Āsayeh-é-Zendegāni – Bakh-é Dovom: Tabākhi-é Irāni va Farangi* (Tehran: Tab'i Ketab Publishers, 1938), p. 71.

'Broiling is the poetry of cooking': The Imaginative Symbolism of Gridirons and Broiling in Nineteenth-Century British Food Writing

Lindsay Middleton

In a *London Magazine* review of William Kitchiner's cookbook *Apicius Redivivus, or, The Cook's Oracle* (1817), the reviewer describes broiling food: 'The lyre-like shape of the instrument on which it is performed, and the brisk and pleasant sounds that arise momentarily, are rather musical than culinary.'[1] The instrument being described is the gridiron, and this review captures how British nineteenth-century recipes and food writing viewed the gridiron as more than a cooking implement. Not simply a grid of parallel iron bars with a handle, held over the fire to broil meat, the gridiron is elevated in nineteenth-century writing to become an imaginative cultural emblem which symbolized multiple things explored in this paper, including literary and cultural history, British national identity, and masculinity.

While histories of food and the kitchen from scholars like Andrea Broomfield and Sara Pennell outline how cultural and social changes altered the way foods were cooked, eaten, and thought of, there has been less attention paid to how food writing turned kitchen implements into symbols which expressed those changes.[2] In terms of culinary writing, critics including Susan Zlotnick, Margaret Beetham, and Natalie Kapetanios Meir have recognized the role cookbooks played in integrating ideologies like imperialism, domesticity, and cultural taste into the nineteenth-century home.[3] This scholarship, however, tends to focus on the discussions cookbook authors included in the paratextual written material that surrounds recipes, rather than considering the literary strategies at play within recipes themselves. This paper builds upon existing scholarship by arguing that recipes enlisted cultural discourses and literary techniques to interpret changing foodways via interactions with culinary implements. Taking the gridiron as a case study, I show how gridirons were depicted imaginatively in recipes. In turn, I unravel the wider discussions recipes engaged in, highlighting that perceptions of culinary technologies and culinary writings are both inherently imaginative. That is, the meanings ascribed to kitchen implements and the written ways those meanings are communicated are dependent on acts of imagination: the creation of stories which give significance to the humblest parts of domestic life.

The evidence my paper draws upon is gathered from a survey of thirty nineteenth-century recipes which address broiling food on the gridiron.[4] This process was prevalent in cookbooks, and typically involved holding a gridiron over a hot fire, greasing its bars with fat, placing a cut of meat like a chop on it, and turning the meat on the gridiron until cooked. Paying attention to the tropes common to broiling recipes, as well as the literary techniques like allusion and satire they employ, allows for a nuanced understanding of how they function as individual texts, seemingly written to instruct readers how to broil food. It also illuminates the places where authors gesture outside the recipe to other texts or sources. This happens in one of two ways. First, within a recipe the author may refer to other sections within the overall text, be that periodical or cookbook, as when Eliza Acton writes: 'the fire, as we have already said in the general directions for broiling [...], must be strong and clear'.[5] This directs the reader to another point in the cookbook, so they gain a complete understanding of the broiling process. Second, authors explicitly or implicitly allude to external sources, items, texts, or historical figures in their recipes. This could be as simple as Alexis Soyer suggesting that 'a little Harvey's or Soyer's sauce is an improvement' in his recipe for broiled mushrooms and steering the reader towards the purchase of a condiment.[6] Yet allusions can also be as far-reaching as Isabella Beeton's lobster recipe in *The Book of Household Management* (1861), where she notes that when 'this fish was to be served for the table, among the ancients, it was opened lengthwise, and filled with a gravy composed of coriander and pepper. It was then put on the gridiron and slowly cooked'.[7] Beeton's instructions are infused with historical resonance, so the reader following the recipe pictures themselves dining with 'the ancients' and the recipe envisions a world, and time, beyond the page. In this paper I focus on the latter form of expansion, highlighting instances in broiling recipes where authors employ allusion or engage with historicity. I utilize evidence from multiple recipes and cookbooks throughout and focus a portion of my paper on an article called 'Chops' from a periodical edited by Charles Dickens, *All the Year Round*, to reveal how gridirons became embedded in nineteenth-century culinary imagination.

Broiling's Fading Functionality

As Beeton's 'ancient' broiled lobster suggests, what emerges from a close literary analysis of recipes is that nineteenth-century writers frequently used food and cooking to situate themselves within culinary and literary histories. These discussions often referred to how the materials and tools used for cooking changed over time. Food writers created teleological histories whereby changes to cooking demonstrated their distance from or connection to the past. In another section of *Household Management*, for instance, Beeton contrasts the use of fire cookery by the Ancient Greeks with the 'simplicity of the primitive ages', declaring that 'the use of fire, as an instrument of cookery, must have coincided with this [Greek] invention of bread'.[8] The use of heat and 'instruments of cookery' are framed by Beeton as things that distance Greeks and nineteenth-century readers from 'primitive' peoples, which speaks to a proliferating self-consciousness about food as a means of cultural separation from the past. Similarly, when discussing baking, Alexis Soyer describes the 'air-tight chambers, called ovens, the best of which have the same form as in the time of the Egyptians', while Arthur Gay Payne declares that global food trade is 'the history of civilisation itself' and asks 'how our ancestors did so well without' tinned foods, in the introduction to *The Housekeeper's Guide to Preserved Meats, Fruits, Vegetables, &c* (1880).[9] Nineteenth-century recipes and food writing are peppered with historical comparisons, and cooking and kitchen implements thereby came to symbolize a person's place in civilization.

When nineteenth-century recipes are concerned with the gridiron, their literary workings take on an intriguing temporal nuance. Gridirons had been cooked on in Britain since at least the fifteenth century, but during the nineteenth century open-fire cookery was gradually replaced for much of the population by enclosed ranges and stoves.[10] These ranges required money and space, meaning they were not a viable option for the poor and working classes or those in rented accommodation. But when they could be afforded, ranges were more efficient in terms of fuel and heat use than hearth cookery; they directed heat around ovens and stovetops so it was not lost into the kitchen.[11] In terms of broiling, seventeen of the thirty recipes that make up the sample for this paper mention how 'bright' and 'fierce' a broiling fire had to be. If the fire was not hot enough it would smoke, charring the meat. Burning a fire until it was 'fierce' required large amounts of fuel for adequate heat, and the author of *Mrs Beeton's Everyday Cookery and Housekeeping Book* (c.1900) noted that broiling was 'not an economical mode of cooking, as a great deal of fuel is needed for a good broiling fire, the meat loses weight, and only the best kinds can be submitted to this process with satisfactory results'.[12] 'Losing weight' refers to fat which dripped from the meat through the gridiron bars and into the flames, resulting in the loss of valuable flavour and nutrients, as well as undesirable smoke.[13] The expense required for broiling and the potential for food waste meant cooking on gridirons became increasingly uneconomic as the nineteenth century progressed. Indeed, in an article called 'Grilling and Devilling' in the *Girl's Own Paper* (1899) Dora de Blaquiére wrote:

> I have taken the trouble to look in the dictionary for the word 'grill,' and I find it is derived from the French word 'grille' – a grate or gridiron. But to-day, in point of fact, grilling is rarely performed in this manner, few people having the gridiron; and if not done in the oven, it is performed in an open frying pan.
>
> I have begun with this piece of information because some of my readers may say on seeing the word, 'Oh, we can't grill! We have no means of using a gridiron!'[14]

While this refers to grilling rather than broiling, and the notion that the author had to look up 'grill' adds a satirical tone, the publication of this piece during the last year of the nineteenth century signifies that cooking on gridirons was becoming less common. Here, kitchen implements still signified advancement from the past, but the gridiron was depicted as a primitive tool that was being left behind.

Despite their implied decline, however, gridirons remained prevalent in cookbooks and recipes until the century's end – even cookbooks aimed at middle-class readers who probably owned ranges. But if using gridirons was so impractical, why did they keep appearing in texts? And what else did broiling on gridirons signify that made it a lasting process? Pennell suggests that '[f]or every domestic manual cautiously welcoming technological change in the mid-Victorian kitchen […] there was an influential defender of the flame, who trumpeted the taste as well as the traditions of food cooked over an open fire'.[15] The notions of taste and tradition are pertinent to the gridiron, and broiling recipes show that gridirons were imaginatively woven into numerous traditions which the rest of this paper explores.

Gridirons, Historicity, and Imagination

In his popular cookbook, *The Modern Housewife, or, Ménagère* (1849), Alexis Soyer includes a section on broiling which immediately engages with historicity: 'Broiling is, without doubt, the earliest and most primitive mode of cookery, it being that which would present itself to man in a state of nature. It is one of the easiest parts of cookery, and therefore should be done well.'[16]

Like Beeton, Soyer uses 'primitive' to describe a cooking process. Here, however, it is not a disparaging remark indicating lack of civility but instead highlights how longstanding broiling has been in culinary history. This timeline connects the nineteenth-century reader to what is depicted as a masculine history of self-sufficiency through the reference to 'man in a state of nature', evoking images of ancient man cooking their quarry over open fires. The second part of Soyer's evaluation refers to broiling's simplicity. By simultaneously emphasizing the age and ease of broiling, Soyer implies that because broiling has been done for centuries it must be a straightforward process.

Other nineteenth-century recipes, however, posit that broiling was not easy. In the fourth edition of *The Cook's Oracle* (1822) William Kitchiner wrote in his broiled rump steaks recipe that '[i]t requires more practice and care than is generally supposed to do Steaks to a nicety; and for want of these little attentions, this very common dish, which every body [sic] is supposed capable of dressing, seldom comes to table in perfection'.[17] This is a revision from the first edition, which lacks the statement about practice and care, meaning Kitchiner has expanded his instructions between cookbook editions to emphasize how difficult broiling is. Then, in an edition of *Warne's Model Cookery* published in 1890, the author Mary Jewry writes that 'much care, niceness, and skill are required to broil properly', and so even seventy years on, cookbooks were still warning readers that broiling was not uncomplicated.[18] In an article called 'Leaves from the Mahogany Tree' in *All the Year Round* (1868), Charles Dickens writes that 'Broiling, to tell the truth, however, requires no common mind […] a thousand impish difficulties surround the broiler'.[19] These references to skill, intellect, and instinct highlight the challenges that faced the cook attempting to broil on a gridiron. Meat burnt if it stayed over the fire too long; it stuck to the gridiron bars if they were not rubbed well with fat; dripping fat caused smoke that marred the meat's taste; and, if a gridiron was not closely monitored, it only took seconds to ruin a dish. Indeed, the fact that instructions for broiling were so prevalent in nineteenth-century cookbooks accents that it was difficult, despite being longstanding. The precarious nature of cooking on the gridiron was perhaps another reason their popularity faded over the nineteenth century. But regardless of whether authors thought it was easy or difficult, it is telling that their discussions of broiling and gridirons repeatedly engaged with historicity, demonstrated by Soyer's primitive man. In most nineteenth-century recipes, however, this was not just a general history of cooking but a distinctly British history.

In 'Chops', published in May 1869, Dickens plays with familiar recipe tropes to simultaneously illuminate and poke fun at the significance ascribed to broiled meat in nineteenth-century food writing. Unlike cookbook recipes which are typically numbered blocks of text, or separated by line spacing, this recipe is part of the article's continuous prose. While it is a functional recipe, containing instructions on how to select and cut a chop, attend a fire and service your gridiron, it is clearly written to entertain. The recipe contains satirical jibes and comic instructions, as when Dickens declares it 'is generally a dangerous thing to touch the fire during cooking', and 'The cook that would turn a chop by sticking a fork into it, and so letting out all its most delicious gravy, ought to be treated in a precisely similar manner, and then broiled over a slow fire'.[20] These farcical remarks are woven throughout instructions that otherwise read as if they have been lifted directly from a cookbook. For instance, Dickens notes that 'our chop should be put down over a bright, clear, and somewhat fierce fire', mimicking the language used in serious broiling recipes, as when Beeton writes that 'the cook must have a bright, clear fire'.[21] Sometimes Dickens intentionally contradicts himself. He remarks that cooks are 'not to let a drop more of these doubly valuable juices escape us than is absolutely unavoidable', but later tells the reader to make sure the 'gridiron is placed well slanting forward, so the fat may trickle along the bars and drop into the fire away from the chop'.[22] This latter instruction is in direct opposition to Dickens's other mentions of fat, and to most broiling recipes. Kitchiner writes that 'Gridirons should be made concave, and terminate in a trough to catch the Gravy and keep the Fat from dropping into the fire and making a smoke, which will spoil the Broil'.[23] Dickens's playful inversion of the typical broiling recipe makes a mockery of the detailed, even pedantic instructions that are recycled and repeated between cookbooks. But something needs to be culturally resonant to be laughed at, and so by satirizing these features Dickens draws attention to the literary patterns that recipes rely upon for functionality. Recipe writers created and utilized a recognizable culinary vocabulary that was suited to their context. A nineteenth-century reader would know that a 'bright' fire referred to the fierceness of flame, and that dripping fat was to be avoided. It was these tropes and writing traditions that gave Dickens the material for pastiche, and the article that surrounds the recipe similarly plays upon the common discourses that surrounded broiling, foregrounding literary and culinary history.

Striking intertextual references and allusions dominate Dickens's 'Chops' article. He opens it with an exchange between Portia, Antonio, and Bassanio from Shakespeare's *The Merchant of Venice*. Situating Shakespeare's characters in London, Dickens places them in 'the coffee-room of the Cock, in Fleet-street' and has them ordering broiled chops.[24] This allusion sets the tone for a discussion of chops that transcends culinary boundaries and transforms the chop from a cut of meat into a national emblem.[25] Dickens then satirizes Shakespeare's characters, writing that 'Portia is unhappily in delicate health – indeed, she never quite recovered from the fright that horrid Jew gave her'.[26] This refers to Portia's encounter with Shylock, when he demands 'a pound of flesh' from Antonio, but characterizes Portia as a sensitive, delicate woman.[27] Dickens uses bodily descriptions to draw comparisons between broiled chops and the mutilation that nearly befalls Antonio in the play, writing that 'the bare mention of' chops 'had frozen the very marrow in Antonio's bones, and curdled every drop of blood in his veins'.[28] Intriguingly, one of the first mention of gridirons in the English language was in *The South English Legendary* published in 1290, where a 'gredire' was cited as a torture device.[29] Dickens therefore takes up the correlation between cooking meat over flames and human torture, and through these subtle yet grotesque allusions to a classic British play, highlights the power food and cooking have in the culinary and literary imagination as something that can instil pleasure and fear in equal parts.

Through his allusion to Shakespeare and mention of identifiable London eateries, Dickens turns broiled chops into a symbol which is both imbued in literary history and framed as an integral part of life in nineteenth-century London. Indeed, though the reference is comical – the idea of Bassanio and Antonio eating chops on Fleet Street in the 1860s is bizarre – it sets the tone for the rest of the essay, which discusses the broiled chop as 'the alpha and the omega, the first and the last, the best and the worst of British dishes'.[30] In keeping with the satirical overtone there is a touch of self-mockery here, as Dickens's repetitive phrasing is reminiscent of 'it was the best of times, it was the worst of times' from *A Tale of Two Cities*.[31] What is pertinent, however, is that this entertainment value uses the cultural ubiquity of broiled chops as its imaginative currency. Readers in 1860s London and wider Britain were so familiar with broiled chops that this comic accentuation of their national resonances would have been amusing. The gag would not operate, however, if broiled chops were not viewed as culturally and nationally symbolizing 'Britishness' in the first place. By relocating characters from a play written and set in sixteenth-century Venice to London, and having them order broiled chops, Dickens is invoking 'the taste as well as the traditions of food cooked over an open fire' to return to Pennell.[32] Though *The Merchant of Venice* had an Italian setting, it was written by Britain's most famous playwright, and by merging the cultural cachet of Shakespeare's name with London's chophouses, Dickens emphasizes that British eaters were consuming a food that has been part of Britain's culinary identity for centuries.

The satirical tone that accompanies Dickens's description perhaps implies that as 'the last' and 'worst' of British cuisine, broiled chops marked the end of culinary prowess, suggesting a stasis in the development of new dishes or food trends. This may also be a satirical critique of the demise of British theatre since Shakespeare. But nevertheless, Dickens groups Shakespeare and broiled chops together as representations of quintessential Britishness. Moreover, the imaginative nature of Dickens's recipe and article demonstrates that even if broiled chops were occasionally the 'worst', they were still significant to both culinary and cultural imagination in nineteenth-century Britain. Dickens also emphasizes this national importance in 'Leaves from the Mahogany Tree', writing that 'To broil, is to perform an operation which is the result of centuries of experience acquired by a nation that relishes, always did relish, and probably always will relish, broils'.[33] This statement invokes the history of broiling food on the gridiron, and simultaneously suggests that broiled foods would always have resonance in terms of British cultural heritage and identity. Not only is broiled meat imbued in literary history via Shakespeare then, but also in culinary, national, and masculine history – the food of successful men who symbolized British success and would 'probably always' relish a broiled chop.

As Dickens's satire elucidates, many texts and recipes that addressed broiling enlisted an imaginative engagement with nationalistic historicity. In *Buckmaster's Cookery* (1874), Charles Buckmaster notes that '[t]he national beef steak and mutton chop have made us the best of broilers' with his use of 'national' laying indisputable claim to broiled chops, steaks, and the broiling process as a symbol of Britishness.[34] Beeton also ties chops to England's national identity, declaring that 'the beef-steak and mutton chop of the solitary English dinner may be mentioned as celebrated all the world over'.[35] An article by 'an Epicure' in *The National Magazine* (1857) notes: 'If a steak feeds one, it has its moral uses also; it suggests country, and calls to mind whole pages of Thomson, and Clare, and Carrington, and Tom Miller.'[36] This notion of 'country' and 'moral uses' together with the mention of poets suggests that consuming broiled foods is nourishing on a symbolic as well as nutritional level: to eat broiled steaks is to consume the essence of Britain. Once more broiled meats, famous men, and literary culture are aligned, and the humble steak signifies British intellectualism and masculinity. This article also includes the gridiron in its adulating praise: 'See the gridiron, with its geometric bars checking with black lines the ground-colour of incandescent charcoal; the steak itself nicely lined with oleaginous bark, frizzling for your good, and gradually changing from sanguinary red to palatable brown; then how the gravy runs from it in luscious streams.'[37] The repeated references to colour and shape in this description, paired with evocative, onomatopoeic words like 'sizzling' and 'luscious', have an ekphrastic effect on the image of the gridiron, elevating it to become an imaginative instrument or tool which creates art. Indeed, this phrasing is reminiscent of the *London Magazine* quotation that opened this paper, which continues its praise of broiling by stating, 'We are transported at the thought of the golden gridiron in the beef-steak club, which seems to confine the white cook in his burning cage, which generates wit, whim, and song, for hours together, and pleasantly blends the fanciful and the substantial in one laughing and robust harmony.'[38] While the flowery language in both articles again suggests satire, the gridiron is given symbolic weight, becoming a conduit for the imagination. Here, the 'golden', lyre-like gridiron evokes myth, with the reference to beef and lyres perhaps referring to the Olympian god Hermes. In Homer's *Hymn to Hermes*, the child Hermes creates a lyre from the shell of a tortoise and the innards of cows and sheep, before stealing Apollo's cattle and 'cutting their fat-rich / meat, / Transfixed on wooden spits he roasted together the flesh'.[39] This sensuous description becomes an in-joke that only those well-versed in the classics can enjoy. The gridiron is thus framed as a signifier of knowledge, and is transformed into an instrument the nineteenth-century reader can use to access the centuries of civilization that gridirons have been involved in. This mythical history is then tethered to British eating practices through the mention of the 'beef-steak club', much like Dickens's chophouse, and so the imaginative framing of the gridiron and broiling once more extends into British cultural belonging. All these texts, whether recipes in cookbooks or in satirical articles, use literary and historical allusions and nationalistic claims to carve a distinctive, symbolic place for gridirons and broiled meat in the nineteenth-century culinary imagination.

Conclusion

The writers discussed did not frame broiling or the gridiron as merely a cooking process and its accompanying implement. Instead, their recipes and discussions approached both things with inherent imagination. Broiling food on the gridiron is elevated in these writings to represent art, civilization, myth, national success and belonging, and the epitome of British cuisine. Broiling remained so prevalent in nineteenth-century food texts because it was a cooking process repeatedly imbued with nostalgia and national pride. By placing broiled meats on a symbolic, imaginative pedestal, both food writers and eaters in the nineteenth century could indulge in nostalgia for simpler times and uphold the connotations of strength, culture, and literary history that they inscribed onto broiling and its spoils. A cooking process that has been around for centuries carries with it a sense of proliferation, which can be translated into a sense of stability – even though broiling itself was anything but stable. Dickens, Kitchiner, and Jewry were among many writers who highlighted the precarity of using a gridiron within a discussion of the national identity of broiled meats. This suggests that while food writers acknowledged the difficulties of the process, they also sought to safeguard broiled meats and gridirons as cornerstones of British cuisine.

What this study ultimately shows, then, is that gridirons, broiling, and broiled foods are inextricable from imagination – imagination which bound the cooking process to narratives of nationalism, historicity, masculinity, and literature. Through the creation of teleological histories, food writers established alternate realities where broiled foods and gridirons retained their place in British cuisine due to their symbolic resonances, despite fading from use. By embroiling this cooking process in their own versions of history, nineteenth-century food writers highlighted the symbolic power food has, and the way this symbolism was meticulously crafted in texts to signify, capture, and establish a place in time. Culinary imagination is thus not limited to the invention of the new but can turn to history and tradition to present a seemingly simple cooking process as a nuanced cultural symbol. Imagination is present in the simplest acts of cooking, and in the literary workings of the recipes which describe them. When we pay close attention to these corners of culinary history, it becomes clear that there is potent imagination behind even the most unassuming broiled chop.

Notes

1. 'The Cook's Oracle', *London Magazine*, 4.11 (October 1821), 432-39 (p. 436).
2. See Andrea Broomfield, *Food and Cooking in Victorian England: A History* (Westport: Praeger, 2007); Sara Pennell, *The Birth of the English Kitchen, 1600-1850* (London: Bloomsbury, 2016).
3. See Susan Zlotnick. 'Domesticating Imperialism: Curry and Cookbooks in Victorian England', *Frontiers: A Journal of Women Studies*, 16.2/3 (1996), 51-68; Margaret Beetham, 'Good Taste and Sweet Ordering: Dining with Mrs Beeton', *Victorian Literature and Culture*, 36.2 (2008), 391-406; Natalie Kapetanios Mier, '"A Fashionable Dinner is Arranged as Follows": Victorian Dining Taxonomies', *Victorian Literature and Culture*, 33 (2005), 133-48.
4. While in North American English the word 'broiling' is still used today, the word has faded and become archaic as a cooking term in British English. In nineteenth-century food writing it referred to cooking meat over an open flame, using a gridiron.
5. Eliza Acton, *Modern Cookery for Private Families* (London: Longman, Green, Longman and Roberts, 1860), p. 186.
6. Alexis Soyer, *The Modern Housewife, or, Ménagère* (London: Simpkin, Marshall & Co, 1849), p. 322.
7. Isabella Beeton, *The Book of Household Management* (London: S O Beeton, 1861), p. 139.
8. Beeton, p. 26.
9. Soyer, p. 68; Arthur Gay Payne, *The Housekeeper's Guide to Preserved Meats, Fruits, Vegetables, &c* (London: Crosse & Blackwell, 1880), p. iv.
10. Though stoves or ranges often gave the user some access to open flame, they were comprised of ovens and used enclosed fire to heat the stovetop.
11. Pennell notes: 'By the end of the eighteenth century, the fully closed range (with the fire shut away in a fire box), supplemented by an oven on one side and water boiler on the other, took the closure of the hearth to its logical conclusion.' There were exceptions to this rule, however, and later Pennell notes that cooking over flames in smaller hearths remained important for the poor and those living in lodgings (pp. 67, 78).
12. Isabella Beeton died in 1867, though publishers continued to use her name to sell cookbooks; *Mrs Beeton's Everyday Cookery and Housekeeping Book* (London: Ward, Lock & Co, [1877] c.1900), p. lxv.
13. Some gridirons were designed with slanted bars or reservoirs to collect juices from the meat. Many broiling recipes still warn against gravy loss however, suggesting it was a common problem.
14. Dora de Blaquière, 'Grilling and Devilling', *The Girls' Own Paper*, XX.1023 (August 1899), 710-11 (p. 710).
15. Pennell, pp. 69-70.
16. Soyer, pp. 72-73.
17. William Kitchener, *Apicius Redivivus, or, The Cook's Oracle* (London: A. Constable, [1817] 1822), pp. 201-02.
18. Mary Jewry, *Warne's Model Cookery and Housekeeping Book*, people's edn (London: Frederick Warne and Co, [1879] 1890), p. 20.
19. Charles Dickens. 'Leaves from the Mahogany Tree', *All the Year Round*, 20.482 (July 1868), 127-31 (p. 129). As there is no author attributed to the *All the Year Round* articles or the recipes within them, this

paper credits them to Dickens.
20. Charles Dickens. 'Chops', *All the Year Round*, 1.24 (May 1869), 562-64 (p. 564).
21. Dickens, 'Chops', p. 563; Beeton, p. 264.
22. Dickens, 'Chops', pp. 563, 564.
23. Kitchiner, p. 107.
24. Dickens, 'Chops', p. 562.
25. For scholarship on meat and British identity, see: Nadja Durbach, 'Roast Beef, the New Poor Law, and the British Nation, 1834–63', *Journal of British Studies,* 52 (2013), 963-89; Nadja Durbach, *Many Mouths: The Politics of Food in Britain from the Workhouse to the Welfare State* (Cambridge: Cambridge University Press, 2020); Nick Fiddes, *Meat: A Natural Symbol* (London: Routledge, 1991), p. 16; Ben Rogers, *Beef and Liberty: Roast Beef, John Bull and the English Nation* (London: Vintage, 2004); Julia Twigg, 'Vegetarianism and the Meanings of Meat', in *The Sociology of Food and Eating: Essays on the Sociological Significance of Food*, ed. by Anne Murcott (Aldershot: Gower, 1983), 18-30.
26. Dickens, 'Chops', p. 562.
27. William Shakespeare, *The Merchant of Venice*, in *The Complete Works of William Shakespeare* (Ware: Wordsworth Editions, 2007), pp. 388-415 (p. 410).
28. Dickens, 'Chops', p. 562.
29. 'Gridiron', in *The OED Online* < https://www-oed-com.ezproxy.lib.gla.ac.uk/view/Entry/81386?rskey=AbhEn8&result=1#eid> [accessed 22 July, 2019]
30. Dickens, 'Chops', p. 562.
31. Charles Dickens, *A Tale of Two Cities*, ed. by P. Merchant (Hertfordshire: Wordsworth, [1849] 1999), p. 3.
32. Pennell, p. 70.
33. Dickens, 'Leaves from the Mahogany Tree', p. 129.
34. Charles Buckmaster, *Buckmaster's Cookery* (London: George Routledge and Sons, 1874), p. 203.
35. Beeton, p. 264.
36. 'An Epicure's Steak', *The National Magazine*, 1.5 (1857), 335.
37. 'An Epicure's Steak', p. 335.
38. 'The Cook's Oracle', p. 436.
39. Homer, *The Homeric Hymns*, trans. by M. Crudden (Oxford: Oxford University Press, 2001), p. 47.

The Spiritual in the Sensual, the Sensual in the Virtual: Modern-Day Spirituality through a Community-Supported Farm

Caitlin B. Morgan

Introduction

I was sitting in an apartment on the Upper West side of Manhattan, listening to an elderly woman tell me about the community-supported agriculture (CSA) farm of which she is a member. It was a beautiful, multi-bedroom home in a tall apartment building, and I imagined she had owned it for a long time, as the New York City housing market is ferocious, and she was living on a fixed income. Outside were high-rises and traffic noise, but we were talking about fresh greens and farm-made sausage. Every week, thanks to paying an upfront subscription, this woman receives a crate or two of food from a diversified farm 300 miles upstate. She can technically eat entirely from the CSA share, as the farm offers herbs, fifty varieties of vegetables, apples and berries, dairy, eggs, lamb, chicken, beef, pork, animal and vegetable fats, local oats and flours and cornmeal, and maple syrup. This 'full-diet' share has meaning for her, even beyond the fresh and high-quality products that she can select and have delivered. She is Jewish and believes strongly in political action as part of her faith. Supporting the farm has become a social justice practice for her. 'I'm in it now,' she told me, 'through an ethical belief...I cannot back out.'

The farm in question is Essex Farm, 1100 agricultural acres in rural, mountainous Essex County, New York. It was established in 2003 when a farmer and a journalist, Mark and Kristin Kimball, moved to the sparsely populated and economically depressed region and began raising food. In 2010, Kristin wrote a best-selling memoir, *The Dirty Life,* and the farm gained international recognition.[1] She wrote a sequel, *Good Husbandry*, in 2019.[2] Both Kimballs became sought-after public speakers. In the intervening years, the farm has grown from a two-person operation with six CSA members to employing up to twenty-five people during the summer months and providing the 'full diet' for around a hundred families. Some of those families now include members in New York City, a five-hour drive south, many of whom have never been to the farm. Thanks in part to the Kimballs training young farmers who then move on, Essex County, which previously contained only dying conventional dairy farms, now boasts at least twelve small diversified and specialized craft farms.[3]

I conducted a comprehensive case study of Essex Farm between 2018 and 2020. My fieldwork included ethnographic participant observation of farm labour and interviews of twenty farmers and fifteen CSA members. One of the primary things I found was that through Kristin's writing – and through Mark's secular, ecological evangelism – the farm has become a source not only of food, but of place-based spiritual communion for its members and farmworkers. This is true even for CSA members in New York City, whose only knowledge of the farm-as-place comes in the form of emailed newsletters and Instagram photos. The elderly New Yorker I spoke to had taken $7000 out of her savings to pay for her annual CSA share. Her upstairs neighbour, also a member, reads Kristin's weekly Farm Note email to stay up-to-date on the farm and said, 'It really makes a huge difference to me to know details about what's happening on the farm. It may seem like a small thing, but it is not. It means that I appreciate the food on a different level.' Both are very involved and committed to this place – but neither have ever been there. The first woman asked me if there were migrant labourers working on the farm, because she did not know who was raising her food. Such lack of transparency is not unusual in the US food system generally, but it is an unexpected contradiction in a community-supported farm, where local members often visit weekly, and for whom distant members are willing to dedicate so much of their time and money in mutual support. At Essex Farm, the desire to connect to the sensed experience of the farm, whether through taste buds or through social media, is part of a larger web of desire for connection that undergirds the entire farm community. The meaning of the farm is a daily experience, but a virtually-mediated one.

A History of Agricultural Spirituality: Modern CSA Farms

To understand the patterns of commitment, spirituality, place, and agriculture present at Essex Farm, we have to go back about a century. Between the late 1800s and mid-1900s, the United States saw a wave of homesteaders and back-to-the-landers who inspired others with their writings on nature, farming, and rural life. For homesteaders Scott and Helen Nearing, for example, working and living close to the land was about sacred economy: simultaneously resisting spiritual evil and its economic corollary, capitalism, by modelling an alternative way of living. As Rebecca Kneale Gould writes in her ethnography *At Home in Nature: Modern Homesteading and Spiritual Practice*, people made 'pilgrimages' to famous homesteads, but did not necessarily adopt the lifestyle themselves: 'For some, the idea of nature, or its accessibility through texts and occasional visits, was enough [...] readers could vicariously experience an intimacy with the natural world.'[4] Similarly, Richard Robbins, an anthropologist and also a member of Essex Farm CSA, writes that the founders of western organic farming in the late 1800s shared five key aspects in their work: emphasis on soil health, a spiritual orientation to nature, appreciation of indigenous or peasant agriculture, motivation for social reform and resistance of technology, and conviction that farming methods reflect both the state of society and of the health of its members.[5] All these aspects show up on Essex Farm.

Since and during the back-to-the-land movement, agricultural and rural landscapes changed enormously in the US. In the early twentieth century, the country had many small, diversified farms; farming was labour-intensive; and half of Americans lived in rural areas. Now, farming is concentrated in an ever-decreasing number of large and specialized farms; technology has replaced much human labour and increased farm productivity; and less than a quarter of Americans live in rural areas.[6] Many US farmers have recently turned to sustainable practices in one form or another, motivated by policy supports, personal beliefs, and/or increased price share for products such as certified organic. CSA farms in particular are often part of alternative agriculture's stand against agrochemicals, monoculture production, and industrial methods.[7] They are a form of community-embedded risk-sharing, where the customers usually pay farmers in advance in a subscription service, often at a rate lower than market price, so that farmers and members can both benefit from mutual support in producing food. The ideal is for CSAs and other forms of 'civic agriculture' to promote environmentalism and citizenship through active engagement with physical place and community.[8]

Thus, for some, small-scale farming is a contemporary way of stepping back from those 'evils' inherent in participating in the dominant economic system. The Kimballs follow other contemporary farms, notably ones across the lake that divides NY from Vermont, who wanted to change the world through organic and values-based agriculture.[9] But the Kimballs go further – or, rather, further back, to established traditions. As a group, Essex Farm farmers and members embody a naturalized spirituality that exists in contrast with mechanical processes of modern scientific agriculture.[10] They do so in the tradition of homesteaders. And yet, they do so through commercial, not subsistence, agriculture, and in increasingly technological and physically distant ways.

Spirituality, Sensuousness, and the Imagination of Connection
Spiritual Connection Through Embodied Cycles

Farmers and members of Essex Farm CSA use sensual engagement with farm labour, cooking, and eating as a form of spiritual connection to place. The seasonality of work and of produce connects them to landscape and life cycles. In a global food system designed for maximum, year-round choice, many members derive pleasure from the changing availability and the connection to seasonal rhythms. For people willing to deal with the August glut and winter limitations, the evanescence of both leads to a deeper appreciation of foods when they are in season. One former member spoke fondly of freezing and canning as part of the whole experience: 'I like the seasonality. I liked those weeks in the late summer when you're preparing for the fall and the wintertime. I like that sense.' Here, sense is the bodily knowledge of where one is in the year's cycle, firmly planted in one season, expecting another.

For farmers, connection to the system is about deep knowledge of the landscape. 'It was a never-ending cycle of longing and fulfilment, directly connected to our work, and learning to live this way was like hearing a tune I had known once and forgotten. It just felt deeply right,' writes Kristin.[11] Sensing a landscape, knowing a system, can be done not only through eating but also through work, which is itself 'a way of knowing nature; it requires an engagement of the senses and attention to the micro-geographies of landscape'.[12] As part of the case study, I ran a small PhotoVoice project, in which participants took photographs that represented their motivations for being part of the CSA. One new farmer, reflecting on her series of photos, described a feeling of deep kinship to place and to farm lifeforms:

> this is where I need to be. These photos capture my love of animals, my adoration of tiny sprouting plants, and my kinship with the people that surround me. I work at Essex Farm because I feel a raw sense of truth and belonging every day. I love farming because I feel a deep connection with the food I consume and the land that I live on. I farm because this work makes me feel alive.

Not all of this connection is to the life of plants, animals, and seasons, however. Some of it is explicitly about the death of each. In her first book, Kristin tries to identify a way of eating that does not involve suffering and comes up short, even for vegetarianism: 'Don't let anyone tell you that growing vegetables is not a violent act. The muted sound of a plow tearing through roots is almost obscene, like the sound of a fist meeting flesh.'[13] In an ethnography of contemporary religious agrarian communities in the United States, Todd LeVasseur argues that the embodied act of farming brings with it wisdom, meaning, and well-being through contact with the cycle of life and death that are larger than any one farmer.[14] For people I spoke with, working directly with death, rather than avoiding it, was an important facet of how the farm expanded their consciousness. As one farmer wrote, 'Being in a work environment that so explicitly deals with the realities of life and death is refreshing, compared to the isolated nature of city life, when life and death are more related to crime instead of nature.' Multiple PhotoVoice participants sent me a photo of animal carcasses in response to why they worked on or were a member of the CSA.

An additional way that people tap into senses, knowledge, and attendant meaning is through how Kristin and Mark communicate about these things, which functions as a form of agnostic, agricultural evangelism. The farm exists thanks to its social relationships; Mark and Kristin have convinced people to engage in their particular agricultural endeavour. It's common knowledge at Essex Farm that if someone expresses even minute interest in the share, Mark will immediately be on the phone with them, for as long as it takes to get them to sign up. He consistently suggested that I quit graduate school to work for him full time. He is, according to Kristin, a 'true believer' in sustainable farming as a method to combat environmental degradation and loss of rural culture. Or, as a member put it, Mark is 'a very typical charismatic leader' of the type you might see in communal or religious communities. At a Friday party for the members, Kristin said she had realized that the reason Mark farms is to share the connection between 'the sun, the soil, the water, and the work': it's a 'direct portal'.

Where Mark's evangelism is spoken, Kristin's is written. As Gould notes, many modern homesteaders come from upper- and middle-class backgrounds, which affects what they consider to be purposeful work and creates a desire to 'articulate a moral vision for the self, and, in some cases, to "evangelize" this vision with the hope of reforming American culture'.[15] Religious imagery and mystical language suffuse Kristin's writings about the farm. Descriptions include praying to farm deities they don't believe in; Adam from the Bible; the reverence of corn; and how children can interrupt an interior, spiritual life. She also writes about 'alchemical' agricultural processes; eggs as a 'special kind of magic'; and transformation 'in the cauldron of an animal's stomach'.[16]

This focus is perhaps strengthened by the absence of formal religion and thus a need to find meaning elsewhere. The farm has replaced the church. Consider a quote from Kristin's first book: 'I cooked and ate it with a reverence that comes from understanding the whole picture, an appreciation that can be expressed equally well, I decided, with a ceremonial sage or with the careful preparation and enjoyment of an exceptional sage *stuffing*.'[17] Holism, connection, reverence, and ceremony come together through the cooking and eating of food from her own farm. Kristin's first impression of the empty-seeming land that became Essex Farm was that it had 'no soul'. Mark insisted that it was not vacant but sleeping, because it was not being used. Agriculturally fallow land is spiritually fallow land, and the converse is that a farm with people working it is an alive farm with soul.

Global Ecological, Religious, and Culinary Imaginaries

While we might expect seasonal eating to connect people to place, sensually, members also identified knowledge and awareness as primary ways of re-integrating themselves into a larger, more sustainable food system – not only their local one. The farm operates with a vision of health, rotating up in scale from soil to planet: their motto – '[h]ealthy soil, healthy plants, healthy animals, healthy people, healthy planet' – conceptually connects their own land practices and stewardship to the wider systems in which they exist, across scales.[18] Again, such imagining can be seen as a way of tapping into meaning that is larger than oneself and even than one's immediate community.

In some cases, people's connection to the farm is overtly religious, rather than allusively so, and connects to long lineages and wide geographies of faith. The elderly Jewish member became interested in alternative agriculture as part of her religious social justice beliefs and traced the connections back to scripture, where 'religion actually melds with farming'. She articulated spiritual connections to Native American beliefs about bison, a Mexican relative's food-decorated altar, Taiwanese religious celebrations with food, and Arab altars appearing akin to Jewish ones, all in reference to cultural expressions of gratitude for crops and livestock. She sees her food choices as part of an inclusive, global web of spiritual and religious tradition. One of the farm's managers, a devout Christian, similarly pointed out 'really all of scripture is agriculturally referenced' and told me that 'being here, and being part of this team, and specifically supporting Mark and Kristin, is as tangible of a [way] of the living out of my faith in Christ as I can find'. This was his answer to the guiding question of 'what does it mean to follow Jesus in everyday life?' that Amish communities use to determine meaning and action, an especially strong association given that several Amish families also work on the farm.[19]

Connection to the global is underlined by how some people prepare their Essex Farm meals. Kristin writes that one way to deal with having limitations on what they can eat – because they do not purchase much food from the store – is to follow recipes from international cookbooks and bring some of the wider world into their geographically-constrained farm and kitchen. One member in Manhattan is Colombian and uses Essex products to make traditional meals from her homeland. The Jewish woman on the Upper West side called herself a 'Chinese cook', by which I think she meant she cooks primarily Chinese dishes (although she did not say why). A thoroughly global understanding of cuisine, culture, and environmentalism emerges from these life choices, literally grounded in the soil of one place, but imaginably circling outwards in its relations and obligations.

Disconnections

Although all these ways of connecting across scales – to place and landscape, to the global ecosystem, to the universal – are present on the farm, there are also separations. Amish employees are deeply religious in a more traditional sense and do not interact more than necessary with the 'English' (non-Amish) farmers. Amish practices are dedicated to the physical world. Through work, their beliefs become embodied in social practices that reproduce religious views, a dynamic that can be seen on Essex Farm generally, as beliefs in sustainability, health, community, and even spirituality become embodied and reinforced through shared practices of farming, cooking, and eating. At the same time, in Amish culture, evangelism of belief is mostly eschewed, as it is seen as a repudiation of humility.[20] Their stability, quietness, and rejection of outward-facing promotion stands in contrast to Essex Farm's social fluctuations – as new farmers arrive and leave regularly – and its visibility as a model for sustainable agriculture. The commitment to work, land, and community is shared between the Amish and English; the verbal and visual expression of what that commitment means in daily life could not be much more different.

There are also real differences between the embodied knowledge of farmers and the members who visit to pick up their food or receive it in a box. The dissonance is especially stark for New York City members, who live in a different landscape and a warmer climate. Social media and the Farm Note newsletter cannot make up for the lack of direct experience for members whose only concept of the farm is imagined, through pictures, descriptions, and meals, instead of being cultivated through physical presence. NYC members might ask for things like flowers in the spring while the farm is still blanketed in snow or lamb meat while ewes are still pregnant. They may feel like they know the farm, but one farmer characterized it as 'misunderstanding': because most of them have never visited, 'they don't know what we're actually working with. Where, I think a lot of our local members [do] see it […]. They're experiencing the same weather'. City members do not occupy the same place as local members, and the sociality of the share has fragmented somewhat as a result. One farmer described this as a disconnect in the 'C' of 'CSA.'

The Limits of Extended Sensing

In other words, there are limits to one's ability to sense vicariously through others' accounts. There is a small body of sensory literature on how media can extend our senses – technology is not merely a method of disseminating information, it is itself sensory, allowing for different presence and qualities of experience.[21] At Essex Farm, the technological extension of senses works both in producing and sharing food, and it makes the entire endeavour possible. By texting his workers, Mark can lengthen his managerial reach to know about and weigh in on things happening across 1100 acres. Instagram and the Farm Note allow members a way of 'seeing' the farm. For local members, the internet can be a way of calling for help – for example, with a sudden crop of perishable strawberries that require volunteer pickers. The images, captions, and stories convey a sense of being on the farm, knowing what is happening by the season, creating a connection that would be difficult or impossible without smartphones and email. As an interesting twist in the lineage of material mysticism, the farm, which many farmers see as an escape from office life and computer work, has become a 'digitally mediated' workplace.[22]

The limits to sensing show especially when it comes to who must do the work. Despite the reliance on computers for communication, the farm operates in a relatively low-tech manner compared to contemporary industrial agriculture, and it requires much more manual labour. Again, being physically absent, city members require even more labour from the farm. They have to process and cook food, but it is selected and packed for them, unlike for locals, who do this themselves. The knowledge, and perhaps some of the appreciation, gained in sensing through labour is completely obscured.

Lack of physical presence has also changed the social connections between people involved with the farm. The initial CSA community, which was a small group of people living close by, was a 'spiritual community. We're all tied together, kind of an ethos. As in most religious communes', said one long-term member. And in many communes, membership eventually wanes, as it has with Essex Farm's local membership, in part because the group feeling has dissipated, and the priorities seem to have shifted towards serving far-away members. Mark appears to have an ambivalent relationship with this kind of fervour for the farm, 'when people literally talk about us almost the way they talk about their churches, right, as born-again Christian…how do we put [the farm's driving principles] in words in a way that doesn't sound like religion, or maybe does'. The deep belief is part of what keeps people with the farm despite it being a more difficult lifestyle than if they went grocery shopping – but the fervour is not necessarily permanent.

Interestingly, I did not sense that the relative lack of embodied knowledge of the farm landscape necessarily limited how spiritually connected people felt they were through it. Echoing conversations I had with other members and farmers, the woman in Manhattan told me that 'once you have an ethical feeling and the feeling for nature, it doesn't matter if you have an organized religious affiliation. But I think once you're sensitive to nature, that is spirituality'.

Tapping into this, the CSA share is an aspirational imagining of the food of the future (sustainable, community-based) through the past (low-input farming practices and connection to land) and the present (joyful, sensual, and culinary engagements). All this comes together at an intersection of seemingly juxtaposed modern trends in social media and CSA farming, and through continual reimagining of a nostalgic modernity.

Through food and farming, one may cross the boundary between embodied action and spiritual signals. Notions of transcorporeality – the porous boundaries of human bodies, in constant exchange with the environment – may here expand past the physical to the metaphysical.[23] Gould argues, 'Physical ingestion becomes a means of incorporating one's deepest values and commitments into one's spiritual self.' Eating a certain way can be 'an embodied practice leading toward spiritual experiences of transcendence or communion'. Homesteaders (and, I would argue in this case, CSA participants) 'are particularly apt to embrace – indeed, to celebrate – embodiedness, this-worldliness, and the materiality of the natural world. Yet operating alongside these explicit gestures embracing the body and the earth are other gestures of resistance, gestures that suggest a certain longing for immortality, even while mortality is being affirmed as the most natural of processes'.[24]

The geographer Edmunds Bunkše describes the idea of connection by arguing that imagination is the most important human ability to sense and interpret landscape. By this token, eating (tasting) from a place and imagining that place (perhaps through virtual aids) can connect what Bunkše refers to as the interior and exterior landscapes of human life. The result is connection, or 'being at home in the world'.²⁵ At Essex Farm, and perhaps in other values-based agricultural projects, personal and collective meaning-making is the motivation for continuing in a labour-intensive lifestyle that contradicts broad trends of convenience and access in contemporary food systems. To fully understand what such farming systems bring forward in our modern world, we may need to look past the ecological and social to the mystical and universal.

Notes

1. Kristin Kimball, *The Dirty Life: A Memoir of Farming, Food, and Love* (New York: Simon & Schuster, 2010).
2. Kristin Kimball, *Good Husbandry: Growing Food, Love, and Family on Essex Farm* (New York: Scribner, 2019).
3. 'Hub on the Hill – Adirondacks', *The Hub on the Hill* <http://thehubonthehill.org/> [accessed 24 March 2017]
4. Rebecca Kneale Gould, *At Home in Nature: Modern Homesteading and Spiritual Practice in America* (Berkeley: University of California Press, 2005), pp. 111-36.
5. Richard Robbins, 'The Transcendental Meanings of Organic Food', in *Organic Food, Farming, and Culture: An Introduction,* ed. by Janet Chrazan and Jacqueline Ricotta (London: Bloomsbury Academic, 2019), pp. 227-40.
6. USDA ERS, 'Farming and Farm Income', *Economic Research Service–United States Department of Agriculture,* 2020 <https://www.ers.usda.gov/data-products/ag-and-food-statistics-charting-the-essentials/farming-and-farm-income/> [accessed 16 November 2020]
7. Ryan E. Galt, 'The Moral Economy Is a Double-Edged Sword: Explaining Farmers' Earnings and Self-Exploitation in Community-Supported Agriculture', *Economic Geography*, 89.4 (2013), 341-65 <https://doi.org/10.1111/ecge.12015>
8. Laura B. DeLind, 'Place, Work, and Civic Agriculture: Common Fields for Cultivation', *Agriculture and Human Values*, 19.3 (2002), 217-24 <https://doi.org/10.1023/A:1019994728252.>; K. Brandon Lang, 'The Changing Face of Community-Supported Agriculture', *Culture & Agriculture,* 32.1 (2010), 17-26 <https://doi.org/10.1111/j.1556-486X.2010.01032.x>
9. Amy B. Trubek, *The Taste of Place: A Cultural Journey into Terroir* (University of California Press, 2008).
10. Robbins.
11. Kimball, *Good Husbandry,* p. 27.
12. Cheryl E. Morse and others, 'Performing a New England Landscape: Viewing, Engaging, and Belonging', *Journal of Rural Studies,* 36 (2014), 226-36 (p. 228) <https://doi.org/10.1016/j.jrurstud.2014.09.002>
13. Kimball, *The Dirty Life*, p. 170.
14. Todd LeVasseur, *Religious Agrarianism and the Return of Place: From Values to Practice in Sustainable Agriculture*, Suny Series on Religion and the Environment (Albany: SUNY Press, 2017).
15. Gould, p. 221.
16. Kimball, *Good Husbandry,* pp. 11, 12, 46, 168, 19, 61, 48.
17. Kimball, *The Dirty Life,* p. 42, original emphasis.
18. 'Our Farm', *Essex Farm* <http://www.essexfarmcsa.com/about-us/> [accessed 3 May 2017]
19. Donald B. Kraybill, Karen Johnson-Weiner, and Steven M. Nolt, *The Amish* (Baltimore: Johns Hopkins University Press, 2013), p. 64.
20. Kraybill, Johnson-Weiner, and Nolt.
21. See for example Sarah Pink, *Doing Sensory Ethnography,* 2nd edition (Los Angeles: Sage, 2015).
22. Pink, p. 119.

23 Stacy Alaimo, 'Trans-Corporeal Feminisms and the Ethical Space of Nature', *Revista Estudos Feministas*, 25.2 (2017), 909-34 <https://doi.org/10.1590/1806-9584.2017v25n2p909>
24 Gould, pp. 77, 75, 87.
25 Edmunds Valdemārs Bunkše, 'Feeling Is Believing, or Landscape as a Way of Being in the World', *Geografiska Annaler: Series B, Human Geography*, 89.3 (2007), 219-31 <https://doi.org/10.1111/j.1468-0467.2007.00250.x>

The Cookbook Whisperer: How Maria Guarnaschelli's Powers of Imagination Redefined Recipes

James Oseland

In the recipe for roast chicken with bread salad that appears in *The Zuni Cafe Cookbook*, the book's author, the San Francisco-based chef Judy Rodgers, translates a signature dish on her restaurant's menu for the home cook. From the first lines, it's clear that it is not an average recipe.

'The Zuni roast chicken depends on three things,' Rodgers explains in the page-long headnote:

> beginning with the small size of the bird. Don't substitute a jumbo roaster – it will be too lean and won't tolerate high heat, which is the second requirement of the method. Small chickens, 2 ¾ to 3 ½ pounds, flourish at high heat, roast quickly and evenly, and, with lots of skin per ounce of meat, they are virtually designed to stay succulent. Your store may not promote this size for roasting, but let them know you'd like it.[1]

Rodgers applies the same calm authoritativeness and attention to detail to the prepping of the chicken. It should be patted 'very' dry, inside and out, and she explains why: 'a wet chicken will spend too much time steaming before it begins to turn golden brown'.[2] When it comes to the cooking, Rodgers urges readers not to just put the chicken in the oven and walk away, but rather to stay alert and use their senses to better appreciate what's occurring inside that hot box: 'Place [the chicken] in the center of the oven and listen and watch for it to start sizzling and browning within 20 minutes. If it doesn't, raise the temperature progressively until it does.'[3]

At one point in the recipe, Rodgers refers the reader to a multipage section called 'The Practice of Early Salting'.[4] In it, she tells the story of how, when she was a young cook in a Paris restaurant, she was won over by the technique of salting certain foods well ahead of cooking them. She also describes in technical yet colourful detail the many different varieties of salt chefs use, from *fleur de sel* to kosher salt, and how home cooks can learn to use them too.

In the end, this recipe, which clocks in at nearly five pages, isn't just a guide to making the most delicious, crackly-skinned roast chicken that you've ever eaten. It's a thorough but friendly invitation to become a more knowledgeable cook. No wonder it has become a cult classic.

Published in 2002, Rodgers's cookbook – the only one she'd write – went on to win every major American cookbook award in the categories in which it was nominated. A few years later, after I had become the editor of *Saveur*, I had the good fortune to have a meal with her in San Francisco. We talked about the book's decade-long creation. 'It was a labor of love with Maria,' she told me over appetizers. She was referring to Maria Guarnaschelli, the legendary American cookbook editor who was the book's shepherd. 'She expected a lot, but in the end I had the great advantage to have her.'

In 2001, Guarnaschelli – who had recently joined W.W. Norton, the publisher where she'd spend the last part of her career – bought a proposal I'd submitted for a book called *Cradle of Flavor*.[5] It was to be a comprehensive exploration, through recipes, of the culinary links between Indonesia, Malaysia, and Singapore, a part of the world where I had lived off and on for years. It was my first book. Naively, I thought I would finish it within a year or two. Instead, under Maria's demanding tutelage, the process of researching recipes, developing them, and writing three radically different drafts took nearly six years.

Maria was unlike any other editor I'd worked with. Her physical presence was forceful, but her opinions, delivered by way of a sharp baritone, were even more so. She insisted on a level of discipline and detail in my writing that was a jolt to a first-time book author like myself. She told me again and again to consider my reader. She wanted me to imagine someone who had never been to rural Java but, through the precision of my writing, would be able to master an authentic *opor ayam*, a definitive Indonesian curry. 'How can you translate such mysterious cooking for a person who knows nothing about it?' she once asked me.[6]

Among the award-winning cookbooks that Maria edited in her decades-long career are such diverse titles as *Gran Cocina Latina* by Maricel Presilla, *The Cake Bible* by Rose Levy Berenbaum, *The Splendid Table* by Lynne Rossetto Kasper, and *The Food Lab* by J. Kenji López-Alt, along with literally scores of others. Maria's influence on culinary publishing over the last five decades – and on my own work as a writer and editor – is immeasurable. Her death in February of this year inspired me to reconsider what it was that gave the books she edited their magic.

In 2004, around the time that I was wrapping up the last draft of *Cradle of Flavor*, the writer and cooking teacher Molly Stevens was publishing *All About Braising*, also edited by Maria. Like so many of the volumes that Maria had a hand in, it went on to win every major cookbook award in its category. And as with many of Maria's collaborations, the process to get there was intense. I asked Stevens to tell me about it.

'I think I realized from the beginning what a master class I was getting,' she said. 'Maria would pick a recipe that was particularly troubled, or that was an illustrative example, and then she'd go deep on that one.'

One recipe Stevens proposed was initially called 'Chicken Legs Braised with Prunes, Green Olives & Lemons'. Upon my prompting, she searched through her archives and unearthed three separate manuscript drafts of that recipe, each scrawled with Maria's theatrical yet always clear handwriting. Seeing those pages brought on a rush of memories from the years I worked on *Cradle of Flavor*. I practically broke out in a sweat.

Poring through those manuscript notes, I instantly recognized a fundamental trait of Maria's editing style: She pushed her writers to make their own improvements, refusing to rewrite the book for them. Consider the fate of this anecdote Stevens included in the first draft about how the lemony chicken recipe had been inspired by one in the *Silver Palate Cookbook*: 'While I applaud the inclusion of green olives in the Silver Palate original,' Stevens's original headnote read, 'I've always wanted something less sugary (it contains 1 cup of brown sugar).'[7]

Maria's note, written in the manuscript's left margin, doesn't mince words: 'This sentence makes no sense if you don't know [that] recipe at all. Please fix and briefly get to your point.' The anecdote is absent in the second draft.

Stevens explained to me what she took away from that edit: 'Going back and looking at these pages reminded me of something that I still struggle with as a food writer.' She said:

> This whole thing about *The Silver Palate Cookbook*, it doesn't matter to the reader and it doesn't help them. I had it there because it's how I got to the recipe. So much of my early process is my internal process: How did I get to this recipe? But as a food writer, your internal process is not necessarily something you need to share with everybody. That might not be what's helpful to them to bring them into a recipe. Maria said that without really coming out and saying it, which is indicative of how she edited.

In her second-draft notes, Maria is even more direct. Here's one of her handwritten edits to the revised headnote: 'wordy detailing of chef-y balance/taste/whatever stuff will have your readers turning the page before they discern how quick it is in the end para!'

Maria frequently tells her author she needs to communicate more precisely. In one note, the editor recommends replacing the generic-sounding verb 'give' with the subtler 'lend', 'impart', or 'contribute'. She dismisses the phrase 'seems just right' as 'too vague'. Always anticipating the questions a typical home cook might ask, Maria takes aim at Stevens's suggestion of serving the chicken with buttered egg noodles: 'Will the noodles soak up the sauce?' Another note admonishes Stevens for being less than totally precise about which cut of chicken to use: 'Wherever you can be concrete it helps! Vague general comments are NOT good.'

Stevens recalled that Maria's edits pushed the author to focus on her own basic knowledge of the dish:

> Maria always reminded me that I was writing this book because I'm an expert. One of the things she said over and over in her notes was 'Get rid of the waffling. We're here because you know and we want to learn from you.' When I was working with her, very rarely would I say 'I don't know' to her because that was not a good answer. Every question had to be answered.

The pursuit of precision continues in the third draft, where Maria writes in response to the now-twice-rewritten headnote, 'You're being somewhat ponderous, over explaining every element, yet we still don't have a clear picture. Can you get the prunes and olives to one sentence?' By now, the recipe's name has been changed from the wordy original to 'Quick Lemony Chicken with Prunes and Green Olives.' The title telegraphs two of Maria's prime imperatives: First, emphasize the recipe's ease and deliciousness, then highlight its versatility. Much of the information in the original headnote has been relocated to a Cook's Note at the end of the recipe, a hallmark of Maria's structural style.

'I feel like Maria saw value in annotating text, having sidebars and appendices, information that made it feel like it was very much a resource,' Stevens said. 'I think she was also sensitive to information buried in a headnote that was an actual tip or takeaway. She loved 'aha!' moments. If she learned something from your text, she'd be so excited about it, so she was always looking for new bits of information.'

In the end, Maria and Stevens got the headnote down to a concise and friendly sixty-seven words. Here's the published version:

> This easy chicken braise simmers on top of the stove for about 35 minutes, making it ideal for a quick weeknight dinner. But don't let that stop you from making it for company. The winning combination of sweet prunes and green olives in a lemony braising liquid makes it distinctive enough for a fancy dinner party. Serve with mashed potatoes, a potato gratin, or buttered egg noodles.[8]

While concision was important to Maria, length in and of itself was not. 'If it was just padding, she'd get rid of it,' Stevens recalled. 'But at the same time, if you needed to write a three-paragraph instruction procedure on how to cut chicken thighs, she was like, 'Write as long as you need to there.' She always encouraged specificity in the instruction. There's a lot of work that goes into writing a recipe that makes a reader go, 'Oh, I really want to make that.' Especially when they're just starting out as a cook. It takes a lot of work to get something that feels neat and tidy and effortless.'

Another book that Maria edited was the 902-page *Gran Cocina Latina*, an encyclopedic guide to the food of Latin America written by the Cuban-American scholar and chef Maricel Presilla. The book was published in 2013, nearly twenty years after Presilla and Maria had initially discussed it. Presilla and I recently talked about the book's long road to publication.

'I met Maria in Spain in 1992, after I gave a talk about Latin America at a conference we were both attending,' she said. 'In 1993, I went to her office and I brought her the idea I had for a cookbook, starting with where I come from. Immediately, Maria said, "This is too narrow." She asked to see the material that I had on Latin America, and she loved it and said, "This is the book that we should write."'

The method by which that book came to exist was unusual, to say the least. 'We developed this process where I would pick her up from her apartment in Manhattan and then we would drive out to her house in Pennsylvania,' said Presilla. 'We would be there for the whole weekend. I would write a chapter and print two copies, and then I would read it to her, and she would say, "Okay, let's change this, let's change that."'

At Maria's behest, the two agreed early on that the book should not be structured around individual chapters exploring each country in Latin America; organizing the book in that fashion wouldn't be useful to the average reader looking for a weeknight recipe. Instead, Presilla divided the recipes into chapters with titles such as 'The Tamal Family' and 'Tropical Roots and Starchy Vegetables'.[9] Not bucketing the recipes by country also allowed Presilla to highlight the interconnectedness of the region's diverse food cultures, showing readers, say, the difference between Guatemalan tamales made from nixtamalized corn and fresh corn tamales from the Mexican state of Michoacán.

'Maria understood the consumer,' Presilla told me. 'She understood that Americans, for whom this book was written, want categories, and that would be the clearest way to present the food. That master plan worked really well. But she understood that I didn't just want to do a book of recipes. The scope was always going to be larger. She trusted me because I was an academic.'

Like other authors that Maria worked with – including me – Presilla was surprised by the level of detail her editor demanded. When Presilla began working on the book, she was not a professional recipe writer trained to create super-precise instructions. Maria required that she measure every single item in every single test and, as with Stevens, write each step in a way that would make sense even to relatively inexperienced cooks.

'She liked my writing, but she thought that I needed to go deeper into each recipe,' Presilla said. 'She demanded so much detail from me. What kind of pot? What's the size? What's happening inside the pot? Is it burbling or is it not? I had to measure everything. I would say eight ears of corn and she would say, "What do you mean eight ears of corn? How big are the ears?" She drilled me on that. She made me go deeper.'

Presilla completed the first draft of *Gran Cocina Latina* around a decade after she and Maria had first discussed the book; the manuscript was more than 2000 pages long and was delivered to Maria's office in multiple boxes. The next step was to edit it down to a publishable length. 'We cut three things that I saw as essential: a beautiful chapter with pizzas and pastas, a much bigger chapter on ingredients than what was published, and a 40-page bibliography,' Presilla said.

Despite sacrificing that material – or perhaps thanks to doing so – Presilla and Maria went on to create one of the best books of their respective careers. Maria's guidance was essential in helping Presilla interweave personal experiences with recipes, science, geography, history, and rigorously researched culinary information in order to bring all of it together in a vital mosaic of pan-Latin American cooking. At the outset it had seemed an impossible task, but they nailed it.

Even as culinary publishing entered the social-media era, when so many publishers are seeking to parlay a writer's Instagram following into a flash-in-the-pan success, Maria knew how to take a creative gamble on first-time authors whom she sensed had something enduring to contribute to the lineage of American cookbooks.

One such author was J. Kenji López-Alt, a columnist for the website *Serious Eats* who sold Maria his proposal for a book called *The Food Lab*. 'Maria was one of the last people to make an offer,' López-Alt told me. 'But she was the first person I talked to who seemed interested in the book beyond a business move. A lot of other people I talked to said things like, "Oh, we can package it this way and it'll look like this." Maria said, "This is a special book proposal. I want this book, and I'm not going to take no for an answer."'

As with Rodgers, Stevens, and Presilla, Maria worked intimately with López-Alt to bring his book to life. Over the five-year writing and editing process, *The Food Lab* went from the 350 pages that López-Alt originally envisioned to a nearly 1600-page draft that the two considered publishing in two volumes. That idea was quashed by W.W. Norton, and the manuscript was ultimately pared down to comprise a single volume of about a thousand pages.[10] The format worked: the book made the *New York Times* Best Seller List and won a James Beard Award.

'I was always afraid Maria would say no to me,' López-Alt said. 'But usually it was the opposite – she would say, "Do more."' He recalls that she was always encouraging – and always willing to get on board with new ideas, no matter how unusual they were.

'Maria was good at identifying people with unique perspectives,' López-Alt continued. 'She had a very good sense of what was going to work before the rest of the cookbook world knew that it was going to work. I think she knew what readers wanted before they knew they wanted it.'

That same uncanny foresight almost certainly played a role in Maria's decision to take a risk on me and *Cradle of Flavor*. After all, what other established cookbook editor would've taken on a newbie whose topic was one of the world's least-understood culinary regions? And yet, I like to think that it was her genuine personal curiosity and imagination, as much as any crystal ball, that ultimately drove her to acquire a book.

Molly Stevens had a similar take. 'I think Maria was the reader,' she told me:

> She learned to cook through the books that she edited. She cooked more of my recipes than anyone I ever worked with. I always knew that when I was turning something in that she might take that recipe home and make it, and if it didn't work, I was in trouble. She was the ultimate user of the book. And that's why she was so intense about not underestimating the reader, but also not assuming they have your knowledge.

It is marvelous to think that this erudite and well-traveled Manhattanite whose books have won dozens of awards was, in the end, her own 'everyreader'. From initial proposal to final galley proof, she was intent on placing herself inside the reader's experience, even if it meant turning on the stove and pulling out the pots and pans.

Back when I was working on the second draft of my book with Maria, she deduced how much I was struggling to explain these foreign cuisines to American readers.

Virtually everything I was writing about – from basic cooking techniques to core ingredients such as palm sugar and tempeh – was a potential minefield of unfamiliarity for the typical home cook here. 'You should teach cooking classes,' Maria suggested at one point. 'That way you could better understand how to translate these things.'

Within weeks, I'd acted on her advice, signing on to teach Indonesian-Malaysian-Singaporean cooking classes at New York's Institute for Culinary Education and the New School. Many of the courses took a hybrid format: I would meet students at an Asian market I liked – an opportunity to show them how to identify and choose ingredients that might otherwise be mysterious – and then we would go back into the kitchen classroom and make dishes from those ingredients. I quickly began to see first-hand the sorts of things that were confusing to my students. They would ask simple yet utterly logical questions like, 'Is this paste ground finely enough?' or 'Is this bok choy fresh or not?'

Maria's advice had been spot-on. In fact, it was one of the best suggestions I've ever been given about anything I've undertaken in my life. All of a sudden, I knew who I was writing my book for.

Notes

1. Judy Rodgers, *The Zuni Café Cookbook: A Compendium of Recipes and Cooking Lessons from San Francisco's Beloved Restaurant* (New York: Norton, 2002), p. 342.
2. Rodgers, p. 343.
3. Rodgers, p. 345.
4. Rodgers, pp. 35-39.
5. James Oseland, *Cradle of Flavor: Home Cooking from the Spice Islands of Indonesia, Malaysia, and Singapore* (New York: Norton, 2006).
6. James Oseland, *Cradle of Flavor* (unpublished draft with notes).
7. Molly Stevens, *All About Braising* (unpublished drafts with notes). Subsequent references also come from this source.
8. Molly Stevens, *All About Braising: The Art of Uncomplicated Cooking* (New York: Norton, 2004), p. 131.
9. Maricel E. Presilla, *Gran Cocina Latina: The Food of Latin America* (New York: Norton, 2012).
10. J. Kenji López-Alt, *The Food Lab: Better Home Cooking Through Science* (New York: Norton, 2015).

New York's Artisanal Oyster Farmers: Creating the Wild(ish) Oyster

Charity Robey

In Jonathan Swift's phrase, the first bold man to eat an oyster did so many thousands of years ago – joined by so many other bold men and women that, by the twentieth century, most of the oysters in the world were no longer wild, but farmed.

Today, cultivated oysters account for at least 95% of the oysters consumed in the US, and an intense culture of connoisseurship has grown up around them. In New York, historically the largest oyster-consuming American city, restaurants and bars take pride in offering oysters from a list of local producers, opening and serving them live as a separate course. Discerning patrons pay attention to the oysters' flavour profiles, places of origin, size, shape, and colour.

The taste may evoke a stormy ocean beach, but these bivalves are decidedly not wild. This paper takes a look underneath the water, before the oysters are harvested and shucked, to uncover the art and technique that Long Island's artisanal farmers employ in the creation of cultivated oysters.

Long Island oysters are sold with a completely transparent chain of identity and responsibility. A person eating an oyster at eight p.m. in Greenwich Village would have no trouble the next day tracing the origin of that oyster to the bay where it grew and

Figure 1 (left). A New York oyster cart, circa 1890. Figure 2 (right). An oyster saloon next to the Academy Hotel in New York, 1876-1914. Images courtesy of the New York Historical Society.

the farmer who planted and tended it from the time it was spat. This paper uncovers how, at every stage of cultivation, farmers intervene to shape the development of their bivalves toward an ideal of shape, size, flavour, and fragrance that is unique to their location and brand – the oysters of their imaginations.

History of Oyster Farming in New York and the Rise of Connoisseurship

> Down by the sea lived a lonesome oyster
> Every day getting sadder and moister
> He found his home life awf'lly wet
> And longed to travel with the upper set
> — Cole Porter[1]

In the nineteenth century, New York was the centre of the oyster-eating world, with twelve million oysters sold in markets annually by 1860. Gnarly, muddy piles of wild and farmed oysters were sold and slurped in great quantities at oyster shacks, and shucked oysters were served in bars and saloons as well as fine restaurants (Figures 1 and 2). Everybody, high and low, ate oysters, which were cheap and abundant, especially in the winter months, when keeping oysters cool enough to transport from oyster bed to oyster bar was easier.[2]

In the early twentieth century, oysters were wild and sexy-looking things, often long and banana-shaped with a substantial meat that could be more than a mouthful. Most were harvested using mechanical dredges that hauled up clumps of oysters that had grown together into reefs. Individual animals were broken off with hammers, and those that could not be separated were shucked in situ and then canned or bottled (Figure 3).

As is true today, New York oyster eaters were often served at stand-up bars or from outdoor carts, the curved part of the oyster's shell serving as plate and bowl. In the 1870s and 1880s, wealthy people enjoyed oysters served as a first course on exquisite plates that replaced the unsightly shells (Figure 4). Banquets sometimes featured centrepieces replicating entire oyster reefs, with the shells opened, resembling conjoined twins.

Large-scale oyster consumption and industrial pollution caused such a decline of the oyster population in New York waters that, by the time Edward

Figure 3. Processing reefs of wild oysters. Image courtesy of the Southold Historical Society.

Ingersoll wrote *The Oyster Industry* in 1881, Long Island commercial oyster producers relied on bedding oysters from the Chesapeake Bay that were only finished in New York waters. 'Little distinction is made by the warehousemen in buying in respect to locality,' he wrote 'The rule is: the deeper the water, the better the oyster.'[3]

When Sandy Ingber, executive chef at the Grand Central Oyster Bar, started buying oysters for the restaurant in the 1980s, there were only a handful of oyster producers left in New York, and the most recognizable New York oyster, the Blue Point, was no longer raised in the waters of the Great South Bay.[4] Ingber has presided over the last thirty years of oyster-eating history, including the astonishing rise of oyster connoisseurship and, along with it, a new kind of artisanal oyster-farmer:

Figure 4. Oyster platter. Courtesy of Museum of the History of New York.

> In the 90s I would go to the Boston Seafood Show in March, and if I came back with one new oyster it would be a complete success. In summer, we had a very difficult time finding oysters that were not spawning. I had maybe two kinds. And then the dot coms crashed and everyone went into artisanal oyster farming. Come 2000, oyster farmers were popping up all over the place. By 2005 I had 25 different oysters on my menu, two-thirds East Coast, one-third West Coast.[5]

Characteristics of Great Oysters

All the characteristics of a great oyster (meaning an oyster that pleases a human being) occur naturally in wild oysters. Farmers marry their understanding of how oysters develop and thrive with artifice and expedients to bring out the best in the oysters they raise. Humans have mindfully influenced shellfish development for as long as we have been eating them. Some of the modern farmer's techniques, such as encouraging larval oysters to set on sand or shell, are ancient, while new ones have been developed, particularly in the genetic manipulation of oyster seed.

Oyster farmers start with seed, and those who farm on Long Island mostly buy seed by the hundreds of thousands at a time from one or two of a handful of seed-producers in coastal Connecticut; on Fisher's Island, NY; and in Southold, NY. These seed producers all grow the same species, *Crassostrea virginica*, and breed for disease resistance (Figure 5).

Physical Characteristics of a Supremely Edible Bivalve

With oyster connoisseurship in the United States came a preference for small oysters whose shell was thick at the shucking end to avoid the heartbreak of disintegration during the opening. Today most American chefs and home-shuckers prefer a bivalve of about eight centimetres (three inches). Easy to open, they can be eaten in one slurp. 'My philosophy is get three-inch oysters. You put half a dozen on a plate and it's beautiful,' said Ingber. 'I go with the wow effect.'

Also desirable is a deep cup of an inch or more, and meat that is slightly firm and tender but not watery. As the cup grows deeper, the oyster's body grows down into it. When the shell grows shallow or long, the body of the animal spreads out, creating a less appealing shape (Figure 6). Harold McGee describes a good oyster as one of 'the sea's tenderest morsels, the marine equivalent of penned veal or the fattened chicken, which just sit and eat. [...] It's big enough to make a generous morsel, has a full, complex flavour and suggestively slippery moistness; and its delicacy is a striking contrast to the encrusted, rocky shell'.[6]

The ideal Sandy Ingber looks for is 'a beautiful round thick body with great mouth feel; that's how you get the full flavor of the oyster'. Related to cup depth is the ratio of meat to shell, which Ingber calls coverage: 'If you open the oyster and there is a big shell and a long skinny, thin oyster that's not much coverage.'

For the six weeks or so when oysters are spawning, they are unpalatable. An entire farm will generally spawn at the same time, triggered by water temperature. During this period the oysters' bodies swell and remain flabby until they release the eggs and sperm, after which they are thin and watery for several weeks until they regain their form. Oysters can switch genders at will, as M.F.K. Fisher explained delightfully in her 1941 book *Consider the Oyster*:

Almost any normal oyster never knows from one year to the next whether he is he or she, and may start at any moment, after the first year, to lay eggs where once he spent his sexual energies in being exceptionally masculine. If he is a she, her energies are equally feminine, so that in a single summer, if all goes well, and the temperature of the water is somewhere around or above seventy degrees, she may spawn several hundred million eggs, fifteen to one hundred million at a time with commendable pride.[7]

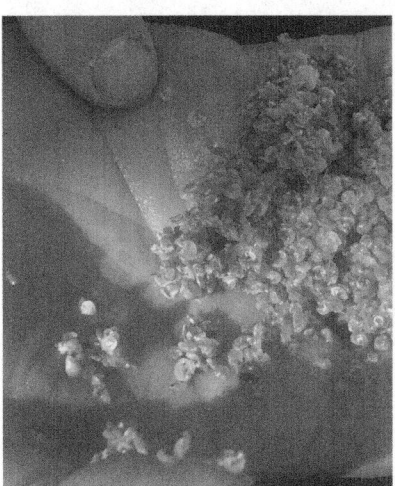

Figure 5. Oyster spat attached to grains of sand.

Light grey meat is considered the ideal. Dark meat can be a sign of post-spawn exhaustion. And oyster meat with a green cast is the specialty of a handful of farms with specific growing conditions: a pond-like environment and the right kind of algae. Green oysters (meat, shells, or both) are unfamiliar to Americans, and the East Coast farmers who produce them rarely market them (Figures 7 and 8).

But as Ingber notes, 'I would never in the past sell oysters with a green tint. It's only in the last year or two people are starting to think that they are sexy. Sometimes the Martha's Vineyard oyster has a green tint and we return them.'

'Meroir': The Environmental Effects of Water Temperature, Salinity, and Plankton on the Life Cycle of the Oyster and on Its Flavour and Aroma

> 'Connoisseurs, consumers, and experimental taste panels often differ on which oysters tend to be saltier, stronger flavoured, finer flavoured, and even whether they are distinguishable. This is just another manifestation of the predictable unpredictability, which itself is something to be savored.' – Harold McGee[8]

There is no generally agreed-upon ideal of flavour and aroma for an oyster, yet no subject brings out the oyster knives faster. Because the taste of an oyster is a direct reflection of its environment, debates about what flavours are most palatable quickly get personal, as in 'my hometown waters taste better than yours'.

There are myriad factors pertaining to taste that farmers must either accept or exploit, depending on their imagined ideal of oyster flavour. Foremost among these factors is the level of salinity, which is about 35 parts per thousand in ocean water and less in the bays and brackish creeks in which oysters are often grown. To tolerate a saline environment, the tissues of most marine animals make chemical adjustments. McGee writes that 'their body tissues adjust mainly with sugars and dissolved amino acids, notably taurine, sweet glycine and alanine, bittersweet proline, and bitter arginine. In addition, the shell liquor that they retain when harvested begins as a sample of the water they grow in. So, the taste of oysters is more intense in oysters from high-salinity waters'.[9]

Water temperature is also a factor in oyster-growing. As the temperature of seawater increases, salinity decreases, affecting the flavour profile of oysters who grow there. Also, oysters growing in deeper, colder waters grow

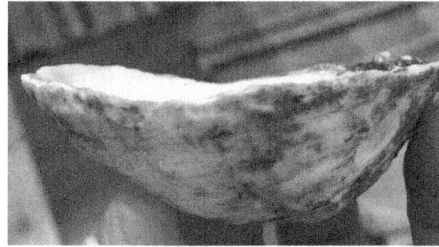

Figure 6 (top). Deep cup, strong shell. Figure 7 (bottom). A Fin de Claire Verte from the Oysterator web site.

New York's Artisanal Oyster Farmers

Figure 8. *In early spring Oysterponds oysters can be a little green around the gills.*

much more slowly than the same animals in warmer water.

Another factor is the depth at which oysters are grown. The plankton that oysters filter and consume occur in greater numbers in light-filled shallow waters, and more species of plankton are available to oysters that live where sea water circulation is greatest.

The oyster's diet is reflected in the flavour and aroma of its body. Phytoplankton (consisting of microscopic plants) contribute fruity, sweet, or grassy flavours to the tissues of an oyster who consumes them. The particular smells of oysters, McGee writes, come from 'molecules that produce the "green" smells of crushed leaves, that scent melons and cucumber, that create mushroominess. Strange, that they should also be prominent in sea animals, so that oysters can smell like cucumber'.[10]

'A Great Oyster Has a Great Name'

The perception of oyster flavour and aroma is so complex and so subjective that oyster-eaters who can choose often look for a recognizable name. 'A great oyster has a great name,' according to Ingber. 'And for New York oysters, Blue Point is the most common name, the best known. We sell five times as many Blue Points as any other oyster. They are also the least expensive oyster on our menu. Personally, I like oysters with more brine than a Blue Point.'

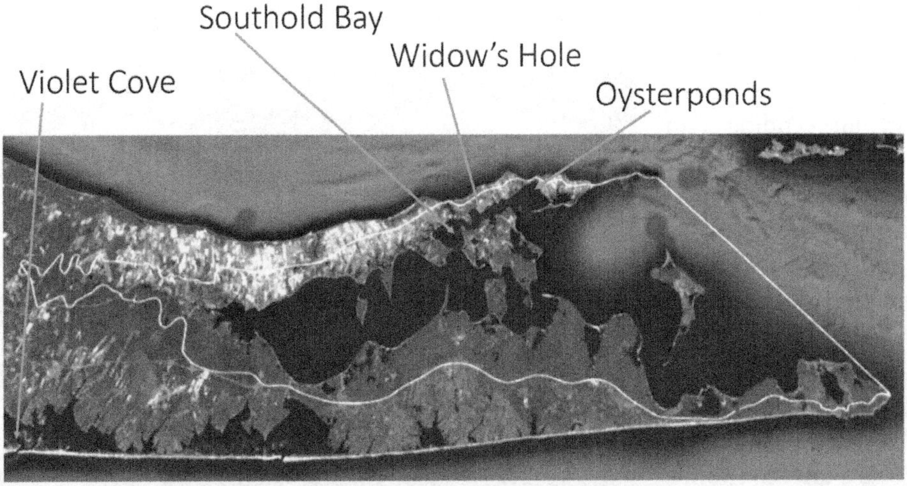

Figure 9. *The two forks of the East End of Long Island embrace a series of bays that are home to about 30 oyster farms. The locations of the four oyster farms discussed here are marked; Southold Bay, Violet Cove, Oysterponds and Widow's Hole.*

Before the rise of oyster bars and oyster connoisseurship in New York around the year 2000, the only names that most customers could recognize were Wellfleet, Cape Cod, Kumamoto (a West Coast oyster), and Blue Point. Now there are many more, and a memorable and evocative name that refers to the place where the oyster was grown has become essential to the ideal oyster.

Four Artisanal Oyster Farmers and How They Use Art and Science to Influence the Attributes of Their Animals

The cultivation techniques used by artisanal oyster raisers in New York waters to create distinct oyster brands from genetically similar animals take a number of environmental and geographic factors into account. Some farms are located in deep, cold water, and others in shallow, relatively warm water. Some farms use mechanical devices to trim and shape their oysters, and others use wave action. Some farms are flooded at times and dry at others, and some experience more water flow than others. In the following case studies, I describe how four oyster farmers use different techniques and ways of managing their animals to achieve the ideal oysters of their imaginations (Figure 9).

Ben Gonzalez of Southold Bay Oysters
The Perfect Oyster Is Raised Deep and Briny, with the Full Flavours of Southold Bay

Ben Gonzalez had a successful career in marketing before he and his partner, Dave Daly, took up oyster farming in 2013. Their farm is located in the Southold Bay, part of the Peconic Bay system, in about twenty feet of water. The bottom is sandy, the water cooler and the algae less abundant than in shallow water, so the oysters grow for up to two years, more slowly than in shallow-water farms. The oysters grow in steel cages that Gonzalez and Daly haul out of the water with a crane attached to their boat *Pulpo* and transport to the land-based part of their farm for tending and harvesting. A shallow tidal creek flows around their boat dock, and its quiet, relatively warm waters serve as an interim grow-out area for oysters that are too small to go into cages: 'The smaller ones I keep in the creek, a little more controlled environment.'

Every four weeks, Gonzalez puts the entire

Figure 10. Ben Gonzalez holding an oyster with new growth (left) and one that has had the growth broken off by the tumbler (right).

farm through the tumbler, a device that looks like a doorless, front-loading washing machine that sorts the oysters by size while washing and tumbling them against each other. This process breaks a thin layer of new shell off the lip of the oysters, stimulating the animals to grow a deeper cup and denser meat. He explains that 'in a way, we are sculpting a live animal' (Figure 10).

Gonzalez takes advantage of the growing conditions on his farm to produce oysters that are full-flavoured, briny, and the right size: 'Three inches is a mouthful for most people, and they don't want to cut the oyster with a fork and knife.'[11]

Sue Wicks of Violet Cove Oysters
The Perfect Oyster Is Raised with Individual Attention and Care

Sue Wicks was born and raised on the Great South Bay of Long Island, the daughter and granddaughter of baymen. After a long professional career that landed her in the Women's Basketball Hall of Fame, she returned to the water in 2016 and began farming oysters.

Violet Cove Oysters is one of three farms located in the shallow waters of the Great South Bay, wedged between a fast-moving current in the navigation lane and the shoreline of undeveloped public land. The depth of the water in the farm fluctuates from 71 centimetres to two metres (28 inches to six feet.) She remembers, 'My dad used to scratch [rake] razor clams on this spot.' On the May day I visited, the water temperature was about thirteen degrees Celsius (55°F). Wicks expected a spurt of growth as soon as the water got above sixteen degrees (61°F), an ideal temperature for growing oysters.

Wicks does not use mechanical tumblers or other tools to keep the oyster's growth trimmed and pruned. Her oysters grow in floating mesh bags, attached with clips to allow movement, and anchored to the sandy bottom so as to rise and fall with the tide. In this setup, she explains, 'I create a gentle tumble for the oysters. Everything matters, the size of the bags, the weight of the clips, the floats that keep the bags at the surface and increase the wave action' (Figure 11).

Wicks grows about 750,000 oysters in a year on a few acres of bay bottom, which is pretty good productivity for a boutique oyster farm. In the spring she tends her oysters at low tide, walking around to check each bag without taking it off the line: 'I'm looking to see if they have grown. I get out of the boat and walk,

Figure 11. Sue Wicks tending her farm at low tide.

checking every single one. It's a nice way to farm. We'll have warm weather this week, and then they will explode. It's like magic.'

Wicks plants three times a year and harvests according to size and stage of development. When the oysters are harvested affects their taste:

> Some say the best time to eat them is January because they are filled with glycogen, but if you like that grassy finish, next month, June will be the time for some of these. Then in July, all their energy goes toward making babies, and then they are tired and then they regenerate. When you open up that little seven-centimetre [2.75 inch] Violet Cove, in the fall, it's going to have a lot of meat. Not long and wonky. Deep cup, thick shell, a lot of meat with a creamy nutty middle flavour, from the muscle. That oyster will have complexity and meat.

Some years Wick's oysters develop a purple stripe in their shell, for which she named the farm: 'You sometimes get that purple colour in the summer with a healthy well-fed oyster, and it seems to persist here. The nutrients here make the purple more pronounced. We are over springs, that may be why, and I like the name Violet.'

Wicks likes this scale of production: 'This is a boutique farm. I have that luxury of paying attention to every single one. I touch them five times before I sell them. Sorting them, harvesting them, maybe I take fifty and the rest go back. That's part of getting a perfect oyster. I don't want to do it mechanically.'[12]

Phil Mastrangelo of Oysterponds Oyster Company
The Perfect Oyster Is the One that Chefs Covet

Phil Mastrangelo worked on Wall Street for twenty-five years before leaving in 2013 to farm oysters full time, but for him that was less of a shift than it seems: 'Oyster farming is where capitalism meets environmentalism. There are very few things that I could go into that would satisfy me on both counts.'

The farm produces just under a million oysters a year, with about three million at different stages of development at any time. They start their filtering career in a shallow tidal creek, where the baby oysters grow in bags in a few feet of water until they are moved to nearby Pipe's Cove to finish in about twenty-five feet of water. Mastrangelo says his mantra is, 'You have to have flow.'

During the growing season, every oyster goes through a mechanical tumbler where it is sorted and its new growth is trimmed, resulting in the firm shell, deep cup, and compact meat that chefs want (Figure 12). 'The tumbler shocks the oyster, and improves the shell coverage of the meat,' Mastrangelo said. 'If you looked at one that we missed you'd see the meat is translucent and loose, not dense. If you try to shuck an oyster and the shell crumbles, that's a sign that the oyster was not tended to properly.'

Oysters are living things, but the chefs Mastrangelo works with are seeking a steady and reliable supply of oysters, consistent in size and quality. He explains, 'Our high season is the summer, and all the oysters on a farm spawn at the same time according to the temperature.'

Figure 12. Oysterponds bivalves go through frequent tumbling to encourage a deep cup, strong shell and compact meat.

To avoid a six-week hiatus in harvesting oysters during the spawn, Mastrangelo purchases seed for a variety of *Crassostrea virginica* that does not reproduce, called a triploid.

When the oysters are big enough, Mastrangelo moves them from the tidal creek to the bay to continue growing, in part to increase their brininess: 'The salinity of the creek is twenty-eight parts per thousand and the bay is just under thirty parts per thousand. Baby oysters prefer brackish water, but I prefer the brininess. You get that in the bay in twenty feet of water.'

Sometimes in the spring, the oysters growing in the creek turn green, with a grassy taste from feeding on shallow-water algae that are photosensitive. The response to the green oysters varies: 'One spring, when we had a lot of green oysters, and I got a call from a restaurant saying, I'll take as many as you have up to 40,000 for St. Patrick's Day. I didn't have anywhere near that many. I've also had them sent back to me. One chef asked me to come to the restaurant to take back an entire shipment. He had it placed in an area for hazardous materials.'[13]

Mike and Isabel Osinski of Widow's Hole Oysters
The Perfect Oyster Is Jewel-Like

Mike and Isabel Osinski got into oyster farming when they discovered by accident that they owned a few acres of bay bottom adjacent to their summer home in Greenport, NY. It was 2001, their kids were young, and they were ready to move on after making a bundle writing the mortgage securitization software that helped create the 2008 financial crisis.

The Osinskis set out to produce the most beautiful oyster possible, show it to chefs at the most refined New York restaurants, and establish a consistent and enduring brand they called Widow's Hole after a tiny creek adjacent to their home and farm.

Sue Wicks, whose Violet Cove Oysters could be considered competitors to Widow's Hole, respected Mike Osinski's pitch: 'He'd walk in to a chef and say, look at this, it's perfect, it's not a wild thing. It's going to look great on a tray.'[14] Two decades later, some of the best-known restaurants in New York are customers, including the Grand Central Oyster Bar and Le Bernardin. 'We don't clean those,' Mike Osinski said, and pointed to a tray of pristine oysters just before shucking them for me to taste. 'That's how they come out of the water.'

Mike and Isabel Osinski work in shallow-water and use a system of floating bags like the farms in the Great South Bay, but their oysters are grown with a difference. The bivalves tumble in purses with floats that accelerate the wave action. The purses snap onto lines, and the lines snap onto a cable that is suspended over the water on wooden beams

Figure 13. Widow's Hole oysters are grown in bags that rock on the waves, suspended by a system of cables and beams.

(Figure 13). The oysters feed at the surface where algae are abundant. When the weather is mild enough, the suspension system allows the purses full of oysters to dry as the tide goes out. Allowing the oysters to dry out eliminates most predators and enhances the spotless appearance of the shells by burning off the algae.

Eliminating predators also allows the Osinskis to grow a few of their oysters for much longer than the typical eighteen months or so. These so-called knife-and-fork oysters are five years old and prized by New York chefs.

Inspired by a Japanese technique called Kusshi (which means 'precious' and creates a small bonsai-type oyster), the Osinskis' son, an engineering student at Yale, designed the farm setup in part because he thought running a boat around a more conventional bag system was too much work for his parents.

Mike Osinski estimates that their revenue from oyster farming over the years has amounted to enough income to pay for their son's tuition at Yale as well as their daughter's at Cornell.[15]

Nostalgia, Landscape, and Culture Expressed in the Bodies of Oysters

Creating the perfect oyster certainly involves science, but the small-yield oyster farmers working in New York waters are artists too, coaxing nature to achieve a distinctive vision of oyster perfection that is different for each farmer. Oysters are sophisticated products of each farmer's craft and labour as well as imagination.

Farmers take great care in controlling the shape and colour of the shell in part because the consumer's experience is enhanced by eating from a shell that seems connected to the landscape. When farmers try to avoid a greenish shade in the flesh of their oysters, they are holding to local tradition and the tendency of Americans to avoid unfamiliar-looking seafood. Even the name of the oyster, monikers such as Pemaquit or Blue Point, express nostalgia for a pre-industrial time when oysters were ubiquitous and wild.

The way that oysters have inspired the likes of Jonathan Swift, Cole Porter, and M.F.K. Fisher testifies to the hold they have on the human imagination. As Eleanor Clark wrote in *The Oysters of Locmariaquer* (winner of the National Book Award in 1964), 'You are eating the sea, that's it, only the sensation of a gulp of sea water has been wafted out of it by some sorcery, and are on the verge of remembering you don't know what, mermaids or the sudden smell of kelp on the ebb tide or a poem you read once, something connected with the flavour of life itself…'[16]

Notes

1. Cole Porter, 'The Tale of the Oyster', *Fifty Million Frenchmen*, Music and Lyrics by Cole Porter, Book by Herbert Fields, 1929.
2. Mark Kurlansky, *The Big Oyster: History on the Half Shell* (New York: Random House, 2006), p. 184.
3. Edward Ingersoll, *The Oyster Industry*, Jan 1881.U.S. Government Printing Office, pp. 99-100.
4. Rowan Jacobsen, *The Essential Oyster* (New York: Bloomsbury, 2016), pp 135-51.
5. Interview with Sandy Ingber, Grand Central Oyster Bar, New York, New York, April 2021.
6. Harold McGee, *On Food and Cooking: The Science and Lore of the Kitchen* (New York: Scribner, 2004), p. 227.
7. M.F.K. Fisher, *The Art of Eating* (Hoboken, NJ: Wiley, 2004), p. 125.
8. Harold McGee, *Nose Dive: A Field Guide to the World's Smells* (New York: Penguin, 2020), p. 394.
9. McGee, *Nose Dive*, p. 392, original emphasis.
10. McGee, *Nose Dive*, p. 382.
11. Interview with Ben Gonzalez, owner of Southold Bay Oyster, Southold, New York, April 2021.
12. Interview with Sue Wicks, owner of Violet Cove Oyster, East Moriches, New York, 26 May 2021.
13. Interview with Phil Mastrangelo, owner of Oysterponds Oysters, Orient, New York, May 2021.
14. Interview with Wicks.
15. Interview with Isabel and Mike Osinski, owners of Widow's Hole Oysters, Greenport, New York, May 2021.
16. Eleanor Clark, *The Oysters of Locmariaquer* (New York: Harper, 1964), p. 6.

The Birth of a Legend: *Mole de Guajolote* and Mestizo Identity in the Imaginary of Post-Revolutionary Mexico

Ana Karen Ruiz de la Peña Posada

Legends about *mole de guajolote*, one of the most typical dishes of Mexican cuisine, were written in a context in which the post-revolutionary elite sought to construct an imaginary that defined Mexican cuisine. This imaginary was underpinned by the mestizo discourse that gave the national cuisine its identity, with *mole de guajolote* as its crowning jewel.

Mexican cuisine has its roots not just in the history of Mexico, but also in the imaginary, constructed over the life of the country by men and women eager to take meaning and identity from their own context. To speak of the identity of Mexican cuisine, the imaginary surrounding it and its typical dishes, requires understanding the process by which it came about as well as the factors that contributed to it.

Constructing Mexican national identity and identifying what is considered Mexican was a process that took several centuries. Colonial ties to Spain, a war of independence, several foreign interventions, and a generally unstable political outlook meant that the official discourse and ordinary Mexicans alike found it difficult to say what defined Mexico as a nation. There were several attempts to conceptualize Mexico during the nineteenth century, after achieving independence, but the real opportunity to debate what would thereafter be considered Mexican came after the Mexican Revolution. The movement that did away with the regime of Porfirio Díaz – who had been in power for more than thirty years – made nationalist discourses prevalent during the first decades of the twentieth century.

The ruling elite began to define how this nationalist discourse would encompass all domains of Mexican life, including its cuisine.[1] Cuisine seemed an excellent representation of what was considered Mexican; however, at the time it was difficult to even conceive of a unified national cuisine given to the regional differences in a country as large as Mexico. Given these differences, some saw the importance of a dish that could bring together the characteristics of what was beginning to be thought of as Mexican cuisine in the imaginary of the era, and they found it in *mole de guajolote*, or turkey *mole*.[2] The roots of *mole de guajolote* go deep in the history of Mexico, and its base component was an ingredient that distinguished Mexico in the collective imaginary: chilli peppers. This history goes back to the Mesoamerican era but more

The Birth of a Legend: *Mole de Guajolote* and Mestizo Identity

immediately to the colonial era, the source of another idea central to Mexican identity: *mestizaje*, the mixed identity resulting from the collision of European and Indigenous people. *Mole de guajolote* became seen as a dish that represented the meeting of two worlds; with a series of ingredients brought from different corners of the globe, it was not just mestizo, but also cosmopolitan.

The transcendence of *mole* exceeds its tangible elements, which in and of themselves make it a wonderful dish. Its preparation method, particularly the use of the *metate*, has roots in indigenous cultures.[3] Its enormous variety of ingredients combine local products, including dried chillies, tortillas, chocolate, and turkey, with others from all over the world, including spices like cloves, cumin, and cinnamon. The dish has a central presence in daily life and is a key feature of holiday celebrations. But even more important than these tangible elements is the mythology that was created around this dish. For *mole* to be considered representative of Mexican cuisine, it first had to be given a story, a history worthy of being told.[4] Creating legends about the origin of *mole de guajolote* – and popularizing those legends – gave *mole* the privileged place it occupies in the pantheon of Mexican cuisine.

Imaginary and Imagination

Studying legends about *mole de guajolote* requires conceptualizing the imaginary, which this paper will define using the work of Dominique Kalifa, who has argued for integrating the concept of the imaginary into the study of history. According to Kalifa:

> The imaginary, such as it is understood by historians, is composed of facts that can be observed, analyzed and measured using real, very material sources. It is a part of the history of *representations*, a term which refers to tangible, material forms of expression that are part of cultural history, shaped by broadcast media and by media limitations and techniques.[5]

From this perspective, the imaginary corresponds to the myths, stories, and even dreams as privileged media in which it is expressed. The world of the imaginary to which myths and legends belong is also a significant part of how our ideas about reality are constructed, because it is influenced by the cultural, political, and social context of the time in which it is created, in such a way that collective imaginaries expressed through this sort of narrative are a reflection of how different groups of humans that make up societies perceive themselves and the elements thereof.[6]

According to Kalifa, the theory of the historical imaginary includes both the temporal and spatial concepts of the imaginary, two key concepts in the study of history. In the temporal imaginary, Kalifa focuses on chrononyms, artificial divisions of time that allow a period with certain characteristics to be defined:

> these denominations of time, particularly when they take the form of chrononyms (the Renaissance, the Middle Ages […]), bring with them an entire imaginary,

a theatricality, even a 'sense of drama'. To unravel a temporal imaginary [...] is to understand how societies care for, interpret and occasionally reinvent entire segments of their past.

In this way, Mexico's post-revolutionary period, beginning with the promulgation of the Constitution of 1917 and culminating in the 1940s with the consolidation of Mexican political institutions, is a chrononym.[7] The imaginary of the post-revolutionary period fits with this definition because reinventing a chapter of the past is exactly what the creators of the different versions of the *mole de guajolote* origin myths did.

Concerning the spatial imaginary, Kalifa argues there are 'places [that] are vested with social appropriations (in the sense that they produce social interactions), giving them strong historical significance (and are therefore shifting, inscribed in a diachronic movement and can be analyzed historically)'. Such places imply beliefs, representations, and practices. In the collective imaginary of Mexico, convent kitchens are considered a melting pot, places for dialogue between Spanish and indigenous cuisines that resulted in mestizo cuisine which, in the discourse and imaginary of these post-revolution period authors, was the basis of the national cuisine.

The Legends

Legends are powerful tools for transmitting the culture of a country or society. In the case of Mexico, legends associated with cuisine and food left a profound mark on the collective imaginary and paved the way for the construction of what has come to be thought of as Mexico's national cuisine. One of the first legends that arose with regard to this national cuisine was about *mole de guajolote*, which is now a symbol of Mexico.

The invention of the legend of *mole de guajolote* is commonly attributed to the chronicler Artemio de Valle-Arizpe; however, more recent investigations have shown that the Poblano chronicler Carlos de Gante published the first legend about this dish in the newspaper *Excelsior*, and that later versions are based on his work.[8] In a piece titled 'Santa Rosa de Lima y el Mole de Guajolote', de Gante gave a nun, Sor Andrea de la Asunción, credit for the creation of the renowned dish that was garnering more and more prestige.[9]

According to the legend, Sor Andrea, who was known in the Santa Rosa convent and in Puebla, the second most important city in New Spain, for her skill in the culinary arts, was charged with coming up with a dish to honour bishop Manuel Fernandez de Santa Cruz, who was visiting the city and had to be impressed with a unique delicacy that distinguished the cooking of the nuns of the convent from that of other convents. During the colonial period in Puebla, the different convents in the city set up a competition to create the best dishes for important guests, both from the government and the church, who came through the city. The dilemma of what to serve the bishop was therefore given to the nuns at Santa Rosa. After going back and forth in the kitchen and rejecting all the other sisters' suggestions, Sor Andrea – as if by divine inspiration – gathered a set of ingredients, starting with dried chillies, spices from Europe and Asia,

The Birth of a Legend: *Mole de Guajolote* and Mestizo Identity

turkey native to America, pork lard, and chocolate, and she began to combine them as the other nuns looked on, flabbergasted, as *mole* was born before their eyes. The *mole* was then served to the clergyman, who was quick to sing its praise. Carlos de Gante's story shows the intimate relationship between cuisine and religious inspiration, an idea that would be reproduced in other legends about *mole de guajolote*.

Spatial and temporal imaginaries play an important role here. The spatial imaginary is represented by two types of spaces: the convent, as a space for culinary experimentation, and Puebla, considered one of the most important cities in the colonial era. Puebla was already illustrious for its cuisine, and it was a well-travelled meeting point between various cultures, as not only did people from both indigenous and Spanish cultures live there, but it was also a stopover for those traveling east to west. During the colonial era, the kitchens of convents, both of monks and of nuns, became a sort of laboratory for experiments with the full range of native and foreign ingredients that were available, and as a result these kitchens created the most extraordinary recipes to impress locals and foreigners alike. One of the main duties of these kitchens was to put on celebratory spreads for important guests to the city, the viceroys and bishops who held the highest positions in the social hierarchy of New Spain. It is also thanks to convent cuisine that the first written recipe books of New Spain were preserved, making these spaces important across time as well. The recipes in these books have transcended generations, seeping through the brick-built convent walls, first to be enjoyed in the high-class houses of New Spain and eventually being cooked and reinterpreted in every home of what is now Mexico. This narrative about convent kitchens was useful to post-revolutionary Mexico as it lent credence to the idea that the identity of Mexican cuisine and Mexicans themselves was mestizo.

Mestizaje is an important matter that should be discussed in this context. As mentioned above, according to researcher Agustín Basave, post-revolutionary nationalist ideology regarding both biological and cultural *mestizaje* resulted from the process of constructing the national identity.[10] This national identity holds that Mexico is a mestizo nation, the result of the encounter between the White world, especially the Spanish, and the Indigenous world. The ideal mestizo Mexican was a reflection of the most authentic elements of the amalgam of the two peoples: they spoke Spanish, their political views were liberal, they sought prosperity and the modernization of the country according to European precepts, and they were also Catholic, but not to the extent of idolatry which went against the era's enlightenment thinking. From the Indigenous cultures, they possessed a sensibility for the arts and were the descendants of the ancient traditions of the Indigenous peoples, who the elites now marginalized and aspired to do away with by integrating them into the seemingly superior mestizo race.[11] The legend of *mestizaje* resonated in the minds of the intellectuals hungry to define their roots, so they said that Mexicans were the result of 'an unprecedented case of integration between colonizing peoples and colonized peoples and blessed by the equally unprecedented miracle of the Virgin of Guadalupe'.[12] In this context, the invention of *mole de guajolote* could be interpreted as an allegory of how Mexican mestizo identity arose; the religious identity is made manifest in the holy hands of a White nun who used the best foreign and local ingredients to make the most typical dish of what is today Mexico's national cuisine.

In another version of the legend in the book *La típica cocina poblana y los guisos de sus religiosas*, Melitón Salazar Monroy tells the tale of how the convent recipes came to be appropriated by the Mexican pueblo: 'Sor Andrea de la Asunción had triumphed mightily with her invention of *mole*. Other convents asked for the recipe for so exquisite a dish, which quickly became a vogue in the houses of the rich, and then reached the masses who made it a mainstay at celebrations.'[13] Here Salazar Monroy is expressing another idea about *mole de guajolote* that would remain engraved in the collective imaginary: that it is a holiday dish. Today, *mole* is considered part of the Mexican diet, it can be found in supermarkets where industrially produced versions are sold, and in markets and cornershops, but *mole de guajolote*, still prepared using traditional methods, continues to be associated with big family celebrations, weddings, *quinceañera* parties, and baptisms; it is eaten at patronal festivals and celebrations such as Día de los Muertos, where *ofrendas* dedicated to the departed often also bear *mole*, and at Poblano tables at Christmastime.

Legends about *mole* express stereotypes about Mexico that began to dominate the thinking of many figures in post-revolutionary Mexico. In the version by José Miguel E. Sarmiento, *mole de guajolote* is accompanied by other foods that are typically Mexican, such as *tamales* and beans. It is also significant that it is served on a Talavera plate: Talavera is a pottery technique brought to Puebla by Spanish settlers of Muslim heritage that has since been made an important Poblano handicraft. Again, cuisine appears in a role charged with significance in the imaginary of the origin of *mole*. The kitchen of the Santa Rosa convent represents, in the imaginary of Mexicans, principally Puebla natives, the place where a nun was inspired in an act of God to create the national dish. It is noteworthy that it was not just any kitchen, but a kitchen lined with Talavera tiles, the same material as the plate on which the *mole de guajolote* was served to the world (Figure 1).

The collective imaginary has given credit for the *mole de guajolote* origin myth to Artemio de Valle-Arizpe, but Carlos de Gante was in fact his precursor. Valle-Arizpe changed the version created by de Gante to make the guest honoured by the *mole de guajolote* Viceroy Tomás Antonio de la Cerda y Aragón, giving the first man to taste the national dish a higher political status, and thereby according the dish itself a greater role in the nascent pantheon of Mexican cuisine. In his tale, the chronicler lists the dishes that other convents in Puebla sent to dignify the Viceroy. His description of the dishes sent out by a convent whose name he does not mention is striking: 'from another, platters of *molotes* with enchiladas, with *chalupas*, with quesadillas, with *tostadas* of various compositions, and with flawless *pambazos* made with unambiguous flair'.[14] All the dishes mentioned here are now considered representative of authentic Mexican cuisine. The majority of them are made of maize and considered part of what are commonly known as *antojitos*.[15] We can therefore say that these dishes were already

The Birth of a Legend: *Mole de Guajolote* and Mestizo Identity

part of the national culinary universe in the imaginary of Artemio de Valle-Arizpe.

The tale goes on to describe the nuns' dilemma over which dish was worthy to be served to the Viceroy. María Elsa Guadalupe Hernández y Martínez notes that 'Sor Andrea wanted to send His Excellency a delicious, exquisite dish, with the spirit of Mexico beating in all its alluring fineness within it'.[16] This version of the legend is adorned with literary language that beautifies the story and gives it a halo of mysticism, elevating the serendipitous creation of *mole de guajolote* to the Mexican imaginary.

Legends about *mole de guajolote* and their creators reinforced narratives of *mestizaje* planted by the elite. These narratives privileged the virtues of the White Spanish like religiousness and bravery; it also glorified the historic Indigenous peoples with their vast empire, embodied in the imaginary by the Mexica culture, but spurned and subjugated actual existing Indigenous peoples. The fact that in the imaginary of authors it was the nuns who created *mole de guajolote* was no accident: in their caring hands the turkey was purified, and the indigenous elements were transformed in this chilli-based dish by giving it a sweet edge that would please the palate of any person in power. The narratives about *mestizaje* were a somewhat simplistic way of interpreting the process by which Mexican identity and its cuisine were constructed, since they ignored the fact that political, economic, and social factors contributed to the construction of Mexican identity more than racial factors. This simplification is also reflected in the legends themselves, since they only tell us about one of the many complex varieties of *mole* that actually exist in the country.

Finally it is worth mentioning that even though we cannot be certain that Sor Andrea de la Asunción was the first to breathe life into *mole de guajolote*, as no historical proof demonstrating the existence of this nun has ever been found, we can say with certainty that Carlos de Gante, Artemio de Valle Arizpe, and all of the other authors that told and retold this fantastic story, and not Sor Andrea de la Asunción, are the ones who left their mark on the post-revolutionary imaginary and gave Mexican cuisine one

Figure 1. The Santa Rosa convent kitchen decorated with Talavera tiles. Picture taken by the author, 1 June 2021.

of its greatest origin myths. *Mole* was, and still is, one of the most refined and elaborate dishes in the oeuvre of Mexican national cuisine, but its most significant impact has been to make visible the immense value of made-in-Mexico cuisine.

Notes

1. Because the prevailing imaginary of the time was not wholly formed in all of society, the ruling elite had the power to influence the imaginary of the epoch. This idea is supported by the work of Juan Camilo Escobar Villegas, who argues that the domination of a social class fundamentally depends on imaginaries (*Lo Imaginario: Entre las ciencias sociales y la historia* (Medellin: Fondo Editorial Universidad EAFIT, 2000)).
2. *Mole de guajolote* is just one of many varieties of this dish that exist in Mexico: almost every state has one typical *mole*. Varieties of *mole* include *mole negro*, *mole verde*, *mole amarillito*, and *mole de caderas*. The *mole* about which the legends were written is known today as *mole Poblano* and was originally an accompaniment to Mexico's native poultry, turkey. The mix of sweet and spicy flavours in *mole Poblano* make it stand out from other *moles*.
3. The *metate* is a cooking utensil similar to a mortar and pestle used in Mesoamerican cultures to grind grain, seeds, and other ingredients and is still an essential tool in traditional Mexican cuisine.
4. María Elsa Guadalupe Hernández y Martínez, *El mole poblano, platillo prehispánico logra su inmortalidad en el siglo XVII* (Puebla: Benemérita Universidad Autónoma de Puebla-Dirección de Fomento Editorial, 2017), p. 83.
5. Dominique Kalifa, 'Escribir una historia del imaginario (Siglos XIX-XX)', *Secuencia*, 105 (2019) <http://secuencia.mora.edu.mx/index.php/Secuencia/article/view/1757/1905?fbclid=IwAR0UA2yFt_6XHmnffLYA0WWysHW3dLUv2AiYrmGT6GFsgbf-_hOTcxRNJLY> [accessed 20 May 2021] All translations by the author.
6. Ángel Enrique Carretero Pasín, 'La relevancia sociológica de lo imaginario en la cultura actual', *Nómadas*, 9 (2004) <https://www.redalyc.org/articulo.oa?id=18100906> [accessed 20 May 2021].
7. Luz María Uhthoff López, 'La construcción del Estado Posrevolucionario en México. Una aproximación desde la administración pública', *Diálogos Revista Electrónica de Historia*, 20.2 (2019) <https://www.redalyc.org/jatsRepo/439/43959529005/html/index.html> [accessed 20 May 2021]
8. Few texts concerning legends about *mole de guajolote* acknowledge the contribution of Carlos de Gante. One of the most recent works that unearths this legend is by the researcher José Luis Juárez López, 'La leyenda de la creación del mole de guajolote de Carlos de Gante', *AAPAUNAM Academia, Ciencia y Cultura*, 10.2 (2018), 124-29.
9. Carlos de Gante, '*Santa Rosa de Lima y el mole de guajolote*', *Excélsior*, México D.F., 12 December 1926, pp. 4-5
10. Agustín Basave, *México mestizo. Análisis del nacionalismo mexicano en torno a la mestizofilia* (Mexico City: Fondo de Cultura Económica, 2002), p. 14.
11. Federico Navarrete, *México Racista. Una denuncia* (Mexico City: Grijalbo, 2016), p.121
12. Navarrete, p. 99.
13. Melitón Salazar Monroy, *La típica cocina poblana y los guisos de sus religiosas* (Mexico City: Impresos López, 1945), p. 145.
14. Artemio de Valle Arizpe, '*El mole*', in Hernández y Martínez, pp. 91-97.
15. *Antojitos* are a type of Mexican street food, generally eaten as an appetizer and made of maize. They range from a high-fat fast food to a more nutritious meal.
16. Hernández y Martínez, p. 93.

Food Reimagined: Diasporic Identity and Authenticity

Shayma Owaise Saadat

When does our collective sense of culinary consciousness begin? Was it in the womb, when my mother's mother fed her pregnant daughter hot *parathas*, sprinkled with sugar, and dollops of chilled *malai*? Or perhaps it was nine years later, when my mother sent me to school with my lunch box? Two *shami kebabs*, scented with clove and cinnamon, made with poached beef and lentils, formed into patties, dipped into egg wash, and shallow fried till crisp. When cool, she sandwiched them between mayo-slathered bread and crisp lettuce leaves. Into my lunchbox it would go.

Food, Nostalgia, And Identity

The instructions are clear: to ½ kilogram of ground beef, I am to add 20 black peppercorns. Roll them into small orbs, and gently transfer into the cumin- and turmeric-spiced tomato-yoghurt sauce. Allow to simmer. Serve warm, with *sufaid chawal* and *raita*. This recipe for Pakistani-style *koftay* was created in the kitchen of Zubaida Sultana, my mother's mother, born 1922 in Lahore, Pakistan. The same recipe made its way to America with my mother, who crossed the ocean as a young bride, to make her new home in America, with my father and me, her almost-two-year-old daughter.

This kind of matrilineal recipe helped foster a sense of continuity for my Ami, my mother, in a new country. For Ami and the women who became my beloved Aunties over the years, a collective cultural memory of food and their respective mothers' traditional recipes tethered them to their past and to their homeland – Pakistan. The recipes they made in the kitchens of their suburban Washington, DC homes were not reimagined. Their recipes were traditional and replicated, in memory of what they had left behind.

As Razia Parveen shares about her own mother and friends who migrated from Punjab, Pakistan to Lockwood, UK:

> They repeated the cultural practices of the homeland in the diaspora and, through this repetition and the process of mimicry, alongside the transmission of these practices from the homeland to the diaspora, made a significant contribution to the maintenance of their cultural life and to the formation of an identity. By their very nature, memory and nostalgia are individual but through the presence of a community with a shared history the memory and nostalgia became *collective*.[1]

For older generations, such as Ami and the women she met upon her arrival to a new country, replicating recipes in their adopted homes allowed them to anchor themselves in the past, but also affirm their identity in the present: this recreation affirms 'narratives [that] weave together a fragile identity within a community, thereby bringing cohesion to a disparate group of people'.[2]

Cooking remains a way for communities in the diaspora to participate in original cultural practices to preserve and recreate a sense of belonging with the home they left behind. Interestingly, Parveen refers to the 'fossilisation' of cultural practices; in which the old generation wants to preserve intact, but the new generation, influenced by popular culture, wants to change. Does this mean that the culinary identity the older generations strived to create in the diaspora dissipates, or does it continue to evolve? There is that gentle but constant push and pull between old and new generations, in what Parveen refers to as static versus dynamic culture – a struggle over which aspects of the homes we left behind to maintain.[3] As such, the food that many of us from the new generation make reflects modern influences and our views on what sets the parameters for traditional food.

Reimagined Homes

Though food can be seen as a marker of identity, it reveals the romanticization and mystification of the past; the longing for a time and place that may not exist anymore, what Salman Rushdie calls 'Imagined Homelands'.[4] These nostalgic interpretations of the past show in the longing for a dish, a method of preparation, a tool, and a landscape – which may not even exist anymore.

By idealizing the past, we are looking back at it through fragments, through a broken mirror, as Rushdie writes emotively. This lends a soft light to the past, with nostalgia recreating a home which may not have existed in the manner that it is remembered. Fragmented, these food memories are reconstructed and pieced together to recreate the home that has been left behind, to find comfort in one's adopted home. As Rushdie explains:

> it was precisely the partial nature of these memories, their fragmentation, that made them so evocative for me. The shards of memory acquired greater status, greater resonance, because they were *remains*; fragmentation made trivial things seem like symbols, and the mundane acquired numinous qualities. There is an obvious parallel here with archaeology. The broken pots of antiquity, from which the past can sometimes, but always provisionally, be reconstructed, are exciting to discover, even if they are pieces of the most quotidian objects.[5]

On Authenticity, Orientalism, and Colonialism

When I arrived in Canada in 2009, I intended to cook all the matrilineal dishes that were passed down to me through an oral tradition. I was not to modify these recipes; like children who learn multiplication by rote, I was to do the same with these recipes.

Food Reimagined: Diasporic Identity and Authenticity

Changing them meant loss: loss of identity. It meant I was disrespecting the women of my Pakistani-Afghan-Persian heritage. I was not to reimagine or recreate; I was meant to replicate and preserve.

But unlike my mother, who had lived in Pakistan till she married my father and moved to Washington, DC, I had lived all over the world as the daughter of an international banker. The flavours of my childhood, though predominantly influenced by my heritage, were a confluence of the pantries and landscapes of the countries I had lived in: Bangladesh, Italy, Kenya, Nigeria, and the UK. The way I cooked reflected those experiences.

As an aspiring food writer, when my first article was published in a prominent food magazine in Canada, I proudly shared it with my mother. She looked at the recipe, which her mother, my Nani Ami, had created. Perfunctorily, she said, 'But these are not Ami's *koftay.* Ami never added paprika.' My Ami disapproved of my dish, because I had added an extra ingredient to her Ami's dish. I had tampered with its authenticity.

This pursuit for the authentic, based on notions of nostalgia, becomes a marker for cultural identity in the diaspora. The dish is not to be contaminated with extraneous ingredients. In his study on authenticity, anthropologist Dimitrios Theodossopoulos explains that there is a presupposition that authenticity is something inaccessible inside us, something that, according to Rousseauian philosophers, cannot be contaminated by the modern world.[6]

But this puritanical pursuit of authenticity exists outside of the diasporic community, too, in which food is judged through the white gaze, in the quest of others to find the best and most traditional version of a dish. And though aspiring to create authentic recipes has been a way for children of the diaspora to pay homage to the recipes of our ancestors, having to follow a perceived idea and taste of authenticity also stifles our creativity and constrains our sense of self. This reductionist notion of authenticity risks replicating the colonialist trope of a demure, exotic woman in her decrepit kitchen in Punjab, dust on the windows, rolling pin in hand, forming perfectly round *chapatis*, as the aromas of ginger and garlic rise from the *karahi* on the stove, with the sounds of a *rickshaw walla* outside.

The construction of these stereotypes, which Edward Said critiqued in his classic work *Orientalism*, delved deep into the Occident's (the West's) views of the Orient's (the East's) people and cultures as backwards and submissive.[7] It is this view through which food of the diaspora is still widely scrutinized, judged, and (mis)understood in a false binary of authentic versus inauthentic cuisine, with the West romanticizing the food and the people of the East. Restaurants serving Chinese or Pakistani food are often declared inauthentic, or not authentic enough, based on narratives like that of the woman rolling *chapatis* in the kitchen or some archetype of nineteenth-century stories. This othering of our food and culture falsely creates an image of a faraway, magical place, flattening the experiences and talent of food made and sold throughout the diaspora in homes and restaurants.

As our food is relegated to otherness, Orientalism still exists as the lens through which the recipes and culinary creations of the diaspora are wrongly judged. When we reflect on the complex structures in society, the question arises as to who has agency: are these Orientalist views of culinary othering being applied to the gastronomic lives of the diaspora? Colonialism has worked not only through conquest and armies, but through exoticizing the East and relegating it to a caricature of otherness. This sort of discourse has further emphasized that the binary of authentic versus inauthentic food is false. As John Paul Brammer argues:

> Heritage and tradition are important, there's no doubt. But it's also important to free our imaginations from the tyranny of authenticity. That's not entirely possible in a consumer culture, of course. But in looking at our lives through a different lens, a lens that is more our own, we can give ourselves more room to be. We can see something that is closer to the truth.
>
> Our culture – any culture – isn't static. It is a living thing. It pulls from its surroundings to adapt in a world that in equal turns marginalizes and fetishizes it. The truth is, I see myself more in Taco Bueno, in my abuela sacking the salsa bar, in the Parmesan crispy taco, than I do in whatever Yelpers think is authentic.'[8]

The murky definition of authenticity circumscribes what immigrant cooks are expected to serve in their restaurants.[9] Demands for authentic cuisine places undue pressure on immigrant cooks, who have to tend to this idea of recreating a far-off, exotic land, in a modern day New York restaurant kitchen. It places the burden on the immigrant cook, to live up to racialized myths, and recreate an environment for the customer, who wants to feel like the tourist, meandering through the ancient streets of Lahore, in search of the *puri halwa* serving *karak chai* eaten by the roadside, overlooking the Badshahi Mosque. These expectations play into pre-existing biases and stereotypes of the food of diasporic communities. Theodossopoulos believes:

> discovering authenticity in the far away often involves a certain obstacle, a hurdle or a self-afflicted rite of passage: long-distance travel to inaccessible (perceived as isolated) communities, infiltration into backstage realms of social life, and/or penetrating self-analysis and introspection.[10]

Change and Immigration

> When immigrants adapt to their new surroundings, the most immediate way this happens is through the food they make: They look around at what's available and try to make it into something they can recognize. – Soleil Ho[11]

When Navreet K came to Canada as a student at Centennial College in 2019, from Punjab, India, she was in awe of all the different types of tomatoes she saw at the farmers' market. 'I saw six different varieties,' she exclaimed, 'it opened up my world, I imagined all the different tomato chutneys I could make – even a unique yellow one!' When I asked her how she felt about innovating the dishes she learnt from her grandmother back in India, she grew more enthusiastic, and explained, 'My Biji [grandmother] would be disappointed, because their emotions and values are tied to these dishes, they cook to remember their mother, and their mother's mother. But I am in Canada, and I am excited about the produce here, and I can still bring the taste of India to the table. I just use local ingredients.'[12]

Navreet went on to talk about risk, and how the women in her family labour hard in the kitchen, but they seek comfort, whereas Navreet wants to experiment. 'I want to take risks and make a *bhujia* with purple broccoli. Just don't tell my Beji,' she laughs. The first time I met Navreet, she was a student in a course I was teaching, 'Recipe Research, Development, and Writing'. She created a typical Punjabi dish of a velvety, roasted aubergine called *baingan ka bharta*, but she added slices of Italian buffalo milk mozzarella on top. She pushed it under the broiler, after which the dish emerged with a bubbly, bronzed crust, perfect to scoop with naan or crackers. 'Through food, I want to open up my world,' Navreet enthused. Soleil Ho explains:

> Unlike 'fusion,' which is often focused on aesthetic innovations and mashups, these immigrant dishes are more like culinary fugues, organically building upon a kernel of a memory over the course of generations and developing into a complicated and layered narrative. Like with any immigrant story, this style of cooking is all about telling the story of a family through its subtle gestures, quirks, and out-of-place ingredients.[13]

For the newer generation, the children of the diaspora, times have changed. We have reimagined the recipes of our ancestors. Harleen K, a production chef at a Toronto-based catering company, also came to Canada in 2019, in the hopes of carving out a culinary career for herself. 'I just created a Vegan Tofu *Tikka Masala* and Butter Chicken Pot Pie, I will bring it for you,' she told me with great pride. Harleen was my student in the Post-Graduate Food Media Certificate programme at Centennial College. I asked her how she felt about making changes to the recipes of our ancestors. As a fellow Punjabi, she understood what I meant. 'Food is art. It is not one thing. It is not one recipe,' she started to explain, 'our culture isn't diluted because we made a pie out of a classic Indian dish. We have to infuse our flavours into local dishes, to make the dishes more inclusive.' I nodded my head over our Zoom call, and we laughed, sharing a cup of cardamom tea over the ether.

This is how I cook, too, adding the knowledge I inherited from my Ami and my Khala, my mother's sister, to create the dishes in the place I now call home, Canada. I thought of a pot pie I could make with my mother's classic Pakistani-style ginger chicken. Harleen reminded me of *gulab jamun* cheesecake, which is so popular on Instagram right now. In her enthusiastic tone she quipped, 'everyone loves a good, creamy NY cheesecake, and add a rosewater-fragrant *gulab jamun* to it, well, now you are tasting two cultures'.[14] As Marina de Camargo Heck argues:

> The transformation and adaptation of recipes follow strange trajectories and

the origins of certain foods becomes, at times, difficult to pinpoint. The style of cuisine fixed in the recollections of some of the interviewees has been difficult to reproduce. New ingredients, the daily contact with another food culture, the evolution of the family embracing other ethnic groups creates a peculiar style of cuisine. Traditional recipes and food habits are often modified through this process of negotiation and incorporation. Often the legacy of an immigrant cuisine is a pot-pourri of cuisines encountered by the family during their collective history and their recollection of the trajectory of their experience in settling down in a new country.[15]

The idea that innovation dilutes our identity is one that we should reexamine. 'And what would your Mumma think of this, Harleen?' I teasingly asked. 'Back in India, Mumma has vanilla ice cream with *gajar ka halwa,* that's not very traditional now, is it?' Harleen laughed.

For this younger generation, innovation and creativity takes precedence over replicating the classic recipes they grew up learning to make in their mothers' and grandmothers' kitchens. It is their way of saying, we are here. 'Being respectful of the tastes and flavours is important. But don't stop innovating. That's why I came to Canada, to learn, to share my knowledge, and to create new dishes,' Harleen confidently stated. As Edward Said argues in *Culture and Imperialism*, identity is, after all, dynamic:

> No one today is purely one thing. Labels like Indian, or woman, or Muslim, or American are not more than starting-points, which if followed into actual experience for only a moment are quickly left behind. Imperialism consolidated the mixture of cultures and identities on a global scale. But its worst and most paradoxical gift was to allow people to believe that they were only, mainly, exclusively, white, or Black, or Western, or Oriental. Yet just as human beings make their own history, they also make their cultures and ethnic identities. No one can deny the persisting continuities of long traditions, sustained habitations, national languages, and cultural geographies, but there seems no reason except fear and prejudice to keep insisting on their separation and distinctiveness, as if that was all human life was about.[16]

Bashir Munye is a Toronto chef and food advocate who dislikes labels. 'I believe that flavours and spices are imprinted in my DNA, and though cultural anchors are important, I don't like labels like traditional and authentic,' he said emphatically. 'Because if the way we cook is changing, and if recipes are changing, this is a good thing. I like the intersection of local and tradition.'[17] Bashir migrated to Canada in 1994, and he believes that food must evolve: 'Food is very fluid [...]. It is like a river; it constantly changes direction and evolves.'[18] His innovative dishes incorporate the flavours of his childhood in Italy, and his mother's pantry in Somalia. His identity, like so many other Canadians today, is not monolithic; he uses local ingredients to create dishes which reflect his past and present:

These recipes travelled with me, as a young boy at boarding school in Italy, and after moving to Canada – over two decades ago – they remain a part of me. At the end of the day, I need to eat food that is culturally appropriate to me. I want deliciousness from fresh ingredients.[19]

Given how, for many of us in the diaspora, identity is tied to the stories and recipes of our ancestors, I asked Bashir if he worries about losing this sense of identity. He confidently responded by saying what is most important to him is to be part of the local environment and to eat food which is culturally appropriate to him: 'There is no reason why I cannot support local food without losing my own identity.' When I asked Bashir what authenticity means to him, he replied: 'To me, authenticity is caring about my local environment, and bringing the flavours of my heritage into these dishes.'[20] Bashir sent me a photo of a salad he made using local Ontario vegetables: okra (a vegetable he ate in Somalia), pepper, tomato, onions, and fresh chillies. As Bashir weaves stories of his life into his dishes, that is about as authentic as it gets.

I was born in Lahore, Pakistan. My father is half-Afghan and half-Pakistani, with Persian heritage on his mother's side. My mother is Pakistani. I grew up all over the world: Washington, DC; Lagos; Nairobi; Lahore; Cambridge; Dhaka; Rome – and now I call Toronto my home. Lahore is also my home, and to me, food has been reimagined as a way to belong in my multi-hyphenated identity as a Canadian. As a food writer and recipe developer, my work focuses on culture and identity. Like Bashir, I create dishes using the spices of my heritage, paired with local produce. It is perhaps my mother's biggest nightmare, these reimagined dishes, like Ontario peaches grilled with ghee and a scattering of cardamom, this mishmash of the old and new in my kitchen! But I am not seeking security from my past, rather, I am looking for positive change, and growth – tied to my fluid identity as a multi-hyphenated Canadian. As Priscilla Parkhurst Ferguson reminds us:

> Because it is a social construct that is of our making, 'authenticity' is not the property of an object as such. Which is precisely the dilemma of national identity. What is it? Who fixes it? Then, how does identity accommodate change? If clear definitions provide security by the same token they arrest change.[21]

Conclusion

I do wonder if, with innovation and creativity, we will lose what was, along with our culinary identity, and I think about my mother – and all the women before her – who preserved our heritage. But if we are to look at identity as something which is dynamic and fluid, this will be ever changing. I spent several years in Italy before I moved to Toronto. I lived on one of Rome's seven hills, in Aventino, and would walk down to the butcher in Testaccio to buy chicken for making my Ami's *murghi ka saalan*, her chicken and tomato curry. I had all the ingredients, the fresh ginger, garlic – I even went to Piazza Vittorio to buy fresh coriander – but the Roman tomatoes, sweet and candy-like, did not make for a good Pakistani-style curry. At the market one day, in Testaccio, I asked the *fruttivendolo* to help me with my mother's dish. The tomatoes cannot be sweet, I told him. He placed three large green tomatoes in a paper bag and smiled, 'Tell me how the curry tastes when you come back next Tuesday.' That night, I made Ami's *murghi ka saalan*. The colour was a dull green; it looked wrong. But the taste was perfect, with a hit of acid from the tomatoes.

When we cross borders, we reimagine our cuisine in ways we have never had to do before. This dish structured memories of home for me. As borders have blurred, with it, our culinary identities have evolved and changed, too. As de Camargo Heck writes:

> The adaptation of their native culinary habits, as well as the adoption of new eating habits, has consequences regarding the food of the immigrant families, but at the same time, it intervenes in the host community, mixing and modifying both culinary cultures.[22]

For those of us in the diaspora, being able to reframe what authenticity means has allowed us to reclaim our culinary narratives. Perhaps our generation is more secure in ourselves, we are here; we are strong. Being a part of the diaspora is a privilege, it expands our worlds. It also provides me with that sense of belonging that perhaps my young, twenty-seven-year-old mother didn't feel at the time she came to Washington, DC. Maybe we are tired of talking about our trauma and loss and want to move forward. I know that I want to talk about food and my identity, but I don't want to talk about the trauma of my childhood otherness – and the lunchboxes – anymore. Maybe by talking about reimagining our food and our recipes, we have also reimagined our world. And with adaptation and adoption of our cooking and eating habits, we are expanding our world, and making it a more delicious place.

My identity and sense of belonging is, as Edward Said wrote shortly before he died, like a cluster of flowing currents:

> I occasionally experience myself as a cluster of flowing currents. I prefer this to the idea of a solid self, the identity to which so many attach so much significance. These currents, like the themes of one's life, flow along during the waking hours, and at their best, they require no reconciling, no harmonizing. They are 'off' and may be out of place, but at least they are always in motion, in time, in place, in the form of all kinds of strange combinations moving about, not necessarily forward, sometimes against each other, contrapuntally yet without one central theme. A form of freedom, I'd like to think, even if I am far from being totally convinced that it is. That skepticism too is one of the themes I particularly want to hold on to. With so many dissonances in my life I have learned actually to prefer being not quite right and out of place.[23]

Notes

1. Razia Parveen, 'Recipes and Songs as Tools for Solidarity: Women's Oral Texts, Diaspora and Communal Identity' (unpublished doctoral thesis, University of Huddersfield, 2013), p. xi <http://eprints.hud.ac.uk/id/eprint/23690/> [accessed 31 May 2021]
2. Parveen, p. 2.
3. Parveen, pp. 3-4.
4. Salman Rushdie, *Imaginary Homelands: Essays and Criticism, 1981-1991* (London: Granta, 1992).
5. Rushdie, pp. 11-12.
6. Dimitrios Theodossopoulos, 'Introduction. Laying Claim to Authenticity: Five Anthropological Dilemmas', *Anthropological Quarterly*, 86.2 (2013), 337-60 (p. 338).
7. Edward W. Said, *Orientalism* (New York: Penguin Random House, 2014).
8. John Paul Brammer, 'I'm from a Mexican Family. Stop Expecting Me to Eat "Authentic" Food', *The Washington Post*, 20 May 2019 <https://www.washingtonpost.com/outlook/2019/05/15/im-mexican-american-stop-expecting-me-eat-authentic-food/> [accessed 31 May 2021]
9. Jenny G. Zhang, '"Always Be My Maybe" and the Trap of "Authentic" Cooking', *Eater*, 4 June 2019 <https://www.eater.com/2019/6/4/18652061/always-be-my-maybe-asian-food-authentic-cooking-netflix-ali-wong-randall-park> [accessed 31 May 2021]
10. Theodossopoulos, p. 342.
11. Soleil Ho, 'Let's Call It Assimilation Food', *TASTE*, 26 June 2017 <https://www.tastecooking.com/lets-call-assimilation-food/> [accessed 31 May 2021]
12. Navreet K., interview conducted by the author, 25 May 2021. Last name withheld by request.
13. Ho.
14. Harleen K., Interview conducted by the author, 27 May 2021. Last name withheld by request.
15. Marina de Camargo Heck, 'Adapting and Adopting: The Migrating Recipe', in *The Recipe Reader: Narratives – Contexts – Traditions*, ed. by Janet Floyd and Laurel Foster (New York: Routledge, 2003), pp. 205-18 (p. 215).
16. Edward W. Said, *Culture and Imperialism* (New York: Vintage, 1993), p. 336.
17. Bashir Munye, interview conducted by the author, 25 May 2021.
18. Wayne Roberts, 'This Somali Chef Shows the Potential in Toronto's Food Scene', *Torontoist*, 8 August 2016 <https://torontoist.com/2016/08/bashir-munye-somali-chef-toronto/> [accessed 31 May 2021]
19. Munye.
20. Munye.
21. Priscilla Parkhurst Ferguson, 'Culinary Nationalism', *Gastronomica*, 10.1 (2010), 102-09 (p. 105) <https://doi.org/10.1525/gfc.2010.10.1.102>
22. de Camargo Heck, p. 208.
23. Edward W. Said, *Out of Place: A Memoir* (New York: Vintage, 1999), p. 295.

'Bileti' to 'Desi': Global Foodways and the Re-imagining of Bengali 'Modern' Cuisine in Late Colonial Bengal

Samapan Saha

In the late nineteenth and early twentieth centuries, several iconic Bengali-language cookbooks were published, and this paper explores the cultural amalgamations that led to their creation. From the mid-nineteenth century, Calcutta, the capital of British India, began to flourish as a major center for education, trade, and commerce and provided opportunities for employment to college-educated youth. Many Bengalis migrated to Calcutta from their villages and made the city their home.

The robust print culture in nineteenth-century Calcutta facilitated the discussion of cuisine among the educated Bengali middle class. The Bengali middle class, or *bhadraloks*, was mostly comprised of Hindus and Bramhos, many of whom belonged to fixed-income groups. Bengali-language periodicals played a crucial role by helping to create the consciousness of shared food habits among this community. Bengali cuisine was being 'modernized' through a process of inclusion, adaptation, and circulation of English culinary knowledge along with vegetables and staples from the New World, and most importantly through new recipes. Innovative authors like Bipradas Mukhopadhyay and Prajnasundari Devi introduced these ideas through their writings and attempted to construct a 'Modern cuisine'.[1] Their writings were subsequently compiled into Bengali-language cookbooks which preserved the cultural identity of the community. The desire of the Bengali middle class for global tastes found representation through new Bengali-language cookbooks.

The authors had multiple roles in the process of cookbook writing. They were the mediators between global ideas and local traditions and customs. They had a deep understanding of Hindu culinary philosophy and local Bengali taste and preferences. These authors liberally borrowed recipes and traditions from traditional Indian high cuisine and put an innovative spin on them by incorporating novel 'foreign' vegetables such as potatoes (*Solanum tuberosum*) and tomatoes, which had recently become local staples as a result of India's colonial encounter. The naming of new hybrid Bengali dishes in these Bengali cookbooks highlighted the role of the authors as mediators. The authors emphasized global influences by using adjectives like 'French', 'English', 'Jewish', and so on to re-imagine humble, everyday middle-class Bengali food as a 'cosmopolitan' cuisine and to signify a 'refined taste'.[2] The original and hybrid recipes combined with local and global elements led to the creation of innovative dishes such as Devi's '*Armmani* Pudding' (Armenian Pudding) and '*Ingraji Arhar Dal*' (English Yellow Split Pigeon Peas) and Mukhopadhyay's '*Ihudi Machh Bhaja*' (Jewish Fish Fry) and '*Aloor* French Ball' (French Potato Balls).

However, this turn towards a global platter required the gradual inclusion of several prohibited food items in the household kitchen. During this time, the traditional Bengali (Hindu) intelligentsia was constantly under pressure to maintain food habits that adhered to existing notions of restrictive caste (*varna-jati*) traditions and taboos. New-fangled recipes, with their foreign elements and ingredients, often challenged the strict orthodoxy of the Hindu palate. Assessing Bengali-language sources raises critical questions about the cultural politics of taste emerging during this period.

Due to the paucity of primary evidence on domestic eating habits, the Bengali-language cookbooks examined in this research are important sources to evaluate the transition to 'modern' Bengali cuisine. These cookbooks represented a formalization of Bengali cuisine. The dietary habits of the Bengali (Hindu) community can be drawn from the list of ingredients mentioned in the cookbooks. Some sense of the market can be gained when the authors mention commodity prices. The food history of this period as evidenced by the new cookbooks bears within it the markers of gradual yet lasting social change in colonial Bengal, seen most prominently in embracing of formerly-prohibited food items as staples of the turn-of-the-century, urban, middle-class Bengali kitchen.

Public Print Culture and Recipe Writing Traditions in Colonial Bengal

In the late nineteenth century, as Calcutta became one of the major urban centres of the British colonial empire, the flourishing popular Bengali print culture created space for the circulation of colonial scientific knowledge.[3] The Bengali intelligentsia was actively involved in the process of 'modernizing' themselves. This process required recipes to track the evolution of local Bengali tastes and also involved changes in household management.

In 1863, Umeshchandra Dutta began publishing a periodical called *Bamabodhini Patrika* to educate and modernize the Bengali community.[4] *Bamabodhini Patrika* was one of the earliest Bengali-language periodicals to address issues related to Bengali women, and many female authors regularly published articles on domesticity, cooking, and recipes. Other journals were also being published in Bengali, and many had a separate column for recipes. A recipe column first started appearing in *Bamabodhini Patrika* in 1884. *Mahila* and *Antahpur* had dedicated food columns from 1895 and 1900, respectively.[5] In 1883, Bipradas Mukhopadhyay, a graduate of Calcutta's Sanskrit College, started publishing a monthly journal entitled *Pak-Pranali* (*Culinary Methods*).[6] In 1886, he published a cookbook, in three volumes, with the same title.[7] He was also the editor of a periodical on domesticity called *Grihasthali*, first published in 1884. In 1897, a journal called *Punya* (*The Virtue*) was published by Prajnasundari Devi. She was the editor for the first two editions and wrote recipe columns for them. In 1900, she published a collection of recipes, along with a long introduction, as a cookbook titled *Amish o Niramish Ahar* (*Non-Vegetarian and Vegetarian Foods*) – which remains one of the most circulated and widely read cookbooks in the Bengali language.[8] *Pak-Pranali* and *Amish o Niramish Ahar* represent a new tradition of cookbook writing.

The *bhadraloks* did not limit themselves to writing about domesticity and recipes. They wrote extensively to popularize scientific agricultural practices and especially on New World crop and vegetable cultivation. Journals like *Krishitatva* (*Theory of Agriculture*), *Krishak* (*The Farmer*), and *Krishi-gazette* (*The Agriculture-Gazette*) concentrated on news and information related to agricultural science, promoting agricultural experiments with New World crops and seeds. They also focused on publicizing the health benefits of these new crops and vegetables. Bipradas Mukhopadhyay, the editor of *Krishitatva*, was also involved with Calcutta's Paikpara Nursery, an initiative by Bengali individuals who experimented with New World crops and seeds and blamed *bhadraloks* for the poor condition of farmers of India.[9] In one such piece, the author criticized the *bhadraloks*' apathy towards agriculture and their general disdain of cultivation as a menial job.[10]

High Cuisine in Nineteenth-Century Bengal

The flourishing Bengali print culture in the late 1870s facilitated the reprint of an important manuscript cookbook, *Pakrajeswar: arthaṯ amishadi bibidha drabya paka karaṇera niyama* (*The Emperor of Cooking or How to Cook Nonvegetarian and Various Other Materials*). The first edition, published in 1831, has now been lost, but in 1873, a second edition appeared, followed by the third edition with an appendix in 1880. Since the first edition has not yet been found, there is confusion over authorship from the second edition onwards. In 2004, Nikhil Sarkar, a prominent Bengali social historian writing under the pseudonym Sripantha, argued that the original author of *Pakrajeswar* was Bisweswar Tarkalankar, and that the second edition was compiled by Gaurishankar Tarkabaghish, who worked under the patronage of the Raja of Bardhaman. It is difficult to determine whether Tarkabaghish, while compiling the second edition, modified the original content from the first edition.[11] *Pakrajeswar* not only represents the high cuisine of nineteenth-century Bengal, but it also reflects the earlier tradition of Bengali-language cookbook writing.

In the late nineteenth century, the Bengali-language cookbook went through a major transformation. The publication of recipes or collection of recipes was not a new phenomenon in Bengal, though as Arjun Appadurai explains, 'while there is an immense amount written about *eating* and about feeding, precious little is said about cooking in Hindu legal, medical, or philosophical texts.'[12] The new cookbooks attempted to change this earlier tradition by introducing the idea of 'modern' culinary science. The authors of the new cookbooks used English-language cookbooks and household management guides as a source for learning the discourse of European culinary science. These English-language cookbooks and household manuals circulated in the English-speaking world from the seventeenth century on, culminating in one of the finest examples of this tradition, Isabella Beeton's *Book of Household Management*, which first appeared in 1861. With the foundation of British Raj in India (after the rebellion of 1857), there was a gradual transformation in English-language cookbook writing as more *memsahibs* started coming to India, a trend accelerated by the opening of the Suez Canal. Several prominent household guides were written for the 'Eastern Empires' to educate the *memsahibs* on how to run an efficient and hygienic kitchen – a kitchen capable enough to produce sophisticated European recipes.

Global Ideas on Domesticity and Restructuring the Bengali Kitchen

English-language household management guides followed the method of separating the culinary space into smaller units (kitchen, storeroom), and listing utensils necessary for day-to-day cooking as well as for preparing special recipes.[13] English-language domesticity was modified to fit the available spaces, climate, and local conditions of India, and this process of restructuring the Bengali household is reflected in Bengali-language cookbooks. The Bengali household culinary space was to be divided into the kitchen and storeroom.

The kitchen, or cooking space, was defined differently in these cookbooks, and these differences in how the kitchen was defined reflect the different culinary approach of each cookbook. *Pakrajeswar* begins with a kitchen or 'cookhouse', but it provides very little information about the space itself, except that the *chullah* should be facing east or west and there should be a window for smoke to escape.[14] The common fuel for cooking in Calcutta was charcoal, which generated so much smoke that maintaining proper ventilation was essential.[15] However, the influence of European culinary science is evident from Devi's projection of a clean hygienic kitchen.

The storeroom was defined as a separate space to store staples, spices, and pickles.[16] It should be located in close vicinity to the kitchen to allow smooth, efficient functioning of the kitchen.[17] Any household that could not spare a room for storing the supplies could use 'chest[s] made out mango wood' as an alternative.[18]

The list of cooking utensils mentioned in *Pakrajeswar* is exhaustive. The list is categorized according to the health benefits of the metals used to make these utensils (except earthenwares), and it explained which metal was suitable for specific cooking methods. However, the intended reader of *Pakrajeswar* was the nobility: the gold and silver utensils indicate that it was written to cater for the royal household, not for the urban middle-class household.[19] In contrast, the list of cooking utensils mentioned in *Pak-Pranali* indicates that Mukhopadhyay's intended audience was the *bhadralok* household. The list of utensils is followed by the health hazards and health benefits associated with every material and instructions on how to clean and maintain the utensils' durability.[20] Devi's uniqueness as an expert in culinary science is reflected through her list of prescribed utensils and equipment. Unlike the other two authors who had different motives for writing the cookbooks, Devi explained the minute details of all the equipment which might come in handy for any Bengali household.[21]

Making 'Modern' Bengali Cuisine
Including New World Vegetables in Bengali Cuisine

The authors of new cookbooks introduced New World vegetables like potatoes and tomatoes into the Bengali *bhadralok* cuisine through their cookbooks. The potato was widely available in Calcutta by the 1860s, but whether it was widely consumed by the Bengali community or not remains a major question.[22] In the second edition of *Pakrajeswar*, there is no mention of potato. But the third edition includes two recipes with potatoes: *aloo'r dum* (Steamed Spiced Potato) and *aloo'r kofta* (Potato Kofta).[23] In Bipradas Mukhopadhyay's *Pak-Pranali*, several potato recipes are included, and Prajnasundari Devi includes more than twenty. Within two decades, the use of potato had increased manifold, and it was incorporated into Bengali household kitchens.

Tomato, known as '*Bilayti begun*', was gradually becoming a part of Bengali cuisine by 1880.[24] Devi mentions two recipes cooked with tomato as an ingredient to bring tartness – '*bileti begun'er ambal*' and '*bileti begun patla ambal*' (Light Tomato Tart Soup).[25]

Including new vegetables into the cookbooks went through a process of negotiation shown in the adoption of common linguistic identifiers. The authors also compared the new vegetables with similar-looking ones already widely used within the community. In the case of potato, it was compared with vegetables like *sakarkand aloo* (sweet potato) and introduced as '*gol aloo*' (round-shaped potato).[26] The health benefits and methods of preserving the vegetables were also elaborately discussed.

Including and Naming New Recipes

Naming new recipes was a very important aspect of the new cookbooks, and the process of naming reflects the ingenuity of the authors. It reveals the connection between the author's understanding of the taste preferences of the intended audience. For instance, *Pakrajeswar* did not mention any European recipes, except '*firang roti*' or '*pao roti*' (Tandoor-Baked Chapati).[27] A taxonomy of food items shows that Mukhopadhyay included Mughlai or Muslim dishes, European dishes like crab cooked in the British style, Italian meatballs, English Kebab, German stew, and Irish stew. He named some foreign dishes in Bengali like '*topeshe machher* english fry' – 'they [the British] call it mango-fish' – or '*aloor french* ball' (French Potato Ball).[28]

However, Devi's *Amish o Niramish Ahar* stands apart from the other two works. Her work suggests her involvement with food and her deep understanding of culinary science as well as her ability to innovate new recipes. Her style of naming recipes like 'Rammohan *Dolma Polau*' signifies her commitment to Bengali heritage and history.[29]

The Culinary Philosophy of 'Modern' Bengali Cuisine

These three cookbooks represent a period of transition. *Pakrajeswar* represents an older tradition of cookbook writing. In that tradition, the authors were simply compilers of recipes and gave little or no instruction about the cooking itself. However, whether recipes were included in these cookbooks depended on whether they were in use in the royal kitchen. The new cookbooks represented a very different objective.

Bipradas Mukhopadhyay helped shape the formative phase of Bengali 'Modern cuisine'. New World vegetables were gradually being received within the community. Based on the limited recipes on potato and absence of recipes on tomatoes, a hypothesis can be drawn that the Bengali community was gradually learning the use of these vegetables and experimenting with them. Mukhopadhyay's writing indicates that his inclusion of recipes was more symbolic than practical. Although Mukhopadhyay claimed that his intention was to 'educate' Bengali women in the art of cooking, he hardly did so, apart from introducing new vegetables and recipes into the cuisine of Calcutta. The recipes mentioned in the text operate within the social and religious boundaries of traditional Bengali (Hindu) society, except some minor relaxations, like the inclusion of fowl. Some communities of Bengali Brahmins prohibit the consumption of birds; Mukhopadhyay's inclusion of fowl indicates the softening up of traditional social norms. However, he still used traditional medicinal texts (*Vaidyashastra*) to prescribe fowl as a diet for the sick.[30] Similarly, when describing a fish recipe, he mentions that 'consumption of fish on Sunday is prohibited by the Hindu scriptures'.[31] His introduction covered several subjects relating to food, ranging from the role of women in cooking to healthy eating habits.[32] Mukhopadhyay's primary concern was to address the well-being of the Bengali body through food.

Prajnasundari Devi's intervention is represented through her understanding of culinary methods as scientific knowledge. Her writing uses simple, descriptive, language to contextualize the cooking of each recipe. Unlike Mukhopadhyay, who wrote in a prescriptive style to 'educate' Bengali women about cooking, Devi's perception was to teach women the methods of cooking and introduce them to both regional Bengali and European recipes.

Devi belonged to the family of Noble Laurate Rabindranath Thakur; she believed in the idea of a global humanity and had a liberal, tolerant worldview. Her religious philosophy of Brahmo monotheism is reflected in her approach to cuisine and culture. She propagated theories on the ancient origins of food and emphasized the ritual significance of Fire (*Agni*), claiming that the Vedic *yajna* ritual paved the way for cooking.[33]

Devi is one of very few Bengali food writers to claim that meat-based dishes are as integral to Indian cuisine as vegetarian dishes, although, referring to Hindu Vedic texts, she constructed a binary that connected vegetarianism with *Devata* (God) and non-vegetarianism with *Asura* (Demon).[34] By connecting the origins of food with Hinduism, she tried to emphasize that cuisines have much in common, differentiated mainly by method.[35] Referring to Vedic food habits to legitimize her claims, she blamed India's climate for the 'unpopularity' of meat-eating. She rejected the claim that meat-dishes are the cuisine of the '*melachhas*'; instead, she argued that meat-based dishes are not just a part of Indian cuisine but also that these dishes, including several for pork, had gradually circulated to Europe and Central Asia.

She tried to establish this common link between India and the West (*Praschatya*) through linguistic similarities. She compared examples from Sanskrit vocabulary with English and German words, and she noted that words like 'dinner' and 'breakfast' can be found in the Vedic text of *Grihasutra*, where they are called '*shaymash*' and '*prataras*' respectively.[36] She also tried to find a common link between Vedic society and Islam, and connected Vedic ritual and monotheistic practices with the Zoroastrians of ancient Persia.

Devi attempted to bridge the gap between vegetarianism and non-vegetarianism through her interpretation of the Vedas. She sought her legitimacy from the scripture and preserved the cultural tradition of the time, yet she forged a connection between diverse and distinct food habits and tried to bring different communities together through food. Her non-discriminatory and inclusive approach to food makes her one of the most remarkable people of her time.

Conclusion

This paper has attempted to look into the making of a cuisine by an emerging colonial middle class through the prism of culinary history. In the late nineteenth and early twentieth centuries, anti-colonial nationalism was gradually becoming more dominant in Bengal and India as well. The paper has argued that the process of 'modernization' of Bengali cuisine went through multiple mediations, in which the Bengali language itself played a crucial role. This modernization was not westernization but rather a negotiation between global ideas and commodities and local traditions and taste.

Notes

1. The term is borrowed from historian Rachel Laudan (*Cuisine and Empire: Cooking in World History* (Berkeley: University of California Press, 2013)).
2. Utsa Ray, 'Eating "Modernity": Changing Dietary Practices in Colonial Bengal', *Modern Asian Studies*, 46.3 (2012), 703-30 <https://www.jstor.org/stable/41478327>
3. Anindita Ghosh, *Power in Print: Popular Publishing and the Politics of Language and Culture in a Colonial Society, 1778-1905* (New Delhi: Oxford University Press, 2006), pp. 19-25.
4. Bharati Ray cites the term 'Brahmo youth' in this context (*Nari o paribar: Bamabodhini patrika (1270–1329 Bangabda)*), ed. by Bharati Ray (Kolkata: Ananda Publishers, 2002, repr. 2014), p. 1.
5. Jayanta Sengupta, 'Nation on a Platter: The Culture and Politics of Food and Cuisine in Colonial Bengal', *Modern Asian Studies*, 44.1 (January 2010), 81-98 (p. 93) <https://doi.org/10.1017/S0026749X09990072>
6. Ishani Choudhury, 'A Palatable Journey through the Pages: Bengali Cookbooks and the "Ideal" Kitchen in the Late Nineteenth and Early Twentieth Century', *Global Food History*, 3.1 (2016), 24-39 (p. 25) <https://doi.org/10.1080/20549547.2016.1256186>
7. Bipradas Mukhopadhyay, *Pak-Pranali* (Calcutta: Bipradas Mukhopadhyay, 1887; repr. Kolkata: Ananda Publishers, 1987; repr. 2007).
8. Prajnasundari Devi, *Amish o Niramish Ahar* (Calcutta: Prajnasundari Devi, 1900; repr. Kolkata: Ananda

9   Rajendranath Das, Rajendralal Singha, and Radhashyam Gui were a few of the Bengali individuals involved with this nursery, and they regularly contributed to *Krishitatva*; for their critiques of the *bhadraloks*, see *Krishitatva*, 4.1 (1288-1289 B.S./1881-1882), pp. 125-28, 167-70, 193-96.
10 Instead, they argued that Indian agriculture can only prosper — and only then can the country prosper — if the educated and wealthy actively took part (Anonymous, 'Chash chashar Kaaj', *Krishitatva*, 4.1, pp. 21-25).
11 Sripantha, 'Introduction', in Bisweshar Tarkalankar, *Pakrajeswar o byanjan-ratnakar*, ed. by Sripantha (Kolkata, 2004 [1879]), pp. 12-14.
12 Arjun Appadurai, 'How to Make a National Cuisine: Cookbooks in Contemporary India', *Comparative Studies in Society and History*, 30.1 (1988), 3-24 (p. 11) <https://www.jstor.org/stable/179020>
13 See for example Isabella Beeton, *The Book of Household Management* (London, S.O. Beeton, 1861), pp. 25-38 <https://archive.org/details/b20392758/page/n9/mode/2up> [accessed 30 March 2022]
14 Tarkalankar, p. 1.
15 See for example F.A. Steel and G. Gardiner, *The Complete Indian Housekeeper and Cook: Giving the Duties of Mistress and Servants the General Management of the House and Practical Recipes for Cooking in all its Branches* (London: William Heinemann, 1909 [1898]), p. 41 <https://archive.org/details/b21528640/page/n9/mode/2upp> [accessed 30 March 2022]
16 Mukhopadhyay, p. 39.
17 'The storeroom should be located close to the cookhouse. It will be convenient to cook if the storeroom is stocked properly' (Mukhopadhyay, p. 39; my translation).
18 Devi, p. 66.
19 '*Earthenware* is the cheapest and most affordable and it also has major health benefits. Unlike the utensils made from *iron* which can have serious health hazards but in the absence of earthen ware, it can be used. *Bell metal* is also considered good for cooking and keeping food. Pure *copper* utensils should be avoided at all cost as it may cause ulcer. Utensils made from *gold* and *silver* are recommended for the rich household. Wares made from wood also mentioned but only selected items like sweetmeat, green leafy vegetables, ghee/clarified butter should be kept in it' (Tarkalankar, pp. 1-4; my translation and emphasis).
20 Mukhopadhyay, pp. 40-41.
21 Devi included rural households as well (pp. 60-62).
22 K. T. Achaya, *A Historical Dictionary of Indian Food* (New Delhi: Oxford University Press, 2002), p. 194.
23 Tarkalankar, pp. 109-10.
24 Devi, p. 364; Achaya, p. 253.
25 Devi, p. 264. Chitrita Banerji notes that 'ambals will provide the refreshing touch of tartness to make the tongue anticipate the sweet dishes' (*Life and Food in Bengal* (London: Weidenfeld and Nicolson, 1991), p. 19).
26 Tarkalankar, p. 16; Mukhopadhyay, p. 43.
27 Tarkalankar, p. 43.
28 Mukhopadhyay, p. 199.
29 Devi, p. 102. The name was her tribute to Raja Rammohan Roy, a social reformer from nineteenth-century Bengal.
30 Mukhopadhyay, p. 56.
31 Mukhopadhyay, p. 197; my translation.
32 Mukhopadhyay, p. 27.
33 Devi cites historian Romesh Chandra Dutt to corroborate the significance of ritual fire (p. 36); p. 40.
34 Unlike the meat-eating *Asura*, the vegetarian *Devata* consumed fruits, *som rasa*, milk, and ghee (Devi, p. 26).
35 Devi, pp. 52-53.
36 Devi, pp. 32, 39.

'Coming from a Place of Impossibility': Imagining a World without Taste

Anna Seecharan

Food and Imagination: for any food-lover, merely the mention of these two words together surely elicits a pulse of anticipation at the manifold forms of creativity food inspires. This is the power of imagination. And yet, we tend not to question the physical status of food as the substance to which imagination is applied. When our ability to access the materiality of food is taken for granted, it's easy to assume that food is, unproblematically, the basic matter to which we add layers of meaning, transforming it through imagination. In this paper I challenge the idea of imagination as an 'added extra', proposing instead that imagination underpins the very foundation of our sensorial engagement with food. To illustrate this, I invite you to imagine what food would be like if imagination were stripped away – to go on a journey into a world without taste.

During the summer of 2018, I interviewed thirteen people about their experiences of smell loss and the impact of this condition on their relationship with food. The general term referring to the loss or lack of sense of smell – anosmia – fails to reflect the diversity of olfactory disorders, which include both congenital and acquired anosmia, and ranges from total loss to sensory reduction, distorted smell/taste, and even 'phantom' smells.[1] The loss can be permanent; however olfactory nerves are sometimes able to regenerate, and may do so in unpredictable ways. While no two experiences of anosmia reported to me were the same, it quickly became clear that losing or lacking one's sense of smell nonetheless affects how food is experienced in a fundamental way.

In 2018 anosmia was a doubly invisible condition. Not only is smell loss literally unseeable and particularly difficult to convey to others, but it was also at that time absent from medical and public discourses. Participants reported feeling dismissed by medical professionals and that there was neither much information available nor wider recognition in the public sphere. In 2020 much changed. As one of the three defining symptoms of Covid-19, the incidence of smell/taste loss increased exponentially alongside the pandemic: almost overnight the world became aware of smell/taste disorders. Since then, a steady stream of news articles on smell loss have been published.[2] While the recent rise in case numbers and visibility will inevitably impact health services and professionals dealing with anosmia as a medical condition, my research aims to supplement medical knowledge through an anthropological approach which can illuminate the often life-changing impact that losing sense of smell can have on one's relationship with food.

I first share accounts of what it is like to live in a world without taste. As Grace explained, this experience is so hard to convey that 'it's kind of a futile exercise to try and talk about it [...]. I am now at a point where I realize that it's coming from a place of impossibility'.[3] I then consider current theories of memory and apply these to how we experience food through the senses. In doing so, I challenge the concept of taste. While flavours are often understood to be objective, inhering in the material properties of food and accessed via our senses, I propose that what we think of as 'tasting' actually happens inside our heads. The brain mentally stores combined smell/tastes as flavour memories, so when we identify a flavour, we do so by accessing these memories. As psychologist Charles Fernyhough argues, remembering is a process of imagination – thus, in a very literal sense, imagining constitutes tasting.[4] Finally, I consider how we imagine ourselves and our social worlds through food. I explore the inextricable connection between memory and imagination and how, together, they constitute our sense of self. That flavour memories are both powerfully emotional and autobiographical suggests a role for food as an important contributor to identity. Far more than simply a means of survival, our ability to smell/taste shapes our sense of who we are. Lived experiences of anosmia illustrate how the loss of this ability – both to experience food flavours and to access the sensory worlds attached to them – can affect sufferers in profoundly personal and emotional ways.

The Impossibility of 'Tasting' without Smell

To understand the roles imagination and memory play in how we taste food, we must first define what we mean by taste. The chemical senses are comprised of three systems: the olfactory system (sense of smell); the gustatory system (sense of taste); and the trigeminal system (which detects noxious stimuli and allows us to feel the sensations of heat from chillies or coolness from mint). In the strictest sense, taste refers only to the five taste sensations (salt, sweet, bitter, sour, and umami) on the tongue. Though it's common to talk about how foods 'taste', we are really referring to the flavours of food, which are almost entirely dependent upon our sense of smell. In contrast to tastes on the tongue, aromas are the volatile molecules of physical things in the world which break free from objects and disperse into the air, where they may be inhaled into the nose. When we smell something, it is because inhaled odour molecules reach the top of our nasal cavity, where they are dissolved into the olfactory epithelium and transmitted via olfactory nerves to the olfactory bulb. The unique chemical patterns of these molecules are encoded by the brain, which stores them in the memory for later recognition.[5]

In humans our airway is not separate from the foodway, which means that when we chew, air forces aroma molecules up the back of the throat (in a process called *retronasal olfaction*) so that they reach the olfactory epithelium via an alternative route. Food molecules are therefore processed simultaneously by the smell and taste centres of the brain, and it is this combined smell/taste that we experience as flavour. As omnivores with generalist food habits, our ability to identify flavours allows us to differentiate between a wide array of potential foods. Psychologist Paul Rozin notes that 'the challenge of procuring food, and selecting a balanced diet, with a low level of toxins, was surely one of the major selecting forces in early human evolution'.[6] Smelling is crucial for safety since it aids identification of potentially harmful foods before we put them into our mouths. When our senses of smell and taste function seamlessly together, we are largely unaware of the importance aromas play in determining flavour; however when sense of smell is lost or absent, the magnitude of its role in how we experience food becomes clear. According to a leading UK Consultant ENT Surgeon, Professor Carl Philpott, 'true gustatory (taste) dysfunction is rare. Although many [anosmia] patients complain of a "loss of taste", this is actually due to their loss of retronasal olfaction, where 80% of the flavour of food is derived from its aroma.'[7] Briget, who suffered total anosmia following a car accident, is keen to emphasize the distinction: 'I'm always emphatic and a bit pedantic about when people say you still have some residual taste…you don't. I can detect […] sweet and salt and bitter and sour and umami – I can detect them. But detecting isn't the same as tast[ing] at all.'[8]

The experience of losing access to the flavours of food can vary dramatically depending on the type and duration of smell disorder.[9] Amanda suffered from a total and permanent loss of sense of smell following surgery on a brain tumour. One year later she was still learning to navigate the loss: 'Everything smells like air. Sometimes I try and…like this cup of coffee – I'll try real hard, and I'll think I can smell it, but I think I'm just hallucinating…I can't smell it. It's so sad; it's like I'm living, but I'm looking through a window.'[10]

Kate also suffered total, permanent smell loss from head trauma, and after seven years of living with anosmia she still struggled with the change every day. While Kate and her husband used to share their passion for food and cooking, now she says that for her 'a risotto with loads of beautiful flavors in…it's…it's just nothing. It's nothing. It's nothing. Do you know what I mean? It's just…desperate'.[11]

The total and permanent loss of sense of smell described above often occurs when olfactory nerves are severed and unable to grow back; however it can also be possible for olfactory nerves to regenerate, though they do not always do so uniformly.[12] In the case of parosmia, aromas may still be detected but are experienced as distorted. In one extreme case, Sandra had experienced only unpleasant (e.g. rancid, rotten, fetid) flavours for sixteen years: 'It's horrible. Nothing smells good; at best it smells of nothing. I am virtually anorexic. I live on whole milk and chocolate chip cookies. […] The milk makes me feel full, and I only drink it at night [because it] helps me get off to sleep.'[13]

The interconnected sense of smell/taste also drives our desire to eat. My research suggests that appetite and satiation are not governed, as one might expect, by physical hunger. Rather than seeking food when we need energy and feeling satiated when we have consumed sufficient calories, appetite appears to be strongly influenced by our anticipation of eating something that will please us. Satiation is the pleasure reward (in the form of dopamine released by the brain) that we get when the flavour experience matches up to our expectation. Smell and taste therefore make a much wider range of edible foods not only palatable but, more importantly, pleasurable.[14] Without either the stimuli of food smells or the guarantee that the flavour experience will deliver, we are less likely to be prompted to eat. John noticed that 'when I'm eating, I don't get that kind of "tasty smell". I never really feel that hungry. I do sometimes go to bed realizing that I haven't eaten anything all day'.[15]

The human olfactory system has evolved uniquely for our survival, and the physical pleasures (and displeasures) of eating are often taken for granted, yet without a sense of smell the materiality of food is experienced in a fundamentally different way. The biological imperative of staying alive demands that we consume food daily; however for anosmia sufferers this process can be fraught as they are forced to engage with food even when the act of eating provides little pleasure, as Briget observes: 'If you watch, say, a farming programme, [the animals] just get this food dumped down, and they just eat it, and they carry on. I think that's how my eating habits are – the food is there, I eat it, and I carry on.'[16]

Smell, Memory, and Imagination

The ability to detect aromas has clear implications for our physiological engagement with food, and yet for human beings the deeper significance of food goes beyond the physical, speaking to the profound interrelation between flavour memories and psychological and social well-being. The human sense of smell combines dual aspects which are both objective and subjective. Aroma molecules possess objective chemical properties which can be identified, catalogued, and even synthetically reproduced, and Harold McGee's recent *Nose Dive* is surely the authoritative 'field guide to the world's smells', achieving the truly exceptional task of taxonomizing what he delightfully calls the 'osmocosm'.[17] Here, however, I consider what happens when odour molecules are encoded by the brain, taking us into the slippery realm of the subjective.

In their examination of scent memory, Caro Verbeek and Cretien van Campen analyze Proust's 'madeleine moment' from a neurological perspective, explaining why the act of smelling is intrinsically subjective.[18] Smell memories, they argue, are highly individualized because aromas are processed via episodic (or 'autobiographical') memory structures.[19] Specific chemical odour patterns are encoded with auxiliary information about the episode during which they were experienced, such as the time, place, context, people we were with, and our emotional state at the time. The meanings we attach to certain smells – or in this case the 'sense' that we make of food flavours – are personal and unique because they connect us sensorially to the events and emotional experiences of our lives. Flavours are not, then, inherent in odour molecules, but are unlocked by our own biographies: we each consult our own memories when we recognize food flavours and recall what they mean to us. Furthermore, research suggests that a particularly strong emotional intensity is attached to remembered smell episodes so that olfactory stimuli, more than any other sense, evoke memories which are emotionally felt, rather than simply cognitively recalled.[20]

It is important to note, however, that smell memories can only be recalled in the presence of a stimulus; without the stimulus, an important means of accessing those memories is lost. If flavours call to mind particular events in our lives, what are the implications for anosmics who can no longer access them? As Briget explains,

> When you smell something it's never just the smell, it links to memories…you'd remember the time that you did something, and "do you remember when…?", and you're making all those links. How do you get those memories back? They're still in there, and perhaps something else would make me think those things, but perhaps it never will, so actually it's like that didn't happen, and that memory, and that either sad or happy feeling that you would have had, has disappeared.[21]

In his work *Pieces of Light: The New Science of Memory*, Fernyhough examines the links between memory and imagination. Current theories in neuroscientific research speculate that a key function of memory may be its role in allowing us to conceptualize and carry out short- to medium-term future actions. If this is the case, then the same neurological processes which allow us to mentally visualize our past could also be implicated in how we mentally visualize the future. Imagining is the physiological means through which we do this.[22]

Fernyhough returns to Proust and his madeleine, yet considers in a different light the moment in which the 'immense edifice of memory' is invoked.[23] He notes that the flavour of the madeleine dipped in lime-blossom tea does not by itself summon up the memory of Aunt Léonie, but, rather, it prompts a cascade of remembering in which pieces of the memory are sought out until the whole is recalled together.[24] Challenging traditional understandings of memories as static records which are archived in the brain as 'snapshots' for later retrieval, Fernyhough instead supports recent reconstructive accounts of memory according to which each time we remember, we reassemble memories anew.[25] A memory may include semantic information (factual), episodic information (relating to an event), and sensory information (visual, auditory, tactile, olfactory, or taste sensations), as well as information about our affective emotional state at the time. Rather than being stored together as one 'complete' memory, the reconstructive view proposes that different components are stored in separate parts of the brain.[26] Each of these fragments may prompt linkages to other snippets of relevant information which are all reassembled in the present moment. Remembering, then, is an imaginative process which is fundamentally spatial rather than temporal, since instead of going back to the past, the memory is reconstructed in the present upon the 'stage' of the imagination.[27]

Accepting remembering as a process of imagination challenges the common conception of taste. The nature of aromas is that we cannot experience a smell (or flavour) from recollection alone; we can only recognize them in the presence of a stimulus. In order to taste something, then, two fundamental processes are necessary: both that we detect the aroma molecule, and that we process its molecular pattern by re-assembling our sensory memory of it. This suggests that we do not taste first and then add imagination: rather, tasting and imagining are one and the same. While fleeting flavour memories may seem like a series of ethereal or insignificant moments in themselves, they constitute a flavour landscape of our personal histories. Being able to connect to the places and times in which meals were eaten, and the contexts within which they were imbued with personal and social meanings, reinforces our sense of who we are. This is important not only for our individual identities, but also for our roles within the wider structures of family and friends and for our place in the world. In what follows, I consider how we imagine our worlds through food, and what happens to sense of self when access to this ability is lost.

Imagining Worlds through Food

To illuminate the extent to which memory and imagination constitute our sense of self, I put forward the argument that we imagine ourselves through food. That flavour memories are not only powerfully emotional but also autobiographical suggests a role for food, through imagination, as an important contributor to personal identity. Food isn't everything – there are undoubtedly many other identity factors which shape how people understand themselves – but it is nonetheless both a daily necessity and a primary means through which people relate to each other, making it 'a highly condensed social fact, [...] well suited to bear the load of everyday discourse'.[28]

Fernyhough argues that memory is autobiographical because it holds together our sense of our self unfolding through time.[29] Past experiences contribute to our understanding of who we are in the present. What makes memories 'ours' is the distinctive feeling of ownership that we have over them – they feel real to us because we were there.[30] Encounters of people, places, sensations, and emotions in the present prompt recollections of similar past events, and, each time we remember, the significance of that memory is reinforced. The more important memories are to us, the more likely they are to become sedimented as part of our identities; thus, our personal store of memories is what makes us who we are. Imagination is the bridge that provides a sense of continuity to our personal story. When we remember in the present, our imagined self not only looks back to the past but also projects into the future: the current sense of 'who I am' unpins the personal agency with which we approach the world and enact our future-oriented goals and desires. In the context of food, when we access flavour memories, the recognition of a smell/taste as meaning-laden reinforces our sense of ownership over the associations to which it connects us. While a particular flavour and the recollections it revives will be unique to each of us, we take for granted that all bodies contain innate experiential knowledge of the 'magic' smells possess to transport us through space and time – that unexpected immediacy with which the madeleine incites Proust's reverie. And yet, without the stimulus of smell, the 'immense edifice of memory' is not evoked, and flavour memories may remain buried forever.

Losing one's sense of smell can have a profound impact upon emotional well-being. What is lost is not only the ability to experience flavours, but the ability to access the personal worlds of meaning previously imagined through 'tasting' flavour memories. When acquired anosmics are suddenly deprived of the capacity to taste, a fundamental way of engaging both with the external world and with their inner lives is curtailed. This loss is a daily lived reality for anosmics who, with every mouthful, remain detached from their own autobiographies.

After surgery for a rare head and neck cancer which directly affects the olfactory nerve, Grace, a lawyer with a young family, began to suffer from panic attacks:

> My daughter likes to read a book about chocolate cakes and it describes the chocolate cake smell. I start to get panic attacks when I read that book just remembering what having a sense of smell is like [...] because I think my body just starts trying to navigate itself around – 'oh, where's the smell? [...] Hang on a minute, there's something really wrong here... you don't have a sense of smell anymore.'[31]

Flavours are not simply a tool through which we physically navigate the world, but also an instrument through which we enact our personal and social identities. Many of my research participants reported that they had reduced the range of interactions they have with food, such as shopping or cooking, and few would now choose to go to a restaurant as a social activity. When an important part of your identity is practiced through food, more than simply the eating is taken away, as Grace relates:

> Three or four months in, [I] was cooking pies for the family…my family loves my chicken pies. I would set the timer, but I would generally go by how it smelled to work out when the crust was ready. Obviously I didn't have that trigger anymore so I burnt the pies, and for me that was one of the most horrifying little events that happened post- the operation. You know – this is something that is the way I express my love for my family.[32]

Participants with total, permanent anosmia often described their condition using the language of grief. Kate, who didn't 'hit the wall with it' until about three-and-a-half years in, tells me of her relief when the specialist head injury nurse advised her to treat it as a bereavement: 'it just absolutely resonated [...] because it really is that big.'[33] Like a bereavement there is a process of acceptance and adjusting to the loss can be a difficult journey, and one that takes time – perhaps a lifetime – to come to terms with. As Kate explains, when you smell:

> you actually hold in your head 'you'. And that's gone. Right at the heart of the

matter, there's no 'you' anymore.... Deep down there's a change, psychologically. It's quite big. [...] Whichever way you angle your thought process, it's there – it's there. And I'd be fibbing if I didn't say I didn't mourn the loss every day. And I guess the fact that you do have at least three meals a day, it's kind of like a reminder that just creeps in, yet again.[34]

For those with parosmia who experience distorted flavours, the sense of total loss, like a bereavement, was not as marked. However, being unable to engage positively with food nonetheless had a significant impact on self-confidence and emotional stability, as Samantha, a teacher, told me: 'I'm not a depressed sort of person, but [...] I just felt like my world was falling apart. You think, "It's just food," [but] it plays such a huge part in everything you do.'[35]

For Sandra, having experienced only disgusting smells for the last sixteen years continues to affect her deeply. In conversation she comes across as highly intelligent and engaging – now 67, she had recently taken up steampunk as a new hobby and had started dressmaking for costume events. And yet, her outlook for her own life was overwhelmingly despondent:

> The way I see it, if you look at your life as being a funfair, I'm at the funfair now; I've been on all the rides I want to go on.... I'm having an okay time watching everybody else, but if they come and say 'right, time to close the funfair....' Fine. I'm happy to go. No reason to stay. [...] Every morning I wake up, I breathe in and breathe out and my eyes open, so I know I'm still alive and, yeah – we'll get through today and see how today goes, but I don't make vast plans of what I'm going to do in the future because I don't really care if I'm here or not [...]. I'm not a miserable person and I don't, you know, worry about my coffin and my shroud and all that. It's just...I want out.[36]

Sandra told me that she has considered asking for surgery to remove her olfactory bulb completely so that she won't be able to smell anything at all, but she hasn't pursued this idea because of a phantom smell which she occasionally experiences:

> Every now and again, and it doesn't happen that often these days [...] I can smell somebody cooking the most wonderful cinnamon apple pie. I can smell this pie, and I'm the only person in the room who can smell it: I hyperventilate because I'm taking in every molecule of the scent because it's such a treat to smell something nice and then, eventually, it just...[trails off]. So, if I were to have my olfactory bulb completely removed, would I still get my phantom smells? Because as disappointing as they are, – it's kind of like being shown a picture of your childhood and you look at it and go, 'oh yeah, I remember when...That day on the beach...' and then...it's just the memory and that's what my apple pie is. But I can't eat apple pie now. It's just not nice.[37]

That she is willing to put up with so much to keep her one good smell memory, even when she knows that the sensation is illusory, shows just how important food flavours are psychologically for our sense of bodily and emotional integrity.

Conclusion

Lived experiences of smell disorders illustrate the intricate link between the sensory capacities of the body and the ability to experience food. These testimonies demonstrate that 'tasting' is not a function of our sense of taste (on the tongue), but rather it is the sense of smell that enables us to access the flavours of food. The way the brain processes aromas as episodic memories is key to how smells, and specifically food flavours, connect us to the events of our lives in uniquely autobiographical and emotional ways. Rather than taste preceding imagination, I have argued that when we recognize food flavours we undergo a process of remembering which is itself imaginative. Imagining, therefore, constitutes tasting. Finally, I have elaborated on the role of tasting in informing identity, as the flavours which are most meaningful to us link our past, present, and future selves, shaping how we engage with the world. For those living with acquired anosmia, loss of sense of smell not only makes it impossible to materially access the flavours of food, but also prevents them from being able to re-imagine personal and social worlds through smell/taste memories. Without access to these memories, the impossibility of living in a world without taste has far-reaching implications for their sense of themselves.

Acknowledgements

I am most grateful to Miles Seecharan for his comments on an early draft. For their invaluable feedback I should also like to thank Nese Ceren Tosun, Theodore Charles, Anna Colquhoun, Jessica Fagin, Zoë Goodman, Katharina Graf, Celia Plender, and Professor Harry G. West.

Notes

1. I don't explicitly discuss the rare condition of congenital anosmia in this paper, though it did affect one participant. Congenital anosmia can be experienced very differently to acquired anosmia; the specific challenges of negotiating food for those born without a sense of smell warrant further research.
2. For examples, see Brook Jarvis, 'What can Covid-19 Teach Us About the Mysteries of Smell?', *New York Times Magazine*, 3 January 2021 <https://www.nytimes.com/2021/01/28/magazine/covid-smell-science.html> [accessed on 21.10.21]; Vincent Deary and Duika Burges Watson, 'COVID Smell Loss Can Have Profound Effects on Your Life, from Weight Change to Intimacy Barriers', *Conversation*, 24 September 2021 <https://theconversation.com/covid-smell-loss-can-have-profound-effects-on-your-life-from-weight-change-to-intimacy-barriers-168300> [accessed on 21.10.21]; and Liz Darke, 'Covid took my sense of smell. A year later I'm doing smell training to get it back', *Independent*, 23 April 2021 <https://www.independent.co.uk/life-style/health-and-families/covid-loss-of-smell-lockdown-b1829760.html> [accessed on 21 October 2021]
3. Interview 13, Grace, 8 March 2018. Pseudonyms have been used throughout to protect the anonymity

4   Charles Fernyhough, *Pieces of Light: The New Science of Memory* (London: Profile Books, 2013), ch. 7.
5   Unlike other senses which are processed via the thalamus, olfactory stimuli are processed via a shorter neural pathway direct to the hippocampus; see Fernyhough, p. 53.
6   Paul Rozin, 'Food is Fundamental, Fun, Frightening, and Far-Reaching', *Social Research*, 66.1 (Spring 1999), 9-30 (pp. 12-13).
7   Carl Philpott, 'Smell and Taste Disorders in the UK: First Experiences with a Specialized Smell and Taste Outpatient Clinic', *Bulletin of the Royal College of Surgeons of England*, 96.5 (2014), 156-59 (p. 156).
8   Interview 11, Briget, 8 February 2018.
9   According to Irfan Syed and Carl Philpott, 'The most common cause of anosmia (60%) is Chronic Rhinosinusitis; 10% of cases are acquired as a result of head trauma. Congenital anosmia is estimated at 1 in 5000-10,000 population' ('Hyposmia', *British Journal of Hospital Medicine*, 76.3 (2 March 2015), 41-45 (p. 41)).
10 Interview 5, Amanda, 24 July 2018
11 Interview 6, Kate, 30 July 2018
12 Olfactory nerves are the only part of the human nervous system which is directly exposed to the external environment, and are the only nerves which have the ability to regenerate.
13 Interview 10, Sandra, 1 August 2018
14 For a discussion of flavour 'images of desire', see Bee Wilson, *First Bite: How We Learn to Eat* (London: Fourth Estate, 2015), p. 91.
15 Interview 2, John, 10 July 2018
16 Interview 11, Briget, 2 August 2018
17 Harold McGee, *Nose Dive: A Field Guide to the World's Smells* (London: John Murray, 2020).
18 Caro Verbeek and Cretien van Campen, 'Inhaling Memories', *The Senses & Society*, 8.2 (2013), 133-148.
19 See Verbeek and van Campen, Figure 1. Concise Classification of the human memories, p. 136.
20 Rachel Herz, *The Scent of Desire: Discovering Our Enigmatic Sense of Smell* (New York: HarperCollins e-books, 2007), pp. 66-89.
21 Interview 11, Briget.
22 Fernyhough, p. 149.
23 Marcel Proust, *In Search of Lost Time. The Way by Swann's. Volume 1* (London: Penguin, 2003 [1913]), p. 50.
24 Fernyhough, pp. 50-52.
25 Fernyhough, pp. 7-8.
26 Fernyhough, pp. 118-19.
27 Fernyhough, p. 150.
28 Arjun Appadurai, 'Gastro-Politics in Hindu South Asia', *American Ethnologist*, 8.3 (August 1981), 494-511 (p. 494).
29 Fernyhough, p. 178.
30 Fernyhough, pp. 100-01.
31 Interview 13, Grace.
32 Interview 13, Grace.
33 Interview 6, Kate.
34 Interview 6, Kate.
35 Interview 9, Samantha, 1 August 2018.
36 Interview 10, Sandra.
37 Interview 10, Sandra.

Have It Your Way: Elizabeth David and the Problem of Norman Douglas

Laura Shapiro

One of the most influential figures in the life of the great British food writer Elizabeth David was Norman Douglas, the man she considered her mentor, whom she met in 1939. Although they spent relatively little time together before his death in 1952, she wrote about him frequently and with enormous admiration, making clear how much in her culinary sensibility she owed to him. She knew, as did everybody in his enormous circle of friends, that he was an open and active pedophile; but she never alluded to this in anything she published. The 'Norman Douglas' who appears in her books and journalism was a work of the imagination.

During the miserable British winter of 1947, Elizabeth David found herself stuck in a provincial hotel, unable to get back to London while floods ravaged the countryside. Day after day, the food that showed up was even worse than the weather. Rationing was still in force, and every meal – flour and water soup, dehydrated vegetables – was a monument to deprivation. During the war she'd been in France, Greece, and Cairo, and as her mind travelled back to those years in the sun, she could practically taste the lemons, the olive oil, the figs, the apricots. She picked up her pen and started to write. At the time it was hardly more than a list of what she longed to eat, but three years later it had become the first of her now-classic works, *A Book of Mediterranean Food.*

Elizabeth herself was the first to tell this origin story: it appeared in the *Spectator* in 1963 titled 'How It All Began'.[1] Since then, journalists and historians have evoked it countless times; it's now an indispensable touchstone in any account of Elizabeth's career. A painstaking writer, and deliberately elusive when the subject was herself, she would have taken great care in composing this anecdote. Hence it's worth noting exactly how she situated herself in relation to the Mediterranean – that is, at a vast, unbridgeable distance. There she was in a bleak and hungry England, summoning to the page an array of entrancing ingredients so definitively out of reach that the only way to taste a dish was to imagine it. What's clear now, looking at *Mediterranean Food* and much of the work that followed, is that she expected readers, too, to use their imaginations. Invariably she set recipes in a captivating swirl of history, literature, and storytelling, as if to signal that cooking was not the only way to bring this food to life.

But to understand more fully 'how it all began', we have to pair this origin story with another one. A year earlier, also in the *Spectator*, she had published a piece called 'South

Have It Your Way: Elizabeth David and Norman Douglas

Wind' – an homage to her beloved mentor, the novelist and travel writer Norman Douglas (1868-1952), on the tenth anniversary of his death.[2] Courtly and charismatic, Norman was based in Capri and had a deep familiarity with food and cooking across the region. He was seventy when they met in 1939; Elizabeth was twenty-five, still just a young food-lover and adventurer. The culinary sensibility we associate so strongly with her, a sensibility steeped in landscapes and people and traditional ways with food, a sensibility persistently at war with the ersatz – all this was activated in the course of walks and talks and meals with Norman Douglas. She owed him a great deal and honoured him for the rest of her life – but obliquely, for he was famous in his time as an open, avid, and indeed proud pedophile.[3]

How, then, was she to memorialize him in print? With an extraordinary degree of tact. Today we would call it compartmentalizing. She never alluded to his sex life, though he himself paraded it cheerfully, showing up to meet friends in cafes with one or another young boy in tow. Rather, she portrayed him as a wry, contemplative source of timeless wisdom on food and life. The 'Norman Douglas' she created for the *Spectator* – and expanded upon in later articles – was a work of the imagination, true to her sense of him while at the same time profoundly incomplete. I've called him her mentor, and he did ignite the intellectual passion that would become her career. But he was also, in a way, her talisman. Norman lived at a delightful – to him – distance from the conventions he scorned, setting an example that Elizabeth cleansed of abusive sexuality and held close.

It's more than likely they never would have met at all, if Elizabeth and her then lover, a sometime actor and writer named Charles Gibson Cowan, hadn't made the truly dumb decision to sail a ramshackle yacht from England to Greece during the summer of 1939. By the time they reached Marseille in September, the Second World War was underway. Two months later they managed to get to Antibes, and there they settled in for the winter. While they sorted through the problems and possibilities now facing them, Charles took the opportunity to make some money by helping a friend pick up a boat in Venice and sail it back to Antibes. Elizabeth stayed in Antibes, socializing with friends in the expat community, and before long she was spending as much time as she could with one of the most notorious expats on the Riviera, Norman Douglas.

'Always do as you please, and send everybody to Hell, and take the consequences. Damned good Rule of Life.'[4] This was the inscription Norman scrawled in Elizabeth's copy of his book *Old Calabria*, and she was charmed by the advice, so much so that she quoted it right at the start of a warm tribute to him she published in *Gourmet* in 1969. Fifteen years later she selected the *Gourmet* piece for inclusion in her essay collection, *An Omelette and a Glass of Wine*, and it is via this appealing portrait that most readers nowadays encounter Norman Douglas for the first time. Elizabeth may have been unaware, when she took to heart his 'Rule of Life', that Norman himself jettisoned this rule whenever it was about to become a nuisance. Yes, he always did what he pleased – but he scrambled like mad to avoid the consequences.

Born to a wealthy Scottish family, owners of an immense cotton factory in Austria, Norman grew up near Bregenz as well as in Scotland and England. He hated his various schools and ended up largely self-educated, with an early passion for natural history that led to his publishing several articles in scientific journals. Eventually he decided on a career in the British diplomatic service and was posted to the embassy in St. Petersburg in 1894. At the time he was still having affairs with women, one of whom was an aristocrat from the powerful Demidov family. When she told him she was pregnant, he finagled his way out of the diplomatic service in a hurry and left for Naples, never seeing her again. Soon after, he married his cousin, Elsa FitzGibbon, in London; and the two of them lived mostly in Italy and Austria for the next few years while two sons were born. The marriage ended in a vicious divorce, with Norman winning custody of the boys chiefly because the British judicial system favoured the husband. He had no intention of raising his sons – once the court had ruled, he handed over the two children to friends in England and made his own home in Capri.

Around that time he began to focus on writing as a way to support himself, and over the next several decades turned out more than twenty books, most of them heavily researched and clogged with obscurantist references to history, literature, and mythology. The books drew some attention in their day and earned a number of admiring reviews, but he never won a lasting readership, and fairly quickly his work dropped out of sight. His only genuine success was *South Wind*, a novel satirizing the bohemian expats on Capri, which came out in 1917 and sold well for many years. Light-hearted amorality was the driving feature of *South Wind*; and it was given a warm welcome by the Bloomsbury circle and other free spirits of the time.

But far more than work, what preoccupied him was the pursuit of boys and occasionally girls. Southern Italy and especially Capri were popular destinations for pedophiles, and Norman had no difficulty – legally or socially – living just as he wished. Around 1912, however, he ran short of money, so he accepted an editorial job at the *English Review* and moved to London, where he was based for the next five years. One day he picked up a sixteen-year-old schoolboy in a museum, took him to a tea shop for cakes, and brought him home. Afterwards the youth reported him, and Norman was arrested. Rather than face trial, he jumped bail and fled to Italy. In 1937, he again ran into trouble with the police, this time over a young girl in Florence, and quickly escaped to France, where he hoped to stay only until the Italian authorities forgot about him. This plan collapsed with the outbreak of war, and that's when Elizabeth showed up. She was entranced immediately.

Norman was on the lam, but he certainly wasn't an outcast. In Antibes and everywhere else, he had an enormous circle of friends and admirers. Some of them loved his work, others respected his wide learning, and they all relished his general air of hedonism. Many were writers, including Joseph Conrad, D.H. Lawrence, Graham Greene, Rebecca West, Compton Mackenzie, E.F. Benson, and Sybille Bedford. Several were rich – the radical activist and philanthropist Nancy Cunard, the arts patrons

Muriel Draper and Brigit Patmore – and he tended such friendships with special care. It's possible he categorized Elizabeth as another of these women with money, despite the somewhat raffish way she and Charles were living, for her upper-class speech and bearing were unmistakable. At any rate, he was happy to welcome her to the entourage.

Elizabeth used to say she was twenty-four when they met, and he was seventy-two or seventy-three. Actually their ages were a bit closer – twenty-five and seventy, as we've seen. This was an uncharacteristic mistake on her part, for she was scrupulous about facts, but perhaps she let the age difference expand in memory. The many years that separated them were fundamental to the way she felt about him, and to the way she evoked him after his death. She rarely portrayed him as an equal; more often she cast him as an oracle, a kind of culinary zen master with herself as the disciple.

Their immediate point of contact was food – a safe space, morally speaking, where she had no need to acknowledge his disquieting sex life. Food was also a world she had been eagerly exploring on her own for some time. Although she had grown up on the stodgy meals favoured in many affluent British households, once she left home she began acquiring cookbooks and teaching herself to cook. On her frequent trips abroad she made a point of stockpiling notes and memories of local meals, and before long she had enough of a recipe collection to assemble a handwritten cookbook for a flatmate. She continued gathering recipes during the voyage with Charles, and she managed to turn out impressive meals from their galley kitchen even when wartime shortages became acute. There was a chicken *en casserole* for Charles's birthday, a lobster mayonnaise when they managed to acquire a lobster, and one day she came back on board with half a goat, which was the only meat she'd been able to find. She cooked her way through it for the next week.

Norman himself rarely cooked, but when it came to the raw materials, the flora and fauna that are the elements of cuisine, he was at home. A lifelong fascination with natural science gave him the habit of acquiring his knowledge of place from the ground up, hiking and exploring, investigating a pond or a grove of trees or a flutter of insects for everything they could tell him. That was also the way he picked up his knowledge of kitchen traditions – by being there, in the restaurants and markets, and paying attention. Elizabeth had mastered the basics on her own; now she learned to think about food more deliberately, as Norman did, and to focus on it as an expression of time, place, and people.

Apart from a couple of coy, faux-erudite collections of aphrodisiac recipes, Norman's books touched on food only sporadically. His idiosyncratic expertise emerged in talk – the observations, advice, and rants for which he was famous among his friends. Charles, who took copious notes throughout his trip with Elizabeth, recorded a typical outburst about the pasta in a local café:

'Muck, my dear, muck! Every day I tell them that spaghetti must be cooked exactly twelve minutes and then allowed to stand for a further three minutes in its own water, no more. Good God! It's simple enough. They don't have to start till we get here, but the barbarians think that it can be cooked in the morning and heated up. Muck, that's what it is, muck.'⁵

After she and Charles left Antibes in May 1940, Elizabeth didn't see Norman again until she visited him in Capri in 1951. He died a year later. By then she had published *A Book of Mediterranean Food* and *French Country Cooking*, and she was at work on *Italian Food*, which would appear in 1954. The following year she published *Summer Cooking*, and in 1960 *French Provincial Cooking*. Norman popped up frequently in these books – she quoted him, thanked him, acknowledged him – in fact she mentioned him so often in the first draft of *Mediterranean Food* that readers of the manuscript had to persuade her to cut most of the references. During this spectacularly productive decade she was also contributing regularly to *Harper's Bazaar, Vogue, House and Garden*, and the *Sunday Times*. She had become the most acclaimed food writer in England, and the very sight of her name evoked the European cuisines of the sun.

Then her life took a sharp turn. Early in the 1960s, a long-time lover suddenly revealed that he had become engaged to another woman, and the news was devastating. Soon after, she suffered a mild stroke and temporarily lost her sense of taste. But even while she was recovering from these setbacks she launched an entirely new enterprise – Elizabeth David Ltd, the kitchenware shop she opened in 1965 with four partners. There she held court regularly, chatting with customers and dispensing advice in a salon-like setting that she greatly enjoyed. It turned out to be an excellent restorative. Meanwhile, back in 1961 she had started writing regularly for the *Spectactor*, long a showcase for some of England's best minds in politics and culture. Elizabeth quickly proved that she belonged in their company. The editor had no interest in traditional recipe stories but encouraged her to pursue any aspect of cuisine, past or present, that fascinated her. What fascinated her, she discovered, was England. In 1970 she published her first book in ten years: *Spices, Salt and Aromatics in the English Kitchen*.

The voice was still that of Elizabeth David – unmistakably so, in the wit and the easy-going intellect, the depth of the research, the delight with which she offered gleanings from centuries' worth of texts – but the sources of inspiration were different. It was as if she had gone back to that provincial hotel room and started dreaming of pickled ox-tongue instead of saffron and basil. And indeed, despite the different culinary terrain, *Spices, Salt* had a great deal in common with *Mediterranean Food*. Once again she was taking the first steps in an exploration that would go on for years as she searched the archives for the wandering ways of culinary history. Once again the recipes were not meant to be an end in themselves but rather to carry on the conversation. And once again she included an affectionate tribute to Norman, though he was somewhat out of place in this book, since he openly despised England and its food. She managed it by putting him in the 'Savouries' chapter, where she praised his knowledge of herbs, spices, and other ingredients from the ancient world that had contributed to English cookery.⁶

Have It Your Way: Elizabeth David and Norman Douglas

During this decade – the decade in which her interests were veering so markedly away from his – Elizabeth began writing about Norman in greater depth. Journalism was the vehicle she chose for this project, rather than inserting notes about him into cookbooks. She seemed intent on establishing an image of him that would exist outside the books, like a statue in a public square. 'South Wind,' the 1962 piece for the *Spectator*, appeared first; then came articles in *Wine & Food* and *Gourmet*. There was a fair amount of recycling from one piece to another, but together they amounted to the 'Norman Douglas' she favoured for posterity.

Creating this portrait, she focused directly on his speaking style, for it conveyed just what she wanted to emphasize: his homegrown wisdom and the charm of his company. In a cafe, she wrote, he would pull out from his pocket a handful of basil and send it to the kitchen for the pasta sauce. '"Tear the leaves, mind,"' he would instruct. '"Don't chop them. Spoils the flavour."'[7] When she brought him a basket of figs one day, he asked which market stall she had visited. He knew the nearby fig trees, he knew the soil, he knew who picked the figs too early and who picked at just at the right moment. '"Next time, you could try Graziella. I fancy you'll find her figs are sweeter; just wait a few days if you can."'[8] When she saw mussels on a menu and considered ordering them – '"Mussels? Of course, if you want to be poisoned […]. You know what happened to the consul in Naples, don't you? […] But have it your way, my dear, have it your way."'[9]

One of her tenderest accounts of their relationship appeared in *Wine & Food* in 1964, where she described taking a trip to Capri after Norman's death. She wrote that she didn't stay long at his grave but made her way to his favourite table at a tavern among the lemon trees. There she ate a chunk of bread with olive oil, drank a glass of local wine, and thought back on everything she treasured about Norman. A particular memory came to her, a remark that Norman had made many times, and Elizabeth quoted it with such passionate conviction you can almost see the highlighting on the page: '"I like to taste my friends, not eat them."'[10]

It's a peculiar image, and rather an unpleasant one, but the meaning is clear: Norman would never pry into anyone's intimate life, and he expected people to avoid prying into his. There could be absolutely no 'idle questioning, meddling gossip and rattling chatter' around the subject of Norman Douglas. Small wonder Elizabeth applauded this dictum: she guarded her own privacy ferociously, as many an interviewer had learned, and she wouldn't dream of crossing that line with Norman. 'The few who failed him in this regard did not for long remain his friends,' she added.[11] She would remain a loyal friend as long as she lived.

Elizabeth had chosen the Norman Douglas she wished to believe in, and the portrait that emerged in her journalism of the 1960s was a work of love as well as art. This Norman was an independent soul, the very embodiment of personal integrity, a man true to himself who simply ignored those standards of behaviour and achievement for which he had no use. It's not a version of Norman Douglas that would strike many of us as credible today, but it was credible to Elizabeth. And it was necessary. Being with him in Antibes had taught her what mattered in life, and visiting him in Capri, as he neared death, made those lessons still more compelling. His sensibility inspired her recipes; his voice was always with her; he had a permanent place at that famous kitchen table where she did her writing. Those of us who tell the story of her life can't leave him out even if we wish we could – because the one good thing he ever did was give us Elizabeth David.

Notes

1. Elizabeth David, 'How It All Began', *Spectator,* 1 February 1963, p. 146.
2. Elizabeth David, 'South Wind', *Spectator,* 16 February 1962, p. 218.
3. For background on Norman Douglas, see two major biographies: *Norman Douglas*, by Mark Holloway (London: Secker & Warburg, 1976) and *Unspeakable: A Life Beyond Sexual Morality*, by Rachel Hope Cleves (Chicago: University of Chicago Press, 2020).
4. Elizabeth David, 'Norman Douglas', *Gourmet*, February 1969, p. 28.
5. Charles Gibson Cowan, *The Voyage of the Evelyn Hope* (London: The Cresset Press, 1946), p. 56.
6. Elizabeth David, 'Savouries', in *Spices, Salt and Aromatics in the English Kitchen* (London: Penguin, 1970), pp. 227-28.
7. Elizabeth David, 'South Wind', p. 218.
8. Elizabeth David, 'South Wind', p. 219.
9. Elizabeth David, 'South Wind Through the Kitchen', *Wine & Food*, Autumn 1964, p. 27.
10. Elizabeth David, 'South Wind Through the Kitchen', p. 31.
11. Elizabeth David, 'South Wind Through the Kitchen', p. 31.

Making the Ordinary Exotic: The Role of Literary Imagination in the Rise of Gastronomic Tourism in Early Twentieth-Century France

Richard Warren Shepro

Food and Imagination can describe the conscious, creative process of inventing new dishes, bringing to mind Brillat-Savarin's comment that 'the invention of a new dish adds more to human happiness than the discovery of a new star'.[1] I would like instead to focus on the literary and rhetorical imagination that can transform diners' perceptions of traditional, often regional, dishes from something mundane to something transcendent, making the ordinary exciting or even exotic, and shaping a country's tastes in new ways.

In late nineteenth-century and early twentieth-century France, both in fiction and in prose works about gastronomy, writers used their literary imagination to paint vivid pictures of dishes that had previously been viewed as ordinary or known only as eccentric or folkloric regional dishes. This, I argue, may have done as much or more to encourage the rise of gastrotourism and the appreciation of those dishes as did the fledgling Michelin guide.

Michelin

A conventional view is that the major impetus for gastrotourism were the guidebooks created by the Michelin tire company to encourage people to drive more, specifically to distant restaurants.[2] Undoubtedly, Michelin's extraordinarily popular red guides did influence the new dining population. Its denizens were a new kind of visitor, known by a new word – *gastronomade* – now more commonly thought of as a gastrotourist. *Gastronomades* were drawn to provincial restaurants where invention may have been limited but expert preparation of regional dishes pulled automobile drivers from far away. The Michelin guide created its own evocative and novel symbolism and mythology – stars, a firmament, reasons to take journeys – but literary flair and storytelling by a few writers may have fired the imagination before the automobile boom began, filling in the essential details drivers needed to take an interest in the Michelin recommendations. An increased recognition of dishes and regions that had been unappreciated or marginalized was a prerequisite to the Michelin recommendations being credible to gastronomes.

In 1900, the fledgling Michelin tire company began handing out to automobile drivers a free booklet containing maps of thirteen provincial French cities and advice on

Figure 1 (left). Perhaps the first appearance of the character who became known as Bibendum, 1900. 'Now, it must be drunk!! To your health. The Michelin tire drinks the obstacles.'
Figure 2 (right). Advertisement for the 1920 Guide Michelin, *with another early appearance by Bibendum, the Michelin man, now with a more recognizable face.*

how to travel without problems (Figures 1 and 2). That year, a journalist writing in a new magazine *L'Auto* noted that he had driven from Paris to Marseille in four days and only came across two other cars.[3] The guide gradually expanded its coverage and in 1923 began to alert drivers to restaurants in a few provincial cities, categorized by three and then five levels of quality, from '*premier ordre*' (first rank) through '*modeste*' and later '*simple mais bien tenu*' (simple but well maintained). In 1932, it reclassified its ratings into three levels of stars, * for '*très bonne qualité*', ** for '*d'excellent qualité*', and *** for '*fine et justement renommée*' (fine and rightly renowned), now covering all of France except Paris. In 1933, it began to cover Paris as well and listed restaurants using the categories still essentially in use today: * '*une bonne table dans la localité*', ** '*cuisine excellent, mérite le detour*' (worth a detour), and, what became a revered ultimate award, *** '*une des meilleures tables de France, vaut le voyage*' (worth a special trip).[4] There were initially twenty-three three-star restaurants, six of which were Paris.

The seventeen three-star restaurants outside of Paris were not particularly fancy or formal. For more than a century, French food had been written about and categorized, principally into the categories of the refined '*cuisine de cour*' or '*haute cuisine*' and two categories of '*cuisine populaire*': '*cuisine bourgeoise*' and '*cuisine régionale*'. There was also a category of '*cuisine des pauvres*'.[5] Two of the classic dishes of the *cuisine bourgeoise* relevant to our discussion are *pot-au-feu* ('boiled' beef, actually long-simmered, not using tender cuts, with a variety of vegetables, served with its broth) and *blanquette de veau à l'ancienne* (long-simmered chunks of veal, less tender cuts from the neck, shoulder, or shin, combined with a creamy sauce made from the broth, simple mushrooms, and separately cooked pearl onions, generally served with rice).[6] Although the *Guide Michelin* at the time gave no descriptions of restaurants or their food other than the judgements indicated by the stars themselves, some of the restaurants outside Paris exemplified these (comparatively) simpler styles of food and regional cooking.

The Disparagement of Regional Food

At the turn of the century in 1900, regional cooking was not respected by the sort of people who could afford automobiles. There was pride in the richness of French agricultural produce, including specialties of each region. These were omnipresent in school classrooms using the characteristic maps of French regional specialties created by Deyrolle, the family also known for taxidermy and their museum-like shop on the Rue du Bac in Paris (Figure 3). But regional foods, in general, were looked down on as peasant food suitable only for the backward people who lived deep in the regions and even disparaged by regional elites. There was a sense in sophisticated circles that bourgeois, rural, and regional food were not gastronomic or worth examining except, perhaps, as anthropological curiosities. Moreover, there had long been in France a tension between regionalism and nationalism. It has been argued that appreciation of regional foods emerged around the time of the French Revolution as an increasingly centralized government reorganized regional boundaries and emphasized pride both in the nation and in the community, and that pride may have sparked the idea that some regional foods could be a success in Paris. There is even a year attached to the first Parisian appearance of the Provençal fish-stew *bouillabaisse*: 1786, when the aptly named brothers Provençaux moved to Paris and introduced *bouillabaisse* and its simpler cousin *brandade* to the capital.[7] But their success introducing sophisticated Parisians to a particular provincial novelty does not mean that rural or distant provinces began to be widely respected, and it is unlikely that the popularity of the automobile and the allure of ratings

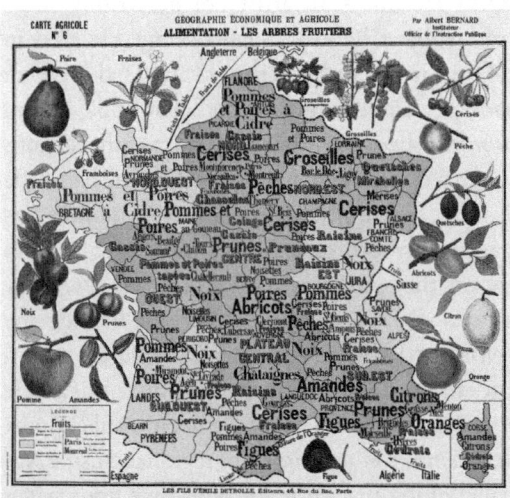

Figure 3. The Deyrolle map of French agricultural specialties.

in an attractive guidebook were sufficient to change attitudes and assure the success of these restaurants and the popularity of their styles of food.

The stereotype of the food of southwestern France, for example, was not focused on images of the luxurious partridges, truffles, foie gras, and Bordeaux wine that later led to parts of the southwest being viewed as a mythical land of Cockaigne, but instead on deprivation, misery, and the omnipresence of garlic as the principal vegetable eaten by people either very poor or entirely undiscerning.[8] In *The Three Musketeers*, Alexandre Dumas presents the three southwestern musketeers and their friend D'Artagnan as eager, ambitious country bumpkins, unsophisticated but gallant and courageous, who drink wine immoderately and savour coarse but hearty foods.[9]

Far from celebrating bourgeois or regional French foods, mid-nineteenth-century French writers often presented characters who were dazzled by foreign and exotic delicacies that were not even French. When the Count of Monte Cristo hosts a dinner party intended to be breathtaking, Alexandre Dumas has him emphasize the exotic and the expensive. The fish are imported, still alive, from southern Italy and from the Volga river in Russia, and there are fruits from China and Japan.[10] In Flaubert's *Madame Bovary* (1856), the Normandy dinner party and ball that so transformed Emma Bovary's life was not full of local specialties one might admire in Normandy today (local seafood, cheeses and cream, apple products) but imported exotica: pineapple, pomegranate, Spanish wines, and Rhine wines. A pharmacist is made to seem small and provincial when he criticizes Parisian restaurant meals he has never eaten that 'aren't worth as much, no matter what they say, as a good *pot-au-feu*' and declares he prefers '*cuisine bourgeoise*, it's healthier'.[11]

Alexandre Dumas was a serious gastronome himself, and like the composer Rossini he finished his life after astonishing youthful success as an artist not by writing more novels or operas but as an encyclopedist of a subject he loved, gastronomy. He died in 1870 with his huge encyclopedia unfinished, but it was published in 1873, based on what he had completed, as the *Grand Dictionnaire de cuisine*. It is a magnificent book, full of fascinating details of thousands of *haute cuisine* dishes, with drawings from early editions of Taillevent, the first French cookbook writer. Voluminous, it suggests Dumas had little interest in *cuisine bourgeoise* or regional cuisine. It does not mention *pot-au-feu* nor discuss the simple regional dishes that people began to travel to eat a half-century later, such as *cassoulet* in the southwest and *bouillabaisse* on the southeast coast. As to *blanquette de veau*, the *Grand Dictionnaire* describes 115 veal dishes including three that include the term *blanquette de veau* that are actually glorified leftovers – roast veal done up with a separately made creamy sauce, and a variant enriched with truffles. As Dumas was at the time the gourmand of gourmands and very serious about his *Dictionnaire*, it would appear that the interest of gastronomes of the time in *cuisine bourgeoise* or in regional cuisine was essentially nonexistent. Similarly, a practical cooking magazine for bourgeois housewives started in 1893 called *Le Pot-au-feu: Journal de cuisine pratique et d'économie domestique* gave strictly practical advice and did not particularly celebrate the dish *pot-au-feu*.

The Role of Literary Imagination in the Rise of Gastronomic Tourism

A Literary Change?

Attitudes began to change, however, with some writers later in the century. Guy de Maupassant wrote evocatively about an old country aristocrat and the details of his presiding over a dinner at which *becasses,* tiny birds locally hunted as game, were eaten, one small bird per person. The heads with their distinctive needle-like beak are then recooked by the host and eaten as part of a story-telling game after the rest of the flesh has been consumed as a main course:

> He took them one by one and grilled them on the candle. The grease crackled, the browned skin smoked, and the randomly chosen one crunched the richly cooked head, holding it by the neck and letting out exclamations of pleasure. And each time the diners, raising their glasses, drank to his health.[12]

This is a rustic, country meal, with a hint of savagery, not at all like Brillat-Savarin's more stately discussion of his refined pairing of roast pheasant and fine Burgundy, presented as special, and delicious, but not particularly unusual in the eyes of the participants, emphasizing a rural tradition but describing the dish in a vivid way that intrigues the reader.[13] In contrast to Flaubert, Maupassant does not appear to be satirizing the ways of these rural characters.

Two other late nineteenth-century fiction writers, Alphonse Daudet and Émile Zola, wrote extensive and memorable descriptions of simple and regional food. Like Maupassant, Daudet wrote a story about hunting, but his was written from the perspective of the red partridges and quail being hunted![14] His other writings about food included vivid descriptions likely to be enticing to any reader. His description of a marine harvest in a Breton fishing village anticipates the enthusiasm of twentieth-century gastrotourists: 'You can't really find anything more delicious, more secluded, than this small village lost in the middle of the rocks, interesting by its dual marine and pastoral side.'[15] In a three-part story in the same volume, called 'Gastronomic Landscapes', Daudet submerges himself in local colour and shows his appreciation for both the highs (in Provence and Corsica) and lows (in Sardinia) of local food, beginning with *bouillabaisse*:

> When the fishing was over, we landed among the high gray rocks. The fire was quickly lit, pale in the bright sun; large slices of bread cut on small plates of red earth, and we were there around the pot, the plate outstretched, the nostril open ... Was it the landscape, the light, this horizon of sky and water? But I have never eaten anything better than this *bouillabaisse* of *languoustes*. And what a good nap afterwards on the sand! A sleep full of the rocking of the sea, where the thousand shining scales of the little waves still fluttered with closed eyes.

And in the Provençal specialty of aioli, variants of which are found around the Mediterranean but which to a nineteenth-century Parisian might merely have reeked of garlic, Daudet found this magic:

> Inside the hut where a fire of woody vine shoots shone, clear and sparkling, the

cook religiously pounded the cloves of garlic in a mortar, letting the olive oil drop, drop by drop. We ate aioli around our eels that had just been skinned, seated on high stools in front of the little wooden table [...]. Around the tiny room one could discern an immense horizon crossed by gusts of wind, hasty flights of traveling birds [...] while the surrounding space could be measured by the bells of the herds of horses and oxen, resounding and sonorous, grew faint in the distance, arriving like lost notes, blown away in a blast of the mistral.

Or as an even more star-struck gastrotourist in Algeria, eating a dish which was called at the time, in French, *kousskouss*:

From the large stately tent [...] we could see a night of semi-mourning descending, a black-violet in which the purple of a magnificent sunset darkened; in the freshness of the evening, in the middle of the half-open tent, a Kabyle candlestick in palm wood raised at the end of its branches a motionless flame which attracted night insects, the rustling of fearful wings. Squatting all around on mats, we ate silently; There were whole sheep dripping with butter which were brought at the end of a spit, pastries with honey, musky jams, and finally a large wooden dish where chickens were spread out in the golden semolina of the kousskouss [...]. I thought that the Arab national dish might well be that miraculous manna of the Hebrews spoken of in the Bible.

His Sardinian main dish, by contrast, he found sadly wanting. Polenta, made of milled chestnut rather than maize, 'is awful. Poorly crushed chestnuts have a moldy taste; it looks like they had spent a long time under the trees, in the rain'.[16] However influenced he may have been by the settings, Daudet was not undiscerning.

Émile Zola was less of a gastrotourist and more a chronicler of naturalistic scenes, particularly in his early novel, *The Belly of Paris* (1873), which contains detailed descriptions of markets and foods. One of his more famous dinners appears in his 1888 novel, *L'Assommoir*, in which Gervaise, the mother of Nana (who grows up to be the protagonist of a later novel), decides to splurge on a special multi-course dinner, largely beyond her financial means. In addition to a roast goose, one of the dishes being considered is the *cuisine bourgeoise* classic (still a favourite today in polls of most-loved dishes by the French populace): 'Tall Clémence suggested rabbit, but that was what they ate every day . . . Gervaise had a mind to do something more distinguished; when Mme Putois mentioned a *blanquette de veau*, they looked round at one another and started to smile.' Later, they decide to prepare the *blanquette de veau* the day before because, as modern cooks also know, 'those dishes are better if reheated'.[17] However, the characters know that only the basic stew is best done in advance; the sauce is to be completed at the last minute. Presumably the garnishes of pearl onion and of mushrooms that define the *à l'ancienne* version of the dish are also completed at that time: Gervaise and her friends do not prepare a dish of this sort often, but they are careful and particular, and the description of the cooking process suggests an art form.[18] The dinner ends in chaos, but Zola shows appreciation and respect for the dish.

In his 1903 novel *Histoire comique*, Anatole France has a character remark that the *fond*, or thickened broth of *cassoulet*, the decidedly regional southwestern bean and meat dish that many at the time would have viewed as heavy and vulgar, had a depth and savour that reminded him of treasured Venetian Renaissance paintings.[19] In a more matter-of-fact way, the enormously popular mystery writer, Georges Simenon, had his main character Inspector Maigret, in seventy-five different novels, take frequent pleasure in the anticipation of the unapologetically *cuisine bourgeoise* dishes his wife makes. Every evening, while hanging up his hat, Inspector Maigret would use his skills at ratiocination to work out what dish would be served: perhaps a *blanquette de veau*? Inspector Maigret's culinary ruminations are frequent, evocative, and brief, showing deep respect for the simple, traditional dishes he eats at home and at simple bistros. *Le Monde* food critic Robert Courtine, a champion of French traditional and regional dishes wrote a popular cookbook to bring to life Inspector Maigret's brief but endearing ruminations.[20]

This literary imagination was not just presented in fiction. The non-fiction gastronomic writers of the period also differed from their predecessors' approach. Édouard Nignon, a restaurateur with a great gift for evocative writing and a favourite of intellectual modern French chefs including Michel Guérard and Yves Camdeborde, wrote evocative, detailed literary descriptions of food from 1919 to 1933 with an inspiring delicacy and finesse very different from the curt, instructional directions of Escoffier and others.[21] The southwestern chef Prosper Montagné presented a vivid portrait of southwestern food in his 1928 book, *Le festin Occitan*, and his description of cassoulet and, especially, his description of three styles of the dish and his anointing Castelnaudary, Carcassonne, and Toulouse as the 'holy trinity of cassoulet' were so memorable that it is quoted or paraphrased in essentially everything written about the dish even today. This happened five years before Michelin began urging its readers to make special trips. A decade later, Montagné's *Larousse gastronomique*,

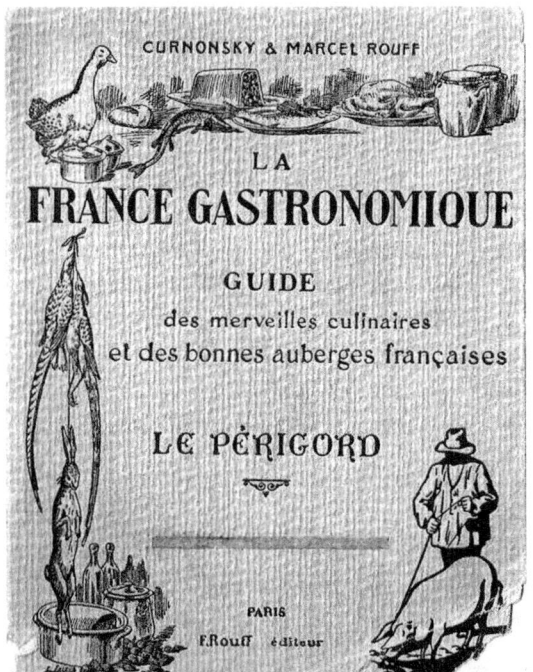

Figure 4. One of the many pamphlets by Curnonsky and Rouff that were compiled to create La France gastronomique, *showing a truffle-hunting pig, some game, some wine (perhaps from Cahors) and a goose.*

the first edition of the first great culinary encyclopedia published since Dumas's, gloriously celebrated a wide range of regional and simpler cooking.

The greatest influence on the popular view of these *cuisine bourgeoise* and regional dishes was undoubtedly a successful writer who abandoned his craft as a novelist but used his literary skills to promote the regional cuisine of France: Maurice Edmond Sailland. He worked as a novelist-for-hire for the famous publisher Willy, the first husband of the writer Colette, who kept her locked up while she ghostwrote his books. Sailland and Colette were the main writers in the Willy *atelier*; Sailland wrote several bestsellers for Willy under the name Perdiccus. In 1908 he went to work writing copy for Michelin under a new pseudonym he claimed to have invented, Bibendum ('now it is to be drunk'), before Michelin applied the name to the Michelin man, the gourmand made of Michelin tires.[22]

Monsieur Sailland did not stay long with Michelin, though, but adopted a final pseudonym Curnonsky, an exotic made-up name in a false Russian style beginning with two syllables in Latin: *Cur Non*. Sort of *Pourquoi Pas*? Or WhyNotSky? This actually fitted with the nineteenth-century tendency in France to equate countries representing eastern exoticism, including Russia, with the heights of gastronomy, instead of the existing, vibrant French regional cuisine that was unknown to many elites. There is some irony in his having adopted this Russian-inspired name and under that name becoming the leading champion of French regional cuisine. This third pseudonym lasted him the rest of his life.

Between 1921 and 1930, Curnonsky, with his friend Marcel Rouff, wrote a series of thirty-two tremendously influential pamphlets about French regional cooking, twenty-eight of which were later compiled as *La France gastronomique*, the first of his many influential books (Figure 4).[23] These were all published by Rouff's relatives at their influential family publishing houses. Curnonsky, a colourful and mysterious man, later became well-known as the 'elected Prince of Gastronomes'. Curnonsky's writing conveys genuine enthusiasm with a flair for the dramatic that also involved self-promotion and an early sense of public relations. When he wrote about a regional dish, like *bouillabaisse*, that may not have been well known outside its region, he had a knack for descriptions that people would remember and could influence their perception of what they ate, such as:

> Bouillabaisse, this golden soup, this incomparable golden soup which embodies and concentrates all the aromas of our shores and which permeates, like an ecstasy, the stomachs of astonished gastronomes [...] and the miracle consists of this: there are as many bouillabaisses as there are good chefs or cordon bleus. Each brings to his own version his special touch.[24]

His writing, at that time, focused on the essence and the excitement of the dishes, not on the restaurants and particularly not on the selection of the best restaurants, although he knew where to eat and where to do his research. He wanted to establish an inventory of the regional treasures of gastronomic France, many of which were little known outside their region. While Michelin told where to go, and began to rate restaurants in a hierarchy, Curnonsky explained unfamiliar dishes with a literary flair that led readers to greater appreciation.

Curnonsky was a showman, easily identifiable in restaurants in his later years, where customers asked him to sign their menus. He admired the food aphorisms that had helped lead people to remember Brillat-Savarin's writing a century before, and Curnonsky's aphorisms helped people remember him, with enigmatic sayings such as 'Cuisine is when things taste of themselves'.[25]

Sometimes tongue in cheek, he even popularized his own myths, claiming, for example, that it was often said that angels carried the first *bouillabaisse* from heaven to nourish shipwrecked saints. Julia Child was enraged (her word) by Curnonsky in his old age for perpetuating a myth (one he may have created) about *beurre blanc*, a regional sauce associated with the Loire, 'how it was a mystery, and only a few people could do it, and how it could only be made with white shallots from Lorraine and over a *wood fire*'.[26]

Marcel Rouff also wrote France's most celebrated gastronomic novel, *La vie et la passion de Dodin-Bouffant* published privately in 1920 and then expanded for a wider audience in 1924. Its most famous chapter describes the dish that Dodin-Bouffant has prepared as the centrepiece of a dinner designed to dazzle his gastronomic rival, the Prince of Eurasia, who has recently hosted Dodin-Bouffant with a lengthy, extravagant display of *haute cuisine*. As a contrast and a lesson in simplicity, Dodin-Bouffant prepares a *pot-au-feu*, merely 'accompanied by its vegetables'. His 'fearsome boiled beef, scorned, reviled, insulting to the Prince and to all gastronomy' turns out to be a triumph, 'carved into slices of […] mouth-melting texture […with] aroma […] of beef like incense with the energetic smell of tarragon'. The Prince cheerfully admits his elaborate cuisine has been bested by a 'humble dish': 'a profound psychologist, Dodin had calculated' the effects of perfect purity and simplicity.[27]

Rouff thus encouraged a change in perception of *pot-au-feu* from that of a meagre dish for the downtrodden into something middle-class gourmands would actively seek out and appreciate for its being, as some began to say, 'at the same time rude and refined'. It could be said that Dodin-Bouffant cheats – this is not a peasant's boiled beef but is enhanced with specially bred chickens, foie gras, and sausages – but Rouff's emphasis in describing the pleasure of the dish is not on those enhancements so much as the simple but profound aromas and tastes, the careful use of herbs, the delicacy of the cooking of the vegetables 'lightly warmed in butter', all together creating a 'quadruple enchantment' for each guest 'to extract […] as his share'.[28] Dodin-Bouffant has transformed the dish by the addition of more luxurious ingredients, but he retains the basic structure of the dish and, most important, had a keen appreciation of its intrinsic taste and goodness.

Conclusion

Changes in gastronomic taste involve many factors, including the desire to pursue novel pleasures, snobbery, the sense of pride in or curiosity about a region or country, and the sense of pleasure in (as Brillat-Savarin noted) the discovery of a new dish – even when the dish is only new to the person trying it for the first time.[29]

With plenty of luxury available in Paris, travelling for food was motivated by a different sort of attraction: what was worth driving for? Before Michelin stars became such a sign of luxury, I suggest, these fiction writers inadvertently influenced taste and behaviour, and these non-fiction writers successfully popularized their views. This is a hypothesis, not a comprehensive examination of French literature and gastronomic writing, but Maupassant, Daudet, Zola, France, Simenon, Nignon, Montagné, Curnonsky, Rouff, and others appear to have imparted to their readers both the information and the evocative literary prose that could lead *gastronomades* to embark on a quest.

The simple can become exotic and exciting. Evocative literary depiction can transform how people think about a dish even as the dish remains the same. These writers helped create a thirst for what others considered the mundane. And sometimes their new appreciation of an old dish itself has led to improvements or refinements of the dish. It is not a coincidence that in 1965 one of the greatest and most poetic of culinary innovators, Michel Guérard, modestly named his first restaurant *le Pot-au-Feu*, indirectly drawing meaning from these literary themes and modern changes in taste, which set him on a path both to celebrate traditional dishes but also to flights of culinary imagination in creating many new dishes in the same spirit.[30]

Notes

1. Jean Anthelme Brillat-Savarin, *Physiologie du gout* (Paris: A. Sautelet, 1825).
2. See, for example, Pascal Ory, *Le Discours gastronomique français des origines à nos jours* (Paris: Archives Gallimard Julliard 1998) pp. 113-42.
3. Jean-François Mesplède, *Trois étoiles au Michelin: Une histoire de la haute gastronomie française* (Paris: Éditions Gründ 1998), pp. 9-13.
4. In 1956 the description of one star was changed to '*une bonne table dans sa catégorie*'.
5. These categories have been discussed since the beginning of gastronomic criticism in France, often thought to have begun with Grimod de la Reynière. A recent compilation of some of his work is *l'Almanach des gourmands, servant de guide dans les moyens de faire excellent chère* (Paris: Menu Fretin 2012), covering his writings from 1803-1812. Some recent examples are Alain Drouard, *Le Mythe gastronomique français* (Paris: CNRS éditions, 2010) and the essays in Francis Chevrier and Laic Bienassis, *Le Repas gastronomique des français* (Paris: Gallimard, 2015). Much categorization of French cuisine has been covered in the many editions of the *Larousse gastronomique*, beginning with the first edition by Prosper Montagné in 1938 through the most recent revision in 2017. The outstanding *Atlas gastronomique de la France* (Paris: Armand Colin 2017) created by Jean-Robert Pitte presents the regional dishes of France in detailed maps, along with the scholarly descriptions and historical analysis for which he is known.
6. See the wonderful short book by Jean-Louis Flandrin, *La Blanquette de veau: Histoire d'un plat bourgeois* (Paris: Jean-Paul Rocher, 2000) and Julia Csergo and others, *Pot-au-feu, convivial, familial: histoires d'un myth* (Paris: Éditions Autrement, 1999). The importance of these dishes, and the myths surrounding them, became subjects for historians in the late twentieth century. See also the discussion of perhaps the third most recognized cuisine bourgeoise dish, *poule au pot* (boiled chicken), by Julia Csergo, 'Entre mythe et utopie: la poule au pot', in *Pot-au-feu*. The chef Alain Ducasse considers *poule au pot* to be, historically and conceptually, a type of *pot-au-feu* (*Dictionnaire amoureux de la cuisine* (Paris: Plon 2003), pp. 406-10). This makes sense when you consider related dishes such as the Austrian *tafelspitz*, which was called *pot-au-feu* at the Imperial Austrian court, and Italian *bollito misto*, which by definition includes multiple meats.

7   Julia Csergo, 'L'émergence des cuisines regionales', in *Histoire de l'alimentation*, ed. by Jean-Louis Flandrin and Massimo Montanari (Paris: Fayard, 1996), pp. 823-41.
8   Philippe Meyzie surveys eighteenth and nineteenth century travelers' accounts in *La Table du Sud-Ouest et l'émergence des cuisines régionales (1700-1850)* (Rennes: Presses Universitaires de Rennes, 2007) p. 357-62.
9   Alexandre Dumas, *Le Comte de Monte Cristo* (1844) <https://www.gutenberg.org/ebooks/17989>. In a sequel, though, one of the musketeers becomes, after long service in Paris, a gastronome able to charm Louis XIV with his food stories. Alexandre Dumas, *Vingt ans après* (1845) <https://www.gutenberg.org/ebooks/13952>.
10 Dumas, *Le Comte de Monte Cristo*, ch. 63-64
11 Gustave Flaubert, *Madame Bovary*, part 1, ch. 8; part 2, ch. 6.
12 Originally published as '*La Bécasse*', in *Le Gaulois*, 5 December 1882, and later compiled as *Contes de la Bécasse* <https://www.gutenberg.org/ebooks/11714>; English translation at <https://madsimonj.wordpress.com/2014/09/29/guy-de-maupassant-the-woodcock/> [accessed 27 March 2022]
13 Brillat-Savarin. See Richard Warren Shepro, '"*Le marriage entre mets et vins*": On the Geographical and Historical Origins of Pairing a Food with a Particular Wine in France', in *Food and Landscape: Proceedings of the 2017 Oxford Symposium on Food and Cookery*, ed. by Mark McWilliams (London: Prospect Books, 2018), pp. 346-58 (p. 353).
14 It should be remembered that hunting was not merely a sport: Alphonse Daudet, '*Les Émotions d'un perdreau rouge*', in *Les Contes du lundi* (Paris: A. Lemerre, 1880), pp. 318-27 <https://fr.wikisource.org/wiki/Les_Contes_du_lundi/Les_%C3%89motions_d%E2%80%99un_perdreau_rouge>
15 Alphonse Daudet, '*La Moisson au bord de la mer*', in *Les Contes du lundi*, pp. 310-17 <https://fr.wikisource.org/wiki/Les_Contes_du_lundi/La_Moisson_au_bord_de_la_mer>
16 '*Paysages Gastronomique*', in *Les Contes du lundi*, pp. 303-09 <https://fr.wikisource.org/wiki/Les_Contes_du_lundi/Paysages_gastronomiques>
17 Émile Zola, *L'Assommoir* (Paris: G. Charpentier, 1879), pp. 250, 252 <https://fr.wikisource.org/wiki/L%E2%80%99Assommoir>. The title is word for a type of drinking establishment without a clear equivalent in English – translated recently by Robin Buss as *The Drinking Den* (London: Penguin, 2000).
18 Flandrin, *La blanquette de veau*, pp. 28-30.
19 Anatole France, *Histoire comique* (Paris: Calmann-Lévy, 1921), p. 224 <https://fr.wikisource.org/wiki/Page:Anatole_France_-_Histoire_comique.djvu/236>
20 Robert J. Courtine, *Simenon et Maigret passent à table: Les plaisirs gourmands de Simenon & les bonnes recettes de Madame Maigret* (Paris: Robert Laffont, 1972); see also Courtine, writing as La Reynière, *Cent merveilles de la cuisine française* (Paris: Éditions du Seuil, 1971).
21 See Édouard Nignon, *Les Plaisirs de la table* (1926, rpt. Paris: Menu Fretin, 2016) and, especially, *Éloges de la cuisine française* (1933, rpt. Paris: Menu Fretin, 2014).
22 Curnonsky, *Souvenirs littéraires et gastronomique* (Paris: Albin Michel, 1958).
23 Maurice Edmond Sailland, *La France gastronomique: Curnonsky & Marcel Rouff. Guide des merveilles culinaires et des bonnes auberges françaises* (Paris: F. Rouff, 1925).
24 Curnonsky, p. 226.
25 Curnonsky, '*Defense et Illustration de la Cuisine simple et des "quatre" Cuisines françaises*', in *Livre d'or de la gastronomie française*, ed. by Édouard Rouzier (Paris: Jacquet & L'Hôpital, 1931), pp. 9-10.
26 Julia Child, *As Always, Julia: The Letters of Julia Child and Avis DeVoto* (Boston: Mariner, 2010), p. 71, quoted by Bill Buford, *Dirt* (New York: Knopf, 2020), p. 353.
27 Marcel Rouff, *La vie et la passion de Dodin-Bouffant* (Paris: Stock, 1924), pp. 114, 116. Translation largely from 'Claude', reprinted in Marcel Rouff, *The Passionate Epicure* (New York: Modern Library, 2002 [1961]).
28 Rouff, p. 115.
29 The great French work of sociology about judgements of taste addresses all these issues, often in terms of choices about food, but does not specifically address gastrotourism: Pierre Bourdieu, *La Distinction: Critique sociale du jugement* (Paris: Les Editions de Minuit, 1979).
30 See Michel Guérard, '*Le petit prince*', in *Mémoires de chefs* (Paris: Textuel, 2012), pp. 86-119 and Michel Guérard, *Mémoire de la cuisine française* (Paris: Albin Michel, 2020).

Food Looks like a Lady: Designing Gastronomy through Ritualized Seduction

Max Shrem

Early nineteenth-century French food writers as varied as Jean-Anthelme Brillat-Savarin, Charles Fourier, and Grimod de La Reynière legitimized gastronomy as a field of knowledge through a highly gendered eighteenth-century aesthetics of pleasure. Dissociating appetite and lust from consumption, these writers repositioned food as an object of intellectual scrutiny. Though they championed Republican ideals of brotherly love and promoted Enlightenment philosophies on the pursuit of happiness, they operated within an ideological framework grounded in libertine strategies of sensual mastery, prioritizing ritual over reason and artifice over nature. The eight volumes of Grimod de La Reynière's *Almanach des gourmands* (1803–1812) not only comprise the earliest restaurant reviews in France, but also the first attempts at conceptualizing eating as an art form.

This paper analyzes a passage from the second volume (1805) scandalously entitled, 'Advantages of Good Food over Women', in which a 'true gourmand' claims that culinary dishes from France are superior to the attributes of the country's most beautiful women. Grimod's treatment of dishes as eroticized body parts paradoxically re-positions *gourmandise* as a scholarly topic to be cultivated. The 'true gourmand' projects an idealized image of femininity onto the French countryside, advancing the notion of *terroir avant la lettre*. This passage is therefore crucial in understanding the role that gender plays in the development of France's first food maps. Analyzing the linguistic overlap between women and food, I study the degree to which Grimod uses the language of seduction to (1) separate the gourmand from the act of gluttony, (2) link the cultural figure instead to refinement, and (3) depict the search for good food as virtuous.

Praising Gluttony by Pairing Comus with Venus

The commodification of culinary pleasure in post-revolutionary France reverted to a metaphysics of pleasure seen in eighteenth-century libertine literature. Nowhere is this more evident than in Grimod's parallel between women and food. Projecting an idealized eighteenth-century notion of femininity onto France's topography, Grimod describes foods as geographical embellishments and decorative objects in a gustatory scenery. This passage suggests that the country is the ultimate lady seductress. Diners are omitted from the gourmand's discourse, and he depicts instead the landscape of France as a referential organism that must be mastered and worshipped. Borrowing from Jean

Baudrillard's study of seduction as a strategy and ritual, this paper analyzes the extent to which Grimod designed France's first culinary maps, and even the notion of *terroir*, as a food iconography in accordance with libertine thought.

Nineteenth-century eulogies to culinary revelry often coincide with hymns of praise to love. In Charles-Louis Mion's *L'année galante* (1747) and Mondonville's *Les fêtes de Paphos* (1758), Comus, the god of festivity, shares the spotlight with Venus, the goddess of love. Grimod's monthly gastronomic journal, launched in 1806 with the members of the Parisian dining society the Dîners du Vaudeville, is therefore fittingly entitled the *Journal des gourmands et des belles, ou, L'épicurien français*. Inspired by his *Almanach*, the journal includes culinary anecdotes, advice, correspondences, recipes, poetry, and songs, most of which Grimod refers to as 'gourmand literature'. However, unlike the *Almanach,* it reads like a songbook; for instance, the first three editions of 1807 contain well over fifty songs written by Vaudeville playwrights and well-known *chansonniers*, including Nicolas Brazier, Marc-Antoine-Madeleine Désaugiers, François-Félix Nogaret, and Armand Gouffé. Whether it's their praises of bacchanalian feasts or the mere attributes of an apple ('Eve's gift to mankind'), they oscillate between homages to women and food.[1] And yet, what makes them stand out from typical odes to festivity (*carpe diem*) from previous periods is not the synchronicity of both forms of pleasure, but the synthesis of Comus and Venus, the fusion of femininity and food.

The writers of this food journal put forth a gastronomic goddess, preceding the culinary mother goddess *Gastérea* from Brillat-Savarin's *Physiology of Taste* (1825). In the January 1807 publication, Gastermann (likely a pseudonym for Grimod who did not want his *Almanach* to be confused with the journal) starts with a portrayal of *gourmandise* as a lifetime companion, comforting man in his old age and perpetually keeping his spirits high:

> Love lasts but an instant, glory is but a flash, the reason for a useless annoyance; but Gluttony remains the faithful companion of old age; supplement of extinct pleasures, comfort of the weakened spirit, relief of the sagging soul, it consoles memories of youth, compensates for the whims of fortune, maintains illusions, and still procures friends by the virtue of a good spread.[2]

Personifying *gourmandise* does not remove the sinful component from gluttony; rather, it reverses the terms to establish the gastronomic event as a virtuous affair. Though the contributors of the journal do not go as far as Grimod in explicitly appraising food over women, they feminize food by associating it with amorous devotion. They also ritualize *gourmandise* by situating it within ceremonial acts and performances; whether feast days, carnival, or fraternal engagements. According to Baudrillard, the feminine poses a challenge to the established order not by objecting to it outright, but instead by shifting its symbols (language) in the opposite direction of their semantic intent: 'Seduction is this reversible form [...] an ironic, alternative form, one that breaks the referentiality of sex and provides a space, not of desire, but of play.'[3] Conceptualizing food as a refined lady censures the 'animalic character' of the glutton thereby civilizing the palate.

Grimod's passage 'Advantages of Good Food over Women' does not subvert the meaning of the signs for women and good food: as the title suggests, it only intensifies their objectification as consumable entities. However, the parallel alters the signifiers, diverting the reader away from the association between foods and the table, the place of consumption, and instead toward dishes and their place of origin. We thus find the gourmand on an impressive roadmap of national gastronomic treasures, rather than confined to the dining room. Grimod's analogy of good food and women is told through an anecdote, in the words of a 'famous gourmand', also referred to as a 'true gourmand'. At a dinner, this character poses a long list of rhetorical questions asking whether a *femme de lettres* and three renowned actresses, all celebrated for their beauty, could be worth as much as France's finest foods:

> Could a woman, as pretty as you suppose her, had she Madame Récamier's head, Mademoiselle Georges Weimer's demeanour, Madame Henry Belmont's enchanting graces, Mademoiselle Émilie Contat's splendour and appetizing plumpness, Mademoiselle Arsène's mouth and smile, be worth these admirable partridges from Cahors, Languedoc and Cévennes, whose divine aroma prevails over all the perfumes of Arabia?[4]

At first glance, it seems as though the 'true gourmand' is personifying the partridges through their association with women. A cursory read of this passage shows Grimod degrading women by reducing them to physical traits and suggesting that they are inferior to meats – pâtés, sausages, and poultry. Yet, the four pages of questions following this initial one prove that the hierarchy of pleasure – appetite over lust – is not actually about choosing one over the other. Instead, the analogy equates the quest for good food to courtship. A deeper analysis therefore reveals the role worship plays in gastronomy's conception. The foods are all geographic indicators in the same way that the women's characteristics are personal adornments, accessories for the actress' spectacle. Whether it's the foie gras from Strasbourg and mortadella from Lyon or sausages from Arles and mutton from the salt marches of Brittany, these delicacies become decorative objects in a gustatory scenery of France.

The meats are analogous to the women's fragmented body parts in that they too are given a superficial description. The dishes are mentioned without any details about the experience of eating them, where to eat them, or how they are prepared. Culinary consumption is strikingly absent. It's as if the 'true gourmand' were moving away from his table and opening an atlas to reveal the correct geographic codes for the finest foods: 'Which city and/or province correspond to each delicacy?' Gastronomy develops into a structured ritual highlighting the semantic links between the French words '*saveur*' (savour) and '*savoir*' (knowledge). Educating the palate requires developing a mental appreciation. The gourmand turns down the seductive finery of women in favour of culinary specialties that have put cities like Strasbourg, Toulouse, and Auch on the map because they bring greater honour to civilization. In a sense there's a reciprocal worship at play. Man pays homage to nature through cuisine and those dishes in turn glorify man by creating a culinary heritage:

> Would you put them [the aforementioned women] in parallel with these pâtés of goose or duck livers, to which the cities of Strasbourg, Toulouse and Auch owe the best part of their celebrity? What is it then compared to these stuffed tongues from Troyes, these mortadella from Lyon, this Italian cheese from Paris, and these sausages from Arles and Bologna, which have brought so much glory to the person from the pig? Can you put a pretty little face next to these admirable sheep from Cabourg, Vosges and the Ardennes, which, by melting in your mouth, become a delectable meal?[5]

When speaking of this gastronomic delineation of landscape, it's important not to confuse the contrast of nature and artifice with contemporary food discourse on organic and commercial. Here we are dealing with the former. The very notion of *terroir* indicates the redesigning of mother earth (*la terre*), crafting at once a consumable and organic view of nature. Although these pâtés, sausages, and mortadellas originate from precise animals in certain regions and then are crafted by charcutiers in specific cities, they do not exist without human intervention. Moreover, in the case of Grimod, these foods are consumed in cosmopolitan Paris entirely removed from their natural origin. Their overwhelming appeal, however, can be attributed to their simulation of nature, allowing consumers to tap into a gastronomic imaginary of France.

Dressing Up Topography in Specialty Foods

In his study of pre-Revolutionary seduction, Baudrillard sets up a binary paradigm, desire/seduction, that allows scholars to make sense of the dialectic of artifice and femininity that are at the core of culinary aesthetics. Baudrillard defines the feminine as a metaphysical force that thwarts and challenges natural desire by converting it into ceremonial artifice and fantasy: 'There is above all, a strategy of displacement (*se-ducere*: to take aside, to divert from one's path) that implies a distortion of sex's truth. To play is not to take pleasure.'[6] Baudrillard contrasts seduction with desire by placing the former in the order of ritual and the latter in that of nature. Furthermore, he argues that what clashes in the feminine and the masculine is not some biological difference but rather these two orders. Operating from this level, gastronomy seduces the signs of *gourmandise* by transforming food into objects of knowledge that divert away from physical appetite and move toward the imaginary. Gluttony is to sex (function, making real, giving meaning) just as gastronomy is to seduction (strategy, making artificial, effacing meaning). Unlike the glutton, the gourmand creates aesthetic systems in which to play with and control the symbolic realm of cuisine. In this case the opposition between the glutton and gourmand could be conceptualized through Baudrillard's contrast between masculine desire and feminine seduction.

Grimod's 'Advantages of Good Food over Women' is subversive because it rejects the notion of consumption as an end in itself (*jouissance comme fin*). Grimod envelops the democratization of the gastronomic sphere within libertine strategies of sensual mastery, luring in his readers, newly enriched citizens of the First Republic and Empire. That is, he plays into their desires to consume culture and increase social rank by evoking a fantasy that eclipses appetite – an image of France submerged in an overflow of delicacies. Bewitching his audience with a seemingly endless geographic catalogue of provisions, the *Almanach* guides the reader through a labyrinth of gastronomic acts – not up a social ladder. In the preface of the first volume, Grimod condescendingly superimposes an historical opposition between himself and his audience, suggesting that the power shift between the Ancien Regime and the Republic represents a movement toward 'purely animal pleasures', or what Baudrillard refers to as 'the work of the body by desire'.[7] Grimod teases the nouveaux-riches' emphasis on capital and desire all the while creating a nostalgia for ritual, what he refers to as the old regime's 'most tender affections'.[8]

To make sense of Grimod's use of eighteenth-century seduction, I turn to Margot, the protagonist from Fougeret de Montbron's libertine novel *Margot la ravaudeuse par M. **** (1750). As a courtesan, the character learns how to transform her body into a 'proud device', an object of display embellished with pomades and rouge and surrounded by sumptuous objects.[9] Her control over the male gaze and power over men's pockets lie in her ability to play with the signs of her own objectification. In fact, when she falls ill, her doctor attributes her sickness to a lack of self-discipline and an overstimulation of the senses, 'the abuse of a too delicious life':

> Your disease, which they knew nothing about, is not an affection of the body, but a disgust of the spirit, caused by the abuse of a too delicious life. Pleasures are to the soul, what good food is to the stomach. The most exquisite dishes become tasteless to us out of habit: they put us off in the end, and we no longer digest them. The excess of enjoyment has, so to speak, disenchanted your heart, and numbed your feeling.[10]

The doctor's medical advice is indicative of the eighteenth-century ontological association between sensuality and the soul. Margot's supremacy, and therefore her sickness, is not one of the body but instead of the spirit. The body is simply a tool with which to enchant and alter the emotions of men around her. The analogy between 'pleasure' and 'good food' emphasizes this conception of the refinement of pleasure as nourishment for the soul: hence, the libertine importance of ritualistic strategy. Grimod's passage 'Advantages of Good Food over Women' reconfigures the above analogy to reverse the connection between 'good food' and the 'stomach'. In Grimod's parallel between women and food, the latter enters this discourse on body as object of ritual rather than object of desire. *Gourmandise* is no longer characterized by an 'affection of the body' but rather by the old regime's 'most tender affections'.

Admission to this culinary fantasy comes with a caveat: the sacrifice of *lady seductress*.

The culinary remapping of France reflects the idealization of a country that naturally gives herself up for consumption. In the sixth volume of his *Almanach*, Grimod includes a drinking song entitled 'Dinners without Women' in which he writes, 'Sweeter goods charm our souls, / Since on this solemn day / Fate unites us without women, / Around a fraternal banquet.'[11] As is often the case with fictional characters, Grimod uses his 'true gourmand', like his 'gourmand poetry', to express provocative and even blasphemous insinuations, daring the reader to replace the lady's splendour with the finery of table. The gourmand's questions show that it's not about fundamentally eliminating women from the table, but rather displacing their enchanting authority. After all, he states that they too are subject to food's transformative powers:

> Who will dare compare them to those unspeakable river calves, from Pontoise and Rouen, whose whiteness and tenderness would make the Graces themselves blush? Who is the gourmand depraved enough to prefer a thin and puny beauty to these enormous and succulent sirloins of Limagne and Cotentin which inundate the one who cuts them up and make those who eat them swoon?[12]

The questions reveal gastronomy's celebratory appropriation of the corporal lexicon that is associated with seduction. The swap of signifiers 'women' for 'good food' gives this absurdly lengthy build-up of food sites a Rabelaisian sense of revelry and intoxication. This passage which Grimod aptly names 'Gourmand Folly' recalls Rabelais's onomastic word plays, from the list of young Gargantua's habits to the catalogue of chefs' names in the *Fourth Book*.

Rabelais often dilutes the importance of the signified with an abundance of phonemes – combining and repeating suffixes and prefixes – creating what François Rigolot calls an 'auditory image'.[13] The words' sonority eclipses their distinct meaning. Similarly, Grimod's reconfiguration of the signifiers, women and good food, creates an image of France that defies the reason and scientific order associated with the very idea of topography. Unlike the Michelin atlas, the first culinary maps drawn up of nineteenth-century France are reflective of Grimod's romanticized *terroir*. Indeed, language is replaced with visual symbols. For instance, in Charles-Louis Cadet de Gassicourt's *Carte gastronomique de la France* (1809), illustrations of a wild turkey and roasted duck are located between the cities Périgueux and Brive-la-Gaillarde.[14] Only the names of the cities are mentioned to help the viewer navigate from one culinary region to the next. Even its mid-nineteenth-century descendant, the *Carte des productions gastronomiques de la France avec ses chemins de fer* (1850), is covered with images of wine barrels, fruit baskets, cows grazing, and rabbits frolicking. These maps appeared in pedagogical travel guides, and, as such, Julia Csergo links them to Grimod's monumentalizing of culinary specialties and promulgating of gastronomic nationalism.[15] I would go a step further and argue that the use of symbols, over words, suggests an even deeper link with Grimod: the worship, cult, of *terroir* by means of a food iconography.

This early nineteenth-century endorsement of geographic culinary markers indicates an evolving ritualistic nationalism around food. A cursory glance at the history of this process can give it an illusion of being scientific, objective, and factual. Yet, Grimod's 'true gourmand' reveals that the topographical edifice of 'researched dishes' is built upon enchantment, one that he claims invigorates the body physically and emotionally. If he uses medical terminology (a typical feature of

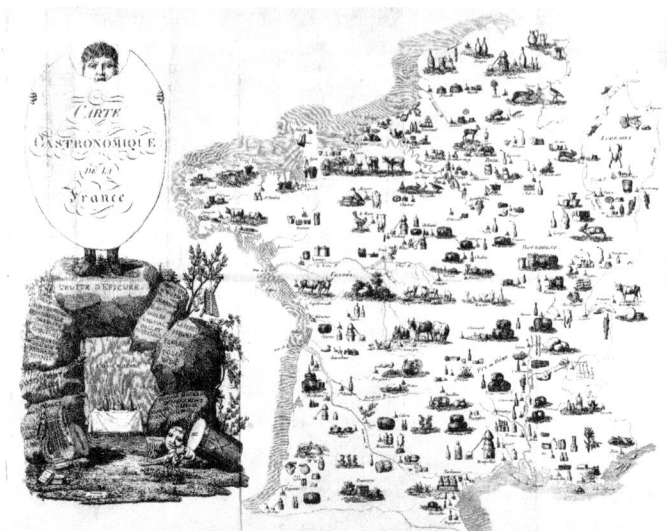

Figure 1. Carte gastronomique de la France. *Source: gallica.bnf.fr (Bibliothèque nationale).*

nineteenth-century gastronomic language), it often reverts to a ritualistic veneration of food, reinforcing its feminization. For instance, the 'true gourmand' highlights the effects of poultry upon the nervous fibres only to suggest its seductive dominance over women:

> What connection can you establish between this prickly, but tired face, and these hens from Bresse, these capons from La Flèche and Le Mans, these virgin roosters from the Pays de Caux, whose slenderness, beauty, succulence, and plumpness exalt all the senses at the same time and wonderfully delight the nervous and sensitive crest of any delicate palate?[16]

Again, the nouns used to characterize the foods from those exact locations ('slenderness', 'beauty', 'succulence', 'plumpness') and their special effects ('exalt', 'delight') reflect those used to describe an attractive woman. Grimod's unusual humour, however, lies precisely in accomplishing the inverse. That is, the woman is described with adjectives that can also apply to food – '*piquante*', translated here as prickly, can also mean spicy, and '*chiffonnée*', translated as 'tired', can mean 'crunchy'. Though he claims that the eighty-four foods are incomparable to women, his entire list is structured by this relentless 'nutritious parallel'. They are neither categorized geographically nor alphabetically. And though he refers to the parallel as 'nutritious', there is never any mention of food as sustenance.

Seeking Mother Gastronomy

Grimod inaugurates a gastronomic world not only structured around seduction but also defined by an archetypal feminine virtue: reflective of eighteenth-century views on women. Grimod's idealized woman projected onto France's finest foods represents Jung's notion of 'mother-love'. Jung defines this archetype as 'the mysterious root of all growth and change; the love that means homecoming, shelter, and the long silence from which everything begins and in which everything ends'.[17] As far as eighteenth-century philosophy is concerned, this archetypal phenomenon is hardly unique to Grimod's writings. Indeed, Enlightenment philosophers were fascinated by the maternal woman; from Joseph Desmahis's esteem for motherhood in his entry *'femme'* in Diderot's *Encyclopédie* and Rousseau's endorsement of maternity in *Émile* (1762) to lesser-known depictions of woman-nurturer, like those in Restif's *La Découverte australe par un homme-volant* (1781). In his *Réflexions philosophiques sur le plaisir*, Grimod praises the upbringing of women in Protestant countries, like Switzerland, where young girls are brought up without being hidden from society in convents. Using the verbs 'enclose' and 'cloister' and advocating for a more liberal child-rearing, he evokes Diderot's critique of convents in *La Religieuse* (1796).[18] Most importantly, Grimod argues that it's precisely this freedom during childhood that maintains a more innocent and virtuous happiness, one that produces a maternal wife and mother.

Rather than connote confinement and oppression, domesticity was venerated as the source – microcosm – of Enlightenment ideals. Assigning feminine authority to the household was, for Grimod, perceived as placing women on a pedestal of virtue. He states that in contrast to their French counterparts, these Protestant women use their seductive authority exclusively in the domestic sphere, embodying a perpetual dispenser of nourishment and exemplifying the womb of life:

> Happy Land, where innocence is the safeguard of morals, where beauty becomes a pledge of virtue, and where even coquetry never departs from decency! [...] A sedentary life devoted to domestic care makes her forget that there are other pleasures. She puts her happiness into making all that surrounds her happy; and convinced that, in her new state [as wife], one would no longer have the same indulgence for her, she observes herself with particular care, and becomes all the more circumspect, since she had been dissipated in her young age.[19]

When Grimod refers to the 'other pleasures', those which the domesticated woman forgets, he is indicating the vices of aristocratic women who he perceives as corrupting society. It's as though the cult of domesticity creates an enlightened feminine dictatorship, a sophisticated form of seduction that mirrors Desmahis's utopian view of maternal intimacy. Desmahis's article on women states, 'She has a character of reserve and dignity which makes her respected, indulgence and sensitivity which makes her loved, prudence and firmness which makes her feared; she spreads around her a gentle warmth, a pure light which illuminates and enlivens all that surrounds her.'[20] By employing a lexicon of noble sovereignty and by repetitively rendering the woman the direct object pronoun, Desmahis reveals femininity to be, at the core, a strategy of objectification and ritualization, a method of enticing devotion, and, as a result, a scheme for controlling and dictating the symbolic realm. In this sense, Desmahis's ethos of feminine dominance in the domestic sphere confirms Baudrillard's theory on seduction during this period.

Gourmandise is like this maternal seductress, generating, as Grimod puts it, 'the face of jubilation, the distinctive character of all children of Comus'. This association is made even clearer in a section from the sixth volume of the *Almanach*, entitled 'Brunette Dinners and Blonde Dinners'. He assigns starters to two distinct culinary categories: dark-coloured dishes and light-coloured dishes. The former corresponds to women with a dark complexion; they consist of ordinary lowbrow meals (rustic cooking) such as meat stews, stewed apples, chopped vegetables, turnip ragout, and braised meat and vegetables. The latter correspond to women with a light complexion; they consist of delicate refined starters (*haute cuisine*), including béchamel sauces, quenelles, chicken fricassee, *poulet à la reine*, and sautés:

> If, on the contrary, he sees that this first course presents a combination of these delicate and fine starters, the colour of which is closer to white than any other […] including the most sought-after fish, the most tender meats, and the most delicate parts of poultry, he will decide that it is a blonde dinner, fruit of the work and the meditations of a first-class artist. It is almost the same with the complexion of women.[21]

By focusing on femininity and the realm of appearances, Grimod reveals that *haute cuisine* involves a ritualistic quest for good food that is analogous to courtship. Like the seductress who initiates men into an ongoing game of devotional proofs, fine foods challenge the chef who displays dedication by transforming them into sophisticated dishes.

The connection between ethics and aesthetics calls to mind Desmahis's discourse on domesticity, most noticeably the lexicon of nobility and reference to a 'pure feminine light'. The passage puts forth two culinary categories: the sinful 'brunette dinners' and virtuous 'blonde dinners':

> With a few exceptions, the colour blonde heralds a distinguished birth, a delicate mind, soft, thin skin, the kind of attraction that lovers treasure most, because it is as sensitive in the dark as it is in light: it is usually the sign of gentleness and all the qualities that please the most in this sex. A blonde seems to be humbly asking for your heart and a brunette seeks to grab it from you. However, we always prefer to receive prayers than orders.[22]

The 'blonde dinners' captivate because they exude 'mother-love'. Grimod compares them to an ethereal angelic woman whose charms are even perceptible in darkness. The contrast of 'brunette dinners' and 'blonde dinners' is inscribed in the semantic contrast between the verbs 'to ask/beg for' and 'to grab', between the nouns 'prayers' and 'orders'. As such, it reflects the Baudrillardian opposition between masculinity (nature/instinct) and femininity (ritual/spirit). 'Brunette dinners' are rough and barbaric; they represent consumption as an end. In the seventh volume of the *Almanach*, Grimod goes as far as comparing the dining table to a virginal bride whom guests approach with admiration. His linguistic framework for gastronomy as idealized femininity is significant because it leads to his rules of gastronomic courtship, rules concerning dining room finery, everything from the appropriate usage of crystal, porcelain, and cutlery to flowers, furniture, and lights.

Grimod's gendered metaphor of fine food as a seductress re-orients the gourmand toward an interiorized space built on rituality, and as a result it undermines the culturally normative depiction of the gourmand as an overweight buffoon. By emphasizing the aesthetics of the table and by omitting (or even condemning) human interaction, it moreover destabilizes the sociability and Christian virtue inherent in the symbolic gesture of breaking bread. The gourmand becomes instead an aesthete dining alone or sitting in his food library. The classical image of sensual pleasure as a Garden of Eden (*honesta voluptas*) is supplanted by a degenerative version of seventeenth-century *préciosité* in which wit and intellect are reserved entirely to the dishes. Not only are the foods treated as props in a performance, but so too are the consumers. Grimod's discourse on the feminine is transgressive precisely because it upends seduction between diners and manipulates the pomp and ceremony of Christian ritual to glorify one of the seven deadly sins. Outrageously ironic and incendiary, Grimod's delivery make him standout from other food writers of his time. However, he is hardly an anomaly when it comes to projecting matriarchal symbolism onto the French nation in the context of gastronomy. Brillat-Savarin builds an entire cult around his imagined gastronomic muse *Gastérea*, reflective of Rousseau's notion of civil religion and evocative of France's lady liberty *Marianne*.

In his *Nouveau monde amoureux* (1816), Charles Fourier also uses religious discourse to create a utopian society that opposes all restraints to corporal desire (monogamy and gluttony). However, his gastronomic system is organized in a way that prioritizes sociability over rituality. Structured by amorous associations, households are reassembled so that people only dine with those whom their heart desires. The dynamic between the gastronomic realm as the seducer and the diner as the seduced may have been explicitly articulated by Grimod, but, afterward, it was also evoked by women gourmands themselves, most notably Elizabeth Robins Pennell and M.F.K. Fisher. Pennell advises the *gourmande* to be swept away by the beauty of cuisine and then to use its magic on others: 'Rejoice in the knowledge that gluttony is the best cosmetic. […] Let her [the *gourmande*] learn first for herself the rapture that lies dormant in food; let her next spread abroad the joyful tidings.'[23]

Conclusion

Libertine discourse on seduction is still at the heart of culinary aesthetics, in particular contemporary restaurant culture. Somewhere between the utopia of eighteenth-century agrarian communities and that of nineteenth-century dining societies, the restaurant emerged as a place to mediate between nature and culture. Falling in love with *terroir* is falling in love with make-believe. By projecting their idea of culinary landscape on their cuisine, chefs contribute to the pastoral imaginary. This comes across most clearly with regional Michelin-starred chefs whose restaurants have become national monuments. These chefs, such as Régis Marcon and Michel Bras, have transformed remote previously unknown villages into food destinations. Soil science aside, *terroir* is a mutable concept. For consumers, the present-day appeal of Marcon's business model lies in its meticulous understanding of the utopian potential inherent in gastronomy, that is its capacity to reconstruct micro-political spheres. *Terroir* is the protagonist of Marcon's natural wonderland, in which he and his idyllic family forage wild herbs and mushrooms. This relationship between fiction and *terroir* originated with the portrayal of appetite as an object of seduction, the table as the site of veneration, and foods as nature's ornaments. As such, Grimod paved the way for the meal itself as performance art.

Notes

1 François-Félix Nogaret, '*Aristenète aux joyeux desservants du Rocher de Cancale*', in *Journal des gourmands et des belles, ou, L'épicurien français*, deuxième année, August 1807, 135.
2 Gastermann, *Journal des gourmands et des belles, ou, L'épicurien français*, deuxième année, January 1807, 6. Unless otherwise noted, all translations are my own. Here I translated 'gourmandise' as 'gluttony', but it could also refer to the pleasures of eating.
3 Jean Baudrillard, *Seduction* (New York: St. Mark's Press, 1990), p. 21.
4 Grimod de la Reynière, *Almanach des gourmands*, 2.29 (1805), 128.
5 Grimod, *Almanach des gourmands*, 2.29 (1805), 129.
6 Baudrillard, *Seduction*, p. 22.
7 Baudrillard, *De la séduction* (Paris: Galilée, 1980), p. 36.
8 Grimod, *Almanach des gourmands*, 1.16 (1804), IX.
9 Jean-Louis Fougeret de Montbron, *Margot la ravaudeuse, et ses aventures galantes* (Munich: Bavarian State Library, 6 December 2011 [Lenoire, 1784]), p. 94.
10 Fougeret de Montbron, p. 169.
11 Grimod, *Almanach des gourmands*, 6.9 (1808), 155.
12 Grimod, *Almanach des gourmands*, 2.29 (1805), 129.
13 '*Rabelais ne forge pourtant pas ses mots de façon arbitraire. On sait qu'il est sensible à l'image auditive qui suggère leur prononciation*' (Francois Rigolot, *Poétique et onomastique* (Geneva: Droz, 1977), p. 89.
14 Julia Csergo, '*La gastronomie dans les guides de voyage: de la richesse industrielle au patrimoine culturel, France XIXe-début XXe siècle*', *In Situ: Revue des patrimoines*, 15 (2011) <https://doi.org/10.4000/insitu.722>
15 Csergo.
16 Grimod, *Almanach des gourmands*, 2.29 (1805), 130.
17 Carl Jung, *Aspects of the Feminine* (Princeton, NJ: Princeton University Press, 1982), p. 121.
18 Grimod, *Réflexions philosophiques sur le plaisir par un célibataire*, 3rd edn (Lausanne, 1784), p. 82.
19 Grimod, *Réflexions philosophiques*, p. 84.
20 Joseph F. Desmahis, '*Femme*,' *Encyclopédie ou Dictionnaire raisonné des sciences, des arts et des métiers* (Paris, 1756), vol. 6, p. 472.
21 Grimod, *Almanach des gourmands*, 6.9 (1808), 128.
22 Grimod, *Almanach des gourmands*, 6.9 (1808), 132.
23 Elizabeth Robins Pennell, *The Delights of Delicate Eating* (Champaign, IL: University of Illinois Press, 2000), p. 13.

Incredible Edibles: American History in Chocolate, Cheddar, and Confectionary Forms

Nancy Siegel

Giant oxen – George and Martha, paraded through the streets of Philadelphia. A mammoth cheddar cheese, a mammoth pie, mammoth beets for Thomas Jefferson! An 800-pound cake in the shape of the United States Capitol, the 2600-pound 'Great Washington Cake', a fifteen-foot-tall sugar monument depicting scenes from the American Revolution, a 1500-pound chocolate statue of Christopher Columbus, and massive Election Cakes made with thirty quarts of flour, ten pounds of butter, and a quart of brandy. Masterpieces from America's farmers, confectioners, bakers, butchers, and home cooks using their imagination to praise and celebrate abundant resources, civic pride, and confidence in the democratic process in the new United States. These public displays, so fantastical in design and proportion while seemingly comedic and bordering on the absurd, actually provided a platform for promoting republican ideals and engraining them in the public consciousness more powerfully than presidential addresses or ratified documents ever could. Since most rural farmers, culinary professionals, and home cooks had little political influence or presence in the establishment of policy or reform, baking a cake in replication of the seat of democracy or producing an historical diorama in sugar was not merely a flight of fancy; rather, such incredible edibles acknowledged and gave form to nebulous ideas such as nationalism and democracy in the years surrounding the Early Republic.[1]

My research posits that culinary creations of astounding size or extravagant ingredients are more than merely humour-driven with their easily recognizable foodstuffs. Commonplace ingredients imbued with ceremonial status contained calculated political messages targeting an audience deeply invested in the political and commercial success of the new nation. As evidenced in newspapers, broadsides, and widely disseminated engravings, the comestibles employed to celebrate the United States and its founding figures expose subtexts that read as political, social, and economic markers. Bakers, cheesemakers, and confectioners of the Early Republic fashioned wondrous, massive food sculptures to manifest political ideals while serving as edible exemplars of American culinary imagination. Within the framework of chocolate, cheddar, and confectionaries, we can unpack and reposition the coded intentions behind such creations which gave material form to public opinion and isolate ingredients that speak directly to the formation of nationhood.

Food and Imagination

Exploring the history of the Early Republic through ingredients and foods that were consumed, valued, and at times, contested, links political and culinary histories. At feasts and fêtes, edible barometers of national pride were eagerly consumed by presidents, politicians, and the general public alike. Whether acknowledged in cheese or chocolate, the domestic language of food was easily understood as part of a widespread but little studied language of political expression. These imaginative creations became increasingly popular from the late eighteenth century on in the United States as a means to communicate caution or approval of political figures, ideologies, and comestibles. From the boycotts of contentious commodities such as tea, prior to the Revolution, to a post-war reappraisal of food and drink in the late eighteenth and early nineteenth centuries, many Americans witnessed a significant change in culinary patterns as professional and amateur cooks increasingly curated and promoted recipes that acknowledged and honoured the new nation. The more outrageous and fantastical the better!

For example, boycotts of everyday consumables including tea were plentiful in protest of the Stamp Act of 1765 and the Townshend Acts of 1767, as were celebrations upon their repeal in the form of politically adorned tableware (Figure 1). Likewise, as tea was dumped into Boston's Harbour at the famed tea party of 1773, recipes for Liberty Tea – a homebrewed herbal alternative included in cookbooks well into the nineteenth century – had already been developed as part of nonimportation movements. From protest to consumption after the Revolution, butchers, bakers, and confectioners – those invested in feeding the new nation – engaged in displays of American culinary prowess. In the field of animal husbandry, cattle, oxen, and sheep became symbols of pride as they made their appearance at numerous patriotic events. In celebration of the formation of the Constitution, a 'Great Federal Procession' took place in New York on 23 July 1788. The butchers of the city processed carrying a linen flag displaying their coat of arms with the motto: 'Skin me well, dress me neat, And send me aboard the Federal fleet', and the striking scene was described thusly:

> A *slaughter-house*, with cattle dressed and killing; a *market*, supported by *ten pillars*, and another 'partly up', under which was written, '*Federal Market*', supported by '*Ten*', in letters of gold; '*Federal Butchers*;' a ship, with smaller vessels. The standard was carried on a stage drawn by four bright bay horses, dressed with ribbons; a boy dressed in white rode and conducted each; on the stage a stall, neatly furnished; two butchers and two boys on the stage at work, splitting the lambs, cutting meats, and arranging this *stall*. This stage was followed by one hundred butchers, (mounted on fine horses,) with clean white aprons, and steels attached to their sides. Then came a band of music, followed with two banners appropriately painted, with their coat of arms and motto – 'Federal Butchers'.[2]

John Lewis Krimmel's 1821 *Procession of Victuallers of Philadelphia, on the 15th of March*, serves as a striking visual complement to this description linking culinary commodities with fanfare and patriotism (Figure 2). Although Krimmel's formal procession salutes

Incredible Edibles: American History in Chocolate

Figure 1 (left). Cockpit Hill Factory, manufacturer, Teapot, 'Stamp Act Repeal'd', 1766. Glazed earthenware, Derby, England, 13.018 cm, Gift of Professor Richard C. Manning, 1933, (121493. AB). Courtesy of the Peabody Essex Museum. Figure 2 (right). Procession of Victuallers of Philadelphia, on the 15th of March 1821. Conducted under the Direction of Mr. William White. Drawn by John Lewis Krimmel, engraved by Joseph Yeager. Aquatint, hand coloured, 49 x 67 cm. Courtesy of the American Antiquarian Society.

the agricultural suppliers of Philadelphia, not New York, the farmers, butchers, and oystermen are similarly heroized. Surely not every cow was treated with such respect as the one pictured on its way to slaughter, but as the motto of the Society of Victuallers declared, 'We Feed the Hungry', the production of food and provisions for the American public was indeed worthy of a parade.

Likewise, from the late eighteenth century through the early decades of the nineteenth, cookbook authors in the former British colony created recipes that acknowledged and promoted the ideals of the new nation linking food to politics thus utilizing a vocabulary of esoteric terms such as 'independence' and 'democracy'.[3] With names such as Election Cake, Independence Cake, Democratic Tea Cakes, Federal Cake, and Liberty Tea, women, in particular, became culinary activists. They authored recipes and cookbooks in praise of the new and fragile nation. These became political ideals that were not only understood, but quite literally consumed. For example, a modest text from 1796, *American Cookery*, was published in Hartford, Connecticut (Figure 3). Its author, Amelia Simmons, is credited with producing what is widely considered the first cookbook written in the United States. Simmons introduced a new 'American' vocabulary of ingredients such as cornmeal for 'American Indian pudding', 'Johny Cake, or Hoe Cake', and dishes for 'pompkin'.[4] Curiously, in her chapter for cakes and sweet breads Simmons provided basic, nondescript recipes for treats such as 'Plain Cake'. But, in a second 1796 edition from Albany, New York, she added strategically-titled recipes such as 'Election Cake' and 'Independence Cake'.

By and large, politically themed recipes are for celebratory foods. While recipes for Election Cake appear as early as 1771 in Connecticut, Simmons's recipe calls for: 'Thirty quarts flour, ten pounds butter, fourteen pounds sugar, twelve pounds raisins, three dozen eggs, one pint wine, one quart brandy, four ounces cinnamon, four ounces fine coliander seed, three ounces ground alspice'.[5] The sheer volume of this ample-sized cake suggests that events such as Election Day were cause for communal celebration and eating. Election days included public gatherings, parades, visiting friends, drinking, and mustering or training exercises when local militia met to train prior to the Revolution.[6] Townswomen made Election Cakes to feed the militia or sold slices on election days at polling places. With its precedent as the English plumb cake, Election Cake is truly a cross between a cake and raisin bread (Figure 4). The massive volume of the ingredients suggests that they were free form and baked, by necessity, on the floor of community ovens. However, as mention of enjoying Election Cake at home often appears in letters and diaries, I suggest that the batter was also separated into smaller cakes and baked at home in numerous pans.

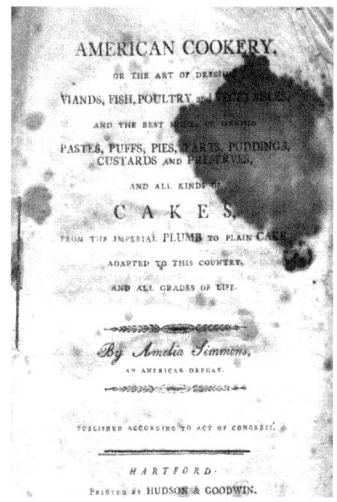

Figure 3. Amelia Simmons, American Cookery, 1796, Hartford first edition (1796 S592a). Collection of the Connecticut Historical Society.

In addition to Election Cake, President's Cake, Federal Cake, Democratic Tea Cakes, Republican Cake, Independence Cake, Freedom Cake, and Liberty Bread, we find reference to important political figures in Franklin Buns, Washington Pie, Jefferson Cake, Lafayette Gingerbread, Madison Cake, Adams Pie, Jackson Jumbles, Van Buren Cake, Harrison Cake, and Tyler Pudding, to name just a few. In fact, there are hundreds and hundreds of politically inspired recipes from both published cookery books and in handwritten receipt books.[7] But let us leave the realm of sweet treats momentarily to talk about cheese. In particular, a 1235-pound mammoth cheese presented to Thomas Jefferson to celebrate his electoral victory. In a letter dated 28 July 1801, a gentleman from Berkshire, Massachusetts wrote to his friend in Albany, New York:

> I have nothing new or strange to tell you, excepting of a MAMMOTH CHEESE which the Cheshire people are making, to present to the *Mammoth of Monticello*. It is now in the press; it measures four feet in diameter and eighteen inches in depth. 'Tis said to weigh from 12 to 1400 pounds. So patriotic were the inhabitants in bringing forward the Curd that, after filling the hoop, there was more than 300 pounds left.[8]

So reads the earliest published reference to what was called the Mammoth Cheese. A Baptist minister, John Leland, presented Jefferson with this widely publicized cheese from his congregation in Cheshire, Massachusetts. Made from 900 cows milked simultaneously (rumour has it), the giant 1235-pound cheese was loaded onto a wagon in the fall of 1801, taken by boat as far as Baltimore, and delivered by wagon to the President's House while crowds gathered and cheered along the way. This was to be 'the Greatest Cheese in America for the Greatest Man in America'.⁹ John Leland was an elder in the Baptist church and a vigorous advocate for religious tolerance. Working with Thomas Jefferson and James Madison, Leland was determined to see religious freedom secured within the Virginia States Constitution. Thus, when Thomas Jefferson became a candidate for president of the United States, Leland became a staunch supporter of his Republican cause, and his congregation desired to show their approval of Jefferson's victory.¹⁰

Although not the first presidential cheese – a 110-pound cheese, 'as big as a chariot wheel', was reportedly delivered to John Adams at the presidential mansion in Philadelphia from the citizens of Rhode Island – great attention was paid in newspapers to the creation of the Mammoth Cheese.¹¹ Once plans for the cheese had been announced, a competitive and satirical spirit emerged among the surrounding towns in the Berkshire Mountains of Massachusetts, pitting Republicans against Federalists. Of particular note was the suggestion to the Ladies of Lenox to bake a 'Mammoth Apple Pye' to accompany the mammoth cheddar cheese.¹² Not only were pie and patriotism proposed, but the baking and delivery processes were explained in great detail. The mammoth pie wasn't the only intended edible of huge proportion; some proposed gifts straight from the garden. Such is the case of the 'Mammoth Beet'. An 'American' from Boston wrote of 'a curious Beet now sent; and have it kept in safe hands, until you learn when the Cheese is to start for the southward; and then, if you think it proper, to send the Beet with it. – I think it a striking specimen of the present government – a truly Republican Beet'.¹³ Weighing over five pounds, this beet would have made quite the travelling companion for the cheese and the pie. Meanwhile, bakers in both New York and Washington planned mammoth loaves of bread, 'the breadth and depth of a large coffin', to be presented once the cheese arrived.¹⁴ The mammoth pie was never baked, but the mammoth loaves reportedly were.

By 5 December, the newspapers in Stockbridge, Massachusetts were reporting '[t]he Mammoth Cheese Afloat'. On 7 December, the *Otsego Herald* reported that the cheese could be seen aboard a sloop in Albany. Along the journey, concerns developed not just about the enormity of the cheese itself, but also about how one would slice it: 'No common instrument will be found sufficient to cut it up; that a guillotine is therefore getting ready, to be employed in this and other service, to which it may be found applicable.'¹⁵ The satirical reference to the multiple uses for a guillotine would not have gone unnoticed, particularly in light

Figure 4. Election Cake. Author's photo.

of Robespierre's Jacobin massacres of recent memory in France. The famous cheese arrived in Baltimore by 12 December 1801. A British traveller, John Davis, who was in the city at the time of the cheese's arrival, commented upon the public's infatuation, 'Baltimore was universally excited; men, women, and children flocked to see the Mammoth Cheese. The taverns were deserted; the gravy soup cooled on the table, and the cats unrebuked revelled on the custards and cream.'[16] Finally, the cheese arrived in Washington on 29 December.[17] On 1 January 1802, the Mammoth Cheese was presented to Thomas Jefferson. *The Republican* reported that the cheese was 'conveyed from a house in Pennsylvania Avenue, on a dray drawn by two horses. We are told it was presented by the Rev. Mr. Leland, who was accompanied by two Clergymen, and many other persons. The president stood on his door to receive it'.[18] Jefferson gave Leland two hundred dollars from his personal account, perhaps to offset the expenses associated with the production and travel of the cheese or to remove any appearance of impropriety related to a gift to a public official.[19]

Critics of Jefferson's administration took the opportunity to use the cheese as a symbol of Republican corruption. The cheese was rumoured to have been full of maggots and rotting away: 'It is confidently said that the Mammoth Cheese is full of skippers. Would to heaven that the Maggots in the heads of certain executive officers were as little detrimental to the public as those in the Cheese.'[20] Republican papers countered this criticism by uncovering what they called the 'maggot plot' unleashed by Federalist papers who used the cheese as a thinly veiled vehicle for their criticism of Jefferson's administration. Newspaper accounts of sightings continued for years. One report is that the cheese was finally consumed at a presidential reception, while still others believe it was dumped in the Potomac River.[21] No one truly knows the fate of the Mammoth Cheese, but to preserve its memory, the town of Cheshire, in 1940, created a concrete replica of the cider press used to form the cheese (Figure 5).

This cheese, however, became iconic of American ingenuity, productivity, and abundance, and other cheeses soon followed. James Madison received a 1522-pound cheese in 1810, also from John Leland's congregation. And, as an act of patriotic good-will, Colonel Thomas Meacham exhibited in Utica, New York a cheese weighing 1400 pounds, made from the milk of 150 cows, to commemorate the presidency of Andrew Jackson. It bore the inscription, 'TO ANDREW JACKSON, President of the United States', along with a 'National Belt', complete with a bust of the President, surrounded by a chain of twenty-four links, representing the unity of the twenty-four states. Larger than Jefferson's

Figure 5. Reproduction of the Mammoth Cheese press, Cheshire, MA. Author's photo.

cheese, Meacham's cheese, sent in late November of 1835, did not travel alone. Colonel Meacham made five other cheeses, each weighing between 700 and 850 pounds. These he inscribed and had sent to Martin Van Buren, the Vice President; one to Congress; one to Daniel Webster; one to William L. Marcey, Governor of the State of New York; and one to the legislature of the State of New York. Each cheese was painted and decorated with 'appropriate scenes', mottos, and declarations. Like the Mammoth Cheese before it, Jackson's cheese was paraded and displayed to much fanfare.[22]

In addition to Jackson's cheese, individuals could show their support for the seventh president by baking Jackson Jumbles ('5 cups of Flour, 3 of Sugar, 1 of Butter, 3 Eggs & tea spoon of Pearl in a cup. Cream. Baked quick').[23] Within this role-call of presidential treats, cookbook authors also responded with recipes to praise the administrations of William Henry Harrison, Zachary Taylor, James Buchanan, and so forth. Harrison, unfortunately, holds the dubious distinction for having delivered the longest inaugural address (one hour and forty-five minutes) yet served the shortest term in office of any American president (thirty-one days). He hardly lived long enough to enjoy the gift of a six-foot-tall, nine-foot-wide, 800-pound cake in the shape of the United States Capitol to mark his presidency.[24] Apparently, this was not the only cake made in his honour. Reports from the Hagerstown, Maryland *Torch Light* reported that a 112-pound cake from the bakery of Mr. William Brazier was sent to Washington to celebrate his inauguration. Its pyramidal sides were inscribed with the words *Liberty* and *Plenty*, along with a bust of Harrison surrounded by twenty-six stars representing the twenty-six states plus an image of the Executive Mansion in miniature. And, 'the whole tastefully iced, capped and wreathed and festooned with evergreens and artificials'.[25] Notably, in 1841, one could serve slices of William Henry Harrison Cake ('5 ½ cups flour, 2 cups butter, 4 eggs, 2 cups molasses, one cup milk, 2 lbs. raisins, tea-spoon saleratus, spice to your taste. Bake it in two middling size forms') or Harrison Pudding on plates adorned with Harrison's figure produced by potters in Staffordshire and exported for consumers in the United States.[26] And, as for Jefferson and Jackson, a cheese was made to recognise Harrison's presidency, but it weighed a mere 194 pounds.[27]

It is important to note that politically inspired recipes had a lifespan. While recipes for Election Cake endured for decades, Madison Cake and Taylor Cake, understandably, came and went. However, the tradition of saluting the achievements of George Washington in the form of Washington Pie or Washington Cake still exist today. In fact, in 1836, 'The Great Washington Cake' was exhibited at the mercantile store of John Pease & Sons in New York City. It weighed 2600 pounds and was twenty-three feet in circumference, *The New York Evening Post* described it thusly:

> Ever grateful for the patronage bestowed upon us by the public and our friends in general, we solicit their attention to the exhibition of our Mammoth Cake for the Christmas holidays, which is now prepared for exhibition. It is one of the most extraordinary delicious compounds that has ever been presented to the public,

consisting of the enormous amount of: 220 lbs. butter, 240 of sugar, 245 of flour, 400 lbs. of raisins, 850 of currants, 160 of citron, 4 each of cinnamon, cloves nutmeg, and mace, and 180 lbs. of eggs. Besides a vast amount of ORNAMENTAL ICEING on the exterior, consisting of 100 lbs. sugar, and the white of 200 eggs, making in all a delectable compound of such gigantic size as to weigh nearly 2600 lbs.; *the largest ever known*. ... and we pledge ourselves that the interior shall be as delicious to the taste as the exterior is gigantically beautiful to the sight.[28]

This certainly puts Amelia Simmons's quantities for Election Cake into perspective. While such presentations, so extravagant in proportion, seem humorous and perhaps even absurd, they reflect much about the givers as well as the recipients. While most citizens were disenfranchised from political power, there was great pride in acknowledging and celebrating the political process. Baking a cake or producing a mammoth cheese were not merely personal gestures, but national ones as well. While food historically serves as a means for communal gathering, these patriotic offerings also communicated approval and celebratory wishes, reflecting support for the nation and its leaders in part through the time and expense required for such undertakings.

This desire for commemorative gestures continued to resonate throughout the nineteenth century. As Manifest Destiny spread and the Civil War approached, cookbooks from the 1850s and 1860s included recipes for Railroad Cake, Ratification Cake, Lincoln Cake, and Union Pudding – meant to be shared with friends and family in celebrations both public and private. Centennials and World's Fairs, too, were ripe for patriotic displays of nationalism including two of the most important cultural events of the latter nineteenth century, the Philadelphia Centennial of 1876 (an obvious anniversary year) and the 1893 International Exposition in Chicago. On display were examples of American ingenuity through scientific and agricultural advances plus some good-natured patriotism featuring culinary invention. At the 1876 Centennial Exposition, Henry Maillard, a manufacturer of 'Fine Confectionary and Chocolate & Cocoa Preparations', presented a large case filled with a fifteen-foot-tall sugar and chocolate monument to American history including scenes from the American Revolution in the Agriculture Hall.[29] Maillard also produced massive chocolate sculptures for the 1893 World's Columbian Exposition, again

Figure 6. Maillard's Exhibit. Trade Card Collection (Col. 9, 04x110.4). Courtesy, the Winterthur Library: Joseph Downs Collection of Manuscripts and Ephemera.

within an agricultural pavilion (Figure 6). The *American Druggist and Pharmaceutical Record* described Maillard's multi-figural installation thusly: 'five figures of heroic size, each weighing about 1500 pounds, and made of chocolate. Four of the figures are at the corners of the pavilion, each pair representing Venus de Milo and Minerva. The fifth one, situated at one side, represents Columbus'. Make no mistake, Columbus and his cohorts did not stand out as the only displays of culinary intrigue. An 11-ton cheese, the 'Mammoth Cheese of Canada' was also present in the Agriculture Building.[30]

While imaginative and curious, massive cakes, cheeses, and sculptures of chocolate or sugar were designated as feats (and feasts) of agricultural, cultural, and commercial success. And, while it is doubtful that Amelia Simmons, pastor John Leland, the home cook making Harrison cakes, or even Henry Maillard ever read the constitution, they certainly understood with profundity the value, enduring significance, and marketability of the American body politic. Who knows what presidential foods await us in future election cycles? But one can certainly begin to imagine fantastic, incredible edibles that pay homage to slices of Election Cake and cups of Liberty Tea.

Acknowledgements

This paper is part of a book-length project titled, *Political Appetites: Revolution, Taste, and Culinary Activism in the Early Republic*. Fellowships from the following institutions have greatly assisted my research: the Smithsonian American Art Museum; Winterthur Museum & Library; the American Antiquarian Society; New England Regional Fellowship Consortium; Radcliffe Institute for Advanced Study, Harvard University; Massachusetts Historical Society; Historic Deerfield; Connecticut Historical Society; Yale University's Lewis Walpole Library; Lilly Library, Indiana University; and the New York Public Library. My extended thanks to Mark McWilliams and the organizers of the 2021 Oxford Food Symposium for producing this important and delicious event.

Notes

1. Two important sources of scholarship on celebrations in the Early Republic are David Waldstreicher, *In the Midst of Perpetual Fetes* (Chapel Hill: University of North Carolina Press, 1997) and Andrew Burstein, *America's Jubilee* (New York: Vintage Books, 2001).
2. Thomas F. De Voe, *The Market Book, containing a Historical Account of the Public Markets in the Cities of New York Boston, Philadelphia and Brooklyn* (New York: Printed for the Author, 1862): vol 1, pp. 316-17.
3. Words such as 'independence' and 'democracy' are faulty at best given the disenfranchisement and persecution of indigenous and enslaved populations.
4. Amelia Simmons, *American Cookery, or, The art of dressing viands, fish, poultry, and vegetables, and the best modes of making puff-pastes, pies, tarts, puddings, custards and preserves, and all kinds of cakes, from the imperial plumb to plain cake, adapted to this country, and all grades of life* (Hartford, CT: Hudson & Goodwin, 1796). See also the Bedford, MA: Applewood Books edition of 1996 for an introductory essay by Karen Hess.
5. My thanks to Ellen Shea at the Radcliffe Institute for Advanced Study for this reference to Hartford Election cake served during the May 1771 election ceremonies; Amelia Simmons, *American Cookery*, 2nd edn (Albany, NY: Charles R. & George Webster, 1796), p. 43.

6. See William Woys Weaver, *America Eats, Forms of Edible Folk Art* (New York: Harper & Row, 1989).
7. A cookbook collection of many of these recipes is forthcoming by the author.
8. 'Extract of a letter from a gentleman in Berkshire (Mass) to his friend in this city', *The Albany Centinel*, 28 July 1801, p. 3. This casual reference predates the 8 August 1801 article in the *Impartial Observer* which was considered the first public mention of the Mammoth Cheese.
9. Burstein, p. 112.
10. For a wonderful discussion of the Mammoth Cheese, see Jeffrey Pasley's chapter, 'The Cheese and the Words: Popular Political Culture and Participatory Democracy in the Early American Republic', in *Beyond the Founders: New Approaches to the Political History of the Early American Republic*, ed. by Jeffrey Pasley, Andrew Robertson, and David Waldstreicher (Chapel Hill: University of North Carolina Press, 2004), pp. 31-56. See also C.A. Brown, 'Elder John Leland and the Mammoth Cheshire Cheese', *Agriculture History*, 18 (1944): 145-53; and Daniel Dreisbach, *Thomas Jefferson and the Wall of Separation Between Church and State* (New York: New York University Press, 2002).
11. Margaret Brown Klapthor, *The First Ladies Cook Book* (New York: Parent's Magazine Press, 1965), p. 28.
12. 'For the Star. A Mammoth Pye', *Western Star*, 14 September 1801, p. 3. Also, a small notice appeared in the *Washington Federalist* recalling the need for the apple pie.
13. 'From the Columbian Centinel. A 'Mammoth' Beet', *The Independent Gazetteer*, 27 October 1801, p. 1.
14. *The Independent Chronicle*, 16 April 1804; 'Extract of a Letter from a Gentleman', *The Repertory*, 6 April 1804. 'Communication. More of the Mammoth', *The New-York Evening Post*, 29 December 1801, p. 3.
15. *Albany Gazette* as printed in *Otsego Herald*, 17 December 1810, p. 3.
16. Taken from L.H. Butterfield, 'Elder John Leland, Jeffersonian Itinerant', *Proceedings of the American Antiquarian Society* 62 (1932): 223 from the original source John Davis, *Travels of Four Years and a Half in the United States of America* (London: [n.pub.], 1803), pp. 329-30.
17. As reported in numerous papers including *The New-York Gazette*, 5 January 1802 and *The Courier*, 13 January 1802.
18. *The Republican or, Anti-Democrat*, 6 January 1802, p. 3.
19. Jefferson's personal account book, entry on 4 January 1802, New York, New York Public Library Manuscripts and Archives Collection, MS 23168 <https://digitalcollections.nypl.org/items/6627be60-82f9-0132-fa97-58d385a7b928>
20. *The Ploughman: or, Republican Federalist*, 1 February 1802.
21. Butterfield, p. 228.
22. 'From the Utica Standard and Democrat', *Connecticut Courant*, 71.3697 (30 November 1835).
23. Handwritten recipe book of Susan H. T. Spalding, widow of Jason Spalding MD c1830, Worcester, MA, American Antiquarian Society Cookbook Collection 1770s-1890s, 15 volumes, vol 5.
24. Klapthor, p. 73, from a report in *The National Intelligencer*.
25. 'A Harrison Cake', appearing in *The Newark Daily Advertiser*, 3 February 1841, p. 2.
26. This recipe comes from a cookbook written by a 28-year-old woman from Boston, c1830s, Washington, DC, National Museum of American History, Dibner Library.
27. Mr. William from Beaverdam, PA, 'The Harrison Cheese', *The Hampshire Gazette*, 1 July 1841, p. 2.
28. *The Evening Post* (New York), 4 December 1838, p. 2.
29. *Chocolate: History, Culture, and Heritage*, ed. by Louis Evan Grivetti and Howard-Yana Shapiro (Hoboken: John Wiley & Sons, 2009), p. 200. Maillard had his manufactory and offices in New York at 114 to 118 W. 25th St. 113 to 117 W. 24th St. and retail stores at the 5th Avenue Hotel and 178 Broadway (Winterthur, DE, Winterthur Library, Trade Cards: (Col. 9) 04 x 110.4).
30. Winterthur Library, Trade Cards: (Col. 9) 04 x 110.4. The trade card depicts 1500-pound chocolate statues of the Venus de Milo and Columbus in the Agriculture Building for the World's Columbian Exposition, Chicago, IL; *American Druggist and Pharmaceutical Record* 23 (July-December 1893), 65.

Reading the Cookbooks of Communist Romania: An Intimate Defence

Adriana Sohodoleanu

A few years ago I read a collection of food memoirs from various Romanian *hommes de lettres*. Reading about a poetess who was reminiscing browsing through old French almanacs as a way of fending off cold and hunger, I remembered my own daydreaming over the 1983 and 1984 editions of the *Almanac of Literature and Gastronomy*. I realized that, decades and living conditions apart, we were both reading recipes to indulge in revery and resist the present. Scholars of Communist food discourse have noticed that the way things were presented in cookbooks was likely to stimulate the imagination, but it might have also activated possible frustrations. The anticipation set in motion when reading recipes leads to excitement that can easily turn into frustration when recipes are impossible to prepare (Bren and Neuberger 2012). And impossible they were in Communist Romania! With the increased pressures around food provisioning that hit Romania in the 1980s, cookbooks became an escapist pastime (Petrescu 2014). Younger readers, such as myself at the time, used recipes as leaps into fantasy land: I was not able to experience the real taste of a fifty-egg Romanian brioche, so I could only imagine the splurge. For some adults, however, the reveries brought back real memories that made a meagre dinner of toast and tea more palatable. To Romanian philosopher Gabriel Liiceanu, born in 1942, 'misery foods' seemed normal during his childhood: he confessed to having no recollection of a feast back then, which caused him to speak of a fall from the culinary Paradise' era in Communism (Parvulescu 2012: 162). However, as I personally observed, something else also took place in the process – education, with cookbooks acting as silent teachers.

Why Study Cookbooks

Food scholars recommend using cookbooks as historical sources because they are not mere recipe collections, but they provide hidden clues about politics, religion, ideology – in a nutshell the prevalent 'world views' of a historical age and social group (Albala 2012, Bracewell 2012, Neuhaus 2014). While Cognard-Black and Goldthwaite view recipes as 'culture-keepers as well as culture-makers, both recording memories and fostering new ones' (2014), for others they are cultural and social cartographies of their worlds (Theophano, 2022: 13), a fact that makes them a suitable medium for a social history study.

Drawing on the existing research on daily life under Communism, this paper starts from the premise that cookbooks are never removed from political and economic realities and that they 'help legitimate the system that put all this bounty on the table' (Bracewell 2012: 170). My research is indebted to Shkrodova's work on Bulgarian Communist cookbooks and Keating's analysis of the culinary discourse as a tool that delivers the knowledge produced by and supports the State's power (Shkrodova 2018; Keating 2018). My analysis also builds on Hofland's discussion around the Soviet Khrushchev regime 'perceiving […] domestic cooking as a public affair' (Hofland 2016: 3). In advancing the theory of the educational role played by cookbooks, this article also relies on the theory that new models of consumption can act as tools for eradicating backwardness and set up a modern society (Massino 2012: 227).

Methodology

In conducting this piece of research my theoretical arsenal is twofold. First, I draw on my own childhood memories and observations as an avid reader and collector of cookbooks. Although there is no consensus on the defining traits of the auto-ethnographic method, I follow Carolyn Ellis's definition: 'research, writing, story, and method that connect the autobiographical and personal to the cultural, social, and political' (Ellis 2004: xix). This echoes Mills's 'sociological imagination' which links the personal to the societal (Mills 1959). The second method I employed is the qualitative coding of over thirty-five cookbooks representative for the analyzed period, mostly from my own bookshelves. Albala notes that cookbooks do not constitute proof of people's eating habits in a given period of time, as they are usually prescriptive in nature. However, he agrees that cookbooks can provide information if the researcher approaches them with a set of methodological tools (Albala 2012). In my research I followed historians' need to address five basic questions to contextualize the information contained, namely 'Who wrote the cookbook? What was the intended audience? Where was it produced and when? Why was it written?' Content analysis and coding were also conducted on a collection of memoirs about food under Communism.

A Brief History of Cookbooks in Romania

Judging by the number of titles, cookbooks were a well-established publishing genre well before the Second World War. By the mid-twentieth century Bucharest was synchronizing with the rest of Europe in terms of culinary books and experiences, with gastronomy becoming a hard-to-ignore marker of civilization (Pirjol 2011). The interwar cookbooks were largely intended for the bourgeois mistress of the house, who employed a cook and a butler and had a refined culinary repertoire (see e.g. Bacalbasa's 1935 recipes for crayfish soup, lobster, and chrysanthemum salad). That changed after 1947, with the new social order imposed by the Communist regime, designed to mimic its Soviet neighbour and guiding star. Part of building the new society was based on erasing the old order, purging 'unhealthy' bourgeois elements. The propaganda machine worked hard to shed a favourable light on the achievements of the Communist 'new man'. Eating and cooking were also subject to this transformation. If the act of food provisioning was always political, cooking was usually relegated to the domestic sphere. Social history recounts peaceful times when food preparation was considered a private affair, an area that escaped the government's interference being relegated to 'the private space of domestic life, far from worldly noises' (Giard 1998: 171). Following the Soviet lead, the Romanian Communist regime perceived 'domestic cooking as a public affair' and actively pursued its alignment to the party's ideology (Hofland 2016: 3). Moreover, who talked about food and how food was talked about and what remained unspoken was a matter of State policy (Annuk 2013). Under Communist rule, food was subject to governmental regulation, and its production, distribution, and prices were strictly controlled by the authorities (Keating 2018). The party understood that power: official communication about food functioned as a semiotic system likely to shape mentalities and ideologies (Net 2014). Such a context turned food consumption into 'a deeply political experience' (Burell 2003: 189).

Communist Culinary Discourse Over Time

The 1950s were based on an 'enforced consensus' modelled on Soviet patterns of nationalization, centrally planned industry, and censorship. The state took control over everything; included printing, so cookbooks too received the call to arms. Culinary literature from that time is brimming with principles of scientific nutrition. A healthy individual meant a healthy worker, therefore a useful citizen. Food became a tool to supply the worker with the necessary calories – it was, after all, the period of the great construction sites: the subway network, the Danube-Black Sea canal, etc. The new workforce (villagers migrated to urban industrial areas) needed to be both educated and fed.

Cooking was approached as part of a wider social endeavour; rational eating was a social responsibility, so cookbooks had extensive opening chapters describing how the human body works, fuelled by the appropriate caloric input. The state advanced the idea of personalized menus, proposing models of caloric intake customized for different age/gender/line of work, with the needs of a mine worker differing from those of a retired senior citizen or pregnant woman. Physiologists were asked to determine precise meal rations; nutritionists were invited to write lengthy introductions. Signs of rationalization and standardization could be found in all cookbooks as they offered pretty much the same recipes, without variation. This consistency was justified by theories of taste that relegate it to the bourgeoisie's mental landscape and define eating as a rudiment of existence, since the primary role of food was feeding, not pleasure (Glushchenko 2010).

The purge campaign that intended to clean the society of retrograde elements extended to cookbooks as well. All traces leading to Western, imperial, or simply decadent foods, foodways, and language were erased. There were also small adjustments of the ingredients, such as tuna becoming generic fish, etc. One study shows that 'quantities and ingredients in traditional recipes were scaled down as the ingredients necessary to make them became more difficult to procure (such as *cozonaci moldovenești*)' (Ghita 2016). This crusade for total renewal was not original, the Soviets did it too, turning '*consommè Printanièr*' into 'stock with roots and greens' (Steila 2015: 5:9). Not all cookbooks renamed recipes; some just adapted their orthography to prefer the Romanian phonetic pronunciation: *sarlota* for charlotte, *bavarez* for *bavaroise*, babe for baba, etc. Others managed to keep the original orthography such as *Bouillabaise* fish soup, butter *à la Strasbourg*, etc. Natalia Tautu's 1975 book gives recipes for *pain d'Espagne, mille feuilles* or *madeleines*, and, if in 1975 Silvia Jurcovan provides instructions for a white sauce, her 1987 edition openly names the concoction *Béchamel*.

The 1960s and especially the 1970s were the golden age of the East trying to catch up with the West (Stone 2012). Social scientists agree that the European Communist countries became 'mass consumer societies' (Crowley and Reid 2010: 11). The State paid attention to the consumer, and the shops were filled with foodstuffs. A new educational goal was set, and cookbooks obliged: a good housewife must be able to entertain at home, an idea which had to do with proving affluence and education, perks of a lifestyle comparable to the West.

However, in 1980 the EEC chose not to renew its trade partnership with Romania. Ceausescu took a highly nationalist approach that culminated with the need to be independent from the USSR and the West. In 1981 he decided to pay off the foreign debt estimated at $10 billion by exporting gasoline, clothing, and basic foodstuffs (Boia 2016). The 1980s meant for Romania the rationing of meat, oil, and sugar; overnight queues appeared outside stores for basic items, with bodies immobilized in food lines (Verdery 1996). Eggs were saved weeks in advance for Easter and Christmas menus. Real coffee was something one would hoard to bribe doctors or any other provider of informal services; otherwise at home, ersatz brewing was the norm. Ceausescu justified these measures on the basis of Romanian sovereignty and in the name of good health, promoting his program of scientific nutrition. Nonetheless, local cookbooks did not follow life's realities. In time, they lost their nutrition-centric approach and ideological weight and started offering substantial numbers of foreign recipes (a 1984 culinary wall-calendar featured recipes from all over the world, including the Western Capitalist World). Culinary literature illustrated a simple but satisfying cuisine, ignoring the reality of food shortage. Some Polish cookbooks, by contrast, did indirectly acknowledge the grim reality of lack of resources by abandoning pretence and publishing austerity-driven recipes that also gave real useful advice on how to make do with limited ingredients (Keating 2018).

Romanian Communist culinary literature is quite rich; I worked on at least thirty-five such books, but there are more of them out there. The most widely known source is Sanda Marin's cookbook, her 1936 first edition being reprinted in abridged form until the late 1960s. Authors are mostly amateur cooks; some volumes do not have an author at all. Titles are generic – 'Cookbook' – or simple and descriptive – 'Practical Advice for the Housewife'. Unless they focus on a single food category, most are exhaustive, compendium-like tomes featuring hundreds of recipes, some reaching or exceeding a thousand. Special diets have dedicated chapters or entire books. Some of them have introductions signed by dieticians in an attempt to give a more professional appearance to the advice being provided.

Just like other researchers dealing with Communist cookbooks, I found recipes to portray a simple, standardized, fairly conservative, and monotonous cuisine. The techniques are basic and so are the dishes; there is no 'ornamental cookery' (Barthes 1972). I noticed the recurrence of the same recipes across volumes, introductions that outline the same science-based advice, and the identical structuring of the universe of ingredients and cooking techniques. Such a single, unified set of recipes thus reflects the propagation of a bureaucratic cuisine, likely to ensure the nation's proper nutrition. This secured both science-approved products and control for a higher uniformity of quality and quantity. The epitome of prescriptive cooking appears to be the national *Standard Recipe Collection for Food Products* intended to serve as the Bible for all restaurants.

Science-based nutrition had a longer history in Romania, though. Local cookbooks had hinted at it well before the Second World War. In 1935 journalist and *bon viveur* Constantin Bacalbașa argued that 'when it comes to feeding, as well as in politics, abuse is anti-constitutional' (2009: 22). In Communist Romania, the woman of the house was to bear the responsibility of understanding the nutritional needs of the family and to meet them at a minimum cost of time, materials, and energy. Set against the background of food penury, this demand opens the door to substitutions and alterations. The results were the so-called economic recipes, cheaper versions of the printed ones. The readers therefore wrote their own alternative cookbooks, by hand, exchanging recipes within their social circle and editing the official ones (Shkrodova 2018). Even some official cookbooks exceptionally included this type of substitute recipes. Probably the most famous is the one for fake fish roe salad. Replacing roe with beans or semolina and adding fish paste resulted in something described as 'imitat[ing] real fish roe well', writes Jurcovan (1975: 60); in her 1987 edition she followed up on her readers' feedback by offering ideas, recipes, and advice on how to use canned meat – a novelty at the time, which she referred to as 'sterilized meat', a much more reasonable and readily available ingredient than fresh or frozen meat. Low-quality or substitute products became staples which prompted humour as a common way of coping; that's when you would hear on Romanian streets about 'chickenware' (wings, heads, and claws) and about 'pork Adidas' (pork hooves). Life acquired a 'gradual redefinition of luxury' (Crowley and Reid 2010: 11).

Reading Communist Cookbooks Then and Now

While reading cookbooks as a child, I'd skip the info on vitamins, proteins, and the like; I saw food items as embodiments of the stories of the world. However, I was obviously attracted by practical examples – which foods should my mother, who worked as a clerk, eat? How should my grandfather, who worked in petroleum extraction and commuted to work every day, be fed at the factory's cafeteria? Well, my cookbooks had no answer to these questions since they do not offer customised menus aside from some general theoretical paragraphs.

Apart from (arguably) educating me about nutrition, my cookbooks also taught me about planning and optimizing the use of resources. There were so many ways one could use a slice of stale bread. However, what really caught my imagination as a kid were recipes for such things as flavoured butters, eggs *à la Strasbourg*, and American lemonade. I remember a complex, butter-rich, decadent French *mille feuille* pastry followed, a few pages later, by economic recipes based on cheaper ingredients like bread, potatoes, starch, and marmalade. Though I did not give it too much thought back then, it now seems like the breeding ground of cognitive dissonance.

There is something else my cookbooks taught me: the value of patience and imagination. Not having enough eggs to spare for recipe testing is how I understood what austerity meant. In the 1980s, Romanian food shops offered mainly toilet paper, Vietnamese shrimp crackers, and canned bean stew displayed skilfully to fill the empty shelves. Therefore, when cookbooks proposed more international and flamboyant combinations, they also became useless or, at least, not functional.

From my cookbooks I learnt that women should cook while men and children eat. Today I simply know Communist cookbooks were highly gendered. Woman, 'this wonderful being who brings us the joy of days spent together through every meal she makes, masterpieces of her work', was, at the same time, the tractor-operating symbol of gender equality in the workforce (Olexiuc 1979: 7; Boia 2016). Despite claims that 'Communism will liberate woman from domestic slavery, so that her life can be richer, fuller, happier and freer' (Aleksandra Kollontaj qtd. by Hofland 2016: 16), cookbooks appear to have promoted this multi-lateral, multi-tasking ideal that adds domestic work on top of official, paid work. Communism legitimized the double workday for women (Miroiu 2014).

Communist culinary literature could also deliver lifestyle content. The gem of my collection is called *Gospodina si oaspetii familiei – The Housewife and the Family's Guests* (Neagu 1968/1977). It is a small, delicate book borrowed by my aunt in the 1970s and never returned to the village's public library. It features menus for specific events such as a small wedding, an anniversary, children's parties, picnics, etc. These come with advice on style, plating, manners, and hospitality as well as lots of sketches showing how to creatively fold a napkin, make a seating card, or decorate a New Year's Eve aspic. Due to its focus on good taste and display it taught me, as a child, that food is not simply about cooking. It is about planning, pairing, and presenting. The author believed the family meal educated participants by providing not only nutritional information but also by honing soft skills such as aesthetics, table manners, and entertaining guests. It showed me a whole world outside the food I knew – and that started a lifelong interest in gastronomy. If cookbooks were meant to educate the masses, this book is a perfect example, especially since it was available in rural public libraries too. Reading this kind of cookbook helped me challenge what I would be told about the material culture of the old world, the denigrated bourgeoisie (dining room versus all-in-one family room, silver cutlery versus nickel, foamy cotton tablecloths, Bohemia crystal glasses, etc.). This is how I learnt about class, inequality, glamour, taste, and political regimes.

Later on, while going back to this book to do my research, the reference to silver cutlery brought up bigger questions – was it a slip, a tacit acknowledgement, or an intentional move, part of the propaganda? Was the Communist party using the kitchen as a (distorted) mirror to cover up shortages and pretend Romania had a normal existence? Was this the way to build the image of a rich, civilized, modern society, similar to if not even superior to any Western one? That is one possibility supported by cookbook authors such as Clementina Petra:

> the rising of lifestyle level is manifested throughout all sectors of our Socialist society and it generates opportunities and superior needs. Eating has changed, aside from the higher caloric intake there is also a form of aesthetic display and consumption. (Petra 1969: 5)

Then again, the empty references to a no longer existent or desirable conviviality model may have been just an element of the Party's strategy focused on painting a cosmopolite, affluent image (Shkrodova 2018).

What I treasure about my old cookbooks even today is the fact that they helped me build culinary capital (Lebescco and Naccarato, 2012). Among hundreds of recipes featuring plain ingredients I was able to effortlessly single out the oddities, meaning the rare-to-nonexistent-and-never-seen-in-real-life recipes. This is how I learnt about parmesan, chocolate, butter, champagne, asparagus, coffee, truffles, sturgeon caviar, etc. Although absent in the pantry, these were present in my books – I found seven asparagus recipes in just one book. The availability of these ingredients in shops before 1947 is documented in culinary and non-culinary literature. I read those recipes with an intellectual appetite, no hunger, no cravings. Decades later, I would smile reading Plesu's poetical definition of a recipe as being able 'to quench hunger, quick and efficiently but also to educate it, to shape it, to celebrate it; through the foreplay of reading and anticipatory imagination the recipe gives an ancillary taste to any dish' (2018).

Part of this educational process was also my familiarity with the Capitalist Other's food early on, even if only in theory. When capitalism officially entered Romania after 1989, I was already versed, theoretically, in the international kitchen lingo. I knew the recipes for French pastry dough, Greek pastry sheets, Viennese *schnitzel*, Greta Garbo cake, ketchup, *vinaigrette*, *choux à la crème*, Chantilly, pizza, etc.

In my personal context the Communist cookbooks I grew up with had a clear educational role, although not the one the State was aiming for. Brought up in an apolitical urban family I was unaware of the bigger picture and took cookbooks at face value. The rational-eating national programme has not proved to be a limitation of personal freedom or food consumption; people developed underground networks of supply, and life followed its course. I understand now that cookbooks were a representation of the regime's duplicity. Responsibility took the basic form of fending for oneself, while planning and optimization allowed for alteration. The state lied; people pretended to believe. The publisher sought legitimation and indoctrination; readers looked for revery, loose inspiration, and maybe the feeling of normality. These different usages somehow managed to coexist.

I brought myself up as a gastronome learning about the (truncated) world around from the official and unofficial culinary literature and practices at hand. There was almost no public legitimacy of indulgence in food and cooking but that did not deter me and others from discovering it. In a Communist context the cookbooks were first an escapist tool, but were later revalued in a personal context as educational tools that eased my immersion in Capitalism. They also laid the foundation of my culinary capital and opened the door to concepts of identity and belonging and difference even if these were only indirectly touched. So even if, just like in other countries from the Eastern Bloc, the cookbook was a tool of 'cultural deceit', it proved to be a useful guide to me in my formative years (Shkodova 2018: 296).

References

Albala, Kenneth. 2012. 'Cookbooks as Historical Documents', in *The Oxford Handbook of Food History*, ed. by Jeffrey M. Pilcher (Oxford: Oxford University Press), pp. 227-40

Annuk, Eve. 2013. 'Culinary Discourse: Organic Food in Estonia', in *Estonia and Poland: Creativity and Tradition in Cultural Communication*, ed. by Liisi Laineste, Dorota Brzozowska, and Władysław Chłopicki (Tartu: Elm Scholarly Press), II, pp. 137-46

Bacalbasa, Constantin. 2009. *Dictatura gastronomica. 1501 de feluri de mancari din 1935*, ed. by Dan-Silviu Boerescu (Bucharest: Editura Trei [1st ed. Bucharest 1935])

Barthes, Roland. 1972. 'Ornamental Cookery', in *Mythologies*, trans. by Annette Lavers (New York: Noonday), pp. 78-81

Boia, Lucian. 2016. *Strania istorie a comunismului românesc (și nefericitele ei consecințe)* (Bucharest: Humanitas)

Bren, Paulina and Mary Neuburger (eds.). 2012. 'Introduction', in *Communism Unwrapped: Consumption in Cold War Eastern Europe* (Oxford: Oxford University Press), pp. 3-26

Bracewell, Wendy. 2012. 'Eating Up Yugoslavia: Cookbooks and Consumption in Socialist Yugoslavia', in *Communism Unwrapped*, ed. by Bren and Neuburger, pp. 169-96

Burrell, Kathy. 2003. 'The Political and Social Life of Food in Socialist Poland', *Anthropology of East Europe Review*, 21.1: 189-95

Crowley, D. and S. Reid. (eds.). 2010. *Pleasures in Socialism: Leisure and Luxury in the Eastern Bloc* (Evanston, IL: Northwestern University Press)

de Certau, Michel. 1988. *The Practice of Everyday Life* (Berkeley: University of California Press)

Cognard-Black, Jennifer and Melissa A. Goldthwaite (eds.). 2014. *Books that Cook: The Making of a Literary Meal* (New York: New York University Press), <http://www.jennifercognard-black.com/all-books> [accessed 31 March 2022]

Danciu, Magda, and Delia-Maria Radu. 2014. *Gastroselves: Expressing Identity in a Hyper-Consumerist Society* (Oradea: Editura Universitatii)

Ellis, Carolyn. 2004. *The Ethnographic I: A Methodological Novel about Autoethnography* (Lanham, MD: Altamira)

Giard, Luce. 1998. 'Plat du Jour', in *The Practice of Everyday Life. Volume 2: Living and Cooking*, ed. by Michel de Certeau, Luce Giard, and Pierre Mayol, trans. by Timothy J. Tomasik (Minneapolis, MN:

University of Minnesota Press, 1998), pp. 171-99
Ghita, Ina. 2018. 'Altering Cooking and Eating Habits during the Romanian Communist Regime by Using Cookbooks: A Digital History Project', *Encounters in Theory and History of Education*, 19 <https://ojs.library.queensu.ca/public/journals/6/content/ghita/index.html> [accessed 31 March 2022]
Hofland, Olaf S.F. 2016. 'Cooking Towards Communism: Domestic Cooking and the Khrushchev Regime's Struggle for the Communist Way of Life' (unpublished master's thesis, Leiden University)
Jurcovan, Silvia. 1975. *Carte de bucate pentru tinerele gospodine* (Bucharest: Editura Tehnica)
Jurcovan, Silvia. 1987. *Carte de bucate,* 2nd ed (Bucharest: Editura Tehnica)
Keating, Marzena. 2018. 'Power of Discourse: Cookbooks in the People's Republic of Poland', Dublin Gastronomy Symposium – Food and Power <https://arrow.tudublin.ie/cgi/viewcontent.cgi?article=1123&context=dgs> [accessed 31 March 2022]
Marin, Sanda. 1936. *Carte de bucate* (Bucharest: Editura Cartea Romaneasca)
Marin, Sanda. 1945. *Carte de bucate,* 11th edn. (Bucharest: Editura Cartea Romaneasca)
Massino, Jill. 2012. 'From Black Caviar to Blackouts' in *Communism Unwrapped*, ed. by Bren and Neuburger, pp. 226-49.
Mills, C. Wright. 1959. *The Sociological Imagination* (Oxford: Oxford University Press)
Miroiu, Mihaela. 2004. *Drumul către autonomie. Teorii politice feministe* (Iasi: Polirom)
Neagu, Draga. 1968/1977. *Gospodina si oaspetii familiei* (Bucharest: Editura tehnica)
Net, Mariana. 2014. '*Vocabularul gastronomic românesc. Recuperări semantice și lexicale*', *Diacronia*, BDD-V151: 313-24
Naccarato, P., and K. Lebesco. 2012. *Culinary Capital* (Oxford: Berg Publishers)
Olexiuc, Nicolae. 1976. *Preparate culinare reci* (Bucharest: Editura Tehnica)
Olexiuc, Nicolae. 1979. *Bucataria practica* (Bucharest: Editura Tehnica)
Parvulescu, Ioana (ed.). 2012. *Intelectuali la cratita* (Bucharest: Humanitas)
Pence, Katherine, and Paul Betts (eds.). 2008. *Socialist Modern: East German Everyday Culture and Politics* (Ann Arbor, MI: University of Michigan Press)
Petra, Clementina. 1969. *Aperitive* (Bucharest: Editura Tehnica)
Petrescu, Dragos. 2014. *Entangled Revolutions: The Breakdown of the Communist Regimes in East Central Europe* (Bucharest: Editura Enciclopedica)
Plesu, Matei. 2018. '*Morfologia bucatelor*', *Dilema Veche* (Bucharest), 1-7 February
Pirjol, Florina. 2011. '*Destinul unui formator de gusturi. De la savoarea pastilei gastronomice la gustul fad al compromisului*', *Revista Transilvania*, 12: 18-26
Podoleanu, Liliana, Emilia Podoleanu, and Mihail Popescu. 1985. *Carte de bucate* (Bucharest: Editura Ceres)
Shkodrova, Albena. 2018. 'From Duty to Pleasure in the Cookbooks of Communist Bulgaria: Attitudes to Food in the Culinary Literature for Domestic Cooking Released by the State-Run Publishers between 1949 and 1989', *Food, Culture, and Society: An International Journal of Multidisciplinary Research*, 21.4: 468-87
Stone, Dan. 2012. 'Responding to "Order without Life?" Living under Communism', in *The Oxford Handbook of Postwar European History*, ed. by Dan Stone (Oxford University Press), pp. 163-82
Steila, Daniela. 2015. 'Food and Cooking in Revolutionary and Soviet Russia', *Journal of Interdisciplinary History of Ideas*, 4.8, 5:1-5:19
Tautu-Stanescu, Natalia. 1965. *Mica gospodina* (Bucharest: Editura Tehnica)
Theophano, Janet. 2002. *Eat My Words: Reading Women's Lives through the Cookbooks They Wrote* (New York: Palgrave)
Verdery, Katherine. 1996. *What Was Socialism, and What Comes Next?* (Princeton, NJ: Princeton University Press)

Stirring Up Historical Imagination: Promoting the Teaching of History through Food-Based Pedagogy

Nicholas Tošaj

Some degree of imagination lies at the heart of any meaningful understanding of history. Through our imagination history can come alive, become relevant and relatable – something that this Symposium has achieved through the passionate discussion of food for forty years. However, anyone who has ever experienced a dry history lecture or an indigestible textbook can attest that stirring up this historical imagination is not always easy. With this in mind, I strive to incorporate food into the teaching of history, sparking a sense of relatability and immediacy for my students by engaging their curiosity through their ability to taste, to smell, to remember, and to imagine. This paper will delve into the role that food has fulfilled in prompting my students to engage their historical imaginations.

I am far from the first person to bring food into the classroom. Ken Albala, Jeffrey Pilcher, and Donna Gabaccia are only a few of the accomplished historians who have successfully integrated food into their formal teaching. Despite these successes, food remains woefully under-represented as a pedagogical tool in history. Using food as a teaching tool is viewed as something of an anomaly, a quirk. While I am under no illusion that food will become a mainstream tool used in all history classes, my goal in writing this article is to reflect upon the role that we can play in raising the profile of food as a means for stimulating learning and to assist in carving a place for food history in curriculum development. My aim is to approach the place of food in the historical imagination, not from the perspective of a seasoned expert, but from that of a junior academic attempting to use food to bridge the gap between theory and practice in historical pedagogy.

This paper touches briefly upon the uses of food pedagogy in academia in recent years before describing my experiences teaching history classes with a practical culinary component. The content of this paper veers intentionally into the informal, relying largely on quotes from student work and anecdotes. My experiences teaching food history have run the gamut from cooking in teaching kitchens with commercial equipment, to improvising a kitchen with a hotplate, cafeteria table, and odds and ends from a thrift store, to supervising pandemic cooking assignments over Microsoft Teams. As such, portions of this paper dwell on the logistical and structural hurdles I have encountered as an educator in my attempts to blend food with formal historical education.

These methodological and structural components serve the same purpose as a stock would serve in a soup: forming a necessary base in which to situate some interesting morsels, the latter represented by examples of student engagement with history through food. Discussions of sensory approaches to food tie into excerpts from student work submitted in my classes in which students discussed topics as diverse as colonialism, migration, industrialization, and globalization through dishes of their choice.[1] Be it Isabelle Menarik hanging arctic char in her suburban garage in order to make traditional *pitsik* or Sherin Thankamma Isac pondering the place of globalization and imperialism in shaping the foodways of Kerala, anecdotes such as these show the value of these personal and striking embodiments of the historical imagination. By encouraging students to dive into history palate first, we not only encourage them to create a sensory bridge between themselves, their ancestors, and important historical events, we also invite students to bring some of the conviviality inherent to sharing a meal into the classroom, even when that classroom is digital. In doing so, history becomes accessible, tangible, and poignant – more relatable in many cases than distant battles and dynastic successions, without being any less meaningful. By promoting the use of food-based pedagogy when teaching history, I aim to connect students to the convivial pleasures that I have experienced at the Symposium and to teach students and educators alike that good food, like good conversation, is best shared.

Teaching with Food: Context and Culture

A significant amount of work has been produced on the place of food in pedagogy and on food as a method for teaching history. Within the academic context scholars such as Deirdre Murphy have expounded upon the use of food as an important base for interdisciplinary studies.[2] In their round table published in the *Radical History Review*, Daniel Bender, Rachel Ankeny, Warren Belasco, Amy Bentley, Elias Mandala, Jeffrey M. Pilcher, and Peter Scholliers discussed the place of food in their courses.[3] Ken Albala's blog has provided us with a wealth of knowledge relating to the use of food, cooking, and kitchens, while Jonathan Deutsch and Jeffrey Miller's chapter 'Teaching with Food' provides important insight into food pedagogy supplemented by pedagogical exercises making use of food in the classroom.[4] Michael Twitty, Paula Marcoux, Ruth Goodman, and Jas Townsend are but a handful of the personalities that have taught historical cookery online, in-person, and on television, creating popular history content that captures the imagination of countless people impassioned by the ways in which food and history intersect.[5]

Anyone who has ever forgotten to write down a recipe can understand that recipes are, at their very core, historical. They serve to record and impart knowledge, to map change and to inform. Recipes, kitchen tools, and accounts of food shine light on lived experiences, providing us with insight into fundamental human existence. As attendees of this Symposium know well, food and history are inextricable. Be it a discussion of Three Sisters agriculture in what we now call Canada, a dive into the origins of wheat in the Fertile Crescent, or French rations in the First World War, food can captivate the imagination. For students who struggle with traditional methods of education, food provides a sensory entry into complex cultural topics. Be it in an academic or popular context, the use of food as a tool through which students can understand history is nothing new. However, despite popular interest in food history, using food to teach history remains relatively uncommon within formal pedagogical contexts. As institutions move to adopt active learning techniques and alternative approaches to pedagogy, the use of food as a sensory tool remains woefully under-represented.

In Quebec, food has drifted out of the pedagogical realm relatively recently, as seen with the absence of Home Economics from the provincial curriculum from the 1997 educational reform on.[6] As these courses were torn out of the provincial curriculum, so too were stoves and kitchen facilities from Quebec schools. Despite the often-problematic nature of Home Economics curricula, mandatory Home Economics courses provided students with an introduction to cooking, an opportunity to fire up ranges, to slice vegetables, and to mingle around food of their own making. In abandoning Home Economics as a mandatory element of the curriculum, educational reforms de-emphasized the importance of food, simultaneously robbing students of basic life skills and the opportunity to question their relationships with food. The removal of culinary infrastructure from educational institutions also meant that other courses that might have made use of kitchens were deprived of the opportunity to do so.

As a member of Quebec's last cohort of students enrolled in a mandatory Home Economics course, I was able to experience, albeit all too briefly, the joys of learning in the stimulating context of a teaching kitchen. Years later as a PhD student at the University of Toronto working with my supervisor Daniel Bender, I had the opportunity to turn the tables when I was given the pleasure of teaching a history course titled 'Edible History' in the Culinaria Research Centre's first teaching kitchen.[7] Though the kitchen was only a dark windowless room, formerly the home of a pizza chain on campus, the experience of sharing the kitchen with students was eye-opening. The discussions, conviviality, and camaraderie within that kitchen space went far beyond anything that I had ever experienced as an educator up to that point.

Students were excited to come to class; one student confessed that he had skipped classes in all his other courses but said that this course, because of the time in the kitchen, was the exception. Students who mentioned that they had a difficult time following lectures claimed that the sensory aspects of the teaching kitchen helped them relate to the course's historical content. The recipes cooked in class were necessarily historical and global in nature, representing a wide range of historical experiences to a diverse and curious student population. A comparison of curries was a popular activity, whereby students cooked British coronation chicken, Japanese battleship curry, and South African bunny chow and were invited to ponder the impact of globalization and colonization on our shared foodways. With access to multiple induction hot plates, a slew of equipment, and a commercial dishwasher, teaching at the Culinaria Research Centre meant that groups of approximately twenty students could be accommodated comfortably, broken into groups of four or five people, each group having its own workstation. The dishwasher made tidying-up relatively painless, allowing us to hold practicums with four different tutorial groups in one day and even hosting a campus-wide pop-up restaurant. After leaving the University of Toronto's teaching kitchen to take a teaching position at CEGEP John Abbott College in my native Quebec I was determined to continue using food as a pedagogical tool.[8]

Food: History and Practice

From a methodological and infrastructure perspective, teaching with food requires overcoming a variety of obstacles to be effective. Historical legitimacy, for instance, can be one of the greatest hurdles to surmount. The fact that tools, ingredients, and cooking methods have all changed over the *longue durée* of human experience is inescapable. Many plants used in cuisine today differ significantly from their historical ancestors. Tools and food systems have changed as well: how accurately can a historical stew recipe making use of factory-farmed lamb and industrially grown vegetables cooked in a stainless-steel pot over an induction burner truly capture the essence of mutton and homegrown vegetables cooked in cast iron over a peat fire? How can anyone claim that bread made of processed modern high-protein flour is an accurate stand-in for the bread of yore made of hand-ground spelt? While careful sourcing of ingredients and recipes can help mitigate some of these issues, even the most judicious of choices cannot guarantee complete historical authenticity. In conversations with fellow food historians, these obstacles have often been discussed, generally with the conclusion that perfect historical reproduction should not necessarily be the goal of historical cookery in the pedagogical context. The impracticality of attempting such perfect reconstructions of historical foods should not lead us to throw the proverbial baby out with the bathwater. This is especially true in a modern, educational setting where the college is unlikely to allow me to dig a roasting pit on its pristine quad in the name of historical authenticity. Instead of defacing the college lawn, I have sought to use these historical inconsistencies as a teaching tool, asking students how they believe that modern kitchens facilitate the cooking of a dish or how the tools which they use might differ from that of the cook who wrote the recipe. In this context, comparisons to campfire cookery tend to strike a chord, while discussions of who did the cooking in different historical contexts have led to interesting discussions on the place of gender and race in kitchens.

In terms of infrastructure, one of the largest hurdles to clear when teaching with food on many modern campuses is the absence of teaching kitchens or community cooking spaces. A kitchen such as that of the Culinaria Research Centre is a rare blessing to anyone wishing to incorporate food into the teaching of history. This was abundantly clear to me when I took up my new position where such kitchen space was lacking – though staff and student interest in such a space may change that. Initially in this kitchen-less context, food simply insinuated itself as a topic into my standard 'History of Western Civilization' and 'Modern History' courses: sugar and its place in shaping the Atlantic slave trade, salt and its importance in preservation, wheat as a cultural marker of Western identity among imperialist nations, all slid easily into a pre-existing curriculum. For some students, these examples were far more relatable than demographic trends, the spread of Christianity, and Papal intrigues. Samples of foods brought to class were useful in demonstrating technological shifts, with sourdough bread made from stone-milled flour standing in stark contrast to Wonder Bread, a testament to the changes brought by the industrialization of our food system. The simple act of bringing food into the classroom made the topics covered in class more tangible and more relevant to the day-to-day experience of students. Three years after I first brought bread to class, former students who have dropped into my office or checked in by email continue to reminisce on the place of food in their lectures.

In aiming to continue to teach with food, I was fortunate to be supported by my institution which has committed to exploring active learning techniques by stepping away from traditional lecturing in favour of alternative forms of pedagogy. The college's openness on this front provided me with the perfect opportunity to propose cooking as a pedagogical tool. It is in this context that my course 'Food: History and Practice' was accepted into the college curriculum. The course, based on a one-hour lecture followed by a two-hour practicum, has been taught for the past three semesters as an evening class offered through our school of Continuing Education. Despite my excitement that the course was accepted into the formal curriculum, the lack of a kitchen – let alone a teaching kitchen – remained problematic.

In the first iteration of the course, adaptation to kitchen-less cooking took the shape of a single two-burner hot plate and some pots, pans, knives, and other tools from the local thrift store and my own kitchen. With a combination of careful negotiation and legal waivers the course was permitted to take place inside the cafeteria dining hall (but not in the kitchens themselves) in order to have access to running water and tables. The initial class was mercifully small, numbering a dozen students who were divided into a rotating roster of roles taking turns prepping, cooking, and cleaning from class to class, with everyone participating in discussion. Though not as streamlined as a course taught in a teaching kitchen, this improvised kitchen space served the purpose of pulling students out of the traditional lecture hall in favour of immersing them in cooking and discussion as they bustled around the hot plate elbow to elbow. Perhaps one of the most striking benefits of such a setup was the shifting of the hierarchy caused by the spatial re-imagining of the class. As we cooked together, blundering through historical recipes side by side, making use of barely functional equipment, an environment of respectful camaraderie emerged, prompting students to feel more comfortable sharing their thoughts and experiences on class readings, recipes, and dishes.

Food, History, and Pedagogy in the Digital Landscape

Unfortunately, my first semester teaching 'Food: History and Practice' in our improvised kitchen was cut short by the rolling tide of the global pandemic. As instructors scrambled to bring lectures online, my course also migrated to Microsoft Teams. This shift presented new complications: how could we share in the conviviality of cooking when we were all isolated? How much would be lost by moving online? How could the sensory elements transition to the online context? The rest of the Winter 2020 semester as well as the Fall and Winter 2020–2021 semesters saw students cooking in their own kitchens, sharing their results via online forum posts, and documenting their historical recipes by taking photos of themselves alongside their dishes. From a logistical perspective, students were provided with lists of recipes one week before the weekly cooking practicum to make sure that they had ample time to secure the requisite ingredients. We would then all gather on Teams for a one to one-and-a-half-hour lecture and discussion period followed by the students diving into their kitchens. Class topics covered the birth of cooking, the Columbian Exchange, food and empire, and even food and the Anthropocene. In order to maintain a level of connection, students discussed the readings and the dishes that they had prepared on a weekly basis and were invited to comment on each other's work, building off of each other's findings. While the move online lacked much of the personal connection which had been so precious in the kitchen context, it did overcome the material issues inherent to our improvised kitchen setup. In addition, there were some unexpected but welcome benefits to students cooking at home, as family members became involved in the course adding a touch of humour and community to a pedagogical context otherwise marred by pandemic isolation.

Shared assignments in the form of online forum posts, classroom discussion, and oral presentations were key to replacing the conviviality of the kitchen when working online. The diversity of student experiences and cultural traditions shone brightly in the recipes that students chose to cook. The setting, though less than ideal, still stirred the students' historical imaginations. Examples from an assignment where students needed to cook a recipe of historical value to them or their family members provided some of the most striking examples. In one case, when asked what her family members knew about the history of the chosen recipe, a student made her favourite soup, Turkish *tarhana*:

> I had to ask my grandmother to answer this question and she said that this dish originates from the Ottoman Empire but there are a lot of different versions of it made in different cultures, for example, in Iran, in Greece, in Armenia or even in India. I couldn't find which period it is from, but I asked my parents and grandmother and they all said that in Turkey, it's known to be one of the oldest 'instant' soups ever made […] plenty of women from the town would gather up together and make it for their families with the help of others. This dish was also an easy way to make a lot of, and it would also help with giving energy and it is also known for keeping people warm so it would come in handy in the old times during winter.[9]

In discussing *tarhana*, the student was able to dive into themes of gender, labour, and technology, tying resource management and subsistence to today's convenience foods. In another case a student described the experience of preparing boiled arctic char. In her essay she reflected on indigeneity and alluded to the traumas of colonization, as well as to some of the changes wrought upon indigenous food systems in Canada's North:

> Our diet has changed a lot, especially my parents and grandparents. But country food is still very much preferred. Most people just simply cook without spices because they are not used to them. It is hard to talk for my family about history. I cannot really say much because they never really talked about their history. All I can say is that my ancestors were hunters and gatherers. [...] Before colonialism, my ancestors did not know any other food, other than what was available to them. Their diet started to change when colonizers or explorers came to their land. And the way they hunted changed.[10]

In another semester, the topic of arctic char and indigenous identity also surfaced in the work of Inuit student Isabelle Menarik. Menarik, who was raised on the island of Montreal, related the experience of learning about *pitsik* from her grandmother, describing the history of the dish:

> It is difficult to find an explanation of the process to make *pitsik* because like with most Inuit and other Indigenous histories, it is passed on orally through the generations. After receiving fish (typically Arctic char), caught by the men of the community, the women would remove the bones, filet the fish with the skin still intact, rub salt on it, then hang it to dry by the tail of the fish. *Pitsik* is a country food (food 'harvested locally') that can be easily made even by those living outside of Nunavik. Through the Hunter Support Program and Makivik Corporation, hunters in Nunavik are paid to provide meat such as caribou, char, and seal to those living in the south. This enables those living in Montreal to enjoy food that connects them with their culture, spirituality, and the land/nature.[11]

When presenting her recipe to the class, Menarik explained that she had never made the dish before and how speaking to her grandmother about *pitsik* and preparing it brought her closer to her culture. She also described some of the challenges that arose when making *pitsik* outside of the traditional context. These challenges included purchasing arctic char in Montreal, hanging the fish to dry in her suburban garage, and foiling her beloved cat's attempts at making a meal of the *pitsik* before Isabelle did.

For Sean Timermanis, one of the most striking attributes of making celebratory Latvian *piragi* was the place of the family matriarch in making *piragi* and the labour involved in the process:

> [...] in every Latvian family the Oma (Latvian Grandma) is and always will be the *piragi* guru. The only common denominator in the making of *piragis* is that

the Oma will tell you that you are only done kneading the dough once your forearms and shoulders feel like they are about to fall off, and then you need to continue kneading for another ten minutes.[12]

Timermanis's attempts to track down the roots of the dish also taught him about the complications inherent to conducting historical research:

> The history behind the *piragi* is clouded and unsure although the history of the *piragi* through the Timermanis family is one of incredible family memories and one of love, it is a tradition that the Timermanis family will continue for years without an end in sight.[13]

This lesson was also learned by Joey Bujold-Généreux when attempting to trace the roots of Quebec's version of shepherd's pie called *pâté chinois*:

> Although we don't know exactly when shepherd's pie was created. One of the most thought hypotheses is that it was created in the late 19th century while Chinese workers were working on the railways in Canada due to the strong beef livestock and crops of potatoes and corn. While this theory might make sense and easy to believe, it may not be entirely true […].[14]

For Sherin Thankamma Isac the assignment provided an opportunity to ponder the place of the food systems that had led her grandparents to grow cassava in Kerala:

> My great Grand Parents were farmers and tapioca was one of the common crops they cultivated and traded between other farmers in exchange for other crops. Polyculture was a common practice at that time. Banana, coconut, and pineapple were cultivated alongside tapioca. Thus, tapioca was the main food in all meals served in a variety of ways depending on the availability of different food sources in that period and the common way of serving back then was mashed tapioca with sardine fish curry (which was comparatively less expensive fish in that period) and a red chili shallot dip.[15]

In discussing tapioca and fish curry, Thankamma Isac's essay delved into the history of cassava's arrival in India from South America and the place which the staple came to occupy as an affordable substitute for more expensive rice, especially in times of hardship. In her work, Thankamma Isac described how tapioca was stigmatized as the food of the poor, being associated with toddy shops and the workers who frequented them.

Themes of hardship and migration also surfaced in the work of Eli Côté-Ryshpan. Côté-Ryshpan described how her family recipe for apple pie, dating from her grandparent's emigration to North America from Poland in the years prior to the First World War, bore reminders of a time and place where sugar was an expensive luxury rather than a ubiquitous additive:

> As the first world war began, food was now in short supply and my zayde's

mother would be damned if some pesky government issued rations were going to stop her from fattening up her family. So, she improvised. They lived on a farm and so would trade their eggs with neighbours for things like flour and butter, but sugar was hard to come by. So, in the summer and fall, she would send the kids off to pick wild berries and cherries from the orchard and she would boil them down and create a syrup to use in her recipes in the place of sugar. She had rationed out her sugar and added just a touch to each batch to sweeten it up. She would store these in the cellar, and they would keep all year round. Of course, it would add a little berry taste to anything she baked, but my dad says my zayde preferred it that way and strongly disliked any dessert that didn't have that hint of a berry taste.[16]

In today's industrialized food system, it can be difficult to imagine a context in which fresh berries were more accessible than refined sugar. Such insights into how rapidly the North American food system has changed in slightly over a century were shocking to Eli's classmates, providing an example of changes to our ways of life that were far more striking than statistics. Sharing such information, even online, provided accessible narratives through which students could engage with history, gaining more insight into each other's cultures and a more democratic understanding of how historical trends changed the lives of everyday people.

Conclusion

These excerpts testify to how food can help students reframe their personal experiences within history. Students not only learned fundamentals of historical education by working on their historical thinking skills, learning the basics of proper citation and honing their critical thinking skills, they also learned to relate wider historical trends and changes to their day-to-day existence. Discussions arising from student research, though sometimes difficult, fostered a climate of awareness, cultural openness, and exchange that encouraged students to share insights and perspectives, exchanges which would likely not have surfaced as easily in a traditional history lecture. While I am under no illusion that food pedagogy will become the norm in historical education, it is my belief that food serves as a deeply important tool for any educator willing to roll their sleeves up and get cooking, be it in a teaching kitchen, a cafeteria dining hall, or in the comfort of their own homes.

Acknowledgements

I would like to acknowledge the work of my students who not only bravely signed up to both 'Edible History' and 'Food: History and Practice' and took alternative approaches to learning in stride but whose keen participation allowed these courses to succeed beyond my wildest expectations. Their participation has made teaching an immense pleasure. I would also like to thank the administration, faculty, and staff at John Abbott College, especially Jocelyne Duchesneau, Jeanne Kunz, and Bill Russell, for making 'Food: History and Practice' possible despite logistical hurdles. Most of all, I would like to thank the students who allowed me to cite their assignments. Their wonderful and insightful work is the foundation of this paper: without their drive to learn and to question, their ability to think critically, and their insight, this paper could never have been written.

Notes

1. Student work is used with consent. In cases where students asked to remain anonymous, their work is only referenced broadly. Quotations from student work are featured here without references to better integrate them into the body of the text but have otherwise not been edited, preserving their writing in its original state to capture their unique voices.
2. Deirdre Murphy. 'Toward a Pedagogy of Mouthiness: The Essential Interdisciplinarity of Studying Food', *Transformations: The Journal of Inclusive Scholarship and Pedagogy*, 23.2 (2013), 17-26 <https://jstor-jac.orc.scoolaid.net/stable/10.5325/trajincschped.23.2.0017> [accessed 28 May 2021].
3. Daniel Bender and others, 'Eating in Class: Gastronomy, Taste, Nutrition, and Teaching Food History', *Radical History Review*, 2011.110 (2011), 197-216 <https://doi.org/10.1215/01636545-2010-035>
4. Ken Albala, *Ken Albala's Food Rant*, 2021 <http://kenalbala.blogspot.com.html> [accessed 28 May 2021]; Jonathan Deutsch and Jeffrey Miller, 'Teaching with Food', in *The Oxford Handbook of Food History*, ed. by Jeffrey M. Pilcher (Oxford: Oxford University Press, 2012), pp. 191-208.
5. 'Afroculinaria', *Afroculinaria* <https://afroculinaria.com/> [accessed 28 May 2021]; Paula Marcoux, *Cooking with Fire: From Roasting on a Spit to Baking in a Tannur, Rediscovered Techniques and Recipes That Capture the Flavors of Wood-Fired Cooking* (North Adams, MA: Storey, 2014); 'Ruth Goodman – Historical Consultant', *Ruth Goldman*, 3 February 2011 <https://www.ruthgoodman.me.uk/> [accessed 28 May 2021]; 'Townsends', Townsends <https://www.townsends.us/> [accessed 29 May 2021].
6. Ministère de l'éducation du loisir et du sport, *Le Renouveau Pédagogique – Ce Qui Définit Le 'Changement'* (Québec : Government of Quebec, 2005), Collections Bibliothèque et Archives nationales du Québec <https://numerique.banq.qc.ca/patrimoine/details/52327/51343?docpos=2> [accessed 26 May 2021].
7. 'Culinaria Research Centre', *University of Toronto* <https://www.utsc.utoronto.ca/culinaria/food-studies-university-toronto> [accessed 29 May 2021].
8. CEGEP refers to the *collège d'enseignement général et professionnel* system which is a publicly funded college that bridges the gap between high school and university. Distinct to Quebec, CEGEP resembles the sixth form/college in the UK or the last year of high school and first year of university in the rest of Canada and the US. As such, 'Food : History and Practice' is comparable to an introductory course at the university level.
9. Anonymous Student 1, 'Final Exam submitted to "Food: History and Practice"', Winter 2020 (unpublished exam, John Abbott College, 2020).
10. Anonymous Student 2, 'Final Exam submitted to "Food: History and Practice"', Winter 2020 (unpublished exam, John Abbott College, 2020).
11. Isabelle Menarik, 'The History of Inuit Pitsik' (unpublished paper, John Abbott College, 2020), p. 1.
12. Sean Timmermanis, 'Piragi: the Sassiest Pastry' (unpublished paper, John Abbott College, 2020), p. 2.
13. Timmermanis, p. 3.
14. Joey Bujold-Généreux, 'Pâté Chinois (Shepherd's Pie) and its Mysterious History' (unpublished paper, John Abbott College, 2020), p. 2.
15. Sherin Thankamma Isac, 'Flavors of Kerala: Mashed Tapioca, Fish Curry and Chili-Shallot Dip' (unpublished paper, John Abbott College, 2020), p. 2.
16. Éli Côté-Ryshpan, 'Not-So-Sweet Apple Pie' (unpublished paper, John Abbott College, 2020), p. 2.

Food in Sabbath Table Hymns: A Taste of the World to Come

Susan Weingarten

Many traditional Jews today sing together at table during their family Sabbath meals, a practice which goes back to medieval times. While the songs that are sung have varied over the ages, a canon of accepted Sabbath songs, *zemirot Shabbat*, has grown up, mostly in Hebrew and Aramaic but also in Yiddish, Ladino, and Spanish.[1]

There are many different tunes for each song, some having been passed down through the generations of a particular family, others influenced by local popular music. The songs belong to a genre of Hebrew poetry called *piyyut* (pl *piyyutim*), from the same Greek root as English 'poetry'. *Piyyutim*, first found in late antique Palestine, are sacred poetry which became part of prayers in the synagogue. *Zemirot* form a different sub-genre, as they belong in the home.

As well as being sung during the three mandatory Sabbath meals, *zemirot* often include allusions to food, such as the wine and bread traditionally blessed before the Sabbath meal. But the *zemirot* also refer to other foods as well. In this paper I shall be looking at food as it appears in these *zemirot*: how much of it is real and how much imaginary.

It is unclear how many *zemirot* are extant today: there is a generally agreed core, but variations on its periphery. I shall be taking as my base the twenty-five *zemirot* discussed by Naphtali Ben-Menahem in his book *Zemirot shel Shabbat* (*Zemirot for the Sabbath*) mostly in Hebrew, but including five in Aramaic.[2] I have excluded prose passages and psalms.

Origins of *Zemirot*

The late antique Midrash Esther Rabbah writes: 'When Israel eat and drink and are merry, they bless and praise and glorify God.'[3] There have been attempts to relate *zemirot* to the 'song for the Sabbath day' (Psalm 92) sung in the Temple, which the Mishnah explains as a song for 'the future to come', 'a day which is all rest and eternal life'.[4] The earthly Sabbath, indeed, is imagined by the rabbis as a 'foretaste of the eternal Sabbath of the World to Come'.[5] We shall return to this later. Meanwhile, I have found no hint that Psalm 92 was ever a table hymn, and it does not mention food.

The earliest identifiable *zemirot* are medieval, although we have no way of knowing how long they had been in use before their first written appearance in northern France, in the compendious prayer book known as *Mahzor Vitri*, which dates from the eleventh century. It is inevitably difficult to date individual songs, and would have been even

Food in Sabbath Table Hymns: A Taste of the World to Come

more difficult had it not been for the habit of Jewish poets to sign their works by including their own name in acrostic form at the beginning of each line.[6] Thus we can identify *Tzama Nafshi* (*My Soul Thirsts*) as written by the Sephardi Rabbi Abraham ibn Ezra (born in Tudela, 1089–1164) or *Barukh El Elyon* (*Blessed be God on High*) as written by the Ashkenazi Rabbi Barukh bar Samuel of Mainz (*c.* 1150–1221). But there are a number of writers whose signature we cannot identify: for example, there are two poets who sign themselves simply as Moses and another as Menahem. And there is at least one case in which the acrostic signature of a popular rabbi seems to have been forged. Rabbi Isaac Luria (known as the 'Divine Rabbi Isaac,' or the Ar"i, after his Hebrew initials) was a leading kabbalist in the Holy City of Safed in Galilee in the sixteenth century. He apparently wrote and signed three *zemirot*, one for each Sabbath meal, each preceded by *Atkinu Se'udata* (*Prepare the Meal*) in Aramaic.[7] But this was not enough for his followers: they took the popular *Yom zeh leYisrael* (*This is a Day for Israel*) signed simply 'Isaac', and added more verses with the acrostic 'Luria'. However, the shorter version of this song – with 'Isaac' but without 'Luria' – was included by Moses b Jacob of Kaffa (d. *c.* 1520) in the Kaffa prayer book before Isaac Luria was born in 1534.[8] This original *zemer* appears to have been written by Isaac Handali, and it became popular with rabbinic and Karaite Jews alike.[9] There are also a number of *zemirot* identified by their inclusion in collections of poetry of well-known authors, for example R Judah haLevi or R Solomon ibn Gabirol. *Zemirot* are found in many prayer books, and in the last few decades little booklets containing the most popular songs, together with the long Grace after Meals, have become a common memento given to guests at wedding meals (although they are not sung at such meals).

The Sabbath
Sabbath in the Bible
These *zemirot*, then, are sung at all three Sabbath meals, and many of them refer to food. Before examining these references, let us first set these table hymns in the cultural context of the Jewish Sabbath and the ways Jews observed it through history, beginning with the Hebrew Bible. The first Sabbath in the Bible belongs to God: it was the seventh day of creation when God rested from his work of creating the world, as told in Genesis chapters 1-2. The description of the second Sabbath, celebrated by the Israelites even before they received the laws of the Sabbath as part of the Ten Commandments, centres on food: manna, the miraculous bread from heaven with which God fed his people for forty years in the wilderness.[10] Every day they received a portion of manna calibrated for their needs, but on Friday they received a double portion to include the Sabbath meals. No manna fell on the Sabbath, so they did not have to work gathering and cooking it. The Ten Commandments given afterwards on Mount Sinai then tell the Israelites that they must always keep the Sabbath holy by refraining from work: 'Remember [observe] the Sabbath day to keep it holy. Six days you shall labour and do all your work: but the seventh day is a Sabbath to the Lord your God: in it you shall not do any work' (Exodus

20.8-10/Deuteronomy 5.12). The prophet Isaiah tells us that all people who keep the Sabbath will be rewarded by God: 'Thus says the Lord: keep judgement and do justice, for my salvation is near to come [...]. Happy is the man that does this [...] that keeps the Sabbath and does not profane it' (Isaiah 56.1-7). He then adds: 'If you restrain your foot because of the Sabbath, from pursuing thy business on my holy day; and call the Sabbath a delight [*oneg*] [...] then shall you delight yourself in the Lord, and I will [...] feed you' (Isaiah 58.13-14).

Isaiah's Sabbath observance has progressed here from passive refraining from work to active enjoyment, *oneg*. Both the double portion of manna for the Sabbath, and the concept of *oneg*, enjoyment – usually by eating – on the Sabbath, form part of the observance of the Sabbath through the ages and are referenced in the *zemirot*.

Sabbath in the Talmuds

Both Talmuds each have a whole tractate, *Shabbat*, devoted to the Sabbath, with instructions for observing it. We concentrate here on Babylonian Talmud (BT) Shabbat, pages 113a-119b, looking at the food in particular. Citing Isaiah 58.13, the text then expands on it: 'honouring' the Sabbath means washing, and changing to special clothes and walking differently, as well as not pursuing business. The discussion then moves to the biblical character of Ruth, who was the ancestor of the royal House of David, and therefore will be the ancestor of the Messiah. Not only is Ruth reported to have washed herself and changed her clothes, but she is said to have eaten, to have been satisfied and to have left food over (simply 'left' in the AV).[11] The rabbis expound: '*She ate*: in this world; *she was satisfied*: in the Messianic age; and *she will leave over*: in the World to Come.'[12] Sabbath food here is thus linked to Ruth, with a foretaste of the Messianic age and the World to Come – when there will be enough food for everyone to leave some over.

Later in this passage the rabbis rule that eating three meals on the Sabbath is obligatory. They promise rewards: those who join these meals will be saved from the travails of the Messiah and the wars that will precede his coming. The table should be set, they specify, before the Sabbath begins. At these meals, breaking and blessing the bread should be done over two loaves, in memory of the miraculously doubled portion of manna God sent his people in the wilderness.[13] And if we 'delight' in the Sabbath, God will reward us by feeding us (Isaiah 58.14 above), and will give us our hearts' desire (Psalms 37.4). This leads to a discussion on the meaning of the word 'delight' (*oneg*): 'It refers to the delight (*oneg*) of the Sabbath. With what do you show your delight in it? – Rab Judah son of R. Samuel b. Shilat said in Rab's name: With a dish of beets, large fish, and heads of garlic. R. Hiyya b. Ashi said in Rab's name: Even a trifle, if it is prepared in honour of the Sabbath, is 'delight'. What is [the trifle]? – Said R. Papa: *Casa de-harsana*.'[14] The rabbis make it clear here that the delight, *oneg,* of the Sabbath comes through enjoying good food. Their definition of good food may not be ours, but it is not confined to luxury foods such as 'large fish': if you intend to honour the Sabbath by eating, you can even do it by making *casa de-harsana*. This dish, made of tiny, smelly fish, seems to have signified the smallest amount of and/or the cheapest food (for example, once, when someone arrived at an inn unexpectedly, there was no food at all – not even a *casa de-harsana*).[15] So even the poorest foods, if made with the intention of honouring the Sabbath, can be part of 'delighting' in it.

The text then continues to detail the servile work various rabbis did 'to honour the Sabbath'. Many of them are connected to preparing food: 'R. Safra would singe the head [of an animal]. Raba salted shibuta fish. R. Huna lit the lamp. R. Papa plaited the wicks. R. Hisda cut up the beetroots. Rabbah and R. Joseph chopped wood. R. Zera kindled the fire [...].'[16]

The Sabbath, which begins at sunset on Friday, was greeted as a Queen or Bride: 'R. Hanina robed himself and stood at sunset of Sabbath eve [and] exclaimed, "Come and let us go forth to welcome Queen Sabbath." R. Jannai robed himself on Sabbath eve and exclaimed, "Come, O Bride, Come, O Bride!"'.[17] This personification of the Sabbath became extremely popular among the sixteenth-century kabbalists of Safed and was incorporated into Sabbath eve synagogue services everywhere, as well as into many *zemirot* in the home. Sabbath meals are thus metaphorized as the banquet of the Queen/Bride.

These Talmudic discussions I have cited are taken up and alluded to in the Sabbath *zemirot*, written some hundreds of years after the Babylonian Talmud, but relating to the same aspects of celebrating the Sabbath. Below is a description of a fictional Sabbath eve meal in a nineteenth-century Jewish novel, which sums up for us the context of the Sabbath atmosphere, the food, and the songs.

Israel Zangwill's Sabbath

Israel Zangwill's *Children of the Ghetto* (1892) depicts the transformative power of the Sabbath in the lives of the Jewish poor of Victorian London, in his chapter 'The Hebrew's Friday Night'. '[R]eturning from synagogue', the rabbi 'dropped into a delicious reverie – tasting in advance the Sabbath peace. The work of the week was over. The faithful Jew could enter on his rest – the narrow, miry streets faded before the brighter image of his brain. '*Come my beloved, to meet the Bride, the face of the Sabbath let us welcome.*' The rabbi here creates his Sabbath in his brain, oblivious of the harsher reality outside, aided by the imagery of the quoted Sabbath hymn. This quotation, ringing in the rabbi's head, is descended from the Talmudic text we saw above, and belongs to a hymn written by R Solomon Alkabetz, another sixteenth-century kabbalist from Safed, which is still sung today in the synagogue service which precedes the Sabbath meal. Weekday cares are left behind: 'Tonight his sweetheart would wear her Sabbath face, putting off the mask of the shrew, which hid not from him the angel countenance [...]. A cheerful warmth glowed in his heart, love for all the wonderful Creation dissolved him in tenderness.' Zangwill notes the Sabbath loaves on the table: 'with a curious plait of crust from point to point and thickly sprinkled with a drift of poppy-seed; and covered with a velvet cloth embroidered with Hebrew words.' On the table also stand a 'flask of wine and the silver goblet'. There is soup at this meal and 'fried fish made picturesque with sprigs of parsley,' but no meat is mentioned. The transformative power of the real food combined with transcendent song is made clear: 'after a few mouthfuls the Pole [a poor guest] knew himself a prince in Israel.' Zangwill relates to the *zemirot* specifically, on a slightly apologetic note: 'When supper was over, grace was chanted and then the *Zemiroth* was sung – songs summing up in light and jingling metre the very essence of holy joyousness – neither riotous nor ascetic [...]. For to feel the "delight of the Sabbath" is a duty and to take three meals thereon is a religious obligation.'[18] Zangwill even provides the text of three *Zemirot*, with their stress on meat, wine and fish; comfort for sorrow, and the rebuilding of the Temple to come. Zangwill's Sabbath, then, replaces and transcends weekday cares.

Foods Mentioned in the *Zemirot*
Bread and Wine
With this in mind, we turn now to look specifically at the food in the *zemirot*. We saw that the rabbis of the Talmud noted the formal blessings over wine and bread that begin the three Sabbath meals, and the required double portion of bread in memory of the double portion of manna. Real wine and two breads would thus be on the table of Jews celebrating the Sabbath with food and song, since they had become religious requirements.[19] So it is hardly surprising that they are mentioned frequently in many *zemirot,* where they form both the *halakhic* (religious regulatory) and the spiritual context. For example, *Menuhah veSimhah* (*Rest and Joy*) cites the two loaves and the *qiddush* (blessing) over the wine, as does *Yom zeh Mekhubad* (*This Day is Honoured*), and many other *zemirot*.

Other Foods
Would the other foods mentioned in the *zemirot* have been reflections of what was on the real table in front of the singers? In some cases we can safely assume that the food vocabulary in these songs alludes back to the Bible and Midrash. *Yom zeh Mekhubad* (*This Day is Honoured*) clearly alludes to the feasts of the book of Nehemiah (8.10) in 'eating sumptuously and drinking sweet beverages', and the 'savoury dishes', *matamim*, of many of the *zemirot* would have reminded the singers of the 'savoury dishes' made of 'two good kids of the goats' prepared for the patriarch Isaac by his wife Rebecca in the book of Genesis (27.1-41), and the many elaborations of this dish in rabbinic exegesis.[20] The *zemer*, *Tzur MiShelo Akhalnu* (*Rock from whose Stores we have Eaten*) begins with a verse which is repeated as a refrain:

> Rock from whose stores we have eaten,
> Bless Him, O constant companions,
> We have had sufficient and have left over,
> Just as the Lord has commanded.[21]

These lines echo the story of Ruth: she too ate of God's food, was satisfied, and left some over.

Food in Sabbath Table Hymns: A Taste of the World to Come

We saw how the two loaves on the table echo the double portion of manna in the wilderness. There too, and later in the Temple, the priests would set out twelve shewbreads as part of the ritual of the Sanctuary.[22] So shewbreads appear in *Ki Eshmera Shabbat* (*As I Keep the Sabbath*), and some hassidic families actually have twelve Shabbat loaves, rather than just the required two.[23]

Other foods mentioned in the *zemirot* which relate back to the Bible include the swans, quails, and fish of the refrain to the *zemer, Ma Yedidut Menuhatekh* (*We Cherish the Rest that Comes with You*). Swans are mentioned in a feast of King Solomon and were certainly seen as royal food in medieval Europe (they still belong to the Queen in England).[24] Quails, like manna, were miraculously provided for the Israelites in the wilderness.[25] Let us look at the context of this *zemer,* known from the sixteenth century, to hopefully understand better what is happening here:

> We cherish the rest that comes with you, O Sabbath Queen
> Run to greet you: Come, O royal Bride.
> Wearing our best clothing we light the Sabbath lamp with a blessing
> When all our labours are completed and mundane work forbidden,
>
> To delight in delights [*oneg*] – swans, quail and fish
> On the Sabbath eve we prepare all kinds of savoury dishes [*matamim*]
> While it is still daytime fattened fowl are made ready
> To be served with a variety of dishes, drinking spiced wines
> Thus to indulge in delicacies during all three meals,
>
> To delight in delights – swans, quail and fish

The following verses talk of both rich and poor honouring the Sabbath, and how, while business and money-making are forbidden, it is permitted to arrange marriages, teach children from books, and to sing, as well as to rest 'as if on a bed of roses'. The final verse says:

> Sabbath rest is a taste of the World to Come
> Everyone who delights in it will have much happiness
> And be spared the travails of the Messiah
> When our redemption will flourish and all sadness and sorrow be banished,
>
> To delight in delights – swans, quail and fish

It seems clear that few of the foods in this *zemer* are in fact the foods which would have been on the tables of those singing: it is unlikely that many – or any – Jews ate the 'swans and quails' of the refrain, or even the 'fattened fowl' of the second verse, although they may have had fish on their table in some form. Nor would everyone have had access to the costly 'spiced wines'. Recognizing this problem, one modern prayer book translates the refrain as: 'It is indeed a day of joy filled *with the likes of* succulent poultry, quails and fish.'²⁶ Moreover, some foods which would usually have been on the table are conspicuous by their absence – like the substantial Sabbath stew kept hot overnight (called *cholent* in Yiddish, or *adafina* in Ladino) which does not, to my knowledge, appear in any *zemirot*.²⁷

Other foods mentioned in the *zemirot* are simply metaphorical. Rabbinical literature, and especially medieval Hebrew poetry, was full of complex wordplays, so it is scarcely surprising that the *zemirot* often play on words connected to food and eating. Inevitably some go back to the Bible. Thus the love of God in *Yedid Nefesh* (*Beloved of the Soul*) tastes better than *nofet tzuf*, a honeycomb, referring to 'The Law of the Lord is perfect […] sweeter than honey and the honeycomb' (Psalms 19.8-11), while Isaac Luria in *Azamer beShevahin* (*I Will Sing with Praise*) prays for honey, alluding to the words of God 'like honey in the mouth' (Ezekiel 3.3). In *Yom Shabbaton* (*Sabbath Day of Rest*), the Sabbath is remembered like a 'sweet savour', an allusion to the 'sweet savour for God' of the offerings in the Sanctuary, mentioned in the Torah many times.²⁸ These allusions join the singers' awareness of the good smell of the real food on their table. Indeed, the rabbis wrote that, since the destruction of the Temple, the Jewish table has taken on some of the functions of the altar.²⁹

Some *zemirot* cite an earlier metaphorical wordplay: when R Joseph Caro wrote his code of Jewish law in the sixteenth century, he called it *Shulhan Arukh* (the *Prepared Table*), and a later commentary on it was called the *Mappah* (*Tablecloth*). Thus the mention of the 'prepared table' in a number of *zemirot* is bi-valent: referring both to the real table, which the Talmud specifies was to be prepared before the Sabbath, and to the metaphorical 'table' of laws, including Sabbath laws.

Meat

Meat is mentioned frequently in the *zemirot*. It is cited repeatedly together with the other delightful foods (*oneg*) – the double portion of bread (or manna), good wine, fish, and 'all savoury dishes' – in a number of *zemirot*. It was clearly very desirable, which does not mean it was always there. But the Hebrew word *basar* (meat) refers not only to the dead animal food we eat, but also to living human flesh. Thus the anonymous undated *zemer*, *Hai Adonai uBaruch Tzuri* (*May God live, and My Rock be Blessed*), quotes Psalm 136.25: God 'gives bread to all flesh.' But in a *zemer* written by the medieval Spanish poet, Abraham ibn Ezra, the play on 'flesh' is turned into an almost metaphysical conceit. Thus *Tzamah Nafshi* (*My Soul Thirsts*) begins: 'My soul thirsts for the Lord, for the living God', alluding to Psalm 63.3: 'O God […] my soul thirsts for thee / My flesh longs for thee in a dry and thirsty land.' Ibn Ezra does not actually quote the second half of the verse in the psalm, but takes up its content, the 'flesh' of the psalm, and uses it in his refrain, sung after every verse: 'My heart and flesh will sing to the living God.' Thus the flesh-and-blood living human both sings of and (sometimes) eats flesh of dead animals. Of course, the human will also die: ibn Ezra contrasts the cemetery, final 'home of all living', with the ever-living God. And he stresses that both eating and singing are done with the mouth, while the hand of God both holds the 'soul of all living' and contains food to feed the living.

Fish

Fish also appear frequently in the *zemirot*. We saw that the rabbis of the Talmud distinguished between eating desirable large fish and '*casa de-harsana*', a much less desirable dish which may have only come in small quantities. But if it was intended to honour the Sabbath, it was the intention which counted. Herring would have been as good as carp, although neither merit a mention as such in Talmud or *zemirot*. The rabbis of the Talmud do mention more legendary creatures: the large fish on which Joseph-who-honoured-the-Sabbath spent his last penny, and when cut open proved to have swallowed a large pearl, which rewarded Joseph with the means to honour many more Sabbaths. Joseph reappears in the *zemirot* too: in *Yom Shabbat Qodesh hu* (*The Sabbath Day is Holy*):

> Meat, wine and fish
> Should not be missing from our delights.
> And if these three are displayed before him,
> This will be his reward
> Whom [the King] delights to honour:
> Joseph cut a fish in half
> And found a pearl in its flesh.

We note here that the presence of the meat, wine, and fish is not to be taken for granted: if they are there, their presence is a reward from God.

Apart from the food, the *zemirot* relate to other aspects of the Jewish Sabbath: rest from work and weekday cares, as well as hopes for the future: both mundane hopes of marrying off the children, and eschatological hopes of the rebuilding of the Temple and the coming of the Messiah. Most of the *zemirot* traditionally sung on the Sabbath eve end with some sort of reference to these future hopes, including hopes of the World to Come. Thus *Menuhah veSimhah* (*Rest and Joy*) ends:

> With two loaves and blessing over wine,
> With many savoury dishes [*matamim*] and a generous spirit,
> Those who delight [*oneg*] in [the Sabbath] will see much goodness,
> In the coming of the Redeemer and the life of the World to Come.

There are indeed several midrashim which refer to the banquets to be enjoyed by the righteous in the World to Come.[30] God is said to have killed and salted the female Leviathan, a gigantic fish, to preserve her flesh for the righteous.[31] Thus mentions of the World to Come often imply food to come as well.

The Audience

It is clear from the *zemirot* we have considered that their learned authors were thoroughly familiar with biblical and Talmudic texts. What of their audience? How many of the ordinary Jews who sang understood what they were singing about in Hebrew (and sometimes Aramaic)? Albert Kohn proposes that singing *zemirot* was originally an elite rabbinical custom, which gradually penetrated ordinary Jewish homes: small booklets with collections of *zemirot* begin to appear from the fourteenth century.[32] Some *zemirot* were translated into German, at least from the mid-seventeenth century, while translations into the vernacular Yiddish aimed at women exist from at least 1854.[33] That women were singing we know from seventeenth-century rabbinic complaints disapproving of this custom, even at family meals.[34] But how many women – or men – were literate in any language? We can perhaps infer that certain keywords in the Hebrew texts should have been comprehensible to many from the prayers – the Sabbath, God's name, rest, the Messiah, the Temple, Eden and the World to Come – as well as food words – wine and bread, and possibly also fish and meat.

Transitional Genre, Transitional Space

Modern scholarship on Sephardi Hebrew poetry from medieval Spain points out that there existed a tension between traditional *piyyutim*, sacred synagogue poetry, and newer Arab-influenced poetry whose content included songs of wine and love, even homoerotic love.[35] I should like to propose here that in some ways *zemirot* (both from Sephardi as well as Ashkenazi contexts) can be seen as middle ground, a transitional genre. They are indeed sacred Sabbath songs, but they also deal with the material world, with foods, clothes, matchmaking, as well as more spiritual aspects. The foods they mention often refer to real foods on the table in front of the singers which they bless and eat, but the foods are also often idealized. As noted, there is no *cholent* or *adafina*, no herring or sardines, but savoury dishes, sometimes mythical ones, with the likes of swans, quails, and fattened fowl along with spiced wines. Thus the *zemirot* sung on the Sabbath are transformative: they convert the material world to a transitional space.[36] The real food on the table and in the mouth combine with the imagined foods of the songs to create a fantasized sacred bubble outside weekday time and space, giving the singers a taste of the future 'World to Come', a hint of the banquet of the righteous in the celestial Garden of Eden.

Notes

1 *Zemirot*, songs, *zemer* in the singular.
2 Naphtali Ben-Menahem, *Zemirot shel Shabbat* (Jerusalem, 1949).
3 Midrash Esther Rabbah iii, 13. For a brief explanation of the Talmudic literature, see Susan Weingarten, 'Nuts for the Children: The Evidence of the Talmudic Literature', *Nurture: Proceedings of the 2003 Oxford Symposium on Food and Cookery*, ed. by Richard Hosking (Bristol: FootWork, 2004), pp. 264-72.
4 MTamid vii 4.
5 BTBerakhot 57b.
6 Acrostics exist in Hebrew poetry from the time of the Bible, where some psalms (e.g. Psalms 145) were written with each line beginning with a different letter in alphabetical order. In the Middle Ages it became popular for poets to sign their works in acrostic form by beginning each line with the letters

7   These *zemirot*, based on kabbalistic concepts from the *Zohar*, are sung today by Hassidic Jews.
8   *Yom Zeh leYisrael* also appears in *Mahzor Aram Tzova* published in Venice in 1527: see Y. Weingarten, *HaSiddur haMefurash haShalem* (*The Complete Annotated Prayerbook*) (Jerusalem, 1991), who also notes that the attribution to Luria is impossible.
9   Kaffa is present-day Feodosiya in Crimea, once a port at the end of the Silk Road: LJ Weinberger, *Jewish Hymnography: A Literary History* (Oxford: The Lippman Library of Jewish Civilization, 1998), pp. 343, 348.
10 Exodus 16.11-35; Numbers 11.1-9.
11 Ruth 3.3-6, 2.14.
12 BT Shabbat 113b.
13 Exodus 18.1-36.
14 BT Shabbat 118b.
15 BT Bava Batra 60b: see Susan Weingarten, 'Fish and Fish Products in Late Antique Palestine and Babylonia in Their Social and Geographical Contexts: Archaeology and the Talmudic Literature', *Journal of Maritime Archaeology*, 13.3 (2018), 235-45.
16 BT Shabbat 119a.
17 BT Shabbat 119a.
18 Israel Zangwill, *Children of the Ghetto* (New York: Macmillan, 1899 [1892]), pp. 222-26.
19 Sometimes no more than raisin 'wine': on allowing it for Passover if ordinary wine is unavailable, see Rabbi Elazar Vormensis, *Oratio ad Pascam*, ed. by Simcha Emmanuel (Jerusalem, 2006) p. 110.
20 See for example *Barukh El Elyon* and *Menuhah veSimhah*, among others.
21 Trans. in Zangwill, p. 226, and adapted by the author.
22 Leviticus 24.5-9.
23 Some families braid their two loaves with six strands of dough each for the same reason.
24 I Kings 5.3; others translate 'geese; as 'succulent poultry'.
25 Numbers 11:31-34.
26 *Siddur Avodat HaLev* (New Milford, CT: Rabbinical Council of America, 2018).
27 See Claudia Roden, *The Book of Jewish Food: An Odyssey from Samarkand and Vilna to the Present Day* (Harmondsworth: Penguin, 1997), pp. 125-28, 365-68. *Schalet* (=cholent) does appear in Heine's poem *Prinzessin Sabbat*, but as a satire on Schiller.
28 Leviticus 1.9 and many parallels.
29 BT Berakhot 55a; for a suggestive analysis of the table setting, albeit in an earlier period, see Jonathan Brumberg-Kraus, Susan Marks, and Jordan Rosenblum, 'Ten Theses on Meals in Early Judaism', *Meals in Early Judaism: Social Formation at the Table,* ed. by Susan Marks and Hal Taussig (New York: Palgrave Macmillan, 2014), pp. 13-39.
30 See Jordan D. Rosenblum, 'Dining in(to) the World to Come', in *olam ha-zeh v'olam ha-ba: This World and the World to Come in Jewish Belief and Practice*, ed. by Leonard J. Greenspoon (West Lafayette, IN: Purdue University Press, 2017), pp. 105-14.
31 BT Bava Batra 74b.
32 Albert E. Kohn, 'A History of the Jewish Custom to Sing around the Shabbat Table (1200-1600)' (unpublished master's thesis, Jewish Theological Seminary, 2018), p. 27. I am grateful to Albert for his discussion of *zemirot*.
33 J. Buxtorf, *Judenschül* (Basel, 1643), ch. 10; *Siddur Qorban Minhah* (Vilna, 1854).
34 Joseph Yuspa Seligman, *Yosif Ometz* (Frankfurt-am-Main, 1927–1928), p. 134.
35 Ross Brann, *The Compunctious Poet: Cultural Ambiguity and Hebrew Poetry in Muslim Spain* (Baltimore: Johns Hopkins University Press, 1991).
36 My concept of 'transitional space' owes much to the 'relational space' discussed by Y. Rotman ('The Relational Mind: In Between History, Psychology and Anthropology', *History of Psychology*, 24.2 (2021), 142-63 <https://doi.org/10.1037/hop0000175>).

Teaching Cookery Gets Personal: Harnessing Imagination to Feed the Will to Learn

Nikki Werner

It's quite a cringey story but we were driving to my auntie's house in England and we were in a traffic jam and I saw this big truck. It had a picture of a pig on it and said 'Veganism: thinking of me as a some-one, not a some-thing', and that made me feel really sad.

My sister was veggie and I'd always talked about it but I loved meat too much to ever actually do it. So I decided after that Christmas lunch, which we were on the way to, I would try my best to go vegetarian. To be honest, I did not think I would last, but now I've been veggie for three years.[1]

This was the first story Molly told me. Molly was fourteen years old when she joined me on a journey of cooking and learning (on both our parts) for this paper. Before starting out we didn't know each other well at all – we were acquainted through her parents – but I did know she was vegetarian, because I remembered this story.

'The reason you remember and enjoy stories,' says Gillian Judson, 'is because they make you feel feelings'.[2] Judson is a scholar of and an advocate for imagination in education, as is Kieran Egan, whose book *Teaching as Storytelling* started me on this journey. Egan defines imagination as 'the capacity to think of things as possibly being so; it is an intentional act of mind; it is the source of invention, novelty, and generativity; it is […] a capacity that greatly enriches rational thinking'.[3]

As a teacher of cooking I became interested in the capacity to imagine as a way of showing not just how to chop an onion, but also why anyone might want to do so in the first place, because my reasons for cooking come from a place of meaning far removed from stainless-steel surfaces or chef's whites.

That said, the Netflix series *Chef's Table* features chefs around the world who tell their stories through their cooking.[4] A simple mechanism often applies: the memory of a much-loved dish serves as the springboard for reimagining it and the story behind it connects the two.

The same mechanism is at play when memories of Sunday coffee with my grandfather (that live on in my imagination) seal my allegiance to his *Kugelhupf* recipe yet at the same time inspire me as a sourdough baker to reimagine it without chemical leavening, which in turn improves my baking skills.

But why should this mechanism be limited to my family cookbook or to fine-dining chefs who use it to turn the lights on in their diners' eyes? What chefs can never give their diners is the essential finishing seasoning: the memory itself.

If each person possesses their own finishing seasoning, a memory that stirs emotion and provides meaning, then why not work with that to turn the lights on in the eyes of those who might not otherwise feel moved to learn how to cook?

After the radical changes required of teaching during lockdown, advocates for alternative education models see an opportunity to move away from a one-size-fits-all approach and towards prioritizing creativity and critical thinking for lifelong learning.[5]

Similarly, I was curious to see what would happen if teaching cookery started in a different place. In the spirit of 'what if', this paper is not a proof of concept but a proof of possibility: could engaging imagination, with the learner as the protagonist, fuel curiosity and drive acquiring skills?

The Role of Imagination in Lifelong Learning

On considering meaning making in the landscape of South African dining, someone who moves storytelling-through-food beyond his own story is Tapiwa Guzha. He describes Tapi Tapi, his Cape Town shop where he sells the ice cream he makes, as an educational initiative.

Flavours such as *bonongwe* (amaranth), okra and plum, or boiled peanut open the door for conversations about ingredient origins, personal origins, and food culture. As does the art he creates on and for the walls, which is rooted in African mythology and cosmology. On asking how Tapi Tapi became a means of shifting consciousness, Guzha explained:

> I made baobab, Mazoe Orange, and maputi, so popped maize [ice cream]. And that was the first time I tasted ice cream that I connected with [.... S]ure you can have a nice ice-cream memory but that was the first time I was [...] connecting to my childhood [...] and I realized, 'Oh there's actually a nice emotional connection to this experience'.
>
> And then I did a few events and [...] people were reacting very emotionally to the representation. And that's when it started morphing into this rehabilitative tool and also educational tool [...] trying to inspire the people to do whatever work they do with the continent in mind.[6]

Acknowledging the integral role of emotion in learning is the focus of Mary Helen Immordino-Yang's work (referenced by Judson), which brings together education, psychology, and neuroscience. She writes, 'the aspects of cognition that are recruited most heavily in education [...] are both profoundly affected by emotion and in fact subsumed within the processes of emotion.'[7]

On the role of imagination, Peter van Alphen draws a line from Kieran Egan to Rudolf Steiner: 'Both theorists argue that teaching needs to integrate intellect with emotion for learning to be meaningful in schools, and that by means of imagination this integration can be achieved.'[8] Steiner founded the first Waldorf school, and one of the defining principles of a Waldorf education is that craft work and art are not only integrated with academic study, but they are also seen as necessary for developing a 'living thinking'.[9]

As van Alphen expounds, when fully experiencing a subject, learners create flexible concepts, which can develop with them as they mature. By contrast, a concept reduced to facts or skills, presented as pre-digested material (textbooks) and adopted by the learner (memorized), can remain fixed even in adulthood.[10] Van Alphen, the founder of the Centre for Creative Education in Cape Town, describes a teacher's focus as: 'How do they bring out the meaning, how do they bring out the values, how do they get children completely immersed […]'.[11]

Cooking is naturally immersive, and regularly cooking a beloved dish deepens understanding with each return, until movements and decisions become second nature. If a finished recipe is a fixed concept, reimagining a dish might create a flexible concept that evolves with the learner through their life.

Learning as a lifelong pursuit is central to *Peripheral Visions* by cultural anthropologist Mary Catherine Bateson, who writes of complex mythology learned through relationship in San culture.[12] The art of sharing knowledge through imagination and storytelling goes back to the Indigenous peoples in South Africa.[13]

Egan describes stories as a culturally universal way of making sense of our experience.[14] In the context of food, we all have stories because eating is a biological necessity, yet in an industrialized reality our stories are often divorced from both the eating and the cooking.

To use storytelling as a tool for engaging the imagination, educators look for the story in existing curriculum content, and food education programmes such as The Edible Schoolyard Project do include lessons that explore food memories.[15] The fundamental differences in my approach are:

1. The food memory is the starting point.
   The original dish is the portal to meaningful learning and the reimagined dish the hook on which learning hangs, allowing for further reimagining in years to come.
2. The learner's story informs the content created for learning.
   This gives the learner a reason to learn how to cook from the first lesson because they need to acquire the skills to realize their vision, which tells their story.

The Age for Conceptual Thought

The earliest age for which the task of reimagining might be the right fit and facilitate learning as a life's work appears to be fourteen years old. In Egan's five stages of understanding, there is the opportunity for 'Philosophic' understanding to develop during the teen years, where discovering laws and theories that make sense of the world brings together what previously seemed disconnected.[16] In Waldorf education adolescence is a time for developing independent thinking.[17] As teacher Torin Finser writes:

> Around age fourteen, the more formed cognitive and intellectual thinking life of the teenager begins to develop strongly. Now the student works with teachers who are specialists in their fields. [… T]here awakens a quest for the truth, and this pursuit of truth takes them on journeys as profound as those of King Arthur's knights seeking the Holy Grail.[18]

Cooking with Molly

Molly and I worked through five two-hour lessons, meeting roughly once a week, mostly in my home kitchen. Before we began Molly referred to our time together as 'an adventure', which was prescient given the story arc that took shape.

Lesson One: Finding the Story

'I'm quite nervous,' said Molly, as she stood in the middle of my kitchen, 'because I don't know how to cook'. Her honesty was disarming. 'So am I,' I admitted, 'this is new for me too', and that set the tone for us finding our way together.

We were both in unchartered territory and no matter how compelled I felt to plan and prepare all possible answers, this process demanded improvisation. As Bateson writes, 'my own greatest resource as a teacher is the learned willingness to wing it in public […]. This is the challenge – improvising, learning on the job – that my students will confront all their lives.'[19]

To create a space where imagination could thrive and all contributions were valid, we started by affirming Molly's fourteen years of accumulated knowledge and skill that lay ready to be awakened in a new context: cooking. Applying knowledge and skills in such new contexts is what Bateson calls 'the generation of novel performances from underlying competences'.[20]

I handed Molly a journal to document what she felt was important in a way that worked for her: a gesture of my invitation and her acceptance to explore the world of cooking together.

We brainstormed her favourite dishes and food memories to see where they intersect and selected one to work on. This is how Molly described her dish and the story behind it:

> Bacon-lentil-potato is the kind of meal you eat from a bowl sitting on the couch on a Sunday night. My mom would make it without me even asking for it. Like if I'd had a hard day at school, I would come home and it would just be there. It's not the kind of dish you make for a dinner party but it's so comforting.
>
> She started making it before I was vegetarian but now, without the bacon, it doesn't taste the same, because then it's basically just lentils and potatoes. So she doesn't really make it any more because we haven't found the right bacon substitute.

Lesson Two: Exploring Ingredients and Cooking Methods

Molly's overarching narrative had a clear challenge: bringing a much-loved dish underpinned by bacon into her new context as a vegetarian. So we had the constraints necessary for imagination to be generative. As Rist and Schneider elaborate, 'mere wealth of imagination has no value. It must connect with given conditions, with the external situation and with inner experiences, if change is to constitute progress.'[21]

In equipping Molly to reimagine, I presented ingredients and relevant cooking methods, and we tasted and discussed with Molly quickly finding her way to a dish of her own.

It developed around an aromatic base of caramelized onions and garlic (in keeping with her love of the bulb) and an equal ratio of lentil to potato. 'It's quite nice using garlic so it isn't one of the actual main ingredients,' commented Molly. 'It's more a side thing, like salt, just to add flavour.'

Her caramelized onion idea, she later explained, was because she imagined them to be sweet but also crunchy and was inspired by thoughts of maple-cured bacon and bacon with maple syrup. One area where I consciously steered the process, with Molly's blessing, was that rather than adding a meat substitute we recreate what bacon contributed: salty, smoky, umami, crisp.

When analyzing what she loved about the dish, Molly led with texture:

> I think it's just everything working together. The lentils are squishy but they're not as squishy as canned lentils, so you still have to chew them. And the potato is soft so it's easy to bite into but then the bacon is always really, really crispy. So [...] you have every single texture in your mouth at once.

After tasting different varieties Molly chose green lentils because of their resistance to the bite and we tested bringing in a crisp element with the potatoes, which she suggested roasting to different degrees of doneness:

> Having a few soft potatoes, then a few that just crunch is quite nice. So you can make them together but take some off earlier and continue half of them so it's like two different ingredients [...] then it also doesn't take up any extra time and space.

When evaluating the flavour of floury versus waxy potatoes, the term umami needed explanation, so we returned to a story Molly had shared in the first lesson of her friends daring one another to taste a piece of seaweed when out surfing. This experience framed our exploration of the fifth taste. This is one example of how Molly's personal narrative and purpose in achieving her outcome determined where the content needed to go, creating stories within the story.

The dish continued to evolve in the third lesson when, while peeling potatoes, Molly suggested we fry the peels for extra crispness. She opted to finish with flaky sea salt, again to boost crunch, and I sourced smoked salt to bring us closer to bacon.

It was not in thinking that Molly needed my support but rather in the mechanical skills, the necessary link between imagination and the physical world that could bring her reimagined dish to life.

Lesson Three: Learning to Cook

Our first cooking session was a baptism of fire for both of us. Molly persevered in wrangling two large onions while becoming accustomed to the feel of a knife in her hand, her eyes stinging with tears. I realized how much I'd taken for granted as a seasoned cook inured to allium fumes.

My ability to apply pressure to keep an onion together while chopping was different than hers, which highlighted the extent to which physical learning needs to be informed by the learner too. It required rethinking how I chop and making it work for her.

We tried dividing the cutting into two stages and then switched to the same weight in baby brown onions so the relative size gave Molly more control. Showing what aspects were flexible in figuring out a solution reinforced the core principles that weren't: the fan cuts, even-sized pieces, and the claw grip.

The need to rationalize lesson hours by ticking off the techniques covered exposed the unlearning I have to do to instil the kind of mastery Rist and Schneider call practical consciousness.[22] In this case, that might be observing at what point gently caramelizing onions develop butterscotch aromas or how to hold a knife to use it effectively while conserving energy.

Molly was up for the challenge. My challenge was allowing her to lead fully, hone her instincts, and make mistakes if necessary when I know so well what to do.

Lesson Four: Practicing Skills

Molly had expressed how much she loved our garden, so we resumed our onion chopping under the lemon tree. Just as we started almost every lesson, I brewed her a pot of loose-leaf rooibos tea and poured it from a teapot with a knitted cosy. Molly had pronounced it the best tea she'd ever tasted, and I like to think it may have illustrated the beauty of ritual.

The raw honey that sweetened her tea became a talking point, again because of how delicious she found it, which led to a tasting at our local honey purveyor where the beekeeper showed how different flowers influence flavour, highlighting the role of provenance.

When Molly asked, 'Do you wear an apron every time you cook?', I realized approaching cooking as a practice might be modelled rather than spelled out explicitly. These touchpoints, none of which were planned with content in mind, underlined the power of showing, or tasting, over telling.

It also underscored teaching as the transmission of a way of being, something long understood by the Khoi and the San, who are recognized as the traditional knowledge holders of the use of *Aspalathus linearis,* the plant from which rooibos tea is made.[23]

Lesson Five: Coming Home to the Table

Molly's home had the air of an imminent feast. She had set the table with flowers, linen napkins, and the bowls reserved for bacon-lentil-potato. For the final lesson she would cook her reimagined dish in her kitchen and present it to her family with the story behind it.

Molly put on music, and we settled into the preparations. When her parents wandered in while she was mincing garlic, she asked if they knew how to remove the germ from a clove and proceeded to show them. It reminded me of organizational psychologist Adam Grant's words, 'the best way to learn is to teach someone else'.[24] When frying, Molly urged her sister to try the puffed, golden potato peels. And after lunch she brewed us all a pot of rooibos tea.

Lunch had turned into a lentil tasting menu of sorts as I'd been inspired to develop a dish of my own and Molly's mum joined in cooking her original. It also happened to be Mother's Day. Molly, given the option of any medium to tell the story, had chosen to write a poem. She finished reading it to joyous applause and dewy eyes. Her story, the all-important bridge between the past and who she is now, had brought us back to emotion. This is as Molly presented it:

Mum's Milestone Meal Reincarnated
So the dish I made is a reincarnation of my mom's dish, which she used to make for me. I can't eat it anymore because it had meat in it, so I decided to remake it vegetarian. This fits perfectly with Mother's Day because as I was making it, it reminded me of all the good memories I had with me and my mom, some of which I didn't even know I had.

'One Special Meal'
One special meal
Turns a house to a home
One special dinner
Makes you feel less alone

The bacon sizzling
Fills the kitchen with its smell
A nostalgic feeling
That's very personal

The lentils boil
And so does anticipation
But mom slaps away your hand
Cause she needs to work on
Preparation

The potatoes frying
As they're stirred around

Teaching Cookery Gets Personal:

Everything added together
To make a compound
You take your bowl
And go and take a seat
The feeling of love
Fills your heart as you eat

Sadly through the years
The meal disappeared
So here I am to tell you
I've made it reappear

The steps might be different
And some ingredients too
But I promise you mum
This meal is for me and you

Reflecting on Molly's Feedback

The journey had a fairy-tale ending. If actions speak louder than words, a high point was seeing Molly standing at her kitchen island casually demonstrating the rocking cutting technique for parsley that she had mastered to make her dish. This was Molly's feedback:

Nikki: How did you find the whole experience?

Molly: I found it really, really fun […]. I was nervous […] because I didn't personally […] think I was very good at cooking, I didn't really find an enjoyment [in cooking] before I did this, but when we were doing it I kind of realized that anyone can […] cook if you're in the right mindset of doing it, then it was very practical, which made it a lot more fun.

Nikki: Did you have a highlight moment?

Molly: Well, I really, really enjoyed on the first day when we went through meals and a lot of meals and memories that I'd forgotten about kind of came back, so that was definitely a highlight moment. And then in the actual practical when we were cooking there were kind of lots of little ones, especially when we first did the deep frying, I found that really interesting, I don't why but that really stuck with me.

There is validation of intent in that Molly initiated frying the potato peels whereas other techniques, like roasting the potatoes, were simply presented as tools for her to work with.

When asked about her greatest learning Molly returned to the brainstorm, which is where we found the meaning:

Nikki: And did you feel like you had a […] light-bulb moment?
Molly: I kind of had a light-bulb moment when we were talking about it, it was kind of like, whoa, this really clicked something and cooking is really more than just […] warming up food, putting stuff together and eating it, it's a lot more about the mindset.

Molly leading with how this affected her thinking is undoubtedly a positive outcome in terms of igniting a lasting relationship with cooking.

That first lesson effectively generated a table of contents for Molly's own book of cooking knowledge, and her journey can continue with or without me. She picked up on this:

Nikki: […] How did you find the book […] was it helpful?
Molly: [...] My book [holding up the journal]? It was very helpful […] especially the first page with the brainstorm of food, now I'm remembering a lot of these meals and I'm […] seeing that some of them are really simple and that if I could have made like bacon-lentil I can definitely go back and figure out my own way for the others.

The ease with which Molly made connections, came up with ideas and asked pertinent questions goes some way to confirming fourteen as an appropriate age for this rich kind of learning. As the educator I didn't anticipate the extent to which my own imagination would come to life. The content flowed naturally and aligned with ease. The difficulty lay in prioritizing.

Going Forward

The promising result is motivation for further exploration. There is much work to be done on how this approach could have greater reach, play out with a group of learners, be culturally relevant, and benefit learners for whom food and the associated memories are not positive.

If the by-products of forging a connection with cooking include a sense of agency and a path to selfhood, perhaps there is also a higher aim of rewriting personal narratives and connecting with our true stories. It is only in strengthening our individual stories that we may contribute to a robust collective food history.

Acknowledgements

Thank you to Molly and her family; Rob Siebörger (Emeritus Associate Professor, School of Education, University of Cape Town) for sharing insights and education books, specifically *Teaching as Storytelling*; the Centre for Creative Education for library access; Tapiwa Guzha, Peter van Alphen, and Michael Oak Waldorf School teachers Vincent Message, Gillian Mathew, and Graham Scannell for interviews; and Vincent for lending *Educating through Arts and Crafts*.

Notes

1. Quotations from the sessions with Molly (whose last name is withheld for privacy) come from edited transcripts of recorded conversations in April 2021 and a recorded WhatsApp video call on 15 May 2021.
2. Gillian Judson, 'Engage Emotion, Engage Imagination: Cognitive Tools at Work', *TED*, September 2017 <https://www.ted.com/talks/gillian_judson_engage_emotion_engage_imagination_cognitive_tools_at_work> [accessed 26 October 2021]
3. Kieran Egan, 'A Very Short History of Imagination', *Imaginative Education*, last paragraph <http://ierg.ca/wp-content/uploads/2014/04/History-of-Imagination.pdf> [accessed 26 October 2021].
4. *Chef's Table*, Netflix, 2015-2019 <https://www.netflix.com/za/title/80007945> [accessed 1 November 2021].
5. Bethan Staton, 'Educators Around World Seek to Take Axe to Exam-Based Learning', *Financial Times*, 22 January 2021 <https://www.ft.com/content/9d64e479-182c-4dbd-96fe-0c26272a5875> [accessed 1 November 2021].
6. Guzha is Zimbabwean and describes these ingredients as part of universal experience in Zimbabwe (excerpt from transcript of recorded interview, 13 April 2021).
7. Mary Helen Immordino-Yang and Antonio Damasio, 'We Feel, Therefore We Learn: The Relevance of Affective and Social Neuroscience to Education', *Mind, Brain and Education,* 1 (2007) 3 -10 (p. 7) <https://onlinelibrary.wiley.com/doi/10.1111/j.1751-228X.2007.00004.x>
8. Peter van Alphen, 'Imagination as a Transformative Tool in Primary School Education', *Research on Steiner Education,* 2 (2011), 16-34 (p. 32) <https://www.rosejourn.com/index.php/rose/article/view/71/99> [Accessed 26 October 2021].
9. After completing and documenting the qualitative research, I became aware of discriminatory remarks in Rudolf Steiner's original and complete works. I wholly and emphatically reject those remarks, and all discriminatory views and beliefs. This paper seeks to promote more effective ways of learning for the whole of humanity by extracting the practical value of teaching methodologies that put imagination at the forefront. The Waldorf institutions mentioned were approached for their inclusionary stance; Michael Martin, 'The Influence of Work on Thinking', in *Educating through Arts and Crafts,* ed. by Michael Martin (Sussex: Steiner Schools Fellowship Publications, 1999) p. 206.
10. Van Alphen, p. 24.
11. Excerpt from transcript of recorded interview with Peter van Alphen, 7 April 2021.
12. Mary Catherine Bateson, *Peripheral Visions: Learning Along the Way* (New York: HarperCollins, 1994), p. 203 < https://archive.org/details/peripheralvision00mary> [accessed 8 April 2021]
13. An archive of stories shared by ǁkabbo and other contributors forms part of The Digital Bleek and Lloyd collection (listed in UNESCO's Memory of the World Register) <http://lloydbleekcollection.cs.uct.ac.za> [accessed 1 November 2021].
14. Kieran Egan, *Teaching as Storytelling* (London: Routledge, 1988), p. 2.
15. Egan, *Teaching as Storytelling;* The Edible Schoolyard Project <https://edibleschoolyard.org> [accessed 28 May 2021]
16. Imaginative Education Research Group (IERG), 'Kinds of Understanding and the Process of Imaginative Education', *Imaginative Education*, para. 13 of 22 <https://ierg.ca/about-us/a-brief-guide-to-imaginative-education/> [accessed 26 October 2021]
17. Roy Wilkinson, *Commonsense Schooling* (England: Robinswood Press, 1990), p. 28.
18. Torin M. Finser, *School as a Journey* (Hudson, NY: Anthroposophic Press, 1994), pp. 231-32.
19. Bateson, p. 212.
20. Bateson, p. 208.
21. Georg Rist and Peter Schneider, *Integrating Vocational and General Education: A Rudolf Steiner School* (Hamburg: UNESCO Institute for Education, 1979), p. 149 <https://unesdoc.unesco.org/ark:/48223/pf0000036368> [Accessed 26 October 2021]
22. Rist and Schneider, p. 164.
23. Natural Justice, 'The Traditional Knowledge of the Khoikhoi and San Acknowledged through the

Benefit-Sharing Agreement for Rooibos', *Natural Justice*, 1 November 2019 <https://naturaljustice.org/the-traditional-knowledge-of-the-khoikhoi-and-san-acknowledged-through-the-benefit-sharing-agreement-for-rooibos/#> [accessed 26 October 2021]

24 'A New Education Story with 5x15 and Big Change', *5x15 Stories,* 29 April 2021 <https://www.youtube.com/watch?v=XY3TXdpOnQo> [accessed 26 October 2021]

A Short History of Science Fiction and Fantasy Tie-in Cookbooks

Shana Worthen

In *Alice in Wonderland,* how can a cook recreate what little Alice consumed at the Mad Hatter's tea party? The text provides limited evidence (tea with milk, bread and butter, a discussion of treacle), but the authors of cookbooks inspired by *Alice* offer a great variety of proposed recipes in answer. Those cookbooks, responding to the text of *Alice in Wonderland,* or later media (films, graphic novels, games) based on it, are tie-in cookbooks. They are a means to attempt to experience first-hand a flavour or sensation which was previously in an untasteable medium, such as a book or film. They are marketed to both those who are already fans of the fictional source material, as well as to those who had always assumed the Turkish delight in C.S. Lewis' *The Lion, the Witch, and the Wardrobe* was a purely fictional confection. Tie-in cookbooks range from ones that only use the name of a well-known brand for promotional purposes to others that intentionally expand the details of a constructed, fictional world. Tie-in cookbooks began to be published in 1969, with the subgenre thriving in the 2000s and beyond, as evidenced by dedicated publishing imprints and the sheer variety of published titles. Focusing on science fiction and fantasy, which most benefit from the expanded worldbuilding which these cookbooks can provide, this paper will document the development of these tie-in cookbooks in greater detail.

Methodology

The work for this survey was primarily done as a bibliographic survey, compiling a list of over 230 tie-in cookbooks in order to examine the overall patterns which emerged. The survey is an initial foray into this data; there are still many cookbooks not yet located, even more are being published, and many other themes in the data could benefit from further exploration. The methodological approach presents several challenges.

Firstly, to what degree is the absence of pre-1969 tie-in cookbooks a result of the lack of ISBN numbers, rather than an actual absence? On this front, the most reassuring evidence is the numerous recent tie-in cookbooks for inspirations from the 1960s and earlier, including the 'Hollywood Hotplates' series from the 1990s.

Secondly, it is unsurprising that small-circulation fannish productions are incompletely catalogued. This survey has used the generous work done by fans on fanlore.org in compiling evidence, but it is unavoidably incomplete.[1] Furthermore, new fan cookbooks are being produced all the time. One frustration of this project was catching glimpses of the many small-circulation fandom-themed foodzines. Anyone failing to support a one-off foodzine in the six weeks when it is available for purchase misses out entirely.

Thirdly, this bibliography only comprises English-language cookbooks thus far. The English language corpus is the largest available, but a multilingual approach would be more indicative of global trends in the long run.

Fourthly, there are works whose qualification for inclusion is ambiguous when copies of the books themselves have not all been checked for verification. A cookbook written for a science fiction convention may or may not include tie-in recipes. Consider *The Conflux Cookbook: Five Historical Feasts*. Written for a science fiction convention, the feasts were intended by organizer Gillian Polack to be straightforward historical recreations.[2] Yet such was the context, many of the attendees processed them as a lens for experiencing aspects of historical fiction instead. As fantasy author Garth Nix wrote of the feasts, 'while we may not become Elizabeth Bennet or Mr Darcy, we can, if we are very lucky, eat their food.'[3]

Finally, all of these works can be interpreted as part of more than one genre, and the complexity of that overlap means that this survey often simplifies when pigeonholing where a given recipe collection belongs. Consider that the earliest tie-in cookbooks are also children's cookbooks, that children's cookbooks are just as often targeted at parents instead of the children themselves, and that cookbooks named after famous individuals are also celebrity cookbooks. It could therefore be constructive to consider *The Pooh Cookbook* as a children's celebrity cookbook targeted at adults, with Winnie-the-Pooh as the celebrity.

1969 and the 1970s

Children's cookbooks begin to be widely published in the late 1960s, both in English and in the wider world.[4] In part because of that, the late 1960s are also when tie-in cookbooks first begin to be published, with both the child's fantasy-based *The Pooh Cook Book* and the comics-based *The Peanuts Cook Book* first printed in 1969.[5] Precursors to the tie-in cookbooks include storytelling children's cookbooks, such as 1912's *The Mary Frances Cook Book*, and the 1965 comic-strip based recipe ('cookstrips') collection, *Len Deighton's Action Cook Book*, which established an early association between comics and cookbooks.[6]

Television programs for children inspired several cookbooks in the 1970s. Children were the target audience for a growing number of tie-in cookbooks, such as those featuring Peter Rabbit, the Mighty Marvel Superheroes, and Sesame Street.[7] But they were not the only audience.

In 1973, *Cooking Out of This World* was published by Ballantine Books, a collection of recipes by science fiction authors, with commentary. (For example, Alfred Bester wrote: 'People have been kind enough to admire the originality of that novel [*The Demolished Man*]. I'm proud of that but even prouder of a recipe for striped bass which I invented at the same time [...].')[8] While not explicitly a tie-in cookbook, its audience was primarily adult fans of those authors' works, and it is worth considering it as an early instance of the community cookbooks produced by science fiction and fantasy fans, many of which were tie-ins. It is a good example of how some cookbooks are ambiguous in terms of their eligibility for this project.

Edited by science fiction author Anne McCaffrey, *Cooking Out of This World* was suggested by press co-founder Betsy Ballantine specifically as a way to help McCaffrey publish more in the wake of her divorce.[9] It came out of the tradition of community cookbooks, whose roots lay in the post-US Civil War fundraising cookbooks. These earliest ones were fundraisers for war victims, but their successors used the format to fundraise for other, increasingly varied, causes.[10] By the twentieth century, community cookbooks were numerous, and published to support a panoply of organizations, often churches, but also fan groups and science fiction conventions by the second half of the century. The advent of home computing and home printing affected how independent fan productions were produced, increasingly replacing their mimeographed antecedents.

1980s

In the 1980s, cookbook authors and publishers experimented with subject matter, from *The Wind in the Willows* to Hallmark's publication of *Muppet Picnic Cookbook*.[11] *The Doctor Who Cookbook* was published in 1985, while the television series was still actively being produced, an official tie-in and celebrity cookbook both, even if it does predate the use of the word 'official' in tie-in cookbook titles.[12]

Many tie-in recipes in the 1980s are found in companion volumes to fiction and sourcebooks for role-playing games. One often fondly discussed for its recipes is *Leaves from the Inn of the Last Home* (1987), edited by Margaret Weis and Tracy Hickman.[13] The book is an Advanced Dungeons & Dragons supplement, designed to be used as an in-game book, written from within the fictional role-played fantasy world. *The Dragonlover's Guide to Pern*, an official companion to McCaffrey's science fictional world, also contains recipes which lay the groundwork for later Pern fan cookbooks.[14]

1990s

In the early 1990s, Abbeville Press put out a series of movie tie-in cookbooks, under the series title of 'Hollywood Hotplates'. These six volumes started with *Gone with the Wind* (1939) and included *The Wizard of Oz* (1939) and a lone television series, *I Love Lucy* (1950s).[15] At the time, the most recent of the sources were over thirty years old. The 1990s saw increasingly creativity in the variety of sources which inspired authors. Narnia, *The Secret Garden*, and Patrick O'Brien's Aubrey and Maturin adventures all had cookbooks exploring their culinary worlds.[16]

Single recipes which expanded an author's own worldbuilding could sometimes be found in community cookbooks, such as *The Bakery Men Don't See* (1991) and *Her Smoke Rose Up From Supper* (1993), organized by Jeanne Gomoll to help fund the Tiptree Award (now the Otherwise Award).[17] Other authors began to help write more extensive collections of tie-in recipes.

One of the best-known authorized cookbooks from the late '90s was *Nanny Ogg's Cookbook*, a compendium of recipes and advice, often tongue-in-cheek, from the eponymous fictional witch, a recurring character in Terry Pratchett's Discworld series.[18] Written from Nanny's garrulous and excessively honest perspective, the recipes include a straightforward (for those with access to Stilton and tinned, smoked oysters) Carrot and Oyster Pie, as well as frog-free Dried Frog Pills. Both Discworld and two late '90s *Star Wars* cookbooks were official publications, claiming the sales opportunity and preempting whatever fannish recipe work was already flourishing in harder-to-find places.[19] Fannish recipe collections grew in parallel, published on photocopy machines or as computer printouts, and often moving to Print On Demand in recent years.

Two unofficial *Farscape* fan cookbooks were also fundraising community cookbooks. The goal of *Foodscape: What the Frell is That? And Foodscape 2: We're So Skewered* was to raise awareness of the television show in the hopes of it being brought back for at least one more season.[20] Not long after the second cookbook came out, the show was indeed revived, the producers creating one more four-hour miniseries. Fan works are in dialogue with their source material.

Early 2000s

During the first decade of the 2000s, authors increasingly began to publish culinary surveys of multiple, unrelated books and other media in collections which provided a single recipe from each source. *The Book Club Cookbook* (which paid tribute to book clubs as much as it did food inspired by books), *Literary Feasts: Inspired Eating from Classic Fiction*, and *The Manga Cookbook* have collectively had numerous subsequent successors.[21] Other new cookbooks' topics included, variously, the comics-based *Chas Addams Half-Baked Cookbook*, *Green Eggs and Ham*, and *Shrek*.[22]

Many of the fan-created cookbooks of the early 2000s were done collaboratively through mailing lists, Usenet groups, or transient websites now preserved only by the Internet Archive. These include ones for McCaffrey's Pern books (website), Robert A. Heinlein's *Stranger in a Strange Land* (website), and *Ma Kosti's Cookbook*.[23] The last was compiled collaboratively in 2002 by members of a Lois McMaster Bujold mailing list.

Prolific bloggers and YouTubers have in particular helped to shape the modern tie-in cookbook market, building up demonstrable markets for science fiction and fantasy-themed foods. Although not specific to any genre or recipes, the *Cake Wrecks* blog, begun in 2008 profiled daily cakes which had gone wrong, accepting submissions from its fans and followers.[24] By frequently highlighting tie-in themed cakes (even if terrible ones), it helped to establish the existence of widespread interest in science fiction and fantasy-based cakes, amongst other themes.

A Short History of Science Fiction and Fantasy Tie-in Cookbooks

2010s

Around 2010 is when tie-in cookbooks really begin to come into their own as a genre, with Adams Media's foray into the genre cementing its importance. Adams Media – acquired by Simon and Schuster in 2016 – began publishing tie-in cookbooks in 2010, starting with Dinah Bucholz's *The Unofficial Harry Potter Cookbook: From Cauldron Cakes to Knickerbocker Glory*.[25] The book is further notable for potentially being the first tie-in cookbook with the word 'Unofficial' in its title. It is explicitly a work of creative interpretation. Plenty of other tie-in cookbooks came out in 2010, including *The Moomin Cookbook: An Introduction to Finnish Cuisine*, *Chef Mickey* from Disney's ongoing cookbook range, and *Love at First Bite: The Complete Vampire Lover's Cookbook*.[26]

In the early 2010s, cookbooks tied in to non-roleplaying games start to appear with *Angry Birds: Bad Piggies' Egg Recipes*, based on the mobile game, and *Wood for Sheep: The Unauthorized Settlers Cookbook*, based on the *Settlers of Catan* board game.[27] By the end of the decade, there would be official cookbooks for games including *Overwatch*, a team-based shooter, and *Destiny*, a first-person shooter, in addition to plenty more for role-playing games, which inspired some of the earliest tie-in cookbooks.[28] The official cookbooks for *Street Fighter* and *Tomb Raider* came out later, in 2021.[29]

Super Mario Brothers was the video game which inspired Rosanna Pansino, a professional actress, to begin recording episodes for her now-enormously popular YouTube show, *Nerdy Nummies*, in 2011, starting with a Mario-themed cake.[30] Pansino continues to specialize in video game, science fiction, and fantasy-inspired baking. Her published cookbooks, the first of which came out in 2015, are recipe collections based on multiple different franchises and secondary worlds.[31]

George R.R. Martin's *A Song of Fire and Ice* series contains lavish food descriptions. In 2011, bloggers Chelsea Monroe-Cassel and Sariann Lehrer started The Inn at the Crossroads blog in order to more systematically adapt historical recipes to honour Martin's on-page meals.[32] The blog was begun a few months before the television series based on the books first aired. So successful were the bloggers, the books, and the television series, that the authors secured a contract to write the official tie-in cookbook. *A Feast of Ice and Fire: The Official Game of Thrones Companion Cookbook* came out in 2012 and launched a career in tie-in cookbook development for Monroe-Cassel.[33]

Several more still-influential blog- or video-based recipe developers began in their channels in 2011 and 2012. Feast of Fiction's YouTube channel was launched in December 2011, with Jimmy Wong and Ashley Adams beginning with a dish from *Skyrim* (a role-playing video game) and continuing with *Harry Potter*, *Minecraft*, and *Lord of the Rings*.[34] Their first published cookbook was released in 2020.[35]

In 2012, Chris-Rachael Oseland began self-publishing unauthorized cookbooks, beginning with *Dining with the Doctor: An Unauthorised Whovian Cookbook*.[36] Like many tie-in cookbook developers, official or unofficial, she built up a community of her own fans around her blog and website, *Kitchen Overlord*.[37]

Oseland's second recipe collection was a collection of steampunk-themed drinks, entitled *Steamdrunks* (2012), and collections of tie-in drink recipes begin to proliferate in the mid-2010s.[38] Although Cassandra Reeder's first multi-genre tie-in cookbook in 2015 was broader, a later one, *The Geeky Chef Drinks* (2018), focused specifically on drink recipes.[39]

The bibliography on which this work is based included around 230 dated tie-in cookbooks. The halfway point on this list, the point after which fully half of the cookbooks were released in whatever form, is the year 2014. That shows how quickly the genre has grown in recent years in commercial viability and helps to explain why official cookbooks for older commercial properties are only appearing now. (That halfway point on the list may well not fully represent the full numbers of earlier fan cookbooks, given their more-limited distribution methods.)

Insight Editions became a major publisher of tie-in cookbooks in 2016 beginning with *World of Warcraft: The Official Cookbook*, written by Chelsea Monroe-Cassel, her first of several for them.[40] Imprint, which specializes in 'literary portals for fans', soon followed up with official tie-in cookbooks for other commercial properties, including *Adventure Time, The Walking Dead,* and *Teenage Mutant Ninja Turtles*.[41]

Adams Media, beginning in 2010, and Insight Editions, in 2016, have done an enormous amount to raise the awareness and commercial viability of tie-in cookbooks, but at least as notable is the sheer variety of other different presses which have published tie-in cookbooks over the years. The inventoried books have come from 95 different publishers, most of which are major brands. Even if many of those were published before the rise of partially or wholly dedicated imprints, a broad variety of presses continue to take on publishing them.

2020-2021

The last couple years have been the heyday of tie-in cookbooks thus far, with astonishingly large numbers of titles published. Recent patterns include more cookbooks based on games, online and off; more based on work done on social media platforms, including blogs, YouTube channels, and now podcasts; more crowdfunded publications; and more cookbooks mining older intellectual properties for inspiration.

In the late twenty-teens, Diana Ault wrote and co-wrote a variety of media-themed recipe fanzines, including ones inspired by *Pokémon* and the video games *Legend of Zelda*.[42] These fanzines were largely funded by subscription or fundraising, much as the original *Kitchen Overlord Cookbook* and *The Unofficial Zelda Cookbook* were.[43] On the basis of that work, Ault was contracted to write *Cook Anime: Eat Like Your Favorite Character* (2020), based on a variety of popular Japanese animation series.[44]

Many recent cookbooks have been productively inspired by older media works. The *Back to the Future* films came out between 1985 and 1990, but *Back to the Future: The Official Hill Valley Cookbook* was published in 2020.[45] In 2020, the official *Wonder Woman* cookbook came out, from a franchise which dates back to 1941.[46] This gap between inspiration and cookbook occurred even with the earliest examples. The first

Winnie-the-Pooh cookbook (1969) corresponds to when Disney first made movies about the character (1966, 1968, and so on), rather than when the book first came out (1926). The recent proliferation of cookbooks has, however, given new culinary life to older, still-popular properties and fandoms.

The genre of science fiction and fantasy cookbooks is going strong these days. There have been at least twenty tie-in cookbooks published in 2020, and plenty more which have or will come out in 2021, including *Marvel Comics: Cooking with Deadpool*.[47] The genre has also caught the attention of other scholars, including Gillian Polack, Ginger Thomason, and Madison Magladry, and the recent academic essay collection edited by Carrielynn D. Reinhard, Julia E. Largent, and Bertha Chin, *Eating Fandom*, is a cultural and sociological study of the topic.[48]

This initial survey of a fascinating and wide-ranging variety of tie-in cookbooks and drink recipes has one major common theme: the recipe collections all grew out of fantasy or science fiction-based media, whether games, television shows, films, or books. The earliest tie-in cookbooks may have been authorized publications targeted at children, but the genre encompassed far more than that within just a few years. The work of countless fans, aided in recent years by numerous publishers, including specialists Adams Media and Insight Editions, have increasingly helped bring the flavours of fiction to life.

Acknowledgements
This paper has been much improved by feedback from Gillian Polack and the attendees at the 2021 Oxford Symposium on Food and Cookery.

Notes
1. 'Category: Food & Recipes', *Fanlore*, <https://fanlore.org/wiki/Category:Food_%26_Recipes> [accessed 28 May 2021]
2. *The Conflux Cookbook,* ed. by Gillian Polack (Culcairn, New South Wales: Eneit Press, 2011).
3. Garth Nix, 'Prefix', in *The Conflux Cookbook*, ed. by Polack, p. 7.
4. Caroline Nyvang, 'Cooking with Kids: Danish Cookbooks for Children 1847–1975', in *Food and Age in Europe, 1600-1800*, ed. by Tenna Jensen and others (New York: Routledge, 2002).
5. Virginia H. Ellison, *The Pooh Cook Book* (Dutton Books for Young Readers, 1969); Charles M. Schulz, *Peanuts Cook Book* (Determined Productions, 1969).
6. Jane Earye Fryer, *The Mary Frances Cook Book: Adventures Among the Kitchen People* (Philadelphia: John C. Winston, 1912); Len Deighton, *Len Deighton's Action Cook Book* (London: Jonathan Cape, 1965).
7. Arnold Dobrin, *Peter Rabbit's Natural Foods Cookbook* (London: Frederick Warne and Co., 1977); Stan Lee, *Stan Lee Presents the Mighty Marvel Superheroes' Cookbook* (New York: Simon & Schuster, 1977); Pat Tornborg and Robert Dennis, *The Sesame Street Cookbook: Featuring Jim Henson's Muppets* (New York: Platt & Munk, 1978).
8. Anne McCaffrey, *Serve it Forth: Cooking with Anne McCaffrey* (Helicong, PA: Wildside Press, 1996), p. 27.
9. McCaffrey, 'Foreword', *Serve it Forth*, p. xiii.
10. Jan Longone, 'Introduction to the Feeding America Project', *Michigan State University Libraries*, 2002

<https://d.lib.msu.edu/fa/introduction> [accessed 29 May 2021]

11. Arabella Boxer, *The Wind in the Willows Country Cookbook: Inspired by the Wind in the Willows by Kenneth Grahame* (New York: Scribner Book Co., 1983); *Muppet Picnic Cookbook* (London: Hallmark, 1981).

12. Gary Downie, *The Doctor Who Cookbook* (Secaucus, NJ: Carol Publishing Corp., 1985). My thanks to Gillian Polack for observing the intersecting categories of celebrity and tie-in cookbooks (private correspondence, 2021).

13. *Leaves from the Inn of the Last Home: The Complete Krynn Source Book*, ed. by Margaret Weis and Tracy Hickman, vol 1 (Seattle, WA: Wizards of the Coast, 1987).

14. Jody Lynn Nye and Anne McCaffrey, *The Dragonlover's Guide to Pern* (New York: Del Rey Books, 1989).

15. *Gone With the Wind Cookbook: Famous Southern Cooking Recipes* (New York: Abbeville Press, 1991); Jennifer Newman Brazil and Vicky Wells, *The Wizard of Oz Cookbook: Breakfast in Kansas, Dessert in Oz* (New York: Abbeville Press, 1993); Sarah Key and Vicky Wells, *The I Love Lucy Cookbook* (New York: Abbeville Press, 1993).

16. Douglas Gresham, *The Narnia Cookbook: Foods from C. S. Lewis's The Chronicles of Narnia* (New York: HarperCollins, 1998); Amy Cotler, *The Secret Garden Cookbook: Recipes Inspired by Frances Hodgson Burnett's The Secret Garden* (New York: Festival, 1999); Anne Chotzinoff Grossman and Lisa Grossman Thomas, *Lobscouse and Spotted Dog: Which is a Gastronomic Companion to the Aubrey/Maturin Novels* (New York: WW Norton, 1997).

17. *The Bakery Men Don't See*, ed. by Jeanne Gomoll (Madison, WI: SF3, 1991); *Her Smoke Rose up from Supper*, ed. by Jeanne Gomoll (Madison, WI: SF3, 1993).

18. Terry Pratchett, Stephen Briggs, and Tina Hannan, *Nanny Ogg's Cookbook* (Yellow Springs, OH: Corgi, 1999).

19. Robin Davis, *The Star Wars Cookbook: Wookiee Cookies and other Galactic Recipes* (San Francisco: Chronicle Books, 1998); Ethan Phillips and William J. Birnes, *Star Trek Cookbook* (Hoboken, NJ: Prentice Hall, 1999).

20. 'Guide to the Save Farscape Auction Collection', *The University of Iowa Libraries* <http://collguides.lib.uiowa.edu/?MSC0371> [accessed 31 May 2021]

21. Shaunda Kenney Wenger and Janet Kay Jensen, *The Book Lover's Cookbook: Recipes Inspired by Celebrated Works of Literature, and the Passages That Feature Them* (New York: Ballantine, 2003); Judy Gelman, *The Book Club Cookbook* (New York: Tarcher, 2004); Sean Brand, *Literary Feasts: Inspired Eating from Classic Fiction* (New York: Atria Books, 2006); Chihiro Hattori and the Manga University Culinary Institute, *The Manga Cookbook* (Saitama: Japanime Co., 2007).

22. Chas Addams, *Chas Addams Half-Baked Cookbook: Culinary Cartoons for the Humorously Famished* (New York: Simon Schuster, 2005); Georgeanne Brennan, *Green Eggs and Ham Cookbook* (New York: Random House Books for Young Readers, 2006); Lindsay Kent, ed., *Shrek Cookbook* (London: DK Children, 2007).

23. Menai, 'Pern Cookbook' <https://www.angelfire.com/on2/menai/cookbook.html> [accessed 17 May 2021]; Kate Gladstone and others, 'Stranger food, some SIASL recipes for The Heinlein Cookbook', *NARKHIVE* <https://alt.fan.heinlein.narkive.com/zSCRGrvz/stranger-food-some-siasl-recipes-for-the-heinlein-cookbook> [accessed 19 May 2021]; 'Ma Kosti's Cookbook: Recipes from the Lois McMaster Bujold Mailing List', *WebArchive* <https://web.archive.org/web/20080112125936/http://www.rojizodesign.com/makosti/> [accessed 25 May 2021]

24. *Cake Wrecks* <http://www.cakewrecks.com/> [accessed 27 May 2021]

25. John Maher, 'S&S to Acquire Adams Media', *Publishers Weekly*, 15 Nov 2016 <https://www.publishersweekly.com/pw/by-topic/industry-news/publisher-news/article/72041-s-s-to-acquire-adams-media.html> [accessed 25 May 2021]; Dinah Bucholz, *The Unofficial Harry Potter Cookbook: From Cauldron Cakes to Knickerbocker Glory* (Avon, MA: Adams Media, 2010).

26. Sami Malila, *The Moomin Cookbook: An Introduction to Finnish Cuisine* (London: SelfMadeHero,

A Short History of Science Fiction and Fantasy Tie-in Cookbooks

2010); Pam Brandon, *Chef Mickey: Treasures from the Vault & Delicious New Favorites* (New York: Walt Disney Theme Park, 2010), and Michelle Roy Kelly and Andrea Norvill, *Love at First Bite: The Complete Vampire Lover's Cookbook* (Adams Media, 2010).

27 Bonnier Kurjat Oy, *Angry Birds: Bad Piggies' Egg Recipes* (Espoo: Rovio Mobile, 2011); Chris-Rachael Oselund, *Wood for Sheep: The Unauthorized Settlers Cookbook* ([n.p.]: [n. pub.], 2013).

28 Chelsea Monroe-Cassel, *Overwatch: The Official Cookbook* (San Rafael, CA: Insight Editions); Victoria Rosenthal, *Destiny: The Official Cookbook* (San Rafael, CA: Insight Editions, 2020).

29 Victoria Rosenthal, *Street Fighter: The Official Street Food Cookbook* (San Rafael, CA: Insight Editions, 2021); Tara Theoharis, *Tomb Raider: The Official Cookbook and Travel Guide* (San Rafael, CA: Insight Editions, 2021).

30 Rosanna Pansino, 'Super Mario Cake – Nerdy Nummies', *YouTube*, 17 June 2011 <https://www.youtube.com/watch?v=IE5eB4vghlY> [accessed 31 May 2021]

31 Rosanna Pansino, *The Nerdy Nummies Cookbook: Sweet Treats for the Geek in All of Us* (New York: Atria, 2015).

32 Chelsea Monroe-Cassel and Sariann Lehrer, *Inn at the Crossroads*, 2016 <https://www.innatthecrossroads.com/> [accessed 31 May 2021]

33 Chelsea Monroe-Cassel and Sariann Lehrer, *A Feast of Ice and Fire: The Official Game of Thrones Companion Cookbook* (New York: Bantam, 2012).

34 Jimmy Wong and Ashley Adams, 'Feast of Fiction', *YouTube*, 25 November 2020 <https://www.youtube.com/user/feastoffiction> [accessed 31 May 2021]

35 Jimmy Wong and Ashley Adams, *The Feast of Fiction Cookbook: Recipes Inspired by TV, Movies, Games & Books* (Taftsville, VT: Countryman, 2020).

36 Chris-Rachael Oseland, *Dining with the Doctor: An Unauthorised Whovian Cookbook* ([n.p.]: [n.pub.], 2012).

37 Chris-Rachael Oseland, *Kitchen Overlord* <https://kitchenoverlord.com/> [accessed 25 May 2021]

38 Chris-Rachael Oseland, *SteamDrunks 101: 101 Steampunk Cocktails and Mixed Drinks* ([n.p.]: [n.pub.], 2012).

39 Cassandra Reeder, *The Geeky Chef Cookbook: Real-Life Recipes for Your Favorite Fantasy Foods* (London: Race Point Publishing, 2015); Cassandra Reeder, *The Geek Chef Drinks: Unofficial Cocktail Recipes from Game of Thrones, Legend of Zelda, Star Trek, and More* (London: Race Point Publishing, 2018).

40 Chelsea Cassel-Monroe, *World of Warcraft: The Official Cookbook* (San Rafael, CA: Insight Editions, 2016).

41 Jason Boog, 'Insight Editions Marks 15 Years of Publishing for Fans', *Publishers Weekly*, 15 Dec 2017 <https://www.publishersweekly.com/pw/by-topic/industry-news/publisher-news/article/75661-insight-editions-marks-15-years-of-publishing-for-fans.html> [accessed 25 May 2021]; Jordan Grosser, *Adventure Time: The Official Cookbook* (San Rafael, CA: Insight Editions, 2016); Lauren Wilson, *The Walking Dead: The Official Cookbook and Survival Guide* (San Rafael, CA: Insight Editions, 2017); Peggy Paul Casella, *The Teenage Mutant Ninja Turtles Pizza Cookbook* (San Rafael, CA: Insight Editions, 2017).

42 Diana Ault and Bryan Connor, Hyrule: Taste of the Wild (2018); Diana Ault, Pokécafé, (2019).

43 'Kitchen Overlord's Illustrated Geek Cookbook', *Kickstarter* <https://www.kickstarter.com/projects/396707778/kitchen-overlords-illustrated-geek-cookbook> [accessed 23 May 2021]; 'The Unofficial Legend of Zelda Cookbook', *Kickstarter* <https://www.kickstarter.com/projects/aimeewoodworks/the-unofficial-legend-of-zelda-cookbook-break-kickstarter> [accessed 23 May 2021]

44 Diana Ault, *Cook Anime: Eat Like Your Favorite Character* (New York: Tiller Press, 2020).

45 Allison Robicelli, *Back to the Future: The Official Hill Valley Cookbook* (San Rafael, CA: Insight Editions, 2020).

46 Briana Volk, *Wonder Woman: The Official Cookbook* (San Rafael, CA: Insight Editions, 2020).

47 Marc Sumerak and Elena Craig, *Marvel Comics: Cooking with Deadpool* (San Rafael, CA: Insight Editions, 2021).

48 Carrielynn D. Reinhard, Julia E. Largent, and Bertha Chin, *Eating Fandom: Intersections between Fans and Food Cultures* (New York: Routledge, 2020).

Contributors

Volker Bach, a freelance translator and historical cooking instructor, is the author of *The Kitchen, Food, and Cooking in Reformation Germany* and the forthcoming *Landsknecht Cookbook*.

Vidya Balachander is a food journalist and researcher based in Dubai. Her work explores the intersection of food and anthropology, particularly its relationship with politics, society and culture.

Janet Beizer is a writer and Professor of French Literature and Culture at Harvard University. She works on culinary matters in literature and the visual arts. She is finishing *The Harlequin Eaters: Leftovers and the Patchwork Imagination in Nineteenth-Century Paris*.

Astrid Böhm is a research assistant at the Centre for Information Modeling at the University of Graz. She specializes in historical script and manuscript studies.

Paul Brummell is a career diplomat and current UK Ambassador to Latvia. He has previously served as UK Ambassador to Turkmenistan, Kazakhstan (and concurrently Kyrgyzstan), and Romania, and as High Commissioner to Barbados and the Eastern Caribbean.

Anthony F. Buccini is an historical linguist and dialectologist who taught at the University of Chicago. As a food historian, his research focuses on the Mediterranean and Atlantic World. He is a two-time winner of the Sophie Coe Prize in Food History.

Noel Buttigieg is an academic researcher at the University of Malta, specializing in cultural heritage with a particular interest in food culture.

Mary Margaret Chappell is an American food writer and editor who lives on the coast of Brittany in France.

Rareș Augustin Crăiuț is a PhD candidate at the University of Babeș-Bolyai and an associated artist-researcher with the Brussels a.pass research center. His academic and artistic research projects, collected at performingfood.com, delve into food performative texts and acts.

Gill Eastabrook recently completed a Masters by Research on food and northern English identities in the mid-nineteenth century at Leeds Beckett University.

Contributors

Julia Eibinger works as a student assistant at the Centre for Information Modeling at the University of Graz. Her focus is on semantic annotation of medieval cooking recipes and data science.

Suzanne Evans, a member of the Culinary Historians of Canada, is an independent scholar whose writings focus on women and war. Her most recent book is *The Taste of Longing: Ethel Mulvany and her Starving Prisoners of War Cookbook*.

Caroline Favre is a young scholar specializing in Russian history. Her main interests are Franco-Russian cultural relations in the late modern period with an emphasis on food studies.

Rebecca Fils-Aimé, a program evaluator and researcher based in the United States, holds a Master's in Public Health from Emory University. An aspiring herbalist, she has a passion for culturally-inclusive nutrition, food justice, and highlighting Africa's role in culinary history.

Len Fisher is a scientist, author, and broadcaster, particularly interested in the applications of science to gastronomy. In addition to his academic work, he has written for the *Guardian* newspaper and contributed a chapter and a recipe to Heston Blumenthal's *Big Fat Duck Cookbook*.

Lindsey Foltz is pursuing a PhD in Anthropology at the University of Oregon with a specialization in Food Studies. She has conducted research with farmers in Oregon's Southern Willamette Valley and with people who practice food self-provisioning and preservation in Bulgaria.

Kevin Geddes, a PhD candidate at Edinburgh Napier University, researches the history and development of television cooking programmes in Britain 1936-1976. Kevin has published several articles on the topic, and a biography of the memorable celebrity Fanny Cradock.

Sudha Gopalakrishnan, one of the founders of Sahapedia, holds a PhD in comparative drama and was instrumental in gaining recognition of Indian heritage expressions as UNESCO Masterpieces of the Oral and Intangible Heritage of Humanity.

Christopher Grocock teaches Latin, Greek, and Ancient History at the Bedales School, and is the author and editor of a number of medieval Latin texts and articles on aspects of ancient and medieval life.

Andrea Gutiérrez is Assistant Professor of Instruction at the University of Texas at Austin. In addition to researching South Asian food history using Sanskrit and Tamil sources, her secondary specialization is animal studies in South Asia.

Contributors

Adrienne Harrington, who studied Irish Food Culture at University College Cork, is the Head of Enforcement, Legal and Governance at Ireland's Central Statistics Office.

Jenny L. Herman is an FWO doctoral fellow in fundamental research and a PhD candidate in Cultural Studies at KU Leuven in Belgium. Her research focuses on the identity-building aspects of food, concepts of *terroir*, and culinary cultural heritage.

Peter Hertzmann is an autodidactic polymath with a strong contrarian bent who likes to provide an alternative approach about all aspects of food. His three books are *Knife Skills Illustrated: A User's Manual*, *A Perfect Mouthful* and *50 Ways to Cook a Carrot*.

Jennifer L. Holm is an independent scholar with a PhD in French. Her research focuses on contemporary French gastronomy. She is currently working on a book project entitled *Comfort Food: Gastronomy and National Self-Fashioning in Contemporary French Literature and Film*.

Ragini Kashyap, a seasoned educational professional, is interested in the food of conflict and displacement, which led to her supper club series 'Bordered'. She is a lecturer on food politics in India and hosts the podcast 'More than Masala'.

Méliné Kasparian-Le Fèvre is a doctoral student in American Literature in the CLIMAS Laboratory at the Université Bordeaux Montaigne.

Anke Klitzing lectures at the Technological University Dublin in food culture, literature, and media. Her PhD research focuses on developing the paradigm of gastrocriticism – the theory and methodology of understanding the nexus of food and writing.

Helmut W. Klug works at the Centre for Information Modeling at the University of Graz. A senior post-doc researcher in digital humanities and food history, he is interested in the recipe as a cultural heritage object.

Bruce Kraig is an emeritus Professor of History, author and editor of a bunch of books and articles on food history, and since 1985 an Oxford symposiast.

Michael Krondl is a food writer, culinary historian, cooking teacher, and artist. His books include *The Taste of Conquest: The Rise and Fall of the Three Great Cities of Spice* and *Sweet Invention: A History of Dessert*.

Paul Levy is the Chair Emeritus of the Oxford Symposium on Food and Cookery.

Priya Mani is a Copenhagen-based designer and cultural researcher. She has worked with large corporates on the role of foodways, consumption, diabetes, and obesity. She is currently writing a *Visual Encyclopedia of Indian Foods* combining over two decades of field work.

Mark McWilliams, Professor of English at the United States Naval Academy, has served as Editor of the Oxford Symposium on Food and Cookery since 2011.

Emily Martin is pursuing a PhD in history at the University of California, Berkeley studying late nineteenth-century US food culture.

Keri Matwick is a lecturer at the Language and Communication Centre, Nanyang Technological University, in Singapore. As a linguist, she researches food, language, and culture in the media, particularly television cooking shows, cookbooks, and Instagram.

Nader Mehravari is a Research Associate at the College of Agriculture and Environmental Sciences, University of California, Davis. His work explores the history, principles, and practices of ancient and contemporary Persian cookery and associated foodways.

Lindsay Middleton, a PhD candidate at the University of Glasgow and the University of Aberdeen, focuses on the literary and technological form of the nineteenth-century recipe. She is also working with the National Trust for Scotland to include food history in heritage properties.

Caitlin B. Morgan serves as a social scientist for the USDA ARS Food Systems Research Unit. She wrote this symposium paper while working as a postdoctoral researcher at the University of Vermont.

James Oseland is the author and editor of *World Food: Mexico City* and *World Food: Paris*, part of his new book series for Ten Speed Press. He was the editor-in-chief of *Saveur* for nine years, and his *Cradle of Flavor* won a James Beard Award.

Charity Robey writes for the *Shelter Island Reporter* and the *New York Times* covering the food, culture, and history of Long Island. A programming chair for Culinary Historians of New York, she lives on Shelter Island, New York.

Ana Karen Ruiz de la Peña Posada is a food historian and history graduate from the Universidad Nacional Autónoma de México in Mexico City. She is currently working on her thesis about *mole* and the role it played in solidifying the idea of Mexican cuisine.

Shayma Owaise Saadat is a cook, recipe developer, and food photographer and stylist. She has written for *Bon Appetit*, *BBC*, *Food52*, *Globe and Mail*, *New York Times*, *Toronto Star*, and *Wine Enthusiast*.

Contributors

Samapan Saha is a PhD candidate in the Department of History at Ashoka University. His research interest lies in understanding South Asian communities' complex relationship with food and his dissertation focuses on the history of Bengali cuisine in colonial South Asia.

Anders Sandberg is a lapsed computational neuroscientist researching emerging technology, global disasters, and the very long-term future at the Future of Humanity Institute at University of Oxford.

Anna Seecharan is a food anthropologist and PhD researcher at the University of Exeter, UK. She conducts embodied sensory ethnography which explores the role of smell/taste memory in creating relationships between sensory perception, the body, food, identity and belonging.

Laura Shapiro is a journalist and culinary historian. Her most recent book is *What She Ate: Six Remarkable Women and the Food That Tells Their Stories*.

Richard Warren Shepro is both an international lawyer and a food scholar. He teaches at the University of Chicago and has now authored seven Oxford Food Symposium papers. He is a former editor of the *Harvard Law Review*.

Max Shrem is an independent scholar whose research explores the evolution of the cultural figure of the gourmand and the relationship between gastronomy and the fine arts. He also works seasonally on an organic goat cheese farm in France's Ardèche region.

Nancy Siegel, Professor of Art History and Culinary History at Towson University, specializes in American foodways of the eighteenth and nineteenth centuries. She is completing a book project, *Political Appetites: Revolution, Taste, and Culinary Activism in the Early Republic*.

Adriana Sohodoleanu completed her PhD in Sociology at the University of Bucharest; her thesis focused on the New Romanian Cuisine movement. Her research interests lie in the broad area of food studies, and she shares her findings through lectures and food-centric projects.

Nick Tošaj is a Professor of History at John Abbott College, where his work focuses on bread, staple carbohydrates, and colonialism, primarily in the modern French colonial empire. Nick is also interested in food-oriented pedagogy.

Susan Weingarten is a food historian and archaeologist living in Jerusalem. She is the author of *Haroset: A Taste of Jewish History*.

Contributors

Nikki Werner shares her understanding of food and cooking through teaching and writing, and she can't help looking for the story in whatever she cooks.

Shana Worthen holds a PhD in the History and Philosophy of Science and Technology from the University of Toronto. Her research interests include Medieval and Early Modern technologies.